CIM

TUTORIAL TEXT

Diploma

Strategic Marketing Management: Analysis and Decision

by Dr David Pearson
and Professor Ashok Ranchhod (CIM Examiner)

First edition 1999
Second edition September 2000

ISBN 0 7517 4111 1 (Previous edition 0 7517 4091 8)

British Library Cataloguing-in-Publication Data
A catalogue record for this book
is available from the British Library

Published by

BPP Publishing Limited
Aldine House, Aldine Place
London W12 8AW

www.bpp.com

Printed in England by DACOSTA PRINT,
35/37 Queensland Road, London
N7 7AH (0207 7700 1000)

The authors are grateful to CIM tutors and students for their contributions, and also to Marketing Tactics and Nottingham Trent University.

Page

Page

Clerical Medical Investment Group Ltd (June 2000)

PREFACE

The exam

The Diploma awarded by the Chartered Institute of Marketing is a management qualification which puts a major emphasis on the practical understanding of marketing activities. At the same time, the Institute's examinations recognise that the marketing professional works in a fast changing organisational, economic and social environment.

Strategic Marketing Management: Analysis and Decision is one of the two compulsory CIM Diploma papers. It is compulsory as the marketing professional is expected to be a *manager.* Knowledge and skills in analysis and decision, together with an appreciation of the role of marketing in the corporate structure, are essential ingredients of managerial competence in this field.

This BPP Tutorial Text (September 2000 edition)

The secret of exam success is effective study material which is focused and relevant to the exam *you* will be sitting. This is the philosophy underpinning this Tutorial Text, which has been especially written for candidates sitting this case study examination. It is divided into five parts.

A Background knowledge relevant to analysis and decision

B The CIM case study examination

C How to analyse the CIM case study (including the Senior Examiner's recommended 6 stage approach)

D Examination techniques: planning your examination

E Learning from experience: ensuring you pass. This includes detailed step-by-step analyses of two recent case studies *(Acclaim Entertainment Inc (12/99)* and *Clerical Medical Investment Group Ltd (6/00)).* You will view a variety of approaches to the material, which will help you set up a good file of data to take with you into the examination room. This approach helps you to take a reasoned, methodical approach to the case material which, by its nature, reflects the uncertainties of the commercial world.

The authors

Dr David Pearson, is a former Senior Examiner for Analysis and Decision, a former Senior Examiner for Marketing Planning and Control and the previous CIM Co-ordinator for all Diploma subjects. Dr Pearson has accumulated a total of 12 years experience in examining CIM Diploma subjects and continues to mark Analysis and Decision papers, also providing student feedback. **Professor Ashok Ranchhod** is the current Senior Examiner for Analysis and Decision with a career background in lecturing, consultancy and examining. Ashok brings some refreshing new approaches to this subject.

Help us to help you

Your feedback will help us improve this Tutorial Text, so please complete and return the *Review Form* at the end of this Tutorial Text; you will be entered automatically in a free prize draw.

A final word

This Tutorial Text offers a professional solution to your needs in preparing for this challenging exam!

BPP Publishing
September 2000

Other elements in the BPP study package for CIM exams, including *Solo Cases*, are listed on the *Order Form* at the back of this Tutorial Text.

For information about all the products and services offered by the BPP Holdings plc group, visit our *website*. The address is: www.bpp.com

HOW TO USE THIS TUTORIAL TEXT

1 What is the CIM case study?

There is no formal syllabus for the CIM's examination **Strategic Marketing Management: Analysis and Decision**. Instead the examination is based on a case study normally comprising 30 to 40 pages of narrative, charts and tables and issued to examinees by post about **four weeks in advance of the examination**.

The issue of the case study some four weeks in advance allows time for considerable analysis and discussion.

The case study is a **practical** test of the candidates' knowledge of marketing (gained in Certificate and Diploma, or equivalent, studies) and their ability to apply it. Normally candidates will also have some practical experience in marketing to bring to bear.

At the same time, some background knowledge is necessary. Those who are coming to the case study 'cold' will find the theoretical underpinning a useful complement to their practical experience. This is provided in Part A of this Tutorial Text. Some current issues in marketing of general relevance are also described here. The background material indicates the examiners' views as to what is relevant for the Analysis and Decision paper.

Whilst case study methods vary according to the institution and lecturer concerned, a particular model embodying a comprehensive 28-step approach is detailed in this Tutorial Text.

2 Discussing the case study

Students are strongly advised to conduct in-depth discussion with colleagues on the case study analysis and its issues. This is often accomplished at colleges by the forming of **syndicate groups** of four to six people and the holding of frequent **plenary sessions** where all candidates gather together. In this way, a syndicate member not only hears the view of his or her syndicate, but also those of other syndicates. In this way a much more balanced, integrated and secure approach can be developed. Students who forgo this sort of discussion are likely to fail, no matter how individually clever at analysis they might be.

Having said this, candidates should not copy out word for word **group answers**: these will be failed. Candidates must offer their own **individual** work on the day of the examination.

3 The examination

There are a number of different methods of dealing with case studies and students are exposed to some of these in Parts B and C of this Tutorial Text, so as to promote a reasonably wide appreciation of the subject. However, some method eventually needs to be chosen, and the one recommended has been thoroughly tried and tested, and has been found to achieve a high degree of success in the CIM examinations.

One of the key success factors in case study examination (apart from being thoroughly prepared) is to be well organised in the exam room itself, freeing the mind to think more calmly and clearly about the exam questions. Students are advised to study Part D on exam techniques very thoroughly.

4 Practice

Part E contains two recent case studies, examination questions and marking guides for self-assessment. You are strongly recommended to conduct a practice run on at least one of these previous case studies together with a mock exam and to get your answers assessed against the frameworks provided. This is the most effective way of preparing yourself for the problems you will eventually have to face in the examination room.

A note on pronouns

On occasions in this Tutorial Text, 'he' is used for 'he or she', 'him' for 'him or her' and so forth. Whilst we try to avoid this practice it is sometimes necessary for reasons of style. No prejudice or stereotyping according to sex is intended or assumed.

SYLLABUS OVERVIEW

Analysis and Decision

This Analysis and Decision paper tests a potential candidate's ability to demonstrate knowledge from different areas of marketing in order to develop appropriate strategies plans and innovative solutions for organisations. Many of the cases presented will draw from all areas of marketing from the CIM syllabi up to and including Diploma level.

As each case is different, candidates should possess the capability to draw upon some of the key topic areas from across the CIM syllabus that will need to be refreshed in order to tackle case studies effectively. There will be a heavier emphasis on the syllabi for Integrated Marketing Communications, Planning and Control, and International Marketing Strategy.

Strategic thinking ability, coherence of argument, absorption of detail and clear justification of any solutions offered will be measured outcomes of the effective understanding of the case studies.

Aims and objectives

Objectives of the Analysis and Decision module are outlined below and students will be expected:

- To utilise the practical and marketing skills which are pre-requisites for analysis of the case and engage students in justifying their strategic recommendations.
- To analyse the case within given constraints and understand possible barriers to implementation.
- To apply the marketing processes within a wide variety of market sectors.
- To develop the ability to cross reference knowledge from other Diploma subjects.
- To develop creative and innovative applications of knowledge of strategic marketing.
- To be able to apply relevant marketing planning models and display critical analytical and decision making skills within the case study examination.
- To comprehend and resolve a wide variety of marketing problems and provide realistic and innovative solutions.

Learning outcomes

Students will be able to:

- Demonstrate an in-depth understanding of the strategic marketing planning process and to develop a creative and innovative strategic marketing plan.
- Critically evaluate case studies using a wide variety of marketing techniques, concepts and models and an understanding of contemporary marketing issues.
- Understand and apply competitive positioning strategies within a given case study.
- Critically evaluate various options available within given constraints and justify any decisions taken.
- Demonstrate the ability to analyse numerical data and management information and utilise it to make decisions about key underlying issues within the Case Study.
- Synthesise various strands of knowledge from the different Diploma subjects effectively in the context of the Case Study examination.
- Apply both practical and academic marketing knowledge within a given Case Study.
- Comprehend and resolve a wide variety of marketing problems.
- Develop appropriate control aspects and contingency plans.

SENIOR EXAMINER'S VIEW OF THE PAPER

1 Overview of the area

The Analysis and Decision paper is the culmination of all the marketing subjects covered at all levels, but especially the Diploma and the Advanced Diploma. For this reason, there is no specific syllabus for this paper. The new Planning and Control syllabus now gives a clear strategic focus. This type of expertise will be needed to tackle the Case Study paper. It is also clear that it will not be possible to tackle the Case Study without a clear grasp of the fundamentals of Marketing Communications and International Marketing. In this sense, for all students, the Case Study is a culmination of the application of all the marketing knowledge they have gained over several years.

The title of the paper 'Analysis and Decision' implies that the candidates are competent enough to analyse problems within a marketing context and subsequently take appropriate decisions to implement marketing strategies for an organisation. In order to achieve competence in this area, prospective candidates will need to be conversant with all aspects of marketing, as strategic marketing problems do not come in neat packages. A comprehensive grasp of the basic subjects at the Certificate and Advanced Certificate level together with the key subjects of International Marketing and Marketing Communications is needed. The Planning and Control Paper is an integral part of the preparation for this paper.

2 The changing focus of the paper

- Marketing as a subject area is undergoing major changes. These changes are taking place as a result of dramatic shifts in technology, demographics, globalisation, systems of production, logistics and ecological issues. The paper, in future, therefore will be designed to reflect more of these contemporary issues in addition to the knowledge base mentioned above.
- The case studies will also be designed to develop strategic marketing issues which can be operationalised and implemented within realistic constraints (June 1998 case). It is often forgotten that marketing is not just about positioning and growth, but also about **effectiveness** within **given constraints** within most organisations. These constraints mean that strategies have to be sensibly evaluated and chosen, with hard decisions being made. When particular strategies are chosen, it is clear that the constraints could be many and varied. Constraints, for instance could be financial, organisational (both employee and culture related), marketing (image, size of markets, branding, distribution systems, networks) and, if the organisation is a division of large entity headquarter-imposed constraints.

Globalisation

- The rapid changes in technology are far reaching as they are changing the normal paradigms of marketing. The four P's cannot be discussed with certainty. The nature and direction of marketing strategies, necessarily have to take into account the massive computing power available and the advent of business on the Internet. Many multi-nationals have operated globally for decades, but technology is changing the patterns of production and consumption.
- For instance, global brands are available anywhere and production facilities may be located in a myriad of different countries (December 1998 case). For smaller companies, the Internet holds the promises and pitfalls of operating in a global arena.
- The introduction of the Euro means that Pan-European marketing strategies have to bethought through in a different manner. The changing nature and the growth of

south Asian markets has an enormous impact on the marketing strategies of organisations. The nature and strength of the American market is often forgotten in many marketing cases. The case studies will reflect these changes and will embrace many different sectors of industry.

Organisational issues

- When developing marketing strategies it is important that the culture and nature of the organisation is taken into account. Marketing strategies often succeed and fail as a result of inappropriate personnel, inappropriate structures or climates within organisations. Organisations are therefore always striving to create the appropriate structures and develop appropriate cultures to meet the demands of the marketing place.
- The customer is king and marketing strategists have to place the level of market orientation at the centre of their thinking.

Sustainability

- Marketing literature has for long been concerned with growth and market share. It is important that issues surrounding the constraints imposed by the environment are taken into account. The world is facing an enormous challenge in terns of the availability of resources and the needs of the population. In some respects a challenge posed to marketing strategists is the need to consider constraints and responsibility.

Financial issues

- Financial issues will also play a key role in developing strategies.
- A good knowledge of basic financial statements such as P&L accounts, balance sheets and cashflow statements is required.

Knowledge of contemporary marketing issues

- Each case is different and will therefore test some knowledge of contemporary issues. Students therefore need to be encouraged to read journal articles pertaining to the case study.

Application of previous knowledge

- The need to apply models for analysis will continue. However, a more critical approach in applying these techniques will be needed. The paper will reflect the need for both academic and practical knowledge as a true marketer needs to have experience of both areas for developing sensible strategies.

Issues of implementation and control

- An awareness of the clear decision making and implementation strategies will be tested. As will be strategic positioning, innovation and branding in the context of implementation and control

3 Links with other papers

This paper deliberately has no syllabus. The paper is the culmination of all the knowledge gained at the Advanced Diploma and Diploma levels. The foundations laid by the Marketing Communications Strategy, International Marketing Strategy and Planning and Control syllabi underpin the Analysis and Decision Paper. In addition to this, the Planning and Control syllabus offers the fundamental underpinning knowledge needed to undertake strategic analysis. In tutoring and preparing students for this paper, tutors need to be aware of the linkages with other areas and they need to be able to draw from a variety of literature sources in order to enhance and improve their analytic and decision making skills this is particularly important for both large and small organisations as amply demonstrated by the **Philips** and **Biocatalysts** case studies. In each case there is an emphasis on understanding international issues as well as communications issues thoroughly.

The examiners are looking for candidates to demonstrate analytical ability, interpretive skills, insight, innovation and creativity in answering questions. They are also looking for candidates to take clear and sensible decisions within the context of the case study. A critical awareness of the specific issues involved, relevant theoretical underpinning, attention to detail, coherence and justification of strategies adopted will also be assessed.

To perform well on the paper, candidates will have to exhibit the following.

- A need to concentrate on the strategic aspects of marketing underpinned by the necessary detail.
- The ability to identify 'gaps' in the case study and to outline the assumptions made.
- The ability to critically apply relevant models for case analysis.
- The ability to draw and synthesise from any of the diploma subject areas as relevant.
- Concentration on the question set rather than the pre-prepared answer.
- The ability to answer in the report format with comprehensive sentences rather than providing simplistic lists.
- The judicious use of diagrams for illustrative purposes.
- The ability to draw disparate links together and give coherent answers.
- The use of interesting an useful articles from journals in their answers.
- Innovation and creativity in answering the questions.
- Demonstration of practical applications of marketing knowledge.
- Sensible use of time and an ability to plan the answer within the set time.
- A good understanding of the cases study set.
- Draw up a comprehensive and convincing marketing plan with accompany costs and schedules.
- Suggest appropriate control mechanisms and contingency plans.

Part A

Background knowledge relevant to analysis and decision

1 Strategic Marketing Management: Planning And Control

This chapter covers the following topics.

Introduction

The case study examination *for Strategic Marketing Management: Analysis and Decision* is intended to bring together and to test all your previous studies and knowledge of marketing. It would be impossible to cover all that here in just one part of one book. To do this, you would need to consult the CIM's full list of recommended publications. However, it is possible to review here a number of key subjects and to revise with you those elements which are most likely to be required for the case study examination. These key subjects are considered to be the following.

(a) The other diploma subjects of:

- (i) Strategic Marketing Management: Planning and Control (this chapter)
- (ii) Integrated Marketing Communications (Chapter 2)
- (iii) International Marketing Strategy (Chapter 3)

(b) Other relevant material including:

- (i) a discussion of financial information and its use (Chapter 4)
- (ii) a brief description of some significant current issues (Chapter 6)

This chapter will revise the syllabus for *Strategic Marketing Management: Planning and Control,* stage by stage. Rather than focusing on the detail required for the Planning and Control examination, it will however concentrate on those syllabus items **most relevant to case analysis and decision**. Theoretical detail is deliberately excluded in favour of practical application, for our purposes. (In other words, the material here will not be sufficient for you to pass that paper: buy the BPP Study Text for that subject if you are taking it.)

1 INTRODUCTION TO PLANNING AND CONTROL: OVERVIEW

1.1 Planning and control are required at all levels of management. For our purposes we are concerned with the top level of marketing management, the level responsible for the critical **strategic decisions**.

1.2 However, **marketing cannot be managed in a vacuum**. Marketing directors and managers cannot take strategic decisions on their own without reference to the Managing Director and the Directors of other functions - ie corporate management as a team. True marketing orientation is found, after all, where everyone in the company from top to bottom accepts the marketing concept, and believes in customer sovereignty.

1.3 Nevertheless, **marketing can be claimed to be the key activity in an organisation**. As Drucker points out, a basic objective of any organisation is to **survive**. Organisations cannot normally survive without selling goods or providing services to people (customers) and this involves marketing.

1.4 A commercial organisation's long term survival usually rests on ensuring that revenue earned exceeds costs incurred and it is marketing managers' role to market profitably. The definition of **marketing** by the Chartered Institute of Marketing is: 'The **management** process which identifies, anticipates and satisfies customer requirements **profitably**'.

1.5 The marketing plan is only one of the functional plans which make up the total plan or corporate plan.

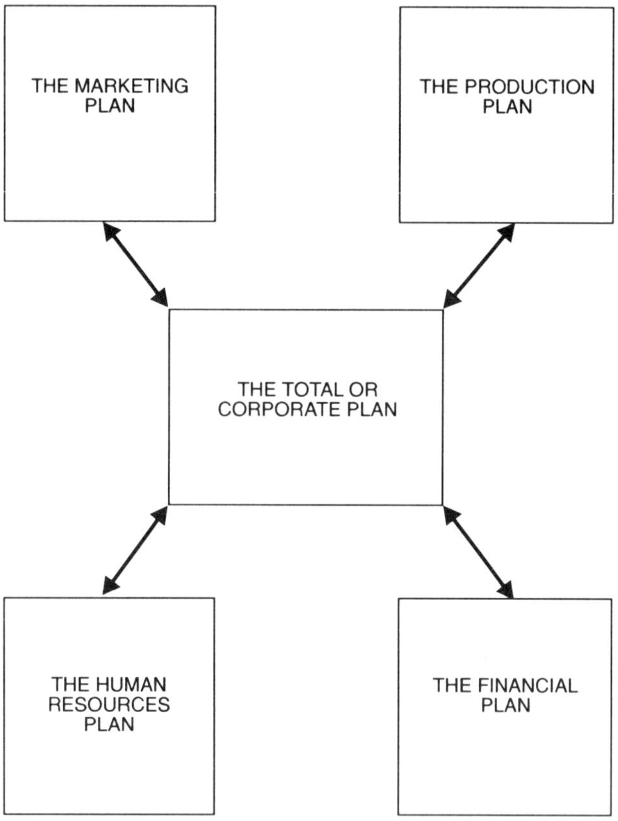

1.6 **The marketing plan leads the other functional plans**. Only after sales volumes have been forecast and agreed can the other functional plans be drawn up. Sales volumes determine the amount of goods that are to be produced in most industries (although in some industries, the costs of shutting down the production may be so huge so as to justify continued production).

1.7 The above figure reminds us of the importance of people. Again Drucker suggests that the art of management is 'getting things done through people'. It does, therefore, involve a **process** (getting things done) and **people**.

1.8 'Getting things done' is however an insufficient description of a manager's role. A manager has to 'do the right things' (strategy) and 'to do things right' (tactics) to be effective.

1.9 In order to **do the right things**, managers need to examine the organisation's current position, to understand how it got there, and to decide where they would **like** the organisation's future position to be.

Strategies and tactics

1.10 In deciding where the organisation can be in the future, rather than where they would like the organisation to be, managers have to assess the **feasibility** of the desired state of affairs, which in turn means examining options for achieving it and constraints on reaching it.

1.11 There will be many **options** or ways of getting to where the organisation wants to be, each of which will entail barriers and costs. **Comparing these options** and deciding which is best is clearly a key management role.

1.12 Having decided on the right things, managers have to '**do things right**' and this involves technical planning, implementation and control.

1.13 All plans drawn up by managers can be said to follow a broadly similar process.

Where are we now?	AUDITING
	↓
Where do we want to be?	DECIDING OBJECTIVES
	↓
Which way is best?	DECIDING STRATEGY
	↓
How do we get there?	DECIDING TACTICS
	↓
Getting there!	IMPLEMENTING
	↓
Ensuring arrival	CONTROLLING

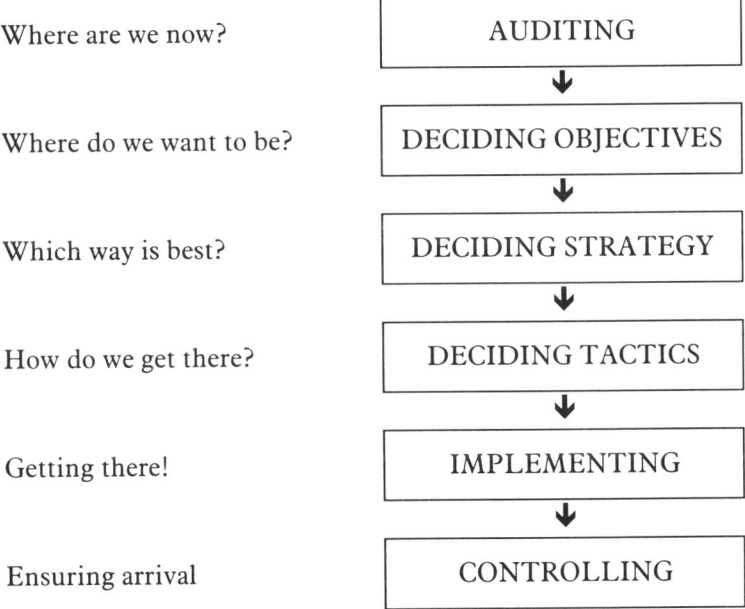

1.14 Marketing management can therefore be seen to have a great deal in common with other functional management.

1.15 Students often find it difficult to relate marketing objectives clearly to corporate objectives and even more difficult to distinguish clearly marketing objectives from corporate objectives. The latter is hardly surprising since corporate objectives are really marketing objectives. **There can be no corporate plan which does not involve products/services and customers.** The following diagram from Kotler clearly expresses the interactive two-way relationship between marketing plans and strategic business planning.

Relationships between marketing and corporate planning

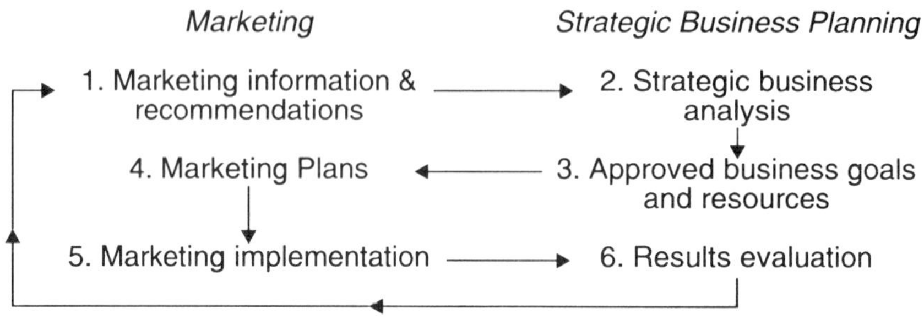

1.16 A good way to achieve greater understanding of marketing in a corporate setting is to recognise that there is no real separation. **Corporate management** does not exist on its own. The only corporate manager is the Managing Director or Chief Executive and even then he or she will have come from a functional background.

1.17 The word corporate is derived from corpus, meaning the body. The body corporate is the body **whole.** The body consists of parts - the trunk, arms, legs, head etc. It does not exist on its own, it is the sum of the parts.

1.18 **Corporate objectives can be said to be largely concerned with achieving growth (ie in size, in the number of activities, in profitability) consistent with limiting risk.** The **stakeholders** in an organisation (ie all those, not only shareholders, who have an interest in what the organisation does) would not normally support high growth objectives which demanded the taking of very high risks. The prospect of an immediate growth of 300 times in the liquid capital of an organisation might sound attractive, but not if it was based on betting the organisation's liquid capital on a 300 to 1 outsider in the Grand National.

1.19 **The pursuit of growth takes many forms** - growth in number of employees, outlets, customers, profit, profitability etc. In a way growth itself, if achieved in a steady way, reduces risk. Not to grow and certainly to decline is seen within the organisation as a threat to an organisation's survival. Normally some profit (surplus of income over expenditure) is needed just to stand still, since assets can depreciate more than planned, employees will hope to improve their earnings and investors will want to see a return on their capital.

1.20 **Corporate management** in seeking to grow profitably and reduce risk will **deploy the functional activities of the business to these ends**. For example **marketing activities** can be deployed to increase (profitable) sales, the production function to reduce unit costs, the finance function to secure funding at lower rates and human resources to employ less people or recruit more productive/effective people. All these measures could help to increase profit and reduce risk. In this scenario, therefore, the functions are deployed **strategically** to meet corporate **objectives** since the functions are means to achieve the corporate ends.

1.21 Once you understand this, we can move on to see that, for a **marketing director growth in profitable sales becomes the marketing objective.** It derives from, and is consistent with but not separate from, the corporate objectives.

1.22 The **marketing strategy is the way in which the marketing function organises its activities to achieve a profitable growth in sales.** It could for example seek to do this by introducing new products/services (Ansoff's growth strategy of product development) or by seeking new customers (Ansoff's marketing development). At a marketing mix level, sales might be increased profitably by increasing/decreasing prices, by expanding the sales force, investing more money in advertising etc.

1.23 It is important to recognise that both **strategy and tactics are means to ends, in other words, ways of achieving objectives.** The difference between strategy and tactics is simply one of detail and depends on the level from which you are looking. To a marketing director, the cleanliness of a room will be a mere detail. To the office cleaner it will however be an objective and entail a plan. The cleaner will:

Step 1. Audit (take stock, decide what state of cleanliness the room is currently in)
Step 2 Decide objectives (what state the room needs to be in by a given time)
Step 3 Decide broad strategies (vacuuming, tidying, dusting)
Step 4 Decide tactics (where to start, what to use)
Step 5 Schedule the order of actions

1.24 Once you realise that the **difference between strategy and tactics is a movable line** you should feel a great deal more comfortable when drawing up your marketing plans for the case study. You do not really need to be precise in your categorisation. The word 'tactics' does not really need to be employed at all. You could move from objectives to strategies (using the Ansoff growth matrix) to the marketing mix. In drawing up your plans for the marketing mix you should move from the general to the particular. For example a marketing communications manager will decide the balance between **pull and push** strategies, before getting down to the detail of which particular exhibitions to show the firm's wares in.

1.25 It is very important to get your thinking clear about this, otherwise your marketing plan and its relationship to the corporate plan will appear confused and your proposals will lose their credibility. To help you further in your thinking please examine and reflect upon the following table.

Eight ways to distinguish between Strategic and Tactical Decisions

1. **Importance:** Strategic decisions are significantly more important.
2. **Level at which conducted:** Strategic decisions usually taken by top management.
3. **Time Horizon:** Strategics = long term. Tactics = short term
4. **Regularity:** Strategy formulation is continuous whereas tactics are periodic.
5. **Nature of problem:** Strategic problems are unstructured and often unique, involving considerable risk and uncertainty. Tactical problems are more structured and repetitive with risks easier to assess.
6. **Information Needed:** Strategies require large amounts of external information much of which is subjective and futuristic. Tactics depend much more on internally generated accounting or marketing research information.
7. **Detail:** Strategy is broad. Tactics are narrow and specific.
8. **Ease of Evaluation:** Strategic decisions are more difficult to make and evaluate.

Source: adapted from 'Strategic Marketing' Weitz and Wensley (ex George Steiner and John Miner)

1.26 You should now have a clearer understanding of how the marketing planning process relates to the corporate planning process. It is therefore appropriate here to return to the other aspect of marketing management namely 'getting things done through people' (as mentioned in Paragraph 1.7).

Human resources issues

1.27 Writers such as Nigel Piercy have rightly pointed out that the marketing manager's plans are often frustrated by other people in the organisation. These 'blockers' can be people in the marketing department but are more likely to be people in other departments. The less an organisation is truly marketing orientated, the more likely it is that marketing plans are ineffective.

1.28 **In the case study it is vital to look at your role and your relationships with other people in the organisation.** You cannot do everything yourself and therefore have to rely on 'getting things done through other people'. Sometimes you may be cast in the role of a consultant, when you can only advise. Sometimes you will have only a **staff authority** (ie the authority to advise but not to direct) and need to **persuade.** At other times you may have **line responsibility** and be in a position to **command**.

1.29 Whatever your role in the case study, you will need to recognise the importance of **internal marketing** and **relationship marketing** in getting things done. You might also have to recommend ways of improving the marketing orientation of the organisation in the case. You will find some useful additional notes on these items in the final chapter of this book headed 'Significant Current Issues'.

Information

1.30 This introduction to Marketing Planning and Control would not be complete without some mention of information inputs for decision outputs. Marketing makes a particularly important input to the corporate planning decisions in the following ways.

(a) The **environmental audit** reviews the organisation's position in relation to changes in the external environment (sociological, legal, economic, political and technological) and provides information which directly affects the setting of corporate objectives.

(b) The **competitor audit** provides competitor intelligence, competitor response models and so on which again influence corporate objectives, strategy and contingency planning.

(c) The **customer audit** assesses the existing and potential customer bases to provide information as to whether to develop new markets.

(d) **Product portfolio analysis** provides input for decisions as to whether to drop particular products and/or add new ones.

(e) The **sales forecast** provides the basis for all other functional activities as well as marketing.

1.31 We have already seen how the corporate plan breaks down into the marketing plan and the other functional plans. Information inputs to the **corporate** planning decisions as suggested above perform a double duty in that they also provide the bases for deciding marketing objectives and strategies.

1.32 However marketing research is vital to **all stages** of the marketing plan. We need information in order to make sensible decisions on the marketing mix, for example product research, pricing research and advertising research. We also need information in order to implement and control the marketing plan and to assess the extent to which marketing objectives have been achieved.

1.33 **Marketing research** and an effective **marketing information system (MkIS)** are therefore essential components of the marketing planning process. You will find the outline of a marketing research plan in Chapter 7 (the methods recommended by the CIM senior examiner).

1.34 Further outline notes on marketing research and MkIS are given in Section 6 of this chapter.

1.35 Before moving on to the next section of this chapter it is felt appropriate to present a **concise** framework for the marketing plan which is our ultimate aim in the case study. Like all concise frameworks it suffers from omissions but many of our students have welcomed the following single page approach as a means of achieving an overview. You will find it on the next page.

2 STRATEGIC AND MARKETING ANALYSIS (WHERE ARE WE NOW?)

2.1 This is of course an area very relevant to the case study **analysis** and decision.

2.2 The actual case study on which you will be examined is unpredictable and the nature of the case study will change over time. It is thus in your best interests to **revise the marketing audit thoroughly.**

The marketing audit

2.3 **The marketing audit** is a thorough examination of all the external and internal factors affecting the marketing planning and control process. A useful way of portraying these factors is by reference to the various environments which surround the **customer**, the customer being the focus of our marketing plan.

2.4 The **external variables** are often referred to as the **uncontrollable variables** as opposed to the more controllable variables represented by the internal factors. It is in the external environment that opportunities and threats can be found which help to forge long-term strategy whereas the marketing mix decisions are internal, of a shorter term and are more tactical in nature.

2.5 Although the external variables are said to be uncontrollable, they can and must be anticipated and modelled. Having done this marketing planners can find ways to exploit opportunities and avoid threats. In this way the external variables become more controllable.

2.6 The more **comprehensive** the marketing audit, the clearer is the picture that emerges of the current situation and the better placed the company is to set **realistic** objectives for future achievement.

2.7 **Ideally speaking the marketing audit should examine every item exhaustively.** For example, an audit of advertising effectiveness should not only cover the detail of media, timing, copy platform, size, advertising research data, but also **changes** made over the past years and a similar examination of each **competitor's** advertising in the same period. Only in this way can a really thorough understanding be achieved the pay-off for which will be gained in better advertising plan decisions.

A CONCISE FRAMEWORK FOR A MARKETING PLAN

1. *ANALYSIS OF CURRENT SITUATION* (Using Marketing Research)

1.1 THE MARKET

	98	99	00	01	02	03	04	05	06	07	08
Mkt size (units)											
Mkt share (units)											
Mkt size (cash)											
Mkt share (cash)											

Mkt trends/forecasts
Company strengths/weaknesses and key features of marketing mixes
Brand strengths/weaknesses and key features of marketing mixes
Competitor strengths/weaknesses and key features of marketing mixes
Customer profiles, buying behaviours, needs
Company sales forecasts

1.2 DISTRIBUTION

Available channels
Sales by outlet
Competitors' distribution methods

1.3 ENVIRONMENTAL FACTORS

2. *BUSINESS MISSION/OBJECTIVES*

What business are we in?
What business would we like to be in 5-10 years hence?
Corporate objectives - profitability, growth, risk reduction.
Marketing objectives - market share, sales.

3. *STRATEGIES* - ANSOFF

	Existing Products	New Products
Existing Markets	Market Penetration	Product Development
New Markets	Market Development	Diversification

SEGMENTATION

- Bases
- Characteristics and measurement
- Strategy

4. *TACTICS/OPERATION PLAN* - MKG MIX PROPOSALS

4.1 PRODUCT DECISIONS

- Objectives
- Branding
- Packaging
- Pre/After sales service

4.2 PRICING DECISIONS

- Objectives
- Strategy - penetration v. skimming
- Discounts

4.3 DISTRIBUTION DECISIONS

- Objectives
- Channels
- Intensive/selective/exclusive distribution

4.4 PROMOTION DECISIONS

- Objectives - roles
- Salesforce size/organisation/motivation
- Sales promotion/PR, merchandising
- Advertising expenditure
- Media - target audiences
- Copy/creative platforms
- Agencies

5. *BUDGETS*

Sales forecasts, Sales budgets
Periods - 1-5 years
Costs - selling, marketing, advertising etc

Different environments impacting upon the satisfaction of customer needs (adapted from Buttle)

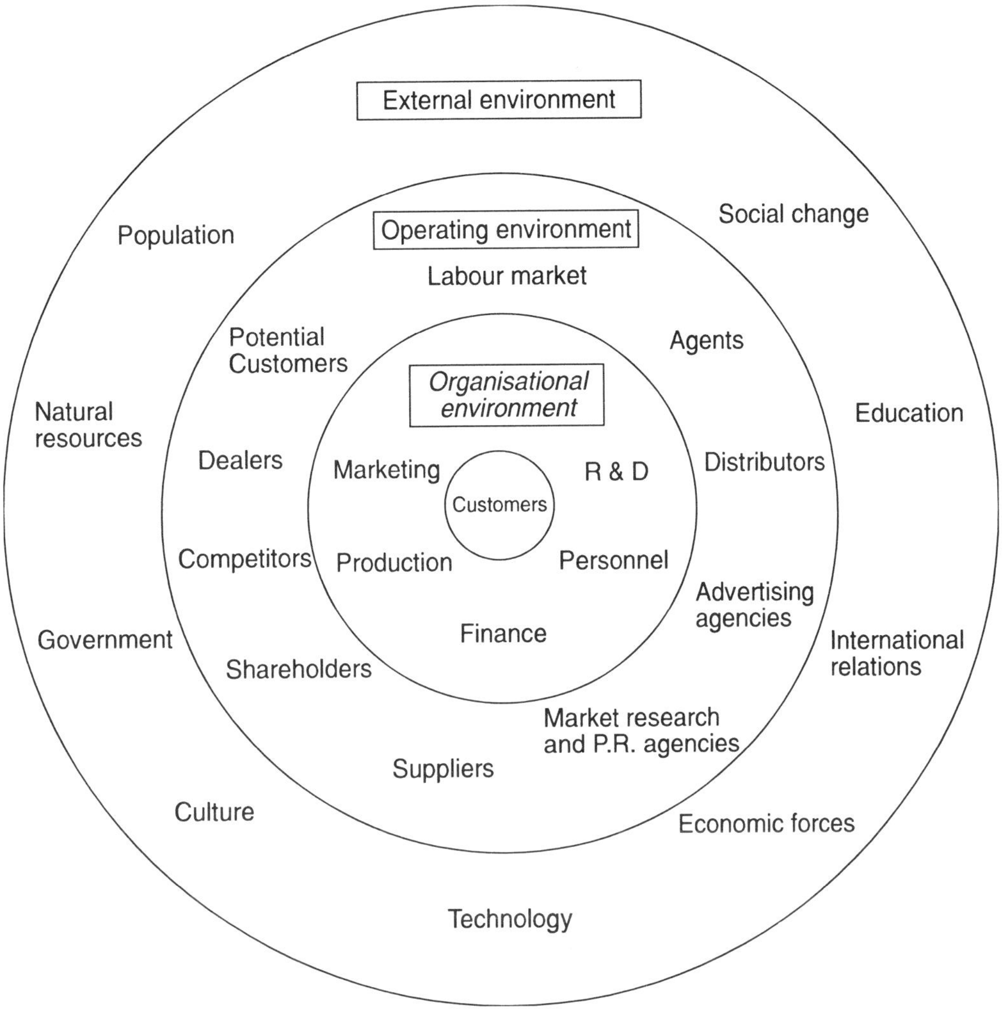

Internal checklist

2.8 (a) **Current position**

(i) **Performance**

(1) Total sales in value and in units
(2) Total gross profit, expenses and net profit
(3) Percentage of sales for sales expenses, advertising etc
(4) Percentage of sales in each segment
(5) Value and volume sales by area, month, model size etc
(6) Sales per thousand consumers, per factory, in segments
(7) Market share in total market and in segments

(ii) **Customers**

(1) Number of actual and potential buyers by area

(2) Characteristics of consumer buyers, eg income, occupation, education, sex, size of family etc

(3) Characteristics of industrial buyers, eg primary, secondary, tertiary, manufacturing; type of industry; size etc

(4) Characteristics of users, if different from buyers

(5) Location of buyers, users

(6) When purchases made: time of day, week, month, year; frequency of purchase; size of average purchase or typical purchase

(7) How purchases are made: specification or competition; by sample, inspection, impulse, rotation, system; cash or credit

(8) Attitudes, motivation to purchase; influences on buying decision; decision making unit in organisation

(9) Product uses - primary and secondary

(b) **Products**

(i) **Firm's current product information**

(1) Quality: materials, workmanship, design, method of manufacture, manufacturing cycle, inputs-outputs

(2) Technical characteristics, attributes that may be considered as selling points, buying points

(3) Models, sizes, styles, ranges, colours etc

(4) Essential or non-essential, convenience or speciality

(5) Similarities with other company products

(6) Relation of product features to user's needs, wants, desires

(7) Development of branding and brand image

(8) Degree of product differentiation, actual and possible

(9) Packaging used, functional, promotional

(10) Materials, sizes, shapes, construction, closure

(ii) **Competitors**

(1) Competitive and competing products

(2) Main competitors and leading brands

(3) Comparison of design and performance differences with leading competitors

(4) Comparison of offering of competitors, images, value etc

(iii) **Future product development**

(1) Likely future product developments in company
(2) Likely future, or possible future, developments in industry
(3) Further product line or mix contraction, modification or expansion

(c) **Distribution**

(i) **Current distribution position**

(1) Current company distribution structure

(2) Channels and methods used in channels

(3) Total number of outlets (consumer or industrial) by type

(4) Total number of wholesalers or industrial middlemen, broken down into areas and by types

(5) Percentage of outlets of each type handling product broken down into areas

(6) Attitudes of outlets by area, type, size

(7) Degree of cooperation, current and possible

(8) Multi-brand policy, possible or current

(9) Strengths and weaknesses in distribution system, functionally and geographically

(10) Number and type of warehouses; location

(11) Transportation and communications

(12) Stock control; delivery periods; control of information

(ii) **Competitors**

(1) Competitive distribution structure; strengths and weaknesses
(2) Market coverage and penetration
(3) Transportation methods used by competitors
(4) Delivery of competitors
(5) Specific competitive selling conditions

(iii) **Future developments**

(1) Further likely and possible developments in industry as a whole or from one or more competitors

(2) Probable changes in distribution system of company

(3) Possibilities of any future fundamental changes in outlets

(d) **Promotional and personal selling**

(i) **Firm's position**

(1) Size and composition of sales force

(2) Calls per day, week, month, year by salesperson

(3) Conversion rate of orders to calls

(4) Selling cost per value and volume of sales achieved

(5) Selling cost per customer

(6) Internal and external sales promotion

(7) Recruiting, selection, training, control procedures

(8) Methods of motivation of salesmen

(9) Remuneration schemes

(10) Advertising appropriation and media schedule, copy theme

(11) Cost of trade, technical, professional, consumer media

(12) Cost of advertising per unit, per value of unit, per customer

(13) Advertising expenditure per thousand readers, viewers of main and all media used

(14) Methods and costs of merchandising

(15) Public and press relations; exhibitions

(ii) **Competitors**

(1) Competitive selling activities and methods of selling and advertising; strengths and weaknesses

(2) Review of competitors' promotion, sales contests, etc

(3) Competitor's advertising themes, media used

(iii) **Future developments** likely in selling, promotional and advertising activities

(e) **Pricing**

(i) **Firms' current pricing**

(1) Pricing strategy and general methods of price structuring in company

(2) High or low policies, reasons why

(3) Prevailing pricing policies in industry

(4) Current wholesaler, retailer margins in consumer markets or middlemen margins in industrial markets

(5) Discounts, functional, quantity, cash, reward, incentive

(6) Pricing objectives, profit objectives, financial implications such as breakeven figures, cash budgeting

(ii) **Competitors**

(1) Prices and price structures of competitors
(2) Value analysis of own and competitors' products
(3) Discounts, credit offered by competitors

(iii) **Future developments**

(1) Future developments in costs likely to affect price structures

(2) Possibilities of more/less costly raw materials or labour that would affect prices

(3) Possible competitive price attacks

(f) **Service**

(i) **Firm's current service**

(1) Extent of pre-sales or customer service and after-sales or product service required by products

(2) Survey of customer needs

(3) Installation, education in use, inspection, maintenance, repair, accessories provision

(4) Guarantees, warranty period

(5) Methods, procedures for carrying out service

(6) Returned goods, complaints

(ii) **Competitors**

(1) Services supplied by competitive manufacturers and service organisations

(2) Types of guarantee, warranty, credit provided

(iii) **Future possible developments** that might require a revised service policy

(g) Organisational points (eg design of marketing organisation, sales, production or marketing orientation)

External checklist

2.9 (a) **Environmental audit: national and international**

(i) Social and cultural factors likely to impact upon the market, in the short and long term

(ii) Legal factors and codes of practice likely to affect the market in the short and long term

(iii) Economic factors likely to affect market demand in the short and long term

(iv) Political changes and military action likely to impact upon national and international markets

(v) Technological changes anticipated and likely to create new opportunities and threats

(b) **Marketing objectives and strategies**

(i) Short term plans and objectives for current year, in light of current political and economic situation

(ii) Construction of standards for measurement of progress towards achieving of objectives; management ratios that can be translated into control procedures

(iii) Breakdown of turnover into periods, areas, segments, outlets, salesmen etc

(iv) Which personnel required to undertaken what responsibilities, actions etc when

(v) Review of competitors' strengths and weaknesses, likely competitive reactions and possible company responses that could be made

(vi) Long term plans, objectives and strategies related to products, price, places of distribution, promotion, personnel selling and service

2.10 We are now in a position to revise the various specific tools, frameworks and techniques relevant to particular sections of the checklist above.

The environmental audit

2.11 Nearly all the case studies are positioned in an environmental situation of considerable change which represents both an opportunity and a threat. Here are some examples.

(a) For *FirstrATE Europe* (June 1995), the setting was an industrial one and the main environmental threat/opportunity was technological change.

(b) In *Leffe* (December 1995) there were sociological and legal overtones.

(c) In the case of *Gravesend Town Centre* (June 1996) which was set in the public sector, almost the full raft of environmental issues applied.

(d) In *Mistral (December 1996)*, demographic factors and changes in public sector procurement policies had an impact.

(e) In *Sentinel Aviation* (June 1997), the firm was competing in a global market and had to be alert to technological change.

(f) In *The Philharmonic* (December 1997), an orchestra faced social change and its effect on the demand for classical music.

(g) Technological change and its effect on competition was also covered in *De La Rue Fortronic* (June 1998) and in *Philips* (December 1998).

(h) Social attitudes towards genetically modified foods were a factor in *Biocatalysts* (June 1999).

(i) Competition and technological change featured heavily in *Acclaim Entertainment Inc* (December 1999).

2.12 All these changes posed threats but also offered opportunities, the analysis of which greatly affected the choice and viability of marketing strategies.

2.13 In both deciding 'where we are now' and indeed 'where we want to be in the future' the environmental audit is therefore instrumental. The analytical framework commonly used for the environmental audit is given by the PEST acronym (political, economic, social, technological) but SLEPT as given below is perhaps more searching.

S = Socio-cultural
L = Legal
E = Economic
P = Political
T = Technological

2.14 Sometimes it is difficult to say whether a factor such as privatisation is political or legal. It is in fact politically led but legally (by Act of Parliament) implemented. However, **the exact category an item falls under is less important than identifying it in the first place so do not waste time splitting hairs**. Analytical tools and techniques do in any case need to be adapted where necessary rather than dismissed as unsuitable because of a little difficulty in applying them.

2.15 A review of recent **major** changes under the above framework, which are likely to affect marketing strategies in case studies is given below.

(a) **Socio-cultural trends**

(i) People in the UK are increasingly cohabiting before marriage or in place of marriage.

(ii) People in the UK are tending to have babies at a later age.

(iii) The UK population is living longer and ageing in profile.

(iv) Unemployment is relatively low in the UK, but higher in Europe. Also, there is now greater mobility of labour throughout the EU.

(v) More people are seeking higher education.

(vi) Ethnicity is changing in the UK and throughout Europe.

(vii) There is an increasing awareness of consumer rights.

(viii) The importance of corporate culture is reflected in mission statements, TQM, internal marketing and relationship marketing.

(b) **Legal factors**

(i) Trade Descriptions Act
(ii) Consumer Credit Act
(iii) Product liability legislation

(iv) Sale of Goods Act
(v) Law of Contract
(vi) Law of Agency
(vii) Data Protection Act (eg limits use of customer databases)
(viii) Changes in the presentation of company accounts
(ix) Restrictions on parking (for sales people, distributors etc).

To legal changes must be added an increasing proliferation of **EU regulations** and the non-legal but closely allied **Codes of Practice** (eg Banking Code of Practice) which constrain marketing decisions.

(c) **Economic factors**

(i) The UK appears to have avoided recession. Growth is picking up in Western Europe and remains strong in the USA ... but a 'crash' is awaited, given over valued stock markets.

(ii) The economies of south-east Asia and Japan have suffered recession since late 1997, but recovery is evident. Firms suffer liquidity problems. Russia's economy is still in difficulties.

(iii) The UK has been part of the single European market for some time. This has culminated in the **single European currency**. The UK has not joined yet.

(1) At time of writing sterling is at a high level in relation to the Euro, more than is justified by the economic fundamentals.

(2) If the UK does eventually join EMU, what will be the impact on marketing programmes, particularly pricing? There will be price transparency, but less volatility in the exchange rate.

(d) **Political factors**

(i) Centre-left governments in Europe
(ii) A lack of strong political leadership in the USA
(iii) A decrease in the relative power of trade unions
(iv) Increased opportunities for political lobbying
(v) The use of sanctions against 'offending' countries (eg in trade policy)
(vi) Political instability in the Balkans, Africa and Russia
(vii) New entrants (from eastern Europe) and constitutional change in the EU

(e) Technological factors

(i) The Internet and e-commerce: b2b (business-too-business) or b2c (business-to-consumer). Who will succeed: new start-ups (that use up cash) or old-established brands with physical assets too. Some argue that the greatest change will be in b2b markets (not b2c) markets.

(ii) Biotechnology: public opposition to genetically modified foods adds tension to the debate, although scientists will plough ahead.

(iii) Digital television: this could herald the fragmentation of channels traditionally used to reach a mass market.

(iv) New materials.

(v) New production processes.

2.16 Some examples of the impact of environmental forces on marketing mix decisions are given in the box below. We have selected two examples, legal and economic factors. To get you thinking about these issues yourself, you might like to do a similar task for socio-cultural, political and technological factors.

Factor	*Mix element*	
LEGAL	PRICE	Laws against agreements which lessen competition. change advertising descriptions, illustrations, ban slush funds etc.
	PROMOTION	Laws on labelling, packaging, publicity, sales promotion, lotteries, selling door to door etc.
	PRODUCT	Laws on safety, function, 'fitness for use'
	DISTRIBUTION	Laws on monopoly, foreign markets, restricted sales (eg drugs through certain outlets) opening days/times, parking etc.
ECONOMIC	PRICE	Intensity of competition, credit restrictions, consumers' willingness to spend.
	PROMOTION	Features emphasised eg cost savings.
	PRODUCT	Recession increases competition and pressure to reduce costs, and add features
	DISTRIBUTION	In recession there is more direct marketing and foreign markets are sought after.

SWOT analysis

2.17 **SWOT analysis** is one of the most useful tools in deciding 'where are we now?' in terms of Strengths, Weaknesses, Opportunities and Threats. Strengths and weaknesses are those of the organisation (ie internal and are controllable). Opportunities and Threats emanate from outside the organisation (ie external variables).

(a) Organisations should of course **exploit opportunities** for which their **strengths are** particularly **suitable, correct weaknesses** and **avoid threats.**

(b) In many ways, therefore, the organisation's **strengths and weaknesses are a blueprint for the short-term operational or tactical plan** whilst **opportunities and threats influence the nature of longer-term strategic planning.**

(c) It does however need to be emphasised that the SWOT analysis is a **subjective** technique. Whether an item is categorised as a strength or a weakness depends both upon the circumstances and the analyst's point of view. Taking a consensus of the organisation's staff (or a case study syndicate) helps to remove some of the subjectivity and clarify the individual's thinking.

(d) In the case study *Leffe* one of the key issues was that of gaining critical mass for the brand in the UK market. How best to achieve this entailed a choice from a number of evaluated options. An opportunity existed to achieve market growth in the premium lager market but others might have seen Leffe as better positioned outside this already fragmented and highly competitive market. Weaknesses existed in the poor penetration of the brand and the lack of promotional funds.

(e) A format for the SWOT analysis is given in Chapter 8 (the examiner's recommended methods of analysing the CIM case study).

(f) When analysing strengths, weaknesses, opportunities and threats, a greater degree of sophistication may be achieved by scoring each item as being **major, medium** or **minor** and then whether that item is of **high, medium** or **low importance**.

A **major strength** can be of relatively **low importance** in terms of the opportunities and threats facing the firm. A strength of high importance needs to be capitalised upon and play a key part in strategy formulation. For example, a major strength in the domestic market may be unimportant if there is a strategic imperative to expand into overseas markets.

2.18 **SWOT and issues analysis.** The findings of the SWOT analysis help to define the basic issues underlining the case study situation. In the case of **Leffe** (December 1995) some of these were as follows.

(a) Should all promotional expenditure continue to be below-the-line?
(b) How should Leffe be positioned in its chosen markets?
(c) What should be the best distribution outlets for this brand.

We cite Leffe so as not to give you any clues for the real case studies following.

2.19 *Ratio analysis*

(a) Ratio analysis can play a major role both in deciding where the company is now and in quantitatively defining where the company would ideally like to be in the future. This analysis can also be applied to competitors.

(b) Most case studies contain Profit and Loss Accounts and Balance Sheets which lend themselves to this form of analysis. Other case studies might actually present some ratios to you. To help you to familiarise yourself with this form of analysis, a section giving more detail has been included in Chapter 4.

2.20 **Productivity analysis** is a type of ratio analysis given here by way of example.

(a) Probably the simplest way of defining the productivity of marketing is:

$$\frac{\text{Marketing outputs}}{\text{Marketing inputs}}$$

(b) This can then be applied to individual marketing activities, eg:

(i) $$\frac{\text{Increase in numbers aware of products}}{\text{Cost of advertising}}$$

(ii) $$\frac{\text{Units shipped through distribution channel X}}{\text{Cost of distribution channel X}}$$

(iii) $$\frac{\text{Number of redemptions}}{\text{Cost of sales promotion}}$$

(c) As can be seen, productivity analysis and ratio analysis are closely related. However, care needs to be taken between efficiency and effectiveness. For example, sales **efficiency** might be increased in terms of numbers of orders taken by the sales force but if they are very small orders or mainly orders for a product with a relatively low contribution then **effectiveness** in terms of profitability may be reduced.

(d) The case study data will often encourage you to seek to improve the organisation's effectiveness in terms of sales.

3 STRATEGIC DIRECTION AND STRATEGY FORMULATION (WHERE DO WE WANT TO BE?)

Auditing the present and forecasting the future

3.1 It is only **when we have a clear picture of where we are now** (and how we've come to arrive here) that **we can decide** realistically where **we want to be in the future.** This relationship between auditing and forecasting can be seen in the following figure.

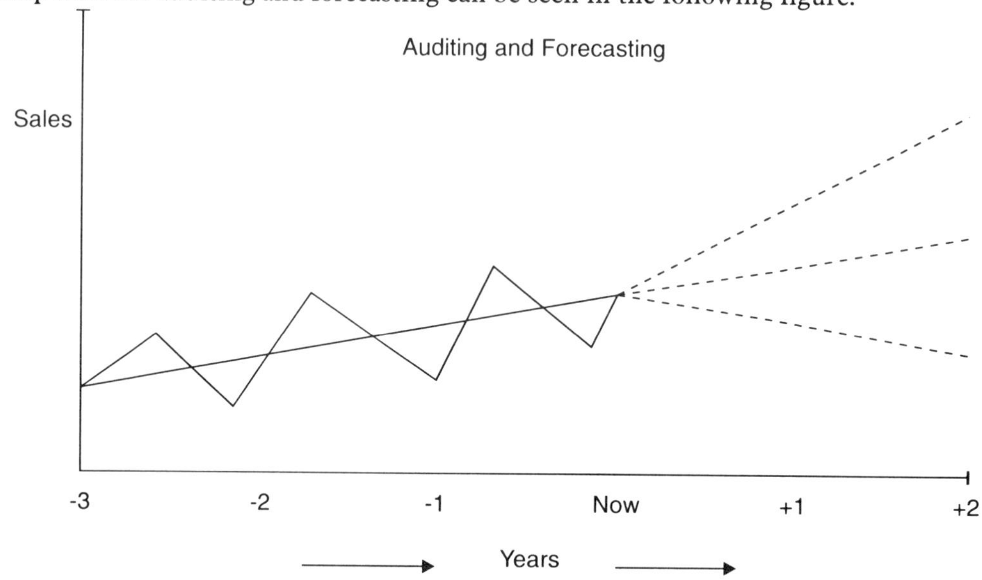

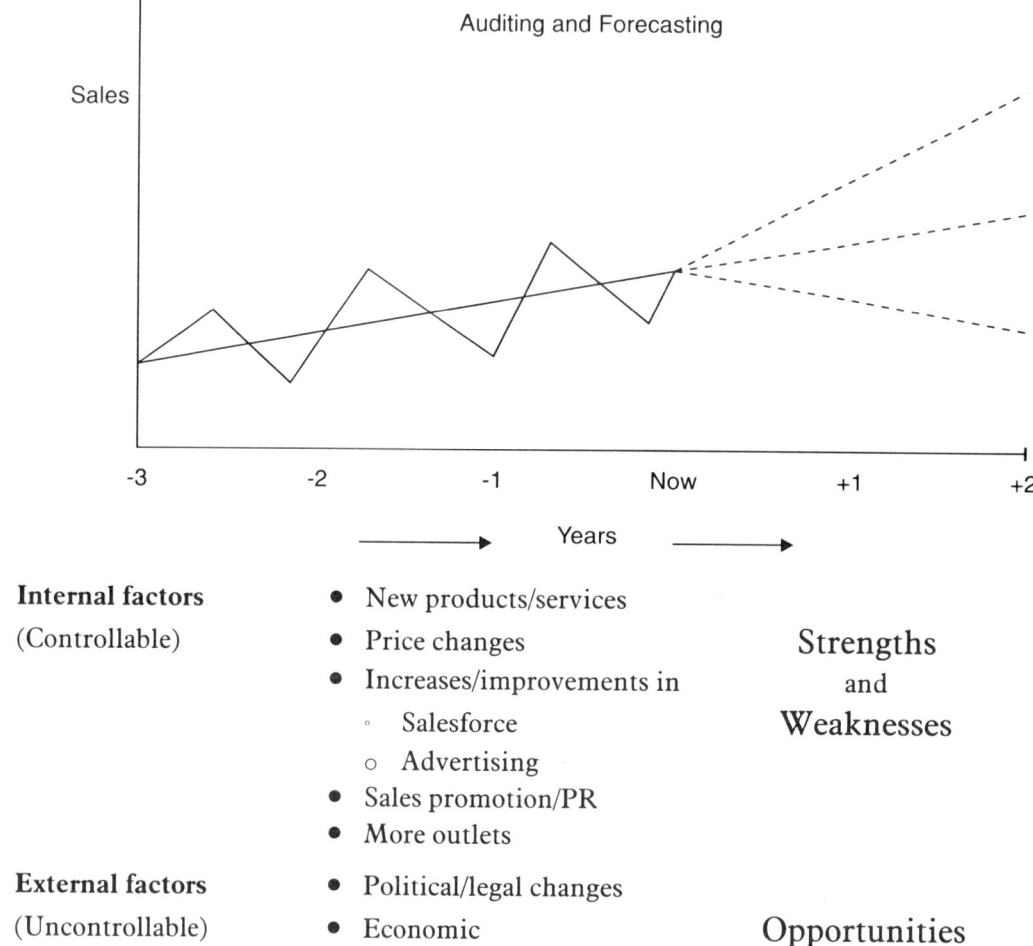

(a) **Internal factors** (Controllable)	• New products/services
	• Price changes
	• Increases/improvements in
	  ◦ Salesforce
	  ○ Advertising
	• Sales promotion/PR
	• More outlets
		Strengths and Weaknesses

(b) **External factors** (Uncontrollable)	• Political/legal changes • Economic • Sociological • Technological • Competition	Opportunities and Threats

3.2 Referring to the above figure we can see how sales can be plotted for previous years and use statistical techniques or simply 'the line of best fit' to establish the base trend. This straight line trend can then be extended or extrapolated to indicate where (all things being equal) we are likely to be in the period which lies ahead.

3.3 However, all things are not equal. Some people might argue that the **more recent** past is a more reliable indicator of the future than the more distant past and so weight the last year accordingly. Furthermore one or **more of the external environmental factors** may be on the **verge of radical change**, for example Europe going into recession or (in the case of *Gravesend Town Centre*) the siting of the Channel Tunnel rail link. Finally your company might be planning to increase the size of the sales force, introduce a major new product, reduce prices or take other actions that will significantly affect future sales.

3.4 Now is perhaps a good time to **revise forecasting**. In your exam case study you are likely to be presented with a **set of accounts** for previous years which will include sales and costs of sales. You can therefore use these to **extrapolate into the future** as indicated above. Your environmental analysis will suggest upward or downward variations on this extrapolation and your marketing plans will do likewise. You can also take actions to reduce or increase the costs of sales and therefore forecast future profit. If for example you were planning to introduce a major new product next year, this could add significantly to costs but not impact significantly on sales until say the year after.

Sales forecasting

3.5 **Sales forecasting can be defined as an estimate of the anticipated volume of sales which the business expects to make over a given period of time.** Its purpose is to reduce to a minimum the risks and uncertainties involved in making decisions affecting the future. The sales forecast is central to decisions on all aspects of business.

- Production schedules
- Human resources
- Purchasing requirements
- Financial requirements
- Price determination
- R & D priorities
- Promotional effort

3.6 **Considerations for sales forecasting**

(a) The international situation (and its likely effects on both exports and government policy at home)

(b) The national situation (expanding or stagnant).

(c) The industrial situation (which may show contrary trends to the above, eg electronics likely to expand even in a stagnant economy).

(d) The company situation (better or worse than competitors).

(e) The product situation (growing and declining products).

(f) The internal situation (current orders, stock levels production capacity).

3.7 **The time period for the forecast**

(a) **Short-term** is the most common, usually one year or less depending on purchasing patterns for the production capacity to current order and stock levels.

(b) **Medium-term** is from one to three years ahead. This will guide decisions on budgets, salesmen's quotas etc, and will require information on market trends.

(c) **Long-term** is up to 10 years ahead. This guides decisions on capital expenditure, research and development programmes, new product development. Information on growth trends, changes in taste, movements in population etc is required.

(d) In addition we can add **long-term objective forecasts:** will we be in business with our present products in ten or twenty years time? This will require information on all major trends - technological, social ethical and economic. It will aid decisions on diversification, capital expenditure etc.

3.8 **Factors influencing the forecast**

(a) Those **outside** the company's control (including SLEPT and competitive factors). Information can come from published data and commissioned field research.

(b) Those **within** the company's control (including, for example, product range, distribution, advertising, selling and pricing). Information will come from internal documentation.

Forecasting techniques: subjective and objective

3.9 **Subjective techniques of forecasting**

(a) **Sales force opinion.** This is a composite company forecast based on individual salesmen's estimates of sales in their respective termination.

(i) **Advantages**

(1) Close acquaintance with customers.

(2) Helps salespeople's morale.

(3) Allows a detailed forecast to be made - by salesperson/customer/product or product group.

(ii) **Disadvantages**

(1) Few salespeople are objective.

(2) They may have a narrow view of life - eg may be unaware of broader economic and technical trends.

(3) The salesperson is paid to sell - not to forecast.

(iii) Its **main use** is in situations where the company has few customers, there is close liaison between customers and the salesperson and orders are large and rare.

(b) **Executive opinion** is a forecast made by obtaining the opinions of those inside the company (Board or senior managers) and also some outsiders (eg banks, brokers etc).

(i) **Advantages**

(1) It is cheap and quick.
(2) A range of views is represented.

(ii) Disadvantages

(1) It is more likely to be based on opinion than fact.
(2) It is only useful for aggregate forecasts.

(c) **Surveys of buyers' intentions**. Forecasting is essentially anticipating what **buyers** will do in a given set of conditions, so why not ask them what they will be buying, how much, when and from whom?

(i) **Advantages**

(1) Information comes straight from the horse's mouth.
(2) Information is detailed.

(ii) **Disadvantages**

(1) You may not always know who your customers are (eg what about new customers?). In a consumer market you cannot contact **all** buyers.

(2) Will your customer tell you what you want to know? Buyers may not be willing or able to provide the correct information eg defence buyers. Buyers may deliberately mislead.

(3) There may be difficulties in discerning who makes the buying decisions.

3.10 **Objective techniques of forecasting** generally involve some form of **statistical analysis.**

(a) **Time series analysis** is a method of forecasting the future on the basis of what is happening now and what happened in the past. Data are analysed in an attempt to discover any pattern that may help to predict future sales.

(i) Extending graphical curves into the future is complicated by short and long term fluctuations in the curve. A number of techniques exist to 'smooth out' these fluctuations.

(ii) Statistical trends show only **what** has happened not **why** it happened. Extrapolating from past sales implies that past situations will be exactly repeated in the future - an unlikely occurrence.

(iii) Historical data is required - but is not available in new firms or for new products.

(iv) Statistical trends have limited value for short term forecasts.

(b) **Correlation analysis** is a measure of relationship between two or more variables, one dependent on the other. For example a cloudy sky is the independent variable, rain is the dependent variable (as without clouds there will be no rain, but you can have clouds without rain).

(i) It is often possible for a firm to isolate an independent variable on which its future sales will depend. For example if national income goes up 1%, then car sales will go up $2^1/_2$%. Thus, forecasts for national income can be used to predict car sales.

(ii) **Problems**

(1) Ensuring that the relationship is real and rational and not merely **coincidental**.

(2) The independent variable itself may be difficult to forecast.

(3) The relationship might change.

Technological forecasting

3.11 For organisations in CIM case studies such as *Sentinel Aviation* or *De La Rue Fortronic*, technological advances can present major opportunities and threats which you need to take into account when developing your future marketing strategy. For example Sentinel faced the threat of systems integrators and De La Rue Fortronic faced the threat of SMART cards. **The ability to predict future technological change may therefore be a critical success factor.** How?

(a) Panels of experts or 'think tanks' can be asked to build future **scenarios** and assign probabilities.

(b) The **Delphi technique** uses individual experts to make initial predictions which are then circulated to other individual experts in the group. Individuals are then asked whether they wish to modify their predictions in light of the other experts' opinions. This process is repeated until modifications become marginal.

(c) **Competitor intelligence** can range from the planting of 'moles' or electronic surveillance devices to simply asking the sales force to keep their ears and eyes open.

(d) Other research activities, such as checking Patents Office registrations, attending exhibitions in developed countries, subscribing to published industry forecasts and enlisting specialist agencies or consultants.

Corporate planning

3.12 **The corporate plan describes a plan for the total future activity including resource allocation of a business, usually for a period of about five years.** More detailed plans are developed to cover annual operations. It might be based on a **long term sales forecast.** We will not go into detail here, but merely say that marketing issues affect the plan, and that marketing activities are determined by it. **Marketing's first concern is to take part in the planning process by contributing an assessment of what the marketing opportunities** are likely to be. Once the corporate objectives have been agreed, the plans for carrying them out will include tasks for the marketing side of the business. These are embraced in the marketing plan. The corporate plan clarifies tasks of the marketing department.

(a) What is our current situation?
(b) Where are we heading if no action is taken?
(c) Objective - where should we be heading?
(d) Strategy is about the broad ways of achieving objectives.

Marketing budgets: the purpose of budgets

3.13 It is likely that you will have to draw up financial data to support your marketing proposals. **The resources available to you are determined by the corporate plan,** but now is perhaps a good time to sharpen up your knowledge of the **budgetary implications of where you want to be at the completion of your marketing plan.** Budgets are compiled for three main reasons.

(a) Assist and express planning

(b) Control expenditure

(c) Calculate the cost of products at standard cost and enable priced catalogues etc to be produced and distributed

3.14 Business forecasting is an important element of budgetary control as it forms the basis of the revenue forecast on which the various expenditure budgets depend. A budget may be regarded as the expression of an objective but having prepared a plan it is equally important to watch **performance**. Differences between actual results and the budget are termed **variances** and may indicate the need for corrective action so as to assure the realisation of the forward plan.

3.15 One of the main dangers in the practical use of budgetary control is to regard the budgets as fixed and immutable. The **budget** is a planned course for the future and that course **must be altered as necessary to deal with developments that may arise on the journey.** The budget idea then combines the features of **forecasting,** of **setting objectives** and of **control** over activities.

3.16 Budgets also aim to secure co-ordination of effort in all the various departments towards the common end. One of the best ways to achieving this is to form a Budget Committee, comprising all the departmental heads responsible for carrying out the various budget activities, under the chairmanship of the Financial Director or the MD. (See Paragraph 3.34 below.)

3.17 **Definitions relevant to marketing**

(a) 'Budgetary control is an exact and rigorous analysis of the past and the probable and desired future experience; with a view to substituting considered intention for opportunism in Management'...*International Management Institute.*

(b) 'A comparison of forecast cost and income objectives, with actual results achieved at sufficiently short intervals to allow remedial action to be taken'...*College of Marketing.*

3.18 **Production, sales and finance functions are often in conflict.**

(a) Often the production function wants a minimum of variety in the goods with long runs, whilst the sales department prefers to cater for every whim of the market with the widest possible range and even with specials produced quickly to individual customers' requirements.

(b) Both sales and production functions may favour large stocks but the finance function might argue for a low stock investment with the maximum return on capital.

3.19 **Budgetary control aims at co-ordinating these conflicting requirements in such a way that the best possible overall result is achieved.** It is fundamentally concerned with the analysis of probable results of alternative courses of action. The result of these considerations is expressed in a budget which can serve in effect as a planned path for the business to follow. If the path is followed the result will be the optimum. Departures from the path are signals for corrective action or a sign of change of circumstances calling for a review of plans. The real value of budgeting in business is not in the figures that go down on paper but in the planning process that they illustrate.

3.20 Budgetary control shorn of its trimmings is a pattern for thinking which removes the unexpected from day to day control of operations and facilitates the process of making decisions in terms of the general good of the business as a whole.

3.21 **Marketing budgets have some unique characteristics.**

(a) Non marketing budgets tend to be a mathematical calculation based on the expected sales volume (eg the purchasing budget). The sales budget contains elements of uncertainty and dynamism.

(b) The conventional **one year period** used as the budget period for other departmental activities and reflected in the annual accounts of the enterprise **is not necessarily applicable to the marketing budgets.** A totally marketing orientated company making use of the brand management principle might need to draw up separate budgets for each product. New products might have budgeted losses for the first three years and their costs will be offset against budgeted profits from **established** products in the annual budget. The marketing budgets for each product could have a variable time base, covering a period from the time of launching through the break-even point and finishing at the anticipated time in the product's life-cycle when the profit return no longer justified production.

3.22 The principal budgets linked with marketing will of course depend on the marketing mix. However, they will be subsumed in the Sales Budget, when this is compared to the other budgets for production, finance, administration, personnel.

Budgets and cost

3.23 **Sales budgets help identify the maximum costs that can be contained within the revenue of the business.** An enterprise can only produce at a given time up to the limit of its existing capacity and it must therefore be able to cover all its cost and make a profit out of the revenue which this output can realise. When output is restricted to a maximum number of units and price is determined by market conditions, the key variable in this situation is the total cost of supplying and selling the product, which must be contained within the **fixed revenue**. The cost structure in this case could be represented by the following diagram

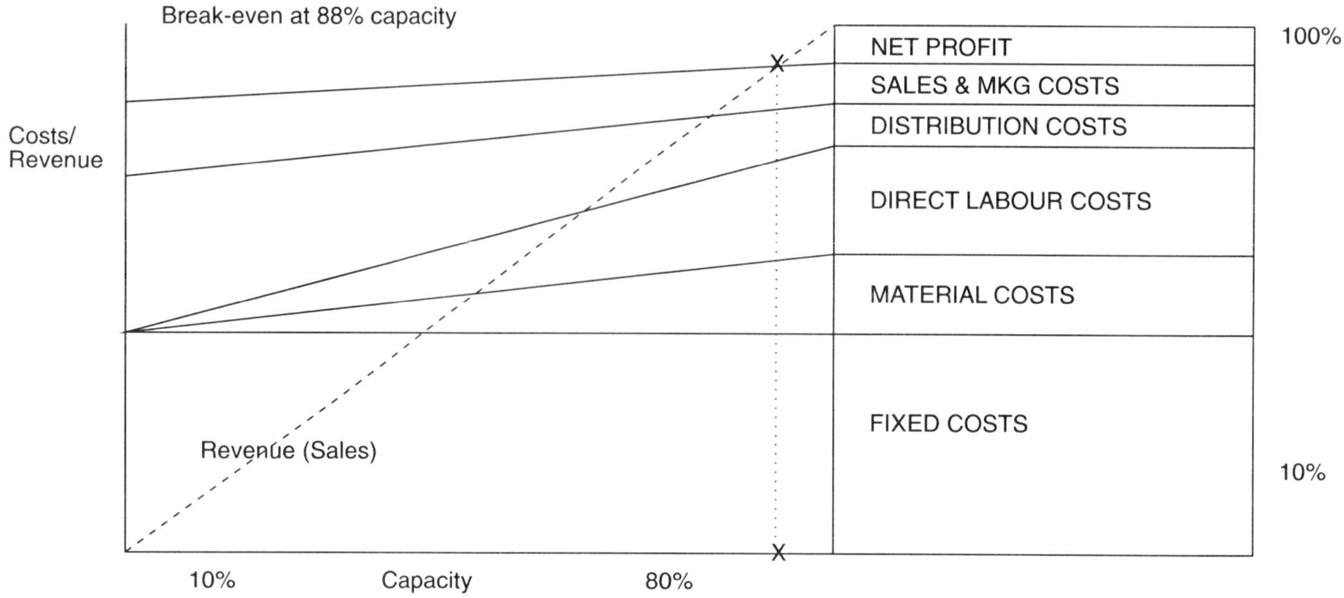

3.24 **Distribution, like selling, helps ensure the realisation of revenue.** The more efficient the distribution of a product, the greater the market which can be profitably reached at a given price. As soon as manufacturers set up their own distribution networks, the budgets for this will be similar to those for production budgets; physical input and output can be estimated with reasonable exactness; a vehicle or depot together with a certain labour complement can be expected to handle a specific quantity of goods, and the financial implications of holding stocks are known.

3.25 After sales service aimed at maximising goodwill must be regarded as a selling cost, even where this is extended through the distribution network. Where customers give top priority to after sales service, the provision of this facility is pre-requisite to credible sales promotion.

3.26 **Analysing marketing costs** is sometimes a matter of judgement.

(a) It is easy to analyse costs on a **functional basis**. For example, the total cost of the advertising department can be easily identified and allocated to the sales and marketing department.

(b) It is also relatively easy to identify some of the **variable costs of selling** (eg sales commission).

(c) **However, it is very hard to do a more sophisticated cost allocation to market segments, product brands, customers etc.** (For example, when a salesman is visiting a town to sell a range of goods, it is extremely hard to estimate accurately the cost of individual calls in that town and the cost of selling particular products.)

3.27 **Cost structure**

(a) **The main difficulty is caused by fixed costs. Fixed costs** do not, in the short run, vary with the volume of production. In a marketing context, fixed costs would be incurred whether you sold one product or one hundred. For example, you may be contracted to pay rent on your warehouse for years ahead. The rent will have to be paid, irrespective of any change in sales level. Fixed costs include warehousing depots, and even advertising, in the short run. (The advertising expenditure is incurred before the products are sold, when those sales are uncertain).

(b) **Variable costs vary with the volume produced**. The amount of dough a baker uses depends precisely on the number of loaves he or she decides to bake. Even so, it is still hard to allocate variable costs sometimes (eg what is the 'cost' of an individual sales call?)

3.28 A useful way of dealing with these problems is of **contribution analysis**. For example in a bakery a different proportion of variable costs to price received might be incurred as seen in the following figure.

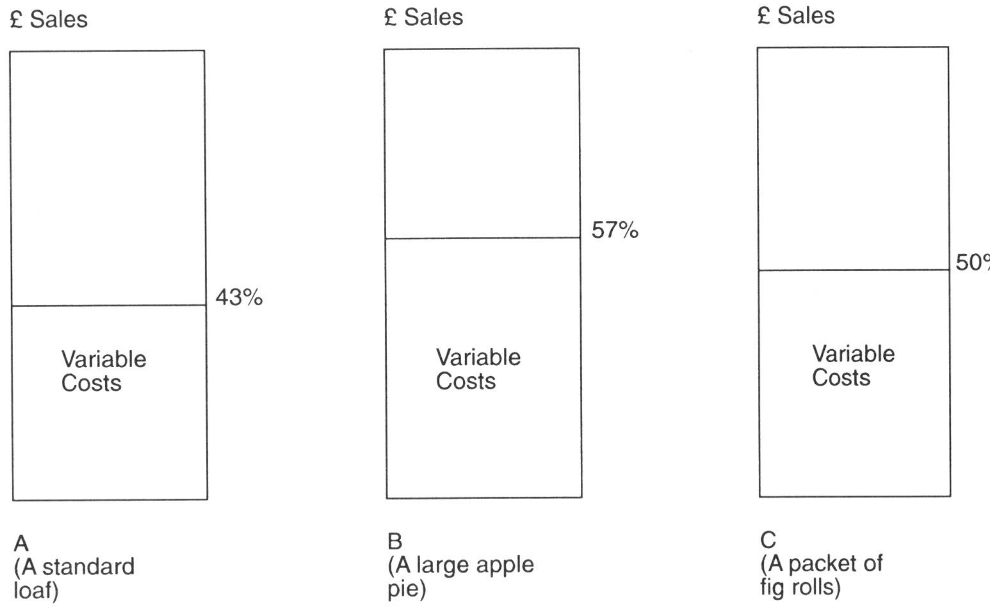

Put another way, Product A makes a contribution of 57% to all other costs and profit. Product B's contribution is 43% and Product C's contribution is 50%.

3.29 The variable costs shown above (those which vary directly and in the short term with the amount of goods produced or sold) are largely those of labour and materials, which can be directly attributed to these products.

Cost ratios

3.30 Ratios can be set between any two sets of functional costs eg advertising to distribution but more importantly they can be set between any functional costs and sales revenue or profit. Any ratio can be selected which is considered likely to improve control of costs (eg advertising to sales, transport to sales, salespeople's expenses to revenues etc).

3.31 **Ratios are means of identifying and controlling trends in inputs and outputs.** Comparisons can be made between:

- The standard ratio and that actually achieved
- One region and another
- One period of time and another
- Various means of promotion and sales
- The ratios for specific segments such as goods, customers, brands etc

3.32 **Ratios are no more sacrosanct than the budget of which they form a part.** The dynamics of marketing make acceptance of changes in the ratios inevitable and a changed ratio will suggest the need for an enquiry into the reasons and into methods of rectifying the situation insofar as possible.

3.33 In order to abandon unprofitable sales, use can be made of the concept of **avoidable and unavoidable costs**. If removal of a product, order or outlet relieves the enterprise of costs in excess of the profits gained from it, then profits will be increased.

(a) The problem is that of identifying those costs which can and cannot be avoided by the elimination of a product, order or outlet. If one product in a range is removed, brand advertising, sales force, depot and transport costs are not likely to be materially affected. If many products are removed then some inroads into these costs will be made.

(b) The expenditure, escapable and inescapable involved in handling products suspected of being unprofitable, may be more profitably used on the rest of the range, on other calls or on new products. The time spent by a representative on an unprofitable call involves not only the loss on the current call but also the loss of **potential** profit on an alternative call (ie **opportunity cost**).

(c) **Nevertheless, a range of products may only be attractive because of its overall content.** To remove products from this range may reduce its attractiveness and thereby diminish profits. (This is especially true where customers are motivated by convenience of purchase and do not want any duplication of buying activity.) Similarly the extra cost of handling apparently unprofitable orders or outlets may be more than offset by economies of scale in manufacturing operations made possible by the total orders.

The budget process

3.34 The principal budgets linked with marketing are of course the sales budget, based on the sales estimate or forecast, the selling expense budgets, the distribution budget and the research and development budget. (They are analysed in detail later on.)

3.35 Determine the **budget period** is the time period to which the budget relates. Except for capital expenditure budgets, the budget period is commonly the accounting year (sub-divided into 12 or 13 control periods).

(a) Sometimes a main budget will be prepared for a twelve months period, with a three month budget in detail.

(b) A **rolling budget** is continually updated and so at defined periods, the budget is changed and the next twelve months is on view. A rolling budget is therefore a 12-month budget prepared several times a year.

(c) Note that certain items do not easily slot into a twelve month time period (see Paragraph 3.22).

3.36 To co-ordinate the budget a **budget committee** is often set up (with the managing director perhaps as chairman). The preparation and administration of budgets is usually its responsibility. The staff work of the budget committee is delegated to a budget officer who is usually an accountant. Every part of the organisation should be represented on the committee, ie there should be a representative from sales, production, marketing etc. The **functions of the budget committee** include:

- Co-ordinating of the preparation of budgets and issue of the budget manual
- Issuing of timetables for the preparation of functional budgets
- Allocation of responsibilities for the preparation of functional budgets

- Provision of information to assist in the preparation of budgets
- Communication of final budgets to the appropriate managers
- Comparison of actual results with budget and the investigation of variances
- Continuous assessment of the budgeting and planning process, in order to improve it
- Issuing of timetables for the preparation of functional budgets
- Allocation of responsibilities for the preparation of functional budgets
- Provision of information to assist in the preparation of budgets
- Communication of final budgets to the appropriate managers
- Comparison of actual results with budget and the investigation of variances

3.37 **The principal budget factor must then be identified.**

(a) The principal budget factor is **usually sales demand**: a company is usually restricted from making and selling more of its products because there would be no sales demand for the increased output at a price which would be acceptable/profitable to the company. The principal budget factor may also be machine capacity, distribution and selling resources, the availability of key raw materials or the availability of cash.

(b) **Once this factor is defined then the rest of the budget can be prepared.** For example, if sales are the principal budget factor then the production manager can only prepare his budget after the sales budget is complete. In other words, the sales department may predict vast quantities of sales, but there may be no production capacity to satisfy them. The volume of activity will thus depend on the production capacity, not demand, in this case.

(c) If production is a limiting factor, then, rather than face unmet demand and the frustration of consumers, the marketing strategy might be adjusted, for example, by raising the price or altering the marketing mix in some other way.

3.38 **The functional budgets are then prepared.**

(a) The production budget, in units produced, is based on the budgets for units sold adjusted for the levels of opening and closing stocks, and manufacturing lead times. From this would be derived budgets for raw materials.

(b) The marketing department, as well as being responsible for determining sales revenue, is also a cost centre. Budgets for selling expenses, advertising and so forth will have to be prepared.

Naturally, the budgets for expenditure will have to be scrutinised.

3.39 A **master budget** is then prepared in which all the functional budgets are integrated.

3.40 An important aspect of budgeting is the balance sheet side. In other words, an estimate is needed of the resources required to fund production, and timing of major items of expenditure or revenue. For example the firm might have to commit a great deal of money 'up front' for production facilities, but only receive the revenue later. The firm might have to borrow money. A **cash budget** shows the inflow and outflow of money. This is vitally important, as a failure to plan the cash properly can encourage a too swift expansion and possible collapse.

The sales budget

3.41 **The practical success of any budget system depends to a large extent upon the accuracy with which future sales can be forecast** since the sales estimate is the foundation for the purchasing and production budgets, the guide to plant-extension requirements and as the prime source of cash receipts, the basis of any plan for financing the business. If the sales forecast is a guess (eg previous years sales plus 10%) rather than a logical researched estimate, the practical value of the budget system may be entirely lost.

Forecast

3.42 As we have seen, there is no standard method of estimating future sales as different businesses demand different methods. However, in every case the estimate must be based fundamentally on a study of **past experience**, modified by anticipated **trade conditions** and proposed **future plans**. The relative emphasis on these three elements will vary considerably from one company to another.

(a) The structure of past/sales may provide a pattern that can be projected into the future with some degree of reliability.

(b) The essence of the forecast may lie on the general economic background, anticipated during the forecast period.

(c) In a third case the key influence may be sales promotion activity with the sales forecast virtually a plan rather than a forecast. The only logical approach to the problem is through an understanding of the factors which affect sales results.

Value and volume

3.43 Once finalised, the sales estimate will show the likely sales quantities for the budget period, as totals. It will have been adjusted according to:

- Profit and earning capacity of the various lines
- Production and purchasing capacity of the business
- Selling and administration expenses involved
- Financial requirements

3.44 **The sales budget will split down these total quantities into quantities for the control periods** - usually monthly or quarterly or both - and to **convert the quantities into value and revenue**.

(a) Thus the sales budget splits naturally into two sections - the **sales quantity (or volume) budget** and the **sales revenue budget**.

(b) In industrial marketing, particularly where long and variable delivery delays are concerned, it is useful to split the sales revenue budget into:

(i) Value of orders received budget
(ii) Value of orders delivered budget, so as better to ascertain the true position.

3.45 The actual money received will of course depend upon the credit period allowed, actual promptness of payment experienced and the amount of bad debts. This is usually the responsibility of the financial departments. For sales budget purposes, the sales revenue budget may be regarded as the **planned value of sales**.

Setting prices

3.46 In order to convert quantities into values it is of course necessary to fix selling prices. Selling prices are ultimately determined by market conditions and the balance between supply and demand. Note that simply deriving sales price as a percentage increase on cost may not work and may be suboptimal.

(a) In the case of a manufacturer basing his prices on prime cost and overheads and a fixed profit margin, when the shop was working at a normal (say 90%) capacity, overheads might be 12.5%; when at full capacity, 10%; and when at 50% capacity, 20%.

(b) In other words when business was good and orders such that the plant was working at full capacity, a reduction in price based on the given formula would merely result in increased orders which could not be met.

(c) On the other hand, when business was slack, increased prices would limit his chances of keeping his share of the reduced volume of business.

3.47 If then, a manufacturer is unwise to base prices on the **cost of production**, by what method should prices be determined? Several firms have found the answer by **price-volume** studies for each product. Price-Volume studies are attempts to forecast the elasticity of demand, so as to determine the probable volume of sales against various price levels and thus to arrive at the optimum price for each product, bearing in mind competitors' prices, to yield the largest net profit.

In this example, the cost of making a unit is £8.00

Proposed selling price	*Expected sales*	*Value of sales*	*Cost of goods sold*	*Surplus over cost*
£	Units	£	£	£
12.50	1,100	13,750	8,800	4,950
12.00	1,200	14,400	9,600	4,800
11.50	1,400	16,100	11,200	4,900
11.00	1,700	18,700	13,600	5,100
10.50	2,000	21,000	16,000	5,000
10.00	2,200	22,000	17,600	4,400

3.48 In the example above it has been assumed that the cost remains at £8 per unit whether output is 1,100 or 2,200 per year. In practice economies would probably result from higher quantities. For example, if you buy materials in bulk you might obtain a discount. This is relevant to differential costing used in special order-industries where contracts have to be tendered for. The principles are these.

(a) There is a cost above which a manufacturer would begin to lose money by accepting an additional order.

(b) The average cost per unit decreases as the volume of output increases, up to a certain level, which enables a manufacturer to charge a lower price on this extra output.

3.49 **Justifying the use of differential costs on a particular job**

(a) Prices on the remainder of the company's output should be unaffected;

(b) The job must represent a definite addition to output that could not be obtained in any other way.

3.50 Suppose a company has established a normal selling price of £6,000 per unit and the sales estimate for the budget period suggests an output of 60 units which represents a production capacity of 80%. (Total capacity is therefore $^{60}/_{0.8} = 75$ units.) It may so happen that the company could secure orders for a further 10 units providing the price was considerably reduced. By consulting the following table of differential costs, the minimum price would be £1,900.

Item	*Cost of 60 units*	*Cost of 70 units*
	£	£
Materials	83,000	91,000
Labour	78,000	85,000
Supplies	30,000	31,000
Variable o/h	56,000	59,000
Fixed o/h	65,000	65,000
Total cost	312,000	331,000
Unit cost	£5,200	£4,730
Cost per extra 10 units (£331,000 – £312,000)		£19,000*
Differential cost per extra unit		£1,900

The company would profit by selling an extra 10 units at any price in excess of £1,900 per unit **providing it maintains its previous price against the normal output quantity of 60 units**. It might be possible to charge different prices in different, perhaps secluded, market segments. It is the existence of such conditions as these which results in the adoption of **dumping policies** overseas by manufacturers with a protected home market.

3.51 In the above example the extra 10 units would bring the output up to 93% of production capacity and enable shop workers to earn higher wages. An alternative policy might be to hire out the additional labour and machine capacity to non-competing manufacturers whose demand exceeds their capacity.

Sales budget: summary

3.52 **Preparing the sales budget**

(a) A preliminary sales estimate based on:

- (i) A study of normal business growth
- (ii) A forecast of general business conditions
- (iii) A measure of the relationship between the company and (ii)
- (iv) A knowledge of potential markets for each product
- (v) The judgement of salespeople, sales management and general management staff
- (vi) A realisation of the effect on sales of basic changes in company policy

(b) The adjustment of the above preliminary sales estimate in light of:

- (i) The seasonal nature of the business
- (ii) From the viewpoint of optimum selling prices
- (iii) The overall production or purchasing capacity
- (iv) The viewpoint of securing even manufacturing loads
- (v) Overall selling expenses and net profits
- (vi) The financial capacity of the business

(c) The adjusted anticipated sales by value and quantity contained in the sales budget should then be classified by commodities, departments, customers, salesmen, countries, terms of sale, methods of sale, methods of delivery and urgency of delivery (rush or normal).

The expense budgets related to marketing

3.53 As a summary checklist, if you are preparing schedules of selling expenses you should concentrate on the following.

(a) **The selling expenses budget**

- Salaries and commission
- Materials, literature, samples
- Travelling and entertaining
- Staff recruitment and selection and training
- Telephones and telegrams, postage
- After sales service
- Royalties/patents
- Office rent and rates, lighting, heating etc.
- Office equipment
- Credit costs, bad debts etc

(b) **Advertising budget**

- Trade journal - space
- Prestige media - space
- PR space (costs of releases, entertainment)
- Blocks and artwork
- Advertising agents commission
- Staff salaries, office costs, etc
- Posters
- Cinema
- TV
- Signs

(c) **The sales promotion budget**

- Exhibitions: space, equipment, staff, transport, hotels, bar etc
- Literature: leaflets, catalogues
- Samples/working models
- Point of sale display, window or showroom displays
- Special offers
- Direct mail shots - enclosure, postage, design costs.

(d) **Research and development budget**

- Market research - design and development and analysis costs
- Packaging and product research - departmental costs, materials, equipment.
- Pure research - departmental costs materials, equipment
- Sales analysis and research
- Economic surveys
- Product planning
- Patents

(e) **The distribution budget**

- Warehouse/deposits - rent, rates, lighting, heating
- Transport - capital costs
- Fuel - running costs
- Warehouse/depot and transport staff wages
- Packing (as opposed to packaging).

Indicative marketing costs

3.54 You will probably be required to indicate the approximate costs of your marketing proposals in your case study examination. Hopefully as a practising marketer you will either be aware of current cost levels or will be able to find out fairly easily. You will not be expected to present **precisely** accurate costs but rather to have an awareness of their scales.

To help you with this, and bearing in mind costs can vary widely between London and other parts of the UK, as well as between the UK and other countries, we are providing some indications as follows. **Note that this data is only approximate, and is for case study purposes only.**

3.55 Of the terrestrial TV channels, three take advertising (ITV, Channel 4 and Channel 5). ITV operates on a regional basis with approximately 15 commercial channels in total, but GMTV provides breakfast broadcasting. There is an ever increasing number of satellite TV and cable channels, some (eg Sky Sports) catering to specialist audiences. Moreover, **digital terrestrial television** will massively increase the number of channels available. digital TV is currently delivered terrestrially by OnDigital, via satellite and, soon, over cable.

	ITV	*Channel 4*
Cost of 30 second advertising break at peak times	£85,000	£56,000
Off peak cost (minimum)	£24,000	£12,000

3.56 **Newspapers.** The cost per full page of some national newspapers and magazines is given below. Circulations refers to the numbers of copies sold per day. Readership, perhaps more subjective, is based on research into the number of people who read each copy. Penetration refers to the proportion of the population reading the paper.

(a) **Daily papers**

			Penetration		*Page cost*
	Circulation	*Readership*	*Men*	*Women*	*black/white*
Title	(millions)	(millions)	%	%	£
Sun	4.1	10.2	29	24	32,000
Daily Mirror	2.5	6.7	23	17	26,000
Daily Express	1.3	3.4	10	9	18,000
Daily Mail	1.8	4.5	11	10	20,000
Guardian*	0.4	1.3	4	2	15,000
Times*	0.6	1.5	3	3	17,000
Independent*	0.3	0.9	3	2	114,000

(b) **Sunday papers**

			Penetration		*Page cost*
	Circulation	*Readership*	*Men*	*Women*	*black/white*
Title	(millions)	(millions)	%	%	£
News of the World	4.8	12.3	29	28	36,000
Sunday Mirror	2.6	8.0	23	20	29,000
Sunday Times*	1.3	3.7	9	7	47,000
Observer*	0.5	1.5	6	4	24,000
Mail on Sunday	1.9	5.8	12	11	28,000

(c) **Some Sunday colour supplements**

	Page cost (black and white)	*Page cost (colour)*
	£	£
Sunday Times*	11,000	16,000
Sunday Mirror	–	25,000
Observer*	7,000	10,000

*Up market, quality press

(d) **There is a very wide choice of women's magazines.**

(i) Weekly

Title	*Circulation*	*Readership*	*Housewives*	*Page cost colour*	*Page cost black/white*
	(million)	(million)	(million)	£	£
Woman's Own	0.8	4.0	3.4	22,000	16,000
Woman	0.8	3.0	2.7	18,000	13,000
Woman's Weekly	0.8	2.4	2.0	12,000	9,000

(ii) Monthly

Title	*Circulation* (million)	*Readership* (million)	*Housewives* (million)	*Page cost colour* £	*Page cost black&white* £
Options	0.2	0.5	0.4	5,000	3,500
Woman and Home	0.4	1.9	1.8	8,000	5,000
Ideal Home	0.2	2.0	1.5	8,100	5,500
Essential	0.4	1.3	1.1	7,700	4,900

3.57 **Radio**. There are over 45 independent stations. At one time, these were only local (eg Capital Radio) but several national commercial radio stations (eg Classic FM) now exist. The cost of a 30 second peak spot might be £4,000, but varies considerably.

3.58 **Cinema** attracts a mainly young adult audience (under 25). A four week campaign might reach 20% of under the 25 age group. The average 'network' cost of a 30 second spot would be £31,000 in such a campaign.

3.59 **Posters**. The average cost of a 48 sheet poster site for one month is £265. A national campaign would require 1,500 - 2,000 of such sites.

3.60 The production cost of an average 30 second TV commercial is £84,000.

Useful analytical techniques and models in deciding 'where do we want to be?'

3.61 There are a variety of analyses, techniques, concepts and models which can help us in deciding our future **marketing** objectives and strategies. These include the following.

(a) The mission statement
(b) Market structure analysis
(c) Buying behaviour analysis
(d) Segmentation analysis
(e) Product life cycle (PLC) analysis
(f) Ansoff's growth matrix
(g) The Boston matrix
(h) Gap analysis
(i) PIMS data base
(j) Critical success factors

3.62 In the same way that Marketing Research helps marketing planning in all its stages, these models/analyses can be applied throughout.

(a) The plotting of product sales to look for evidence of the product life cycle (growth or decline) not only tells us where we are now but also predicts where we are likely to be in the future (up or down) and prompts action where necessary. This is of course also a control mechanism.

(b) Similar remarks could be made with regard to segmental analysis which will show us where we are now (sales by segment) where we would like to be (new segments) and act as a control device (did we get there?)

We are simply dealing with these other approaches now because of convenience and because deciding where we want to be could be said to be the most critical marketing strategy decision of all.

Mission statement

3.63 The mission statement provides a **consensus** between different viewpoints and a **focus** for business activity. The mission statement is likely to have a degree of **generality** so that it can integrate various stakeholders over a long period of time. Stakeholders could be defined as 'any group or individual who can affect or is affected by the achievement of an organisation's purpose'

Market place stakeholders	*External stakeholders*	*Internal stakeholders*
Customers Competitors Suppliers	Government Political groups Financial community Trade associations Activist groups	Owners Decision makers Unions and employers

(a) The use of **open** objectives is appropriate for areas that are difficult to quantify **or** express in measurable terms, eg 'to be a leader in technology'. Open objectives can avoid overformalisation, opposition, rigidity to change and alerting competitors. Although generalised, they can still provide a focus to the activity of the business.

(b) The mission is shaped by five key elements.

(i) The organisation's history
(ii) The current preferences of owners and managers (stakeholders)
(iii) Environmental considerations
(iv) Resources
(v) The organisation's distinctive competences

(c) Examples of some mission statements are given below. These are all quite brief. Often mission statements are much longer.

(i) **What business are we in?**

Firm	*Product view*	*Market view*
Revlon	We make cosmetics	We sell hope
Xerox	We make copying equipment	We help improve office productivity

(ii) RCA. 'To be technological leader again in its core business of electronics and communications.'

(iii) Apple. 'Apple (computers) is not in the game or toy business but in the computer business. What Apple does best is to take a high cost ideal and turn it into a low cost, high quality solution.'

(iv) 'To make a lot of money' is not a mission statement but Toyota's 'Global 10' mission, for example, 'to have 10 per cent of the world auto market by 1990' did give form to its business activity.

Market structure analysis

3.64 Every market will differ in its characteristics so that it is difficult to be specific about structure. However, the following general analytical framework can be applied to most markets.

(a) What are the **market parameters**? In other words, what are its boundaries? The UK domestic market's parameters are the borders of the UK.

(b) How **big** is the market within these parameters?

(c) Is this market **growing**, stable or declining?

(d) How does the market **segment**?

(e) To what extent is **each segment** growing, stable or declining?

(f) Who are the **key players** in the market or segments? (Manufacturers, distributors, others)

(g) What are the **key success factors** in this market or segment?

(h) What are the **buying behaviour characteristics** of this market or segment?

(i) Who are the **major market/segment competitors** and what are their distinctive competencies.

(j) What **future environmental factors** are likely to affect this market/segment?

(k) How easy or difficult is market **and/or segment** to enter or exist?

Buying behaviour analysis

3.65 Buyer behaviour is a topic which connects the consumer's needs wishes and desires - normally studied by the psychologist - with the economic and commercial objectives of a firm. The model below indicates the main issues in buyer behaviour. One of the consequences of a purchase might be to encourage an additional purchase (especially true in service industries). Post-purchase feelings are therefore important.

STEPS IN THE BUYING PROCESS

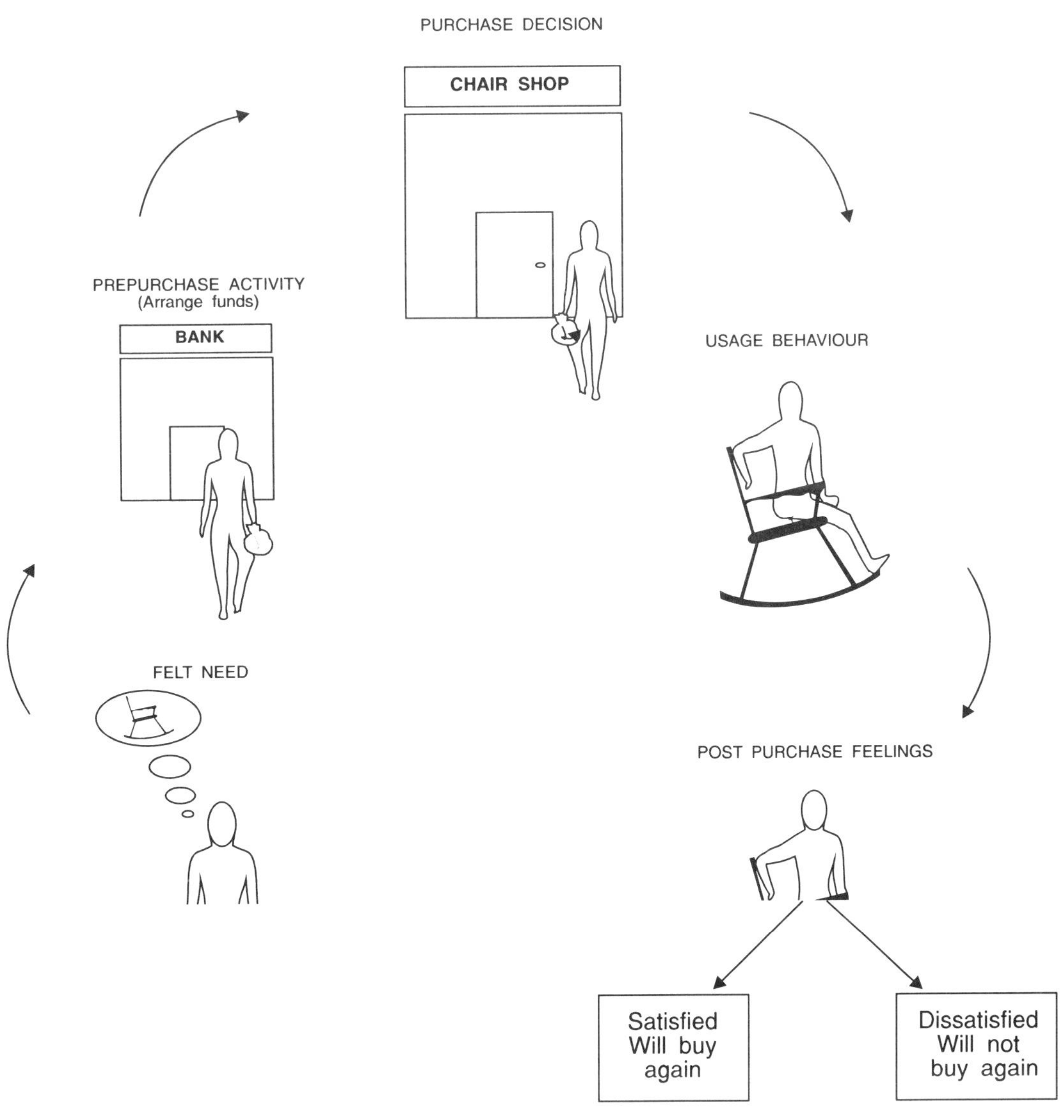

Buying decisions

3.66 The **decision making unit** is responsible for an organisation's purchases. it involves five roles, which may be played by different people. Several individuals may occupy the same role and one individual may occupy more than one role.

Role	Comment
Users	All those in the organisation who use or are going to use the product being purchased. It will include people at all levels in the organisation - thus the decision to purchase a particular type of powered hand-tool may well be influenced by the shop floor workers who tried out the samples.
Buyers	In most organisations, there is a **purchasing or buying department**. Certain members of this department will have formal responsibility and authority for signing contracts for purchases on behalf of the organisation. These are, in this context, the purchasing agents together with any other persons with such authority.
Influencers	This is usually a large ill-defined group as it includes all those who influence the decision process directly or indirectly by providing information and setting the criteria for evaluating alternative buying actions.
Deciders	This is the group with authority to choose amongst alternative buying actions. A buyer is not always a decider and vice versa. Thus when purchasing a very complex product of an advanced technological nature, a group of engineers and scientists may pick or decide upon a particular supplier. Their decisions might then be passed to a purchasing agent to be implemented purely in the sense of drawing up the necessary formal documents to complete the legal aspects of the transaction.
Gate keepers	Any decision-making unit will need, from time to time, to collect some information. Those supplying the information may influence the group's decision by withholding certain information available or by controlling access from personnel in the selling organisation to personnel in the buying organisation. This is not dishonesty or bias, but simply emphasises the fact that time does not usually make it possible to provide all relevant information and selections have to be made or a synopsis provided.

3.67 The principles of the industrial DMU can be applied in consumer goods marketing. Children can influence parents in their food purchasing decisions. For some types of household goods the decision is generally taken by the male and, for other types, by the female.

Diffusion of innovation

3.68 The diffusion of innovation curve is another buyer behaviour model. Take the example of the compact disk player. When first introduced, it was a speciality item. Now, certainly for classical music, it has become standard.

Diffusion of innovation curve: statistical patterns in buyer behaviour

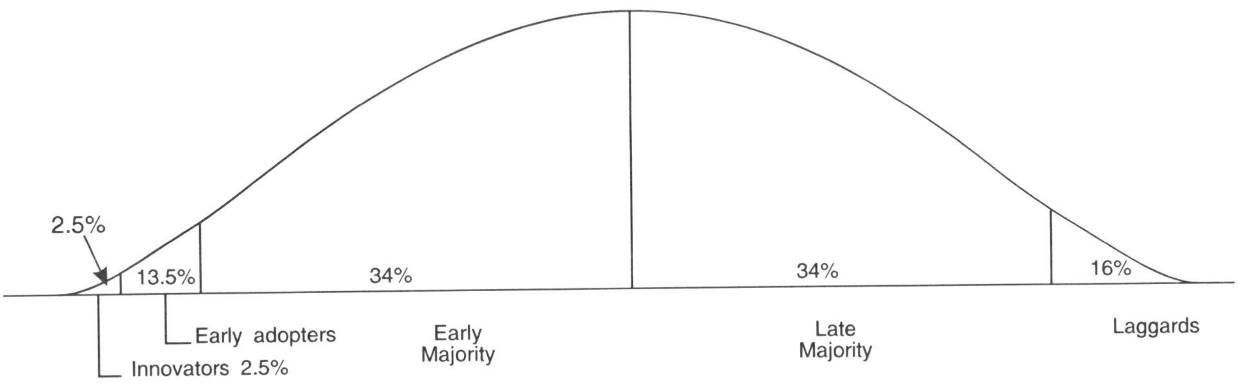

(a) This model can equally be applied to industrial as well as consumer marketing. Some companies (Rolls Royce, aero engines) may be seen and wish to be seen as technological leaders in their field and are, therefore, much more likely to be early adopters of innovations than other industrial companies who may have elected to follow rather than lead in this respect.

(b) In choosing where we want to be we may wish to specialise in meeting the needs of particular customers (the leaders in innovation as perhaps expressed in our mission statement).

(c) At a later stage (in the marketing mix) we will need to take account of how the buying system works, who makes the purchasing decisions and who influences these decisions.

Segmentation analysis

3.69 Segmentation classifies the market so that there are fewer people in a market segment than in the whole market. They have more in common with each other than with others in the wider market. Some writers have said that segmentation and positioning within a segment are at the very heart of modern marketing.

(a) **Segmentation variables useful in deciding why people buy**

(i) **Psychographic (the type of person)**

- Life styles
- Attitudes
- Self concept
- Culture

(ii) **Benefits sought (from the product)**

- Economy
- Convenience
- Prestige
- Services

(b) **Segmentation variables useful in targeting marketing effort**

(i) Demographics

- Age, sex, education, religion
- Social class, occupation
- Residence, life cycle (eg with children)

(ii) Geographic

- Urban, suburban, rural
- Climate

(c) **Usage behaviour.** In other words, what people do with the product. (Do you consider a watch simply as a time piece or as a fashion accessory? This is how SWATCH watches have been marketed.)

(d) **Segmentation variables for industrial markets**

(i) Industrial demographics; industry, company size, geographical location.

(ii) Usage: light, medium or heavy.

(iii) Purchasing criteria: companies seeking lower prices or higher quality, better service etc

(iv) Conditions of purchase: stringent or light?

(v) Company personality: risk taking, loyal, bureaucratic, power seeking etc.

(vi) Ordering characteristics: frequency, size of order, urgency of order etc.

The product life cycle (PLC)

3.70 This product life cycle concept suggests that most products and services, will, over time, exhibit stages of growth, maturity, and decline as follows.

Product life cycle: simplified version

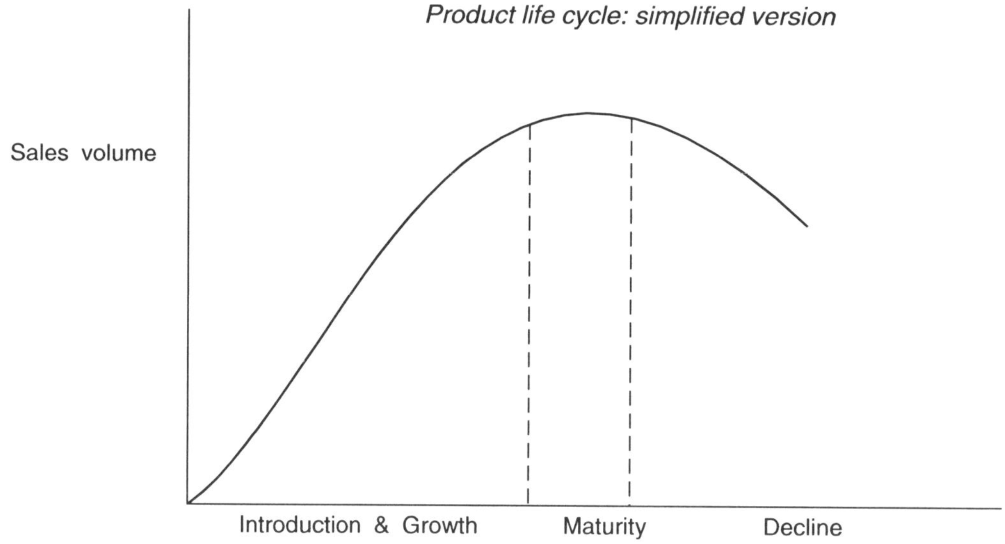

(a) The concept is useful inasmuch as it **draws attention to the need for marketing action to lengthen a product's life, regenerate or replace it**. Whilst some critics argue that the PLC has been responsible for far too many premature product withdrawals and others argue that coal, bread etc. have been in demand for thousands of years, there is little doubt that a great many individual products do exhibit PLC tendencies unless modified. Likewise less bread is eaten in terms of ounces per capita and new varieties (eg slimming breads) have now appeared to challenge the standard British loaf. Hovis is now packaged and available in a sliced variety, more in tune with modern needs.

(b) In practice, some products and services can be re-cycled as in the case of sixties' music and mini-skirts. However, it would be difficult to accept the possibility of a future boom in horse-drawn carriages in place of the motor car as a viable means of modern transportation.

3.71 The utility of the PLC in indicating the need for action is perhaps best demonstrated in the following diagram where it can be seen that unless something is done urgently, the likelihood is that total turnover and profit will radically decline. This is because Product A is in decline whilst Products B and C have reached maturity and are about to enter into decline.

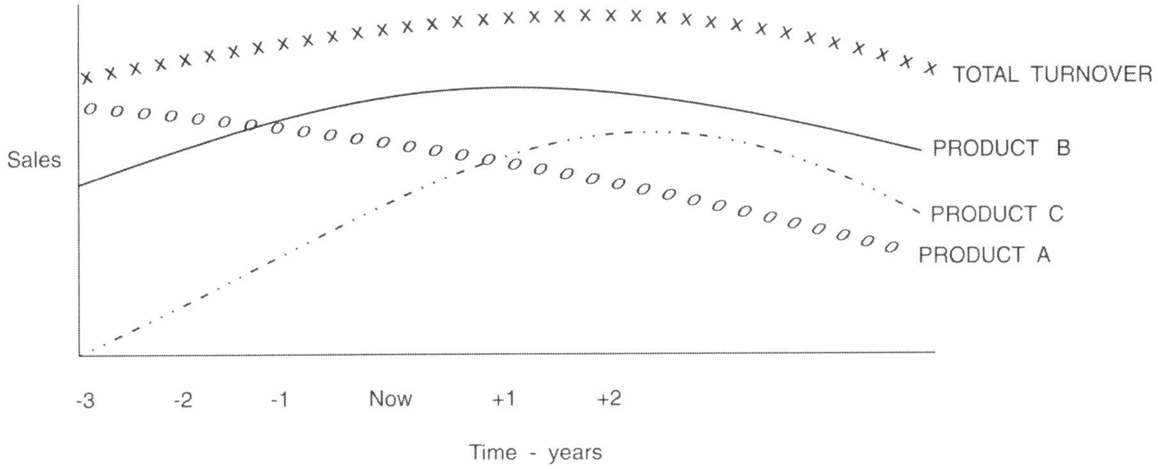

3.72 We can now move to a more sophisticated treatment of the PLC, one that adds the pre-launch and the deletion stages to the picture and paints in the aspects of cash flow and profitability.

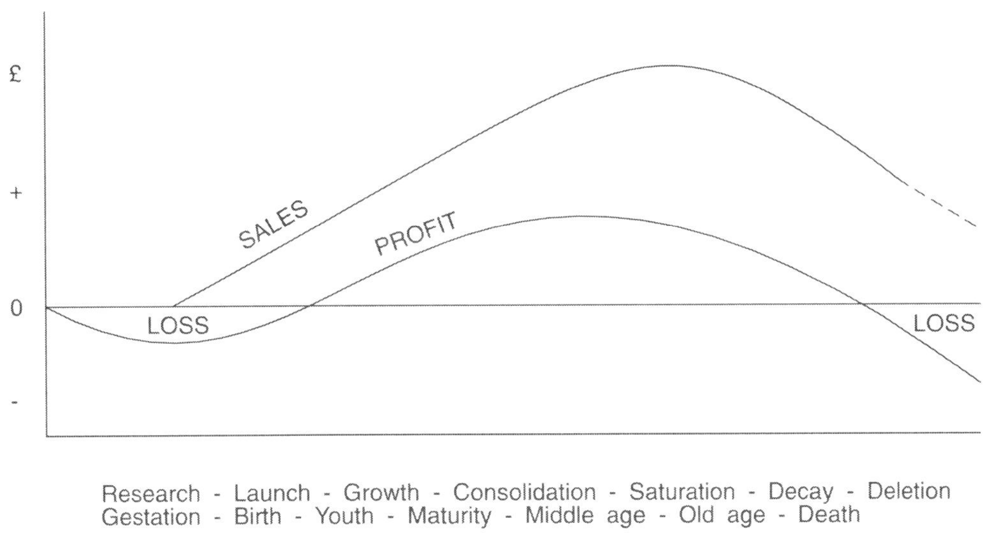

(a) At the **pre-birth stage**, costs are involved in conducting research and product development so that a negative cash flow occurs. This situation tends to worsen on launch, in that heavy promotion and distribution are added whilst relatively few sales are made. However, during the **growth stage**, marketing planners expect to generate positive cash flow and go into profit, a position which should last until a point in the **decline stage** where sales drop below break-even and deletion becomes desirable unless regeneration is possible

(b) In the above diagram that the profit curve is shown to peak before the sales curve. This is often the case when competitors enter what can be seen to be a growing and potentially lucrative market and prices are, therefore, forced down further than can be compensated for by lower costs due to increased sales volume.

(c) Marketing planners can deploy elements of the marketing mix to varying degrees over the PLC so as to enjoy maximum cost benefit relationships. The PLC can also be used as a strategic tool to identify, for example, the need for replacement products and/or product modification, as illustrated in the diagram below.

Marketing mix relative to product life cycle

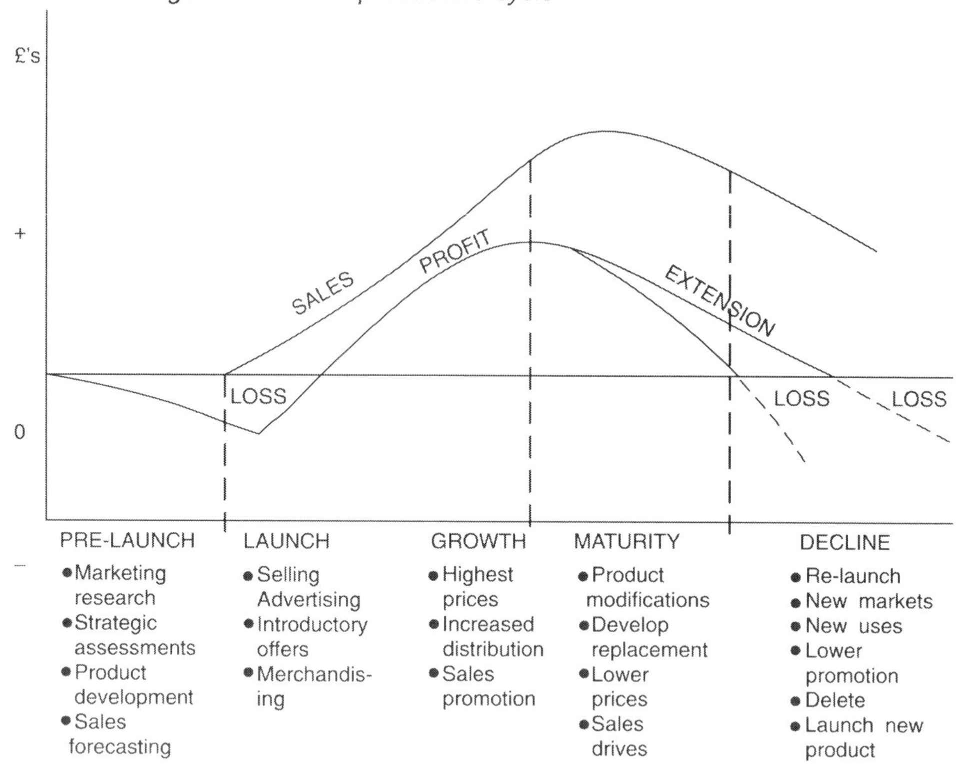

3.73 **New product development, sales forecasting, market research.** Identification of the position of existing products on the life cycle by the simple process of plotting sales will indicate a possible need to re-develop existing product or develop new ones. It also assists in sales forecasting and highlights the potential need for marketing research, particularly at the decay stage of an existing product and/or the generation stage of a new product.

3.74 **Advertising, sales promotion, selling.** The communications job will be particularly demanding at the selling stage of a new products and will continue at somewhat lower levels during the stages of growth and maturity. Lower prices, special offers, development of the existing product, improvement of the service element etc. are resorted to in an attempt to counter decline which, if continued, will lead to efforts to find new outlets, new uses and new markets. If decline continues, promotional support is often removed in order to postpone the point at which the product's sales fall to break-even and efforts to develop a new replacement product are increased.

3.75 **Distribution and pricing.** The planning of increases in the number of outlets in harmony with production (and transport) capacity is particularly important during the growth stage. New outlets, particularly in less sophisticated markets abroad, may be sought during the decline stage. Price levels may be high during the period of high demand in order to recover development costs but may be forced down before sales peak, with the onset of competition.

3.76 **Arresting decline.** Marketing planners can attempt to arrest decline by finding **new users**, perhaps in developing markets overseas. **New uses** may be developed for existing products or they can be **modified** in some way or **perhaps re-packaged.**

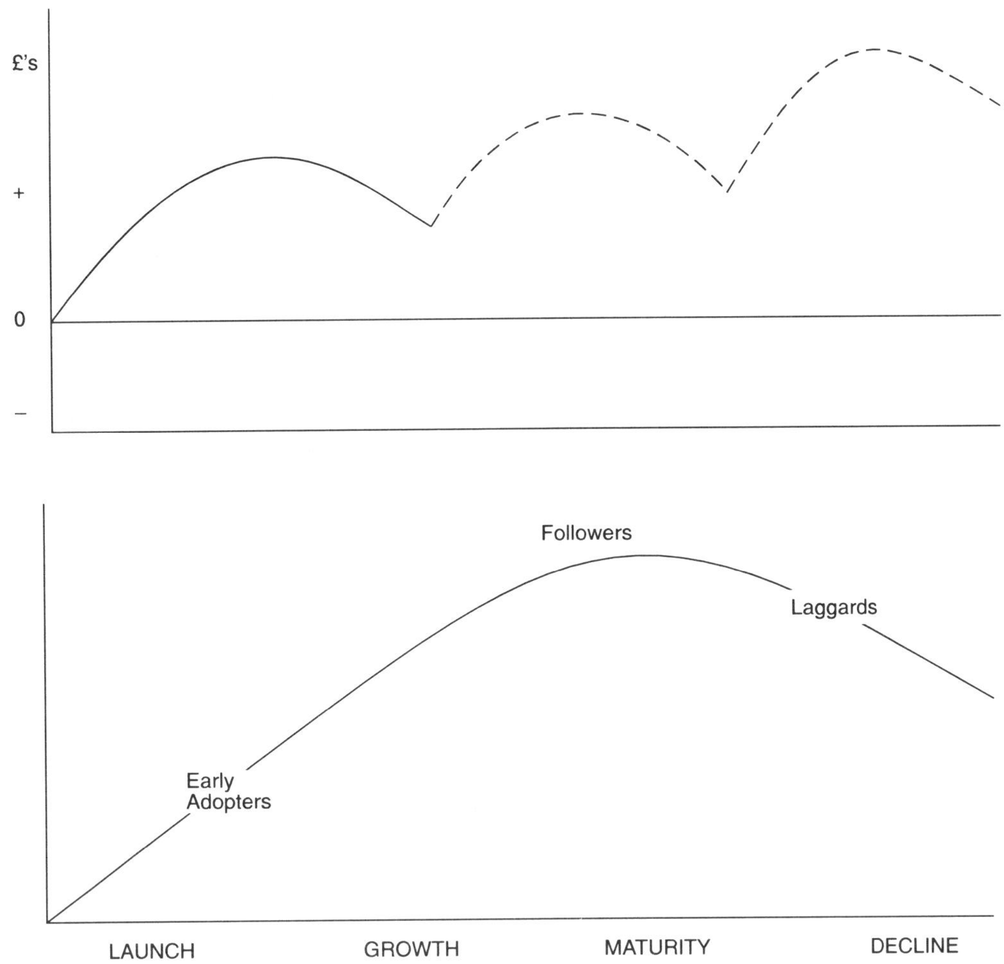

3.77 A further strategic aspect of the PLC is that of considering the **relative buying behaviour** patterns. Studies by Midgeley and Wills, 1974 indicated that relationships between types of buyers and PLC exists in fashion markets, which can be exploited in terms of more accurate targeting of the marketing mix over time.

(a) Thus, at the launch stage, buyers are likely to be the more adventurous, innovative, leader types. Promotional messages, media chosen, pricing and distribution outlets can be targeted accordingly.

(b) At the growth stage, the marketing strategy can move towards mass media and mass distribution outlets with alterations in messages appealing to the followers of the trend setters and opinion leaders (early adopters).

(c) At the decline stage, promotion and distribution strategy can aim at the laggards, ie those buyers who react more slowly than the norm to fashion trends. It is suggested that most buyers of goods exhibit a spectrum of buying behaviour similar to that identified by Midgeley and Wills.

Ansoff's growth matrix

3.78 The Ansoff matrix is used to analyse the appropriate product-market strategies, by the type of product and market. Here are some examples. of the type of strategies that might be used.

	Existing products	*New products*
Existing markets	*Market penetration strategy* 1. More purchasing and usage from existing customers 2. Gain customers from competitors 3 Convert non-users into users (where both are in same market segment).	*Product development strategy* 1. Product modification via new features 2. Different quality levels 3. 'New' product
New markets	*Market development strategy* 1. New market segments 2. New distribution channels 3. New geographic areas eg exports	*Diversification strategy* 1. Joint ventures 2. Mergers 3. Acquisition/take-over

The Boston matrix

3.79 You may find the Boston Consulting Group's analysis of products into stars, cash cows, dogs and question marks quite a useful one. Bear in mind, though that this is simply a *model* and a tool, involving subjective judgements and prone to change over time.

Boston constancy group growth - share matrix

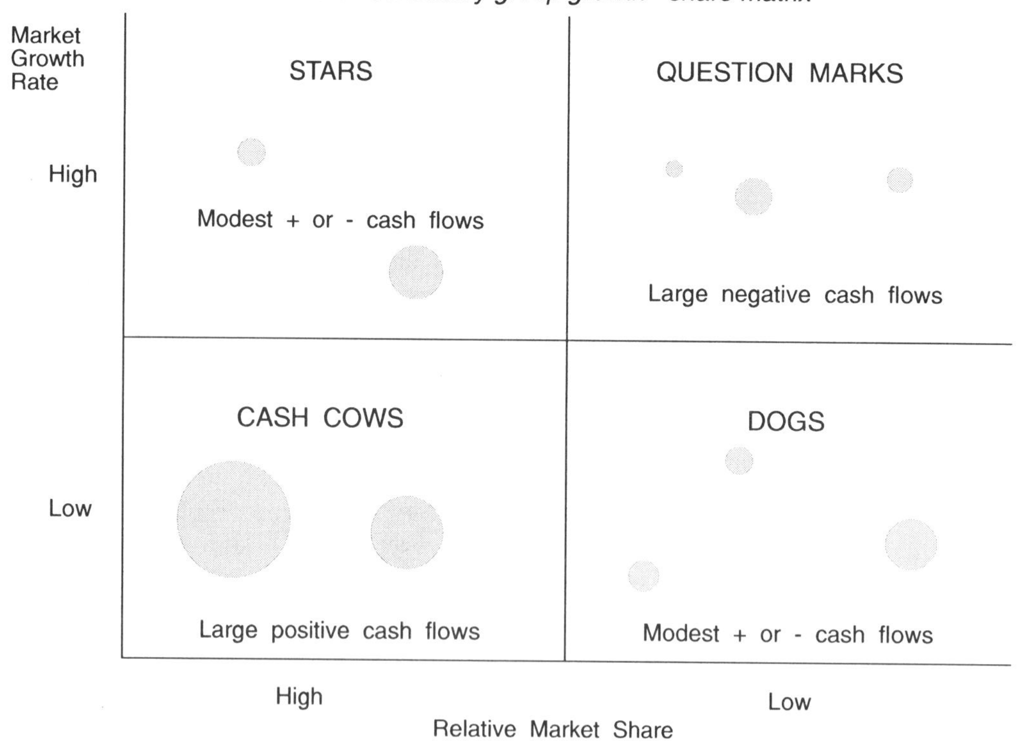

(a) The BCG model can also be applied to a strategic business unit (SBU) within a group or conglomerate particularly where the SBU is a single product manufacturer.

(b) **The idea is to work towards a balanced portfolio.** The Boston matrix is related to the product life cycle analysis in that question marks are often those products in the launch stage, stars are in the growth stage, cash cows are in the mature stage and dogs are in the decline stage.

(c) In the FirstrATE case study the Delta product could be said to be a question mark whilst Omega perhaps is a cash cow in danger of becoming a dog.

Gap analysis

3.80 **By comparing the objectives with the current forecast, it is possible to measure the gap which is the discrepancy between what the firm wants and what it is likely to achieve.** A task of corporate planning is to identify gaps and propose strategies whereby the gaps may be closed. In the diagram below, let us assume that re-examination of the current forecast shows that one of major products will not achieve sales targets (perhaps due to technological developments in market, increased competition etc).

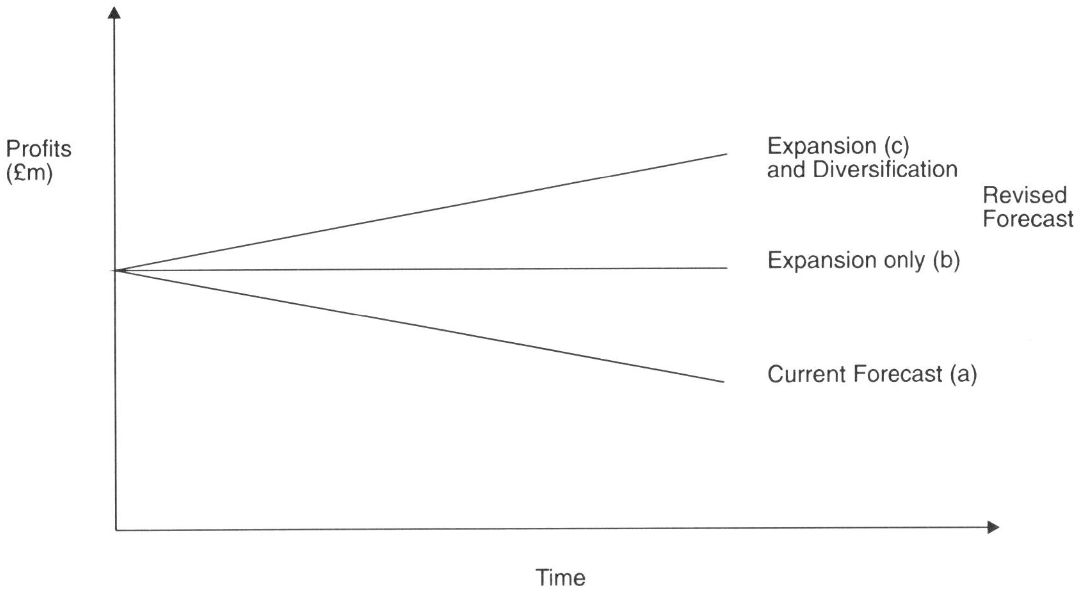

(a) The current forecast indicates that profits will decline in future

(b) Expansion in existing markets, by improving existing products, may maintain level of profits in future

(c) By expanding within existing markets and/or improving existing products and **diversifying** into new markets with new products, a higher level of profit may be obtained.

The PIMS database

3.81 PIMS (Profit Impact of Market Strategy) research is important to the decision of 'where we want to be' in that it uses an analysis of more than 2,800 businesses to identify two key issues.

(a) Product innovation and quality are significant factors in achieving a dominant market share.

(b) Dominant market share is a key factor in achieving high levels of profitability.

If, as in most case studies the objective is to achieve profitable growth, PIMS can be quoted and leadership/innovation strategies proposed as ways of getting there.

Critical success factors

3.82 In the case of FirstrATE, flexibility seemed to be a critical success factor in a rapidly changing technological environment. Fortunately FirstrATE had an advantage in flexibility and this could therefore be developed into a distinctive competitive advantage.

4 STRATEGIC EVALUATION AND CHOICE (HOW MIGHT WE GET THERE AND WHICH WAY IS BEST?)

4.1 The **decision** on which strategy is best is the most **difficult and risky decision** that marketing managers have to take. In the case study **many students find themselves unable to take it**. They want to go on analysing until the decision becomes crystal clear and fail-safe. Forced into it by the question, they will opt for all four Ansoff growth strategies rather than decide which one is best. In real life of course we **have** to take marketing decisions on imperfect and insufficient information and analysis if we wish to take advantage of 'a window of opportunity' which opens for a limited amount of time. Limited resources means that we cannot pursue all available strategies and if we tried to do this, failure would be almost certain.

Risk and reward

4.2 In deciding which of the growth strategies on the Ansoff matrix is best, consideration has to be given to the risk factor associated with each strategy.

	Existing product	*New product*
Existing market	1	4
New market	2	16

(a) The numbers in the matrix indicate **notional levels of risk**. Note, however, that market penetration (existing products and markets), while easy, may be risky in the long term if a new competitor is about to leap in, or if a new technology can render yours obsolete overnight, or if the market you are in is saturated. New products are always risky (research has shown that 8 out of 10 grocery products 'fail'). However, in some situations it can be **more** risky to go into new markets than to launch new products into a market that you know and understand well.

(b) **Trade offs inevitably occur between levels of risk and levels of return**. When considering entering new markets or new market segments for example (Ansoff's market development strategy) the following trade-offs are likely.

	Low exit barrier	*High exit barrier*
Low entry barrier	Low stable returns	Low risk returns
High entry barrier	High stable returns	High risky returns

4.3 There is a variety of **matrix analyses** which can be used. You can invent your own according to your particular product - market situation or better still, the one in the case study. However, here are some established matrices which have a degree of universality as well as a history of success.

(a) The directional policy matrix (George Day)

The directional policy matrix (George Day)

Market attractiveness / Degree of competition	Strong	Medium	Weak
High	PROTECT POSITION • invest to grow at maximum digestible rate • concentrate effort on maintaining strength	INVEST TO BUILD • challenge for leadership • build selectively on strengths • reinforce vulnerable areas	BUILDS SELECTIVELY • specialize around limited strengths • seeks ways to overcome weaknesses • withdraw if indications
Medium	BUILD SELECTIVELY • invest heavily in most attractive segments • build up ability to counter competition • emphasize profitability by raising productivity	SELECTIVITY/MANAGE FOR EARNINGS • protect existing program • concentrate investments in segments where profitability is good and risk is relatively low	LIMITED EXPANSION OR HARVEST • look for ways to expand without high risk otherwise, minimize investment and rationalize operations
Low	PROTECT AND REFOCUS • manage for current earnings • concentrate on attractive segments • defend strengths	MANAGE FOR EARNINGS • protect position in most profitable segments • upgrade product line • minimize investment	DIVEST • sell at time that will maximize cash value • cut fixed costs and avoid investment meanwhile

Degree of competition

(b) Arthur D Little matrix

Stage of industry maturity

Competitive postition	Embryonic	Growth	Mature	Ageing
Dominant	Grow fast. Build barriers. Act offensively.	Grow fast. Aim for cost leadership. Defend position. Act offensively.	Defend position. Increase the importance of cost. Act offensively.	Defend position. Focus. Consider withdrawal.
Strong	Grow fast. Differentiate.	Lower cost. Differentiate. Attack small firms.	Lower costs. Differentiate. Focus.	Harvest.
Favourable	Grow fast. Differentiate.	Focus. Differentiate. Defend.	Focus. Differentiate. Hit smaller firms.	Harvest.
Tenable	Grow with the industry. Focus.	Hold-on or withdraw. Niche. Aim for growth.	Hold-on or withdraw. Niche.	Withdraw.
Weak	Search for a niche. Attempt to catch others.	Niche or withdraw.	Withdraw.	Withdraw.

(c) **Porter's five factor map of segment attractiveness**

Porter's five factor map of segment attractiveness

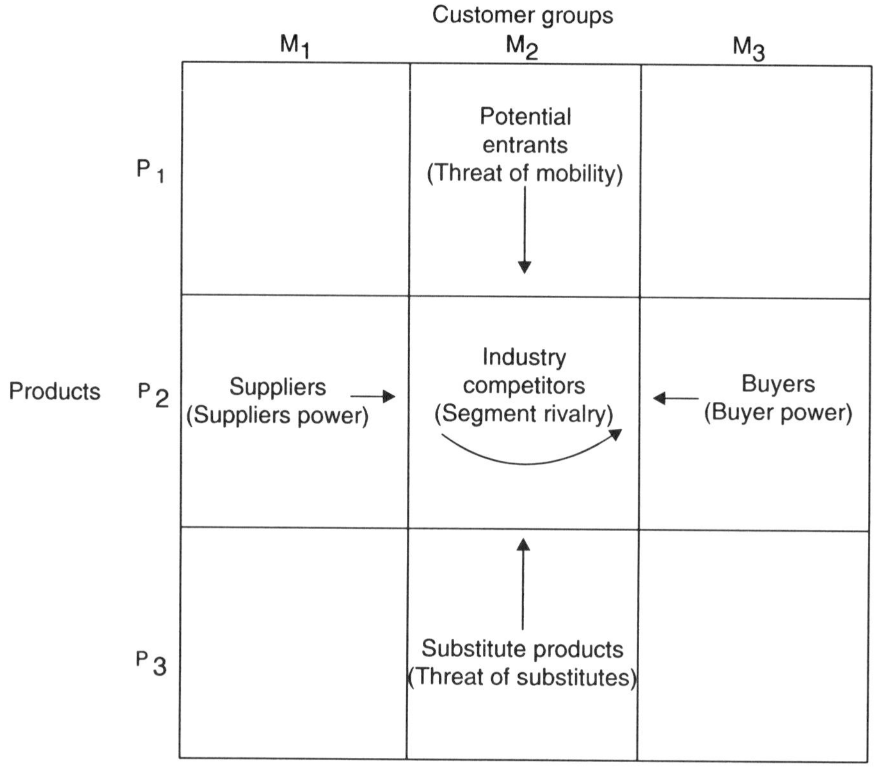

Competitive strategy

4.4 Michael Porter suggests three generic competitive strategies.

(a) **Overall cost leadership strategy**

The business works hard to achieve the **lowest costs of production and distribution**. Less skill perhaps is needed in marketing as the firm which pursues this strategy will **always** be able to compete on price, and will stay profitable for longer.

(b) **Differentiation strategy**

Here the business concentrates on achieving superior performance in some important customer benefit area valued by the market as a whole. It can strive to be the service leader, the quality leader, the style leader, the technology leader etc but it is hardly possible to be all of these things. The firm cultivates those strengths that will give a differential performance advantage along some benefit line. Thus, the firm seeking quality leadership must make or buy the best components, put them together expertly, inspect them carefully and so on.

(c) **Focus strategy**

Here the business focuses on one or more narrow market segments rather than going after the whole market. The firm gets to know the needs of these segments and pursues either cost leadership or some form of differentiation within the target segment.

Leader or follower?

4.5 A firm can choose between a market leader strategy and a market follower strategy.

(a) **Market leader strategy**. This is risky and expensive, especially as innovators do not always reap the rewards of their hard work. This has the following requirements.

- Research-intensive effort
- Major development resources
- Technical personnel (eg scientists)
- Close relationship between marketing and technical staff
- Flexible organisation structure
- Innovative product

(b) **'Follow the leader' strategy.** In this case, the leader is copied quickly. The advantages are that the firm can offer customer benefits over those offered by the leader. Success requires a true marketing orientation: the firm has to pursue customers more fiercely. This strategy is most successful in large volume markets. The requirements are as follows.

- Streamlined organisation
- Rapid response time in product development
- High quality development engineers

(c) **'Me too' strategy** is another follower strategy. Companies follow this because they have to, just to keep up with competition. By this time, the technology will have become more widely available. The requirements are as follows.

- Minimal research and development
- Strong manufacturing function
- The ability to copy designs quickly
- Product modification to reduce production costs
- Competitive strategy based on price and delivery

Competitor response models

4.6 A great deal can be accomplished in understanding competitors by relatively simple numerical analysis, and financial and market review. No business exists in a vacuum and marketing strategists need to assess competitors and their reactions to a firm's plans. Here is a **checklist of questions about competitors** you should find answers to.

Question	*Answer*
(a) How many? (b) Size? (c) Growing or declining? (d) Market shares and/or rank orders (e) Likely objectives and strategies (f) Changes in management personnel (g) Past reactions to: (i) price changes (ii) promotional campaigns (iii) new product launches (iv) distribution drives (h) Analysis of marketing mix strengths and weaknesses (i) Leaders or followers? (j) National or international (k) Analysis of published accounts	

4.7 Adding to the above data obtained from competitor intelligence (observation, asking customers, planting moles etc) and from maintaining comprehensive records of competitors' past behaviour and you can begin to develop **competitor response models.** These attempt to predict for example, what competitor A will do if you launch a radical new product (do nothing, retaliate by non-product means, copy you, develop superior product etc), or what competitor B will do if you raise your prices (nothing, immediately copy, increase theirs less, increase theirs more, wait a bit and then copy etc). Such modelling can be an invaluable aid to strategic choice.

Experimentation and test marketing

4.8 Experimentation is particularly appropriate when applied to the marketing mix. We can experiment with different price levels and study price-volume-profit relationships. We can try out a new sales promotion in a small geographical area, we can ask selected customers to test new products etc. In these ways marketers can avoid the possibly disastrous consequences of a failed strategy. A failure of a new product launch on a national scale is measured not only by unrecovered costs but also in the loss of credibility which can jeopardise future initiatives.

You will learn more about concept testing and test marketing in Section 6 of this chapter which can be put to good use in your case study examination.

The marketing mix

4.9 In terms of marketing, strategy is achieved by deploying the elements of the marketing mix. This essentially entails developing products and services to meet target segments' needs (established by marketing research), communicating their benefits to target audiences and ensuring they are available in the right place, at the right price and at the right time. At its simplest, the marketing mix can, therefore, be defined (after McCarthy) as the 4 P's, namely:

P1 = PRODUCT
P2 = PRICE
P3 = PROMOTION (communications)
P4 = PLACE (Distribution)

Three extra Ps can be added for services: People, Processes and Physical evidence.

4.10 Each of these elements subsumes other elements which might be termed sub-elements or submixes. The exact nature or make-up of these submixes is determined both by the product or service itself and by the marketer's choice. For example, branding may not be a consideration for industrial raw materials, whereas a consumer goods marketer might decide to seek a differential competitive advantage through distinctive packaging, unique product design and style of advertising.

4.11 With these points in mind, we can identify submixes as follows.

(a) **Product submix**

- Pre-sales service
- Product range
- Packaging
- Patenting
- Design
- Positioning
- Warranties
- Demonstration/trial
- Standardisation
- Modification
- Rationalisation
- Innovation
- After-sales services
- Evaluation

(b) **Pricing submix**

- Costings
- Demand
- Profitability
- Competitive pricing
- Promotional pricing
- Product-mix pricing
- Discounts
- Price Increases
- Evaluation

(c) The **promotional submix** consists of four submixes.

Advertising	*Sales promotion*	*Public relations*	*Selling*
Objectives Budget Messages Media Scheduling Evaluation	Literature Incentives (consumer, dealer, sales force) Exhibitions Direct mail Merchandising Trade presentations Point of sale display materials In-house visits Evaluation	Corporate identity Internal communications Publicity Media receptions Evaluation	Sales force size Structure of sales force Remuneration Training Motivation Evaluation

(d) **Distribution submix**

- Channels
- Stocking levels
- Ordering systems
- Speed of response
- Dealer relationships evaluation
- Depots
- Channel costing and evaluation

4.12 These submixes at least form the framework for **marketing operations planning** and control, although the amount of detail can be debated.

4.13 We should also note that the elements of the marketing mix/submixes are, in practice, interdependent and interactive. They need to combine harmoniously to form an integrated and tailored whole, so as to be attractive to the target market or segment.

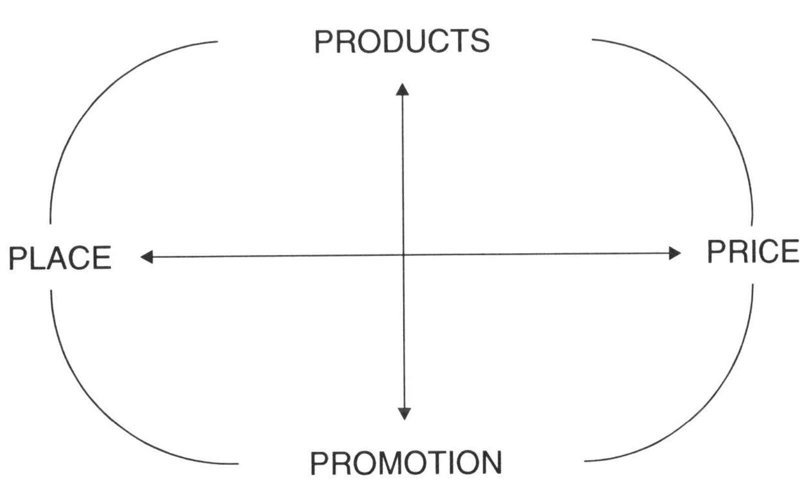

Interrelationships of the marketing mix

(a) **Price is to some extent dependent on product** in the sense that any price below variable costs (labour plus materials) would fail to generate any contribution.

(b) The nature of the product might also determine its method and/or channel of distribution(place).

(c) As an example of interaction, the sales force will refer to advertising support in their personal presentations. Point-of-sale display material will embody the advertising theme and the advertisements themselves might well refer to company benefits in the form of sales force and merchandising support.

(d) Price communicates a degree of value and, therefore, could be considered to be part of the communications mix as well as an element in itself.

(e) Packaging in a self-service environment becomes 'the silent salesman' to the consumer.

Products and services

4.14 Most authors attempt to differentiate between products and service. The unique characteristics of services present special challenges and strategic marketing opportunities to the services marketer.'

(a) **Three fundamental characteristics of services**

- Intangibility.
- A service is an activity rather than a thing.
- Production and consumption are to some extent simultaneous activities.

(b) Service marketing involves three additional 'P's: People, Process and Physical evidence. (See paras 4.18 - 4.20 below.)

4.15 However, most products purchased entail some element of service, if only that of availability, delivery or credit, which facilitate the sale and most services have tangible elements eg dry cleaners provide coat hangers and bags. Cowell concludes that there are four categories.

(a) A pure tangible good
(b) A tangible good with accompanying services
(c) A service with accompanying goods
(d) A pure service

What is a product?

4.16 When marketing goods or services, we should remember the maxim that people do not buy goods or services, they buy what products and services will do for them that they want doing, ie **they buy benefits**. In this context, it can be useful to view the product (for service) as an input-output device, so as to gain a clearer insight of how to communicate product features in the form of user benefits.

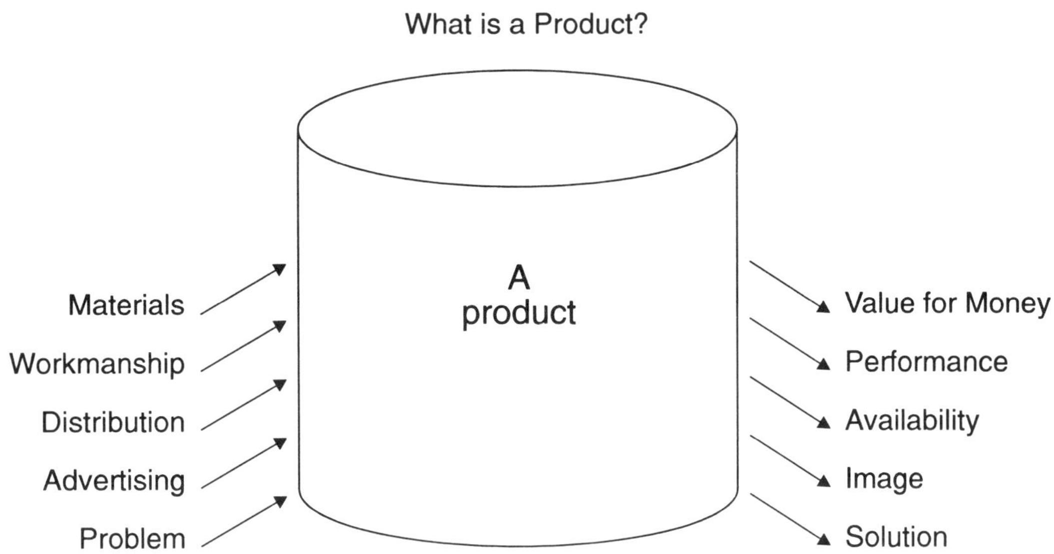

The product as an input-output device

4.17 Extending the above idea, we can now say a product is everything a purchaser gets in exchange for his money, including the following possible 'extras'. It is also useful to acknowledge here that different people seek different benefits, giving rise to market segmentation. In general, people seek new and/or better benefits, such as image enhancement, greater reliability and more convenience, giving rise to new market segments and the concept of product life cycle.

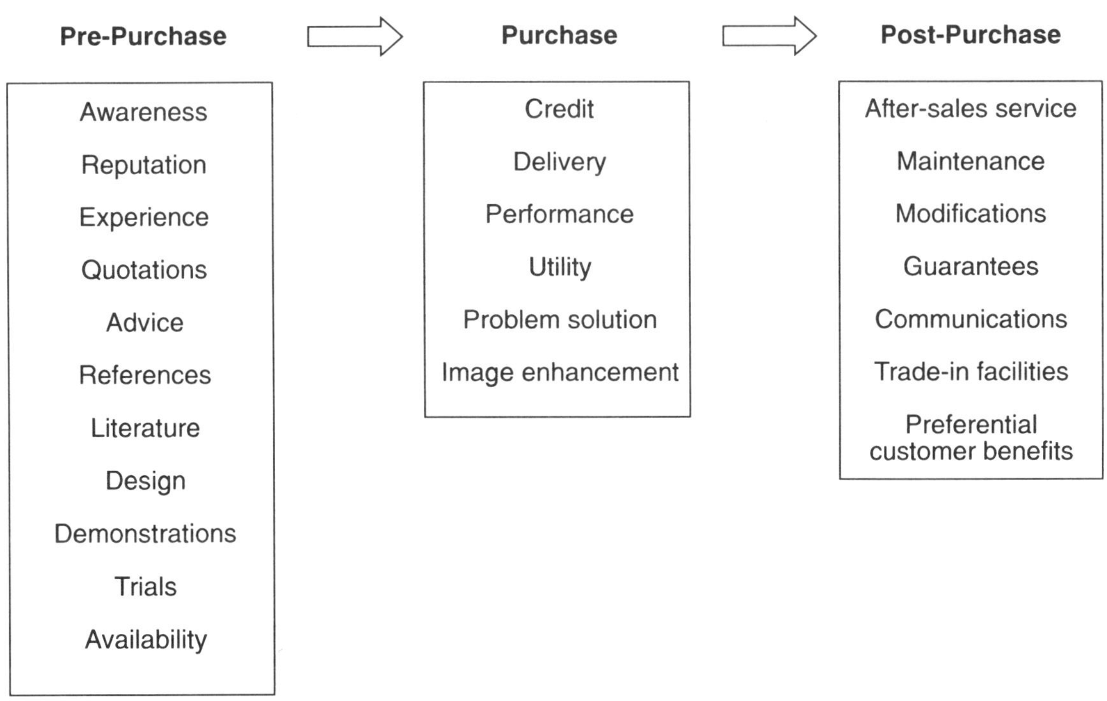

Product inputs-outputs related to the buying cycle

4.18 **People**

(a) **Employees.** For example, if you have had poor service in a shop or restaurant, you may not be willing to go there again. An American retailing firm estimated that there was an identifiable relationship between lower staff turnover and repeat purchases. Managing front-line workers (eg cabin-crew on aircraft) who are the lowest in the organisational hierarchy but whose behaviour has most effect on customers, is an important task for senior management. It involves corporate culture, job design and motivational issues.

- Appearance
- Attitude
- Commitment
- Behaviour
- Professionalism
- Skills
- Numbers
- Discretion

(b) **Customers.** At first sight, having customers here might seem strange. Customers are, after all, the destination of the efforts of the marketing professional. However, customer, values and attitudes are important.

- Behaviour
- Appearance
- Numbers
- Customer/customer contact

4.19 **Process.** Processes involve the ways in which the marketer's task is achieved. Efficient processes can become a marketing advantage in their own right. For example, if an airline develops a sophisticated ticketing system, it can encourage customers to take connecting flights offered by allied airlines. Efficient processing of purchase orders received from customers can decrease the time it takes to satisfy them. Efficient procedures in the long term save money.

- Procedures
- Policies
- Mechanisation
- Queuing
- Information
- Capacity levels
- Speed/timing
- Accessibility

4.20 **Physical evidence.** Again, this is particularly important in service industries, for example where the ambience of a restaurant is important. Logos and uniforms help create a sense of corporate identity.

Environment	Facilities	Physical evidence
Furnishings	Vans/vehicles/aeroplanes	Labels
Colours	Equipment/tools	Tickets
Layout	Uniforms	Logos
Noise levels	Paperwork	Packaging
Smells		
Ambience		

New product development

4.21 The process of new product generation entails three basic stages.

(a) Generating ideas
(b) Screening
(c) Developing the launch strategy

Generating ideas

4.22 Ideas for new products and/or services can come from employees, customers, suppliers, intermediaries, competitors and the general public.

4.23 In recognising the need for a continuous stream of new product ideas, many companies formalise their approach. For example, they may install suggestion boxes at various points within the company and offer rewards for ideas brought to fruition. **Quality circles** are used to seek ideas for improvements from production staff in organised discussion groups. Some of these ideas will give rise to product modification. Other companies scour **complaints files** periodically for product/service improvement ideas.

4.24 **Value analysis** usually involves obtaining a range of competitive products, adding your own and subjecting this combination to a rigorous and detailed critique.

> For example, the following questions might be asked about a range of electric fan heaters. (This list is not exhaustive.)
>
> - Why do we need 3 fan speeds?
> - What price reduction could we make if only 2 fan speeds were offered?
> - Would this modification result in better value?
> - Why use stainless steel screws?
> - Would mild steel screws be almost as good?
> - What price reduction would this make?
> - Would this represent better value?
> - Why use 20 gauge casting which vibrates without reinforcement?
> - Would 18 gauge casting be vibration free without reinforcement?
> - What would be the relative cost of 18 gauge?
> - Would using 18 gauge represent better value?

4.25 Some organisations use **brainstorming** techniques. Individuals are gathered together in groups and are asked to contribute ideas without forethought, embarrassment or inhibition.

(a) Nothing should be held back, however wild.
(b) The greater the number of ideas generated, the higher the probability of a good one.
(c) Ideas should be combined, and interesting ones improved, during the session.

4.26 The **sales force** can be a good source for new ideas, being closer than anyone else in the organisation of customers and competitors. However, formal **market research** can be applied to discover both new needs and existing attitudes towards your own and competitive products, on a number of attributes, in the form of gap analysis.

4.27 Scaling techniques can be applied to discover the perfect mix of a product's attributes and how far existing products fall short of ideal product improvement. For example, research could give us an idea of what customers regard as the ideal or perfect loaf. Its attributes can include taste, freshness, nutritional value, non-staling characteristics etc. Existing types of bread are then tested to see how far they fall short of the ideal. If we could then develop a loaf which comprised a better fit, this would fill a gap in the market.

4.28 Technological forecasting is another way of generating new product ideas, along with the building of 'what if?' scenarios. The process involves an examination of current technological and current research progress (see Paragraph 3.12). The next step is to see what products might be developed. A number of possible applications might exist. There is speculation on what will happen if the gap in the ozone layer widens - what new products/services might be needed?

4.29 How far a new product is in fact **new**, rather than a modification of an existing product, is less important than whether potential customers **see** it as a new product. (Thus, mushy peas in a can were portrayed and accepted as a new product, despite having been available loose or in cardboard containers in chip shops in the UK for decades.)

Screening

4.30 New product ideas need to be screened against a set of criteria in order to prevent expensive failures, but guarding against the premature dismissal of ideas which could turn out to be winners. Here is a general purpose or generic screening model.

General purpose screening model for new product ideas

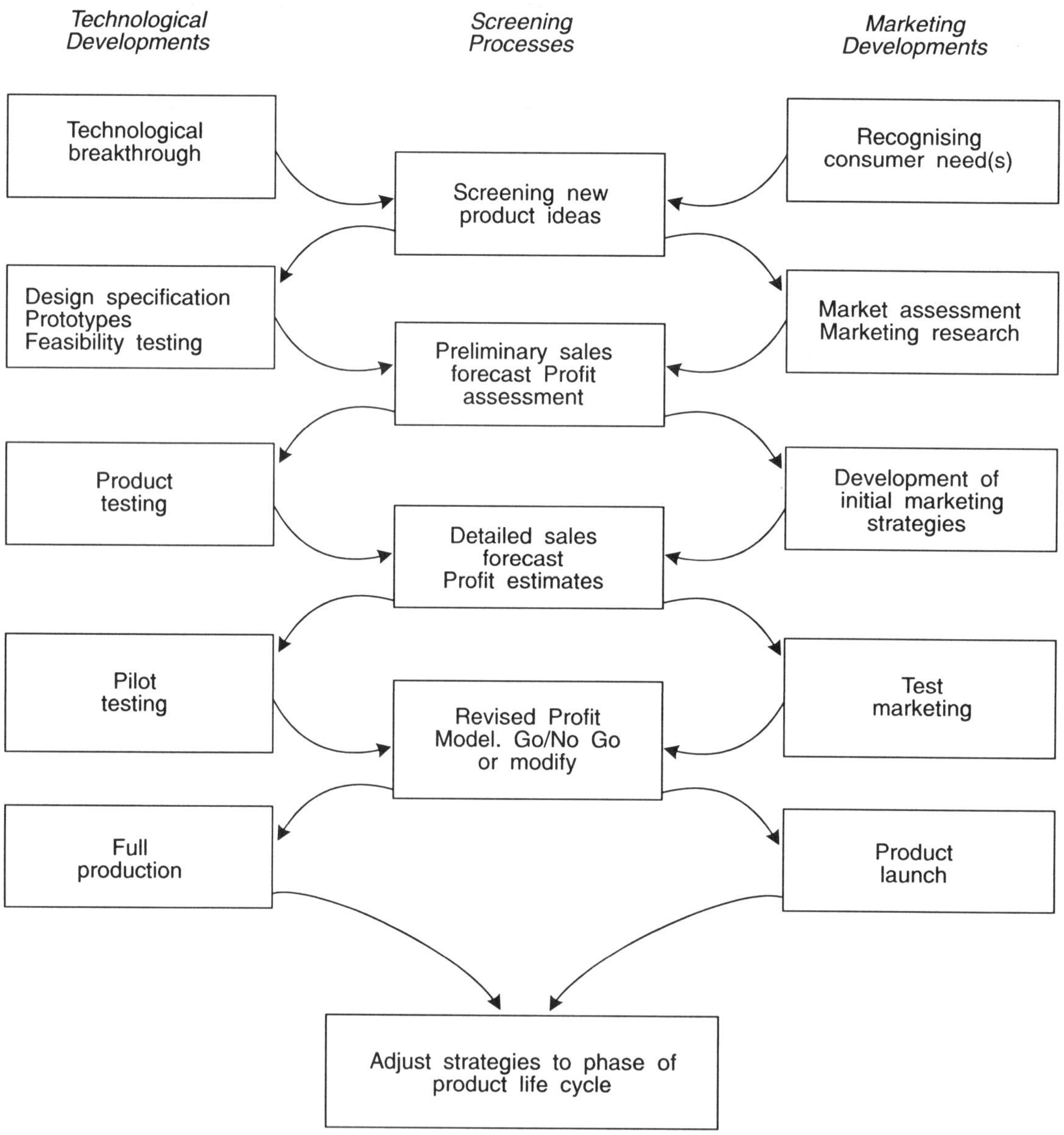

Promotion

4.31 This element is covered in detail in Chapter 2 on Marketing Communications Strategy.

5 STRATEGIC IMPLEMENTATION AND CONTROL (HOW CAN WE ENSURE ARRIVAL?)

Implementation

5.1 Getting things done entails delegating responsibility and granting the necessary authority. In case study exams you may well be asked for action plans and, if so, you are expected to specify not only who is responsible, but also the sequence and timing of the actions. This could be expressed in columnar form as follows.

	Actions in sequence	Person responsible	Timing	Estimated cost (£'000)
1	Conduct full marketing audit	MkIS manager	January 2000	10
2	Summarise situation from this audit	Marketing manager	February 2000	1
3	Agree sales forecast for 2000-2001	Marketing manager, sales manager	February 2000	-
4	Finalise marketing plans	Marketing team	March 2000	3

Control

5.2 **The implementation schedule acts as a control document.** Checks can be made that the action has been carried out by the agreed deadlines and within the agreed cost. More often than not, outline schedules like the example given above, will be backed by more detailed documents which can then contain the control procedures. In addition to budgetary control which has been covered earlier in this chapter (and also in Chapter 4) are the human controls and the contingency plan. **The range of potential control techniques** are as follows.

- Budgetary control
- Ratio analysis
- Cost-volume-profit analysis
- Net present value analysis
- Distribution cost analysis
- Quality controls
- Marketing audits
- Marketing research
- Marketing experimentation and test marketing
- Management science
- Meetings and discussions
- Contingency planning

Most of the above have already been covered or will be covered in subsequent chapters.

5.3 **Management science** is an area of increasing importance. It can relate to systems, in particular control systems, in which control action is built into the very operation of a system (like a thermostat).

(a) It would for example include systems which automatically signal when an event occurred outside the tolerances laid down. (In a stock control system this could be whenever stock exceeds maximum or falls below planned levels.)

(b) Flowcharts, programming, networks, critical path analysis all come under the aegis of management science.

(c) In retailing, systems such as EPOS (Electronic Point of Sale) can be programmed to automatically debit stock and re-order as goods sold are registered by the tills.

5.4 Most companies hold regular (weekly, monthly and quarterly) meetings at which performance is discussed and any remedial action necessary is agreed and documented. Special meetings can be called when for example a competitor action seriously threatens existing plans.

5.5 Events can be predicted, assigned degrees of probability of occurrence and for events most likely to happen **contingency plans** drawn up in advance detailing the actions to be taken. Again, the control action is premeditated.

5.6 It is possible to use ratio analysis in a control system.

$$\frac{\text{Selling expenses}}{\text{Sales revenue}} \quad \frac{\text{Advertising expenditure}}{\text{Sales revenue}} \quad \frac{\text{Below the line expenditure}}{\text{Sales revenue}}$$

$$\frac{\text{Promotional expenditure}}{\text{Net profit before tax}} \quad \frac{\text{Net profit before tax}}{\text{Sales revenue}} \quad \frac{\text{Total marketing expenditure}}{\text{Sales revenue}}$$

5.7 A ratio can be historically assessed and new ratios agreed which can then act as control mechanisms

Total market expenditure	*1996*	*1997*	*1998*	*1999*	*2000*	*2001*	*2002*
% of sales revenue =	5	5.5	6.0	6.5	7.0	7.5	7.5

In the above case, a company bent on gaining dominant share might have to be prepared to increase advertising expenditure, as a proportion of sales revenue as well as expecting sales volumes to rise, so that marketing expenditure would in practice get a double boost. The drawback of this particular form of control lies in the difficulty of forecasting future revenues. A mechanism for partially coping with fluctuating revenues is to agree tolerances. For example in 2000 we would accept a ratio in between 6.8 and 7.2%.

6 MARKETING RESEARCH AND THE MARKETING INFORMATION SYSTEM (MKIS)

6.1 Marketing research and marketing information systems (MkIS) are favourite areas for testing in the case study and so it is often necessary for you to draw up a marketing research plan as part of your examination preparation. A format for the marketing research plan will be found in Chapter 8 paragraph 5.13 of this Tutorial Text.

6.2 **Marketing research** can be defined as follows, either:

(a) research into all aspects of marketing (markets, sales, advertising, products, price, distribution); or

(b) the systematic gathering, recording and analysing of data relating to the marketing of goods and services.

Market research is research into markets (sizes, segments, trends, manufacturer and distributor shares etc) whereas marketing research is research into all elements of the marketing mix (price, product/service, promotion etc) **and** markets.

6.3 **Rationale for marketing research**

(a) The widening communications gap between an organisation and its customers in a modern economy and the need to provide a more informed basis for strategic decisions than mere hunches.

(b) Increasing competition necessitates a detailed knowledge of competitors' activities.

(c) Rapid changes in technology must be noted

(d) Growing affluence creates changes in tastes and purchasing habits

(e) Marketing costs (largely labour costs) are increasing faster than production costs.

Types of marketing research

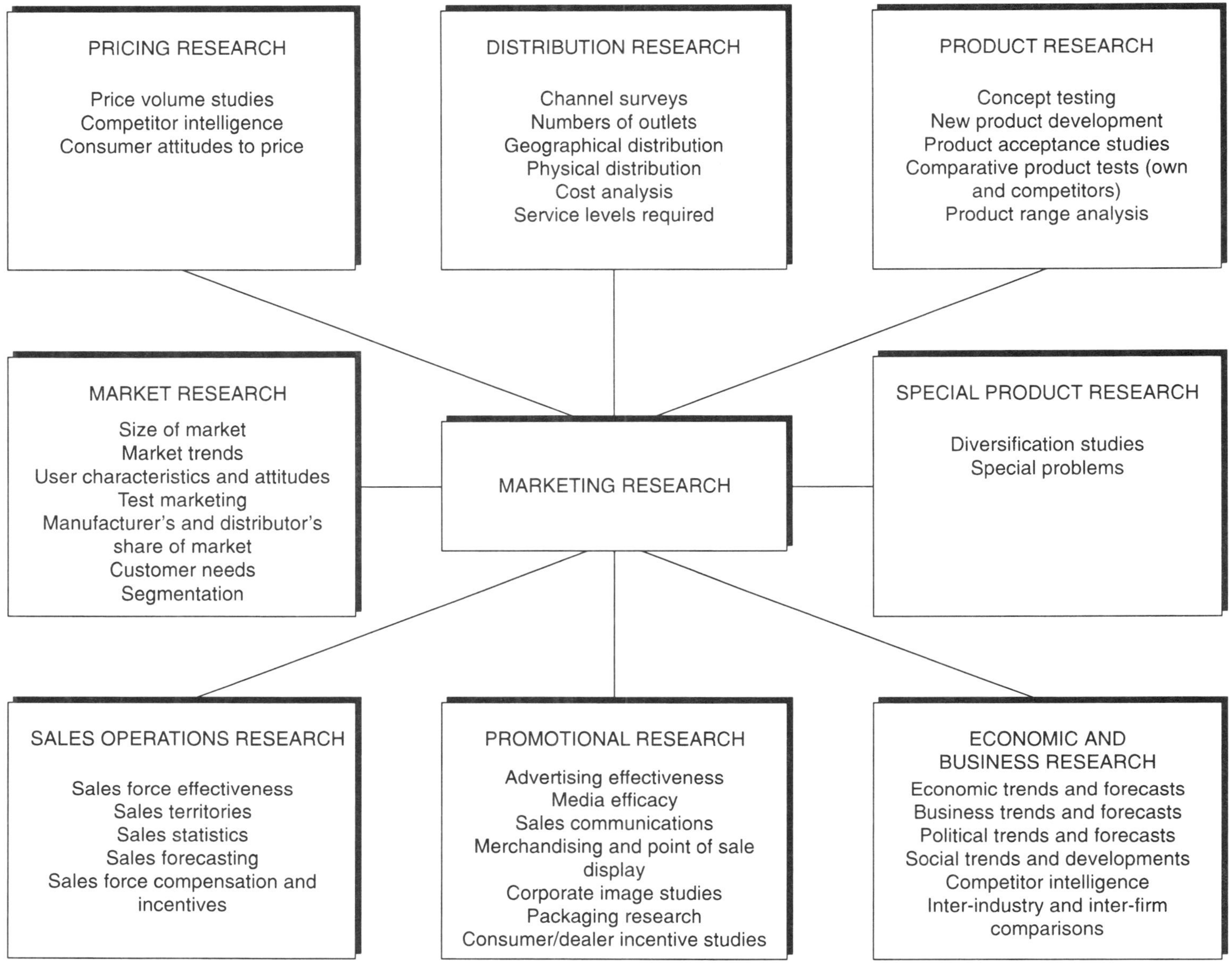
PRICING RESEARCH
Price volume studies
Competitor intelligence
Consumer attitudes to price
DISTRIBUTION RESEARCH
Channel surveys
Numbers of outlets
Geographical distribution
Physical distribution
Cost analysis
Service levels required
PRODUCT RESEARCH
Concept testing
New product development
Product acceptance studies
Comparative product tests (own and competitors)
Product range analysis
MARKET RESEARCH
Size of market
Market trends
User characteristics and attitudes
Test marketing
Manufacturer's and distributor's share of market
Customer needs
Segmentation
MARKETING RESEARCH
SPECIAL PRODUCT RESEARCH
Diversification studies
Special problems
SALES OPERATIONS RESEARCH
Sales force effectiveness
Sales territories
Sales statistics
Sales forecasting
Sales force compensation and incentives
PROMOTIONAL RESEARCH
Advertising effectiveness
Media efficacy
Sales communications
Merchandising and point of sale display
Corporate image studies
Packaging research
Consumer/dealer incentive studies
ECONOMIC AND BUSINESS RESEARCH
Economic trends and forecasts
Business trends and forecasts
Political trends and forecasts
Social trends and developments
Competitor intelligence
Inter-industry and inter-firm comparisons

6.4 What does a firm need to know? An information specification is suggested here.

Information	Comment
Markets	Who are our customers? What are they like? How are buying decisions made? This information is vital to every marketing decision
Share of the market	What are total sales of our product? our sales? competitors' sales?
Products	What do customers think of our product? What do they do with it? Are our products in a 'growth' or 'decline' stage of their life cycle? Should we extend our range?
Price	How do we compare: high, average, low? Is the market price sensitive?
Distribution	Should we distribute directly, indirectly or both? What discounts are required?
Sales force	Do we have enough/too many salesmen? Are their territories equal to their potential? Are they contacting the right people? Should we pay commission?
Advertising	Do we use the right media? Do we communicate the right message? Is it effective?
Customer attitudes	What do they think of our product? firm? service? delivery?
Competitors' activities	All aspects
Environmental factors	(SLEPT factors)

6.5 In seeking data for decision taking purposes marketing managers should follow a logical series of steps, starting with internal sources and ending with the conducting of ad-hoc surveys only as a last step when proceeding sources have failed.

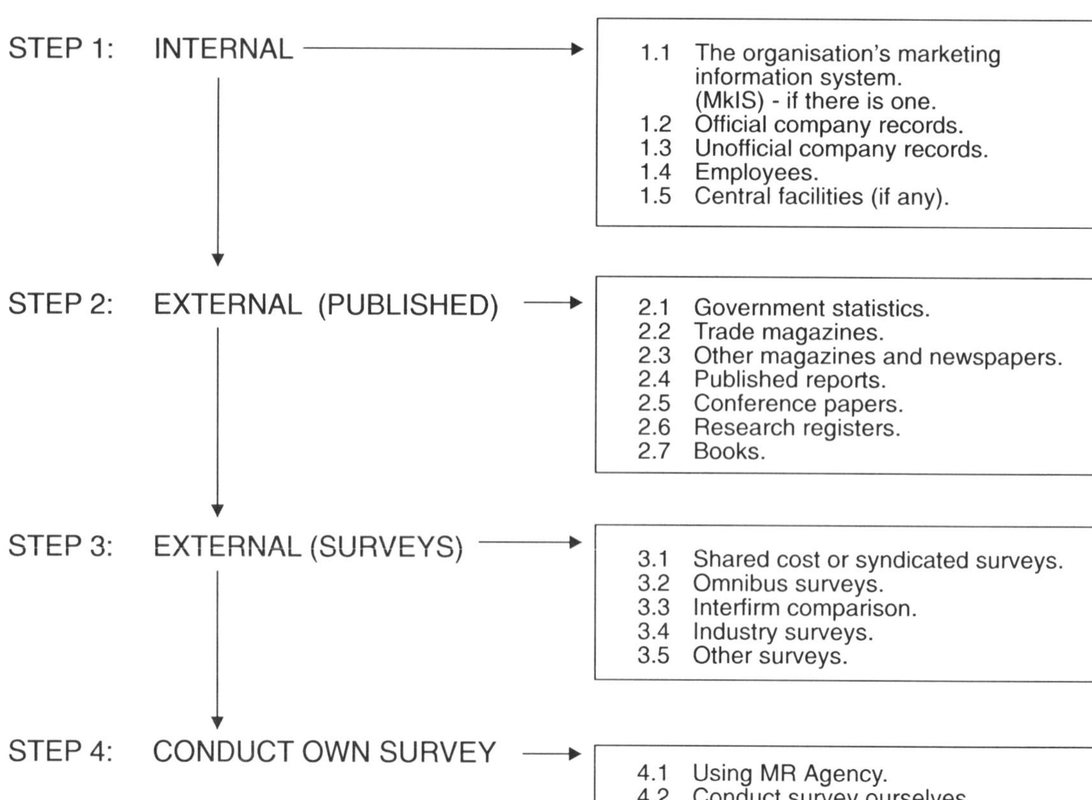

6.6 To fully cover all data sources in detail would take several volumes and be beyond the scope of this book. However the following guide to locations of data should be helpful not only for answering exam questions but also for career purposes.

Sources of marketing research data

6.7 (a) **Government statistics**

Central government has an army of statisticians producing data in the national interest and like everyone else, wanting the results of their labour to be put to use. The *Office of National Statistics* can be reached by contacting, at first instance. The ONS Library (1 Drummond Gate, Pimlico, London SW1 2QQ, phone 0171 533 6262, fax 0171 533 6261, E-mail info@ons.gov.uk) who will provide a free booklet giving a brief guide to sources. Alternatively phone the ONS sales desk on 0171 533 5678). The following more specific statistics are often available in your town/city public library.

- Monthly Digest of Statistics
- Annual Abstract of Statistics
- Population Trends, Economic Trends, Social Trends, Regional Trends
- Family Expenditure Survey and the General Household Survey
- Distribution Monitors (shops and stores) and Transport Statistics
- Production Monitors
- Special Monitors eg Travel and Tourism

(b) **Business directories.** Examples include, although there are many others:

- Kompass Register (Kompass)
- Who owns Whom (Dunn and Bradstreet)
- Key British Enterprises (Dunn and Bradstreet)

(c) Some **digests and pocket books**

- Lifestyle Pocket Book (annual by the Advertising Association)
- Retail Pocket Book (annual by Nielson)
- A to Z of UK Marketing Data (Euromonitor)
- UK in Figures (annual, free from CSO)

(d) **International data**

- Overseas Trade Statistics General Statistical Bulletin (EC)
- Consumer Europe (bi-annual, Euromonitor)
- International Directory of Published Market Research
- Statistics and Market Intelligence Library (DTI London)

(e) **Some important periodicals (often available in the public libraries)**

- Economist (general)
- Campaign (advertising)
- Marketing Week
- Mintel (consumer market reports)
- Retail Business (consumer market reports)
- BRAD (all newspapers and magazines published in UK)

(f) **Some special data bases**

- ACORN (consumption indices by class of neighbourhood)
- PRESTEL (British Telecom)
- TEXTLINE (abstracts articles from c.80 newspapers)
- Marketing Surveys Index (CIM)
- MRS Yearbook (Market Research Agencies and their specialisms)

(g) **Some retail audits and consumer panels**

- Nielsen Retail Audits
- AGB Home Audit
- Television Consumer Audit (TVA)
- Attwood Consumer Panel
- BMRB Target Group Index (TGI)

(h) **Shared cost/syndicated research and omnibus surveys**. Companies and organisations can obtain general surveys they can buy into on a shared cost basis. Some of these are given above (eg the Nielsen Retail Audit). A particular form of shared cost research is the omnibus survey a variety of which are advertised in the Market Research Society Newsletters and range from general weekly surveys done by telephone (eg phonebus) to special sector surveys (eg Omnicar - motoring, Carrick James - children and youth, small businesses etc). The advantage is that for a few hundred as opposed to a few thousand, pounds a company can ask a few questions of a reasonably representative sample and have a report sent within 2 or 3 weeks. Companies can also link up with others in an industry through their federations so as to conduct shared cost marketing research surveys.

6.8 **External assistance.** Few firms can carry out all the research they may find necessary. Employing outside agencies is often the answer and need not be too expensive.

(a) **Government bodies.** The DTI will often advise on these matters and is particularly helpful on export marketing research. Practical and financial assistance will be given in some instances.

(b) **Marketing research agencies and consultants.** Their numbers are increasing in response to demand for their services. The two professional associations in this sphere, the Market Research Society and the Industrial Marketing Research Association both issue lists of agencies and will often recommend a suitable agency.

(c) **Other bodies.** An increasing number of universities have business schools where advice and help can be obtained, often at small or no cost.

Field surveys

6.9 **Field surveys.** Few companies should undertake their own field surveys without expert help in survey design, sampling, questionnaire design and questionnaire administering. As the old saying goes 'rubbish in equals rubbish out'. It would be counter-productive if critical and expensive decisions were made on the basis of faulty research. However, companies should at least be aware of the basics of fieldwork in order to brief agencies adequately.

6.10 Field surveys generally speaking involve posing a number of questions to a **respondent**, who answers them. Respondents can be contacted in several ways. These are now briefly described.

(a) **Personal interview.** This is the most common method. Skilled interviewers attempt to obtain information from selected individuals. Formal questionnaires are usually used.

(i) **Advantages**

- It yields a high percentage of acceptable returns.
- There is a low refusal rate.
- The sample can be an almost perfect cross-section of the population.
- Interviewers can clear up contradictory statements at once.
- Answers are likely to be spontaneous.

- Much information can be obtained.

(ii) **Disadvantages**

- High cost per interview - travel, wages, etc.
- Interviewer bias can occur: the interviewer may influence the answers.
- Inaccuracies in recording can occur.
- The number of interviews per day is restricted.

(b) **Telephone interview.** This is, of course, restricted to samples of people with telephones. Contact is made by telephone and the people are then questioned.

(i) **Advantages**

- Speed.
- Interviewers are easily supervised.
- The cost per interview is low.
- The sample can be widely spread over the country - no travel expenses.
- People who might otherwise be inaccessible can be contacted.
- The respondent hears only one question at a time, so there is no bias due to **subsequent** questions.

(ii) **Disadvantages**

- Telephone subscribers are not always truly representative of the general population.
- Only a short questionnaire can be used.
- Observation is not possible, so no information can be obtained in this way.
- It is difficult to predict suitable times to telephone the respondents.
- Recalls are necessary when a number is engaged.
- Voicemail etc may prevent you getting to the person you want.
- The quality of the interviewer must be very high indeed.

(c) **Postal or mail survey method.** Respondents are contacted by post. Questionnaires to be completed and returned are sent to randomly selected individuals. Follow-up letters may have to be sent to those who have not replied. Sometimes a small gift is enclosed as an incentive to complete the questionnaire. The questionnaire needs to be short and easy to follow. The questionnaires may be enclosed in newspapers, periodicals or attached to some consumer product.

(i) **Advantages**

- A widely spread sample can be reached without increased costs.
- It can be much cheaper than field survey method.
- No interviewer training is required.
- Interviewer bias is avoided.
- Post is the only way to reach some groups.
- The respondent can fill in the form at his or her own convenience.
- Data about several members of a household can be obtained together.
- Information which the respondent has to verify can also be obtained

(ii) **Disadvantages**

(1) Respondents select themselves and are not fully representative of the population.

(2) The refusal rate tends to be very high. Returns will usually fall between 10 and 50 per cent.

(3) Respondents may not understand the questions and no interviewer is there to explain them.

(4) The questionnaire has to be simple and short, which limits the obtainable information.

(5) Up to date address lists are difficult to obtain and maintain.

(6) Returns can dribble in slowly and this stage of the survey can take considerable time.

(7) Personal questions may alienate the respondent and may have to be omitted.

(8) The answers may be influenced by the opinions of other people - there is no way this can be checked. Therefore, they are not appropriate for testing a person's knowledge on a topic.

(9) The wording has to be perfect.

(10) There is no chance to add observational data (eg type of house, the person's appearance, etc).

(iii) **Methods of increasing response rates**

(1) Include a stamped addressed envelope.

(2) Pay great attention to the covering letter.

(3) Use code numbers so you can tell who has not responded. This will need explanation probably in the covering letter. While this may put a few respondents off it is likely that the gains will outweigh the losses.

(4) Follow up to non-respondents ie sending another copy.

(5) Use of incentives - free sample or payment (as in the Family Expenditure Survey).

(d) **Group interview method.** A small, carefully selected group of people is invited to discuss whatever topic is under review. A questionnaire can be used, the discussion can be taped or an observer can take notes.

(i) **Advantages**

(1) Useful for research concerned with motives and opinions where factors such as social status and acceptance are involved.

(2) Reasonably cheap - one observer can handle up to ten people at a time.

(3) The spontaneous discussion may provide information not obtainable by other means.

(ii) **Disadvantages**

(1) Doubtful if such a group can be regarded as really representative of the population.

(2) The information obtained is not usually suitable for statistical analysis.

(3) It is possible that the more vocal members may have some undue influence on the group opinion.

(4) The observer must be a psychologist or similarly trained person. His job is not to intrude, only to keep the discussion to the point.

(e) **Panel method.** A group of people are selected, and their services are retained over a period of time to obtain a series of answers.

(i) **Types of panel**

(1) Consumer purchasing panel
(2) Consumer product testing panel
(3) Retail audit panel
(4) Radio audience panel
(5) Television audience panel

(ii) Recruitment of panels is by personal interview of a cross section of the population. Those chosen are given diaries in which they are asked to enter, for example, all their purchases of the commodities being surveyed. Diaries are returned at regular intervals (often weekly). Alternatively the panel can be interviewed periodically. This has been successfully used for radio, television and opinion research.

(iii) **Advantages**

(1) Because the people involved stay the same over a period of time it is useful for researching into trends eg changing TV viewing habits.

(2) Data gathered over a period of time can be accumulated and factors underlying changes in trends analysed.

(3) Case histories of respondents can be used to provide relevant background material to responses.

(4) The panel, once established, may be used for enquiries on other subjects.

(iv) **Disadvantages**

(1) The membership of the panel is not fixed (death, removal, etc).

(2) Refusal to join the panel may destroy its representativeness. Often the less literate section of the population refuses to join.

(3) The fact that the members belong to the panel may affect their reactions over a period of time. They may become **less** typical.

(4) Recruitment is expensive (a long time before it yields returns).

(5) Much interviewing is necessary to replace lost panel members.

(6) Panel members may have to be visited regularly to check on their activity and reliability. This is costly.

(7) Panel members usually have to be rewarded.

(f) **Observational methods.** An observer simply records what he sees.

(i) **Types of observational method**

(1) **Stock audits** can be made at regular intervals in order to establish sales trends for certain products.

(2) **Passenger counts** are useful if poster advertising is being considered. Counts could involve pedestrians, motorists and passengers on public transport.

(3) **Behaviour observation.** Movements and behaviour of store customers are monitored to check store display and layout.

(4) **Participant observation.** The observer remains with subject for a period of time to see what the subject really does.

(ii) **Advantages**

(1) Respondent mistakes deriving from faulty memory are eliminated.
(2) Interviewer bias is slight and may not occur at all.

(iii) **Disadvantages**

(1) People are not always reliable observers, although sometimes mechanical recording devices can be used.

(2) Only a limited amount of information can be obtained.

(3) The cost may be high.

Briefing a market research agency

6.11 In your marketing research plan you will need to decide whether to appoint an agency and if so how to go about this, and the selection criteria you will use. It is advisable to draw up a shortlist of agencies based on size, location, expertise, recommendation etc and approach, say, three of them for proposals and a quotation. The following notes will help you to draw up a brief.

6.12 **What the market research agency can expect from you**

(a) A statement of the research problems, preferably in the form of a written brief.

(b) A setting of the problem in its general background and context. In some cases, users may be able to define their overall problem within its generalised context but not have the experience to define it in **research** terms.

(c) An opportunity to meet and discuss the problem and its background

(d) An indication of the decisions that are likely to be influenced by the research results and the uses to which the results are to be put (eg whether publication is envisaged).

(e) A broad indication of the budget available for the research project.

(f) A reasonable probability that the project under consideration will actually be commissioned.

(g) If it is the type of project which you feel should be subject to tender, then you should restrict the agencies you approach to a reasonable number (say two to four), and inform them that they are competing.

6.13 **What you can expect from the agency: general.**

(a) Evidence of the background and quality of its research executives.

(b) Details of any specialists (psychologists, statisticians) employed full-time or on a consultant basis.

(c) Evidence of the company's experience that may be relevant to your particular situation; work on similar kinds of problems; work within the same market; experience of using relevant research techniques.

(d) Details of the field operation; selection and training of interviewers; levels of supervision; check on quality and accuracy.

(e) Details of editing, coding, and purchasing operations; quality and training of staff; supervision; checks on quality and accuracy.

(f) Details of analysis and tabulation, computers and machinery used, restrictions on numbers and types of tabulations.

(g) Details of normal standard of reporting; the style and content of reports.

(h) Details of accounting and legal aspects; normal billing procedures.

6.14 **What you can expect from the agency: specific**

(a) It should be obvious from their statement of the research objectives and of the scope of the inquiry, that the agency **understands your problem**.

(b) Detailed descriptions of the research design including:

(i) a statement of the scope and nature of any preliminary desk research, qualitative work, or pilot studies;

(ii) for any quantitative study, a statement of the data collection technique (how the information is to be obtained) population to be sampled (who is to be interviewed). the size of the sample (how many are to be interviewed), the method of sample selection (how the individuals are to be selected).

(c) A **statement of the cost of the project** and a clear indication of the assumptions on which it is based and what is included eg assumptions made about length of interview, assumptions made about degree of executive involvement, whether personal briefing of interviewers is included, the number of copies of the report envisaged, the approximate number of tabulations envisaged; whether there will be a written interpretation of the tabulations, whether visual presentations of results is included.

(d) A reasonably detailed **timetable** for the project and a reasonably firm reporting date.

(e) The name(s) of the executive(s) responsible for the project.

6.15 **A marketing research programme**

(a) **Research brief.** This should define clearly the marketing problems to be investigated (eg the need for machines of a specific capacity, specific formulations of chemicals, likely demand for spares). It may be necessary to make some exploratory enquiries in certain areas of the organisation (eg selling arrangements, publicity methods, pricing structures in order to gain valuable background knowledge). They should agree on the level of accuracy and the required submission date.

(b) **Work plan.** This should specify a simple model of the problem, specify the data to be collected and the methodology. It should give the timing of various operations. It should be shown how the work plan meets the objective of the research.

(c) **Collection of data** is the longest stage, and it is necessary to check the relative efficiency of alternative methods of data collection.

(d) **Analysis and evaluation of data.** Analysis pre-supposes sound data. Data have to be refined by means of tabulations analysis and interpretation. The analysis should ascertain significant relationships between variables. Systems of data storage and retrieval may be incorporated at this stage, with provision for updating and extending the data base as required.

6.16 **Presentation of findings.** Most findings have to be presented to two main groups, general management, and research specialists. Often, therefore, there have to be two reports - a fully documented technical report and a short, detailed account of major findings, conclusions and recommendations, abstracted from the first. The Market Research Society suggests the following minimum acceptable contents of a report should include the following.

Market research report

- Purpose of the survey
- For whom and by whom the survey was undertaken.
- General description of the universe covered
- Size and nature of the sample, including a description of any weighting methods used.
- The time when the field work was carried out.
- The method of interviewing employed.
- Adequate description of field staff and any control methods used.
- A copy of the questionnaire
- The factual findings
- Bases of percentages
- Geographical distribution of interviews.

6.17 A formal layout of an MR report is given below.

1 **Introduction**

- Title of the report
- Name of sponsor
- Title of research organisation
- Date of publication.

2 **Table of contents**

3 **Preface.** (Stating terms of reference and acknowledgement.)

4 **Statement of purpose.** (Elaboration of the terms of reference contained in the preface. It would outline the general nature of the problem and be investigated and specific hypotheses on which the research was based.)

5 **Methodology.** (Outline the stages through which the project passed, a statement of the definitions adopted, research techniques employed, sources of data used, details of sample size and composition, description of the methods of analysis employed, any explanatory observations.)

6 **Findings.** (Abstract of relevant data.)

7 **Conclusion.** (Used on findings.)

8 **Recommendations.** (Based on conclusions).

9 **Appendices.** (Detailed accounts of sample design and its theoretical reliability; copy of the questionnaire and instructions to interviewers; detailed statistical tables; bibliography and glossary of terms; details of any tests of reliability; theoretical proofs.)

(a) In a report intended for the management, conclusions and recommendations follow immediately after the statement of purpose or terms of reference, and methodology could be consigned to the appendixes.

(b) There will usually be a single page statement of the basic purpose and findings entitled Management or Executive Summary.

6.18 **Type of research.** Care needs to be taken to distinguish types of research (product research, advertising research, distribution research) and methods (desk research, field research, telephone research, observational research etc)

Retail audits and consumer panels

6.19 **Retail audits.** A retail audit is a form of market research which provides information for manufacturers about the sales, distribution and stocks of their products and of competing brands.

(a) It accounts for a substantial proportion of total expenditure on market research in this country, being sponsored mainly by manufacturers of food and pharmaceutical products.

(b) Without retail audit the manufacturer has little knowledge of movement of his product from the wholesaler to the retailer and on to the actual purchaser. Thus if ex-factory sales rise it will not be certain whether this is due to an increase in consumer demand or whether it is the result of wholesalers or retailers increasing their stocks. Moreover, a manufacturer's own sales figures tell nothing about how competitors are faring.

6.20 **Special panels for test marketing.** Retail audit panels provide a means for testing a new product in a restricted area before large-scale production and distribution are embarked upon. The product tested might be a completely new one or might only be new to a manufacturer wishing to get into a particular market.

(a) The basic operation in test auditing is to provide sales and market share information for three consecutive periods: before the product is launched, the launch period itself and after the launch.

(b) The object of this type of testing is to avoid making mistakes on a large scale, by confining the initial marketing operation to one area. The area chosen is usually an ITV region

(c) The **test operation** proceeds as follows.

(i) Before the product is launched **audit data are collected to establish the existing market pattern**.

(ii) After the new brand has been launched the immediate impact is observed from the audit figures. Initial sales figures can, of course, be misleading: the auditing operation is therefore continued until the market has settled down to its new equilibrium level.

(iii) The manufacturer, having noted the reception of his product in the test area can decide whether to extend the marketing area or whether any strengthening of the product or of the marketing method is necessary.

(iv) Modifications to the product or to its presentation can be made and their effects measured.

(v) When the product is finally approved and the best marketing strategy has been decided, it is ready for launching over a wider area, maybe on a national scale. This may be up to two years after the initial launch in the test area, reflecting the care and detailed planning necessary when introducing a new product.

(d) **A test marketing area** affords the first opportunity for a manufacturer to observe the reactions of consumers to his product under **actual market conditions.** Such reactions differ from those to other forms of product testing (eg free samples, in that the product is actually purchased over the counter by the consumer).

(e) A test marketing operation also enables the manufacturer to assess the trade's reaction to the new product, in particular to such matters as margins, packaging, display material and advertising.

(f) The test operation consists basically of a 'before, during and after' measurement, principally of market share. The 'before and after' periods should be 'as long as possible' but the actual length is determined as usual by the time and money available. Nevertheless, it is essential that the 'after' period should be sufficiently long to enable the **initial** impact to subside.

(g) The use of a test panel is not confined to the testing of a new product. The effect of changing the packaging, advertising or marketing policy for an established product may also be measured with the same idea of avoiding mistakes on a large scale with consequent waste of money or, worse, damage to the brand image.

6.21 **Limitations of retail audit**. However, the research is based on sampling techniques which depart from random methods, sometimes to a considerable extent. The main dangers are as follows.

(a) Generalising from the sample to a population wider than that from which the sample was drawn (eg assuming that results from stores who do co-operate apply to those who do not).

(b) Attempting to base large-scale marketing strategies on tests made in only one or two towns.

(c) Basing decisions on test figures before the effect of the **initial** launch or advertising impact has died down. (People might try out the product once.)

(d) Competitors might intervene to distort the data obtained.

Retail audit is now a firmly established and respectable form of research with most manufacturers of food, cosmetics, pharmaceutical, and other consumer goods. The money spent checking how a brand is selling against competitors' brands is small compared with the money spent on advertising the brand.

6.22 **Consumer panels.** Bearing in mind that markets are essentially people (ie and their wants and needs) you should want to know more about your actual customers than the retail audit can tell you. This gap is addressed by a representative sample of consumers in the form of a panel or series of panels. These consumers maintain detailed records of what they buy and why they change brand loyalties or store loyalties.

6.23 **Information obtainable from consumer panels**

(a) Who buys?

(i) Socio-economic class.
(ii) Age group

(b) How good is your distribution?

(i) By area
(ii) Town or country?
(iii) How strong is your distribution through every type of outlet?

(c) How frequently do people purchase your product?

(d) Do people buy your product more than just once?

(e) Use of 'size of household' analysis.

(f) Where is your greatest appeal (eg to households with children)?

(g) Does seasonal change affect your sales unduly?

(h) What makes a customer switch brands?

6.24 Advertising/communications research is covered in Chapter 2 on Marketing Communications Strategy.

The marketing information system (MkIS)

6.25 Many marketing decisions are taken on a continuous basis (eg decisions are taken on various aspects of the marketing mix - sales, advertising, sales promotion at least annually). A continuous plan of information is also required for control purposes. A marketing information system (MkIS), normally part of the Management Information System (MIS), meets these needs. A diagram can be found on the following page.

6.26 **Contents of the MkIS**

(a) **Internal reports (and accounts) systems** provides:

- Results data
- Provides measures of current activity performance
- Sales, costs, stock information
- Possible areas for improvement include the timeliness, availability and distribution of reports

(b) **Marketing intelligence system**

(i) **Happenings data** (eg what competitors are doing).
(ii) It provides information on developments in the environment.
(iii) It involves scanning and the dissemination of a wide range of intelligence.
(iv) Possible areas of improvement include:

- Increased use of salesmen as intelligence agents
- Additional intelligence sources
- Purchasing data from special marketing intelligence services
- Processing of intelligence by improving the system for evaluation, abstraction, dissemination, storage and retrieval

(c) **Marketing research system contains** specific studies of marketing problems, opportunities and effectiveness.

(d) **Analytical marketing system (Management science).** This uses models to explain, predict and improve marketing processes. Models may be descriptive, decisional, verbal, graphical or mathematical.

6.27 An MkIS has implications for costs and for the organisation's practices.

(a) Training of existing and new staff.

(b) Staff with specialist skills might be recruited. Job descriptions and specifications might need to change.

(c) **Organisational considerations**

- Reallocation of duties
- The degree to which the system should be centralised

The marketing information system

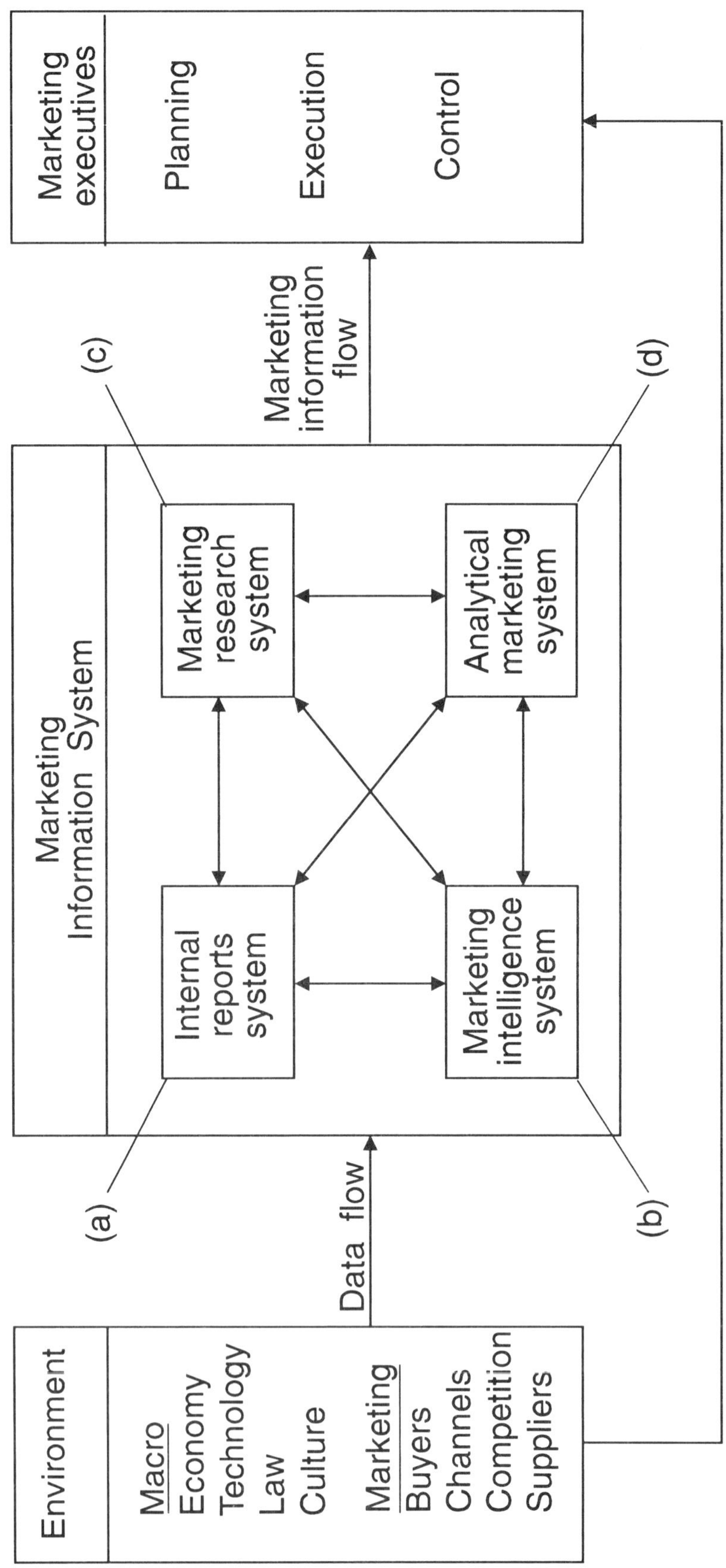

(d) Costs incurred include:

- Specialist staff
- Retraining
- Equipment
- System running costs

(e) Time is needed before the system will display any benefits

6.28 The **design of any MkIS** should:

(a) Recognise user limitations in defining and then fully using information
(b) Ensure users understand the systems and are in position to evaluate and control it
(c) Review the system regularly and improve feedback
(d) Clarify the true meaning and highlight the limitations of information provided
(e) Be flexible
(f) Recognise that a system is only as effective as designers and users make it

6.29 **Points to bear in mind**

(a) Managers may not know what information they need and want.

(b) Even if provided with the information, managers do not always make good use of it.

(c) More communication often means better performance.

(d) The managers do not have to understand how an information system works, but they should get some idea of the benefits it can give them to encourage them to use it.

6.30 The benefits possible with a sophisticated MkIS are outlined in the table on the next page.

Typical applications	*Benefits*	*Examples*
Control systems		
1 Control of marketing costs	1 More timely computerised reports	1 Undesirable cost trends are spotted quickly so that corrective action may be taken sooner
2 Diagnosis of poor sales performance	2 Flexible on-line retrieval of data	2 Executives can ask supplementary questions of the computer to help pinpoint reasons for a sales decline
3 Management of fashion goods	3 Automatic spotting of problems and opportunities	3 Fast-moving fashion items are reported daily for re-order and slow moving items are reported for price reduction
4 Flexible promotion strategy	4 Cheaper, more detailed and more frequent reports	4 On-going evaluation of a promotional campaign permits reallocation of funds to areas behind target
Planning systems		
1 Forecasting	1 Automatic translation of terms and classifications between departments	1 Survey-based forecasts of demand for industrial goods can be automatically translated into parts requirements and production schedules
2 Promotional planning and corporate long-range planning	2 Systematic testing of alternative promotional plans	2 Simulation models, both developed and operated with the help of data bank information can be used for promotional planning
3 Credit management	3 Programmed executive decision rules can operate on data bank information	3 Credit decisions are automatically made as each order is processed
4 Purchasing	4 Detailed sales reporting permits automation of management decisions	4 Computer automatically repurchases standard items on the basis of sales data with programmed decision rule
Research systems		
1 Advertising strategy	1 Additional manipulation of data is possible when stored on computer in an unaggregated file	1 Sales analysis is possible by new market segment breakdowns
2 Pricing strategy	2 Improved storage and retrieval capability allows new types of data to be collected and used	2 Systematic recording of information about past R&D contract bidding situation allows improved bidding strategies
3 Evaluation of advertising expenditures	3 Well-designed data banks permit integration and comparison of different sets of data	3 Advertising expenditures are compared to shipments by country to provide information about advertising effectiveness

Chapter roundup

- This chapter has endeavoured to cover those areas of the Strategic Marketing Management: Planning & Control syllabus relevant to the Analysis & Decision examination. Consequently it has dealt with the practical aspects of the issues you will face, rather than a theoretical examination of them.
- The marketing plan is one of many functional plans, but at strategic level it has a great impact on the organisation's corporate plan. After all, deciding the business the organisation is in (the products and services it provides to its chosen markets) is a corporate as well as a marketing issue. Growth in sales volumes and value is the overall marketing objective. Marketing planning requires:
    - an analysis of the current situation (a marketing audit);
    - an awareness of the business's mission (what business are we in now? what business would we like to be in in 5-10 years time?);
    - objectives, ensuring that corporate objectives are translated into marketing terms;
    - strategies (eg Ansoff, segmentation) for achieving those objectives;
    - tactics (marketing mix proposals: product, price, place, promotion and the three extra Ps for service marketing, people, processes and physical evidence).
- Marketing research and the marketing information system provide essential underpinning to the planning and control of marketing strategies.

Quick quiz

1 Draw a diagram of the planning process. (see para 1.13)
2 What is the difference between strategy and tactics, in marketing? (1.22, 1.23)
3 Who or what is the focus of a marketing plan? (2.3)
4 What is SWOT? (2.17)
5 What subjective techniques of sales forecasting might you use? (3.10)
6 Why are budgets compiled? (3.13, 3.16)
7 What is the importance of the sales budget? (3.23)
8 Describe the expense budgets related to marketing (3.53)
9 What strategies are suggested by the Ansoff matrix? (3.78, 3.79)
10 What are critical success factors? (3.82)
11 What are three generic strategies for obtaining competitive advantage? (4.4)
12 Describe competitor response models. (4.6)
13 Distinguish between products and services. (4.14, 4.15)
14 What is value analysis? (4.24)
15 What control techniques can be used? (5.2)
16 How can ratios help? (5.6, 5.7)
17 What would be contained in an information specification for a firm? (6.4)
18 List some sources of marketing research data. (6.7)
19 At the back of this Tutorial Text you will find a review form which asks you for your comments on this Tutorial Text. How does this rate as MR in your opinion? (Can you improve it?)
20 What are the drawbacks of a MkIS? (6.29)

2 Integrated Marketing Communications

This chapter covers the following topics.

Introduction

This chapter emphasises the practical aspects of marketing communications relevant to the case study. This material will **not** be appropriate for the Integrated Marketing Communications exam: buy the BPP Study Text if you are taking it.

1 MARKETING COMMUNICATIONS STRATEGY AT CORPORATE LEVEL

1.1 Marketing communications are only a part of the total communications output of any company or organisation. Total communications breaks down into:

- External communications (to people outside the organisation)
- Internal communications (to people within it)

Corporate identity

1.2 Any organisation cannot help having a **corporate identity**. The physical aspects of an organisation, eg premises, literature, staff duties, vehicles etc convey impressions or images. A corporate identity relating to the firm is sometimes promoted as distinct from the firm's products. The penalty for not having a good corporate identity is perhaps best expressed by the following statements.

> I don't know who you are
> I don't know your company
> I don't know your company's products
> I don't know what your company stands for
> I don't know your company's customers
> I don't know your company's record
> I don't know your company's reputation
> Now what was it you wanted to sell me?

1.3 The salesperson representing, say, Coca Cola, a company with a recognisable image would be unlikely to have to face the above communication barriers. There are, however, many other **reasons for developing appropriate corporate identities**, including the following.

(a) The increasing importance of **public relations** (eg establishing the right relationships with governments, opinion influencing pressure groups, local communities in the vicinity of offices, factories, distribution centres).

(b) The need to attract and retain **investment**.

(c) The need to attract **labour** of the right kind in the right numbers (depending on the level of employment etc).

(d) The growing realisation of the importance of **good relationships** with suppliers and institutions involved in forward distribution processes: wholesalers, agents, distributors.

(e) The need to foster a feeling of belonging within an organisation-this is particularly in evidence in large, widely spread groups and/or merged or re-structured units.

(f) The realisation of the cumulative impact of multiple repetition.

1.4 You may find the following distinctions (Olms 1989) help to avoid confusion.

(a) **Corporate personality** 'is the soul, the persona, the spirit, the culture of the organisation manifested in some way. A corporate personality is not necessarily something tangible that you can see, feel or touch - although it may be'.

(b) **Corporate identity** 'is the tangible manifestation of a corporate personality.....It is the identity that projects and reflects the reality of the corporate personality'.

(c) **Corporate image** 'is what people actually perceive of a corporate personality or corporate identity'.

We should all be aware that the image actually received is not always that intended by the message sender - hence the need for pre-testing. For example a bank sends messages saying that it is friendly and caring but potential customers might find these messages patronising and insincere.

1.5 **Corporate public relations**. Many companies which recognise the importance of having a good corporate identity manage their external/internal communications by the use of a Corporate PR function or department. The Institute of Public Relations defines public relations (PR) as 'the deliberate, planned and sustained effort to establish and maintain mutual understanding between an organisation and its publics'. **There are eight basic publics for PR.**

(a) The **community** at large - people living near the premises or affected by them

(b) **Employees** and their unions

(c) **Customers** - past, present and future

(d) **Suppliers** - of materials and non-financial services

(e) The **money market** - shareholders, banks, insurers, potential investors.

(f) **Distributors** - agents, wholesalers, retailers etc

(g) **Potential employees**

(h) **Opinion leaders** - all those whose opinions could help or harm the organisation including media editors

1.6 Care needs to be taken therefore to distinguish between corporate PR and marketing or product/service PR. You will find that some authors prefer to use the term 'publicity' to describe the sub-function of PR which seeks to gain favourable editorial publicity in the media about a firm's products and services. More about this comes later in Section 3 on the promotional mix.

1.7 Occasionally, firms use **corporate advertising** to build public awareness of their size and activities. Conglomerates do this for a variety of reasons (eg to purvey an image of ecological friendliness to communicate with shareholders, and influence public opinion).

2 COMMUNICATIONS PLANNING

Integration of marketing communications

2.1 It is essential that **marketing** communications are integrated with **corporate** communications and that all elements of the marketing communications (promotional) mix are also harmonised. All a firm's communications need to say the same thing to avoid confusing and alienating the firm's customers, potential customers, and publics.

2.2 A model of the process is given below.

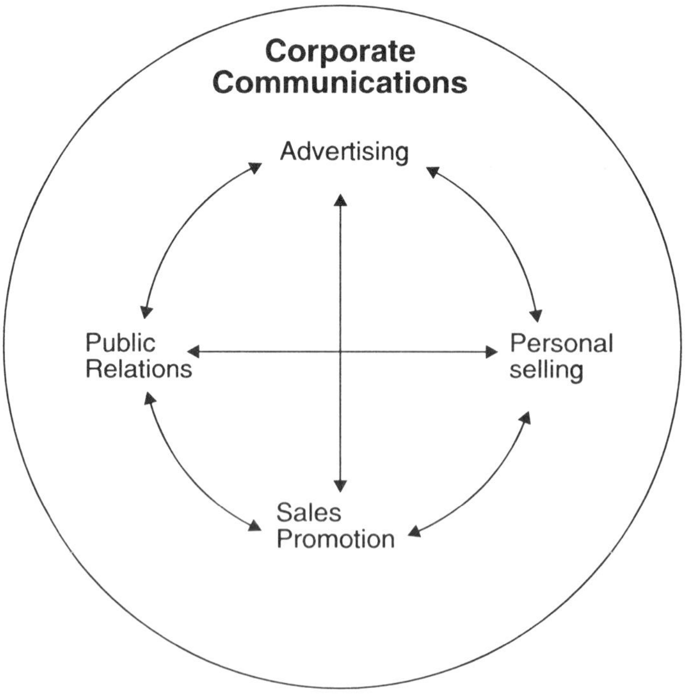

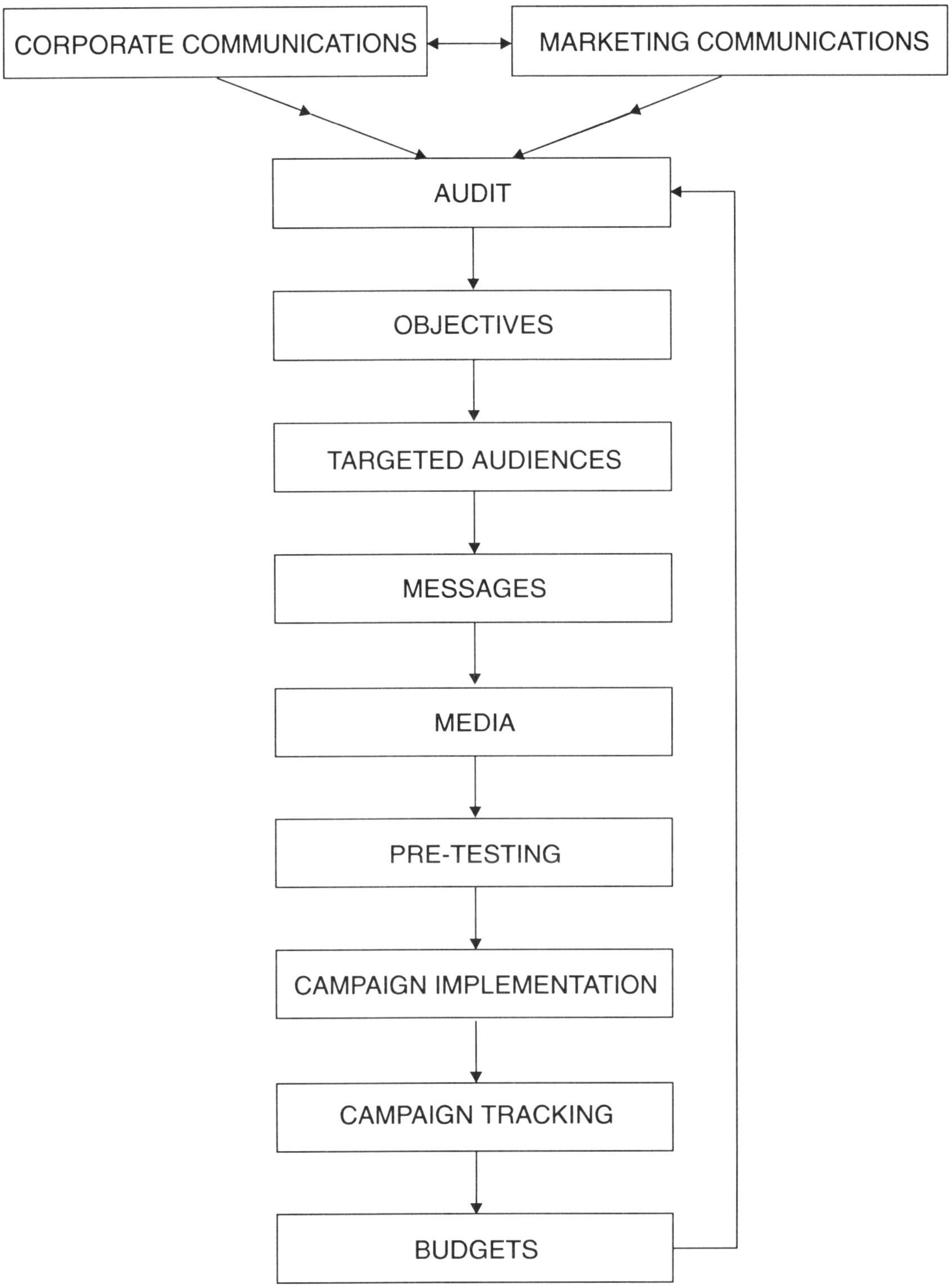

Communications planning formats follow the same general framework of any planning activity with the additional considerations that we need to:

(a) Define clearly the target audiences with which we wish to communicate

(b) Decide the messages we wish to send and the most appropriate media to carry these messages to the target audiences

(c) Pre-test (to ensure the messages will have the desired effect)

(d) Post-track (to ensure the messages have reached the target audiences at the right time, the measure of recall and conviction etc)

Corporate vs marketing communications objectives

2.3 Again we need to distinguish between corporate communications objectives and marketing communications objectives. Examples might be as follows.

(a) **Some potential corporate communications objectives**

(i) Assure the general public that the organisation's policies are environmentally friendly

(ii) Resist take-over by a bidder

(iii) Gain governmental assistance

(iv) Announce changes in the Board of Directors

(v) Promote awareness of the corporate mission

(b) **Potential marketing communications objectives**

(i) **Consumer communications**

- Inform about a new product
- Correct misconceptions about a product
- Increase frequency of use
- Remind people about a product
- Present special offers
- Educate consumers in how to use a product
- Build an image for the product/company
- Build up consumer loyalty

(ii) **Trade communications**

- Provide information
- Inform about promotional programmes
- Present special trade offers
- Avoid stockpiling
- Educate the trade on product usage
- Build patronage motives

(c) Some communications are quantitative (eg numbers of enquiries) and qualitative (eg aimed at changing attitudes).

3 PROMOTION AND THE PROMOTIONAL MIX

3.1 The words promotion and communications tend to be used synonymously but some authors prefer to use the terms **promotion** and **promotional mix** to distinguish marketing communications from corporate communications. The rest of this chapter is concerned with marketing communications.

3.2 **Some benefits of promotion**

(a) **Personal contact is expensive**. Appropriate promotion takes the place of personal contact, and has a lower cost, for example by mailshots.

(b) Promotion helps prepare the ground for personal sales.

(c) Customers are forgetful. Promotion can remind customers or potential customers of the firm's products and services.

(d) Sales visits consume time. Promotion can convey some information in advance, making calls more productive.

(e) Promotion can promote the wide range of a firm's activities.

(f) The morale of staff can be boosted if the firm has a good image.

(g) Promotion can communicate to customers who are otherwise hard to contact.

(h) Promotion can help identify potential new customers, through enquiries received for follow-up.

3.3 Consider also the following example of a buying behaviour model for a retail setting and the effect of promotion (advertising, personal selling, PR/publicity and sales promotion) on the model's outcomes. 'Dupont' is a manufacturer of branded consumer goods distributed through retail outlets.

The Dupont consumer buying behaviour model

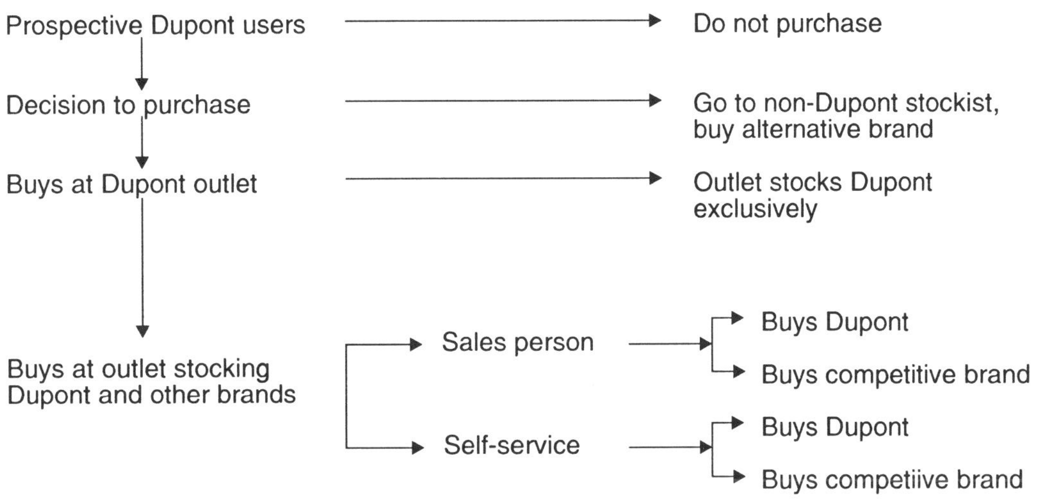

Potentially **beneficial effects of promotion** for Dupont

(a) It increases the number of prospective Dupont users.

(b) It increases the number of outlets stocking Dupont or the number of people using existing Dupont outlets.

(c) It influences more customers to specify Dupont despite what the salesperson may suggest.

(d) It increases the number of salespeople suggesting Dupont.

(e) It increases the number of self-service customers selecting Dupont.

A problem, of course, is that other people are 'promoting' as well.

3.4 Each of the four elements of the promotional mix has its own submix which requires planning and decisions, as illustrated in the following chart.

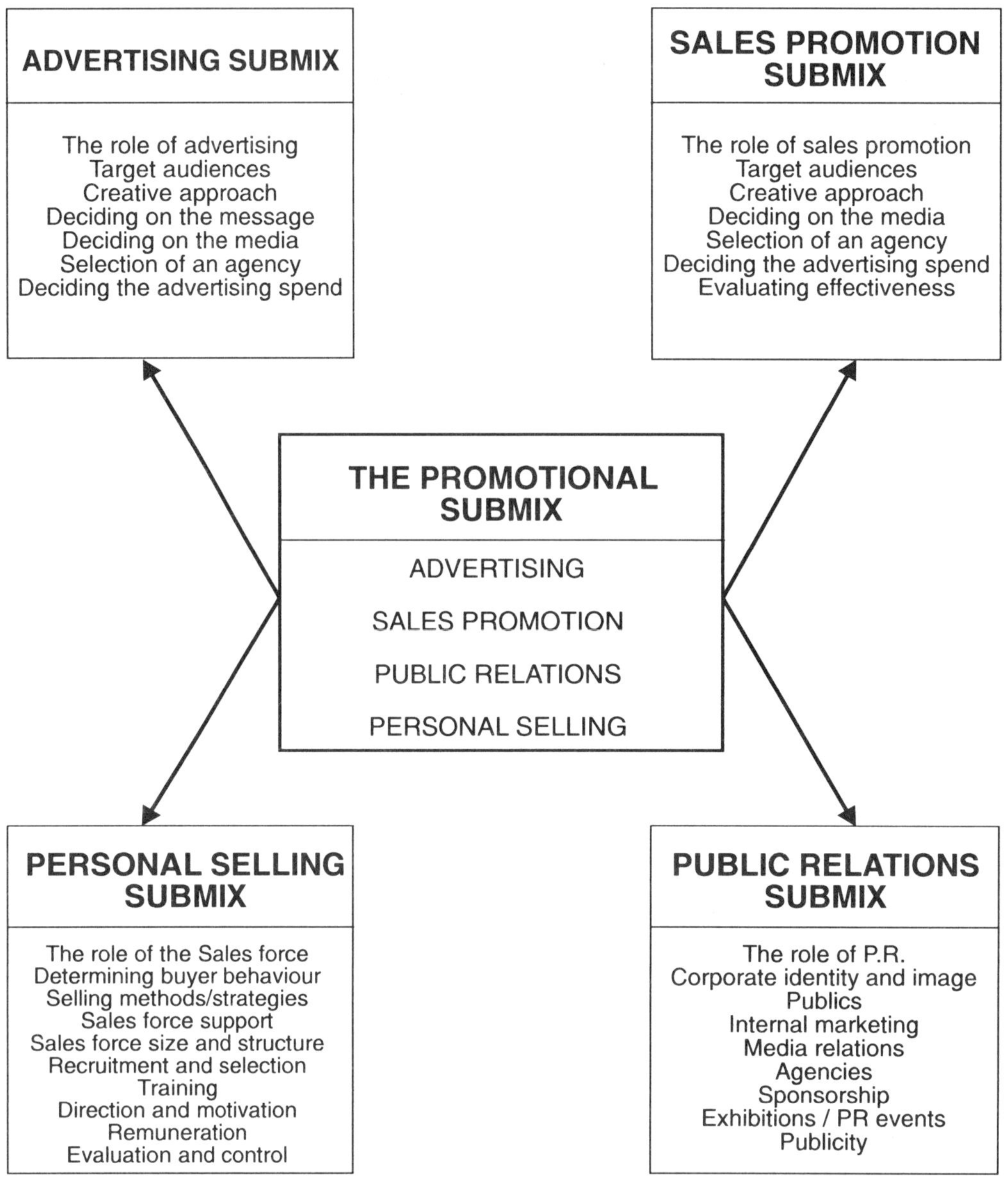
ADVERTISING SUBMIX
The role of advertising
Target audiences
Creative approach
Deciding on the message
Deciding on the media
Selection of an agency
Deciding the advertising spend
SALES PROMOTION SUBMIX
The role of sales promotion
Target audiences
Creative approach
Deciding on the media
Selection of an agency
Deciding the advertising spend
Evaluating effectiveness
THE PROMOTIONAL SUBMIX
ADVERTISING
SALES PROMOTION
PUBLIC RELATIONS
PERSONAL SELLING
PERSONAL SELLING SUBMIX
The role of the Sales force
Determining buyer behaviour
Selling methods/strategies
Sales force support
Sales force size and structure
Recruitment and selection
Training
Direction and motivation
Remuneration
Evaluation and control
PUBLIC RELATIONS SUBMIX
The role of P.R.
Corporate identity and image
Publics
Internal marketing
Media relations
Agencies
Sponsorship
Exhibitions / PR events
Publicity

3.5 The elements of the promotional mix, like the elements of the marketing mix need to be harmonised for maximum productivity.

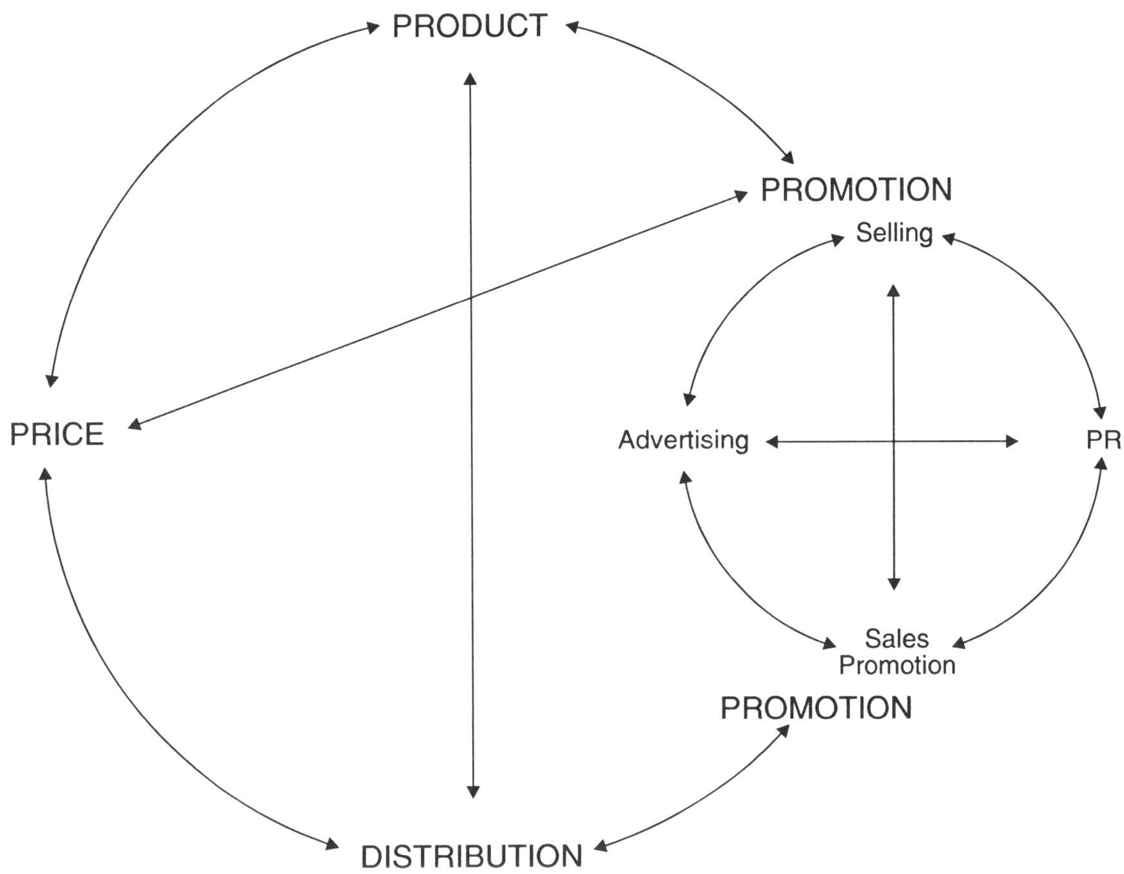

Deciding the right promotional mix

3.6 In trying to increase market share (a marketing objective) using a promotional strategy (rather than a price decrease or new product introduction) we do of course need to decide the right promotional mix. Increases in sales can be brought about by:

- More advertising
- More customer incentives
- Better PR
- Enlarging the sales force
- A mix of all four measures

The decision then becomes how much more advertising, how many more salespeople etc.

3.7 In taking these decisions we ideally want to know the **relative efficacy of each action.** This can possibly be determined by experimentation and/or observation of competitor actions, or indeed similar actions in different markets. Unfortunately for marketing managers, favourable reactions to previous promotional initiatives are not always repeated. This is because markets change, competitors act differently etc. However, you should find the following general advantages and disadvantages of major promotion methods (as proposed by Peter and Olson) helpful in making your decisions.

Advertising	
Advantages	*Disadvantages*
Can reach many consumers simultaneously Relatively less cost per exposure Excellent for creating brand images High degree of flexibility and variety of media to choose from; can accomplish many different types of promotion objectives	Many consumers reached are not potential buyers (waste of promotion expenditure) High visibility makes advertising a major target of marketing critics Advertisement exposure time is usually brief Advertisements are often quickly and easily screened out by customers
Personal selling	
Advantages	*Disadvantages*
Can be the most persuasive promotion tool; salespeople can directly influence purchase behaviours Allows two-way communication Often necessary for technically complex products Allows direct one-on-one targeting of promotional effort	High cost per contact Sales training and motivation can be expensive and difficult Personal selling often has a poor image, making salesforce recruitment difficult Poorly done sales presentations can hurt sales as well as company, product and brand images
Sales promotion	
Advantages	*Disadvantages*
Excellent approach for short-term price reductions for stimulating demand A large variety of sales promotion tools to choose from Can be effective for changing a variety of consumer behaviours. Can be easily tied in with other promotion tools	May influence primarily brand-loyal customers to stock up at lower price but attract few new customers May have only short-term impact Overuse of price-related sales promotion tools may hurt brand image and profits Effective sales promotions are easily copied by competitors
Publicity	
Advantages	*Disadvantages*
As 'free advertising', publicity can be positive and stimulate demand at no cost May be perceived by consumers as more credible, because it is not paid for by the seller Consumers may pay more attention to these messages, because they are not quickly screened out as are many advertisements	Company cannot completely control the content of publicity messages Publicity is not always available Limited repetition of publicity messages; seldom a long-term promotion tool for brands Publicity can be negative and hurt sales as well as company product, and brand images

Pull and *push* promotional strategies in retail marketing

3.8 The following two diagrams illustrate these push and pull strategies.

(a) The **push strategy is one where the producer concentrates on selling in to the channel in the hope that its goods will sell out.**

(b) By contrast the **pull strategy is where the producer advertises heavily and directly to consumers to create demand so that consumers ask for its goods** which the channel is then induced to stock. In fast moving consumer goods most producers employ both policies to gain maximum effect.

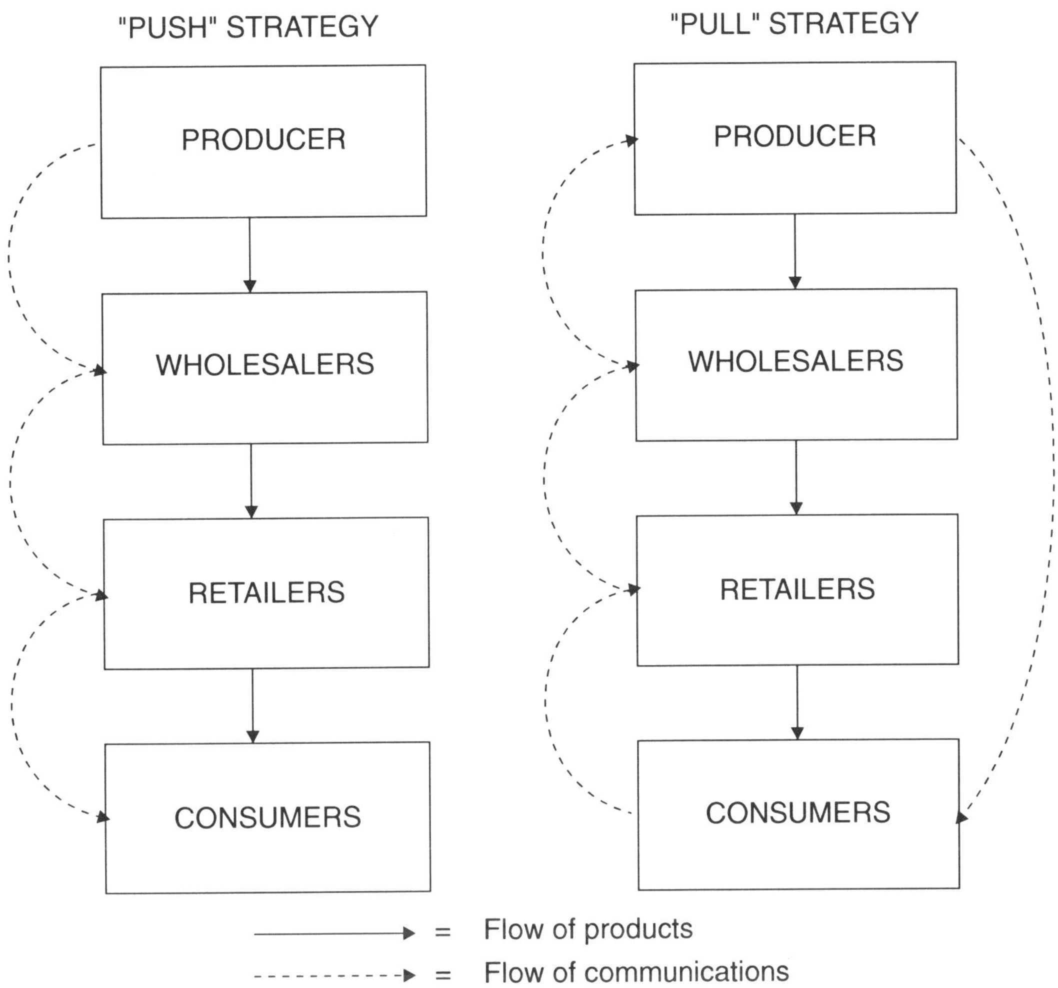

Push versus pull strategies

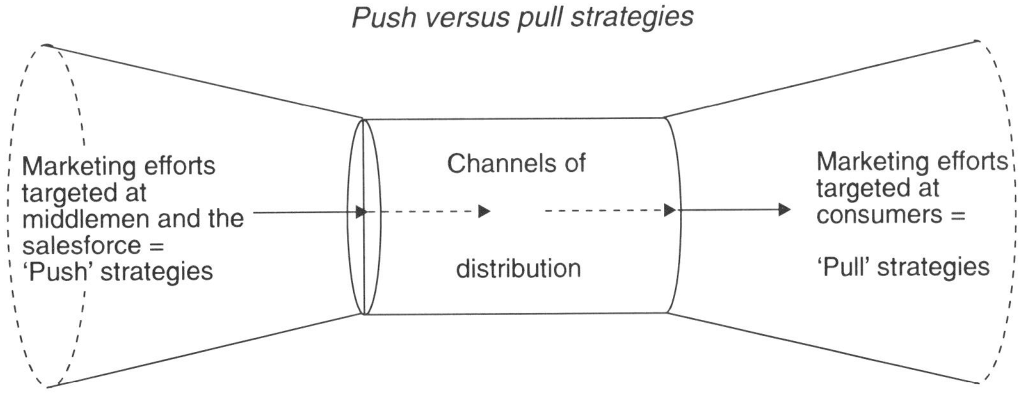

3.9 The use of a push strategy usually requires a sizeable amount of personal selling and sales promotion, whereas the pull policy demands mass media advertising to a larger degree.

Selling decisions

3.10 The most **expensive** and the most **effective** form of promotion is personal selling.

(a) The cost of selling includes:

- Salary
- Meals
- Accommodation
- Car
- Commission
- Supervision
- Administration
- Training

(b) The cost of actual selling time is greater than this because few salespeople spend more than 20% of their time actually selling. On average a salesperson's time can be broken down as follows.

	%
Travelling	40
Meals	10
Waiting	17
General chat	17
Selling	16

(c) Some **alternative forms of selling**

- Commando sales forces conducting 'raids' on particular areas
- Telephone selling
- Agents

(d) The effectiveness of personal selling is high because the salesperson can:

- Vary the approach to suit different customers
- Answer questions and counter objections
- Accept an order on the spot

3.11 The main **sales decisions** are as follows.

(a) Steps in determining the **size of the sales force**.

Step 1. Group customers by turnover

Step 2. Determine the number of calls required per customer

Step 3. Total work load = Number of customers × number of calls required per customer per annum.

Step 4 Determine number of calls a salesperson can make each year.

Step 5. The number of salespeople required =

$$\frac{\text{Total number of calls per annum}}{\text{Average number of calls per sales person per annum}}.$$

(b) **Structure of the sales force**

(i) **By geographical area.** The basis can be either:

(1) Equal potential sales per area (which gives unequal workloads, as one area may be much larger than another, or contain more customers, requiring more travelling); or

(2) Equal workload (which gives unequal potential sales, the corollary of (i) above)

The practical compromise is a mixture of the two.

(ii) **By product** where there are technical problems.

(iii) **By customer** where customer needs differ.

(c) The sales force can be remunerated by:

- Commission only
- Salary only
- Salary and commission
- Salary and bonuses
- Salary and commission and bonuses

Commission is based on each individual sale. Bonuses might be based on the achievement of certain sales targets, and might even be paid on a group basis.

Advertising decisions

3.12 The main advertising decisions are as follows assuming that target audiences have been identified and responses sought have been clarified. (Further notes are given in Section 5 of this chapter.)

(a) **What are the objectives of advertising?** The advertising objectives must be specific and well defined if advertising is to be successful and properly targeted.

- Increase or move consumer through any of the following stages of awareness/knowledge/liking/preference/conviction/purchase
- Image building
- Convey message
- Educate
- Increase sales volume
- Increase awareness
- Create loyalty
- Increase willingness to buy
- As reminder

(b) **Setting the advertising budget**

(i) **Marginal analysis.** This tries to link variances in sales with changes in volumes of advertising, but in practice this is difficult to quantify.

(ii) **Advertising expenditure as a percentage of sales revenue**. This is widely used, being a fixed percentage of forecast sales thus is affordable. is no scientific reason for using a particular % figure. This approach **implies** that advertising is being based on sales, rather than sales being generated by advertising. The amount will fluctuate each year depending on sales revenue - sales revenue falls, perhaps you should increase advertising, not decrease it.

(iii) **Competitive parity.** In this case budget matches or exceeds competitors'. It is useful to know what competitors spend, but this information is not always obtainable. Any way, how do you know that competitors have got it right, or that the 'conventional wisdom' is, in fact, wisdom.

(iv) **Affordable approach**. Firms allocate what they feel they can afford. However, the amount available will fluctuate, and the approach assumes advertising has no effect on its position. The implication is that advertising is low priority - has the entire promotional strategy been properly thought through?

(v) **Budgets based on objectives**, ie the tasks to be achieved (precise quantification of advertising goals, choice of media, etc, and estimation of associated costs forces management to recognise what is needed and its cost).

(c) **Message decisions**

(i) Content (rational, emotional, moral?)
(ii) Structure (draw conclusion? 1 or 2 sided argument?)
(iii) Format (quantity of copy, coloured, size, pictorial?)

(d) **Media decisions**

(i) Reach (how many people exposed to advert?).
(ii) Frequency (of exposure).
(iii) Impact (of exposure).
(iv) Selecting the **media type** you need to consider the following.

(1) **Audience research findings**

- Circulation and readership of newspapers
- Duplication of audience
- Number who would see advert
- Ability to reach target
- Does half or full page make it more noticeable

(2) **Prestige, mood, expertise of each media vehicle**

(3) **Merits of each media type.** For example TV is suitable for movement, for demonstration, sound and visual impact, and is flexible (regional/national). The disadvantages of TV advertisements are the expense of production, the necessity of repetition to achieve awareness and the fact that they are unsuitable for long explanations

(4) The media type's ability to deliver **reach, frequency and impact**

(v) **Choice of specific media**

- Circulation
- Costs for different advertisement sizes
- Colour options
- Advertisement positions
- Cost per thousand
- Credibility
- Prestige
- Reproduction quality
- Lead times
- Audience quality

(vi) **Media scheduling**

(1) Period of campaign?

(2) Timing of adverts?

- Concentrated? (ie for brand launches, seasonal products)
- Continuous? (very expensive)? Intermittent? (widely used, gives concentrated impact periodically)?

(3) Buying efficiency?

- Advertising agency used for everything
- Advertising agency used for creative work
- Own advertising agency or department
- Specialised media broking services
- Limited services creative agencies

(4) Should media timespace be purchased centrally?

(5) How often should the company change advertising agency?

(6) What benefits are there to be gained by changing? Being tied to one agency can be restrictive.

Sales promotion decisions

3.13 **Objectives of sales promotion**

(a) The objective of all promotions is to increase sales, either in the short or long-term. The **specific** objective will condition the strategy (ie persuade as many potential shoppers as possible to try it out).

(i) A new retail product must have the widest trial, so the appropriate methods would be coupons, free samples, in-store trial, banded offers, etc.

(ii) A new product requires a longer campaign than an established product.

(iii) An established product requires a more selective approach in order to concentrate on low user segments with a shorter campaign designed to increase brand loyalty.

(iv) In a highly competitive market (detergents, cereals etc), campaigns can be designed to increase short term sales, knowing that buyers will revert to a former brand or take advantage of a competitive promotion.

(b) Sales promotion is **tactical**, designed to achieve a short term and limited objective, and is normally concentrated at the point of sale. It usually takes place in close association with the dealers who stock the product. Some sales promotion activities (personality promotions for example) do take place in the street or on a door to door basis, but even then, there is usually a strong tie-in with local dealers.

(c) The distinction between advertising and sales promotion roughly equates to the distinction between 'above the line' and 'below the line'.

3.14 **Some typical sales promotion tasks**

(a) **Encouraging dealers to stock.** Dealers need persuasion to take on a new line, they must be convinced that it will be profitable for them, which means that they must be convinced that customers will buy it in reasonable volume. Sales promotion activities can be used to persuade and provide direct cash incentive (eg cash discounts or deals).

(b) **Encouraging customers to sample.** With food products, for example, it is often crucial that customers try the new product. A special price offer, 'two for one' or an exciting display may tempt them sufficiently to make the test. A new brand of tea might be sold with a free packet of biscuits for example.

(c) **Combating competition.** A competitive situation, such as someone else introducing a new product, may call for an intensive short-term promotion of an existing product to ensure that not too many present customers are wooed away, and that, if possible some new ones are gained.

(d) **Improving distribution.** An existing product may have a 'patchy' distribution and sales promotion techniques can be used to fill in the gaps and gain extra dealers in a poorly represented area.

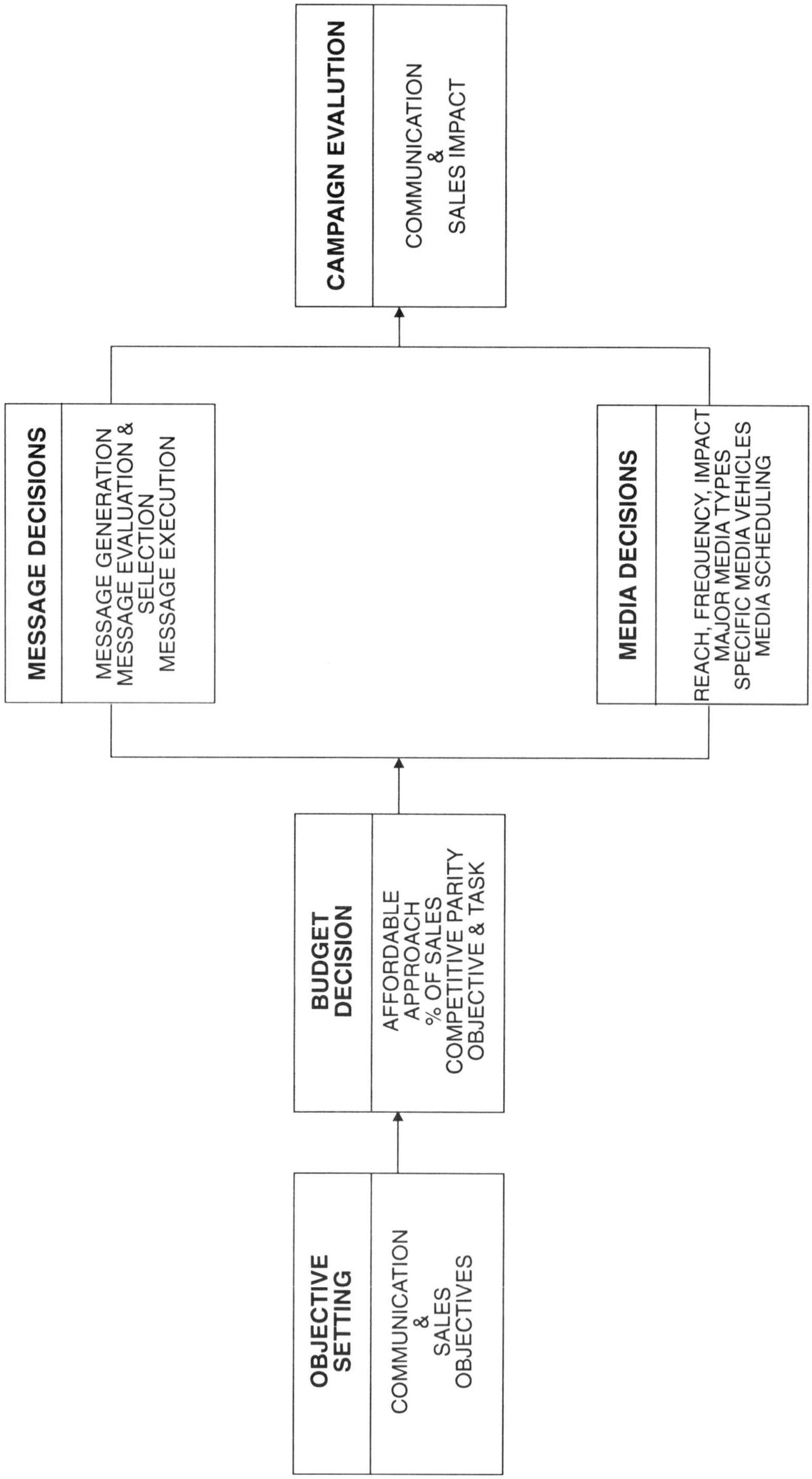

MAJOR DECISIONS IN ADVERTISING MANAGEMENT

(e) A well established product may suffer from over familiarity. Since most people are well aware of it, it can become boring. Sales promotions liven it up again and revive interest in it.

3.15 **Examples of sales promotions in current use**

(a) **Free samples** give the greatest chance of inducing trial. They are the most expensive method, and can only be used for brands with substantial annual sales.

(b) **Off-price labels.** This method is acceptable to consumers and retailers. There is no administration and they can feature the special offer in their advertising.

(c) **Banded offers** come in two forms.

(i) Existing well known brand 'carries' a free sample of another non-competing product (eg soap and toothpaste).

(ii) Two for the price of one.

(d) **Premium offers**

(i) Free gift in the pack (plastic animals in breakfast cereals), attached to it (plastic rose, tea towel), given out at the checkout (china bowls, wastepaper bins, etc) the pack itself (instant coffee in storage jars, to encourage the collecting habit and extend the trial).

(ii) Free, secondary premium. Free gift for proof of purchase.

(iii) Self-liquidating premiums. The consumer sends money and proof of purchase, and secures merchandise, often a leading brand name, at a discount.

(e) **Competitions**

(f) **Personality promotions** (usually with fancy dress). A prize is offered if the housekeeper has the product in the home when the personality calls (Egg-chick, Ajax superman).

3.16 When should you run a promotion? Promotion works best when part of an advertising, product development, or trade incentives strategy, and also when integrated into the overall strategy.

(a) Firstly, you need information. What is the target market for the product? Why do **customers use the product and how?** How frequently is it bought and where? What products are its main competitors?

(b) **Do you run a promotion?**

(i) Determine the priority of the problems facing the product.
(ii) Determine the money available to solve the problems.
(iii) Test and cost all possible solutions.
(iv) Estimate effectiveness of each solution.

(c) **Which promotion do you choose?**

(i) Does the promotion offer an incentive to the people in target audience from **their** point of view?

(ii) What is the likely impact of the promotion on the product's image?

(iii) Which consumer problems can the promotion solve (eg measuring cup, applicators, etc)?

3.17 **Trade promotions.** The trade has to be persuaded to stock the goods and promote them to their customers. 'Dealer loading' may have repercussions on the manufacturer, although there are other situations where the dealer may need to carry higher stocks (eg preparation for a new product launch). You need to make provision for display material. Examples of trade promotions are as follows.

(a) Co-operative advertising schemes (the producer and retailer act together).
(b) Contests for the retailer's sales staff.
(c) Special discounts to retail staff
(d) Special quantity trade terms.

3.18 **Sales force promotions** include incentives to sales staff, eg gifts, holidays, prizes etc.

3.19 **Industrial promotions** include discounts, introductory offers, give aways, diaries, calendars, pens. In addition, firms can supply annual golf or racing parties for customers, yachts, holiday villas to entertain customer's staff, sponsorship of sporting events. There are certain limits, eg relating to business ethics and practices, which must be observed in certain countries.

3.20 **Trade exhibitions** include the Motor show, Ideal Home Exhibition, Packaging Exhibition, Plastics Exhibition. An exhibition is a specialist temporary market place. There is also growing use of individual company exhibitions, seminars and demonstrations, where the audience can be selected more closely at a lower cost.

(a) **Reasons for exhibiting**

(i) The launch of a new product which cannot be demonstrated physically by sales personnel, but can be shown at an exhibition and reported by the press, TV etc.

(ii) New markets can be developed rapidly, customers contacted and an image speedily created.

(iii) Exhibitions help maintain or gain goodwill of sponsoring trade or professional organisations.

(iv) They are sometimes the only way to make initial contact with professional personnel buying on behalf of foreign governments.

(b) **How to ensure the cost effectiveness of your stand at the exhibition**

(i) Invite important customers to the stand

(ii) Make sure the stand accords with the corporate image (size, positioning and lighting)

(iii) Avoid over or under manning

(iv) Provide less costly literature for 'free loaders' rather than serious customers

(v) Provide an eye catching stand design, and exhibit to appeal to target groups (eg working models etc)

(vi) Secure information from people who are interested to enable follow up

(vii) Pay attention to press relations, with suitable releases and visual material

(c) You should discern in advance:

- What kind of people will attend?
- Whether they are a position to buy?
- What results are expected (actual sales, additional publicity, etc)?
- Follow-up action.

3.21 **Direct mail** may be broadly defined as a method of sending unsolicited advertising or promotional material through the post to customers or potential customers at specific named addresses.

(a) **Advantages**

(i) It enables direct contact to be made with specific individuals in the target market group.

(ii) It is highly selective and avoids 'waste' circulation.

(iii) It is not competing at the same time with other advertising messages.

(iv) It is very flexible and can be phased and designed in terms of geographical areas, types of prospects, frequency.

(v) Results are readily measurable.

(vi) It is relatively cheap and quick.

(b) **Response and cost effectiveness.** Response rates depend on:

(i) The user's ability to maintain accurate, up to date lists of potential respondents by appropriate categories

(ii) Mailing packages of appropriate quality, attraction and format interest to appeal to the respondent

(iii) Easiness of replying (eg business reply cards or envelopes included)

(iv) Speedy arrangement of personal and/or other forms of follow-up

3.22 **Point of sale promotions.** The buyer's final decision is made at the point of sale. Showcases, windows, posters, special display material can all be used to persuade people to shop at one location in preference to another.

3.23 **Packaging should:**

(a) Stand out clearly on the shelf
(b) Be clearly identifiable, with strong brand name
(c) Lend itself to displays

3.24 **Factors to help evaluate the success of sales promotion**

(a) The number of 'promoted' units taken up

(b) The number of new users who repeat purchase

(c) The profit per promoted unit, and profit per unpromoted unit

(d) Attitude towards brand among actual and potential users

(e) Ascribable profit from new and former users who have taken up the promotion

(f) Ascribable sales and profits against promotion costs

(g) Distribution and display increases, increases in buying, sales, trade (and consumer) goodwill

3.25 We have discussed the notions of **push** and **pull** promotional strategies in an earlier section. When we examine the role of sales promotion in relation to these two notions in more detail we can observe that its various techniques can be used in both contexts as shown in the figure below.

3.26 When deciding whether or not to stock a new product a distributor can often be swayed by the amount of and quality of **consumer sales promotion support.** This is because the distributor's main fear is that of the product not selling and consumer incentives will help to ensure that products stocked are sold. In this way consumer incentives can help a sales force to sell in to the distribution channel. However, many manufacturers will also offer distributors some special incentives to stock and display a new product or to specially feature an existing product such as base bonuses, special trial offers, special display fittings etc. Sales promotion is thus an important contributor to the selling-in (to retailers) process as well as to that of selling-out (to customers).

Public relations and publicity decisions

3.27 Here are two definitions of **public relations**.

(a) PR practice is the deliberate, planned and sustained effort to establish and maintain mutual understanding between an organisation and its publics.

(b) PR consists of all forms of planned communications inward and outward, between an organisation and its publics for the purpose of achieving specific objectives concerning mutual understanding.

3.28 **Publicity** involves capitalising on specific events or opportunities relating to the organisation or its products/services, so that these are communicated to its defined publics, in line with the corporate or marketing communications objectives. As a result:

(a) PR is invariably a long term activity;
(b) publicity is more frequently short term.

3.29 PR and publicity depend on communications, both internal and external.

(a) Few organisations can avoid publicity whether may want to or not.

(b) PR is **not** free advertising.

(c) PR is not even free. (Somebody has to pay for lunch!)

(d) Every organisation has PR.

(e) PR involves communication with many groups and audiences, not just consumers or potential consumers.

(f) PR is not propaganda - it does not set out to indoctrinate.

(g) PR is a two-way process.

3.30 Communication vehicles used in PR and publicity include:

(a) Personal communication (eg with journalists)
(b) Printed communication:

- Direct mail
- Literature (the press magazines visual communications - photographs)
- Videos/films, television, exhibitions, company logo/house style, airships, radio

3.31 Effective public relations/publicity requires the setting of objectives which should **ultimately** reflect the corporate and/or marketing objectives.

(a) PR, being more subtle, may incorporate corporate objectives which are different from product objectives.

(b) PR is frequently wider based than just Marketing (product marketing).

(c) Its objectives are therefore often long term.

(d) Its effectiveness is difficult to quantify and measure.

But nevertheless, objectives as guidelines and direction pointers are important so that there exists a consistency in communication with the relevant publics.

4 LEGAL AND OTHER CONSTRAINTS

Non-legal constraints on promotion

4.1 Non-legal constraints on promotional decisions are of two kinds.

(a) Consumerism - watchdogs, protest bodies, consumer media programmes and features.
(b) Codes of practice - infringement of which can lead to recriminations by the industry.

4.2 It is increasingly difficult today for large companies operating in consumer markets to escape from bad media publicity in the event of transgressions, whether intended or not, against what is deemed to be the consumer interests. Consumers who feel that they, or indeed society at large, are being badly served will find a variety of newspaper columns, television or radio programmes willing to air their grievances to a wider audience.

4.3 Many organisations have adopted and published codes of practice (eg the CIM and most other professional institutes). These codes bind their members/staff to good practices upon penalty of expulsion or other sanctions. Cynics have said that organisations generally only adopted codes of practice as an attempt to ward off a further escalation in legal constraints.

4.4 In any event marketing managers not only need to observe the law, but also need to take note of consumerist pressures and codes of practice when making promotional decisions.

Legal constraints on promotion

4.5 You will find in the pages which follow some details of the major laws affecting promotional decisions at the time of writing. Please bear in mind that new laws and changes in regulations are likely to occur which you need to take into account when making promotional decisions in the scenario of the case study. Also needed is an awareness that different legal constraints apply in different countries.

(a) **Trade Descriptions Acts, 1968 and 1972**

(i) These acts detail three offences, false or misleading trade descriptions, false or misleading indications of price and false or misleading statements as to services, accommodation or facilities.

(ii) The object of each Act is to protect consumers from misleading claims from retailers. For example, it is an offence to state. 'Reduced to 95p from £ 1.50' when the goods are seconds, specially purchased for the sale. Before reducing goods, the higher price must have been charged for at least 28 days continuously, unless the retailer displays a notice to the effect that these are genuine reductions although they have not been displayed at the higher price for 28 days during the last 6 months.

(iii) It is also an offence to apply a 'false trade description' to goods. The Act defines a trade description under 10 headings.

(1) Quantity, size, gauge.
(2) Method of manufacture, production, processing.
(3) Composition.
(4) Fitness for the purpose, strength, performance.
(5) Special characteristics.
(6) Tests and results of tests.
(7) Approval given by any person or body.
(8) Place of manufacture: Date of manufacture.
(9) Persons by whom manufactured.
(10) Other history, including previous ownership or use.

(iv) Breach of the Act can result in fines of up to £400 or two years imprisonment.

(v) The National Consumer Council analysed 11,000 complaints in first 6 months of 1989. 55% concerned claims and description labels and packaging. 0.5% concerned claims made in advertisements. 44.5% concerned other types of claims and descriptions.

(b) **Supply of Goods (Implied Terms) Act 1973.** This act guarantees the consumer's rights and prevents vendors from entering clauses in contracts waiving the buyer's Common Law rights (unfair contract terms).

(c) **Fair Trading Act 1973.** This Act set up the Office of Fair Trading. Basically the OFT can look into almost any aspect of trading and if they feel it is unfair can put proposals to Parliament.

(d) There are other Acts that relate to the advertising of **specific** merchandise.

4.6 TV and radio advertising are subject to legal control under the terms of the Broadcasting Acts of 1981 and 1990. The ITC (Independent Television Commission) regulates the amount and content and has a Code of Advertising Standards and Practice. Other advertising media are governed by the British Code of Advertising Practice which is almost identical to the ITC code. The Code is run by the Advertising Standards Authority and is self regulatory.

(a) **Television**

- Regulated by ITC
- Subject to statutory control
- Limited to maximum of seven minutes in any 'clock' hour, and an average of 6 minutes per hour
- Should amount to no more than 10% of broadcast time (25% in the USA)

(b) **Radio** advertising

(i) Regulated by its own regulatory body
(ii) Subject to statutory control
(iii) Limited to a maximum of 9 minutes/per hour
(iv) Must be no more than 15% of broadcast time

(c) **Press**

(i) Currently, there is no formal control except by the publisher, although legislation is looming.

(ii) In practice, the ratio of advertising to editorial is around 50% (tabloids) and 50% (glossy magazine).

(iii) 'Freesheets' usually contain 90-100% advertising.

(d) **Posters**

(i) These are controlled by town and country planning regulations (1969).
(ii) Poster advertising has decreased dramatically since 1900.
(iii) Many other countries make more use of poster advertising.
(iv) It can brighten up otherwise dull areas.

(e) **Cinema**

(i) No formal control exists.

(ii) In practice an average of 12 minutes of advertising is shown in a two-and-a-half hour programme.

Control of advertising content

4.7 Two types of statutory regulation of advertising content exist.

(a) Direct legislation, as we have seen.
(b) Indirect statutory control.

4.8 **Indirect statutory control**

(a) The Independent Television Authority (ITA) set up when commercial broadcasting was first permitted; established an advisory code of practice in 1955. Its successor, the Independent Broadcasting Authority (IBA), also produced standards of practice.

(b) The Broadcasting Act (1990) makes it a statutory duty of the *Independent Television Commission* (ITC) to draw up and enforce a code covering television advertising. The Act states that: 'the general principle which will govern all broadcast advertising is that it should be legal, decent, honest and truthful'. Advertisements may not be included in the following.

(i) Religious ceremonies or programmes
(ii) Programmes designed for schools
(iii) Formal royal ceremonies/occasions and appearances of Queen or Royal family
(iv) Some half hour adult education programmes
(v) Some current affairs programmes and documentaries

(c) Viewers sometimes find advertisements offensive, misleading or dishonest despite the controls (eg various campaigns in which women have been portrayed in stereotyped ways). The Broadcasting Standards Commission receives complaints.

4.9 The ITC has also issued a code of advertising standards and practice. The ITC code is modelled closely on the former IBA and Cable Authority Codes which it replaces. It has many points in common with the self regulatory code for the non broadcast media (the British Code of Advertising Practice). The ITC code applies to all television services regulated by the ITC. In the main these are: ITV, GMTV, Channel 4, Channel 5, UK direct broadcast satellite (DBS) services. Separate provisions apply to Oracle Teletext. The enforcement of any self regulatory code is a problem. In this case it is the media owners who have agreed not to accept any advertising from an advertiser who has refused to abide by an ASA decision. The weakness of the scheme has not been in **enforcing** the code, but the willingness of media owners to print advertisements which contravene the Code, rather than upset advertisers. This tends to make the code a 'longstop' rather than a preventative measure.

4.10 Self regulation of advertising and sales promotion. The Advertising Standards Authority (ASA) has responsibility for supervising the advertising industry's system of self-regulation. It is recognised by the Office of Fair Trading and the government as a fundamental part of consumer protection. One of the Authority's specific tasks is to investigate complaints from the public that advertisements are in breach of the British Code of Advertising Practice (BCAP). The ASA is a wholly independent body which operates quite separately from the industry's Code of Advertising Practice Committee. The ASA was set up in 1962, and is a watchdog which oversees all advertisements **except** those on radio or TV. Complaints about radio and television advertising made to the ASA are passed on to the IBA.

4.11 The ASA is a voluntary body. Unlike the IBA it does not have the force of an act of Parliament behind it. In theory, non-broadcast media owners, agencies and advertisers follow the ASA's advice.

(a) The ASA's main functions are to see that the British Code of Advertising Practice is adhered to, and to deal with complaints from the general public. The ASA does, however, check all advertisements for cigarettes before publication, and in practice most advertisements for alcoholic drinks are also pre-vetted. Otherwise, it is clearly impractical for the ASA to vet every press advertisement, every poster and every advertising film before it was used.

(b) Between 7,000 and 8,000 complaints are received each year from the public. If, after an investigation, the complaint is upheld, the Authority seeks an assurance from the advertiser that the offence will not be repeated. Advertisers who do not agree to amend their advertisements in line with the ASA's recommendations are reported to media owners.

(c) The Authority issues a monthly case report which described the complaints received and the action taken. The January 1986 Case Report gave the results of 109 investigations into breaches of the British Code of Advertising Practice which had been completed. The complaints were upheld in 70 cases, and partly upheld in a further three. Many complainers were readers who had been attracted by price offers in advertisements which involved hidden extra costs, or to have suffered increases since the advert.

4.12 The British Code of Sales Promotion Practice (BCSPP, 1982) is published by ASA's Code of Advertising Practices Committee. It aims to regulate marketing techniques, usually used on a temporary basis, to make goods and services more attractive to the consumer by providing some kind of additional benefit in cost or in kind.

(a) The BCSPP covers:

- All types of premium offer
- Reduced price and free offers
- Distribution of vouchers
- Coupons and samples
- Personality promotions
- Charity linked promotions
- All types of prize promotions
- Sales and trade incentive promotions
- Editorial promotions offers
- Aspects of sponsorship.

(b) It **defines** a promotional product as: 'a product which the consumer receives or may receive as a result of participation in a sales promotion'.

(c) The ASA implements the code, but primary responsibility for ensuring the code is implemented rests with the promoter (but in the case of a mailing of a cigarette promotion to a 17 year old girl, the complaint was not upheld, as she had previously completed a coupon declaring she was over 18 years old).

4.13 The British Direct Mail Association (BDMA) introduced a Code of Practice in 1982. It covers direct mail, direct response mail order advertising, other direct response advertising and telephone selling. Members of the BDMA are bound by the BCAP and the BCSPP. The *Direct Marketing Association* was formed in 1992 and issued a code in 1993.

Comparative advertising

4.14 Attitudes are very hard - and therefore expensive - to change. Thus, much advertising is highly competitive, with two objectives; to reinforce the attitudes of existing customers and to change the attitudes (or convert) competitors' customers. One of the most powerful but controversial tools available to advertisers in this respect is comparative advertising, known to the trade as knocking copy.

4.15 The control of knocking-copy and selective comparisons has always been a matter for controversy. Some advertising people have demanded the right to make comparisons in favour of a product advertised. Yet it would then be unfair to isolate one feature of a product and illustrate it in a discrediting way, giving the impression that the exceptional incident is the norm.

4.16 The view of the ASA is that 'knocking-copy' can only bring advertising into bad repute. Secondly, 'knocking-copy' is the refuge of the incompetent or lazy copywriter, who finds it only too easy to knock. Some critics consider that advertisements which make direct comparisons with competitive products or services are undesirable and should not be permitted.

4.17 The BCAP is very explicit on the subject:

'Advertisements containing comparisons ... including those where a competitor is named, are permissible in the interests of vigorous competition and public information,' provided that they comply with five specific clauses of the code. These may be summed up as saying that the comparisons must not be deliberately misleading, that it must be clear what is being compared with what, that the points of comparison must not be so selected as to confer an unrealistic margin of advantage, that price comparisons must use comparable and comprehensible units of measurement and that advertisers should not gratuitously attack one another.

4.18 The ITC Code of Advertising Standards and Practice offers the same guidelines, though in less detail. The five year battle of words between the leading UK manufacturers of hover and cylinder lawnmowers reached the point at which the hover mower manufacturers petitioned Parliament to restrain their competitors, on the grounds that the competitive comparisons were 'unfair', despite the fact that the ASA and ITC were both satisfied that their codes were no longer being breached in any way.

5 CAMPAIGN PLANNING

A campaign planning framework

5.1 From time to time companies will experience a need for a special promotional campaign. This might be to launch an entirely new product or service or to re-launch/re-position an existing product. Such campaigns would normally call for a new creative strategy, the forerunner to which would be a new creative brief. For such an important exercise, it would be highly likely that an advertising agency and/or a creative specialist would be heavily involved at an early stage. The framework for such a special campaign might therefore be as illustrated in the diagram on the following page.

5.2 **Additional issues in campaign planning**

(a) Determine the **objective of the campaign**. This is a task for management and not for the advertising specialist who may, however, cause management objectives to be modified if it is felt they cannot be achieved because of copy, media, budget or other limitations. However, the advertising specialist should be involved in deciding the objectives of marketing communications.

(b) **Determine the message (copy and design).**

(i) Advertisements consist of verbal symbols, illustrations, colour, movement, sound etc. It is the task of the creative personnel in advertising to achieve the mix most likely to accomplish the purpose of the communication taking into account literal and emotional aspects.

(ii) Copy will be influenced by the choice of media as well as the target audiences. In general the most effective copy is that which concentrates on a limited selling appeal, and frequent repetition of a single appeal is a feature of many very successful campaigns. Certainly many campaigns are spoiled by the attempt to cover too many selling points in one advertisement.

(iii) Campaigns may, of course, be planned to cover a number of single objectives over a given time, in line with a multiple communications strategy.

(iv) Advertising can be pre-tested to determine whether the intended message is being communicated, and comparisons of the effectiveness of communication of a number of advertisements can also be made. Samples of prospective viewers or readers are exposed to advertisements, and certain reactions are measured. Sometimes, tests are carried out on specially constituted panels. The tests may be conducted on the basis of aided or unaided recall of advertisements to which the panel or sample member has been exposed. It should be noted that these tests relate to the effectiveness of the communication as such and do not give a measure of sales results.

(c) **Select and schedule appropriate media.**

(i) The extent of **coverage** required to reach potential buyers and its effective cost.

(ii) The comparative **communication effectiveness** of various media (eg the compatibility of the advertising or editorial material with media audiences - an advertisement designed for the popular press might be totally unsuitable in a specialised journal).

(iii) Is there a **medium** or specific newspaper or TV channel to reach your target audience?

(iv) **Location**. Many national media have facilities to enable regional advertising. TV and Radio are obvious. Sunday colour press, TV and Radio Times and many national dailies have regional editions. Is your target market evenly spread?

(v) **Penetration**. A free newspaper may have a larger circulation than the local 'paid for' paper. However, if you are a local advertiser the smaller circulation publication may be better, as it is probably read more thoroughly. Penetration is the proportion of the 'readers' who are registering the message.

(vi) **Timing**. It is important that the advertisement appears at a time when the consumer is most responsive. Obviously, for a new product this is crucial, but it is also important for established products. Sunday newspapers are advertised on TV on Saturday night.

(vii) **Use by competitors**. For example, if six dog food brands are already heavily using TV, would you be better off using a combination of radio, outdoor and press?

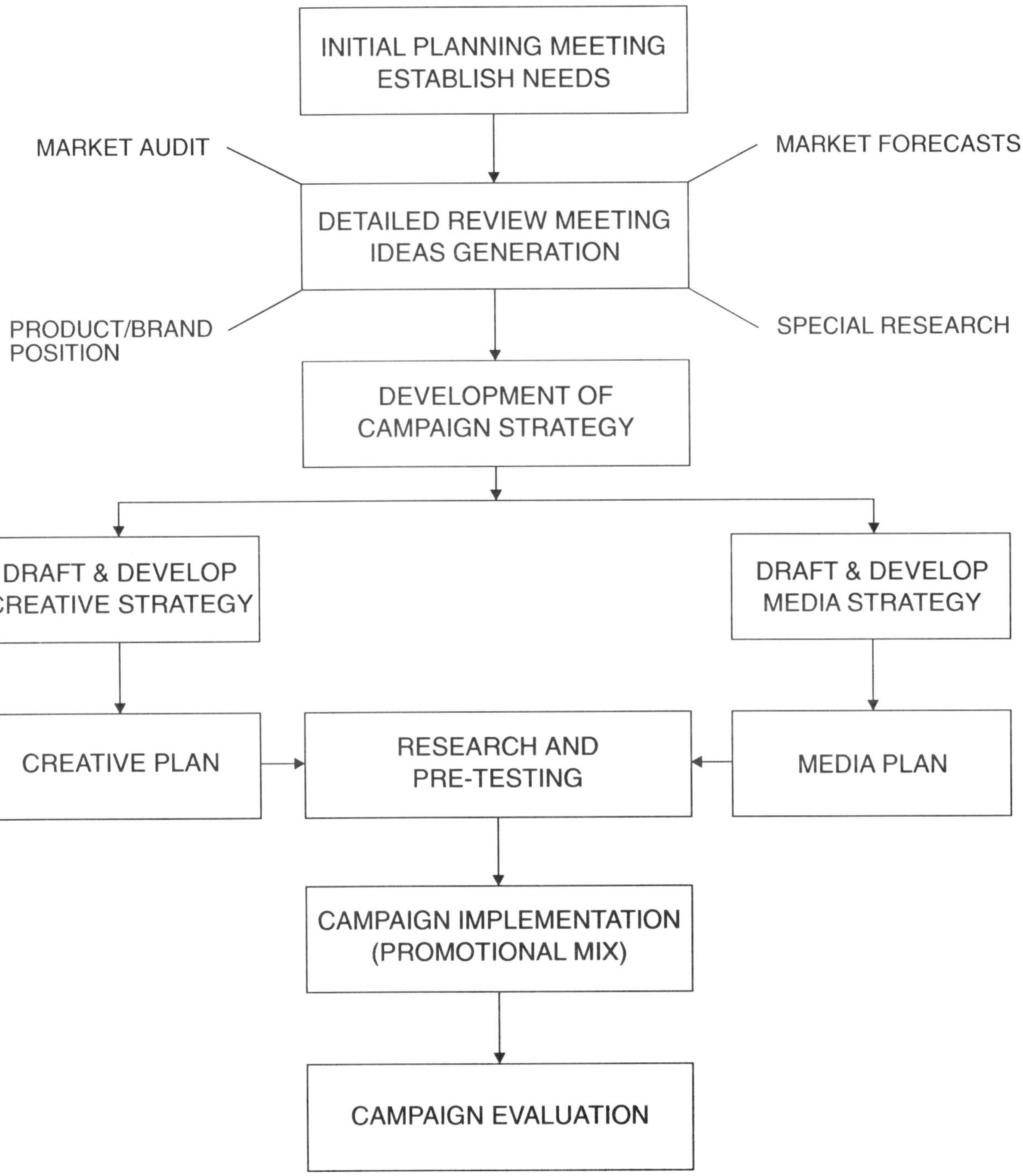

(viii) **Cost**. The media planner must make best use of the budget. Firstly, a small budget will preclude media with high production costs (such as TV or cinema).

(ix) The **administrative**, organisational and operating **requirements** of the media (eg frequency of publication and length of lead time required for placing advertisements).

(x) Consideration of the ways in which **competitors** allocate expenditure to various media.

(xi) The determination of advertising **frequency** - 'opportunities to see'.

(xii) The **size, positioning and/or timing** of advertisements.

(d) Co-ordinate advertising with the total promotional plan. Amongst co-ordination problems would be those of assigning tasks and expenditure to promotions, personal selling efforts, handling and follow-up of enquiries, and public relations.

(e) Determine and control the advertising budget. The size of the budget will, in practice, determine very largely the selection of media, but ideally budgets should be determined by companies after due consideration of the cost of achieving communication objectives.

(f) Media planning. It is all too easy to say, 'that was a good advertisement' without asking, where did it appear, how often, who saw it, when and how often.

Advertising strategy

5.3 **Objectives**. The setting of advertising objectives, the strategy to achieve them, and the measurement of their effectiveness is stressed in the concept of DAGMAR. This concept was first described by Russell H Colley as 'Defining Advertising Goals for Measured Advertising Results'.

5.4 **Testing advertisements.** Everybody believes they can tell a good advertisement from a bad one. If the advertisement is shown to five or six people, the chances are there will be a divergence of opinion. Alternatively they may all like it, but not be able to tell you the name of the product the next day.

(a) When judging advertisements they must be judged against their stated objectives and they should be only tested on the target audience. There are a few characteristics that all good ads have in common.

(i) Does it stop me and make me look?
(ii) Is some element of it unusual or original?
(iii) Is it a pleasing design?
(iv) Is it relevant to the product?
(v) Is it easy to understand?

(b) However, there are two questions we need to answer when testing an advertisement that are far more difficult to answer.

(i) Does it fit the strategy?
(ii) Will it work?

The answers to these questions can be arrived at before or after the advertisement has been run and this is called pre-testing and post-testing.

5.5 Pre-testing techniques normally involve showing the advertisement to members of your target group and soliciting their response. All the methods of doing this have the drawback that it is difficult to recreate the conditions under which they would really see the advertisement (ie passing a poster in a car, thumbing through a magazine, in the middle of a TV programme).

(a) The method normally employed is a discussion group, where a highly trained interviewer asks a number of groups questions that are not leading or rhetorical.

(b) For advertisements the proposed ad can be placed in a folder with alternative or competitors' advertisements and respondents questioned when they have been studied.

(c) Any pre-testing for TV advertisements is more problematical as it involves producing the advertisement before it can be tested and human nature is such that there is a reluctance to abandon an advertisement that tests badly. However, for a big campaign it is worth pre-testing. This is sometimes carried out using low cost story boards, animatics or a low budget video approach.

Defining advertising objectives

5.6 It is important to be able to distinguish between **marketing objectives** and advertising objectives. To increase sales or to increase market share are not advertising objectives but objectives, of the total marketing plan. Advertising objectives are much more specific to the communications process. Example of advertising objectives are given below. In practice, you would aim to **quantify** these objectives.

(a) Maintain the loyalty of existing buyers and encourage their greater usage.
(b) Encourage non-users to sample.
(c) Inform users, especially lapsed users, that the product has been improved.
(d) Develop the belief that it is better than other products for whatever reason.

5.7 Is must also be possible to measure the effectiveness of the campaign against these specific objectives. This can only be done by research before and after the campaign. It is fairly straight forward using 'ad hoc' research to establish attitudes and usage levels amongst users and non-users, within our target market.

Designing advertisements

5.8 The strategy involves two aspects.

(a) Who do we want to communicate with? We will normally want to communicate with our target market. This should be already established as it is **fundamental** to the whole marketing plan.

(b) What are the desired reactions to the advertisement.

5.9 EXAMPLE

Let us take the example of Black and Decker Power Drills aiming at the market segment of new home owners who do not own a power drill.

(a) Consumer reactions might range through the following.

(i) 'Black & Decker is a name I've heard of and know is widely available.'

(ii) 'I've also heard Bosch make drills, are German and make parts for cars so they might be better.'

(iii) 'Power drills are expensive, I could make do with a hand drill.'

(iv) 'I will probably need lots of extras such as drill bits, power leads, etc.'

(v) 'Would I use a power drill enough to make it worth buying?'

(b) The strategy could be to reinforce the positive aspects, to change the negative aspects and to suggest new, previously unconsidered motives.

(i) **Reinforce**

(1) Black and Decker has been established 80 years
(2) It has a wider dealer network (than Bosch)
(3) The guarantees are good
(4) Black and Decker are the most popular in the UK

(ii) **Change**

(1) Black and Decker only make power tools, so are specialist (knock Bosch)
(2) Cable is included and can be used for hedge cutters, strimmers.
(3) Drill bits are included
(4) The power drill can also be used to power sanders, saws, screwdrivers
(5) Prices start at £19.95

(iii) **New**

(1) A drill makes an ideal wedding/Christmas/birthday present
(2) The new model is more powerful

(iv) **Emotional/psychological factors are also often added**

(1) Power-tools are 'macho'.

(2) They satisfy a 'need' to make an impressive home, impress family and neighbours.

(3) They look professional and knowledgeable.

(4) Tool advertisements often use 'the choice of the professional' partly to appeal to the ego but also to reduce perceived risk.

(5) In addition to this, the advertising can give something extra, normally described as 'from the advertising'. In the case quoted, it could be a shot of some impressive shelves (bearing a lot of weight) or some other completed DIY job.

5.10 **Post-testing.** Accepting that the role of advertising is to sell, the obvious post testing method is to measure sales. However, as advertising is only one small part of the promotional and marketing mix, it is normally wrong to credit any change in sales purely to advertising except in very unusual circumstances, where a control is available and every other factor remains constant. This is the philosophy behind **area tests** where the advertisement is run in one area and the sales compared with the rest of the country. This has various drawbacks.

(a) The area chosen may respond to the message differently to the rest of the country.

(b) Obtaining information from individual branches of multiple retailers, who buy centrally, is difficult.

(c) The overlap of TV transmission areas.

(d) The time taken up in receiving results.

5.11 Press advertising has the advantage of enabling the inclusion of a direct response element, such as a coupon.

5.12 If it is difficult to test a single advertisement, it is even more difficult to test a complete campaign or prove that 'advertising works', and most text books completely ignore these topics. As previously stated, research should be used to measure changes in attitudes to the product and such research is probably the only way that we can realistically assess the value of a campaign.

Media buying

5.13 As previously explained, the media space is normally booked by the advertising agency, and it is one of the agency's main jobs to buy well. Personnel in some agencies believe they are so creatively brilliant that their advertisement can be sufficiently effective whenever or wherever they appear. There is a basic conflict between media buyer and seller in that within all media there are spots or positions less popular than others. To some extent this is accounted for by the rate card but even so, it is difficult to fill unpopular spots with advertisements. Consequently, a deal is normally struck that includes good, bad and indifferent spots at an advantageous price.

5.14 The task of converting your media plan into firm orders placed with media-owners is more than simply an administrative task, and here the difference between **media planning** and **media buying** becomes all important. For example, your approved media schedule might show a series of television commercials to be transmitted in various time segments on certain dates. When the plan was drawn up, however, it was impossible to know the programmes that would be transmitted or the viewing figures that would be achieved many months ahead. So a great deal of skill is called for in negotiating the best possible spots at times when your commercial will be seen by the largest number of people in your target market group. Similar detailed negotiations will be necessary with the owners of other media.

5.15 The up-to-the-minute buying function contrasts sharply with the earlier planning stage, which produced only an outline plan to be implemented in the light of subsequent information. Media buying calls for a highly competitive cut and thrust approach which many find more exciting than the abstract planning stage which, in contrast, seems a rather boring mechanical exercise.

Schedule improvement

5.16 Few advertising campaigns ever appear exactly as originally planned, and you should keep your schedule under constant scrutiny and make whatever improvements are possible. A marginal improvement of, say, 10 percent in coverage is equivalent to a 10 percent increase in your appropriation, so you should keep your schedule under review and adjust it in the light of subsequent information.

5.17 With television advertising, schedule improvement is just as important as the original plan. Changes are less frequent with press or other media but the case for schedule improvement is just as valid. The publication of new readership data, the issue of a new rate card or the launch of a new publication, for example, should lead you to re-examine your current media plans.

6 SELECTING AND BRIEFING AGENCIES

6.1 Few companies can entirely satisfy their customers without calling upon other organisations to provide specialist services. Serving customers is a matter of getting the product, promotion, price and place right. In the case of promotion there are three major types of agency as illustrated in the model below. Note that there are four major participants in the communications system.

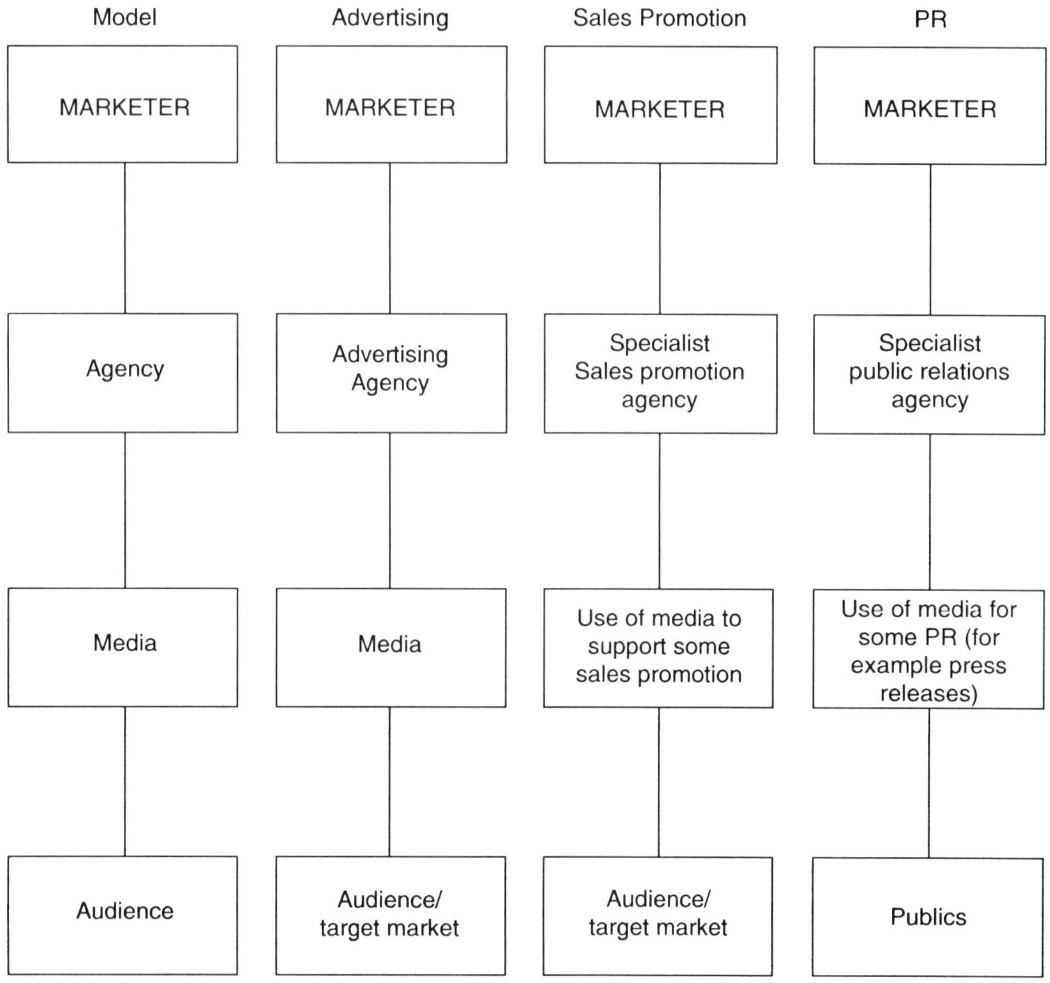

The client

6.2 The advertiser is the party who wishes to advertise a product or a service. Advertising agencies refer to them as clients. Advertising is unusual in that it usually involves other organisations (agencies, media) whereas most marketing functions are carried out internally. Some companies do not use an agency and produce their own advertisements and buy their own media, but this is unusual. More common is an arrangement where the advertiser has a marketing or advertising department and uses an agency. An organisation's **advertising manager** will normally have the following roles.

(a) He or she will represent the sales promotion and advertising function, just as the sales manager will represent personal selling.

(b) He or she will lay down the advertising objectives for the organisation and appeal for the necessary appropriation.

(c) He or she will plan a strategy to make use of the available resources.

(d) He or she will brief the advertising agency and control its activities in the interest of the organisation.

In many companies Product Managers and Brand Managers carry out many or all of the above roles.

The advertising agency

6.3 The main role of the agency is the preparation of advertisements for their clients and the purchase of advertising space. In this section we shall consider:

- The services offered by agencies
- How agencies are structured
- Selecting an agency
- Briefing an agency
- Remuneration of the agency
- Working with the agency
- Alternatives to the agency

The services offered

6.4 Agencies originally worked for the **media owners** to sell space to advertisers. They soon began to help the advertisers prepare their advertisements and today they specialise in preparing advertisements and placing them in appropriate media.

(a) At its most elaborate, the agency offers a full marketing resource and is able to provide assistance in business planning together with supporting show-material, sales literature, sales conferences, etc.

(b) On the other hand there are agencies which specialise in one market (eg often an industrial market). Whatever the size of the agency, they often use sub-contractors to produce artwork and print.

How agencies are structured

6.5 The main parts of most modern agencies are as follows.

(a) **Account management.** The agency functions by allocating an **account executive** to the client (the account). The account executive heads up a team (the account group) made up of specific members of the creative department, a planner and media specialists. Normally the whole team meets the client and get to know client needs and operations. The **account executive** is responsible to the client to ensure that the client is satisfied. The account executive is present at all meetings.

(b) The **account planner's** job is to assemble information about the product and the market, production of the advertising strategy which guides the creative team. The account planner will organise any research into the advertisement and its results. Planners have appeared for two reasons.

(i) The account executive does not have time

(ii) Planners redress the balance away from the creative side to channel the artistic resource in the right direction. This is becoming very important in times when clients are looking for accountability/measurability for the money spent on advertising.

(c) The **creative team** are the ideas people who actually think up the advertisement. The team normally consists of an artist or art director and a copy writer. A traditional stereotype is that they are nonconformist in terms of normal office practice.

(d) **Media**. The **media planner** gets involved from the beginning to decide which media are most appropriate. This enables the creative team to tailor their efforts according to the media. When the creative work is complete, the media planner will draw up the schedule and, when agreed, will go out and buy 'the space'.

(e) The **progress or traffic department** does not usually have a representative on the account team, but oils the wheels, making sure jobs go to and from the right places, on time. This is co-ordination.

(f) Similarly the **accounts** or billing department is not on the team, but is vitally important in keeping the client happy. Charging the client is complicated and advertising is expensive, consequently there is scope for friction. From an agency viewpoint the accounts department is important in minimising cash-flow difficulties.

Selecting an agency

6.6 The Institute of Practitioners in Advertising has over 300 member agencies and represents a wide choice for the advertiser. Apart from new advertisers, existing accounts are often on the move. *Campaign* magazine, which you should dig into from time to time, is often full of news of accounts (and personnel!) moving between agencies. Because of all this activity, it is important for the agency to be able to court and win new accounts, and for the client to be able to assess agencies.

6.7 **Recognition** of an agency by the trade associations that represent the **media owners** confers the automatic right to receive media **commission**. Media commission is not paid to unrecognised agencies or advertisers who deal directly with the media. Most agencies seek to be recognised.

Criteria for recognition include:

(a) Existence in the business (a barrier to entry for new agencies needing media commission to become established)

(b) Professional competence (poorly produced advertisements reflect badly on the media)

(c) Solvency (the most important criterion as the agency is responsible for the client's debts if the client pays late or goes bust)

6.8 Incorporation of an agency is a status awarded by the Institute of Practitioners in Advertising (IPA) as professional associates, so that an incorporated agency can call itself 'Incorporated Practitioner in Advertising'. Criteria for the award of incorporated status include that the agency must be:

(a) Completely independent of media owners;
(b) Agree to abide by the IPA code of conduct;
(c) Agree to abide by the British Code of Advertising Practice (BCAP).

6.9 IPA member agencies (ie incorporated agencies) account for around 40% of the 900 or more advertising agencies in the UK. These 40% of agencies account for a 90% of the total billings of advertising agencies. The larger and more successful agencies are IPA members. Some agencies do not have incorporated status because they choose not to adhere to the second criterion which involves strict rules on competition (ie IPA code).

6.10 The selection of an agency is very subjective and unscientific, but it does pay to approach the problem by first drawing up a shortlist of agencies using the following general criteria.

(a) **Size.** The size of the account should be in proportion to the size of the agency. Small agencies cannot always handle big accounts, and big agencies might not put all their weight behind a small account.

(b) **Track record.** Agencies grow and fail. Try to find a growing one as it will attract the best staff. If an agency has a record of gaining or holding on to other good accounts it is a good sign.

(c) **Compatibility.** Can you get on with the people, do they 'speak your language'?

(d) **Creativity.** All agencies claim to be creative. Look at their past work (are the staff who did the good work still there?). Make sure that the creativity is not so esoteric that it fails to sell.

(e) **Relevant experience.** Assume you are selling cheese. An agency does not need to have handled a cheese account to handle yours, but it may be a help to have handled other food accounts. The agency will know good photographers of food and may be able to get good deals from the media as they have used them before. You may wish to move to an agency which has just lost your **competitor's** account, particularly if the competitor is the market leader. The agency will know your market and your competitors' weaknesses. Agencies rarely take on **conflicting accounts** from competing clients.

6.11 You can start to talk to agencies at this stage to reduce the list still further as you need a final list of no more than four. Discount those who do not appear keen. You will get approaches from other agencies, try to put them off but consider those who are persistent or ingenious. If you need to reduce further, give them all the opportunity of a one hour presentation.

(a) The classic way of choosing an agency is to give three or four the same brief and ask them to present against it, giving them a number of weeks.

(b) There are draw-backs to such a system. It is rather artificial as the timescale is short. The decision tends to be made too much on the creativity of the advertising copy whereas the advertising **plan** is just as important.

(c) From the agency's viewpoint, they can spend £000's on preparing a pitch and get less than nothing as they are giving away their creative ideas. Some of the very biggest refuse to join in.

6.12 When the final decision has been made, a standard letter of terms is drawn up by the agency covering:

- The range of services to be provided
- The basis of payment
- Length of credit
- Copyrights, confidentiality, etc
- Conditions of termination

Briefing the agency

6.13 Guinness's brief to the agencies involved in pitching for their account was 100 pages and probably the most expensive ever produced. Other clients produce two sheets of A4 culminating in the objective 'to increase sales'.

(a) The brief should comprise two parts, information on the company and the advertising objective. The information should include historical sales, financial and marketing information and research into attitudes to the product or brand and its current advertising.

(b) However, a company with limited marketing resources may replace the advertising objectives by a statement of its problems and ask for a complete promotional plan.

(c) There are obvious dangers in too little information but the dangers of the client trying to direct the creative approach are real and equally dangerous.

(d) A 'typical' brief could include some or all of the following.

Brief	
1	Marketing plan - include time scale for advertising guidelines
2	Communication objectives (be precise)
3	Campaign budget - penalties for overspend etc
4	Product profile - in consumer terms
5	Company profile
6	Market analysis - segmentation of market
7	Production schedules - can we cope with created demand?
8	Distribution policy
9	Pricing policy
10	Evaluation criteria (effectiveness of agency and efficiency of the advertising campaign)

Remuneration of the agency

6.14 The amount of advertising undertaken is usually determined by the size of the advertiser's budget. It is important, therefore, to understand how it is paid for. As already stated the agency originally worked for the media owner and this is still where the agency gets most of its revenue. Nearly all media owners give the agency 15% of the cost of the space as a commission. The media outlet bills the agency net of commission and the agency then bills the client for the full amount. This means that the commission is in fact 17.65% on the **cost**. For every £100 the client pays, the agency pays the **media** £85, ie

$$\frac{£15}{£85} \times 100 = 17.65\%$$

6.15 **Calculating media commission**. Assume the rate-card cost of time/space for an item is £10,000, and a standard rate of commission of 15%, which the agency receives if it is recognised. Commission discount on £10,000 is £1,500. The agency bills the client for £10,000. The media owner bills the agency for £10,000 **less** £1,500 commission, ie £8,500. The agency therefore makes £1,500 on the deal.

6.16 The agency also receives a mark-up on work supervised by the agency but bought from external suppliers. Let us assume that a market research survey cost £8,500. However the agency will charge to the client a fee of:

$$\frac{100\%}{85\%} \times £8,500 = £10,000.$$

The agency therefore makes £1,500 on the deal, which is equivalent to a 15% commission discount on £10,000 worth of media buying.

6.17 Whilst the commission system is almost universal, it tends to be replaced for very large or small accounts. If a campaign is very small the 15% will not cover the agency costs. In such a situation the agreement may be that the client pays for all the cost of preparing the advertisement or a flat fee. Alternatively a figure of, say £500, could be set and the client makes up any shortfall that the agency does not earn from commission. The fee system is rarely used however, and the commission system is as already stated above, almost universal.

6.18 As long as the commission system is the norm, agencies **cannot** compete with each other on price (of buying time/space) only on creative flair, management quality, customer service etc **unless** the agencies are willing to pass on to the client some of their commission. This is commission rebating.

Working with the agency

6.19 The agency exists to provide a service that the client needs, and consequently agency and client should work as partners, even if they are not equal. Bearing in mind the hard work involved in selecting a new agency, it is worthwhile making an effort to co-operate. An agency will work better once it is acquainted with the client and the client's marketing staff, and market. Consequently a series of regular reviews is becoming more common. These cover areas such as gaps in performance, the relationship, strategy and campaigns.

Alternatives to the agency

6.20 Alternatives have become more popular. The use of a full-service advertising agency is still the norm, however, particularly in the USA, and creative consultants and media buying shops are at your service. We can distinguish four main types of alternatives to using a full-service agency.

(a) 'Do-it-yourself' or in-house advertising
(b) Use a creative shop (Hot House or Hot Shop)
(c) Use a media independent
(d) Go 'a la carte'

6.21 Whether you do it yourself, or use specialist services, it is down to you to co-ordinate the exercise and this requires skill and a considerable amount of time. The final result of using specialist services or indeed doing the job personally may be a lower paying out cost but will the advertising be as effective'?

6.22 The **media owner** is the independent broadcasting contractor, newspaper or magazine publisher, bill posting contractor, radio company, etc. Media owners normally have a department responsible for attracting advertisers (or agencies), and arranging for the appearance of the advertisements. The head of this department is the advertising manager. It is worth remembering that the media is itself a product and has to be marketed to readers/viewers and to advertisers as its revenue is derived from both.

6.23 We have seen that there are three parties to the relationship shown earlier. We focused on the agency-client relationship, but we must also consider what each party should be doing to nurture the **tri-partite** relationship, including the media owner, the agency and the advertiser.

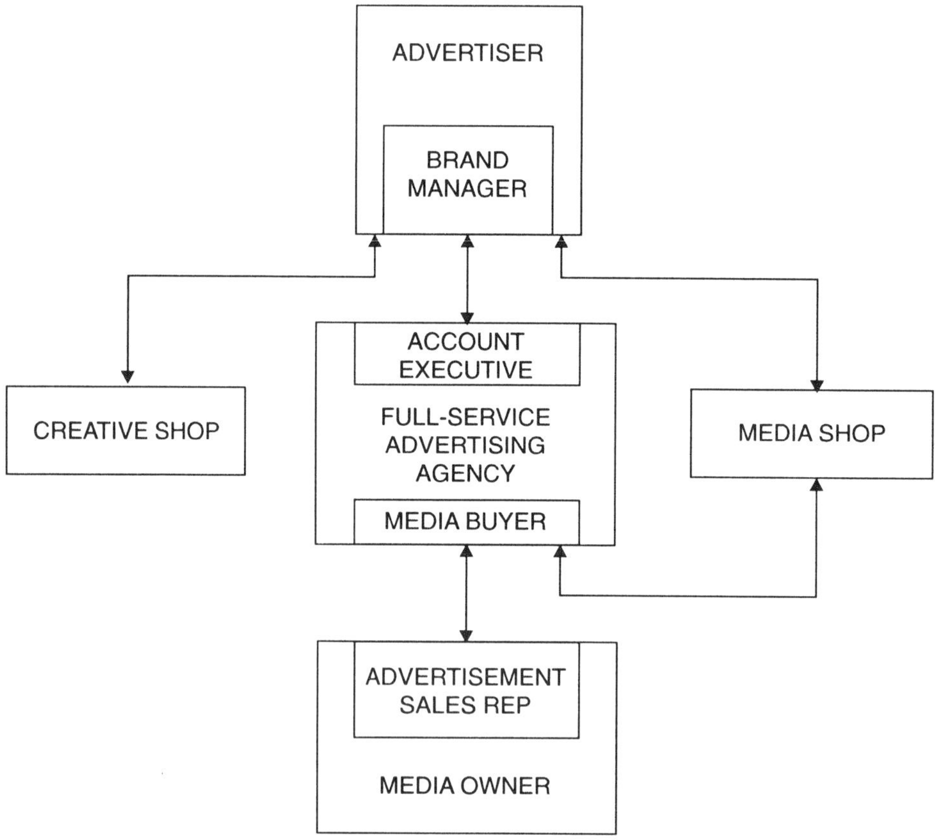

6.24 **What the media owner should do**

- Pay attention to the long-term quality of the media product
- Try to develop media that hit specific target markets
- Work closely with client and agency, keeping both informed about the medium
- Notify agencies in advance of future editorial comment
- Ensure an appropriate balance between editorial and advertising
- Invest in research or relevance to improving the media and its effectiveness
- Not misrepresent the reach of the medium
- Recognise the importance of flexibility, offering as many varied positions as possible
- Not sell time/space to a higher bidder once a firm contact has been signed
- Conduct extensive follow-ups on business already won
- Keep agencies informed of meetings with the clients
- Not quote different prices to agency and client
- Not offer deals cutting out the agency and, therefore its commission earnings
- Should not increase rates without adequate notice
- Should not omit advertisements without prior notice

6.25 **What the advertiser should do**

- Have a good product
- Make messages known to an appropriate audience using the correct media
- Be the expert on the brand and the market
- Be completely clear as to the objectives of the advertising
- Learn and understand media characteristics
- Initiate planning well in advance of campaign date to
- Contribute to the agency's and media owner's knowledge of the market
- Give a clear, easily understood briefing with complete background information
- Involve the agency in the total marketing strategy
- Fix the budget, target audience and media objectives in advance

- Reward the agency and recognise it has to be allowed to make a profit
- Be ruthless in removing business if performance is substandard
- Give the media schedule time to do its job

6.26 **What the agency should do**

- Encourage three-way contact (advertiser-media owner-agency)
- Have close personal ties with the media, to secure time and space, when these are scarce
- Involve the media reps in producing media and market information
- Make full use of media facilities/run/research etc
- Understand overall marketing plans for brands
- Keep clients informed of changes in media, expanding clients' media knowledge
- Remember it is the clients' money (they have the final say)
- Not treat the client like an idiot or dictate to the client
- Periodically review media schedules to ensure the reasons for choice still hold good
- Ensure the payment method allows the agency to be unbiased
- Not object to the client demanding changes provided adequate reason is given
- Explain precisely to the client how media schedules are arrived at
- Do not ignore clients' views on media matters
- Remember that the client understands the needs of customers best of all.

Role of the media independents

6.27 Some agencies, rather than expand by diversifying their departments, prefer to **concentrate** their abilities. Rather than provide the full service of advertisement creation, media planning and buying, and production work, they **restrict their expertise to one of these areas.** These independent companies now form such an important part of the current advertising scene that they merit separate attention.

6.28 What was originally thought to be a temporary phenomenon has turned out to be **substantial and permanent feature of the advertising industry**. These organisations are no longer described, as they were originally, as media-brokers or buying shops. The term 'media independent' is not fully adequate, but does describe these companies which specialise in an aspect of the media side of advertising, yet are independent of the traditional agency structure, and of any specialist creative or production company

6.29 In order to understand why these specialist media planning and buying companies have prospered, we must examine both the service they provide and the clients who use it.

(a) What service is provided? Media independents are specialised and have grown because they are cost-effective streamlined organisations which employ skilled media talent.

(b) Why should any organisation call on the services of a media independent? There is no single answer. A number of advertisers found that conventional full-service agencies did not meet their particular needs or budgets.

6.30 As marketing departments grow more skilful, so they are better able - and are often more inclined - to commission specific tasks, and they now have a far wider range of smaller specialist teams, to perform these selected tasks Some companies use several creative companies to develop different campaigns for different products, and one media independent to place the advertisements.

6.31 One view - held by many independents - is that this trend will mean the end of many traditional agencies, particularly those of a medium size which cannot afford to match the talents available within independents. With a full-service agency, the client might find some services extremely good but others, particularly media, weak.

6.32 The opposing school of thought - found, of course, in the agencies - is that there will always be a need for the superior resources and fertile interconnections of the full-service agency. Companies without internal resources of experienced advertising and marketing staff need all the help they can get in straightening out their advertising strategies and marketing planning.

6.33 The client profile for the media independents now covers the whole gamut of opportunities - advertisers, agencies, creative consultancies and design groups, and even media-owners and management consultancies

6.34 Many small agencies and some medium-sized now place some or all of their media planning or buying in the hands of the media specialists, but it is not only the small firms who do this: quite a few medium-sized agencies enlist outside media assistance, particularly where TV buying is concerned. Media independents are also getting business from new agencies without media dependents. These companies are providing the top creative and account-handling experience that complement the media independents' own services to clients. Added to this, the rise of separate media-buying companies has also opened up the field for the creative consultants, whose work has multiplied over the years.

6.35 The media independents are now in a period of evolution rather than revolution and the 'either/or' syndrome no longer applies so rigidly - advertisers and agencies recognise that the independents have a lot to offer can save time and money and cut down administration costs.

Services provided

6.36 It is interesting to note the wide variety of services now offered. Some independents work in an advisory capacity but do not plan or buy campaigns, while others specialise in international business. Furthermore, the ways in which the media independents are integrating have become increasingly flexible, they co-operate not only with creative consultancies and the new-type agencies but also work freely with advertiser/agency partnerships direct. Some advertisers now use media independents working alongside their existing agencies, rather than seeing them as competitors. the growth of new media opportunities (eg cable and satellite channels), along with the proliferation of selective press media has meant increased demand on the independents' talents.

6.37 There is no longer any need to argue for the respectability of what were called buying shops - it is now firmly established that most media independents are run by professionals. This professionalism was recognised more formally by the formation in 1981 of the Association of Media Independents. In order to establish the calibre of companies seeking membership, the Association checks that applicants meet various criteria as laid clown in its memorandum and articles.

(a) The applicant company must be in the business of media buying, with billings and a client list which show that its capacity extends across major media and that its practice is not unduly restricted. The company must also have received recognition by the various media trade bodies.

(b) The applicant firms are of high professional standing: they must give a written understanding to provide any first-hand client with copies of invoices from media-owners, showing prices at which space or time was bought on their behalf. The applicant firm must also give a formal undertaking to abide by the Code of Advertising Practice.

(c) They should be of sound financial standing and, to this end, must provide the last set of accounts as submitted to one of the recognition bodies.

(d) The applicant company should be independent of any advertiser, agency or media-owner and to establish this independence the applicant company must submit to the Association details of its company share holdings and corporate structure.

7 MEDIA AND MEDIA RESEARCH

Main media types

7.1 There are six main media types available in the UK.

(a) Television (TV)
(b) Press (newspapers and magazines)
(c) Radio
(d) Outdoor (mainly posters)
(e) Cinema
(f) Internet

You will need to consider the reach frequency and impact of the above media when planning a campaign. These aspects will influence your decision as to the best media mix for any given campaign. See the table on the next page.

	TV	*Press*	*Radio*	*Outdoor (posters)*	*Cinema*
Strengths	Creative opportunities Sound and real movement Mass economic coverage Regional (but with national image) Time control Intrusive	Very selective therefore cost efficient Detailed message possible No time limit Personal communication Production costs not excessive	Cheap Flexible Good creative opportunities Precise timing High trade interest	Continuous presence Highly visible Regionally selective High coverage High trade awareness	Selective coverage of your audience Captive audience Sound movement + Big sound Regionally flexible Trade involvement
Weaknesses	Time limit on message No reference back Rarely selective Expensive for both advertising time and production costs	Not intrusive Little control over timing Long lead times - especially colour Regional media have no national image	Sound only Limited geographical cover Limited penetration (variable) Limited research	Creative limitations Best sites committed long term High demand - limited availability High capital outlay High production cost Little reliable research	Low coverage of total population High production costs

7.2 Media are constantly changing. For example electronic media are being increasingly used. Particular instances are outdoor programmable electronic signs (eg a theatre advertising future plays or shows) and indoor videos advertising to queues inside major city post offices. It is important for your Diploma examination and indeed your marketing career that you keep up to date with the latest developments.

7.3 Some references to media research have been made in earlier pages and it is not proposed to go into a great more detail here since it is unlikely that you will be asked a detailed question on this in your case study exam. However you should be aware that media research takes two major forms.

(a) Client or agency research on the media.
(b) Media owners' research on the media's audiences.

7.4 Clearly you would as a client want to know the general advantages and disadvantages of the various media as given on the previous pages. However, you would also want to know:

- Media costs
- Media audiences
- Media reach - geographical, percentages of target audience
- Media images
- Media effectiveness

7.5 Reputable media conduct their audience research on viewers, listeners, readers, passers-by and so on in the knowledge that clients/agencies will be interested not only in the numbers reached but also in the type of persons reached (eg, sex, age, social class, lifestyle etc).

7.6 You may find a knowledge of the following other data sources for media research helpful. Most research is controlled by committees within the governing bodies of advertising, as it is in the industry's interest to be able to provide accurate information and have a co-ordinated scheme providing accurate information and comparable statistics. (These bodies are called **Joint Industry Committees or JIC**'s).

(a) *Audit Bureau of Circulations (ABC)* is a limited company, independent of media owners, advertising agencies and advertisers but which has members representing each. Founded in 1931, it certifies net (per issue) sales figures for newspapers and magazines. These figures are averaged over the six month periods from the end of June and December each year. **Sales** is defined as a copy bought by an individual and not received in any other way ie it excludes bulk purchases for organisations and free copies. The certified figure-is described as the 'ABC circulation' of the publication. These figures are found in BRAD (see (c) below).

(b) *Broadcaster's Audience Research Board (BARB).* Its remit is to commission and supervise TV audience research in the UK. Before BARB was established in 1981, JICTAR (The ITV JIC) and the BBC had independently measured the total TV audience, but their figures rarely tallied due to differences in measurement techniques. BARB is based on a survey of 24,000 households to determine the demographics of the TV area, and who can receive which channels.

(c) *British Rate and Data (BRAD)* is a monthly index of current advertising rates and mechanical data for almost every separate media vehicle available to UK advertisers. Press vehicles also normally include ABC or VFD circulation figures or a publisher's statement of claimed circulation. BRAD is the media buyer's indispensable reference book. (Its American counterpart is Standard Rate and Data.)

(d) JICNARS is the *Joint Industry Committee for National Readership Surveys*. It was set up in 1968 to co-ordinate and commission research into **readership** of UK newspapers and magazines. Readership is the number of people who read (or scan through) the publication. Certain publications are passed onto other readers (Vogue, Cosmopolitan), some end up in waiting rooms (National Geographical, Readers Digest, Country Life) significantly increasing the potential of each advertisement. There is a variation amongst national dailies and the tabloids being read during breaks at work while the more serious titles are taken home to read in the evening.

(e) JICPAR is the *Joint Industry Committee for Poster Audience Research*. In addition there is OSCAR (Outdoor Site Classification and Audience Research).

(i) OSCAR calculates the 'opportunities to see (OTS) rates for every member's sites (95% of all sites) using a mathematical model and a census of sites.

(ii) Gross audience - estimated number of people passing each site.

(iii) OTS are less than the gross audience to allow for factors such as:

- Illumination
- Height and reflection
- Permanent obstructions
- Other poster panels
- Visibility distance
- Angle of panel to sightline

(f) Radio research tells us if the set was switched on during a particular period, and the demographics of the audience. Radio research is less involved partly because it only accounts for 2.3% of advertising expenditure and cannot afford the £1m that BARB costs. The information is collected via a diary scheme giving audience details for 1/2 hour periods, together with demographic details and socio-economic groups. RAJAR (Radio Joint Audience Research) now conducts audience research for both the BBC and independent local radio.

8 BRANDING

8.1 Branding has provided exam questions in recent cases. Firstly, some definitions.

(a) **Brand:** 'a name, term, sign, symbol, or design (or a combination of them) which is intended to signify the goods or services of one seller or group of sellers and to differentiate them from those of competitors'. (Kotler)

(b) **Brand name:** is that part of a brand which can be vocalised or uttered.

(c) **Brand mark:** that part of a brand which can be recognised but cannot be uttered (symbols, design, or distinctive colouring or lettering).

(d) **Trademark**: a brand or part of a brand that is given legal protection because it is capable of exclusive appropriation.

(e) **Copyright:** the exclusive legal right to reproduce, publish, and sell the matter and form of literary, musical, or artistic work.

8.2 From the buyer's viewpoint, a brand tells the buyer something about the product's quality. Brand names contribute to shopping efficiency. Brand names help attract consumers' attention to new products.

8.3 From the seller's viewpoint, brand names help the seller to handle orders and track down problems. Brand names and trademarks give legal protection when there are unique product features, which would otherwise be easy to copy. (Illegal brand copying is a big problem in international marketing.) Branding gives the seller the opportunity to attract a loyal set of customers whose regular purchase give more sales stability and long-run profit. Brands are usually supported by good product quality and promotion. Brand recognition, brand preference, and ultimately brand insistence represent the aims of many companies in FMCG (fast moving consumer goods) markets.

8.4 From the viewpoint of society as a whole, branding has advantages and disadvantages.

(a) Branding leads to higher and more consistent product quality. A brand essentially makes a promise to customers about delivering certain satisfactions. The seller cannot easily tamper with the brand's quality or be careless.

(b) Branding increases the rate of innovation in society. Without branding, producers would not have an incentive to look for new features that could be protecting a product against imitating competitors. Branding gives producers an incentive to seek distinctive product features, and this results in much more product variety and choice for consumers.

(c) Branding increases shopper efficiency, since it provides much information about the product and where to buy it. It enables cost benefits of self selection in large retailing outlets. These benefits can result in higher profits for manufacturers and retailers and/or lower prices for consumers.

(d) Branding leads to higher prices, false and unnecessary differentiation of goods. Branding increases the status consciousness of people who buy certain brands to impress.

Naming

8.5 The essentials of a good brand name are as follows.

(a) Is it distinctive? Does it have individuality? It is different from others in the field?

(b) Does it lend itself easily to display and use in advertising? Short names can be printed larger than long ones.

(c) Is it easy to say? Audi should be pronounced Owdy, but people outside Europe tend to call it Ordy.

(d) It is easy to remember? (eg OXO, Coco-Cola, Rentokil, Yamaha, Heineken). Sometimes new names are adopted, to indicate a change in management, or to overcome the bad associations of the old ones. Think of the motor company of Hillman that became Rootes, then Chrysler, then Talbot, then Peugeot. Morris became BMC, then British Leyland and now Rover.

8.6 The marketing and PR implications of a name are therefore very important. The Japanese car names Cherry and Laurel sound odd in the West where car names usually suggest power or prestige. The *Economist Pocket Marketing* says: 'When Chrysler introduced a new car into the Mexican Market called the Nova it forgot that in Mexico **no va** means "it does not go"'.

Company names

8.7 Choice of a corporate name is important because it will become an identity (including a legal identity) to which will become attached a good or bad reputation forming a corporate image. It will have a character or personality.

(a) Some are based on the founder's name - Ford, Cadbury, Guinness, Lipton and Singer. Others are more general, but perhaps have imposing nature - Premier, National, British, Perfect or Marvellous.

(b) Others based on the product Coca-Cola, or mention the service (eg First Bank of Nigeria)

Some firms use initials (eg BMW for Bayerische Motoren Werke) or form words based on the initials of the company.

(c) Long and difficult names such as Tokyo Shibaura Electrical Company become short, like Toshiba. The Royal Dutch Airlines has a long name in the Dutch language, but the airline has readily been recognised as KLM for over 50 years.

(d) The names of long established organisations may have been chosen haphazardly, or for personal reasons, long before marketing considerations demanded more careful choice of names. Today, one is less able to choose any name because it may already exist. In most countries business names may have to be registered under company law.

Brand names

8.8 Brand names are the specially devised names used to distinguish products. They may also be company names, like, Heinz, Guinness, or Sanyo, but they can be quite different names of which Radion, Persil, Crest, Dove, Marlboro, Sprite, Oasis, or Lion are examples. Such names are usually registered as trade marks by designing the name in a distinctive way.

(a) Unregistered names are usually called trade names.

(b) At the moment there are two Budweiser beers on sale in Europe: the American one and one produced in the Czech Republic (called Budweiser Budvar).

(c) The 'halo' effect operates when a new product benefits from the already established good name of the manufacturer.

9 COMMUNICATIONS RESEARCH

9.1 Advertising research as described above is but one aspect of communications research. As a marketing manager you will be concerned with the following aspects of your decision making.

(a) **Economy** - the need to minimise the cost of inputs.

(b) **Efficiency** - the process of maximising the productivity of inputs.

(c) **Effectiveness** - the extent to which the output generated meets the objectives set for the organisation.

9.2 You will therefore be continuously assessing the effectiveness as well as the relative costs of each element of the promotional mix using research methods.

(a) **Sales research**

(i) What are the selling costs for different customers?
(ii) How can we improve sales presentations so as to obtain more orders?
(iii) Should we have fewer personal visits and more telephone calls?
(iv) Is personal selling more effective than direct marketing?

(b) **Sales promotion research**

(i) What extra sales resulted from the extra costs for these promotions?

(ii) What level of retention of extra sales was there post-promotion?

(iii) What proportion of the budget should go on consumer incentives as opposed to dealer incentives or salesforce incentives?

(c) **PR/publicity research**

(i) How effective is PR relative to other forms of promotion?
(ii) How can changes in image and attitudes be measured..
(iii) How much notice do potential customers take of editorials?

10 INTERNAL COMMUNICATIONS AND THE ORGANISATION

Internal communications and internal marketing

10.1 With the advent of Total Quality Management and its increasing adoption more and more companies have come to realise that without the wholehearted co-operation of all employees (whether in direct contact with the customer or not) any extra marketing effort can be wasted. As previously mentioned you will find additional material on internal marketing in Chapter 5. However you might find the following internal marketing framework helpful bearing in mind that questions on internal marketing have been posed in recent cases.

10.2 Communications within the organisation fall into two types.

(a) **Vertical communication** is mainly formal, and it reflects the organisation hierarchy - in other words it is communication from boss to subordinate and from subordinate to boss.

(i) Organisations are geared to relay orders/instructions regarding specific tasks

(ii) Length of **chain of command** (the number of people the order goes through eg managing director, marketing director, product group manager, brand manager, secretary etc).

(iii) Distortion is a risk especially if communication is verbal.

(iv) There is a need for the provision of upward communication (feedback).

(v) Difficulties can arise if the decision-making area is divorced from areas where the decisions are implemented.

(vi) Authoritarian attitudes can cause resentment amongst subordinates.

(vii) Problems related to co-operation.

(b) **Horizontal communication** is between departments and individuals of the same level. It is often informal.

(i) There is a need to communicate at equal levels.
(ii) It relies on good relations between departments and co-operation to achieve success.
(iii) There are problems related to demarcation of responsibilities.
(iv) Distortion of information can be caused by specialist jargon.

Effective internal communication

10.3 Communication may break down inside an organisation for one or more of the following reasons.

(a) Gaps in transmission, eg between office and field salesforce

(b) Bureaucratic structures with formalisation of communication

(c) The manufacturing and marketing of a large number of different products

(d) The size of the organisation (eg Unilever) may add to its communication problems because of the volume of information to be transmitted

(e) Inflexibility of structures

(f) Isolation of departments (eg legal department within a company)

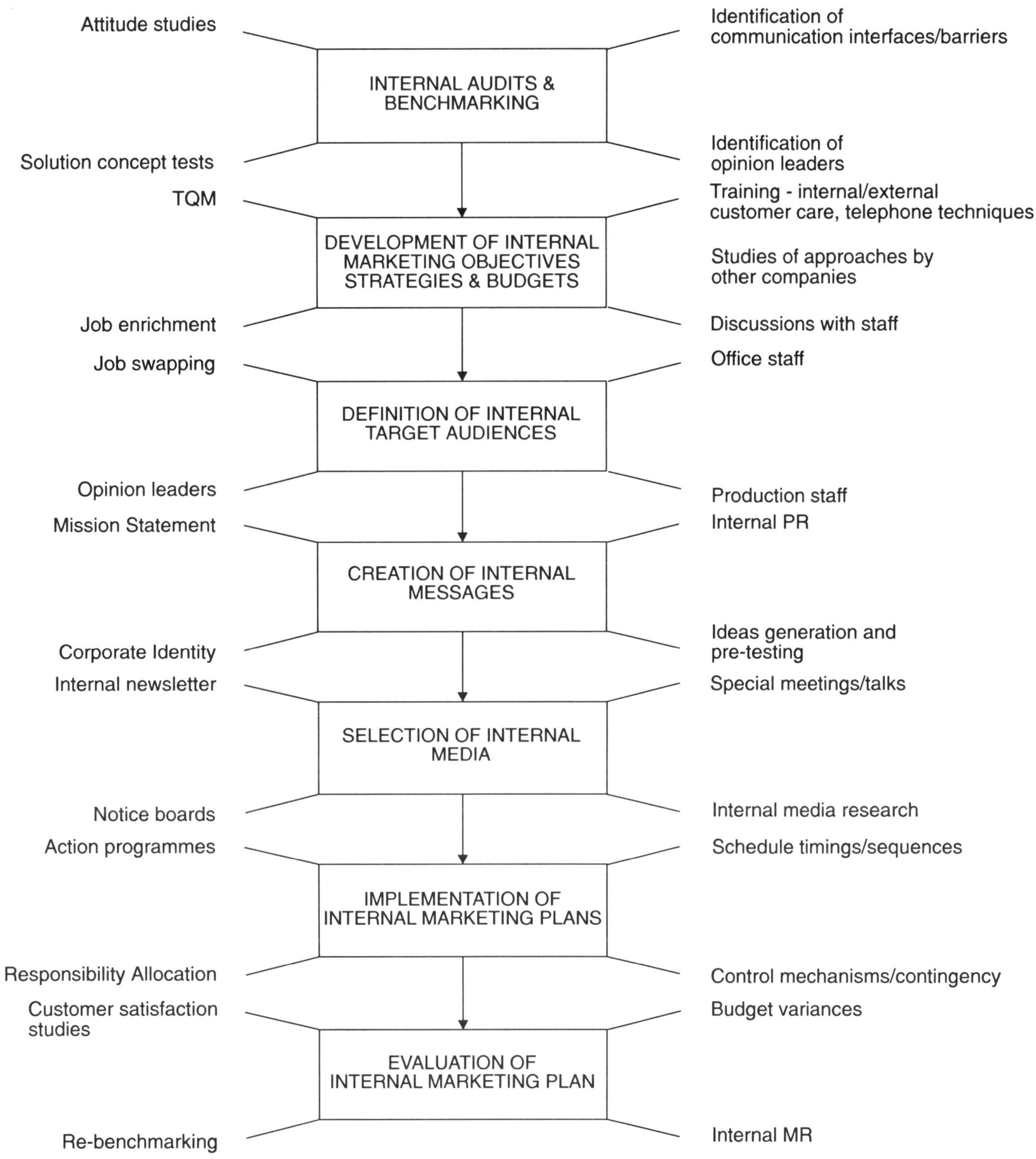
Attitude studies
Identification of communication interfaces/barriers
INTERNAL AUDITS & BENCHMARKING
Solution concept tests
Identification of opinion leaders
TQM
Training - internal/external customer care, telephone techniques
DEVELOPMENT OF INTERNAL MARKETING OBJECTIVES STRATEGIES & BUDGETS
Studies of approaches by other companies
Job enrichment
Discussions with staff
Job swapping
Office staff
DEFINITION OF INTERNAL TARGET AUDIENCES
Opinion leaders
Production staff
Mission Statement
Internal PR
CREATION OF INTERNAL MESSAGES
Corporate Identity
Ideas generation and pre-testing
Internal newsletter
Special meetings/talks
SELECTION OF INTERNAL MEDIA
Notice boards
Internal media research
Action programmes
Schedule timings/sequences
IMPLEMENTATION OF INTERNAL MARKETING PLANS
Responsibility Allocation
Control mechanisms/contingency
Customer satisfaction studies
Budget variances
EVALUATION OF INTERNAL MARKETING PLAN
Re-benchmarking
Internal MR

(g) Reluctance of subordinates to report upwards that some things are not going according to plan.

(h) Misinterpretation of messages (is a **cost reduction programme** the same as redundancy or reorganisation, or what?)

(i) **Shortcomings in communications skills:**

  (i) Low standards of written communication
  (ii) Poor speaking, listening
  (iii) Ambiguity
  (iv) Verbosity, etc.

10.4 An organisation must identify the internal groups with whom it is or ought to be communicating and decide what messages should be sent along which channels to reach them.

10.5 Internal marketing, discussed in more detail in Chapter 5, is a means by which organisations can address these issues.

Chapter roundup

- Promotion is an aspect of an organisation's total communications with its environment. Promotion deals with distinct products and services. Corporate communications promotes the organisation.
- Promotion is necessary because personal contact is expensive and impractical for many products and services.
- The promotional mix includes:
  - advertising;
  - sales promotion;
  - personal selling;
  - public relations (PR).
- The choice of mix depends on the promotion objectives, the competition, the type of product/service and budget. Industrial goods (eg power stations, turbines) are likely to require a heavy degree of personal selling.
- For most campaigns, the services of an advertising agency are required, even though there are also media independents who provide a part of the service. Advertising agencies are generally divided between account management and creative tasks.
- Messages must reflect communication objectives and be tailored to the specific needs of each public.

Quick quiz

1 Distinguish between corporate personality, corporate identity and corporate image (see para 1.4)
2 List some marketing communications objectives. (2.3(b)).
3 What are the benefits of promotion, in the context of buyer behaviour? (3.3)
4 Distinguish between pull and push strategies. (3.8)
5 What decisions have to be taken in an advertising campaign? (3.12)
6 What is a 'false trade description'? (4.5(a)(iii))
7 Draw a framework for campaign planning. (5.1)
8 How would you select an advertising agency? (6.6 - 6.12)
9 What are the pros and cons of TV, press, radio, poster and cinema advertising? (7.1 diagram)
10 What is a brand? (8.1(a))

3 International Marketing Strategy

This chapter covers the following topics.

1 International marketing (IM) and the CIM case study examination
2 The rationale for international marketing
3 Barriers, problems and risks involved in marketing internationally
4 Cultural differences affecting marketing
5 Other environmental factors affecting marketing strategies
6 International market entry options and evaluation
7 International marketing research
8 Planning and organisational aspects of international marketing

Introduction

This chapter does not purport to be a **comprehensive** treatment of International Marketing. In other words, if you are sitting the separate Diploma examination in *International Marketing Strategy* you should buy the BPP Study Text on that subject. This chapter draws on material provided for CIM courses by Dr Paul Fifield and Keith Lewis.

1 INTERNATIONAL MARKETING (IM) AND THE CIM CASE STUDY EXAMINATION

1.1 Most, if not all, of the companies featured in recent CIM case studies have had international interests. Although these interests have been mainly in Europe, there have also been opportunities to market in the wider world. Examples include the following.

(a) *Sentinel Aviation* services major export markets in the USA and Europe.

(b) *De La Rue Fortronic* are looking for advice on entering the People's Republic of China.

1.2 You need to bear in mind that the major part of international marketing is **marketing,** the basics of which have been covered in Chapters 1 and 2.

1.3 All we need to do in this chapter, therefore, is to examine how planning and control and the marketing mix might differ when marketing abroad. We can also confine ourselves to those aspects of international marketing likely to be needed for CIM case study examinations.

2 THE RATIONALE FOR INTERNATIONAL MARKETING

2.1 Some countries are not self-sufficient in food, in raw materials or both. They therefore need to import in order that their populations can survive, grow and prosper.

2.2 The UK is not self sufficient either in food or in all its needs for raw materials. It has traditionally imported a large proportion of its food and some of its raw materials, converting the latter into manufactured goods which have then been exported in order to pay for the imports. The UK is also a major international investor, earning dividends on overseas investments. The UK is also a major provider of services.

2.3 The difference between payments for imports of goods and services and the revenue received for exports of goods and services is sometimes known as the Balance of Payments (current account) and is an important factor in determining the economy of a country. Adverse balances have to be financed by borrowing from overseas investors (even the International Monetary Fund) but in the long term these debts will have to be repaid.

2.4 Some countries have more raw materials or can produce more food than they need and will naturally be tempted to export so as to raise their standard of living.

Comparative advantage

2.5 Ricardo, a 19th century economist, demonstrated that because certain industries enjoyed advantages in certain countries, it would be of mutual advantage for **countries** to trade in those goods where their **comparative** advantage, compared to other countries, was most favourable.

2.6 Ricardo's doctrine of comparative cost (1817) can be illustrated below in this simple example. Compare England and Portugal.

(a)

	England (Cost)		*Portugal* (Cost)	
One gallon of wine	120	hours work	80	hours of work
One yard of cloth	100	hours work	90	hours of work
Total hours work	220		170	

(b) Portugal has an **absolute** advantage in both wine and cloth. Portugal also has a comparative advantage in wine: it is better at producing wine than cloth. England is better at producing cloth than wine. **Despite** the fact that Portugal is more efficient than England in producing cloth, it should still produce wine, and England should specialise in cloth. Why?

(i) Assume that one yard of English cloth is traded for one gallon of Portuguese wine. In other words, for 80 hours work producing a gallon of wine, the Portuguese can import one yard of cloth. Therefore, for the cost of 160 hours of work (one gallon of wine for domestic consumption, and one for export) it can have its gallon of wine (home made) and its yard of cloth (imported), a saving of ten hours work. England fares even better. For the cost of 200 hours work (one yard of cloth for domestic use and one for export) it can have its gallon of wine (imported) and its yard of cloth, a saving of 20 hours of work.

(ii) In other words, it **still** benefits Portugal to produce wine and import cloth, even though it is more efficient at making cloth than England.

(c) Portugal has **absolute** advantage in both wine and cloth but a **comparatively** greater advantage in wine.

2.7 Reasons why industries may benefit from a comparative advantage include the following.

(a) Raw materials industries benefit from the existence of raw material, if it is efficiently produced and constitutes a large part of final product costs for user industries.

(b) Transport , if the effect of transport costs are high in comparison to the value of the product.

(c) Wages and employment structure leads to high labour productivity, but cheap labour can be a source of comparative advantage (in the short term).

(d) Economies of scale. If a market is large enough to permit the establishment of economically sized plants where scale economies are important, this can give an industry an advantage.

(e) Acquired skills: the existence of experience and know how based on historical specialisation can provide advantages.

2.8 The example of fairly simple goods like wine and cloth was chosen because trade in high-tech goods or specialised services is much more complex. This has been demonstrated by Michael Porter in his *Competitive Advantage of Nations*. Cost is only one factor, not perhaps the most important. Porter proposes that the competitive advantage of a country's firms, that is their ability to pursue successfully strategies of cost leadership, differentiation or focus, derives from a country's:

(a) factor conditions (human resources, physical resources, knowledge, capital, infrastructure, divided into basic factors such as cheap labour or raw materials which are unsustainable as a source of long term competitive advantage and **advanced factors** such as proprietary technology);

(b) demand conditions (which determine how firms interpret buyer behaviour: sophisticated domestic consumers are a good discipline for global success);

(c) related and supporting industries (eg suppliers, industries using similar technologies);

(d) competitive rivalry.

2.9 When you are considering international markets, then you need to consider the extent to which your distinctive competences are enhanced by those conditions identified above.

2.10 **Reasons for companies to market internationally**

- Product nearing the end of its life cycle on the home market.
- Excess production capacity and/or surplus production.
- Competition in overseas markets may be less intense.
- To gain economies of scale.
- For prestige purposes and/or patriotic concerns.
- To gain political favour and/or government subsidies.
- To lessen risk (ie wide customer/market base).
- Comparative advantage.
- Saturated home market.
- Organisational ambitions/desires - shareholder pressure
- Perhaps most important of all - the potential for extra profits.
- Survival.
- To compete against overseas firms which are entering the domestic market.

3 BARRIERS, PROBLEMS AND RISKS INVOLVED IN MARKETING INTERNATIONALLY

3.1 Two types of barriers exist in international trade.

(a) Tariff barriers
(b) Non tariff barriers

3.2 **Tariff barriers** are visible and straightforward. They simply consist of a surcharge on all goods described in detail by the special tariff concerned. This can be applied as a percentage of the **value** of the goods or on volume (ie the quantity). There can be different levels of tariffs for different volumes. Both tariff and non-tariff barriers are used by governments to protect home industries but also as a means of discouraging imports so as to obtain a more favourable balance of payments. The EU has a standard 4% tariff for most non-EU imports.

3.3 **Non-tariff barriers** are many, varied and usually less visible than tariff barriers (which attract reprisals from other countries). They may be summarised as follows.

(a) **Technical barriers** can be:

- **Deliberate,** such as noise level restrictions on aero engines or exhaust emission levels in the USA
- **Incidental,** such as electrical supply (different voltages, incompatible equipment etc)

(b) **Administrative barriers**

- **Deliberate barriers** such as bureaucratic 'red tape' delays (such as against Japanese imports to France).
- **Incidental barriers** such as over zealous officials

(c) **Cultural barriers** are dealt with in more detail in Section 4 of this chapter.

(d) **Quotas** are restrictions on the amount of particular types of goods allowed into the country. These may be for limited periods only.

(e) **Prohibitions** are the result of deliberate government policy banning the import of certain goods (eg made from the skins of endangered species).

(f) **Monetary controls** on payments/currency leaving the country, although fluctuating exchange rates can also make exporting difficult.

(g) **Government pressure** ('Buy British' campaigns policies etc).

(h) Other **legal barriers** are described in Paragraph 3.4 below.

3.4 Legal constraints affecting international markets include the following.

(a) **Markets**

- Export controls
- Import controls
- International law
- Treaties (eg GATT/WTO)
- Patents/trademarks
- Regional economic groupings (eg the EU)

(b) **Marketing mix**. Specific country laws govern products/services, pricing, promotion and distribution (too many and varied to cover here).

(c) **Organisation**

(i) Ownership and capital structure

(ii) Permits for:

- Location of plant
- Employment of labour
- Types of product or process
- Monopoly, trusts etc

(d) **Financial**

- Minimum wages
- Expatriation of profits
- Methods of payment

(e) **Legal administration**

- Contracts
- Which law prevails, importing country, exporting country, third country
- Which courts settle disputes

3.5 Although perhaps a little over-detailed for our needs and subject to updating, Beatrice Bondy's (1983) study of protectionism in the 1980s is very revealing. We give below her detailed categorisation of non tariff barriers. Note that there is a movement towards free trade, with the GATT agreement of November 1993 and the founding of the World Trade Organisation 1995. At best non-tariff barriers are being converted into tariff barriers.

3.6 There are of course risks involved in international marketing but depending on the country concerned these may not necessarily be any greater than trading in the home country.

3.7 Many organisations exist to encourage you and give you tangible help when exporting. You could start with the Overseas Trade Services, the Institute of Export and the banks. The following is based on an extract from a brochure detailing Barclays' services offered to all businesses. Such services help you:

(a) Find new outlets and sources of overseas trade, enabling you to develop your sales markets and identify sources of supply by providing you with impartial information about prospective overseas trading partners

(b) Gain efficient access to a vast international market place (by providing you with information about international markets on a scale inaccessible to most companies)

(c) Determine your costs in advance as such services are offered on a fixed cost basis, so that you know exactly how much you will have to pay at the outset

(d) Advertise your products or services (eg on a **worldwide trade opportunity database,** which provides 24-hour exposure to a vast international marketplace)

(e) Find potential trading partners, by scanning the trade opportunity database

(f) Obtain export finance, foreign currency accounts, documentary credits, foreign exchange hedging contracts and options

4 CULTURAL DIFFERENCES AFFECTING MARKETING

4.1 There are approximately 200 different countries each of which contains many different cultures, each with a myriad of beliefs, norms and taboos. It is helpful for us to have a framework used on CIM courses showing the major categories as follows.

Non tariff trade barriers in detail

Formal trade restrictions

A *Non tariff import restrictions (Price related measures)*

Surcharges at border
Port and statistical taxes
Non discriminatory excise
Taxes and registration charges
Discriminatory excise taxes
Government insurance requirements
Non discriminatory turnover taxes
Discriminatory turnover taxes
Import deposit
Variable levies
Consular fees
Stamp taxes
Various special taxes and surcharges

B *Quantitative restrictions and similar specific trade limitations (Quantity-related measures)*

Licensing regulations
Ceilings and quotas
Embargoes
Export restrictions and prohibitions
Foreign exchange and other monetary or financial controls
Government price setting and surveillance
Purchase and performance requirements
Restrictive business conditions
Discriminatory bilateral arrangements
Discriminatory regulations regarding countries of origin
International cartels
Orderly marketing agreements
Various related regulations

C *Discriminatory freight rates*

Administrative trade restrictions

D *State participation in trade*

Subsidies and other government support
Government trade, government monopolies, and granting of concessions or licences
Laws and ordinances discouraging imports
Problems relating to general government policy
Government procurement
Tax relief, granting of credit and guarantees
Boycott

E *Technical norms, standards and consumer protection regulations*

Health and safety regulations
Pharmaceutical control regulations
Product design regulations
Industrial standards
Size and weight regulations
Packing and labelling regulations
Package marking regulations
Regulations pertaining to use
Regulations for the protection of intellectual property
Trademark regulations

F *Customs processing and other administrative regulations*

Antidumping policy
Customs calculations bases
Formalities required by consular officials
Certification regulations

Administrative obstacles
Merchandise classification
Regulations regarding sample shipments return shipments, and re-exports
Countervailing duties and taxes
Appeal law
Emergency law

A cultural framework

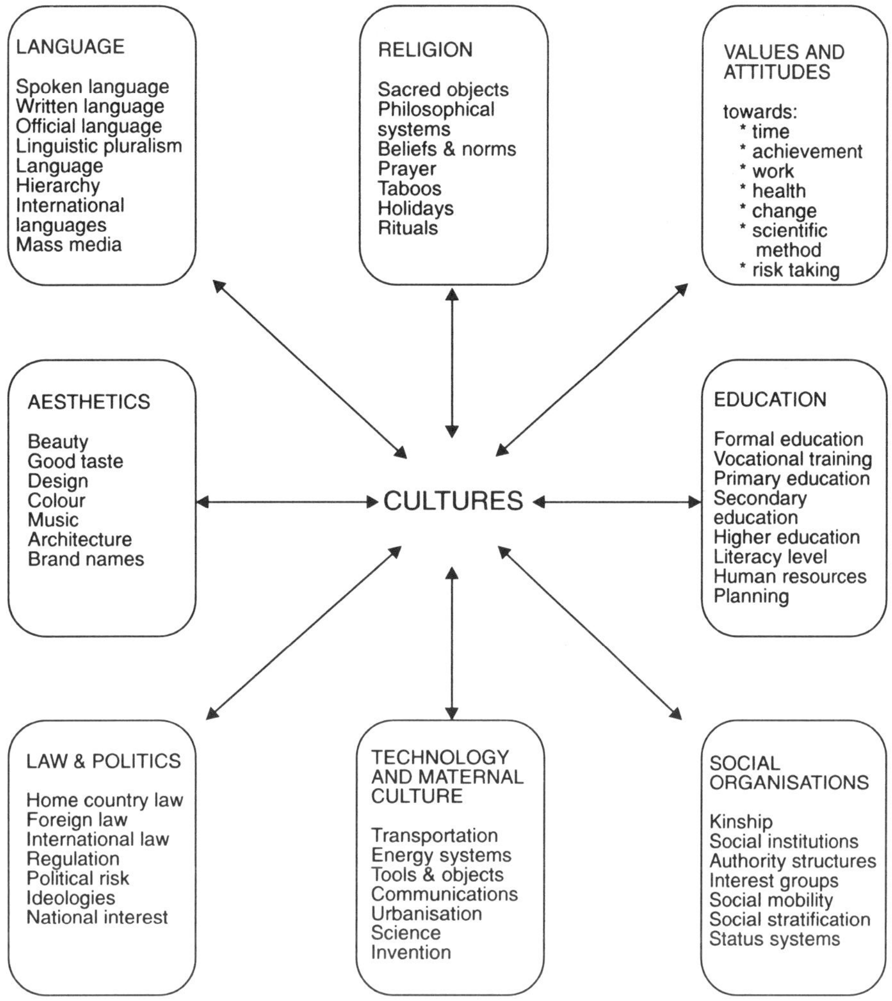

4.2 It is of course impossible for us to cover the above without reference to specific countries, specific sub-cultures, specific religions etc. However just taking the example of religion, this can affect market entry (religious conflict) marketing organisation (days of prayer) goods (type of clothes worn, types of food eaten) promotion (images shown), methods of doing business (eg Islamic banks) and so forth.

5 OTHER ENVIRONMENTAL FACTORS AFFECTING MARKETING STRATEGIES

5.1 We have already touched upon some of the cultural and legal factors affecting marketing decisions. We can now look in more detail at some of the **political, technological** and **economic** factors as follows.

5.2 **Political factors**

(a) **Role of government** in the economy

(i) Participator and/or regulator

(ii) Trade, prices, wages, budget process

(b) **Ideologies and dominant political ideas**

(c) Political stability assists long term planning

(d) **International relations** between home and host governments and between different host governments

(e) **Major trends**

(i) Central planning - democracy?
(ii) Environmental pressures: the 'Green' dimension
(iii) Fundamentalism

5.3 **Technological factors**

(a) Basic technology levels (Including infrastructural support, electrical power, skills available etc).

(b) Industrialisation (Importance of agriculture, manufacturing base, industrial growth or decline, level of automation etc).

(c) Investment (political supports, sphere of influence, international dependency etc).

5.4 **Economic factors**

(a) **Market size**

- Population size and growth
- Population density and concentration
- Population age and distribution
- Disposable income and distribution
- GNP

(b) **Nature of the economy**

- National resources
- Topography
- Climate
- Economic activity
- Infrastructure
- Energy and communications
- Urbanisation
- Inflation
- Role of government
- Financial factors (eg currency controls)

5.5 It is also possible to identify the marketing characteristics relating to the country's **stage of economic development**, although this model will not hold for all markets.

(a) **Self sufficiency**. The country is largely a farming economy. The marketing characteristics are:

- The use of barter
- The exchange of basic necessities
- The limit of exchange to the immediate area (ie local markets)

(b) **Emergence**. Economic wealth has increased.

- Expanded local markets
- Supply surplus of basic goods
- Developing trade specialists and intermediaries
- Product orientation
- Money-based economy
- Moderate consumption
- Developing middle class

(c) **Industrialisation**. The country builds factories for mass production. More people live in towns, and fewer on the land. The marketing characteristics are:

- Trade in national and international markets;
- Product differentiation;
- Market segmentation;
- Consumer orientation;
- Modern technology;
- Rising levels of consumption;
- Rapid growth of middle class.

(d) **Mass consumption and post industrialisation?** The marketing characteristics are:

- Economic affluence;
- Credit based economy;
- Mass application of technology;
- Pervasive middle class;
- Growing concern for quality of life, environment and conservation.

5.6 **Geographic factors**

(a) **Infrastructure/topography.** (Distribution planning, logistics, damage in transit considerations, handling/packaging methods etc.)

(b) **Distance**. (Delivery dates, product life deterioration, management control etc.)

(c) **Climate.** (It affects product quality/life, colour, fading, infestation etc.)

5.7 All the above factors affect international marketing strategies in the choice of suitable markets/market segments and the marketing mix.

The international marketing mix

5.8 The question then arises as to what extent marketing mixes need to be modified to cope with overseas market conditions. Distribution strategies are obviously affected. Different packaging methods and materials may be required and the channels of distribution in overseas countries are unlikely to replicate those in the UK.

5.9 Because of the greater distances entailed in trading in international markets compared with home market operations, transportation costs will no doubt be higher. Such extra costs may however be offset by lower production costs gained by greater economies of scale. Ways in which some of the SLEPT factors might affect **international pricing strategies** are listed below.

SLEPT factor	Effect on price
Social	Customer's perception of product and its quality. Customer's preference for purchasing eg haggling. Customer's perception of country of origin. Social/cultural elements with influence price. Reference groups, lifestyles, beliefs etc.
Legal requirements	Pricing and redistribution decisions Margins in distribution network Prices to be printed on packaging Price promotions

SLEPT factor	Effect on price
Economic	Number of competitors Role of price competition in marketing mix Potential response to price competition Pricing strategies pursued General economic changes and their implication for price
Political	Presence/absence of resale price maintenance Level of sales or value added taxes Role of trade associations in pricing decisions 'Consumer Association' lookalikes and their influence on consumer price perceptions
Technological	Recent developments in distribution technology Recent development in communications

5.10 **Promotional strategies** will also be affected to some degree by the prevailing environment and market conditions in different countries as suggested below, in relation to advertising.

(a) **Environment** (eg culture; literacy levels; readership details; response to symbolism; general attitude to advertising; details of buyer, decider; influencer patterns; market segments; demography.)

(b) **Competition** (eg identification of competitive advertising practices and their expenditure and ratio to sales over a period. Research into strengths and weaknesses of competitors' advertising policies.)

(c) **Institutions** (eg total advertising expenditure in country; media available and growth in expenditure patterns; technical facilities. Media details: circulations, readership and segments, media costs, frequency; code of advertising.)

(d) **Legal system** (eg trade description legislation, special rules pertaining to various products (eg cigarettes, drugs, fertilisers), law limiting expenditure.)

(e) **Economics** (eg levels of consumption, disposable incomes, ownership of radios and TVs, readership of newspapers and magazines, socio-economic class structure, degree of social mobility.)

(f) **Language** (eg translation and 'back translation' of copy etc.)

(g) **Technology** (eg availability of satellite/cable communications etc and levels/organisation of research methodologies' microcomputer applications.)

5.11 **Distribution strategies** are affected by:

- Physical infrastructure (extent, condition)
- Existing distribution channels (eg large supermarket chains, small retailers)
- Warehousing
- Competitors' dominance over distribution

5.12 This leaves us with the extent to which the product will need to be modified to suit overseas markets. The answer depends upon the type of product and the nature of the market. If we accept the marketing concept we will conduct research to establish needs before making the decision. Having said this the example of Coca Cola is often quoted as an example of successful global **standardisation.**

6 INTERNATIONAL MARKET ENTRY OPTIONS AND EVALUATION

6.1 Modes of entry to overseas markets

(a) Indirect exporting
(b) Direct exporting
(c) Overseas production

6.2 Indirect exporting without overseas involvement is usually by one of the routes below. The firm itself does not get involved in the process of exporting.

(a) **By default**. Goods sold to other home market manufacturers may find their way into overseas markets and ultimate users may then come to you for spares/replacements. (Eg you make electric motors which carry your nameplate and are bought by many engineering companies marketing say compressors, generators, pumps etc overseas).

(b) **UK buying offices**. These may be the subsidiaries of overseas businesses set up in the UK to buy UK goods. They buy from you in the normal way and arrange their own shipments overseas.

(c) **Export houses**. A variation on (b) but not foreign owned. These are often long-established companies set up to exploit demand for British goods. They provide the export services for British manufacturers who did not want the bother of exporting themselves.

(d) **Trade missions**. Overseas trade missions periodically visit the UK to buy goods direct, for example in the fashion industry.

(e) **Piggy backing**. You ask another manufacturer already trading overseas to sell your products along with his own.

6.3 Some advantages of indirect exporting

(a) No language problems or literature translations
(b) Transactions according to British law
(c) Revenues paid through your bank in the normal way
(d) Subject to your conditions of sale
(e) No complex export documentation needed
(f) No risks of non-payment due to foreign government interventions
(g) No need to arrange shipment overseas
(h) Ideal for start-up situations

In summary, there is no hassle but the big disadvantage is that you may miss out on greater opportunities for profit.

6.4 **Direct exporting** is where the producer exports goods directly to the market. There are various degrees of involvement, as outlined below, but to summarise these are:

- Overseas agents
- Overseas distributors
- Overseas sales office

6.5 Overseas agents do **not** take title to goods (exceptions exist). They are restricted territorially and only sell (obtain orders - transmit to UK). The manufacturer delivers. An agent is paid commission and acts in role of substitute sales force. Agents are best suited to 'simple' standardised products, but are not suitable where high marketing involvement is necessary.

(a) **Advantages**

- Little cost involved
- Risk factor low

- Payment by result
- Quick, easy to start
- Market and 'contacts' knowledge, language ability

(b) **Disadvantages**

- Variable quality
- Lack of control
- Conflicts of interest
- Legal complexities (exit strategies)
- Communications
- Motivation
- EC interest in agency agreements (greater complexity)

6.6 **Distributors,** unlike agents, take title to goods buy and sell usually at their price, and absorb risks. They are restricted territorially. They are more involved than agents in the success of the product, and as well as increasing commitment, are likely to give more marketing assistance. **Key factors in managing distributors** are as follows.

(a) Create loyalty
(b) Create involvement and sense of teamwork
(c) Ensure adequate payment, training/development programmes
(d) Determine standards of performance
(e) Evaluation of their performance
(f) Efficient communications

6.7 Setting up an **overseas sales office** perhaps in the form of a subsidiary company offers potential cost savings, gives greater control, and perhaps offers faster feedback. The head office's marketing strategy can be transferred easily.

(a) Drawbacks

- Higher capital costs
- Back up support needed is higher
- Training
- Commitment (long term)
- Continuity (in personnel)
- Organisational and administrative involvement
- Time/speed of entry

(b) Choosing a sales office. The choice depends on:

- Corporate objectives
- The nature of market
- Speed of entry
- The level of marketing
- The scale of effort
- The desired level of control
- Risk
- The degree of the company's experience in international marketing.

Overseas production for overseas sales

6.8 Finally goods which would have been exported from the home country to the foreign market can be made in the foreign market.

6.9 **Licensing** confers a right to the licensee to utilise a company's specific patent or trademark for a defined period of time.

(a) **Benefits to the licenser**

- No capital outlay, as the licensee provides capital for the operation.
- Trade restrictions are overcome.
- Little political risk.
- It is a quick and easy way of producing within the overseas market.
- The licensee has access to local market knowledge.
- Considerable cost savings can be generated (eg saving on freight).

(b) **Disadvantages to the licenser**

- Heavy dependence on licensee;
- Limited returns (usually 2% to 5%);
- A lack of control of licensee (eg in product quality);
- A lack of control of marketing;
- The licensee may learn enough to become a long-term competitor at the end of the licensing agreement

(c) **Managing the licensing agreement**

- Careful selection of licensee if possible
- Careful drafting of agreement (in home language)
- Control of key components/formulation should be retained by licenser
- Limit the geographic area covered
- Register trade marks/patents in licenser's name
- An agreement attractive enough to retain the licensee.

6.10 **Franchising** is a special form of licensing. The franchiser provides a total marketing programme including the brand name, logo, product and method of operation. It usually involves selling a service and is thus open to small investors with only working capital. It allows small, independent, entrepreneurial individuals to enjoy the benefits of belonging to a large organisation whilst retaining owner-manager status. Franchising is fast growing, but not without its problems, which largely centre around standards/service levels, etc and reflect cultural expectations. Examples have included MacDonalds, Kentucky Fried Chicken, Hertz, Manpower, and Holiday Inns.

6.11 **Contract manufacturing** is where products are produced by an independent local company on a contractual basis. The manufacturer's responsibility is limited to production, and, in effect, the international company is 'renting' production capacity. It is different from licensing in legal terms.

(a) **Advantages**

- Avoids import barriers
- Reduces risk
- Can claim to be 'local'

(b) It is suitable for low market volume combined with high tariff situations, and is usually employed where production technology is widely available and where **marketing** effort is crucial to success.

6.12 Assembly involves locating only a part of the manufacturing process overseas, typically the final stages of production. For example, some firms send components or parts from the home country for assembly into finished goods. It can takes advantages of low wage costs in the country of assembly, and lower transport costs. It can help overcome government restrictions, (quotas, tariffs, etc), but many governments are beginning to insist on a set percentage of local content.

6.13 **An overseas joint venture** is a foreign operation in which the international company has enough equity to have a voice in management but not enough to dominate or control. It is fast growing, increasingly important strategic business activity (eg GEC). It is insisted upon by many countries, whose governments wish to benefit from technology transfer.

(a) **Advantages**

(i) Faster development of product, if this process is shared
(ii) Shared costs/risk
(iii) Control over production and marketing
(iv) Market feedback
(v) The venturer gets more experience in international marketing

(b) **Disadvantages**

(i) The need for greater capital investment
(ii) More management involvement
(iii) Cultural conflicts between the partners
(iv) Disengagement problems

6.14 Firms can buy or build factories overseas from scratch. Some also develop their own distribution networks, operating effectively, as domestic firms (a process which Kenichi Ohmae calls **insiderisation**).

(a) **Advantages**

(i) Complete control
(ii) Total commitment
(iii) No 'partner' conflicts
(iv) Profit

(b) **Disadvantages**

(i) May be costly in time and money
(ii) Political risk - expropriation
(iii) Socio/economic risk (eg different management styles)

Which mode of entry?

6.15 Strategic factors affecting mode of entry are given below.

(a) **Factors specific to the firm**

- Goals
- Size
- Product line and nature of product
- Competition

(b) **General factors,** which are relatively independent of firm, include the following.

(i) **Number of markets**

- Different methods give different coverage
- Wholly owned foreign subsidiary may not be permitted
- Licensing may not be possible (no qualified licensees)

(ii) **Penetration within markets**

- Quality of coverage required

- Some markets are more open than others.

(iii) **Market feedback**

(1) It is important that the method chosen provides feedback
(2) Direct methods provide better possibilities for feedback
(3) Management of the distribution channel ensures feedback

(iv) Administrative requirements, including documentation, red tape, management and time can affect a mode's attractiveness.

(v) **Personnel requirements**

(1) These become more complicated with greater involvement.
(2) Managing overseas staff requires skill.
(3) International personnel need to be recruited.

(vi) **Exposure to foreign problems**

(1) New kinds of legislation
(2) Regulation, taxes, labour problems

(vii) Flexibility. The type of involvement might change in the long run

(viii) Risk of the method of involvement (in addition to the risk of the market itself).

6.16 On a broader level still, Paliwoda gives us the following criteria.

- Speed of market entry desired
- Direct and indirect costs of entry
- Degree of flexibility required
- Risk factors involved
- Investment payback period
- Long-term profit objectives

6.17 When evaluating entry options in the CIM case study exam you need to recognise the question's **time constraints** and work from the **broad to the particular** in order to select the more viable options.

7 INTERNATIONAL MARKETING RESEARCH

Exam focus point

When making your proposals in the CIM case study exam, you need to take into account that the stage of economic development of your overseas market may not allow the same degree of sophistication as we might be used to in the UK. For example, telephone research may not be viable if only a small proportion of the population have one. Random sampling using street names and house numbers will be impossible if streets are not named (eg Tokyo) and numbers do not exist. Databases such as Acorn cannot be assumed to be universally available.

7.1 Special problems of international marketing research

(a) **Comparability**

(i) Aggregation of data makes comparison difficult.

(ii) Decision making is made locally, so there may be unique local marketing requirements.

(iii) Comparing of results of decisions.

(b) **Sampling**

(i) Validity of techniques varies from country to country.

(ii) Poor transportation in some countries can affect the viability of the sampling

(iii) Different languages or dialects in the same country reflect cultural or sub-cultural differences

(iv) Different family structures may mean that the person taking the decisions are not the same as in the host structure (ie there is different household buyer behaviour)

(c) **Data collection methods**

- Telephone and mail difficulties in developing countries
- Cultural problems
- Suspicion of interviewers (especially in countries with authoritarian regimes)

(d) **Response error**

- Not-at-home problem/call backs
- Co-operation levels

(e) **Field force**

- Training differences
- Composition. In some countries, female interviewers may not be acceptable.

(f) **Data**

- Lack of historical data
- Few and poorly aggregated statistics may make it hard

7.2 Information sources used by UK companies (%) are as follows.

	%
Feedback from export sales staff	61
Trade associations and chambers of commerce	54
General knowledge	44
Press reports	32
Export departments of banks	29
Local press and journals	20
Test marketing	5
Financial institutions	14
No information base	15

7.3 Most frequently used **government services** in the UK are as follows.

Rank order	*Service*
1	Specific export opportunities
2	Help with overseas visits
3	Tariffs
4	Finding overseas agent
5	Calls for tender
	Economic reports
6	Status reports
	Market reports
	Export regulations

7.4 **Export facilitating agencies** provide a range of service and expertise which can provide a research, entry and promotional basis for the commercial and industrial sectors seeking to expand their sales operations into export markets.

7.5 **Evaluating market opportunities.** Market **opportunities** can be evaluated using the SLEPT factors with particular emphasis in the Social, Political, Economic and Legal dimensions.

(a) **Social**

- Major historical developments
- Population and its composition (age, race, religion, occupation, residence, education)
- Mobility (between jobs, places, social classes)
- Communications (transport and media)
- General way of life and traditions

(b) **Political**

- Major political trends
- Governmental structure and organisation
- Prevailing political philosophy
- Principal government activities
- Annual budgets (eg chief sources of revenue, chief expenditure)
- Policies towards labour, business, agriculture, foreign trade

(c) **Economic**

- Gross national product, but also the **total** and main **components** of personal consumption (eg percentage spent on clothes), government expenditure, foreign trade balance, private investment
- Agricultural production
- Industrial production
- Services
- Construction
- Currency and exchange rates
- Banking system and financial institutions
- Labour force and wage rates
- Incomes and standard of living
- Natural resources

(d) **Legal**

- Main laws affecting business (eg forms of organisation, capital and ownership, permits regarding location, employment, trademarks, patents).
- Tariffs
- Taxes
- Currency and foreign exchange control
- import/export regulations
- Antitrust regulations
- Labour laws

7.6 **Some data sources for international marketing research**

(a) Information relating to the changes in the social, political, economic and legal dimensions can be found from the following.

(i) *The Europa Yearbook* is a two volume compendium providing reviews of every country. It is published annually.

(ii) *EIU World Outlook* annual publication by the Economist Intelligence Unit (an offshoot of 'The *Economist*') gives summary details of the economic and political trends in 165 countries.

(iii) **Clearing banks.** Many of the major banks of the world produce periodic reviews of the performance of each of the countries of the world.

(iv) **Department of trade and industry.** The *Hints to Exporters* series provides synopses of each of the countries of the world, and a wealth of other material.

7.7 **Information relating to the activities of commercial organisations**

(a) *Kompass publications.* Details of companies who subscribe to Kompass covering products and services offered, are supplied with an indication of export/import activities. A wide range of countries are covered but the Americas and Africa are not covered in as much detail (by country) as Europe, Australasia and parts of south-east Asia.

(b) *Thomas Register (TOM-CAT)* is the 'Kompass' equivalent in the USA.

(c) *Trade Association Publications* often provide details of like associations in other countries.

7.8 **Statistics**

(a) *Industrial Statistics Yearbook* is published by United Nations (UN) and details the manufacturing activities of each country. Data is usually two to six years old at time of publication depending on the country concerned.

(b) *International Trade Statistics Yearbook* (UN) contains details of the trade between countries by product (volume and value). Data is usually two years old when published.

(c) *Statistics of Foreign Trade* is published by the Organisation for Economic Co-operation and Development (OECD), and is similar to the UN publication but not as detailed. Statistics are usually one year old when published.

(d) *Eurostat* is published by the EC, and is a comprehensive set of statistics covering the activities of each country of the EC and their trading relationships with the world.

7.9 In addition, information can be supplied by:

- Government
- International institutions (OECD, IMF, WTO, EU)
- The World Bank
- Trade associations
- Professional bodies
- Chambers of commerce
- Market research agencies
- Consultants
- Service industries
- ESOMAR (European Society for Opinion and Market Research).

8 PLANNING AND ORGANISATIONAL ASPECTS OF INTERNATIONAL MARKETING

International marketing planning and control

8.1 International marketing and control is similar in essence to marketing planning as detailed in Chapter 1 with the difference of detail as indicated below.

Transfer pricing

8.2 A word about transfer pricing is perhaps appropriate here, although this decision would normally be addressed at corporate level. Transfer pricing is the term used to describe differences in prices as goods are transferred from division to division both within a country and across national boundaries.

(a) For example, the manufacture of a component might take place within country A, offering comparative advantage in labour and/or materials. These semi-manufactured goods are then transferred at price A to country B where manufacture is completed and the goods are transferred at price B to another division in country B for packaging, stocking and eventual sale to a number of other countries at different prices.

(b) Tensions arise within the company over pricing where divisions operate as separate strategic business units (SBUs). The reason is that if each SBU is supposed to make a profit, they will charge the highest price.

(c) Perhaps more importantly, political tensions arise (governments, consumer bodies, trade unions) when multinationals use transfer pricing to avoid tax. Transferring at a low price from a high-tax country allows a subsidiary in a low-tax country to make a larger profit and is in the interests of the multinational but not necessarily the high-tax country government or population.

Controlling international marketing

8.3 Distances and differences in language and culture affect communications effectiveness and thereby mechanisms for planning and control Other factors previously discussed such as fluctuations in exchange rates and political stability can also adversely affect control systems for international markets. Some potential ways of overcoming these difficulties are given below.

The international marketing planning process

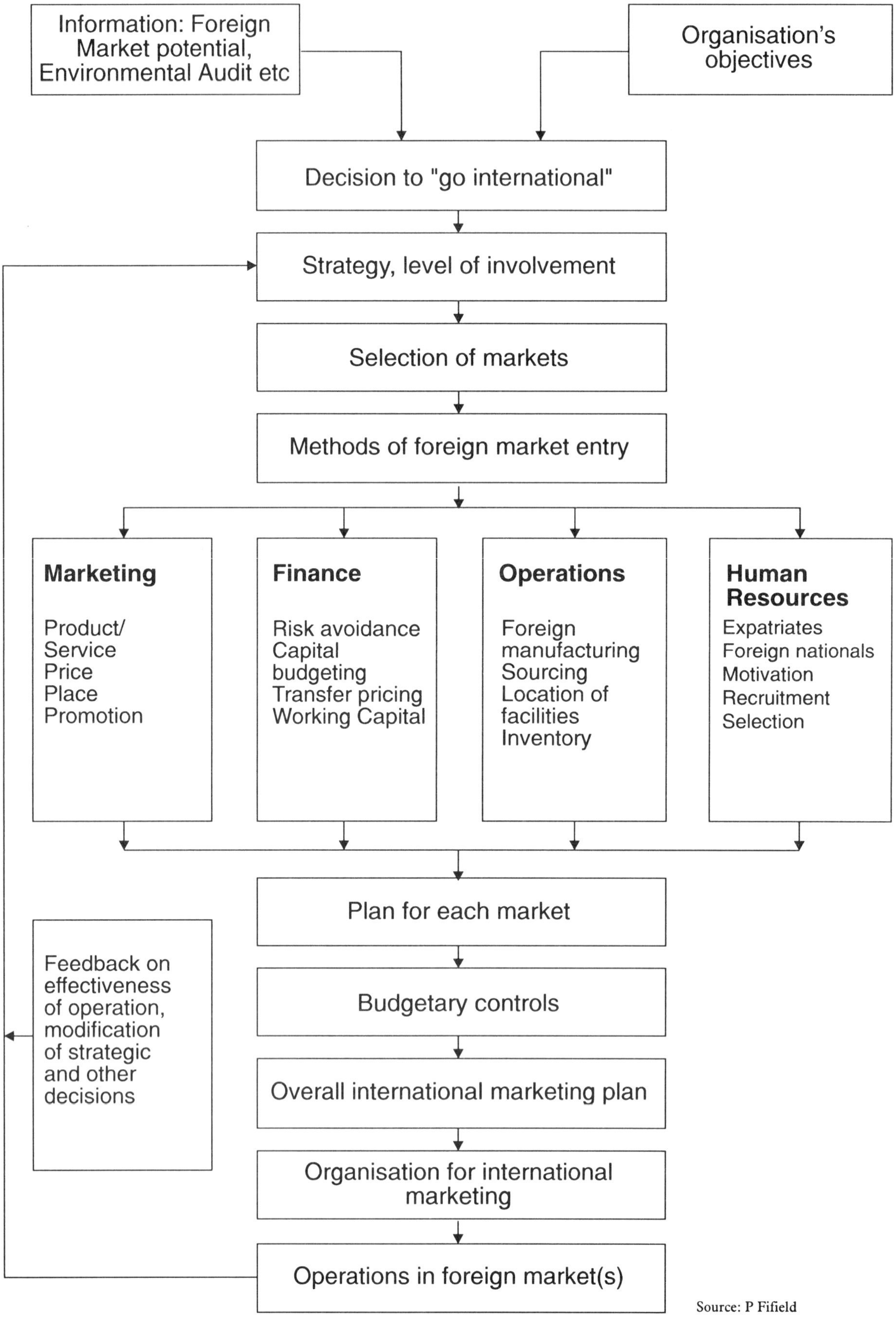

Source: P Fifield

(a) **Methods of integrating international marketing**

- Standard planning system
- Standard reporting system
- International meetings/committees
- International task forces (trouble shooters)
- International marketing publications
- Common marketing support systems
- Rotation of personnel

(b) This can be summarised as follows.

- Centralisation of strategic decision-making (planning)
- A strong corporate culture (loyalty etc)
- Systems transfer
- Personnel transfer

The organisational implications of international marketing

8.4 **Variables influencing organisational structure**

- **Size** of business - overall volume and foreign volume.
- **Number** of markets in which operating
- Degree of **involvement** in foreign markets
- The company's **goals** for international business
- The company's international **experience**
- The **nature** of products - complexity etc
- The nature of marketing **task**
- Political factors, external **and** internal

8.5 Some companies have an international division. In other words, all aspects of overseas activities are collected in **one** division.

(a) **Advantages**

- Centralisation of all specialist skills/expertise
- International business can be focused upon
- Resources can be properly allocated
- Objective analysis of potential markets is provided

(b) **Disadvantages**

- Separation of the two divisions may not mean equality between them
- Sub-optimisation may result from dilution of corporate resources
- Friction between international and domestic divisions

8.6 Structuring the organisation by area means that activities, especially marketing activities, are broken down by region.

(a) **Advantages**

- Easy communications
- Expertise can be grouped
- Area problems can be identified and rectified at the right level
- They reflect existing economic groups (eg EU)

(b) **Disadvantages**

- Duplication $\Rightarrow$ management inefficiency
- Friction between areas and HQ

- Limited communication between areas.
- Gaps emerge between countries in one area (increasing friction).

8.7 Centralisation and decentralisation of operations determine the relative power of corporate head office and local subsidiaries, ensuring a division of labour.

(a) **Corporate HQ** is in charge of international marketing at corporate level. It:

- Sets objectives/policies for world markets
- Plays a major role in planning
- Is a source of ideas and a back-up resource (trouble shooting)
- Co-ordinates and integrates national programmes

(b) The **local subsidiary** has its own roles. It:

- Implements the plan within broad guidelines
- Conducts market research
- Has a 'voice' in product policy and pricing
- Selects and administers distribution channels
- Manages the sales operation
- Directs the promotional programme
- Ideally has dual reporting to local and HQ management

Human resource implications of international marketing

8.8 We need to consider the effects of going international on our standard recruitment and training policies. Should we:

- Recruit from expatriates in the foreign country?
- Use foreign nationals? or
- Use our own personnel recruited and trained in the home country?

8.9 Obviously circumstances alter cases but most companies have found that using a foreign sales force is on balance more effective than sending home country personnel with the accompanying language and cultural difficulties involved.

8.10 Many overseas countries have regulations concerning the proportion of indigenous/ foreign employees for different levels - management, office staff, factory staff which are allowed for foreign companies.

8.11 You may also experience differences in foreign countries concerning the types of training available, laws on hire and fire, salary levels etc.

8.12 Whereas delegation of responsibility may be encouraged in one culture, only the top executives may be allowed to make decisions in another culture (as analysed by Hofstede). Similarly criteria for promotion can vary considerably from culture to culture. Any human resources plan has to be sensitive to these issues.

Chapter roundup

- International marketing is not a unique type of marketing in its own right, but does have specific problems of its own related to the different circumstance of each county and its culture (eg political stability, different levels of development, buyer behaviour).
- Other factors include international financial issues such as exchange rates, and trade liberalisation agreements.
- IM is often more risky than domestic marketing because of the variety of environmental influences involved, and there are additional organisational considerations to be taken into account. Help for exporters is available however.

Quick quiz

1 What is the rationale for a **country** to trade? (see paras 2.2, 2.6)
2 Why do **companies** engage in IM? (2.10)
3 Describe some non-tariff barriers. (3.3, 3.5)
4 What are the distinct marketing characteristics of a country at different levels of development? (5.5)
5 Describe licensing. (6.9)
6 Draw a planning model for IM. (8.1)

4 Financial Aspects of Marketing

This chapter covers the following topics.

1 Financial aspects of the CIM case study
2 The balance sheet
3 The profit and loss account
4 Financial analysis: external ratio analysis
5 Inflation
6 Sources of finance
7 Feasibility and risk

Introduction

The CIM has in the past been criticised for turning out 'financially illiterate' diploma holders. It is now official CIM policy to ensure that marketing managers who become members are able to play their full part in corporate decisions. To do this, they need to know the financial status not only of their own organisation but also those of their leading competitors.

1 FINANCIAL ASPECTS OF THE CIM CASE STUDY

1.1 In this chapter we are examining only those aspects of finance which you are expected to apply to the case study. Almost all case studies have financial accounts which you are expected to analyse and understand. You also need to be able to assess the value of data (including financial data). Not all the data is accurate. This is something you will have to decide for yourself.

1.2 In addition to financial ratio analysis (and of course marketing costs ratio analysis) you are expected to have a basic knowledge of approaches to cost. This is necessary to understand pricing decisions.

1.3 The definition of marketing by the CIM ends with the word 'profitably'. You must therefore be aware of the financial implications of your marketing proposals and the importance of being able to demonstrate a return on investment at least equal to that of competing proposals.

1.4 With the above points in mind please read the following sections 2 to 13 assiduously. It is important not only for your CIM case study exam but also for your career and your own professional standing to have an adequate grasp of these financial aspects.

2 THE BALANCE SHEET

2.1 The balance sheet/position statement is a 'snapshot' of the financial picture/position of the business at a single moment in time (eg 12 o'clock midnight on 31 December). It shows us the total 'value' of the assets that the business owns and how these are represented by the liabilities that the business owes. In this respect the accounts may be looked at as **balancing** assets with liabilities.

2.2 **Assets** are items which have a **value to the company** at the balance sheet date. They may be long term/fixed assets, such as buildings, equipment and motor vehicles, or short term/current assets, such as stocks, debtors (money owed by your customers) and cash.

2.3 **Liabilities** are the **responsibilities** that the business has to pay suppliers for goods received (creditors), to repay loans and to account to the shareholders/investors for the money they originally put into the business, and the profit that has been earned to date but not paid out in dividends. **Share capital** is the money initially invested, **reserves** are the **profit retained**. **Equity** describes the total of capital and reserves.

2.4 **Presentation.** Accountants now use a combined vertical format which allows certain additional information (eg net current assets or working capital) to be readily shown. The general convention is to list assets down the page in descending order of permanence, ie land and buildings first, cash last. This is then followed, but in the opposite way, by liabilities.

2.5 **Historical costs.** The value of a company's assets shown in its accounts reflects the cost to the company **when the assets were purchased,** less of course any depreciation that has been charged so far. There is much debate on whether these historical costs are relevant to the users of accounting documents. (For example, a building may have an historical cost less depreciation of £50,000, but have a market value of £200,000.) Modification to historical costs is sometimes allowed.

2.6 **Tangible and intangible assets**

(a) Tangible assets are those with a physical identity such as buildings, furniture and fittings, vehicles etc. They can be counted and verified each year.

(b) Investments are financial investments in stocks and shares (occasionally in subsidiary companies).

(c) **Intangible assets are not physical assets.**

(i) Development costs of a new product should only be treated as an asset in special circumstances.

(ii) Concessions, patents, licenses, trademarks (**not** brands) should only be treated as assets if acquired for valuable consideration.

(iii) Brands, however, do not count as trademarks. They are 'goodwill' which is a 'combination of factors which is expected to produce enhanced earnings'. Treating brands as **assets** (like a company's head office building) is a very contentious topic, and it is possible that the practice will be so hedged around with restrictions that it will be effectively outlawed.

2.7 Consider though the position of a marketing department that wants to spend £10m establishing a new brand. They will rightly argue that the brand once established will last say five years and the cost should therefore be capitalised and written off over five years. The counter argument is that it should be written off in the first year as no one can say how long it will last or in fact whether it will achieve the desired results in the market place. Also, the value of a brand may suddenly fall: the price of Marlboro cigarettes was reduced in the US, to compete with low price competition, even though the owners of the brand had invested large sums of money in it. Thus the ability of a brand to command a premium price may be restricted.

2.8 Items contained in the balance sheet include the following: this is **not a standard layout**.

Item	*What the item represents*
1 Fixed assets	1 Cost of long-term assets
2 Depreciation	2 Amounts charged to profit up to now to reflect the use of an asset over its life
3 Tangible assets	3 (1) - (2)
4 Current assets	4 Assets that can easily be converted into cash
- Stocks	- Raw materials, work in progress and finished goods
- Debtors	- Amounts owed to firm by customers.
- Cash	- Money in bank or actual cash
5 Current liabilities (under 1 year)	5 Amounts owned by firm (payable during year)
- Creditors	- Amounts owed to suppliers
- Overdrafts	- Owed to bank
- Taxation owing	- Owed to Inland Revenue
- Dividends owing	- Owed to shareholders
6 Net current assets (liabilities)	6 Current assets less current liabilities
7 Net Assets	7 Total assets (fixed assets plus net current assets)
8 Loans (over 1 year)	8 Borrowing, repayable in medium/long term
9 Share Capital	9 Money invested by owners
10 Reserves	10 Profits made, not distributed
11 Equity	11 Total owners' stake

2.9 For companies domiciled in the UK the rules governing balance sheets (and profit and loss accounts, and cash flow statements) are laid down by Act of Parliament (in the Companies Acts) and in Financial Reporting Standards (formerly Statements of Standard Accounting Practice) which can also have a legal effect. Note that the rules only apply to **external reporting**: a firm can arrange its internal management accounting information in any way it likes. CIM case studies may include companies domiciled overseas and therefore subject to other laws.

2.10 A typical balance sheet is given below.

WAY AHEAD INTERNATIONAL PLC
BALANCE SHEET

	19X9		19X8	
	£000	£000	£000	£000
Fixed assets				
Intangible assets		5,000		5,000
Tangible assets		15,840		15,527
Investments		4,908		4,688
		25,748		25,215
Current assets				
Stocks	995		954	
Debtors	1,743		1,375	
Cash at bank and in hand	10,823		7,959	
	13,561		10,288	
Creditors				
Amounts falling due within one year	6,439		4,478	
Net current assets		7,122		5,810
Total assets less current liabilities		32,870		31,025
Creditors: Amounts falling due after more than one year		200		1,371
		32,670		29,654
Provisions for liabilities and charges		521		539
Net assets		32,149		29,115

	19X9		19X8	
	£000	£000	£000	£000
Capital and reserves				
Called-up share capital		1,675		1,675
Revaluation reserve		11,104		11,104
Other reserves		10,230		10,230
Profit and loss account		9,140		6,106
Shareholders' funds		32,149		29,115

Signed on behalf of the Board
Directors

3 THE PROFIT AND LOSS ACCOUNT

3.1 If the balance sheet is a snapshot at a **point** of time then the profit and loss account (or income statement) is a history, as it were, of, what has been happening to the business over a **period** of time, usually a year, a quarter, or a month. By deducting the total of all expenses from the income (revenue earned) a profit or loss for that time period will be left. In practice this is not quite as straightforward as it sounds.

3.2 The **accruals or matching principle**. Revenue and expenses must be matched to the time period to which they relate. The total sales will be the summation of all the invoiced or firm sales in the period. Expenses though consist of the items of expenditure which have been **enjoyed** by the firm **in the same time period**. This can be very **different** to the amounts that have been **paid for**.

(a) Some charges which must be taken into account may not even have been invoiced by the supplier until after the year end. For example the electricity consumed in December might not be billed until February. The accountant therefore has to estimate and provide for or **accrue** these charges, which is why they are called accruals.

Similarly, you might buy and use goods from suppliers at the end of year 1, but not pay them until year 2 (which is why they appear as creditors on the balance sheet).

(b) Similarly some charges such as business rates are paid in advance from April to March. The accountant will therefore deduct a proportion of the total bill before calculating the profit. This is called a **prepayment.**

3.3 **Stock.** A company which manufactures or trades will hold stocks of goods for resale. At the end of the year when the cost of the goods sold is calculated, it is logical that a deduction is made in recognition of the stock that has **not** been sold, but has been made or received. This stock will then become a cost to the business in the **following** year. The calculation is performed as follows.

	£	£
Sales for year		10,000
Opening Stock (1 January 19X0)	900	
Purchases, other production costs etc	7,050	
Total cost	7,950	
Closing stock 31 December 19X0)	(800)	
Cost of goods sold		7,150
Gross profit		2,850

3.4 **Depreciation.** The costs of fixed assets/items which are purchased for use in the business over a long period ie over a year, need to be charged as expenses over the period of time in which those assets are **useful** to the business. The simplest way of doing this is to estimate how many years of life the asset will have and then divide the cost by the number of years.

(a) For example, a computer costs £5,000. Its estimated life before it wears out, becomes scrapped, or whatever, is five years. In each of the five years, £1,000 (£5,000 divided by five years) will be charged as depreciation to the profit and loss account. (The value of the asset in the balance sheet will be reduced by that amount.)

(b) There are a number of other methods of calculating the charge per year. Motor cars for example depreciate faster in the early years of their life and so non-linear methods are used which frontload the charges per year, such as the reducing balance or the sum of the digits method. In other words, most of the depreciation is charged early on.

3.5 Cash based expenses are often straightforward items such as fuel for salesmen's cars which require no adjustments.

3.6 **Profit.** To the economist profit is a straightforward concept, the reward of capital, land, and labour. The accounting concept is slightly different, as accountants analyse profit in several ways.

(a) **Gross profit** is the difference between the sales value and the cost of the goods which have been sold. In Paragraph 3.3 it was £2,850 or 28.5% of sales value (£10,000) **gross margin on sales.** This figure of £2,850 also represents the **mark-up on cost** of:

$$\frac{£2,850}{£7,150} = 39.9\%$$

(b) **Net profit** is the gross profit after deducting all other expenses and is usually shown before deducting the interest payable to the banks and other capital lenders (Net Profit Before Interest and Tax NPBIT) and then after interest but before the deduction of corporation tax. (NPBT).

(c) **Retained profit** is the profit that is left after deduction of the dividend payable to the company's shareholders. It is the money 'ploughed back' into the business.

	£	£
Turnover		10,000
Cost of sales (eg production wages, raw materials etc)		7,150
Gross Profit		2,850
Distribution costs	1,000	
Administrative expenses (eg personnel department)	475	
		1,475
Net profit on ordinary activities before interest and taxation		1,375
Interest payable and similar charges		300
Net profit on ordinary activities before taxation		1,075
Tax on profit on ordinary activities		250
Profit or loss for the financial year		825
Dividends paid or proposed		175
Retained profit		650

SSAP 25 Segmental reporting

3.7 Certain large companies are required, under Statement of Standard Accounting Practice 25 (SSAP 25), to analyse their profit and loss account in more detail, giving turnover and profit figures by:

(a) class of business (defined as 'a distinguishable component of an entity that provides a separate product or service or a separate group of related products or services', which sounds very much like a strategic business unit);

(b) geographical market ('a geographical area comprising an individual country or a group of counties in which an entity operates or to which it supplies products or services').

3.8 Turnover (ie sales) must be analysed by origin and destination and any sales between segments must be identified. Financial reports therefore give additional information about competitors' businesses, both how much they sell and, as importantly, how profitable they are in a particular segment.

4 FINANCIAL ANALYSIS: EXTERNAL RATIO ANALYSIS

4.1 The three financial statements reviewed so far all give **absolute financial values**, which will answer the following questions.

(a) Has a profit or loss been made?
(b) Has it generated or consumed cash?

The historical values may not relate to the market value of the business or its ability to generate cash **in future**.

4.2 To understand more about the company from those statements we need to answer the following questions.

(a) Is the company being run efficiently in comparison with:

- Other firms in the same trade?
- Previous years?

(b) Would you supply goods on credit to that company? Is the company able to continue trading and is it paying its creditors?

(c) Would you recommend investing money in the business in comparison with:

(i) The return from, say, the building societies?
(ii) Other companies with different profits and different share prices?

4.3 To answer these questions we need to use **ratio analysis.** It should be stressed that there are a number of variations of ratio formulae, but whatever format used must be applied **consistently** and to related account headings. For example comparing gross profit to the current liabilities is in itself meaningless but comparing net profit with the total capital employed is useful.

Example

4.4 For the purpose of illustration, study the figures below in relation to the questions posed in 4.2.

		X plc	*Y plc*
		£'000	£'000
Gross profit		30	60
Net profit before tax and interest		20	40
Turnover (sales)		200	500
Capital employed		100	150
Bank loans (included in capital employed)		80	50
Share capital		20	100
Previous years' net profit		18	37
Interest Rate	10%		
Inflation rate	10%		

(a) *Question:* which management team is most effective?

(b) *Question:* which would you invest in?

(c) *Question:* if you were beamed down from Mars into both companies could you tell which was which by observing their marketing strategies in relation to these figures?

Analysis

4.5 Y plc would appear to be much larger than X plc. Turnover is 2.5 times that of Y and net profit is double that of Y. This is as far as the absolute values can take us. By calculating a few simple ratios we can get a much better insight.

(a) **Gross profit percentage**

	X plc	*Y plc*
$\frac{\text{Gross profit}}{\text{Turnover}}$	$\frac{£30,000}{£200,000} = 15\%$	$\frac{£60,000}{£500,000} = 12\%$

X plc is more efficient than Y plc in realising gross margins from its sales. From this level of gross profit we might assume that they are involved in a trade such as food retailing which has similar gross margins. If both companies were buying and selling the same goods at the same prices we might assume that the 3% deficiency of Y is the result of shoplifting, poor stock rotation (selling out of date goods cheap), staff theft, damaged goods (through poor handling) etc.

(b) **Net profit percentage**

	X plc	*Y plc*
$\frac{\text{Net profit}}{\text{Turnover}}$	$\frac{£20,000}{£200,000} = 10\%$	$\frac{£40,000}{£500,000} = 8\%$

Again this is consistent with food retailing. The gap between them has now closed to a difference of 2%. Let us see why.

(c)

	X plc	*Y plc*
$\frac{\text{Operating / admin costs}}{\text{Turnover}}$	$\frac{£10,000}{£200,000} = 5\%$	$\frac{£20,000}{£500,000} = 4\%$

We can deduce these costs as the difference between gross profit and net profit (£10,000 and £20,000 respectively). We can now say that Y plc has lower overheads per £1 of goods sold than X plc. This saving on items such as administration, staff costs, lighting etc may contribute to the lower level of **control** and efficiency highlighted in (a).

(d) **Return on capital employed**

(i)

	X plc	*Y plc*
$\frac{\text{Net profit}}{\text{Capital employed}}$	$\frac{£20,000}{£100,000} = 20\%$	$\frac{£40,000}{£150,000} = 27\%$

This shows that Y plc is getting a better return on the money that has been invested in the business than X plc, because while Y plc net profit is double that of X plc it has only 50% more capital (£150,000 against £100,000). Y plc is making more efficient use of its funds.

(ii) If we now look at the two companies from the viewpoint of a shareholder, we notice that X has a higher proportion of bank loans than Y, 80% capital employed against 33%. If we take these loans out of the capital employed because they carry a 'fixed' interest charge (as opposed to receiving a share of the profits) then we can see that from a shareholder's viewpoint it is far more beneficial to invest in X in comparison with Y.

In calculating the ratios above we have to adjust for the interest charge that the banks will make. The full calculation is as follows.

		X plc	*Y plc*
$\frac{\text{Net profit (after interest)}}{\text{Share capital}}$	=	$\frac{£20,000 - (£80,000 \times 10\%)}{£20,000}$	$\frac{£40,000 - (£50,000 \times 10\%)}{£100,000}$
	=	$\frac{£12,000}{£20,000}$	$\frac{£35,000}{£100,000}$
	=	60%	35%

(e) This effect is the result of **gearing** which is calculated as follows:

$\frac{\text{Fixed interest loans}}{\text{Total capital employed}}$	=	$\frac{£80,000}{£100,000}$	$\frac{£50,000}{£150,000}$

High gearing is not always advantageous! No matter how low your profits are, you still have to pay the interest.

(f) We can see that both X and Y have attractions for the investor. If we assume for the sake of illustration that if we were to invest £1 in either company and that the relative merits had been fully reflected in the share price of the two companies which one should now be chosen?

		X plc	*Y plc*
$\frac{\text{Increase in profit}}{\text{Last year's profit}}$	=	$\frac{£20,000 - £18,000}{£18,000} = 11.1\%$	$\frac{£40,000 - £37,000}{£37,000} = 8.1\%$

Company X would appear to be expanding faster than Y and so this would be the preferred investment. With the inflation rate at 10% the real growth of X at 1.1% looks very modest but Y is not even keeping pace with inflation and so is looking stagnant.

(g)

	X plc	*Y plc*
$\frac{\text{Turnover}}{\text{Net assets = capital employed}}$	$\frac{£200,000}{£100,000}$	$\frac{£500,000}{£150,000}$
	2 times	3.33 times

Here is another insight into the two companies. Y plc is achieving a far greater turnover from its assets. (Net assets are equivalent to the capital employed.) This ratio is probably the most revealing in terms of helping us to understand their different marketing strategies. If these do in fact represent supermarkets it should be possible to identify which one was which from this ratio.

(i) Supermarket Y is probably devoted to a high sales per square foot policy with minimum warehousing but the cramped conditions lead to stock 'drift' and damage.

(ii) Supermarket X, by contrast probably has an uncluttered layout with ample well laid out warehousing. This is speculation of course, but it should be seen that while ratio analysis will not lead to a single definitive assessment of a company it is however a powerful analytical tool which will generate questions and serve as a cross check on the other features of a business.

The management of working capital

4.6 Consider the following additional information at the year end and try to relate it to companies X plc and Y plc.

	X plc	*Y plc*
	£000	£'000
Closing stock	10	22
Debtors	-	-
Creditors	30	80

Ratios can be calculated as follows.

(a) **Stock turnover**

	X plc	*Y plc*
$\frac{\text{Closing stock}}{\text{Cost of sales}\star} \times 365 =$	$\frac{£10,000}{£200,000 - £30,000} \times 365$	$\frac{£22,000}{£500,000 - £60,000} \times 365$
	= 21.5 days	= 14.9 days

⋆ Sales-Gross Profit

Where the stock turnover is low it is easier to think in terms of a number of times per year. A factor of 2.2 times is easier to relate to than 166 **days**. The calculation is simply done the other way round ie $\frac{\text{Cost of sales}}{\text{Stock}}$. This shows the rate at which stock is used.

The turnover rates of 21.5 days (X plc) and 14.9 days (Y plc) helps to explain how Y plc is getting a better asset turnover rate and also underpins the view that we are probably looking at two supermarkets. (Sainsbury's 1990 stock turnover was 18 days.)

(b) **Creditor turnover**

	X plc	*Y plc*
	64 Days	54 Days
$\frac{\text{Creditors} \times 365 \text{ days}}{\text{Cost of sales}}$	$\frac{£30,000 \times £365}{£200,000 - £30,000}$	$\frac{£80,000 \times £365}{£500,000 - £60,000}$

Here X plc is, taking 10 days longer credit from its suppliers than Y plc.

(c) Debtor turnover is not relevant here. As there are no debtors, both businesses are trading exclusively on a cash basis. The calculation would normally be:

$\frac{\text{Debtors}}{\text{Sales}} \times 365$. It shows how long your customers are taking to pay you.

(On the other hand, they could have received money from debtors just before the balance sheet date - but this is unlikely given the other information.)

Liquidity ratios

4.7 The importance of cash to the financial survival of a company was highlighted above. The balance sheet will show what the immediate liabilities are at a certain point in time. The test here is to see if the value of the current (or non permanent) assets of the business will cover the current liabilities. In doing this we take a pessimistic but not implausible view that all the creditors may require payment in full on demand. Note, that in the event that one creditor cannot be paid then the word will quickly get around the other suppliers who will promptly stop supplying goods, effectively preventing the company from trading its way out of a problem.

There are two ratios used.

(a) The current ratio is $\frac{\text{Current assets}}{\text{Current liabilities}}$

Analysts will regard a benchmark of 2:1 as 'healthy'. This recognises that in the event of a sudden liquidation of current assets only a half of the value of those assets might be turned into cash fast enough to satisfy the creditors.

(b) The acid test or quick ratio is:

$$\frac{\text{Current assets - stock}}{\text{Current liabilities}}$$

This ratio reflects the difficulty of realising/converting stocks of raw materials, work in progress and finished goods, to pay liabilities. These items are now excluded from current assets to leave near cash or quick assets. These should ideally be £1 of quick assets for every £1 of current liabilities ie a 1: 1 ratio. (Remember that liabilities that do not have to be paid before 12 months such as bank loans, as opposed to overdrafts, are classed as long term and not current liabilities.)

4.8 '*Wealth*' *warning*. Ratios must not be viewed as rigid indicators. Their calculation, application and interpretation will vary from analyst to analyst and from company to company. It is possible for example for companies to influence or 'window dress' their results for ratio analysis. Consider for example the following.

$$\frac{\text{Current assets} \quad £200{,}000}{\text{Current liabilities} \quad £300{,}000}$$

The ratio of 0.66: 1 would not be considered favourably. However if on the last day of the year a £500,000 overdraft is drawn down and say shares are purchased for short term investment the figures are now:

$$\frac{\text{Current assets} \quad £700{,}000}{\text{Current liabilities} \quad £800{,}000}$$

0.88: 1 appears much more respectable!

Financial ratios

4.9 This final section of ratio analysis examines two aspects of the company's funding picture.

4.10 *Price earnings ratio.* The return to shareholders measured in terms of the profit or earnings per ordinary share compared with the market price of the share, so that the percentage return on purchasing one share can be compared with other similar companies and the risk free market return (eg the return that would be earned from investing money in government stocks ie gilts).

This is the $\frac{\text{Market price per share}}{\text{Earnings per share}}$

Earnings per share is, subject to sundry adjustments = $\frac{\text{Net profit}}{\text{Number of shares in issue}}$

A high PE ratio can indicate shareholders' expectations of growth, low risk etc. A low PE ratio suggest that, despite the high return, investors are not confident in the company.

4.11 Effects of **gearing**. The gearing ratio which looks at the sensitivity of the company's finances to changes in:

(a) the rate of interest levied by lenders on the money the company has borrowed;

(b) the way in which gearing affects profit attributable to shareholders in different trading conditions.

4.12 The gearing ratio is:

$$\frac{\text{Long term interest bearing loans}}{\text{Total capital employed *}}\%$$

* TCE = Long term interest bearing loans + shareholders' funds.

The inclusion of **overdrafts** in the calculation is debatable because overdrafts are usually a short term function of working capital requirements and fluctuate daily. However many companies tend to run a significant and permanent overdraft as part of their overall funding. (Overdrafts are more flexible and sometimes cheaper than fixed interest loans, but they are repayable on demand.)

4.13 The significance of this sensitivity analysis is best demonstrated by means of an example.

Top Gear Plc has the following capital profile.

	£'000	£'000
Commercial mortgage	4,000	
Loan from merchant bank	5,000	
Total loans		9,000
Shareholders funds		
Share capital	500	
Reserves	500	
Total		1,000
Total capital		10,000

This gives a gearing ratio of 90%.

4.14 The profit before interest for 19X1 is £1m and analysts are looking forward to assess the prospects of the company in the following year. Two factors are being considered.

(a) Trade prospects will fluctuate between +10% and -10% of 19X1 levels.

(b) Interest rates will fluctuate between +1% and –1% around the 19X1 rate of 10%.

To demonstrate the impact these factors will have on the shareholders' fortunes calculate the interest payments and shareholders' profit in 19X2.

Scenario	Total profit £'000	Interest payments £'000	Profit to shareholders £'000
1 19X1 results	1,000	900	100
2 Trade prospects + 10%	1,100	900	200
3 Trade prospects -10%	900	900	NIL
4 Interest rates + 1%	1,000	990	10
5 Interest rates- 1%	1,000	810	190

The reality will depend on many other economic and political factors, particularly the underlying asset value of the company (sometimes called the break-up value).

4.15 The volatility induced by the gearing effect is plain to see and it often accounts for the large movements in share prices that affect some companies. The effects can be mitigated by borrowing at fixed interest rates and diversifying across different market segments and in different economies.

5 INFLATION

5.1 Inflation, or the deterioration of monetary value, is a persistent economic phenomenon. The accountancy profession have attempted for a number of years to develop mechanisms to account for its effect on company finances but with little success. The effect of inflation is in essence quite simple. Companies lose money while ostensibly performing more successfully each year.

5.2 Consider the following example. A plc buys a piece of equipment, let's say a crane, to hire out to others. For the purposes of illustration we will assume that in hiring out the crane no expenses are incurred and no margin is levied. It cost £100,000, and it has an expected life of five years to run. Let us say that to replace it at the end of five years would cost £160,000. Inflation is 10% per annum. Also assume that shareholders leave all their money in the business.

The inflation on cranes is not quite 10% unlike the rate of general inflation of which there are a number of measures (RPI, manufacturers headline, underlying etc). The company's turnover revenue is affected by the general rate of inflation.

5.3 Let us now look at what the company will show in its accounts. Depreciation will be provided at £20,000 per annum and the turnover will increase in line with inflation at 10% per annum.

	Turnover from rental £'000	Depreciation on crane £'000	Profit £'000
Year 1	20,000	20,000	NIL
Year 2 (£20,000 + 10% of turnover)	22,000	20,000	2,000
Year 3 (£22,000 + 10% of turnover)	24,200	20,000	4,200
Year 4 (£24,200 + 10% of turnover)	26,600	20,000	6,600
Year 5 (£26,000 + 10% of turnover)	29,300	20,000	9,300
	122,100	100,000	22,100

Each year the company will report a record level of turnover and record profits, but has it made any 'money'? Well, the tax man will think so, charging tax on the £22,100. The shareholders will have a company with more money in the bank than it started with, but can the company continue trading? In other words can it buy another crane? The answer is no, unless it asks the shareholders for £37,900 (£160,000 - £122,100) and whatever the tax man has taken. At this stage it is clear that this is not a sound basis on which to carry on business. The company will argue that it was able to earn money on the original £100,000 and will do so again on the next £160,000. The problem comes when the company cannot raise further sums to keep up with inflation: it then continues with ageing plant and is uncompetitive until it goes broke. The same effect can be seen on working capital items such as stocks and debtors. Each year more cash is required just to `stand still'.

5.4 A more realistic approach might be to provide one fifth of the £160,000 **replacement cost** each year as follows.

	Turnover from rental	*Provision for replacement*	*Profit/ (Loss)*
	£	£	£
Year 1	20,000	32,000	(12,000)
Year 2	22,000	32,000	(10,000)
Year 3	24,200	32,000	(7,800)
Year 4	26,600	32,000	(5,400)
Year 5	29,300	32,000	(2,700)
	122,100	160,000	(37,900)

It would be a brave chairman that presented those results to his shareholders. In any event the rate of inflation may not be constant and the replacement cost could not realistically be predicted. (Try explaining to the customer that you are charging £32,000 pa for a crane they know only cost £100,000!)

5.5 If the provision for replacement is reassessed each year on the basis of **known inflation** then the effect is even more pronounced as there is a cumulative catching up effect.

	Turnover from rental	*Provision for replacement*	*Calculations*
	£	£	
Year 1	20,000	22,000	(£100 × 110%) × $^1/_5$
Year 2	20,000	26,400	(£100 × 110% ×110% × $^2/_5$) – £22,000
Year 3	24,200	31,500	etc
Year 4	26,600	37,200	
Year 5	29,300	42,900	
	122,100	160,000	

This effect of increasing provision is necessary because each year less provision is provided compared to the £32,000 which we know with hindsight **should** be provided.

5.6 These tables and calculations are only shown to demonstrate how inflation causes businesses to go **bankrupt** while **appearing** reasonably healthy. The marketer should bear this in mind when setting prices and analysing business performance. Some companies such as oil retailers do put up prices as soon as replacement costs are known so that their cash flow is preserved but many other companies do not have the power to do this.

6 SOURCES OF FINANCE

6.1 Although as a marketing manager you will not be involved in managing money (other than from sales, of course!), there are occasions when you will need to take account of how you are going to raise money, if your marketing strategy involves expense, and if the company is in a difficult position.

6.2 **Short term sources of finance**

- Delay payments to creditors
- Bank overdraft
- Factoring of sales (getting a bank to collect the debts)
- Export credit guarantee
- Profit (retained in the business)
- Sell investments

6.3 **Medium term**

- Bank overdraft
- Bank loan
- Leasing
- Hire purchase
- Government (and EC) loans and grants

6.4 **Long term**

- Merchant bank loans
- Bond home/overseas
- Debentures/mortgages
- Shares issues
- Retained profit

6.5 Sources of finance will, of course, vary for companies domiciled overseas. Credit can be restricted by a country's government or indeed directly and indirectly by the International Monetary Fund and World Bank. International companies and multinationals are better placed by virtue of their organisation to take advantage of low-cost sources of finance worldwide.

7 FEASIBILITY AND RISK

The financial implications of your marketing plan

7.1 In order to get your marketing plan implemented in real life, you will need to persuade your superiors and peers of its financial viability as well as its marketing feasibility. In the past this has been a weakness in the marketing plans of a high proportion of the CIM case study examinees, some of whom give the impression that they should have carte blanche to spend large sums of money without any regard to a return on these investments.

7.2 In Chapter 8 (Paragraph 5.21) there is a **financial implications checklist**. Please study this carefully. Many students interpret a request for the financial implications in an exam paper as a question on **costs**. Obviously cost is one of the financial implications of your marketing plan but it is **only** one. (Others might be revenues, return of investment, sources of investment finance, exchange rates etc.)

7.3 Consider your plan to increase sales. This will inevitably place strains on the organisation's working capital as you will no doubt be spending more money on raw materials, work in progress, stocks and wages. The increase in working capital needed will require funding and if this is external it will incur interest. If you need to buy new machinery this might be a capital investment: a return on capital employed will be required to justify the purchase. Having purchased the machinery it will be subject to depreciation. The planned increase in sales may have implications for debtors and the creditors (as a result of the increased production) debtors situation which in turn may affect your cash flow.

Risk

7.4 Now what about **risk**? Just supposing your planned increase in sales did not materialise. How would it affect the above issues? Do you need a contingency plan? Would you 'buy' your own marketing plan or is it too risky? Have you done your homework? Are your figures sound? Should you acquire new machinery on a lease and buy-back basis? Are projected increases in sales based upon properly conducted test marketing? What assurances can you give your superiors and peers on this element of risk?

7.5 If you were the finance director and you could obtain an 8% return on investment in securities after one year with very little risk, why should you support your marketing director's costly proposals to venture into new international markets with no prospect of breaking even in the first year? The finance director might suggest a risk premium. In other words, your marketing plan should not only match the return available from investing it, but should perhaps exceed it by a set percentage.

7.6 These and other questions need to be addressed at CIM Diploma level. You need to be able to demonstrate your acumen and grasp of these financial aspects if you are to succeed in your professional marketing career.

Feasibility studies

7.7 Very little appears to have been written specifically on this aspect in the marketing literature. The following guidelines should therefore be found useful in the event of a future question on this matter. The guidelines are based on a specimen answer to a specific question on feasibility in a previous CIM case study.

The form and content of a feasibility (viability) study

1 *Corporate audit*

- Objectives, five year plan,
- Key criteria for project appraisal/evaluation

2 *The scenario or project*

3 *Assumptions*

4 *Feasibility research*

(a) *Experimental/technical research*
Design studies, performance specification, timings, costs.

(b) *Market research.*
Demand analysis, competition, buying motives, pricing etc.

(c) *Commercial potential.* (to include analysis of the feasibility research in terms of timing, cost, human resource needs). Outline income and expenditure analysis.

(i) DCF projections over 5 years, prices, break-even analysis
(ii) Venture capital required
(iii) Cost of capital at current interest rate
(iv) Working capital
(v) Short-term loans/overdraft requirements
(vi) Cash flow projections - funding periods
(vii) Contingencies
(viii) Payback periods and net gains

Chapter roundup

- An awareness of the financial implications of your marketing plans is becoming increasingly necessary for the examination.
- The balance sheet displays what a business possesses (assets) and what it owes (liabilities). The profit and loss account describes how a business has performed over time. A cash flow statement describes how the business has been financed.
- Ratio analysis is a way of using financial information to glean facts about an organisation's performance (eg gross margin). It should be used with care, as financial data is easily manipulated.
- Any profit needs to be assessed for risk, especially new ventures or markets.

Test your knowledge

1 Distinguish between tangible and intangible assets. (see para 2.6)
2 What is the matching principle? (3.2)
3 What rule should be adopted for ratio analysis? (4.3)
4 Distinguish between gross profit percentage and return on capital employed. (4.5)
5 What is the current ratio? (4.7)
6 List some short term sources of finance. (6.2)

5 Significant Current Issues

This chapter covers the following topics.

Introduction

This chapter contains notes on current issues which you should bear in mind in case study work.

1 MARKETING MYOPIA

1.1 The syndrome identified famously as 'Marketing Myopia' by Theodore Levitt in 1960 still exists today in many companies and organisations. Even today some customers seem blind to customers' needs and wants or couldn't care less. We still come across hotels and bars which are apparently run for the benefit of the management and staff rather than customers. Television sets are tuned to the programmes which the staff want to see and left on regardless of whether customers want to watch. Young bar staff play the music they want to hear at maximum volume irrespective of the fact that the clientele are trying to make conversation. Companies priding themselves on technological advance still become entranced with their products to the point when they cease to enquire what the customers really want. These companies push their products before customers and hard-sell benefits which most people may not relate to.

1.2 An innovation concept recently hyped up in the media comprises of a completely robotised hospital trolley which can deliver tea, newspapers etc to hospital beds without human assistance. Great for the hospital management, perhaps, but one wonders whether patients have been consulted.

1.3 Too many candidates fail CIM case study examinations because they do not understand that marketing is first and foremost about **customer pull** as opposed to **product push.** The most significant change in marketing thinking today is (or should be) from chasing a sale to creating and keeping a customer. The movement is towards relationship marketing and achieving a true, lasting marketing orientation: **read on!**

2 RELATIONSHIP MARKETING

2.1 The essence of relationship marketing is stated by Martin Christoper, Adrian Payne and David Ballantyne in their book of this title (Butterworth-Heinemann 1991) to be as follows.

- Focus on customer retention.
- Orientation on customer benefits.
- Long time scale.
- High customer commitment.
- High customer contact.
- Quality is the concern of all.

2.2 It is claimed that gaining a new customer can cost four times as much as to keep an existing one, so that a focus on customer retention makes a great deal of sense.

2.3 The longer term approach can also be said to be eminently suited (to the 1990s when the article was written) in many ways. Studies of successful Japanese companies are likely to reveal an underlying long term strategy. Why?

(a) They will accept losses in the short term in order to gain a dominant market share and lasting profitability in the longer term.

(b) They form long-term contractual relationships with all their staff rather than the 'hire and fire' approach.

(c) They build long-term partnerships with their suppliers in the interests of the customers rather than the 'cheapest price on the day' approach.

(d) Once a Japanese company wins a customer it works hard to build the relationship rather than easing up.

(e) A long-term approach is also taken with regard to location and the development of good relationships with the community.

2.4 Note that in the late 1990s and in early 2000, Japanese firms' long-term success was in question because of:

- Poor profitability
- Poor return on investment

2.5 Relationship marketing's emphasis on high customer commitment is in keeping with the TQM approach being taken by many British companies in the 1990s. There is increasing recognition that internal customers and indirect customer contacts play crucial roles in the quality of external customer service. Put quite simply if someone in the despatch department drops a case rather too heavily on the pallet, a subsequent customer complaint of damaged goods is likely to result. Failure of the works office to respond quickly to a sales office telephone enquiry on progress of a job means a customer is let down and an expensively built-up relationship is tarnished.

3 TOTAL MARKETING: TOTAL QUALITY AND THE MARKETING CONCEPT

3.1 The following is a summary of an article by Barry J Witcher of Durham University Business School published in the Quarterly Review of Marketing (Winter 1990).

3.2 Witcher's main contention is that marketing, as currently understood by management and the marketing profession, is generally too narrow a concept. In fact, it can be argued that the marketing concept has a great deal in common with total quality management (TQM).

3.3 Going back to Kotler, marketing is about identifying customer needs and targeting organisation resources at them in the most appropriate way. Segmentation is an important technique for ascertaining customer needs, although only 47% of UK companies, according to a report published in 1987, can identify their main types of customer.

3.4 Witcher feels that companies still follow rival philosophies to the marketing concept.

(a) Production orientation involves a focus on costs, quality and reliability, 'a pre-deterministic rather than a flexible and responsive approach to customer needs'.

(b) Product orientation involves a concentration of product features rather than customer benefits, leading to a misunderstanding as to the significance of product changes on the competitive offer.

(c) A selling orientation results in an emphasis on promotion and 'a hit-and-run attitude towards the customer which gives a distinctly short-term emphasis to a company's operations'.

3.5 Witcher argues that the marketing concept goes much deeper than ideas about 'segmentation' and 'targeting'. He holds that three conditions must be met for a true marketing orientation.

(a) All aspects of a company's organisation and functioning must be directed to customers. This deals with issues of the marketing environment, keeping in touch with customers etc.

(b) The company must coordinate its efforts and activities with those of its customers. This deals with targeting, segmentation and competitive advantage.

(c) There should be a total marketing environment for the whole company. The marketing philosophy must be embraced by the whole company (eg including the accounts department).

Internal marketing

3.6 In most UK companies, marketing is a separate activity, devoted to outsiders. For the marketing philosophy to be adopted, it must overcome the pattern of communication within the company.

3.7 Some examples by which this can be achieved are:

(a) Internal communication (eg mission statements)

(b) Linking business functions (eg production and marketing personnel should be trained together

(c) Relationships between marketing and staff

3.8 Witcher quotes the example of BT's TQM programme.

(a) A mission statement was drawn up for the company, expressing what was required from the company by its users, in terms of 'customer service, product quality, involvement of suppliers and attainment of a positive market position.'

(b) Cross-functional training and workshops tried to build bridges between different parts of the company.

(c) Full discussion of TQM was encouraged.

Total quality management (TQM)

3.9 'The purpose was to implement planning and management through the use of team working, and by so doing create an understanding which leads to a greater spread of responsibilities, and pro-activity... TQM tries to make the process continuous.'

Relationship marketing

3.10 TQM matches with the concept of relationship marketing. Relationship marketing is concerned with 'more than just a short term event in a market place'. Rather, 'relationships take time to establish, and all long term phenomena which involve complete series of exchanges (however defined). In short, relationship marketing is orientated towards 'strong, lasting relationship with individual accounts.'

3.11 A simple example can be provided in the service sector. A restaurant management will want satisfied customers to return, as repeat custom will be a more important factor in the restaurant's success than new customers.

Business to business marketing

3.12 Marketing to other businesses has a different set of problems than marketing to consumers. Arguably, if TQM is encouraging customers to have a more restricted number of suppliers, then business-to-business marketing, on a relationship basis, will become more important.

Marketing and TQM

3.13 Marketing is perhaps 'too basic to be noticed' and, as it is not considered in the abstract, the marketing department often has little connection with TQM programs.

(a) If 'quality' is fitness for use, then this should be part of internal marketing. Quality is not simply a matter of improving production processes.

(b) If 'total quality management' is to be introduced, so perhaps must 'total marketing' in order that the firm's productive capacity can be tailored to customer needs. This would mean everybody in the firm knowing, or at least considering, 'the demands of customers.'

3.14 Witcher suggests that UK companies are culturally ill-suited to this approach.

(a) The history of adversarial relations with suppliers does not encourage a 'partnership' approach, as noted in Paragraph 3.12 above.

(b) UK firms' activities are compartmentalised, so that there are significant divisions within the company.

3.15 'The insularity of UK-based companies has probably prevented the full application of marketing in its modern sense. This is a British marketing failure. For the future, British companies should look to their corporate cultures, and change them. The marketing concept, like the total quality concept, applies totally and to everything. Both these things must be brought together through training and company identity schemes as a common programme to influence culture. Management have to understand that the marketing idea is not a functional activity but a way of business life. In the Japanese way of stating things, it is an important part of 'continuous improvement. This is not generally understood at the moment, which is why companies do not seem to be implementing modern marketing ideas. The marketing profession must understand it first.'

4 IMPROVING MARKETING ORIENTATION

4.1 Richard Wilson and Noel Fook of Nottingham Business School argue, in *Marketing Business* (June 1990) that the adoption by organisations of the marketing orientation improves their effectiveness in marketing specifically, and then in the effectiveness of the organisation throughout its activities.

4.2 The authors feel that marketing is a process by which 'an enterprise seeks to maintain a continuous match between its products and services'. A more precise definition is that the 'marketing orientation is the process by which an enterprise's target customers' needs and wants are effectively and efficiently satisfied within the resource limitation and long-term survival requirements of that enterprise'.

4.3 However, how far does the marketing orientation actually exist in UK companies? If so, how can you recognise it? The authors suggest that the existence of an **effective marketing orientation** can be identified by the following characteristics.

(a) A 'good understanding of the needs, wants and behaviour patterns of targeted customers'.

(b) The organisation should be concerned with profitable sales rather than just turnover.

(c) The chief executive should be a marketing strategist.

(d) The mission should be market driven.

(e) Marketing should be 'seen as being more important than other functions and orientations'.

(f) The marketing orientation should be recognised as superior.

(g) All managers should use marketing inputs in decision making.

(h) The cost-efficiency of the marketing function should be analysed.

(i) The marketing function should be involved in new product development.

(j) Marketing professionals should be employed for marketing functions.

(k) Marketing is the responsibility of everyone in the organisation.

(l) Decisions with marketing implications are made in a well-coordinated way and executed in an integrated manner.

4.4 Wilson and Fook go on to connect these issues with the 7 S framework (shared values, style, structure, skills and staffing, systems, strategy) outlined by Kinsey.

4.5 Developing a marketing orientation 'is a long term process and needs to be thought of as a form of investment. To a large extent this investment is in changing the organisation's culture, so that common values relating to the need to highlight service to customers, a concern for quality in all activities and so forth, are shared throughout the organisation. This is not an appropriate target for a quick fix.'

4.6 Wilson and Fook suggest the following stages to increase the marketing orientation of an organisation.

(a) Secure the support of senior management with the prestige and authority to push it through and overcome scepticism.

(b) There should be a specified mission relating to the development of the marketing orientation.

(c) A task force should be set up to:

   (i) Identify the current orientation

   (ii) Carry out an analysis of deficiencies between the current orientation and the desired marketing orientation

   (iii) Advise on change and implementation

4.7 Progress must be monitored to ensure that the firm does not snap back into its old ways.

5 INTERNAL MARKETING

5.1 Kevin Thomson writing in *Marketing Business* (September 1991) stated that 'looking at the employee as a valued customer is the focus of the new discipline of internal marketing'.

5.2 'If total customer satisfaction is the responsibility of marketing, then it is no longer good enough for marketing people to simply look at the external customer's requirements. Quality can only come from inside the organisation, so marketing must start to turn its attention this way.'

5.3 Internal marketing is not just the responsibility of training staff (employed by the personnel department) but of marketing personnel because the author suggests that only marketing personnel possess:

- Knowledge of the organisation's overall strategy
- Understanding of the needs of external customers
- Marketing techniques and tools
- Ability to use techniques and tools on internal customers
- Budgets

5.4 Internal marketing is a means to 'reach and teach' the internal customer. Internal products and services include education, information, strategy and planning.

5.5 Internal marketing also can be integrated with a company's external marketing practice. Service businesses in particular, which depend on customers being made to feel welcomed, depend on those personnel dealing directly with the customers. Internal marketers can affect these employees, or indeed, any other aspect of the organisation/customer relationship (eg quality).

5.6 Internal marketing combines:

- Marketing
- Human resources
- Training
- Behavioural science

5.7 It operates at three levels.

(a) It can be integrated at overall policy-making level as one of the objectives of the company.

(b) It is a strategic tool in the planning of organisational change.

(c) It is part of a way of implementing organisational change, or supporting an external marketing effort.

5.8 Internal marketing sees internal communications, and so forth (eg company magazines, services to employees) as products to be 'sold' to customers.

5.9 Internal marketing it is hoped, will provide the right framework for quality management. Internal marketing - identifying and meeting customer needs - can be seen as giving focus to quality control.

6 BRAND MANAGEMENT: CULTURE, VALUES AND CHANGE

6.1 Neil Pickup and John Smith argue, in *Marketing Business* (April 1990) that 'more organisations which have been successful in establishing a brand have directed their attention both inside and outside the organisation; not merely to the external environment within which the business operates, but also to the culture influencing and governing delivery of the package to the customer'.

6.2 Marketing has traditionally had an external focus. However, communicating these external issues to other members of the organisation, has been relegated to standard internal communications 'as the sole means to initiate what may well be major cultural change'.

6.3 Especially in service businesses, creating a corporate brand by which the business is known, and delivering it successfully, often requires changes in corporate culture. The major issues involve:

(a) Corporate culture
(b) Procedures and processes
(c) Organisational design

6.4 If a business's culture is in conflict with customer expectations, then corporate branding is a liability, as it might make claims which cannot be satisfied.

6.5 The authors hold that internal research is necessary, before any attempt is made to set up a corporate brand.

(a) Management and staff need to understand why the organisation exists and the role of the brand.

(b) Management and staff should 'own' the culture.

(c) There should be an 'objective and pragmatic analysis of the culture(s) and values operating within the business'

(d) There should be a 'change management' strategy

6.6 The process of organisational change can be analysed in three steps.

Step 1. This is the 'pre-managerial' phase of a business. It thrives on entrepreneurial flair.

Step 2.. However, this flair needs to be supported by good management if the business is to succeed. Management structures tend to become rigid in this phase.

Step 3. Businesses evolve from formal rigidities to Phase 3 and are held together not so much by procedures as by values.

6.7 In **step 1**, the corporate brand image might be founded on the entrepreneur (eg 'Virgin' is Richard Branson). In **step 2**, a corporate brand might be increased, as it were, from outside and imposed by formal procedures. However, as the brand is not connected with the underlying corporate culture, its claims, compared with the service actually provided, may founder. In **step 3**, the corporate brand will reflect the corporate culture, and will be shared by managers and staff.

6.8 Managing the introduction is a major task as it requires a thorough review of all the behaviour patterns. 'Shared values and agreed standards must become inherent in all management activity, whether routine dealings with external and internal customers or non-routine activities such as management development programs'.

6.9 Corporate branding though required changes in behaviour so that the brand's ideals can be matched.

7 INDUSTRIAL (BUSINESS TO BUSINESS) MARKETING

7.1 A study of the series of CIM case studies will reveal that from time to time, cases will appear which involve companies engaged in business to business marketing eg *Sentinel Aviation* and *De La Rue Fortronic*. Such cases can catch students unawares especially if they have focused their studies entirely on consumer goods marketing.

7.2 It is important to distinguish between industrial and consumer goods in terms of buying behaviour. Such differences affect marketing strategy, the marketing mix and marketing research.

(a) What is **industrial marketing?** A definition from Aubrey Wilson is: 'All those activities concerned with purchases and sales of goods/services in industrial markets and between organisational buyers/sellers.'

(b) What are **industrial goods?** A definition from Professor Baker is: 'Goods which are destined for use in producing other goods or rendering services, as contrasted with goods destined to be sold to ultimate consumers', eg office furniture, fork lift trucks, weaving looms, aero-engines.

7.3 It has been estimated that the total of interfirm sales of industrial goods amounts to about two and a half times the **value** of total sales of consumer goods. This comes about because, for example, Company A will buy copper and make it into copper wire sell it to Company B who will wind it onto a motor which they will then sell to Company C who will use it in, say, a washing machine for final sale to a consumer. In other words, for each consumer sale there will probably have been several transactions within the industrial markets with the same basic product or raw materials (eg copper) changing hands and, perhaps, form in the process.

7.4 **Derived demand**. An important distinguishing factor in industrial markets is that demand for the majority of industrial products is derived, often indirectly, from the final demand for consumer products. Thus the industrialist is faced with the need for providing increased plant, equipment etc for anticipated increases in consumer demand or for curtailing expenditures in anticipation of decreased levels of consumer expenditure. He is also faced with the impact or sales changes at consumer level reflected back through the channel of distribution. These changes are magnified by changes in inventory levels and inventory policy and can even be distorted by time lag - ie with sales moving one way and manufactures' order moving in the opposite direction.

7.5 Industrial market buying behaviour typically differs from consumer markets in the following ways.

(a) **Concentration of buyers.** The number of potential buyers for industrial goods tends to be rather smaller than for consumer goods.

(b) **Scale of purchasing.** The scale of industrial purchasing tends to be considerably greater than consumer purchasing in absolute terms (not always true, however, in relation to disposable assets).

(c) **Complexity of products**. Industrial products tend to be more complex technically thus requiring expertise on part of buyer and salesman.

(d) **Buying motives**. Industrial purchasers must satisfy company objectives of profitability etc. This taken together with the points above tend to lead to more rational buying motives than in the consumer market. This does not preclude emotion from industrial buying nor logic from consumer buying.

(e) **Group buying.** Again, stemming from the scale and complexity of purchases and the need for satisfaction of company objectives. Industrial buying tends to be a group process with some formalised evaluation and decision procedures.

(f) **Negotiation.** Whereas in the consumer market the element of negotiation (or bartering) has almost disappeared it is still an important factor in the industrial market.

The decision making unit (DMU)

7.6 Expanding now on (e) above, there are several different roles in the DMU which industrial marketers need to take into account when planning marketing operations. The two key points are that the buyer may not be the decision taker and even if he is, you can still use other people within the buying organisation to influence the decision your way. The several distinct roles in the DMU which have been identified are users, influencers, buyers, deciders and gatekeepers. Several individuals may occupy the same role and one individual can occupy two or more roles. Let us now expand on these roles.

(a) **Users** exert influence either individually or collectively. The influence can be a positive one, by suggesting the need for purchased materials and by defining standards of product quality, or a negative one, by refusing to work with the material of certain suppliers for certain reasons.

(b) **Influencers** are organisational members who directly or indirectly influence buying or usage criteria. They exert influence either by defining criteria which constrain the choices or provide information with which to evaluate buying actions.

In manufacturing organisations, technical personnel are significant influencers over the purchasing decision. Research and development personnel, design engineers, production engineers and manufacturing personnel may all be significant influences, and may emphasise different factors in the buying decision.

(c) **Buyers** are organisational members with formal authority for selecting the supplier and arranging terms of purchase. Buyers may be the purchasing manager, purchasing agent or buyer or a vice-president manufacturing, an office manager may also have buying authority.

The choice available to the buyer may be significantly limited by the formal and informal influence of the others.

The influence of the Buyer is especially apparent in determining the set of feasible suppliers and selecting suppliers. The Buyer's influence depends on the nature of the buying task, ranging from the simple, routine, clerical operation, through the need to negotiate prices and conditions of sale, to the most complex, where a simultaneous definition of specification and alternative is necessary.

(d) **Deciders**. Organisational members with formal or informal power to determine 'final' selection of supplies. In practice it is not always easy to determine when the decision is actually made and by whom. A purchasing agent may be the person with formal authority to sign a buying contract, he may not be the true decider.

Many purchasing agent's job descriptions place an upper limit on the financial commitments they can make, reserving larger decisions for other members of the organisation.

(e) **Gatekeepers.** Group members who control the flow of information into the group. The purchasing agent or Buyer may often have this function, but salesmen employed by the buying organisation can also be sources of inflation, and similarly technical personnel may perform the role on an informal basis.

Gatekeepers exert influence at the stage of identifying buying alternatives, and hence they significantly determine the outcome of the purchase decision.

7.7 Reflecting on the above, it can be seen why industrial marketing communications strategies depend heavily on personal selling and below-the-line, rather than advertising (fewer buyers, more complex products, rational decision taking, price/terms negotiation etc). Exhibitions and technical literature feature strongly in industrial marketing budgets whilst advertising is usually limited to relatively infrequent appearances in trade magazines.

7.8 Industrial marketing research methodology also varies from that used in consumer markets. Again, respondents are much fewer and more accessible (all on the telephone and usually in the offices or in the factory). The industrial salesforce know their Buyers personally. Information can be obtained face to face either formally of informally relatively easily and cheaply. New product development is usually a participative process between seller and buyer.

8 THE INTERNET AND OTHER SIGNIFICANT CURRENT ISSUES

8.1 It is important that you demonstrate an understanding of the new forces that may be transforming the environment of the organisation featured in the case. In the last two case studies featured in this text, Philips are driven by technological advances which include the Internet whilst Biocatalysts are affected by current consumer resistance to genetically modified food.

8.2 You need to read quite widely and keep abreast of current affairs in order to acquit yourself adequately in this paper when articulating your strategy. For example in a case on insurance a candidate making no reference to direct selling and the Internet would appear out of touch. Equally a case study to do with the health industry would be expected to acknowledge the pressures to reduce costs, increase availability and cope with ageing populations.

Chapter roundup

- These articles suggest some general principles.
    - The marketing approach needs to be involved with all facets of an organisation's relationship with customers, including quality.
    - For service businesses, or in service activities of non-service businesses, the success of external marketing may depend on the spread of marketing values within the organisation.

Test your knowledge

1 What is the essence of relationship marketing? (see para 2.1)
2 What three conditions must be satisfied for there to be true marketing orientation? (3.5)
3 Why should marketing departments be involved in TQM programmes? (3.13)
4 What is internal marketing? (6.1)
5 What sort of research should be conducted before a corporate brand is set up? (6.5)
6 What are the salient characteristics of industrial buyer behaviour? (7.5)

Part B
The CIM case study examination

6 The CIM Case Study Examination

This chapter covers the following topics.

Introduction

The case study method of learning and teaching has played a major part in management education, training and development over the past twenty years. The Harvard Business School in the USA helped both to pioneer and to stimulate the development of the case study method on its senior management courses and quickly gained an international reputation in this field.

It has been demonstrated increasingly that:

(a) case studies make an extremely important contribution to the study, knowledge and understanding of management;

(b) case studies are being used more and more often as an examination technique by professional bodies, and in particular by the Chartered Institute of Marketing (CIM).

It is fitting that the final examination of the CIM Diploma, which once conferred, is in effect a licence to practise, should use this most searching test of management ability.

1 THE CASE STUDY EXAMINATION: RATIONALE AND ROLE

1.1 An understanding of the role of case studies is pre-requisite to being able to learn from them and how to handle them.

(a) A case study portrays, as far as possible, a real world situation and aims through its use to develop a greater ability to analyse, conclude and make decisions.

(b) Case studies are also used the encourage the application of theoretical concepts and techniques in a selective and evaluative way to solve practical problems.

(c) Case studies are often explored on a group basis, as opposed to individuals solitarily reviewing data, so as to develop broader perspectives.

1.2 In business and management education and training, the situation described by a case study is usually one faced by an organisation and would typically include some facts and figures on:

- The organisation's past development;
- Its current situation;
- Financial, marketing, and personnel aspects;
- Competitors.

1.3 A case study can vary from a single page (often termed a mini-case or caselet) to fifty or more pages and appendices.

1.4 Cases also vary in the extent to which they are based on real life situations. Some are based entirely on a real world situation (sometimes distinguished by the term case history).

1.5 On the other hand, a case study might be one that is fabricated by the writer so as better to test particular aspects. Often case writers deliberately distort data so as to preserve confidentiality and will intentionally introduce anomalies, jumble logical sequences and omit data so as to make the case more challenging.

1.6 There is no one perfect solution to a case. Solutions not only depend upon an individual's interpretation of the data (which can in turn be influenced by the nature of the analytical techniques employed) but also upon the role and relationships of the people involved in the case.

1.7 For the foregoing reasons, students can find, on their first introduction to the case method, that case studies are intimidating, irritating and frustrating. However, given the right approach and the benefits of some experience the following advantages from the use of case studies are claimed.

1.8 According to Edge and Coleman *(The Guide to Case Analysis and Reporting)* students can benefit from increased skills in:

(a) Clear thinking through complex situations

(b) The ability to devise credible, consistent and creative plans

(c) The application of analytical techniques

(d) The recognition of the relative significance of information

(e) The determination of informational needs

(f) Oral communication in groups

(g) The writing of clear, forceful and convincing reports

(h) Choice of career paths

(i) Recognising the importance of personal values in organisational decision taking processes and self analysis

1.9 With regard to the last item Wilson highlights individual behavioural differences pointing out that 'the more stakeholders there are, the greater is the scope for differing interpretations and assumptions'. (A stakeholder is a person, group or organisation with an interest in another organisation's performance.) He draws out the following four key propositions.

(a) People have different ways of relating to other people in the world.
(b) People have different ways of gathering and using information.
(c) People have different ways of using information and making decisions.
(d) People attach different priorities to gathering and using information.

1.10 The **implications of these propositions**

(a) Value judgements and other affective issues are essential in defining problems;

(b) The roles people play need to be made explicit, as do assumptions about the people in these roles, and this is part of the learning process. After all management is often held to be about 'getting things done through people'.

Making the most of case studies

1.11 Edge and Coleman place the emphasis on student responsibilities in case learning. Much greater effort and cooperation are needed from students in learning from cases as opposed to lectures.

1.12 A more positive attitude can be encouraged by students working as a team on a real management situation and by role adoption.

1.13 Students need to familiarise themselves with the case in advance of discussion. They should both participate in, and help to manage, the discussion.

1.14 A sense of humour helps groups to relax, to develop a team spirit and to enjoy discussion and feedback.

1.15 When a complex and lengthy case study and analysis takes place over a period of several weeks or sessions, regular attendance is essential. Otherwise a student might become a burden on the group, or be seen as a malingerer.

1.16 Students must respect the contributions made by and feelings of other group members, but at the same time they should be prepared to give and take constructive criticism.

1.17 Some sympathy for the case study leader's role and problems in the overall management of the project will also help.

1.18 Students need to appreciate the likelihood of initial dissatisfaction with the case, the necessity for learning, and the value of keeping an open mind. At the start, **confusion and frustration** will be caused by the following factors.

(a) There is no one best answer.
(b) Information can be ambiguous and/or irrelevant.
(c) Vital information is missing.
(d) The key issues may not be given or identified.
(e) The case study leader does not direct.
(f) The case study leader does not provide solutions.

A constructive attitude should help allay these problems.

1.19 Attention to the two matters below should help students get the most out of their case study group.

(a) The position of chairing syndicate groups and acting as spokesperson in plenary sessions should be rotated so that all concerned develop leadership and communication skills.

(b) The adoption of stakeholder roles (eg one member to act as the finance manager, another as managing director, another as spokesperson for employees' interests) by group members helps to develop greater understanding of the human relations aspects of decision making.

How to handle case studies: an overview

1.20 All writers and most case study instructors recommend a step by step approach to case study analysis. Easton *(Learning from Case Studies)* summarises these as follows.

Step 1	Understanding the situation
Step 2	Diagnosing problem areas
Step 3	Generating alternative solutions
Step 4	Predicting outcomes
Step 5	Evaluating alternatives
Step 6	Communicating the results

However the detailed methods of carrying out these steps can vary according to the nature of the case, its length and how far in advance (if at all) the case is issued.

1.21 Also, time constraints and other reasons may cause the case instructor to concentrate on particular steps. For example, the London Business School use a particular caselet purely for the purposes of generating as many alternative solutions as possible. This helps to encourage groups of mature business people to look beyond the first immediate solution that springs to mind.

1.22 Students being exposed to case studies as part of coursework will normally be issued with detailed guidelines on how to tackle each of the above steps or referred to recommended reading by the course instructor. For the purposes of this Workbook we are concentrating on how to handle case studies being used for examination purposes.

1.23 In the pages which follow, distinctions are drawn between:

(a) the recommended treatments for the unseen caselets (or mini-cases) which are used as part of the format for several Chartered Institute of Marketing examinations; and

(b) the major case study which is issued four weeks in advance and is the sole method of examination for the Institute's Diploma subject *Strategic Marketing Management: Analysis and Decision*.

2 WHAT YOU CAN EXPECT IN THE EXAMINATION

2.1 It is now CIM practice to supply the examination case study in the form of an A4 booklet, printed on both sides of the page. There is not much room therefore for making notes in the booklet and you may prefer to photocopy each page on to A4 single sides for this purpose.

2.2 Typically, the CIM diploma case will be 30 to 40 pages long. It will consist of five to twelve pages of text, usually (but not always) followed by a number of appendices.

2.3 The information contained in the case study is likely to include some or all of the following matters.

(a) Background and historical data on the company featured
(b) Corporate and group organisation
(c) Marketing and sales organisation
(d) Strengths, weaknesses, opportunities, threats (indicative only)
(e) Market size, segments, competitors, trends
(f) Environmental factors
(g) Marketing mix (product, price, promotion, distribution)

(h) Marketing research
(i) Consolidated accounts (profit and loss, balance sheet)

2.4 As is usual in most management case studies, the CIM case will:

(a) Include some information which is not particularly useful and
(b) Exclude some data which you might feel essential

This is to test your powers of discrimination and also to suggest a blueprint for a marketing research plan and or improvements to the marketing information system.

2.5 You are also likely to find some anomalies and contradictions which will oblige you to make assumptions.

2.6 On the inside front cover of the case you will find *Important Notes* for candidates, followed by a page *Candidate's Brief* (see Chapter 8 for details), which you must, of course read thoroughly and have in mind when interpreting the subsequent data in the case itself.

2.7 The examiner reserves the right to issue **additional information** on the case with the examination paper on the day itself. This is to ensure thinking takes place in the examination room and to discourage excessive use of pre-prepared answers. In the most recent examinations, additional information **has** been provided in the examination paper and a proportion of the total marks has been allocated for its use when answering the questions set. Up to 20% of the marks might be allocated for this purpose.

Questions in the examination

2.8 Typically, you may expect three or four questions of unequal marks requiring you to undertake some calculation of how much time to allocate to each question - see Chapter 10 on examination techniques. There is normally no choice and you are required to answer all questions.

2.9 It is normal for these three or four questions to be split between issues of:

(a) Strategy formulation
(b) Strategy implementation

Trends in the examination paper

2.10 The current examiner has made it clear that he wishes (on behalf of the CIM) to encourage the adoption of longer-term strategic planning by marketing management. It is also current policy to try to ensure that future marketing managers are financially literate by asking candidates to state the financial implications of their proposals.

2.11 Finally, the examiner will normally expect candidates to think through the organisational implications posited by the case and to be aware of the contribution that an improved marketing orientation and internal marketing can make to corporate wellbeing.

3 EXAMINATION RULES

3.1 This subject is examined as a three hour 'open book' case study examination. This means you may take as much pre-prepared material, reference books etc into the examination room as you wish, provided this does not interfere with the space and comfort of other candidates. The use of electronic calculators not requiring mains electricity is also permitted providing of course that this does not distract other candidates.

3.2 If you have any doubts on this matter it would be as well to check with the CIM. However, you would be well advised to limit your equipment to that normally required for any examination plus a well-indexed ring binder of pre-prepared analysis (see Chapter 10 on examination techniques). All CIM examinations are held under the jurisdiction of a professional invigilator whose decisions on any point of order must be accepted as final.

3.3 You must of course only start when the invigilator gives permission and you must stop writing immediately you are asked to do so.

3.4 All candidates will be provided with an examination slip which permits entry into the examination room. You will have been allocated an examination number which you must write on the examination script, together with the examination centre and the number of questions attempted, in the order in which they appear in the script. Your name must not appear on the script.

3.5 Additional pages must be securely fastened to the script booklet.

3.6 Answers must only be submitted on CIM script and/or paper such as graph paper supplied by the invigilator. You cannot submit pre-prepared pages and any material suspected of this will be treated as invalid.

4 CANDIDATE'S NOTES

4.1 The Candidate's Notes are amended from time to time but stay broadly the same. The following example was used in the June 1998 case.

Diploma in Marketing: Marketing Analysis and Decision

Important notes

The examiners will be marking your scripts on the basis of questions put to you in the examination room. Questions **may not** carry equal marks and candidates are advised to pay particular attention to the mark allocation on the examination paper. Candidates are advised to budget their time accordingly.

Your role is outlined in the candidates' brief. In the position outlined you may be required to recommend clear courses of action.

You **will not** be awarded marks merely for analysis. This should have been undertaken before the examination day in preparation for meeting the specific tasks which will be specified in the examination paper.

Candidates are **instructed not to conduct research or analysis outside** the material provided within the case study. The introduction of extraneous material in examination answers will gain no marks and serves only to waste valuable time. Although cases are based upon real world situations, facts have been deliberately altered or omitted to preserve anonymity. No useful purpose will therefore be served by contacting companies in this industry and candidates are strictly instructed **not to do so,** as it would simply cause unnecessary confusion.

As in real life, anomalies will be found in this case situation. Please simply state your assumptions where necessary when answering questions. The CIM is not in a position to answer queries on case data whether in writing or on the telephone. Candidates are tested on their overall grasp of the case and its key issues, not on minor details. There are no catch questions or hidden agendas.

Additional information will be introduced in the examination paper itself which candidates must take into account when answering the questions set. Up to 20 per cent of the marks will be allocated for this purpose.

Acquaint yourself thoroughly with the Case Study and be prepared to follow closely the instructions given to you on the examination day. **To answer examination questions effectively, candidates must adopt report format.**

The copying of pre-prepared 'group' answers written by consultants/tutors is strictly forbidden and will be penalised. The questions will demand thinking out in the examination itself and individually composed answers are required in order to pass.

5 CANDIDATE'S BRIEF

5.1 The Candidates' Brief will of course be specific to the particular case and states your role and reporting relationships. It will normally include pointers to the areas for examination questions and is, to a degree, an indication of the stance you should take on the material. The following example has been taken from the June 1999 case.

> *Candidates' Brief*
>
> You are **Joseph Mendes**, a marketing consultant of some repute, who has been appointed by Biocatalysts Ltd. to undertake the development of a marketing report, prior to undertaking a strategic exercise. Joseph's previous work ranged across many industry sectors, but he had undertaken any work in the biotechnology sector. He is keen to understand the sector and the company profile before he develops any plans. As part of his internal and external research he has prepared the following report. At the end of this report are appendices relating to the main body of the text. Joseph has prepared this report for the Managing Director, Stewart North, ready for the next Board Meeting.

6 FURTHER GUIDANCE

6.1 These Guidance Notes are normally updated annually but remain substantially the same over a period of about three years. They contain important information on how to prepare for the examination and should be read carefully. The Guidance Notes are issued to providers of tuition for this subject for passing on to students at the tutor's discretion.

6.2 Tutors are told the following.

(a) Notional taught hours	45
(b) Method of assessment	3 hour written examination
(c) Number of questions	all questions to be attempted (3 or 4)
(d) Pass mark:	50%

Preferred sequence of studies

6.3 The culmination of the Certificate, Advanced Certificate and Diploma course is the case study. The examination has the purpose of ensuring that those who hold the Diploma qualification have not only achieved a certain level of marketing knowledge, but also have the competence to use that knowledge in addressing simulated marketing management problems.

6.4 Any aspect of the entire Certificate, Advanced Certificate and Diploma syllabuses may be applicable and if you have been exempted from parts of the course you should ensure you familiarise yourself with the detailed course requirements.

6.5 This paper should be taken at the end of your course of study.

Case study rationale

6.6 The rationale of the case study as follows.

Aims and objectives

'To extend the practice of candidates in the quantitative and qualitative analysis of marketing situations, both to develop their powers of diagnosis and to create a firm basis in decision making'

By the end of their study students will be able:

(a) to identify, define and rank the problem(s) contained in marketing case studies;

(b) to formulate working hypotheses regarding the solution(s) to problems identified in marketing case studies;

(c) to assemble, order, analyse and interpret both qualitative and quantitative data relating to a marketing case, using appropriate analytical procedures and models;

(d) to describe and substantiate all working assumptions made regarding the case problem(s) working hypothesis and data;

(e) to generate and evaluate the expected outcomes of alternative solutions to case problem(s);

(f) to prepare and present appropriate marketing case reports.

6.7 The CIM Diploma is recognised increasingly widely as a licence to practise. It is in no-one's interests for it to be awarded lightly, as those who have striven hard to attain it will surely agree. The value of the Diploma depends directly upon the quality of the people holding it; in turn the respect earned from peers, superiors and clients depends on the value of the Diploma.

6.8 **Strategic Marketing Management: Analysis and Decision** is quite rightly the severest test in the CIM examinations. The examination is based upon a real-life major case and requires the application of theories, principles and techniques learned in the study of other subjects. It is not an examination to be passed by regurgitating knowledge.

6.9 Candidates must demonstrate beyond reasonable doubt that they are capable not only of in-depth analysis before the exam, but also are able to take decisions and write clear, concise and convincing marketing plans. These marketing plans need to show an understanding of the corporate and financial implications.

Question design and scope

6.10 Questions applied in case studies do not have any standardised format; they will be action orientated, but one inevitable and recurring theme will be the **strategic marketing** of products and services. The examiners are aware of the time constraint of three hours and the questions are designed to enable a candidate to cover them adequately if not well, within that period. Candidates should remember that they are expected to have knowledge equivalent to the syllabuses of the other three Diploma subjects. The whole course (Certificate, Advanced Certificate, and Diploma) is a legitimate source of questions.

Examination approach

6.11 Candidates are required to do what the examiners ask, to answer the question as put and in accordance with any mark allocation which is stated on the paper. This means the management of the time within the examination situation is crucial. In every case, candidates have a human role to play within the structure of either the case, the examination paper, or both, to which they are expected to be able to relate. Usually, this means that they have to respond and restructure their thinking within the examination itself; this is precisely what the examiners are seeking.

Preparation

6.12 There are two basic parts to this paper embodied in its title, Analysis and Decision. There can be no better description of these two parts than the questions put to his students by one lecturer as follows.

(a) What is wrong?
(b) What are you going to do to put it right?

Within the context of management, marketing or otherwise, the second question is the critical one, but cannot be answered without the problem identification implicit in the first.

In the examination (as in real life) more marks will be gained from proposing decisions than will be gained from presenting analyses.

6.13 There will be anomalies in the case, as in real life. Assumptions will therefore need to be made and clearly stated. (The CIM cannot enter into discussion on these aspects, either verbally or in writing.)

6.14 Problem identification will certainly require the application of statistical and financial analytical techniques, and of organisational and behavioural understanding and marketing knowledge. The examiners must know what the problems are, what alternative solutions to them have been considered and which alternative has been chosen by the candidate, in other words:

(a) What is to be done?
(b) In what time period?
(c) By whom?
(d) With what financial and human resource implications?
(e) With what projected outcome?

6.15 There is no such thing as a right answer to these questions. Above all, sensible recommendations are required, supported by reasoned argument. **Lists of problems and regurgitated materials from the case itself do candidates no credit.**

6.16 The evidence is overwhelming that a great many students try to seek refuge in analysis and come to their examination desks hoping that inspiration will suddenly flow to the tips of their ball-point pens! The case study is issued prior to the examination data to enable students to conduct their analysis **before** responding to the situation posed in the examination hall. **A restatement of this analysis is insufficient to pass the examination.** You have to make decisions, and clearly articulate them on the exam day.

Decisions

6.17 There is an apt Chinese proverb which says 'He who deliberates fully before taking a step will spend his entire life on one leg'. The question of taking decisions is a conceptual leap for many students. Since even students in employment will rarely be in a position to take decisions in their company, they need help. In the absence of full information, they have to make assumptions, use their judgement and be prepared to back it up on paper.

6.18 One of the difficulties, which the examiners fully understand, is the lack of knowledge about any particular industry used in the case. Candidates will not be penalised for lack of industry knowledge. Marketing decisions however, are applicable in any environment based on sound principles relevant to the situation. This is what the Analysis and Decision Paper sets out to test.

6.19 The examiners will not tolerate academic essays or deep but fruitless analyses of the material presented in the case. We are looking for the ability to apply marketing concepts and this means that candidates should adopt **management report style** to maximise their chances of success.

Further research

6.20 The examiners can state categorically that there is **no need**'for any candidate to seek additional information outside the case study. There are three reasons for this.

(a) The examiners incorporate within the case itself enough information for the candidate to work on. It is a self-contained exercise.

(b) Some data within the case studies needs to be disguised to preserve confidentiality. Trying to search out the company concerned can thus not only be a waste of time but also lead to confusion.

(c) Access to additional research data is limited, particularly for overseas students.

6.21 Nevertheless, candidates may be expected to be able to state within the examination what additional research information they would seek, for what reason, in what time period, at what approximate cost and by what method. There is every justification for encouraging student research during the course of an academic year in order to have the experience and be able to apply it to the examination case. No students will earn additional marks for external research data introduced in the examination.

6.22 **Creativity and innovation**

The lack of imagination by the majority of candidates in this examination is a major weakness. Marketing is creative; it is one of the means by which companies distinguish themselves or their products from competition. Only on rare occasions are the examiners confronted by some illuminating or different approach and marks then have a tendency to soar!

6.23 **What tutors can, and should, do**

For the purposes of this section, the examiners must assume that students have, at the beginning of the year, the knowledge and skills required by the syllabus. What follows can also only be recommendations; there is no one way to teach case studies, just as there is no one answer.

Chapter roundup

- This chapter has presented you with a sense of the context regarding the case study exam.
- Firstly, you are given information in advance, not all of which will be relevant. You should not research outside information.
- In dealing with the information, group discussion is important.
- You are required to take reasoned decisions within the case's context, not to provide an ideal solution as one is not available. Do your analysis in **advance.** Take decisions in the exam.
- The questions asked in the case can cover topics contained in the **entire** CIM syllabus, from the Certificate, the Advanced Certificate and the Diploma.

Part C

How to analyse the CIM case study

7 How To Analyse a CIM Case Study: a General Overview

This chapter covers the following topics.

1 Case study methodology in general
2 Mini-cases
3 Longer case studies
4 Preparing for study
5 The six stage approach

Introduction

A case study element has featured in your CIM exams already. This chapter identifies the main differences between minicases in other CIM papers and the cases in the Analysis and Decision exam.

1 CASE STUDY METHODOLOGY IN GENERAL

1.1 A number of writers have endeavoured to summarise and express the vast amount of experience gained over many years by a host of institutions using the case study approach to teaching and learning. These institutions include universities, business schools and colleges.

1.2 The following few pages are devoted to introducing you to some of the best practice and custom expressed by these writers. This will enable you to develop a broad appreciation of the ways in which most institutions approach case study teaching.

1.3 Chapter 8 will then explain the specific methods recommended by CIM Senior Examiners for the purposes of the Diploma in Marketing case study examination. These specific methods do, of course, have their roots in the general custom and practice covered in this section.

1.4 Methods tend to vary in general according to the following factors.

(a) The length of the case.
(b) The content of the case.
(c) The culture of the teaching institution.
(d) The abilities of the students.
(e) The personality of the case tutor.
(f) The amount of time available.

2 MINI-CASES

2.1 Candidates used to handling short cases must take care not to assume that the methodology can be successfully applied to the longer case study. Clearly, the shorter the case study, the less is its content and the smaller is the amount of the analysis that can be conducted upon it. Another related criterion is the amount of numerical as opposed to textual data. This affects the nature of the analytical techniques that can be applied.

2.2 For those students sitting other CIM exam papers which feature unseen minicases, a former senior examiner gives this advice

2.3 'It needs to be stated unequivocally that the type of extremely short case (popularly called the mini-case) set in the examinations for Diploma subjects **other** than 'Analysis and Decision' cannot be treated in exactly the same way as the extremely long case set for the subject of marketing analysis and decision. If it could, there would be little point in going to all the trouble of writing an in-depth case study.

2.4 'Far too many students adopt a maxi-case approach, using a detailed marketing audit outline which is largely inappropriate to a case consisting only of two or three paragraphs. Others use the SWOT analysis and simply re-write the case under the four headings of strengths, weaknesses, opportunities and threats.

'Some students even go so far as to totally ignore the specific questions set and present a standard maxi case analysis outline including environmental reviews through to contingency plans.

2.5 'The CIM "mini-case" is not really a case at all, it is merely an outline of a given situation, a **scenario.** Its purpose is to test whether examinees can apply their knowledge of marketing theory and techniques to the company or organisation and the operating environment described in the scenario. For example, answers advocating retail audits as part of the marketing information system for a small industrial goods manufacturer, demonstrate a lack of practical awareness. Such answers confirm that the examinee has learned a given MkIS outline by rote and simply regurgitated this in complete disregard of the scenario. Such an approach would be disastrous in the real world and examinees adopting this approach cannot be passed, ie gain the confidence of the Institute as professional marketing practitioners. The correct approach to the scenario is a mental review of the area covered by the question and the selection by the examinee of those particular parts of knowledge and techniques which apply to the case. This implies a rejection of those parts of the student's knowledge which clearly do not apply to the scenario.

2.6 'All scenarios are based upon real world companies and situations which are written with a full knowledge of how that organisation actually operates in its planning environment. Often, the organisation described in the scenario will not be a giant fast-moving consumer good manufacturing and marketing company, since this would facilitate mindless regurgitation of textbook outlines and be counter to the intention of this section of the examination.

2.7 'More often, the scenarios will involve innovative small or medium sized firms which comprise the vast majority of UK companies and which lack the resources often assumed by the textbook approach. These firms do, however, have to market within these constraints and are just as much concerned in marketing communications, marketing planning and control and indeed (proportionately) in international marketing, particularly the EU.

2.8 'However, as marketing applications develop and expand and as changes take root, the Institute through its examiners will wish to test students' knowledge awareness of these changes and their implication with regard to marketing practice. For example, in the public sector increasing attention is being paid to the marketing of leisure services and the concept of 'asset marketing', where the 'product' is to a greater extent fixed and therefore the option of product as a variable in the marketing mix is somewhat more constrained. Internal marketing has been recognised as essential to the effective operation of TQM.

2.9 'Tutors and students are referred to Examiners' Reports which repeatedly complain of inappropriateness of answer detail which demonstrates a real lack of practical marketing grasp and confirms that a learned by rote textbook regurgitation is being used. Examples would include:

(a) the recommendation of national TV advertising for a small industrial company with a local market;

(b) the overnight installation of a marketing department comprising managing director, marketing manager, advertising manager, distribution manager, sales manager, etc into what has been described as a very small company;

(c) the inclusion of packaging, branded-packs, on-pack offers etc in the marketing mix recommendations for a service.

2.10 'It has been borne in mind that the award of the Diploma is in a very real sense the granting of a licence to practice marketing and certainly an endorsement of the candidate's practical as well as theoretical grasps of marketing. In these circumstances, such treatments of the mini-case, as described above, cannot be passed and **give rise to some concern that perhaps the teaching/learning approach to mini-cases has not been sufficiently differentiated from that recommended for the Analysis and Decision Paper.**'

3 LONGER CASE STUDIES

3.1 With the above comments in mind, it is suggested that the following approaches should be treated as being more appropriate to the longer case study.

3.2 Cravens and Lamb (1986) recommend a six step approach to case analysis along the following lines.

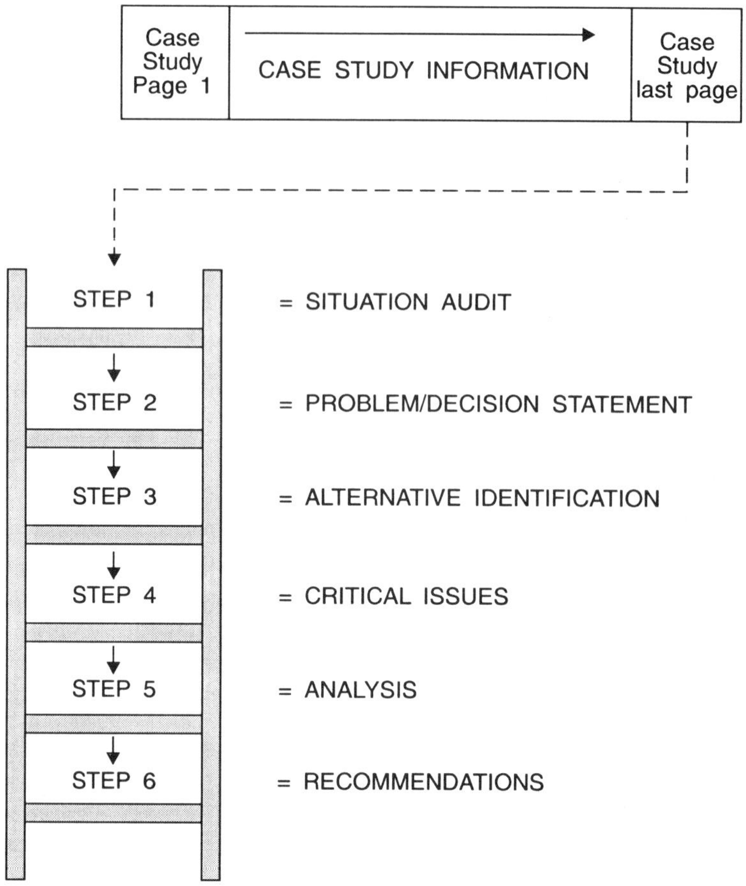

3.3 Whilst not disputing the appropriateness of any of the above steps, this model is insufficiently comprehensive for CIM major case study preparation. It suggests analysis as step 5 whereas analysis has to take place much earlier in the process. Also CIM examination candidates would need to take step 6 (recommendations) a great deal further, for example into costings, budgets, schedules and their financial/human resource implications.

3.4 Edge and Coleman's framework for case analysis also has six steps which are, however, somewhat different in their detail from those recommended by Cravens and Lamb.

1 Comprehend case situation
↓
2 Diagnose problem areas
↓
3 State problem
↓
4 Generate alternatives
↓
5 Evaluate and select
↓
6 Defend implementation

3.5 The Edge and Coleman model adds to that of Cravens and Lamb, particularly in its first and last steps. Defending implementation is another way of saying 'justify your recommendations' which is certainly a necessity for the CIM Diploma case preparation.

3.6 Mention has already been made in Chapter 6 paragraph 1.20, of the Easton (*Learning from case studies* 1982) approach which is similar to the two outlined above but suggests a seventh step, namely that of communicating the results (of the analysis).

3.7 Easton refers to two basic methods of 'teaching' case studies in the classroom.

(a) Traditional Harvard method of open class discussion.

(b) Asking individuals or groups (syndicates) to make formal presentations during each stage or step of the case study analysis, which then may be followed by questions and/or general discussion.

3.8 In the class discussion the case instructor may question individuals rigorously or may simply direct the groups attention to particular areas, issues or anomalies in the case. The case instructor may specify which analytical tools and techniques should be applied.

3.9 The less directive case leader will tend to chair the discussion and control the **process** rather than its **content**, guiding and advising rather than dictating solutions.

3.10 In the case of the CIM Diploma where the case study is given out at least four weeks before the examination, there is time for a structured approach aimed at developing both group and individual solutions, in the form of a complete and professional marketing plan. This is the approach which we shall be recommending in the next chapter.

4 PREPARING FOR STUDY

4.1 It has been the traditional practice for CIM Senior Examiners for the subject *Strategic Marketing Management: Analysis and Decision* to write their own case studies dedicated to the particular standards and teaching/learning objectives set by the CIM and its academic Boards. These case studies are individually tailored to the testing of particular areas of marketing management abilities.

4.2 Over the years a considerable expertise has been built up through extensive dialogue with Course Tutors; by teaching and directing actual case study courses; through student appraisals and not least by the need for case study writers to submit marking schemes, examiner's reports and specimen answers.

4.3 This expertise is synthesised in the following recommendations and in the stage approach adopted in the next chapter.

Objectives

4.4 **Objectives of the case study**

(a) A thorough understanding of the situation and of the key issues should be gained through a rigorous analysis of the information provided in the specific examination case being tackled.

(b) A complete and credible marketing plan should be produced which is appropriate to the specific case study, and which addresses the key issues and is underpinned by the prior analysis.

Rationale

4.5 Whilst it would be unlikely for the examiners to ask for the presentation of this complete marketing plan in the examination paper (owing to time constraints), the questions are inevitably going to invoke **parts** of this plan.

4.6 Rather than gamble on which parts of the plan are likely to be tested in the exam **and therefore run the risk of failure**, it is better to be prepared for all eventualities. Whilst other subjects can be revised relatively easily in the event of failure, each case study is unique. To resit the case examination essentially means **starting again from scratch**.

Basic approach to a case study

4.7 A **group** approach to analysis and decision is recommended. It is extremely unlikely that a person working alone (however clever) will be able to develop the wider perspectives necessary to a thorough understanding of the case. Additionally, the challenges provided by the group to an individual's recommendations constitute an excellent forum for developing appropriate justification. This process also helps to moderate excesses and provide a balanced, reasoned report.

4.8 The **ideal** approach is that whereby a study group is formed consisting of a group of say 24 people who then work in four syndicates each of six people in a programmed way through each of the steps recommended below.

4.9 At the end of each syndicate session, the syndicates should report formally back to the plenary group of 24, through a rotating syndicate spokesperson. Each syndicate's presentation should be open to questions, challenges and constructive criticism from the other syndicates and be followed by general discussion. All sessions should ideally be programmed and guided by an objective case instructor of the less directive nature (see Chapter 7, paragraphs 3.7 to 3.9).

4.10 Continuity, commitment, discipline and organisation within the syndicates is essential to producing the quality of marketing planning required.

4.11 Failing this ideal, candidates working alone are, **as a minimum** urged to discuss aspects of the case with as many colleagues as they can muster and to continually challenge their own assumptions, conclusions and solutions. Analyses of the case are available at modest prices from a number of sources normally advertised in *Marketing Success* published by the CIM. These analyses do at least provide other perspectives, usually generated by a small group of marketing consultants.

5 THE 6 STAGE APPROACH

You can use this as a checklist to monitor your progress.

STAGE ONE - CONFRONTING THE CASE STUDY

Step 1.1 Read the case.
Step 1.2 After an interval, re-read the case.
Step 1.3 Reflect on the instructions and candidate's brief.
Step 1.4 Think yourself into the role and the situation
Step 1.5 Re-read the case and write a précis. Discuss with colleagues.

STAGE TWO - ANALYSING THE CASE STUDY

Step 2.1 Conduct a marketing audit. Discuss with colleagues.
Step 2.2 Do a SWOT analysis. Discuss with colleagues.
Step 2.3 Conduct analyses/cross analyses of appendices. Discuss with colleagues.
Step 2.4 Reconsider your précis, marketing audit and SWOT analysis.
Step 2.5 Conduct a situational analysis. Discuss with colleagues.

STAGE THREE - IDENTIFYING ISSUES AND DEVELOPING STRATEGIES

Step 3.1 Decide key issues. Discuss with colleagues.

Step 3.2 Develop a mission statement. Discuss with colleagues.

Step 3.3 Decide broad aims. Discuss with colleagues.

Step 3.4 Identify and analyse major problems. Develop and analyse alternative solutions. Discuss with colleagues.

Step 3.5 Develop quantified and timescaled objectives. Discuss with colleagues.

Step 3.6 Consider alternative strategies and select those most appropriate. Discuss with colleagues.

STAGE FOUR - DEVELOPING YOUR PLANS

Step 4.1 Draw up detailed tactical plans covering the marketing mix. Discuss with colleagues.

Step 4.2 Draw up a marketing research plan and MkIS (Marketing information system).

Step 4.3 Consider organisational issues and make recommendation for changes towards complete marketing orientation as felt necessary. Discuss with colleagues.

Step 4.4 Consider the organisation's culture and make recommendations for internal marketing programmes as felt necessary. Discuss with colleagues.

Step 4.5 Consider the financial and human resource implications of your plans/recommendations. Discuss with colleagues.

Step 4.6 Assess costs and draw up indicative budgets. Discuss with colleagues.

Step 4.7 Draw up schedules showing the timing/sequence of your plans/recommendations. Discuss with colleagues.

STAGE FIVE - CONTROL AND CONTINGENCIES

Step 5.1 Specify review procedures and control mechanisms. Discuss with colleagues.
Step 5.2 Outline contingency plans. Discuss with colleagues.
Step 5.3 Review your complete marketing plan.

STAGE 6 - THE EXAMINATION

Step 6.1 Draw up your examination plan.
Step 6.2 Practise writing in true report style.

This, then, is the 6-stage approach to a thorough preparation for the CIM examination. It can be seen that this specific approach is necessarily more comprehensive than the more general approaches recommended by other authors. It encompasses many different steps of **analysis** and **decision** which are the basic ingredients of this subject and of marketing management in general. Nevertheless the above steps are only in summary form and need expansion into more practical detail in the remainder of this chapter.

Chapter roundup

- This chapter has introduced you to the contrasts between mini-cases you will encounter elsewhere and the longer case study sat in this paper.
- You have also been introduced to some of the underlying methodologies of approaching a case study.

8 The Case Study Analysis Methods Recommended by the CIM Senior Examiner

This chapter covers the following topics.

Introduction

It has been the traditional practice for CIM Senior Examiners for the subject *Strategic Marketing Management: Analysis and Decision* to write their own case studies dedicated to the particular standards and teaching/learning objectives set by the CIM and its academic Boards. These case studies are individually tailored to the testing of particular areas of marketing management abilities.

Over the years a considerable expertise has been built up through extensive dialogue with Course Tutors; by teaching and directing actual case study courses; through student appraisals and not least by the need for case study writers to submit marking schemes, examiner's reports and specimen answers.

This expertise is synthesised in the following recommendations.

1 STAGE 1: CONFRONTING THE CASE STUDY

Step 1.1. Read the case

1.1 The first thing to remember is not to panic when the actual case study falls through your letterbox. To panic is not good marketing management practice.

(a) Keep calm, remember you have at least four weeks (normally) to prepare and that thanks to this text, you have an excellent game plan. Resist the temptation to drop everything, miss your breakfast, frantically pore over the case and immediately start analysing all the tables.

(b) Choose a time when your brain is receptive. Set aside no more than **one hour** for this purpose. Find somewhere quiet where you will not be disturbed.

(c) Read the case through very quickly twice then put it away, ideally until the next day, when you've slept upon it and your sub-conscious mind will have sifted it through for you and made more sense of it.

(d) **Resist the temptation to read the case slowly and thoroughly because if you do, you are highly likely to become obsessed with the detail and never see the wood for the trees.**

(e) Speed reading tests show that quicker reading not only saves time but also actually **improves** retention of the content (up to a point of marginal returns). Reading very quickly twice, rather than very slowly once, is therefore more effective. Go on, try it. Force yourself.

Step 1.2. After an interval, re-read the case

1.2 This time read the case through **once** very quickly - as you did yesterday, then once again more slowly. Allow yourself a maximum of **two hours**.

Step 1.3. Reflect on the instructions and candidate's brief

1.3 All CIM case studies contain a page of instructions under the heading of *Important Notes* and a further page headed *Candidate's Brief* prior to the text of the actual case itself. Both pages give important clues, need to be read carefully and given close consideration.

(a) The *Important Notes* will tell you that no useful purpose will be served by conducting research or analysis outside the material in the case. So do not waste your valuable time by doing this. They also tell you that you will not be awarded marks for mere analysis. Analysis is expected to have been undertaken between receiving the case and the four week period before the examination. It is to be used in the examination solely for the purpose of underpinning your decisions. The notes will emphasise that you must adopt report format, hence the need for practice. Finally the notes will warn you that pre-prepared 'group' or syndicated answers written out blindly without reference to the actual questions set, will be failed. You really do have to think in the examination itself, **select** data from your analysis, manipulate it and add to it, in order to pass.

(b) The page headed *Candidate's Brief* is equally important since it will not only tell you which role to adopt but remind you of the need to justify the financial and human resources demanded by your proposals, against competing projects. The candidates' brief will often also indicate at least one of the key issues which act as pointers towards possible examination questions.

Step 1.4. Think yourself into the role and the situation

1.4 You will note later in the Examiner's Reports that candidates lose marks for failing to **adopt the role** designated in the Candidate's Brief, for example, writing 'What Irma should do...' when they are supposed to be Irma.

(a) Sometimes candidates are placed in the role of a **consultant**. In this case, it would be unsuitable to adopt the tell style and more appropriate to position yourself in an advisory capacity. The more you can adopt your role and think yourself into the situation described in the case, the better will be your grasp, and the more realistic will be your recommendations.

(b) **Without** re-reading the case, start thinking about it and make strong efforts to adopt the company/organisation as your own. What are the major problems? What business are you in? What is the present position? Where would you like to take the company over the next few years?

(c) **Avoid detail**. You are in the position of an artist trying to decide the nature of your next painting. You decide upon a rural scene, approximate size and **broad** content, sky, water, trees, a hill. This is sufficient for a visualisation, a rough sketch. The details of cloud types, tree varieties, number of leaves etc can come later. **This overview is most important**. The ability to see the most **important** things in the case situation is crucial. You need to see the ball clearly **now** in order to keep your eye firmly upon it in subsequent and more detailed stages.

(d) You will find the précis called for in the next step is a useful technique towards confirming your overall initial grip on the situation.

Step 1.5. Re-read the case and write a précis. Discuss with colleagues

1.5 The pre-précis reading of the case should be a quick one, merely serving as a reminder to you of its contents and to confirm initial impressions of the more important facts.

(a) You are now asked to précis the 30-40 pages of the case in **not more than two A4 sides**. This is a really good way of forcing yourself to decide what is truly basic to the case and what is relatively less important. One case study tutor has remarked that some of his course members, when put to the task of doing a précis, produce one considerably longer than the original text. Let us therefore remind ourselves of what a précis is.

'A concise summary of the essential facts or statements of a book article or other text'.
(Dictionary)

(b) **Stick to the facts.** It is important to avoid putting your own opinions, assumptions or interpretations into your précis. Many people find it difficult to avoid suggesting solutions to problems in their précis, a sign that they will find it difficult to stick to the question in their examination. This is not the purpose of the précis.

(c) **How to do the précis?**

(i) Well, one way is to do it in easy stages. Go through each page and pencil lightly at the side I for important, VI for very important. Try not to treat each page the same. Some pages may have no important information on them and others a great deal.

(ii) You may find you have pencilled about a third. If so you can boil it down still further until you really have condensed it down to two pages or can do so when using your **own** words, rather than those given in the text. Now you can either maintain the order in which the case is printed or you can re-order. You might want to add structure, such as which parts of your précis come under the headings of objectives (or problems or opportunities or indeed the marketing mix), if you think this will help to give you a better grip on the essential facts.

(d) Now, and only now, **discuss** your précis and what you feel to be most relevant important issues, with your colleagues. Remember there is no one wholly correct answer. It is quite normal to find that someone with an **accounting background** will think the **financial data** to be more important than someone from the social sciences. You should find that while there are a number of different perspectives, all should share some common ground and that your own knowledge of the case study has been significantly improved.

2 STAGE 2: ANALYSING THE CASE STUDY

Step 2.1. Conduct a marketing audit. Discuss with colleagues

2.1 What is a marketing audit? Here is Kotler's definition.

(a) 'A marketing audit is a comprehensive, systematic, independent and periodic examination of a company's - or business unit's - marketing environment, objectives, strategies and activities, with a view to determining problem areas and opportunities and recommending a plan of action to improve the company's performance'.

(b) It is, therefore, a pre-requisite to the setting of objectives. If you think about it, the clearer the view of where we are now and how we arrived at this position, the more likely we are to set realistic objectives. The further our actual position is from that imagined, the more unrealistic will be the targets set.

(c) The marketing audit should, therefore be rigorous. It is well worth a considerable investment in time and resources. Wherever possible, comparisons should be drawn with competitors. For example, in discussing advertising you might ask the following questions. How much did we spend on advertising last year? How much did our competitors spend? How effective is our advertising compared with competitors? How do our advertisements compare in terms of media used, size of advertisements, the use of colour, copy platforms etc?

(d) The full marketing audit has two parts, the internal (or micro) audit and the external (or macro) audit, a summary of which follows.

Audit	Comment
Marketing environmental audit	Political, legal, economic, sociological and technological factors. Markets, competitors, distributors, suppliers, publics.
Marketing strategy audit	Mission, objectives, strategies
Marketing organisation audit	Formal structure, functional efficiency, interface efficiency
Marketing systems audit	MIS, planning systems, control systems. Marketing research inputs.
Marketing productivity audit	Profitability analysis, cost-effectiveness, analysis
Marketing function audits	Products/services, price, distribution, selling, advertising, sales promotion and public relations. If services, add people, process and physical evidence (see paragraphs 4.6, 4.7, 4.8 in this chapter).

(e) In the context of the CIM case study we have to adapt models, frameworks, tools and techniques to suit our own purposes. It would, for example, be folly not to examine the financial position of the company in the case bearing in mind we are likely to be required to give the financial implications of our proposals. With this in mind it is suggested that you add audits of other functions as follows.

(i) **Financial audit**. Revenue/profit trends, financial ratio trends, financial accounts.
(ii) **Production audit**. Production facilities, constraints, developments.
(iii) **Personnel audit**. Organisation, training, human resources.

(f) When auditing the case study, it would also be sensible to use a **marketing planning framework** bearing in mind what we are trying to accomplish is a comprehensive marketing plan. We could ask questions such as 'What do we know about the corporate mission? Do we have one? Is it good, bad or indifferent?' etc. A simple schematic approach for this is suggested below.

Auditing the marketing plan - schematic approach

Planning	*Auditing*
Corporate mission	Correct? Understood?
Corporate objectives	Feasible? Being achieved?
Corporate strategies	Appropriate? Have environmental factors changes? What are competitors doing?
Marketing objectives	Feasible? Being achieved?
Marketing strategies	Appropriate? Working? Competitors? (Direct, indirect)
Marketing mix plans	Harmonised? Tailored for each segment? Positioning OK? Check price, place, product/ service and promotion. Internal audits, customer audits
Marketing research plan	Is the right data provided at the right time in the right format?
Budgets/performance measures	Appropriate? Being achieved?
Organisation, integration, co-ordination	Working harmoniously? Is the organisation effective?
Overall	How do we compare with last year and the years before? How do we compare with competitors?

(g) A full marketing audit using the checklist in Chapter 1 (section 2), is difficult to apply on the relatively scant information given in the typical case study. However, you could use this checklist to identify **the information you have not got** but would ideally require and which therefore might constitute part of the information specification for your marketing research plan or marketing information system.

(h) After completing this audit and discussing it with your colleagues, your understanding of the case should have again improved. However, a great more analysis is needed before we can start our decision making process.

Step 2.2. Do a SWOT analysis. Discuss with colleagues

2.2 The following sheet (purposely designed for use on CIM case studies) illustrates the approach used to identify from the comprehensive marketing audit those areas of Strengths and Weaknesses, Opportunities and Threats. You should have come across SWOT earlier. It is a popular analytical tool because it is quick and easy to use and it can form the blueprint for the marketing plan.

(a) Companies can attempt to exploit strengths and correct weaknesses so as to form the basis of a short-term tactical plan. Strengths and weaknesses emanate from within the company and are, therefore, classed as internal, controllable variables.

(b) Opportunities and threats come from outside the company. These variables being external are, to a greater extent, uncontrollable (eg we cannot directly control competitors). Operating in ways to seize and develop opportunities, and so stave off or negate threats, can form the basis of longer term strategic plans.

SWOT ANALYSIS SHEET

STRENGTHS	Ref	Function	WEAKNESSES	Ref	Function
1			1		
2			2		
3			3		
4			4		
5			5		
6			6		
7			7		
8			8		
9			9		
10			10		
11			11		
12			12		
13			13		
14			14		
15			15		
16			16		
17			17		
18			18		
19			19		
20			20		

OPPORTUNITIES	Ref	Function	THREATS	Ref	Function
1			1		
2			2		
3			3		
4			4		
5			5		
6			6		
7			7		
8			8		
9			9		
10			10		
11			11		
12			12		
13			13		
14			14		
15			15		
16			16		
17			17		
18			18		
19			19		
20			20		

(c) **Limitations of SWOT analysis**

(i) It is essentially subjective.

(ii) One person can see an attribute as a strength, whilst another might see it as a weakness.

(iii) Under particular circumstances, a strength can become a weakness and vice versa.

(iv) People have difficulty in deciding whether something is a strength or an opportunity and whether something is a weakness or a threat.

(v) It can produce almost endless lists with variations on themes and so can result in too much detail to be effective.

(d) **Making the SWOT analysis more effective**

(i) Keep strictly to the internal versus external criteria when deciding between strengths and opportunities, weaknesses and threats.

(ii) Categorise all items by function, for example a particular strength as being a marketing strength, or a financial strength and so forth.

(iii) Rank each strength in relative importance on a scale of major to minor.

(iv) Draw up a list to show in descending order of ranks which items are most important.

(v) Take it as read that there are always opportunities to correct weaknesses and exploit strengths.

(vi) Use the broad frameworks of other techniques to develop the SWOT analysis. Here are two examples.

(1) Ansoff: we have a broad opportunity to develop new products/services for existing markets (which new products and for which existing markets?).

(2) SLEPT (Social, legal, economic, political and technological) factors representing opportunities or threats - which particular legal factors? - do these emanate from the national legislation, or Europe or other international sources?

(vii) Do not equivocate. Decide, for the purposes of what follows, how an item should be categorised.

(viii) Keep the SWOT analysis under continuous review.

(ix) Use the ref. column to indicate the page number in the text of the case (p1) and/or appendix number (A10) from which you have extracted each item. This not only underpins your analysis more objectively, but saves time during the discussion periods, and other occasions when disputes may arise.

Step 2.3. Conduct analyses/cross analyses of appendices. Discuss with colleagues

2.3 CIM case study appendices normally considerably enrich the information afforded by the text. However, many of the appendices may be in the form of tables and the data contained therein may need analysis and interpretation in order to extract information for decision-taking purposes. Remember, information which cannot be used for taking decisions is by definition useless as far as we are concerned.

(a) The analysis of numerical and financial data poses two pitfalls.

(i) Many people (usually the more numerate ones) get carried away by figures and will argue endlessly whether the extra cost of switching from hard toilet paper to soft is £2.27 per week or £2.35 per week, depending on whether or not we can negotiate a retrospective volume discount. Quite honestly, such debates waste the valuable time of a group and so the format suggested below is designed deliberately to simplify the data.

(ii) What do the figures **mean**? Without meaning, figures are useless. We must also recognise that some tables may be deliberate red herrings and add very little to our understanding. Be aware that **figures can be interpreted differently**. For example, a series (representing annual turnover net of inflation as an index, 1988 = 100) reading 100, 99.8, 99.5, 99.4 may be interpreted by the more statistically minded person as a declining trend. However, looked at from a marketing management viewpoint the series could, on the contrary, be said to represent a highly stable market.

(c) **Does the appendix corroborate data in the text, in other words, does it strengthen or contradict something in the text?** If so, which is right? You are, in the latter case, entitled to make your own assumptions but if the data in the text emanated from a newly appointed cleaner whilst that in the appendix came from a statistically sound survey, it would be more sensible to opt for the appendix. Data in one appendix can of course corroborate or contradict data in another appendix.

(d) What is the source of the data? How old is it? How reliable is it? Is the data quantitative or qualitative? What value can we place upon it? - are all worthwhile questions to ask.

(e) **Finally on this subject of appendix analysis, look for synergy by cross analysis.** You can often gain valuable extra information by doing so. For example if Appendix 2 reveals that half our customers are female and Appendix 12 that female customers currently spend twice as much on our goods or services as males, then we can deduce that female customers are responsible for about two thirds of our turnover of £300,000 or approximately £200,000.

Case appendices - analysis/cross analysis

Appendix number	*What is it essentially saying?*	*How does it help us?*	*Which other appendices or text can it be related to?*	*If so what other extra information and insights does this reveal?*

Step 2.4. Re-consider your précis, marketing audit and SWOT analysis

2.4 Now is the time to recap on your work so far. It may well be that new knowledge acquired from your appendix analysis would warrant some modifications to your previous outputs. In some instances it may have given you fresh insights and in others, confirmed your views.

Step 2.5. Conduct a situational analysis and draw up a statement. Discuss with colleagues

2.5 The situational analysis can be both time consuming (depending on how well you did your marketing audit) but it is also rewarding. After a great deal of effort, you want to end up with a statement between half and one page long **which puts the case study situation in a nutshell.** It should leave you with a satisfying feeling of command.

> **Example**
>
> Imagine you are a retail stores' group manager. You visit one of your hypermarkets and ask the manager 'What's the situation?' He or she might well reply - 'Well we've had a good month but that's down to the new city festival. Overall, we're down this year to date against last year, mainly on the premium brands. I'm worried about the high rate of pilferage and suspect the back stores have got a racket working. On the staff side, we're struggling a bit and I've worked it out that we've been two down on establishment on average this year. All in all, I reckon that we'll pan out about 98% of budgeted revenue this year but there'll be some compensation from costs of only 96%. We should just about hit targeted profit'.
>
> You can see that the store manager knows the situation very well and has been able to sum it up in just a few sentences. However, to get there will have taken many hours of analysis and enquiry.

(a) The **situational analysis** seeks to bring out the relevant relationships between the often overlapping and contradictory aspects of the **SWOT**. An example would be the importance of purchasing to marketing and corporate success.

(b) The situational analysis builds on the **marketing audit** by adding a time dimension by looking at likely future market trends and by looking for a prognosis (where is the company headed - glorious success, grim survival or somewhere in the middle ground). It establishes factual information and makes value judgements.

(c) **A situational analysis should cover at least the following issues**, concentrating on the areas identified as important. You should have already covered these in your marketing audit, but need to revisit them together with your précis and SWOT in a grand summary.

External	*Internal*
Economic environment Market environment Competitive environment Technological environment	Sales Market share (if relevant) Profit margins Product range and development Price Distribution Promotion

Before summarising you should add further analytical methods and models, wherever possible (eg product life cycle, diffusion of innovation, buyer behaviour models, product portfolio, customer portfolio, profit impact of marketing strategies), to establish understanding of the case material and gain fresh insights on the relationship between different pieces of information. You **should gain a thorough understanding** of **buyer behaviour, competition and competitive strategies, distinctive competences. The more perspectives you can bring to bear on the case then the greater will be your understanding and the higher your payoff in terms of examination marks.**

> **Example**
>
> Take for example, buying behaviour models. You cannot know your markets without knowing your customers and understanding their buying behaviour. In the case study Euro Airport Ltd (June 1992) you would have learned a great deal by constructing a flow chart, depicting the stages through which a typical passenger goes from leaving work or home to arriving at the destination in a foreign country. At many of these stages lie opportunities for gaining, or losing, sales.

Remember that the objective of all this revising, reconsidering and further analysis is to give you a firm and clear command of the situation which you can express in not more than a single page statement. So let's hear it!

3 STAGE 3: IDENTIFYING ISSUES AND DEVELOPING STRATEGIES

Step 3.1. Decide the key issues. Discuss with colleagues

3.1 Any good case study should yield, upon proper and thorough analysis, its key issues and any good examiner should set exam questions around these key issues in order to maintain good faith. So this is it. This is absolutely crucial to your exam success. **Have you done your analysis thoroughly? If not, you have only yourself to blame if you haven't identified the right key issues and therefore the likely exam question areas.**

> **Example**
>
> In a retail situation you might have identified purchasing as a critical success factor, following analysis and discussion. A key issue might then be the method(s) of organising purchasing within the corporate and marketing plan. In Part E of this text you will be able to practise and test your ability to identify key issues in three actual exam case studies. Having identified the key issues we can now proceed to address these in our marketing plan.

As it can get out of hand (eg you could put forward 47 key issues just to be on the safe side) you should limit yourself to a maximum of **six**. Bearing in mind that the exam paper will normally contain three questions, you can see the wisdom in limiting yourself to six key issues. When deciding key issues, look for clues not only in the case study itself, **but also in the Candidates' Brief.** Try not to get carried away. By all means create a list of possible key issues, but then **reject** all those which are not key. You could use a **ranking technique** and you should 'parcel up' minor issues under a major heading eg:

4 Sales force effectiveness
6 Advertising constraints
8 Poor press relations (PR)

might then be parcelled up under the heading of **marketing communications** and allocated a ranking of 3.

Step 3.2. Develop a mission statement. Discuss with colleagues

3.2 The mission statement is an important part of strategy. It has an important role in providing a consensus between different viewpoints and a focus for business activity. It has been covered in detail in Chapter 1, Paragraph 3.63 of this text, but just to recap, look over the following paragraphs.

(a) The mission statement is likely to have a degree of generality so that it can integrate various stakeholders' interests over a long period of time. Stakeholders could be defined as 'any group or individual who can affect or is affected by the achievement of an organisation's purpose'. (eg customers, government, employees).

(b) Open objectives are appropriate for areas that are difficult to quantify or express in measurable terms, eg 'to be a leader in technology'. Open objectives can avoid over centralisation, opposition, rigidity to change and alerting competitors.

(c) The **mission** is shaped by five key elements.

(i) The organisation's history
(ii) The current preferences of owners and managers (stakeholders)
(iii) Environmental considerations
(iv) Resources
(v) The organisation's distinctive competences

(d) An example of a mission statement is one adopted by Apple. 'Apple (computers) is not in the game or toy business but in the computer business. What Apple does best is to take a high cost ideal and turn it into a low cost, high quality solution.'

(e) Note that there are two possible approaches to a mission. Here is an example.

Firm	*Product view*	*Market view*
Revlon	We make cosmetics	We sell hope
Xerox	We make copying equipment	We help improve office productivity

Step 3.3. Decide broad aims. Discuss with colleagues

3.3 Most people find it difficult to proceed directly from a mission statement into quantified and timescaled objectives. They are also perhaps overly concerned with the problems the company in the case study is facing.

(a) For these reasons the step of deciding **broad aims** is often found to be very useful. You do not immediately have to decide by how much and when.

Example

For example, in the Brewsters case your broad aim might be to maintain sales, despite having to sell off a large proportion of your pubs, or to reduce your dependence on the UK market. In the Regional Railways case it might be to change staff attitudes towards customers from negative to positive.

(b) Your broad aims must be **consistent** with your mission statement. (In fact, consistency throughout the different parts of your marketing plan is something you must aim for and continually check from now on.)

(c) Generally speaking broad aims must be **capable of later** refinement into quantified and timescaled objectives, such as to increase sales (net of inflation) from the current £36m in 2000 to £63m by 2005. However, this can be difficult in the case of a broad aim being for example 'to become more marketing orientated'. Nevertheless you could convert this into a marketing objective of 'to be fully marketing orientated by the end of 1999' and go on to suggest strategies and tactics by which this could be achieved. You could also say in what respects the company is not yet fully marketing orientated and the measures you would take at the end of 2005 to check whether your objective has been achieved.

PROBLEM NO.	ALTERNATIVE SOLUTIONS	MAIN ADVANTAGES	MAIN DISADVANTAGES
1.0	1.1	1.1.1	1.1.1
		1.1.2	1.1.2
		1.1.3	1.1.3
	1.2	1.2.1	1.2.1
		1.2.2	1.2.2
		1.2.3	1.2.3
	1.3	1.3.1	1.3.1
		1.3.2	1.3.2
		1.3.3	1.3.3
	1.4	1.4.1	1.4.1
		1.4.2	1.4.2
		1.4.3	1.4.3
	1.5	1.5.1	1.5.1
		1.5.2	1.5.2
		1.5.3	1.5.3

PROBLEM NO.	ALTERNATIVE SOLUTIONS	MAIN ADVANTAGES	MAIN DISADVANTAGES
2.0	2.1	2.1.1	2.1.1
		2.1.2	2.1.2
		2.1.3	2.1.3
	2.2	2.2.1	2.2.1
		2.2.2	2.2.2
		2.2.3	2.2.3
	2.3	2.3.1	2.3.1
		2.3.2	2.3.2
		2.3.3	2.3.3
	2.4	2.4.1	2.4.1
		2.4.2	2.4.2
		2.4.3	2.4.3
	2.5	2.5.1	2.5.1
		2.5.2	2.5.2
		2.5.3	2.5.3

PROBLEM NO.	ALTERNATIVE SOLUTIONS	MAIN ADVANTAGES	MAIN DISADVANTAGES
3.0	3.1	3.1.1	3.1.1
		3.1.2	3.1.2
		3.1.3	3.1.3
	3.2	3.2.1	3.2.1
		3.2.2	3.2.2
		3.2.3	3.2.3
	3.3	3.3.1	3.3.1
		3.3.2	3.3.2
		3.3.3	3.3.3
	3.4	3.4.1	3.4.1
		3.4.2	3.4.2
		3.4.3	3.4.3
	3.5	3.5.1	3.5.1
		3.5.2	3.5.2
		3.5.3	3.5.3

(d) The advantage of deciding broad aims before doing problem analysis is that you have the vision of your mission statement behind you, and are not held back by problems which upon subsequent analysis may turn out to be relatively minor.

Step 3.4. Identify and analyse major problems. Develop and analyse alternative solutions. Discuss with colleagues

3.4 You should now **identify all the problems first** and **then decide** which of these are **relatively minor and which are major**. Generally speaking your tactical plan will address the more minor, short term problems, whilst your strategic plan will focus upon the more major, long-term problems.

(a) Having identified the major problems you must not immediately jump to ill-thought out solutions. The more responsible and managerial approach is to generate alternative solutions and then to evaluate each solution by examining its advantages and disadvantages, in order to arrive at the best selection.

(b) A format for doing this is given on the previous page and it is suggested you set yourself the task of analysing the six most important problems in this way, as a minimum. You should, of course, discuss your results with colleagues and be prepared to change your stance, given sufficient logical argument.

(c) One way in which to decide which are the most major problems is to ask yourself **'Which of these problems most stands in the way of the achievement of my broad aims?'**

Step 3.5. Develop quantified and timescaled objectives. Discuss with colleagues

3.5 Although modern marketing management must allow for some objectives which at first sight may be judged as qualitative, they should, if worked at, be capable of measurement over time. The hard business approach is that unless an objective can be measured over time, there is no accountability and no management objective, only a delusion.

(a) The case study is difficult enough without making a rod for your own back unnecessarily. So choose your objectives carefully and do not parade too many in your answer.

(b) **Remember that for each objective you need at least one strategy and for each strategy you need a set of tactics, a budget and a schedule.** It is better to stick to key or main objectives and (only if you must) then use the subterfuge of sub-objectives to avoid over-complicating your plan.

(c) Many people get confused between corporate objectives and marketing objectives, also between objectives and strategies, which is not surprising since most authors seem themselves confused or are at least incapable of writing clear differentiations.

(d) It may help you to assume that corporate objectives are usually concerned with profitability, growth and risk reduction and to realise that all the functions are deployed strategically towards achieving these objectives. The table below shows the level. The difference between strategy and tactics is one of detail and where you are looking from.

CORPORATE OBJECTIVES (SETTING)

Profitability	ROCE increase
Growth	Turnover, size, prestige
Risk reduction	Increase product base, customer base, market base

FUNCTIONAL OBJECTIVES ARE CORPORATE STRATEGIES

How is the marketing function deployed to meet corporate objectives? (Ask the same of production, finance and personnel functions.)

Say the **marketing objective** is to increase market share from X% to Y% by end of 19X9.

How is this done?
Devise a strategy

- new products
- new customers

These become the objectives for the following.

- New product development manager, to introduce 'N' new products by ....
- Sales manager, to obtain 'N' new customers by ....

TACTICS ARE DETAILS

Advertising objective	=	To increase awareness from X to Y by ....
Strategy	=	Press
Tactics	=	Mirror, Times, 1 page black and white once monthly

Step 3.6. Consider alternative strategies and select those most appropriate. Discuss with colleagues

3.6 Please bear in mind the work 'select' and do not try to pursue every available strategy. Good marketing management is about strategic choice.

(a) Your starting point should be **Ansoff.** Leaving aside diversification for the moment, since this would normally involve corporate management, you need to ask yourself the following questions.

(i) Is the current market saturated, or is there room for greater market penetration?
(ii) What opportunities are there for product development?
(iii) What are the possibilities for market development?

(b) The basic Ansoff analysis should of course be expanded to define which new products and which new markets should be developed and then into more detail such as:

- Product modification
- Re-packaging
- Market segments
- Niche markets
- Positioning

(c) Your strategic choices should also be advised by **competitor analysis.**

4 STAGE 4: DEVELOPING YOUR PLANS

Step 4.1. Draw up detailed tactical plans covering the marketing mix. Discuss with colleagues

4.1 Although some of the broader marketing mix decisions such as pull or push promotional policy, skimming or penetration pricing, overseas market entry etc, are quite rightly seen as strategic decisions by some authors, **for the sake of simplicity we are treating the marketing mix plans here as tactical.**

(a) In the case study answers we may need to go into the tactical detail. If you wish, you can in your marketing mix plans distinguish by headings between promotional strategy and promotional tactics, pricing strategy and pricing tactics and so on, but as was said earlier the distinction depends to some extent upon the level from which you are looking and you are likely to be placed in a more senior role than that of a manager of an element of a marketing mix (such as advertising manager, or sales promotion manager).

(b) To help you in drawing up your detailed marketing mix plans, you will find a reminder of the normal types of decisions and considerations you need to identify, under each of the 4 P's, on the following page. **Since case situations can cover services rather than products, you should consider the '7 P' approach to the marketing services, namely the 4Ps plus the extra 3 Ps of People, Process, and Physical evidence.** These are described in Chapter 1.

(c) You should also look back to Chapter 1 Paragraph 4.30 for the general purpose screening model for new products. Also go back to Chapter 2 Paragraph 3.4 for the elements of the **promotional submix** (eg the mix elements for advertising, personal selling, sales promotion and PR).

(d) Screening sometimes crops up in exam questions and many students seem to lack knowledge of this important process. Screening of new product/service ideas or concepts can be seen as both part of the new product development plan and part of the marketing research process.

Step 4.2. Draw up a marketing research plan and MkIS (marketing information system)

4.2 **Marketing research** is usually dealt with separately by most authors since it does not easily fit into the standard planning outline of objectives, strategy and tactics.

(a) **Marketing research is, however, key to all the planning stages.**

(i) It is needed for the adequate audit of the marketing environment prior to the formation of objectives. Internal data is used together with competitor information and market information when deciding objectives.

(ii) Marketing research is also necessary to decide strategy (eg which new products and/or which new markets?).

(iii) Finally, marketing research should be employed to decide the best marketing mix for given market segments and to check on the progress of the plan in achieving the objectives.

(b) Because of its pervasive importance to marketing planning, marketing research (research into all aspects of marketing) often forms the basis of at least one of the examination questions.

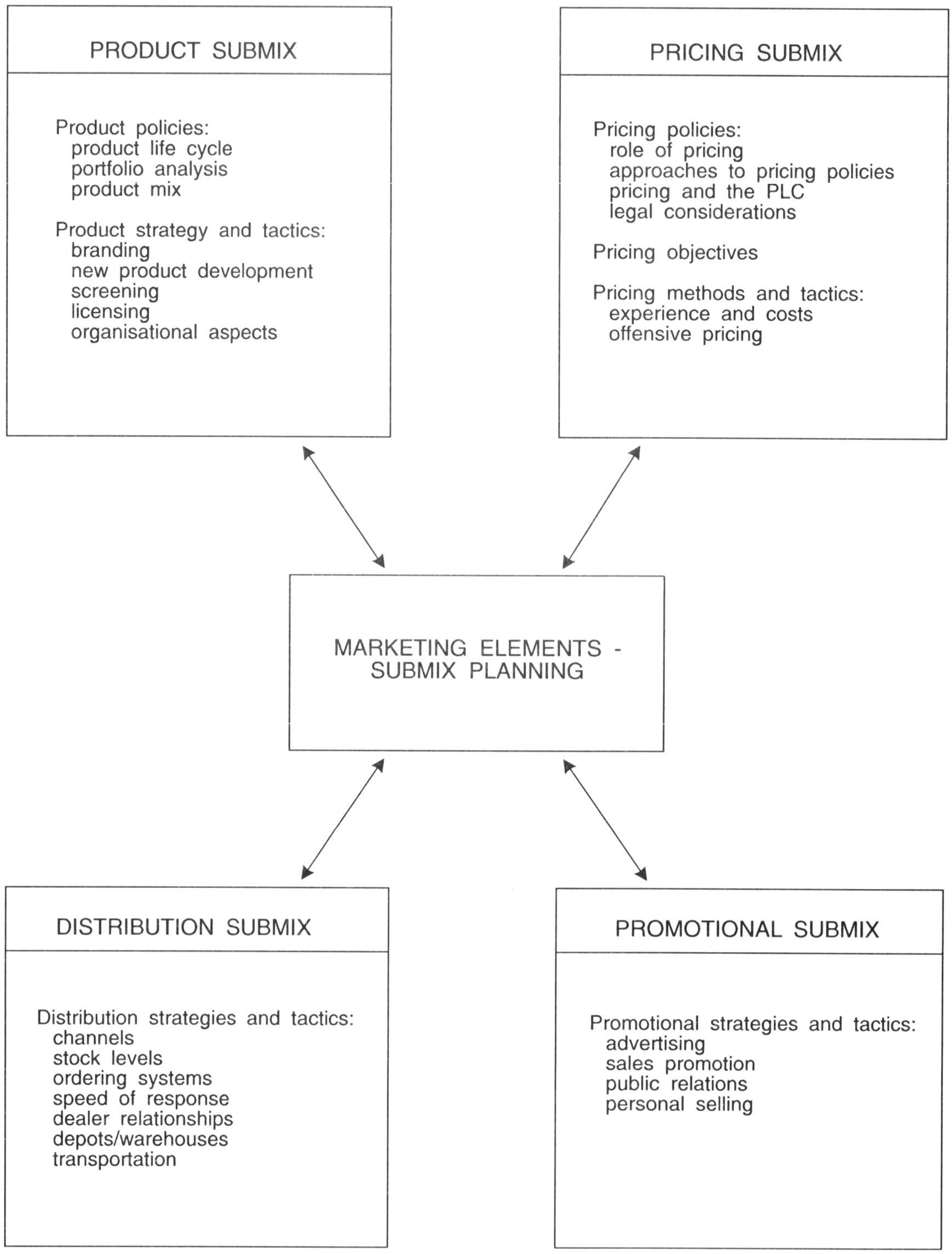

(i) This can be in the form of an information specification eg 'what information is needed in order to determine the best means of entry into mainland Europe?' or an outline marketing research plan itself.

(ii) Occasionally you will be asked to differentiate between information needed for a particular project or sub-plan and that which should be ongoing and part of the company's MkIS (marketing information system).

(iii) You also need to distinguish between:

(1) The detailed information sought (ie the information specification, by type (product, market etc)

(2) The method used (postal questionnaire, personal interview etc)

(c) To help you with drawing up this sub-plan within your total marketing plan, a typical format is given below.

OUTLINE OF A MARKETING RESEARCH PLAN

(a) Research objectives.

(b) The information specification.

(c) Research methods - survey design - desk research, field research (postal, telephone, personal visit, observations).

(d) Questionnaire design - drafting, pilot testing.

(e) Respondent selection - sample size, sample frame, characteristics.

(f) Timing considerations - survey, report, decisions.

(g) Briefings - in-house and/or agencies.

(h) Analysis - method, staff.

(i) Report - format, writer, readers.

(j) Budget - costs of each plan element.

(k) Contingency - for overspend, delays, faults etc.

Step 4.3. Consider organisational issues and make recommendations for changes towards complete marketing orientation as felt necessary. Discuss with colleagues

4.3 You need to remember that the CIM case study is a test of all your marketing knowledge gained in previous studies. Here is a checklist.

(a) To what extent has this organisation adopted the marketing concept?

(b) Do all functions in the company (not just marketing) accept the idea of customer sovereignty?

(c) To what extent does the company work together to satisfy customer needs?

(d) Is the marketing function on an equal footing alongside the other functions in the organisation or is it organisationally subservient?

(e) Is adequate marketing research being conducted to keep the organisation fully in touch with changing customer needs?

(f) Is the organisation structure flexible enough to respond to changing customer needs?

(g) To what extent does the marketing organisation reflect the importance of critical success factors in the particular market (such as in retail marketing - packaging, merchandising, point-of-sale)?

(h) Would the organisation benefit from a matrix approach?

(i) To what extent might brand managers, product managers or market managers be appropriate?

(j) Is the salesforce organisation properly aligned to customer buying behaviour, market segmentation etc?

By the use of these and other questions you might be able to identify ways in which the company could make organisational changes to gain greater competitive advantage and reap dividends in terms of increased sales and repeat business.

Step 4.4. Consider the organisation's culture and make recommendations for internal marketing programmes as felt necessary. Discuss with colleagues

4.4 This step is closely related to the previous one and both steps have been tested recently in examinations, so it would pay you to read up on marketing orientation, internal marketing (under TQM) customer care and relationship marketing. Any organisation can make cosmetic alterations, for example changing the title of the sales manager to sales and marketing manager but these do not themselves result in full marketing orientation. A change of culture will require total commitment from the top and often take several years of careful internal marketing planning and training.

Step 4.5. Consider the financial and human resource implications of your plans/recommendations. Discuss with colleagues

4.5 In order to work effectively within the corporate team marketing managers and directors need to understand the basics of return on investment, cashflow and risk. They also require to be able to interpret a balance sheet and profit and loss account, at least as well as production and personnel managers.

(a) The definition of marketing by the CIM ends with the word 'profitably'. No longer can marketers go on spending money in the hope of increasing market share without recognising the importance of a return on investment and that other projects within the company might return more profit at a lower risk and within a shorter period.

(b) The CIM has made it clear that future members will need to provide evidence of financial literacy and that financial acumen will be tested in the case study. **As a minimum you will be expected to show the anticipated results of your proposals in terms of revenues, costs and gross margins.** Hopefully you would also be able to demonstrate an understanding of how your plans might increase tensions on cashflow, affect rates of stockturn, require capital injections etc. A checklist of financial implications is given below for your convenience.

FINANCIAL IMPLICATIONS CHECKLIST	
Capital investment	Stock
Risk	Liquidity
Revenue	Depreciation
Profit, profitability, break-even	Forecasting
Working capital	Budgets
Cash flow	Financial planning/organisation
ROI/ROCE	Financial control
Creditors/debtors	Costs-staffing etc

(c) Equally you need to be able to show an appreciation of the **human resource implications** of your plans.

(i) Every proposed action will require time by people, time that may not be available. Proposed actions may demand from people skills or knowledge which they do not have.

(ii) Recruitment and training not only cost money but also take time and may not have the desired result. For every basic salary there are considerable related employment costs.

(iii) Changes in personnel have knock-on effects and may adversely affect team spirit and company culture. When proposing action you should at least indicate who is involved in taking it and who will monitor or control results.

Step 4.6. Assess costs and draw up indicative budgets. Discuss with colleagues

4.6 Within the four weeks time available to study the case, it should be relatively easy for marketers to acquire rough costs for advertising, market research, salaries, training etc.

(a) You are not expected to be accurate beyond a 'ball park' figure. For example, it does not matter too much whether you indicate a cost of £1,000 or £1,500 per group discussion in a marketing research plan (they vary anyway) as long as you don't show £100 or £10,000.

(b) The examiner does, however, expect you to have some knowledge of how to construct a marketing budget. Candidates who quote a total promotional budget of £100,000 appear to have plucked this out of the air. If this was supposed to cover everything from a series of exhibitions to an extensive TV advertising campaign they would reveal their ignorance. Far better to show the examiner that you know how this figure is built up viz:

	£'000	£'000	£'000
Literature	6		
Reps display materials	22		
Exhibitions	60		
Trade advertising	12		
		100	
Contingency reserve at 10%		10	
			110

(c) Or if this were an advertising budget

	£'000	£'000	£'000
Local radio	10		
TV	-		
Press*	82		
Cinema	-		
Poster	8		
		100	
Contingency reserve at 10%		10	
			110

* Monthly 1 page black and white advertisements in the Daily Dozen (£42,000), and quarterly full page adverts in the Monthly Review (£40,000).

(d) The typical contents of marketing budgets are given in Chapter 1, paragraph 3.53.

Step 4.7. Draw up schedules showing the timing/sequence of your plans/ recommendations. Discuss with colleagues

4.7 Far too many candidates lose valuable marks by failing to schedule their proposals. Others simply put timings such as X = 6 months, Y = 3 months, Z = 1 year, without indicating their sequence. The easiest and quickest way to indicate schedules in the examination is by means of a Gantt chart similar to that shown below, which enables you to display and schedule activities, which are relatively short-term along with others which are ongoing.

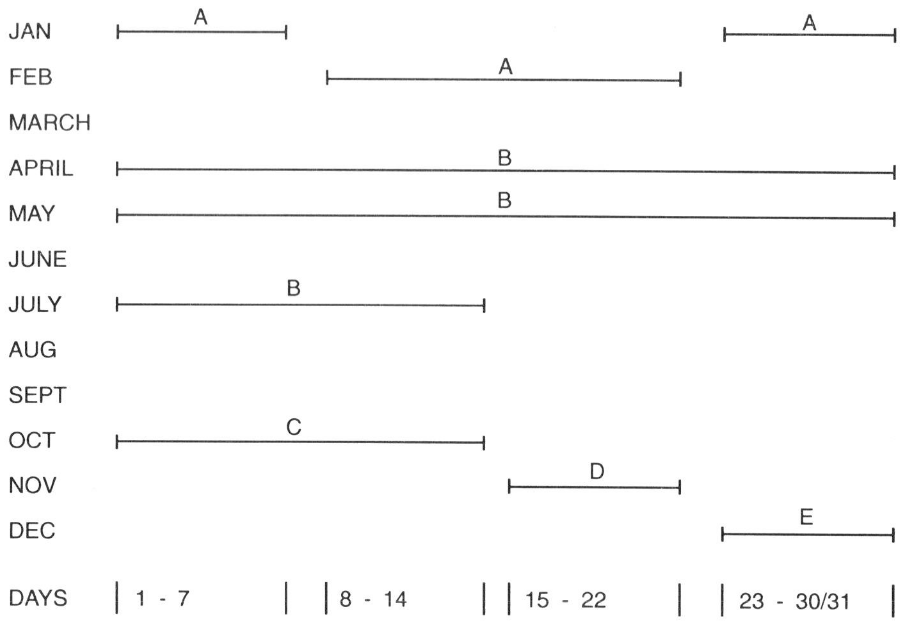

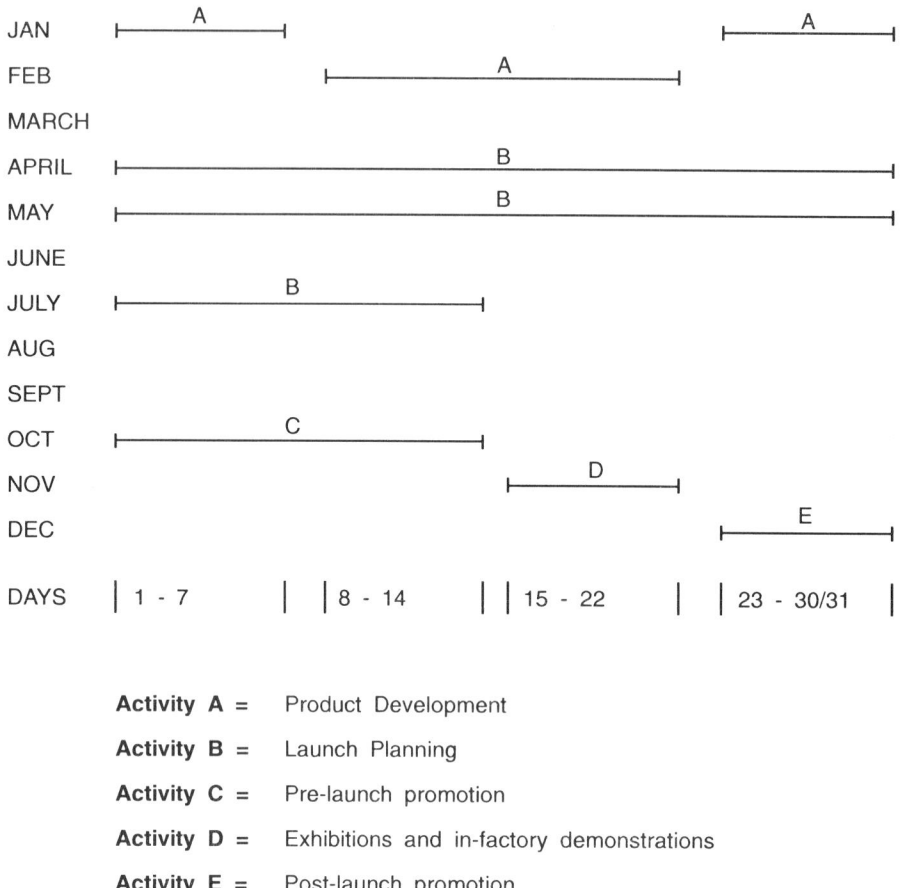

Activity A = Product Development

Activity B = Launch Planning

Activity C = Pre-launch promotion

Activity D = Exhibitions and in-factory demonstrations

Activity E = Post-launch promotion

5 STAGE 5: CONTROL AND CONTINGENCIES

Step 5.1. Specify review procedures and control mechanisms. Discuss with colleagues

5.1 Students' performance is generally weak in this area. Relevant material is covered in Chapter 1 of this text. If you excel here, this might identify you as a distinction grade graduate. It is not enough to simply list items such as budgets, meetings, ratio analysis. You need to indicate clearly which budgets are used, which parts of the management accounting system are involved; which people should attend the meetings, when and for what purpose; and which particular ratios are important and so on.

Step 5.2. Outline contingency plans. Discuss with colleagues

5.2 The CIM examiner reserves the right to introduce extra material into the actual examination paper. Since this right is not always exercised in recent examinations it is as well to think through this contingency.

(a) What sorts of extra information might you, if you were the examiner yourself, introduce? Bear in mind this would have to be modest, fair and not over-demanding.

(b) You should additionally consider one or two 'what if' scenarios which you could cover with an outline contingency plan in your standard answers. For example, what if the EU introduced new competition rules on mail services?

(c) Good modern planning includes contingency planning and you need to show in a modest way that you have covered this in your thinking.

Step 5.3. Review your complete marketing plan

5.3 Does it fit together? Is it consistent? Does it cover everything? Which are the areas of weakness? Can you improve it?

6 STAGE 6: THE EXAMINATION

Step 6.1. Draw up your examination plan

6.1 Now you are satisfied that your marketing plan is complete and satisfactory, it would be a sad folly if you had gone through all that effort simply to fail because of lack of examination technique and planning.

(a) Examination planning should cover everything you need to do between now and when you finally put your pen down as the invigilator calls time in the examination hall.

(b) Many hardworking and clever people fail through lack of examination technique. This aspect is so important that it has been given a chapter to itself (Chapter 10). Please be sure to study it carefully and take the necessary action.

Step 6.2. Practise writing in true report style

6.2 Most of us have been conditioned at school, college and/or university to write essays for both assignments and examinations. However, essays are not the stuff of business communications.

(a) Business needs succinct, clear reports which take the minimum of time to assimilate, rather than elegant but wordy prose. Many candidates are unclear about what true business report style is, simply because they have not received any tuition during studies or training in this aspect.

(b) Marketing managers need to be able to produce good business reports for their colleagues and seniors. You must demonstrate this ability in order to gain the CIM Diploma. Furthermore, you will find it is almost impossible to cover all the points you need to make when answering the case study questions, within the time available, when writing in essay style. So get some practice done. You will find further details on report style in Chapter 10.

Chapter roundup

- You have now reviewed the CIM examiner's recommended method.
- It covers everything from your mental state as you read the study from the first time to writing reports at the end.
- Help yourself succeed, and follow the method.

9 Adopting The Role And Creating The Plan

This chapter covers the following topics.

1 Syndicates

2 Personalities and teamwork

Introduction

This is a guide to working in groups. There are benefits to be had from sharing insights.

1 SYNDICATES

1.1 This relatively short section is really aimed at getting the best out of syndicate work.

(a) Syndicates are an ideal way of enlarging individual perspectives, moderating excesses and producing results in more detail and of a higher quality than could normally be achieved by any individual working alone.

(b) These benefits depend on the collective ability of the members of the syndicate to work as a team, to agree on a division of labour for the more menial and time consuming tasks, and, above all, to be organised and disciplined.

1.2 First of all, an individual syndicate member can adopt the role of **devil's advocate**, deliberately taking an opposing view to test the syndicate's logic. The role of devil's advocate can be adopted by each individual in turn, as can the adoption of the role specified in the candidates' brief. Other syndicate members can in discussion, adopt the role of the person reported to, the managing director, the financial director and so forth.

1.3 For maximum effectiveness a syndicate should elect a **chairperson**, for each session, and a **spokesperson**. Again these two roles should be passed round in turn.

(a) **The chairperson's job**

(i) Ensure the task is completed on time
(ii) Maintain order
(iii) Arbitrate in the case of a dispute

It is not to steamroller his or her views on the syndicate.

(b) Likewise, the **spokesperson's** job is to relay the syndicate's views objectively to the plenary assembly, not his or her own personal views.

1.4 **Groups**

(a) There are occasions when the syndicate should work together (eg on the **mission statement**).

(b) At other times, individuals should work entirely on their own (eg **on the précis**)

(c) Sometimes the syndicate of eight persons, say, for example might be advised to split into four pairs to work on the SWOT analysis for example. One pair could work on strengths, another on weaknesses, a third on opportunities and the fourth on threats. Very little is lost as a result, and a great deal is gained in the amount of items gathered. The team would, of course, come together to amalgamate their work at the end of the session.

1.5 **Writing up**

Many syndicates leave the write-up for the presentation of their work to the very last minute and therefore often do not do themselves justice as a result. **It is strongly recommended that writing up is done as you go along** and this is particularly important when producing overhead projection transparencies.

1.6 Syndicates can also benefit by organising 'swap shops', between syndicate groups, to exchange work. This helps to avoid excessive note-taking during plenary sessions when all come together and encourages maximum debate.

1.7 Extra work outside course hours can also be conducted voluntarily within the syndicates. Alternatively, special assignments suggested by the case study tutor, can be accepted as extra workload.

1.8 Work allocated to syndicates can play to each syndicate's strengths, as can work shared among syndicate members. If a given syndicate contains a large number of people in marketing communications, it might be allocated the task of producing a promotional plan. If within a syndicate there is a person from an accounting background he or she might be asked to analyse the appendix containing the accounts.

1.9 This is not to absolve **individuals** from creating their own personal plans, but merely to make best use of limited syndicate and plenary group time. Individuals can and should sit in critical judgement of other people's contributions, accepting the best, rejecting the poorer and adding their own contributions.

1.10 **Remember that while you can prepare with others, the exam is a test of individual, not group ability.**

2 PERSONALITIES AND TEAMWORK

2.1 Syndicate members will get the best out of their team if they pull together, retain a sense of humour and recognise the value of interplay between personalities. Individuals should endeavour to categorise themselves eg as being too dominant or too quiet and attempt to overcome these faults in their own and the group's interests.

2.2 The following categorisation is offered for self-analysis and with the tiniest pinch of salt.

(a) The **Jumper**. Usually better qualified than the average, this person knows the best solutions instantly and feels that the development of alternative solutions and the weighing up of each solution's advantages/disadvantages before making a choice is a menial task suited to his or her less well qualified colleagues but unnecessary for someone of his or her acumen. 'It's obvious' is the catchphrase, delivered with thinly disguised scorn for those people who cannot see the argument (including the tutor). This person is impatient, quick-thinking and finishes the job in half the time, making other team members feel that it is they who are doing something wrong.

(b) The **Sitter**. This person finds it difficult to come to a decision and sits on the fence equivocating brilliantly on both sides. He or she seems to forget that the subject examined is 'Analysis and **Decision**'.

(c) The **Xerox**. With no strong personal views and no real inclination to hard work, this person copies other people's ideas - unfortunately often those of the Jumper. The Xerox is caught out by the exam questions which puts a slightly different slant on the matter and blindly copies out the pre-prepared answer notwithstanding.

(d) A **Tree** never sees the wood. This person tends to receive the case and plunge into analysis of all tables to the nth degree with calculator smoking. This person works hard and is extremely difficult to beat in discussion since he or she can bring more and more data to bear on the question, endlessly splitting hairs, crossing t's and dotting i's. This person can pass with honours if only he or she would sit back and review objectively what it is he or she is really trying to achieve.

(e) A **Blinker** sees things only from his or her narrow experience. This person tends to have one textbook approach for all situations, and adamantly sticks to this in face of all opposition or evidence to the contrary. This person worships Kotler, or Baker, or Smallbone, or Levitt, and apart from this one, all other authors are idiots not worth reading. Favourite catchphrases are 'I once knew a company which ...' and 'the company I once worked for (usually the Post Office as a Christmas temp) do it this way'. A favourite examination technique is to write out whatever pre-prepared views he or she has on the world, irrespective of the actual exam question or, for that matter, the case study.

Chapter roundup

- This chapter has endeavoured to give you some advice as to how to relate to your colleagues in the syndicates, and how you can get the most out of group work.

Part D

Examination techniques: planning your examination

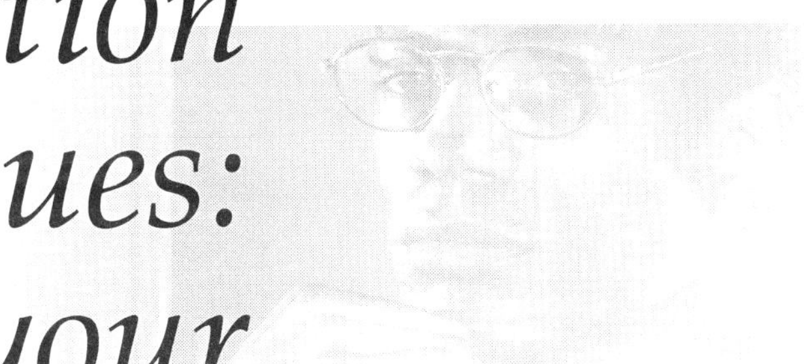

10 Examination Techniques: Planning Your Examination

This chapter covers the following topics.

Introduction

The most thorough preparation beforehand will be wasted if your exam technique is poor. So don't spoil your chances by panic or a lack of foresight.

1 PREPARING FOR THE EXAMINATION DAY

1.1 As a professional marketing manager you should possess two attributes, namely to be able to:

- **Visualise** the future
- **Organise** for it

Please apply these two attributes to preparing for your examination.

1.2 If you are typical of most candidates, **you will have amassed a great deal of paperwork** comprising your analysis and your complete marketing plan.

1.3 What you do now is to reduce it to manageable proportions. None of us likes to throw away the results of our hard work, but you can at least **produce neat, concise summary sheets of each section**. Relegate the remainder to the status of back-up detail, to be consulted and used only if needed. All your work should be placed in an A4 ring binder and indexed for quick and easy access. The best way to index it is to use the framework for your marketing plan since this is the most logical and practical access system for your exam and you are already familiar with it.

1.4 An outline for your index is suggested overleaf but however you organise your ring binder, be familiar with it. **Know exactly where everything is and how to locate it quickly**.

EXAMINATION RING BINDER INDEX: SUGGESTED FORMAT

(a) Analysis

- (i) Précis
- (ii) Marketing audit
- (iii) SWOT analysis
- (iv) Appendix analysis
- (v) Situational analysis
- (vi) Problem analysis
- (vii) Key issues

(b) Mission statement/broad aims

(c) Objectives

(d) Strategies

(e) Tactics/marketing mix

- (i) Product/service plan, packaging
- (ii) Pricing
- (iii) Promotion
  - (1) Advertising
  - (2) Sales promotion
  - (3) Selling
  - (4) PR
- (iv) Place - Distribution
- (v) People
- (vi) Process
- (vii) Physical evidence

(f) Organisation/internal marketing

(g) Budgets/financial and human resources

(h) Scheduling

(i) Control

(j) Contingencies

(k) Ready reckoner (see Paragraph 1.12)

1.5 You will need at least 42 hours to apply the 6 Stage approach recommended in this text to the actual examination case. You have about four weeks to do this; let us say this works out at 12 hours a week. You must find the time and plan it out properly.

1.6 **Take a copy of the case study** - ideally you should enlarge this from A5 size pages to A4 to allow you space to make notes.

1.7 The principles of marketing planning and control should also be applied to your examination scripts. In the Chartered Institute of Marketing's (CIM) major case study examination there are usually three or four questions each scoring a different percentage of marks eg 20%, 30%, 50%, or 15%, 15%, 30%, 40%. Your time needs to be apportioned accordingly.

1.8 A spatial control as well as a temporal control is recommended. How long does it take you to write an A4 page, legibly in essay style and report style? Make allowances for fatigue setting in part way through a three hour paper. For example, you may find you can write a legible A4 page in essay style, in ten minutes, when you are fresh but this increases to twelve minutes when fatigued. The figures for report style become five minutes and six minutes respectively.

1.9 You can now **calculate the number of pages** you should target for any given question (after deducting thinking and planning time) and pencil in a 'spatial control' on your script paper. A three part report for 30% of the market might be allocated a total time of 50 minutes, of which 15 minutes is allocated to thinking and planning, and five minutes for checking what you have written. This leaves 30 minutes for report style writing when fresh, which equals six pages or two pages for each section of your report.

1.10 This sort of planning can of course be conducted before you enter the examination hall to avoid unnecessary waste of precious examination time.

1.11 In the examination room itself, use the following 'ready reckoner' to quickly allocate time proportionately to question marks. Have a copy of this ready reckoner handy in your ring binder and indexed.

1.12 This table shows how many minutes to allocate to each question in a three hour exam, based on the number of marks per question.

Marks	Minutes
5	9
10	18
15	27
20	36
25	45
30	54
35	63
40	72
45	81
50	90
55	99
60	108
65	117
70	126
75	135
80	144
85	153
90	162
95	171
100	180

1.13 Think through and prepare your ancillary equipment for the examination.

(a) Your **exam entry documentation.**

(b) **Pens and pencils, pencil sharpener.**

(c) **Calculator**. Your calculator needs to be silent and should not require mains electricity. You are not likely to need it if you have thoroughly prepared your analysis, but take one in case.

(d) **Rubber/White 'Tippex' fluid.**

(e) Stencils for drawing organisation charts, boxes, or anything that may help you to save time as well as being neat. If you pre-prepare charts do them in black ink on a white background and on an A4 sheet. If you slide these behind your CIM exam script paper you will find they show through sufficiently well for you to copy neatly in double quick time.

(f) Blanks of charts - organisation, Gantt schedules, graphs, pie charts etc in black ink on white paper.

(g) Ruler

(h) The case study itself

(i) Indexed ring binder

(j) Sweets?

(k) Watch/clock

(l) **Marketing text book**. Although you will not have time in the exam to keep looking things up, it is as well to take this tutorial text with you as an insurance policy. Be reasonably familiar with its index and layout.

1.14 Check where the examination centre is and estimate how long it will take you to get there. Allow for contingencies like traffic and parking delays. **You will not be allowed into the exam hall more than 15 minutes after the start.**

1.15 Plan to get there early so that you do not put undue pressure on yourself.

1.16 Plan to get to bed early the night before the examination day and to dress comfortably for the weather.

1.17 Remember that space (ie the desktop and around the desk) will probably be extremely limited.

2 REPORT FORMAT

2.1 **Report style is always mandatory** for the major case study, and is often mandatory or recommended for the mini-case studies as far as the CIM is concerned. You are being examined in Marketing Management and busy managers do not thank you for wasting their time by using too many words to get to the point in essay format, when report format will convey information not only more quickly but more clearly. The use of charts of diagrams is also recommended wherever possible.

2.2 Many of the questions related to planning will require costing and activity scheduling in the answers to score good marks.

2.3 Many candidates are unclear about report style and use a quasi-report style which is really an essay split into sections under headings rather than true report style. Here are a couple of examples. The sections addressed by each relates to the criteria on whether to launch product A.

Quasi-report style: WRONG

'The first criterion is whether this will be profitable over the estimated life cycle of product A. Another criterion which is related to the first criterion is that of estimated volume sales at the proposed price. A third criterion which needs to be considered when deciding whether or not to launch Product A is....'

Report style: RIGHT

> (a) Decision criteria in rank order
>
> (i) Profit (ROI) over product life cycle
> (ii) Sales volume at proposed price
> (iii) ...

Question structure

2.4 Try to structure your answers in the same way in which the question is structured so that there is no doubt as to which parts of your report relate to which parts of the question. An example of how to do this against the *Leffe* Case paper follows.

Example

2.5

> Based on the data you have collected and further consultations with Interbrew and various customers, you have decided to approach the strategic marketing presentation in three parts.
>
> Your presentation, *in report format*, will cover the following:
>
> 1 Propose a clear position for Leffe in the UK market. Describe the rationale behind your decision and explain the brand attributes and values that will be required to establish Leffe as a unique offering against the competition.
>
> 2 Produce a strategic marketing plan for Leffe. Your plan should explain how you will achieve the positioning proposed for the brand by 2005. The plan should include all aspects of the marketing activity except promotional plans (see question 3).
>
> 3 Based on market position and strategic marketing plans for Leffe, produce a strategic promotional plan for the Leffe brand. This plan will form the basis of a subsequent presentation to Interbrew and should cover the next ten years of Leffe's development in the UK market.

2.6 A specimen layout of the report asked for in 2.5 is given below

> LEFFE
>
> FROM: James Burgess
>
> SUBJECT: Presentation on the strategic marketing of Leffe for the divisional board meeting
>
> DATE: December 2000
>
> CONTENTS
>
> (a) *Positioning*
>
> (i) Proposed positioning for Leffe in the UK market
> (ii) Rationale for proposition
> (iii) Brand attributes and values required
>
> (b) Strategic marketing plan (excluding promotional plans)
> (i) Environmental analysis
> (ii) Marketing objectives
> (iii) Marketing strategy
> (iv) Marketing mix programmes (excluding promotion)
> (v) Budgets and controls
>
> (c) Strategic promotional plan
>
> (i) Promotional objectives
> (ii) Promotional strategies
> (iii) Promotional mix
> (iv) Promotional budgets and controls

Succinct writing

2.7 Practice writing succinctly. Critically review your own wording. In fact 'staccato' style is often more appropriate than long sentences.

Example

2.8 Consider the following actual extract from an exam script submitted for a past exam paper.

> (a) Proposals for change in the organisational structure.
>
> (b) Creation of 'strategic business units' centred around each terminal
>
> This would allow each terminal to be represented at board level with each managers having his own operational and commercial staff beneath him. This will involve a huge restructuring of the organisation and individual job roles/responsibilities, however this move is necessary in order that commercial and operations staff work alongside each other and cooperate to solve problems in the most effective way, to the benefit of EAL in serving the needs of its customers. All commercial versus operations conflicts would be solved lower down the hierarchy which will in turn be flattened out as a result of restructuring. Each terminal general manager must have beneath him his appropriate support staff for his commercial and operations roles eg catering manager, retail operations manager, quality control engineers.'
>
> Total words = c 140
>
> Total time = 8 minutes

2.9 Keeping the same heading we might change the section to read as follows.

> Each terminal to become an SBU under a general manager with his own support staff (catering, retail operations, quality control etc).
>
> BENEFIT
>
> Although requiring much restructuring and reformulation of job descriptions:
>
> (a) commercial and operations staff would work together in meeting the needs of the customer;
> (b) all commercial v operations conflicts would be solved lower down the hierarchy;
> (c) each terminal would be represented at board level.
>
> Total words = c 70
>
> Total time = 4 minutes

2.10 Quite apart from the re-wording which **cuts the original word length in half,** it is **easier to understand and mark.** If this saving was replicated throughout the paper there would be at least an extra hour to make extra points and gain extra marks.

2.11 You really do owe it to yourself to work at this if you are the sort of person who writes 'quasi-essays' instead of reports. Not only will you be much more likely to pass the examination but you will also become a more effective communicator for your company.

3 EXAMINATION DAY

3.1 Hopefully, you will have gone to bed the previous evening, risen early, gone through your normal ablutions and breakfast routine and are now feeling organised.

3.2 Check through your exam kit once more and pack it in your brief case if you have not already done so.

3.3 Allow yourself the luxury of a short walk round the block to clear your head and make you feel good.

3.4 Psychology is important. Tell yourself that you are well prepared, you are intelligent, you have a track record of success. Look forward to performing well.

3.5 Try not to feel nervous (although some nerves are normal and can enhance performance). Remember that the examiners want you to pass - all you have to do is to give them sufficient excuse.

3.6 In your mind's eye, imagine yourself in the exam room. Imagine yourself sitting there calm and organised whilst others are fussing about, all 'uptight'. Don't feel intimidated if you see other examinees entering the hall with the equivalent of the Encyclopaedia Brittanica as their case ring binder. Instead, anticipate a glow of satisfaction and superiority once the exam has started and you can see and hear the endless shuffling of mountains of paper.

3.7 Always make it a point of honour not to be the first to start writing. Do all your thinking up front. Plan your answers. Make sure you have read the questions properly and understood them and any instructions.

3.8 Plan your time and stick to it. Allow adequate time for checking. If you have really thought through and planned your answers thoroughly, all the hard work is done. You know you will pass. All you need to do now is to put the flesh on the bones.

4 WHAT NOT TO DO

4.1 **Please do not**:

(a) Write out the questions

(b) Write a lead sheet for each section of the report (just do one at the beginning)

(c) Repeat information from the case (your reader will know this)

(d) Write lengthy introductions, current situations, executive summaries, background information or other time wasting waffle - get straight down to business

(e) Answer only part of the question (a good technique is to pencil in the key words in the question at the start of each answer and stick rigidly to these)

(f) Write endless assumptions

(g) Submit uncalled-for SWOT analyses

4.2 Hopefully you will find the following guide to examination failure both instructive and amusing.

HOW NOT TO PASS EXAMS
SOME KEY RULES

(a) Play it by ear	'Candidates don't plan to fail, they fail to plan'
(b) Don't revise	Do not have a revision plan either
(c) Aim to just pass	That way you won't waste effort
(d) Have no exam technique	Exams are bad enough without having to think about techniques
(e) Do not anticipate questions	You may get it wrong

(f)	Do not read previous papers or exam reports and avoid any student aids like the plague	*You're* no wimp
(g)	Just do the first five questions	They're all as bad anyway
(h)	Write what you want to say. Don't worry about the question	It's more interesting
(i)	Ignore instructions	They only put you off
(j)	Do not check the time	Whilst you're doing this you could write a few more words
(k)	Never check your answers	There'll only be a few minor errors
(l)	Always start with an introduction and finish with a summary	That way you can forget about the middle
(m)	When in doubt - waffle	It will probably con the marker into thinking you know what you're talking about.
(n)	Write illegibly, especially the words that really matter	The examiner will always give you the benefit of the doubt
(o)	Do not structure your answers when it is a multi-part question	Let them guess which part belongs to which - it's what they are paid for isn't it?
(p)	If it is a two-part paper do the last bit first	It shows initiative - makes you stand out from the crowd
(q)	Arrive late and leave early	What's a few minutes between friends
(r)	Be disorganised	You can always ask the invigilator if you can borrow his/her pen, and for the odd toilet break or two
(s)	Have just a little drink before the exam	It helps you to relax doesn't it?
(t)	Don't bother to put the question numbers down	Well it should be obvious shouldn't it and you never know your luck!
(u)	Tell the examiner what a hard life you've had and don't forget the good wishes for Christmas, Easter, the hols etc.	Should earn you a few 'Brownie points'. Well they're only human aren't they?

If all else fails - ignore the above - do not take any action, do not change your ways one iota.

Chapter roundup

- You have by now learned the Senior Examiner's recommended method to approach this paper, and you have revised some analytical techniques.
- You have also been instructed in exam technique. And, should you intend to fail, perhaps for the pleasure of retaking the case study, we have even told you how to manage that as well.
- Now it is time for you to practise some real cases.

Part E

Learning from experience: ensuring you pass

11 Introduction To Past Cases

This chapter covers the following topics.

1 Practice on previous cases

2 Your first steps

1 PRACTICE ON PREVIOUS CASES

1.1 There is no better way to prepare for your examination than to **practise on actual previous** case studies used for CIM exams. This means systematically analysing the case study using the methodology described in Chapters 8 and 9 and then tackling the actual exam questions set using the techniques given in Chapter 10.

1.2 You will then see for yourself how the methodology and techniques work to ensure you pass. This will build up your confidence and of course your expertise. It will help you to avoid making costly errors in the examination paper and to make best possible use of the limited time available.

1.3 To make it easier for you **we shall, after each stage of your analysis, give you examples of other students' analyses**. These are not necessarily the best examples or in any way perfect analyses but rather the sort of acceptable standard you would normally get from a syndicate working under pressure.

1.4 Remember there is **no one correct answer**. Different people interpret the same data in different ways. The purpose of the analysis is to widen your perspectives so as to better understand the case situation and to identify its key issues.

1.5 A good case study should, given competent and thorough analysis, **yield its key issues**. These key issues should normally be the basis on which the examination questions are set, so as to preserve the integrity of the case.

1.6 The first case study you are recommended to practise on is *Acclaim Entertainment Inc* as set for the CIM December 1999 examination and based upon the threats to a consumer gaming firm facing competition and technological change.

1.7 The first step is of course to read the case study which is presented on the following pages exactly how you would have received it through your letterbox about four weeks before the exam.

2 YOUR FIRST STEPS

2.1 You should now turn to Chapter 8 paragraphs 1.1 to 1.5 of this Tutorial Text for full details of how to conduct Stage 1 of the analysis:

- Read the case
- After an interval re-read the case
- Reflect on the instructions and candidates' brief
- Think yourself into the role and the situation
- Re-read the case and write a précis

(NB. Most students need between three and six hours to complete these steps.)

2.2 Good luck!

12 Acclaim Entertainment Inc: Case Study Documentation

This chapter includes the case study information sent to candidates.

INTRODUCTORY NOTE

(a) The first practice case is Acclaim, a company very much involved in the latest technological advances.

(b) The paragraph numbers here have been inserted by BPP for ease of reference. You are unlikely to find such a numbering system in the case itself.

(c) We will remind you of the essentials for each step/stage in panel form. Good luck.

CONSULT THE GUIDANCE NOTES FOR STAGE 1 IN CHAPTER 8 SECTION 1

STEP 1.1 READ THE CASE
STEP 1.2 AFTER AN INTERVAL, RE-READ THE CASE
STEP 1.3 REFLECT ON THE INSTRUCTIONS AND CANDIDATES' BRIEF
STEP 1.4 THINK YOURSELF INTO THE ROLE AND THE SITUATION
STEP 1.5 RE-READ THE CASE AND WRITE A PRÉCIS - IN NOT MORE THAN TWO A4 SIDES

1 CANDIDATE'S BRIEF

1.1 The games industry is a relatively new and growing sector of the market. You are **Sam Lee,** a marketing consultant who made his reputation in the audio and electronics market. You have been appointed by Acclaim Entertainment Inc to undertake the development of a marketing strategy for the future. Prior to an important meeting with the key directors, you have had the chance to prepare this report with key inputs from one of the directors. The report contains a comprehensive analysis of the state of the games industry and the company. At the end of the report are appendices relating to the main body of the text. You are aware that the company is keen to assess its marketing performance. At the meeting you will discuss the report and the directors are likely to ask you to prepare answers to some critical questions facing the company.

2 ACCLAIM ENTERTAINMENT INC: TEXT

The company

2.1 Acclaim Entertainment Inc was founded in 1987 and is incorporated in the State of Delaware. The company was formed by Gregory Fischbach, co-chairman of the board and chief executive officer. Fischbach was president of Activision, a publisher of entertainment software for computers and video games. His background is entertainment law and he left Activision to become president of RCA International, a record company owned by General Electric. His tenure lasted some eight months until RCA was sold to Bertelsmann (BMG). James Scoroposki discovered the computer and video games business as a buyer with the mass merchant retailer, Macy's. He established a sales representative company called Jaymar and his services were retained by Activision, where he met Gregory Fischbach. Their association was rekindled following Mr Fischbach's departure from RCA. At this stage, Mr Scoroposki advised Mr Fischbach that there was going to be a resurgence in video games, after a brief lull, following the demise of Atari. It would be led by Nintendo and as Mr Fischbach had forced a close relationship with Nintendo, he should secure a licensed publishers agreement from the hardware vendor. This signalled the birth of Acclaim Entertainment Inc.

2.2 Having managed to get Nintendo to agree to grant the licence to produce the software, Fischbach and Scoroposki combined their skills to develop Acclaim Entertainment Inc. Entrance to the North American and European markets was realised by licensing finished products from Japanese companies without overseas distribution and adapting them to appeal to western consumers.

The company revenues in the first two years were:

- 1987 $0.9m (from March-August – start-up year)
- 1988 $39.3m

The company then formed a shell corporation, publicly traded on Nasdaq.

2.3 It was soon apparent that the revenues which were derived from Nintendo only products were in danger of decline as Nintendo's market share in dedicated consoles was being eroded by Sega. Hardware vendors recognise that software sells hardware and key software franchises which are exclusive to a system provide competitive advantage. It is not therefore in the interests of a hardware vendor to encourage cross platform exploitation of a title which has the potential to establish itself as a brand.

2.4 Acclaim Entertainment Inc determined to walk a political tightrope, decided to publish on a competing platform without prejudicing the relationship from which Acclaim Entertainment Inc became the first multi-format publisher in the industry. Others swiftly followed suit, (see Figure 4).

2.5 As Acclaim Entertainment Inc was responsible to its shareholders, it felt that the revenue stream would be unnecessarily capped if it only sold Nintendo related products. Thus, around 1990, as a fully fledged games entertainment company, Acclaim Entertainment Inc was recording revenues of $141.5m, expanding its overseas operations by entering the European market, initially in Germany, followed by the UK (1991) and France (1992). These three territories represented more than 70% of international revenues, which accounted for 35-40% of global turnover. Mr Rod Cousens is directly responsible for the expansion of the European and international operations.

2.6 Initially the company's product strategy reflected the lifestyle of the audience, which was demographically weighted towards 12-16 year olds. During this period, the company's strategy was to acquire known licenses from motion pictures, TV programmes and coin-operated games, providing hits such as Terminator 2, Aliens, The Simpsons and WWF Wrestling. The company also recognised the influence of sports on the consumer and acquired the likes of the NFL, the NBA, the NHL and baseball icons.

2.7 As the hardware systems evolved the target audience broadened to cover the 16-25 year olds. At the same time, the systems began to attract a female audience. This shift became really noticeable in the 32-64-bit transition.

2.8 The company understood that:

(a) Acquiring licenses was a fashionable risk and there was no Intellectual Property Ownership therein.

(b) As hardware systems advanced, the ever changing audience was both susceptible to and sceptical of external licenses. This was largely dependent on the age of the consumer.

2.9 In order to mitigate against this dependency, Acclaim Entertainment Inc embarked on a strategy to create its own brands and has successfully introduced Turok, NFL Quarterback Club, All Star Baseball, Foresaken and Shadow Man amongst others into the market. At the same time it has been selectively and tactically picking up external licenses such as South Park to complement the product portfolio.

2.10 Some of these icons emanated from the acquisition of a comic book company, Valiant Comics, Now named Acclaim Entertainment Inc Comics, spawning Turok, Shadow Man and Armorines. The comic section also offers and alternative revenue stream from the publication and sales of strategy guides, in order to assist the consumer through the games. The company has also been able to exploit these brands in other sectors, such as the toy industry where Turok figures have been distributed under a licensing agreement with the toy company, Playmates.

2.11 In order to maximise the hardware potential, the company could no longer rely on its product source from external developers and set about acquiring the captive development studios Iguana in 1993, Sculptured Software and the UK developer Probe Entertainment in 1994. In addition to this, Acclaim Entertainment Inc built up an international advanced technology group and provided it with a motion capture studio in 1994, supporting the in-house development of studio initiative which was then consolidated as Acclaim Entertainment In Studios. This allowed the company, though its engineering resource, to create software tools, technologies and development engines from which games of high quality could be written, allowing ownership of the intellectual property or brand.

2.12 The company invests almost 20% of its revenue in product development, as it believes that internal development resourcing is critical in achieving competitive advantage on progressive hardware systems. The software market is highly receptive to certain genres of products such as sports, driving, action and role playing games. However, in order to achieve brand recognition and sustainability, the approach can be threefold:

- The use of Acclaim Entertainment Inc umbrella brand
- The use of Acclaim Entertainment Inc Sports genre and the NFL Quarterback Club
- The use of the title brand

Eventually, the success of a particular product will determine its status as a brand. If successful the product will yield series and sequels which can form the backbone of future release schedules.

2.13 Acclaim Entertainment Inc together with its subsidiaries is now a worldwide developer, publisher and mass marketer of interactive entertainment software for use with dedicated interactive entertainment hardware platforms (such as Nintendo, Sega and PlayStation) and multimedia computer systems (PCs). The company owns and operates four software development studios located in the USA and the United Kingdom, Germany and France/ The purchase of studios was linked to improving the company's performance, which was poor in the mid-nineties. The company's operating strategy is to develop and maintain a core of key brands and franchises (eg Turok, NPF quarterback Club and All Star Baseball) to support the various entertainment platforms and PCs that dominate the interactive entertainment market at any given time, or which the company perceives as having the potential for achieving mass market acceptance.

An overview of the entertainment industry

2.14 The games software industry us driven by the size of the installed base of entertainment platforms such as those manufactured by Nintendo Co Ltd (Japan), Sony Corporation and Sega Enterprises Ltd and PCs dedicated for home use, (see Appendix 2).

Rapid technological change is characteristic for this industry, as shown by the successive introductions of hardware systems from Nintendo, Sega and Sony, for example.

- The 8-bit cartridge system from Nintendo in 1985
- 16-bit cartridge systems from Sega and Nintendo in 1990 and 1991 respectively
- 32-bit compact disk systems from Sega and Sony in 1995; the 64-bit cartridge system from Nintendo in 1996
- The current planned introduction of Dreamcast (a new 64-bit CD system in Japan). This was released in Japan in late 1998 and is due for shipment to North America and Europe in September 1999
- The development of Sony PlayStation 2

2.15 These successive introductions have created related cycles in software production. So far, there appears to be no single Entertainment Platform or system which has achieved long-term dominance in the interactive entertainment market. Sony Computer Electronics, the division which developed the PlayStation, became the most profitable part of Sony Corporation and is now one of the four pillars of core business for Sony.

History

Phase 1: Atari and the birth of the 4-bit console

2.16 The launch of the Atari VCS 2600 console paved the way for the development of games publishing by providing slots for removable cartridges. Previously, games were 'hard-wired' into the system and it was only possible to play one game. After a slow start, the products started to diffuse through the market place and by 1981 20 million units had been sold worldwide. The games market suddenly had a new sector which had become the most important element within five years. Established toy manufacturers were keen to imitate Atari's success. This pushed up the sector sales. Warner Communications, perceiving a new growth market for copyrights, movie, music and television spin-offs purchased Atari. Sales peaked in 1982 and then the market slumped in 1983 with Atari losing $536 million. Warner sold its stake and the first cycle of boom and bust was over by the mid eighties. Companies such as Sinclair and Commodore produced low cost home computers which could be used for games playing, as this market started to take-off in the early eighties. Many enthusiasts wrote their own games and were to play a large part in the subsequent growth of the games market.

Phase 2: Japanese success with the 8-bit console

2.17 In 1983, the Japanese card manufacturer launched a sophisticated video games console on the Japanese market. The 8-bit processor, more powerful than the Atari processor, was an instant hit in Japan. The games were available on solid state cartridges and also more exciting. The success in Japan, led the company to dip its toe into the US market, launching the Nintendo Entertainment System (NES in 1985. They went national in 1986 and by 1989 they had sold 20m units. Several European launches followed the success in the US. Suddenly the games market was alive and well. In 1986 Sega also entered the market with its own 8-bit console. Although the Nintendo system was technically superior this entry pushed market growth and helped the growth of third party software developers such as Acclaim Entertainment Inc. The market for 8-bit consoles peaked in 1990 in the US and at a variable rate in Europe. The console penetration was greatest in the UK and France.

Phase 3: 16-bit consoles bring a maturing market

2.18 In 1989 Sega produced a 16-bit sophisticated console. This was launched in Japan in 1988, US in 1989 and Europe in 1990, as the Genesis (in the US) and the Mega Drive (in the rest of the world). The new product sales took Nintendo by surprise and they responded with the Super Nintendo Entertainment System.

2.19 However, by that time, Sega has stolen the march on Nintendo. Within five years, 20 million were sold to America with software sales reaching $2 billion. In Europe too, the market grew four times its original size. The demographic range had also expanded. The teenagers who grew up with the 8-bit processors were now graduating to the more sophisticated 16-bit system in their twenties. This phenomenal growth in the hardware market allowed many software publishers such as Acclaim Entertainment Inc to become substantial international players in their own right.

2.20 At the same time, the PC market just kept growing. PCs are now a major competitor to the games console manufacturers as their prices are dropping and their power is more than doubling every eighteen months, following Moore's Law (Moore's Law is based on observations undertaken by a computer specialist), (see Figure 1). The growth in the use of CD-ROMS has meant that the PC is emerging as the global standard for publishers. In

1992, Philips launched its CD-i system (CD-i was a self-standing CD interactive system), broadening the appeal of the 'multimedia' PC systems. This failed.

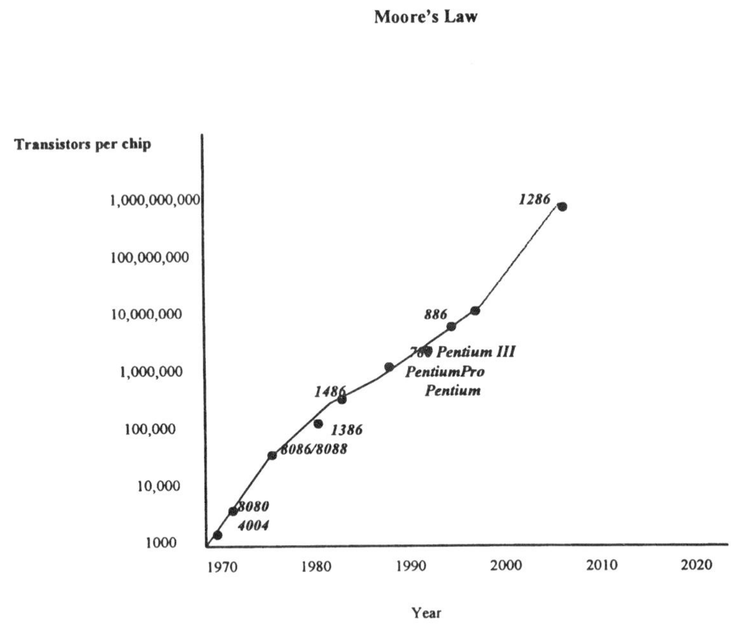

Figure 1

Phase 4: 16-bit and...

2.21 In 1993 and 1994 respectively, the 16-bit console market peaked in the US and Europe. Nintendo and Sega have tried to improve the performances of their respective products through add-ons and greater efficiency. The slump in the console market however has been paralleled by the continuing growth of the PC market.

Phase 5: The next generation

2.22 The end of the life cycle of the 16-bit machines and the lack of penetration of formats such as CD-i created an opening for new console machines. In 1995, Sony launched the PlayStation and Sega, the Saturn. The Sony product was initially priced at £299 and the Sega was at £399. As a new player the market was unsure of the produce. However, by 1997, one million Play Stations were sold in Europe and three million in the USA. By that time Sony had established a lead over Sega. The Nintendo was also late. Nintendo stuck to cartridges instead of the CD format and this has not only made manufacturing more expensive, but has also limited the ability of third parties to develop software. In presenting the PlayStation to the consumers, Sony targeted opinion formers in night clubs and lifestyle magazines with a low circulation. The target market was 20 to 30 year olds. As mass market items, the average age of its consumers is over 20. However the subsequent drop in price has broadened the demographic range. This has been accompanied by games such as *Spiceworld* and the growth in the use of *Turok* and *Lara Croft*.

2.23 During the 16-bit boom, Sega and Nintendo were accused of abusing their power by placing onerous restrictions on any third party wishing to publish a game on their machines. They have changed their stance for current machines as a result of a Europe Monopolies and Mergers Commission into the two companies. The commission's investigation, however, was ineffective and produced no conclusions. Nintendo's policy of supporting its own developers by giving them pre-production access to machines has limited the software support. They also have such exacting standards that many titles do not reach manufacturing stage. Nintendo's biggest selling titles have been developed by the company itself or a company in which it has a stake. *(Mario 64, Goldeneye 007, Diddy Kong Racing.)* Allied to this some quality software from other parties such as Acclaim Entertainment Inc have also done very well (*Turok: Dinosaur Hunter*).

2.24 During this period, the PC platform has been somewhat disappointing for the leisure software publishers from the point of view of margins. Aggressive marketing by a handful of US publishers has driven prices down. The nature of the way in which the PC market changes every eighteen months also creates more complexities for programmers. They only have an eighteen month window or the opportunity and the development time needed is also 18 months! Work on the most advanced machines means that they will then become entry level machines in approximately 12 months. Developers need to learn new skills all the time. Recently, 'multi-play' has become important. This is the need to make games more suitable for many players simultaneously. Games such as *Quake* have created this need. *Quake* can be played by many players over the Internet. This is a boom area. The use of 3D cards adds to the complexity as each new type or brand of card needs more programming instructions. Thus the PC market though massive has its own problems for the software programmers.

Some future developments

2.25 The industry is now considering the new generation of console machines, Sega have come out with Dreamcast – a new generation of hardware designed to generate a new cycle of industry development. This time they have a multitude of technology partners such as Microsoft, Hitachi, VideoLogic and Yamaha. They will be able to offer Windows driven software so that the PC platform can be used. Sony on the other hand is biding its time. For each of the major console manufacturers and the software developers, DVD technology brings a new dimension to the PC. DVDs store more information than CD-ROMs (up to nine times more) allowing developers more space to fabricate sophisticated games with 3D graphics. Currently very few DVD titles are available although current PCs now have DVD drives. There is a one year lag between the US and Europe. The PC market is not massive for entertainment software and it is a risky market as the development cost are high with low sales volumes.

2.26 The platforms have a 5 year life cycle with 128-bit system due for Sony and Nintendo in 2000 and 2001 respectively. The Sony PlayStation will be backward compatible and the Nintendo Dolphin will be driven by DVD. It will also reflect an association with IBM for manufacturing and Matsushita for DVD production. While it is clear that the life of a dedicated console is typically five years, it is also clear that interactive entertainment is here to stay and the long-term players are likely to be Sony and Nintendo.

2.27 Video games also appear in portable form and its market is dominated by Nintendo's Gameboy, first introduced in 1989 with a colour version being launched in 1997. The next generation is likely to be launched in 2001. There have been attempts by Atari and Sega to gain market share, but these have been ineffective. In more recent years, toy companies such as Tiger Electronics with the Gamecom system and Bandai with Wonderswan have entered this market, but have made little impact against Nintendo. Nintendo's first software, Mario, Zelda, Donkey Kong and Tetris ensures that is has ownership of all aspects of the sector. It anticipated maintenance of this through the introduction of Pokemon which has been released in Japan in 1997, USA in 1998 and Europe in 1999. This is destined to be a craze amongst the younger audience.

2.28 The next generation of dedicated consoles will incorporate a portable device such as the Sony Pocketstation, which can receive down-loaded levels of a game for the consumer to carry with them and play, allowing mobility and flexibility.

2.29 The advent of the personal computer for the purposes of entertainment has advanced greatly in recent years due to fast processing power, graphic and sound cards, Windows and falling prices. The ever changing specification poses difficulties for software development, where a typical two-year development cycle is inconsistent with machine configurations, which can advance dramatically within a twelve month period, rendering previous versions obsolete.

2.30 Gaming has evolved from an isolated experience for a single user to a social environment through the Internet, where on-line gaming connects users across the globe to play against each other. As technology advances, so does the style of software that appeals to an audience whose appetite for virtual environments knows no bounds.

The software life cycle

The development phase

2.31 Initially, when systems were relatively unsophisticated, one or two programmers could produce games from scratch. With the advent of 16-bit consoles, the development of a game became a multi-skilled task needing artists, musicians, coders, animators and games designers, with budgets of up to £1.5m being quite common. The games also take up to eighteen months to complete. The new environment created a need for innovative developers with a good track records. They were scarce and in demand. New companies were formed with venture capital and stock market flotation, (Argonaut, Rage and Titus). Many developments financed their work through publisher advances. Many sold up completely and were bought up by companies like Acclaim Entertainment Inc.

2.32 Acclaim Entertainment Inc Studios now incorporate Iguana Entertainment and Probe Entertainment employing more than 425 professionals with locations in Austin, Texas; Salt Lake City; Utah: Glen Cove, New York and two facilities in the UK. These studios have been responsible for many of the popular titles such as *Turok: Dinosaur Hunter, Extreme-G, Foresaken, NFL Quarterback Club 98, WWF War Zone and All Star Baseball 99.* In 1998, 68% of Acclaim Entertainment Inc's gross revenues were from products developed internally.

Cycles of development for software

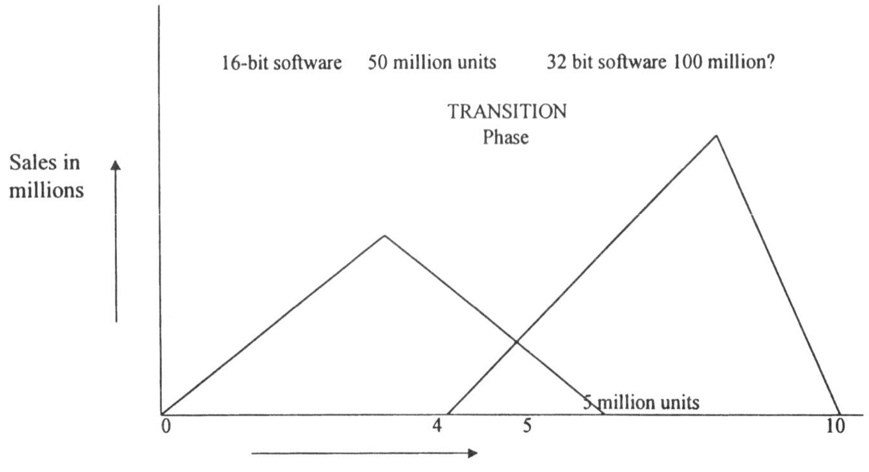

Figure 2

2.33 The transition phase as shown in Figure 2 is often difficult to handle. Publishers such as Acclaim Entertainment Inc are also exposed to great risks in the market place, especially if the hardware format proves to be unpopular. Under these circumstances, market intelligence is of vital importance. The company's software development strategy is driven by:

(a) The hardware platforms that are marketed and/or are anticipated to be on the market in future years.

(b) The time and cost of software development for each platform.

(c) The cost of manufacturing software for a particular platform

(d) The possible gross margins for software.

(e) The development time which is normally between eighteen and twenty four months

(f) Genres such as sport.

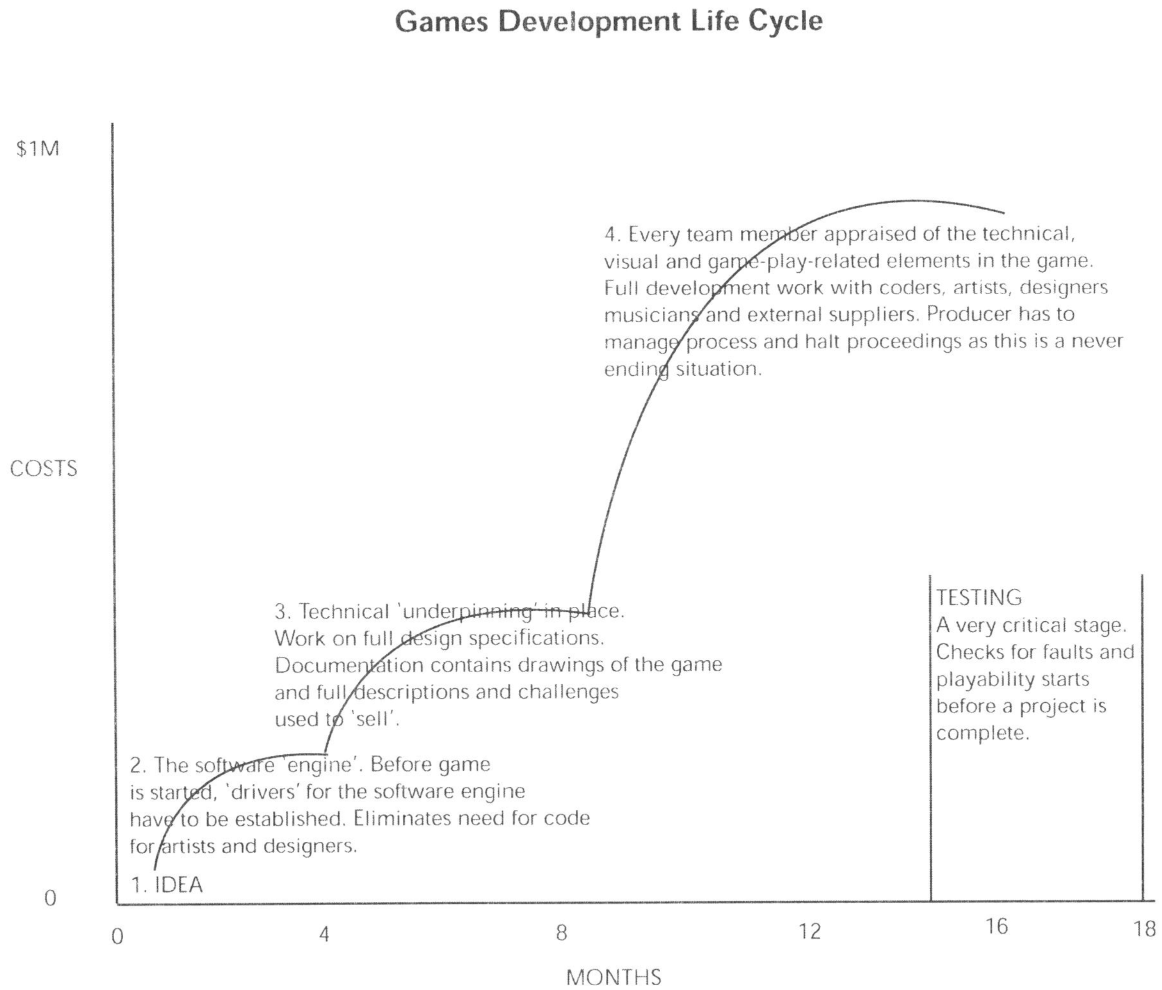

Figure 3

2.34 Publishing, from its humble origins is now a global business. The competition is intense and the number of key players is shrinking. Companies such as Viacom, Bertelsmann, Pearson and Time Warner have attempted to control the market but have failed, nevertheless their movie and music business models have been adopted by the major manufacturers. The key players in the field of publishing are Electronic Arts, GT Interactive, Acclaim Entertainment Inc, The Learning Company, Infogrames, Ubisoft, Eidos, Take 2, Activision, Havas, Mattel and Hasbro. All these key competitors have invested heavily in both development and distribution. The whole area of publishing has become more complex and will need to plan for marketing, public relations and development. Globalisation also creates its own cultural problems for gaming, with scenes having to be tailored for different cultures. For instance, scenes allowed in the UK may be too violent for Germany, It is therefore difficult to produce a pan-European product. In some instances, however, Tomb Raider, Command and Conquer and Formula 1 all had pan-European appeal.

Acclaim Entertainment Inc's position

2.35 Acclaim Entertainment Inc invests in the creation and development of sophisticated programming tools and engines which are used in the design and development of its software. These particular tools and engines help the company to gain a competitive advantage in the creation of new and innovative software. Prior to 1995 and its acquisition of the Studios, it relied heavily on the development of games by independent studios. The change in emphasis allows it to control the creative process, product quality, release timing and the cost of software. At present, approximately two-thirds of the company's employees are involved in the studio operations. The company develops and sells software for the N64, PlayStation, Dreamcast and PCs. The company employs product managers, who are responsible for directing the teams developing the software in the studies, (ie programming, graphic, animation, sound and game play of each title). Individuals hired by the company to oversee software development outside the studio are known as 'producers'. They manage and monitor the delivery schedule and budget for a new title, ensuring that the title follows the approved product specifications. In addition to this they act as facilitators with licensors who s trademarks or brands may be incorporated in the title if necessary, and co-ordinate testing and final approval of the title.

2.36 The company constantly scans the market seeking new sources of brands for using as a base for developing software. Generally, it has obtained such rights from a variety of sources in comic book publishing (eg Batman, Shadow Man and Turok: Dinosaur Hunter), sports (eg NFL Quarterback Club and NBA Jam), arcade (eg NBA Jam Extreme), film (eg Batman and Robin) television (eg South Park) and other areas of the entertainment industry. The contractual arrangements are complex and vary for each brand, ranging from individual property rights to the right to create software based on or featuring particular brands over a period of time.

2.37 The company has well-developed procedures for testing software and eliminating bugs prior to manufacture. The hardware manufacturers also test the software. So far the company's software has not been recalled because of bugs in the system.

Product strategy

2.38 The company's intention is to maintain key core product brands in the games industry, and to introduce new products, as potential for a mass market is established. This strategy is supported by scheduling the introduction on selected new titles. The intention is to develop one or more key brands every year. These developed brands can then be featured on an annual basis in successive titles.

2.39 The life cycle of a particular title could range form one to three months to more than a year. The life cycle is often dependent on the initial success of the title. This initial success is often determined by innovation, write-ups in magazines and other factors such as recent augmentation of the title through TV or film. Actual sales results may vary for each title, however, the sales pull through of a title often peaks 90 to 120 days after introduction. In 1998, Acclaim Entertainment Inc released eight N64 titles, 11 PlayStation titles and six PC titles. In 1999, the company aims to release between 10 and 13 titles for the N64, between eight and ten titles for Nintendo's Game boy portable platform. Within this portfolio are sequels to Turok, Dinosaur Hunter, NFL Quarterback Club, WWF, All Star Baseball, NHL Breakaway and Extreme G.

Platform license agreements

2.40 The license agreements with Nintendo, Sony and Sega vary on the rights to develop and distribute software. The company gets non-exclusive rights to utilise the various names (Nintendo, Sega and Sony) on its products. Current agreements do not guarantee future successful outcomes in negotiating new licenses with the key platform manufacturers. Each company has the right to review and evaluate, under standards set by them, the content and playability of each of the titles produced by Acclaim entertainment Inc. In addition to this they also have the right to inspect and evaluate all art work, packaging and promotional materials used by the company in connection with the software. Acclaim Entertainment In is responsible for any warranty or repair claims with respect to the software. Fortunately, to date there have been no claims. All trademark, patent, copyright and product protection rights have to be covered by Acclaim Entertainment Inc, indemnifying Nintendo, Sony or Sega against any infringement.

Marketing and advertising

2.41 In terms of marketing and advertising, the company faces the complex task of maintaining old titles as well as promoting new ones. The target consumers vary from 15-25 for the platform games, and 15-34 for PC games. The target audience is primarily male. Acclaim Entertainment Inc develops a separate marketing strategy for each title, so that the story concepts and brands are appealing to the imagination of the targeted audience. The marketing campaigns are consistent with this philosophy. Various channels are used for marketing the software such as PR, the Internet, television, radio and magazines. Product sampling offered through the demonstration software distributed on the Net, as are contests and promotions. The company also undertakes publicity activities, trade shows, co-operative advertising with retailers and in-store advertising.

2.42 The ability to promote and market software efficiently is important for success. Some of the key strategies have been discussed earlier (in the section on product strategy). The creation of key brands enables the company to maximise cross-merchandising opportunities and to maximise its investment in tools and engines created for the original title, and to capitalise on the name recognition of the brand or franchise in subsequent releases.

Production sales and production

2.43 In order to disseminate its software efficiently, the company tailors its distribution policy to suit each geographic market. Figure 5 shown how distribution is handled in different areas of the world. The distribution in Europe is handled via the London offices, in order to maximise revenues and profits. Customers (retailers) are offered a warranty policy to provide repair or replacement of defective software for a period of 90 days after sale. In its favour, the company has not experienced significant warranty claims.

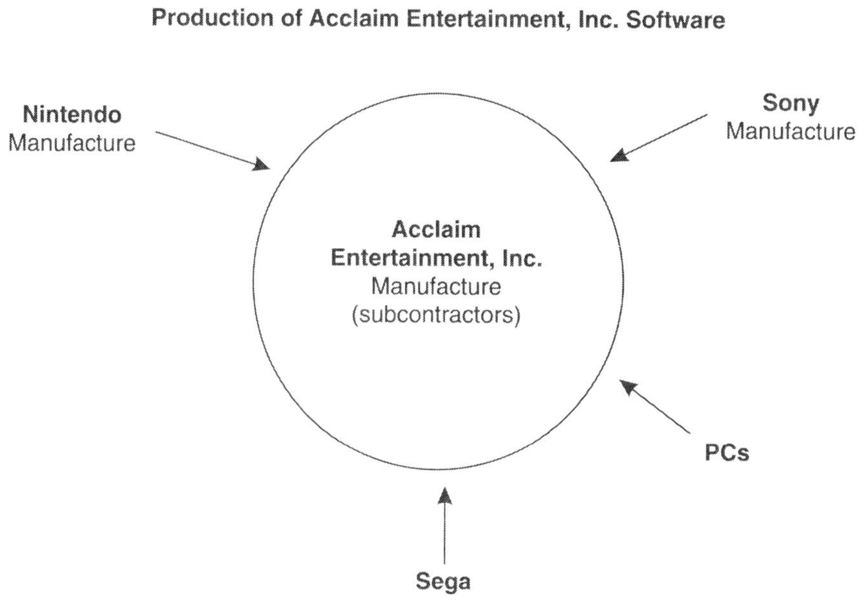

Figure 4

The software developed by Acclaim Entertainment Inc is then manufactured by Sony and Nintendo. In the case of Sega and PCs, Acclaim Entertainment Inc manufacture through subcontractors.

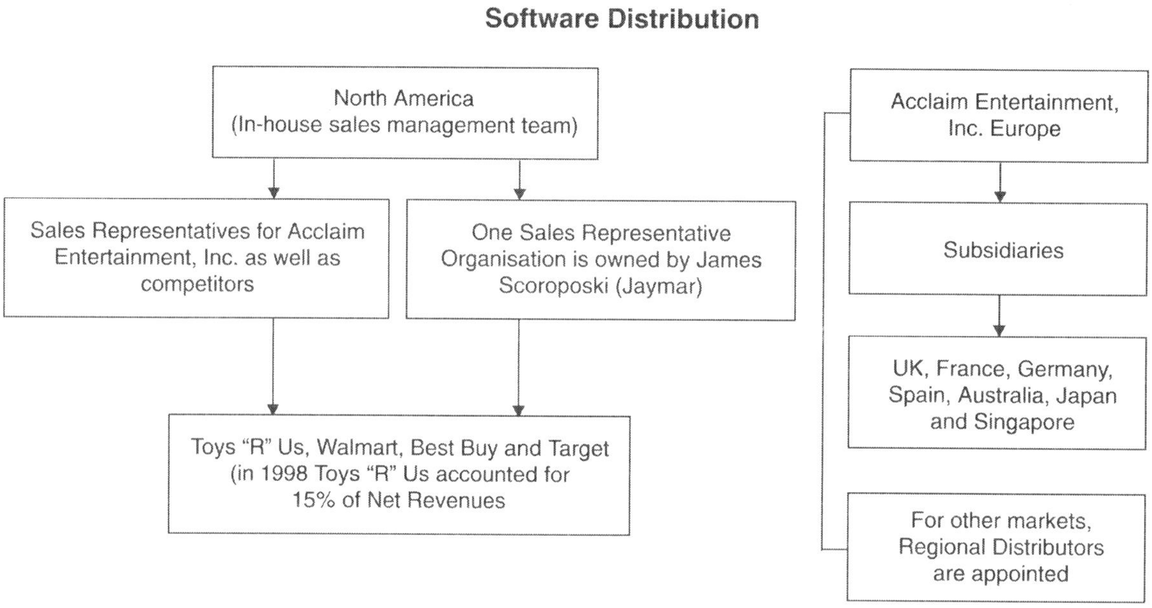

Figure 5

Competition

2.44 The competition in the interactive entertainment industry is intense. Despite producing software for the major platform manufacturers, the company also faces its most intense competition from them (see Appendix 1), and numerous independent software manufacturers. Success in this sector is often dependent on the availability of financial resources, as the costs of developing and marketing software are very high. Acclaim Entertainment Inc's size and position in the US market makes it one of the of the largest independent publishers of software for entertainment platforms, (see Table 1). However, in the more fragmented PC market it has a small share.

Table 1

Toy retail sales tracking service (TRSTS)
Acclaim Entertainment Inc market share for the first three quarters and the last quarter of 1998

	1998 (3/4)	*1998 (4/4)*
Nintendo N64	9.80%	13.40%
PlayStation	4.60%	9.10%

2.45 Competition in this industry is largely based on the quality of the title, access to shelf space, product features, sales of the entertainment platforms (see Appendix 2) for which the title is written, the number of titles available for the Entertainment Platforms and the marketing campaign supporting the title. Acclaim Entertainment Inc's competitive edges are determined by its product quality, marketing and sales ability (see Appendix 1), proprietary technology and product development capability, capital resources, the strength and depth of its worldwide distribution channels, and management experience. From 1994, the company also began to enter into selected licensing agreements with third party publishers to distribute software developed by them in selected markets. In 1997, the company received 9% of gross revenues from software developed by Interplay Productions. Interplay was only distributed in Germany and France.

2.46 The company acquired Acclaim Entertainment Inc Comics in July 1994 and commenced the development and publication of comic book magazines. It appears that Acclaim Entertainment Inc Comics are primarily used for the development of proprietary titles such as Turok: Dinosaur Hunter, Shadow Man and Bloodshot. The company does not seem to derive any significant revenue from the sale of Acclaim Entertainment Inc Comics products (around $4-$5m). It is likely that the section's revenues in the future may depend on the licensing and merchandising agreement of its characters in interactive entertainment and other media such as motion pictures or television.

Industry trends

2.47 As discussed before, the interactive entertainment industry is characterised by rapid technological change mainly due to:

- The introduction of entertainment platforms incorporating more advanced processors and operating systems
- The rapid technological changes taking place in the PC market
- The development of the Internet and new channel delivery systems which are both electronic and digital
- The entry of new competitors into the arena, though there is much consolidation taking place.

2.48 It is clear that there is a never ending battle, with no single entertainment platform achieving long-term dominance (see Appendices 1, 2 and 7). Acclaim Entertainment Inc constantly needs to anticipate and adapt its software to the emerging new platform technologies. The process of developing the software is extremely complex, and with the advent of new and better multimedia features, it is likely that the process will become even more complex and expensive. In the future substantial investment will be required in graphics, sound, digitised speech, music and video.

2.49 The development of the Internet is also likely to create further opportunities and problems for the incumbent software publishers, mainly for the following reasons.

(a) Gaming is stretching the frontiers of on-line technology.

(b) A free section of doom was downloaded onto a staggering 10m PCs!

(c) Players can participate on a worldwide basis.

(d) BT in the UK has built-up an on-line gaming service, lowering the lag time or ('ping' times) between a player depressing a key and seeing the action enacted on screen.

(e) A 'frictionless' distribution system through the Internet, which bypasses distribution and legal problems in many countries.

(f) The development of dedicated games networks, such as the one BT provides in the UK which already has 50,000 members.

(g) The possibility of interacting with consumers on a one-to-one basis.

(h) Testing new games cost-effectively.

2.50 The interactive industry is highly seasonal. Typically, net revenues are highest during the last quarter of the year. The year-end Christmas season seems to show an increased demand for software.

Key issues facing Acclaim Entertainment Inc

2.51 In order to secure its future position in the market place, Acclaim Entertainment Inc is faced with the following issues.

1 Dependence on entertainment platform manufacturers – the need for license renewals

Table 2

Fiscal revenues derived from sales of software

		Platform dependence	
Title	*1996*	*1997*	*1998*
Nintendo-compatible	29%	41%	60%
Sega-compatible	36%	12%	1%
Sony-compatible	19%	28%	30%

Table 2 shown how dependent Acclaim Entertainment Inc is on the platform manufacturers for the sale of titles. The manufacturers tend to limit the number of titles the company can release in any one year. This tends to limit future growth in sales. Success relies on being able to renegotiate contracts every year. The company is also reliant on the platform manufacturers for certain cartridge and CD-ROM software.

2 Reliance on new titles – product delays

Acclaim entertainment Inc's ability to maintain favourable relations with retailers and to receive maximum advantage from its advertising expenditure depends on its ability to provide retailers with a timely and continuous flow of products. Quality assurance procedures and acceptance of new titles by the platform manufacturers may delay production. If titles are rejected by manufacturers as a result of bugs, or if there is a delay in the approval of a product, the company results are negatively affected. In the past Acclaim Entertainment Inc has experienced significant delays in the introduction of certain titles and this is likely to happen again in the future. The market for software is driven by 'hits'. In 1998, 53% of the gross sales were from the top four titles. There is continuous pressure to produce 'hits', yet there is no guarantee that this will always happen from year to year.

3 **Inventory management – risk of product returns**

The company has to manage product returns and also excess retail inventories. Account also has to be taken of discounts, price concessions and estimated returns.

4 **Litigation**

In 1997, the company had to allow $23.6 million in its accounts for claims and litigation settlements

As the company is responsible for litigation settlements and not the platform makers, any future litigations are bound to have an adverse effect on the operating profit.

5 **Increased product development costs**

As a result of acquisition of its Studios in 1995, the company's fixed software development and overhead costs were significantly higher for the following two years, affecting profitability.

6 **Intellectual property licenses and proprietary rights**

Some of the company's software has trademarks, trade names, logos or copyrights licensed by third parties to guarantee economic success. In order to protect its titles and property rights, the company relies mainly on a combination of:

- Copyrights
- Trade secret laws
- Patent and trademark laws
- Non-disclosure agreements
- Other copyright protection methods

The company policy is to get all employees and third party developers to sign non-disclosre agreements.However, these measures may not always be sufficient to protect the company's intellectual property rights against infringement and existing copyright laws only afford limited protection. As the number of titles in the industry increases, Acclaim Entertainment Inc believes that the claims and lawsuits with respect to software infringement will increase.

7 **Sales outside the USA**

International sales represented approximately 41% of net revenues in 1996, 51% of net revenues in 1997 and 34% of net revenues in 1998. It is likely that these sales will continue to account for a large proportion of its revenues. These reveneus are however dependent on the following

- Unexpected changes in regulatory environment
- Tariffs and other economic barriers
- Fluctuating exchange rates
- Difficulties in staffing and managing foreign operations
- The possibility of difficulty in accounts receivable collection.

8 **Dependence on key personnel and employees**

The software industry is characterised by a high level of employee mobility, as the skills are in high demand. This leads to aggressive recruiting in the industry for personnel with technical, marketing, sales, product development and management skills. Successful operations are very dependent on Acclaim Entertainment Inc's ability to identify, retain and motivate such personnel. Gregory Fischbach and James Scoroposki are absolutely vital to the success of the company.

9 **Volatility of the stock price**

Historically, stock prices of companies involved in the software industry have shown significant volatility. This volatility results from:

- Timing and market acceptance of product introduction by the company.
- The introduction of new and innovative products by the company's competitors.
- Loss of any of the company's key personnel.
- Variations in quarterly operating results.
- General changes in the software industry.

It appears that historical trends may have little or no significance for projecting future growth and earnings.

10 Financial performance

Although the net revenues have almost doubled since 1996, the company came into profit in 1998. The losses in 1996 and 1997 were due to the industry transition from 32-64-bit entertainment platforms. The revenues during this period have been considerably lower than in 1995 (around $567 million). Appendix 5 shows the key financial highlights for the company. the rapid technological advances in games systems have significantly changeed the look and feel of software, as well as the software development process. Previous development costs are $300,000 to $400,000, whereas the current estimates show that the costs for developing an entertainment platform title is £1 million and for PCs it is $2 million.

Summary

2.52 Acclaim Entertainment Inc is a substantial player in the world software games market. As a company it has been very successful, but over-reliance on outdated platform games cost it dearly in 1995/96. As it consolidates itself in to a more secure position for the future, numerous problems need to be considered and addressed. These are the growing demand for games on the Internet; the advent of DVD-ROMs with the attendant requirement in design expertise (see Appendix 6); and the continual need for new material and innovative marketing strategies. It enters the millennium with confidence yet with some apprehension as to what the future holds for them

3 ACCLAIM ENTERTAINMENT INC: APPENDICES

Appendix	
1	Major leisure software companies
2	Market data
3	Publicity
4	Financial data
5	Consolidated balance sheet and geographic financial data
6	Newspaper article: DVD
7	Newspaper article: competition

3.1 Appendix 1. Leisure software publishers

Major leisure software companies

Company	Base	Company type	Turnover	Staff	Key products	Key points
The Eldos Group	London, UK	Developer/publisher	£137.2m (Mar 1998)	420	Tomb Raider, Championship Manager	Ambitions to be a global player. On an acquisition trail 5 wholly owned UK: 8 partially owned, UK, FR&US Studios, has publishing links with 9 studios
The company is more interested in content development rather than distribution. In 1997 Tomb Raider 2 was the UK's best selling game o all formats Championship manager was the best selling CD-ROM.						
Infrogrames-Ocean	Lyon, France	Developer/publisher/ distributor	Ffr 1,402.7m (June 1998	800	V-Rally, Tintin, Worms, Asterix, The Smurfs, Alone in the Dark	Europe's largest and world's fifth largest company. Ocean est. 1983 in Manchester. Infogrames in 1983. Sole rights to Looney Tunes characters.
The company purchased Philips Media as a distribution company for $33m in 1997. Worms is a hit game series. It has a very good distribution system in Europe.						
Ubi Soft	Paris, France	Developer/publisher/ distributor	Ffr 632m (Mar 1998)	933	Rayman, POD	1996, 15% of stock offered on French Stock Exchange. Hs subsidiaries in 3 countries including US, Japan, Italy, Spain and China.
The company accounts for 25% of all software sold in France. Exports are 61.4% of sales. POD and Ray man have sold 3.5 m and 2.5m copies worldwide. Development accounts for 46%, licensing for 23% and distribution for 31%.						
Gremlin	Sheffield, UK	Developer/publisher	£27m (Projected, 1998)	290	Actua sports franchise, Premier Manager	Floated in June 1997, raised £10m. Two studies, one in Sheffield and one in Dundee. Now owned by Infogrames.
DMA in Dundee, founded by David Jones, is regarded as one of the world's leading studios – developed Lemmings and Uniracers for Nintendo. In 1997, Grand Theft Auto was published. 56% of sales from the UK, overall 80% from Europe. Distribution deals signed with Interplay, Fox and Activision in the US.						
Codemasters	Southam, UK	Developer/publisher	£20.2m (Apr 1998)	160	Dizzy, TOCA, Micro-machines, Colin-McCrae	Started by David and Richard Darling as teenagers. Very successful and innovative.
The company releases about six titles a year. they have had great success with TOCA Touring Cars, a PlayStation hit. Colin McCrae rally will gross them £20m. An ambitious company which plans to increase its staff to 280. Turnover in 1999 is expected to hit £120m, with expected profits of £45m+.						
Entertainment International Empire software	London, UK	Developer/publisher	£20m (1997)		Pro Pinball, Battleground	An independent company that produced the successful Gazza games.
Success based on Pipemania, a puzzle game licensed to Lucasfilm. Has also produced the military game Battleground and International Cricket Captain, the UK's first cricket management game.						

Major leisure software companies

Company	Base	Company type	Turnover	Staff	Key products	Key points
Blue Byte Software	Germany	Developer/publisher		40	The Settlers, Pro Tennis	Large independent, works with other independents in other countries
Some success on consoles with games such as The Settlers and Pro Tennis Tour. Now focused on the CD-ROM format.						
Titus Software Corporation	France	Developer/publisher/ distributor	Ffr. 132 (1997)	75	Automobili - Lamborghini, Virtual Chess	Sells in well-over 30 countries, Offices in Paris, Los Angeles, Tokyo and London
In 1997 it became a public company and earns 92% of its income from international sales. Recently, it has acquired an American studio Blue Sky Software and Digital Integration in the UK. Took a 54% stake in INTERPLAY						
Rare	Twycross, UK	Developer	£10.5m (Dec 1996)	135	Goldeneye 007, Diddy Kong Racing, Blast Corp, Banjp Kazooie	A significant influence on the Nintendo market. Nintendo owns a 40% stake
In the face of serious competition, Diddy Kong Country single-handedly extended Nintendo's 16-bit life cycle by the improved use of graphics. Goldeneye is another extremely successful title. In 1997, six members of the team defected to Eighth Wonder, a PlayStation developer						
Argonaut	London, UK	Developer	£5m (1997)	140	Star Fox, Croc	One of Europe's oldest development studios. Started with Commodore, now mainly with Nintendo
Produced Starglider, and Star Fox, one of Nintendo's best selling games, (£10m). It has attracted outside cash and management from Apax						
Sony	Japan			406	Tekken, Ridge Racer, WipeOut, Gran Turismo	The Games Division contributes 25% of Sony's total revenues. Heavy investment in development
There is some doubt over its acquisition of UK studios Psygnosis and Millennium. Sony is also a giant in the software business with Tekken, Ridge Racer Final Fantasy and Gran Turismo. These have been derived from publishing deals with Japanese companies Namco and Squaresoft						
Nintendo	Japan				Mario, Donkey Kong,, Zelda	Creator of the modern games industry. Enjoys a huge lead over third party development
In 1997 published the top three best-selling games in Germany, two of the top five in France, and two of the top ten in the UK. Nintendo's stronghold is Japan, under the direction of Shigeru Miyamoto creator of Mario. Currently reorganising its global management systems, with Europe having more autonomy						
Sega	Japan		£60m (European T/O) (Mar 1998)	205 Europe	Virtua Fighter, Sega Rally, Virtua Cop NiGHTs	Key affiliate is Adeline. In March 1997 Sega had losses of $167.3m.
Current performance of Sega consoles is very poor. They are pinning their hopes on the new Dreamcast 128-bit processor and collaboration with Microsoft, Acclaim, Argonaut, GTI, Micropose, Interplay and Midway						

Major leisure software companies

Company	Base	Company type	Turnover	Staff	Key products	Key points
Electronic Arts	US	Developer/publisher	$1.3bn (1988 T/O) $326m in Europe	2,212 601 Europe	FIFA, Road Rash, EA Sports, Need for Speed, Wing Commander	Subsidiaries are Maxis, Bullfrog Westwood, Origin
The world's largest games group, fairly well spread globally. The sports series sell in their million – FIFA Soccer, NHL Hockey, PGA Golf and NBA Live. It is aggressively acquisitive.						
GT Interactive	US	Publisher	$530m (Dec 1997) £97m Europe T/O	1,337 117 Europe	Total Annihilation, Unreal, Abe's Odyssey	Virtually unknown before 1993. One of the world's leading publishers. Now up for sale owing to financial difficulties
Growth occurred as a result of Wolfenstein 3D. Doom has become the most important game of the decade. In 1995 a limited amount of shares were offered to the public. The funds were used for acquisitions such as Wizard works and Humungous. Acquisitive in Europe, buying One stop and Warner Interactive (Europe).						
The Learning Company	US	Developer/publisher	$392m (1997)	1,525 146 Europe	Catz, Dogz, Mavis Beacon, Berlitz, Sesame Street	One of the leading software companies in the world. Ini6tially produce non-games, budget PC products and management of titles in non-specialist stores.
Began purchasing games studios in 1997. In 1998 merged with Broderbund (producers of Riven and Myst – US's best selling games in 1997). Heading for $1bn T/O.						
Hasbro Interactive	US	Developer/publisher	$100m (1997) $22m		Monopoly, risk, Frogger, Trivial Pursuit	IN 1997 published 7 of the US's top 50 titles on PC.
Fourth largest publisher in the US. Europe accounts for 22% of revenue. Many successes based on parent company's board games – Monopoly, Battleships, Risk and Trivial Pursuit. They plan to publish third part titles.						
Activision	US	Developer/publisher/ distributor	$259m (Mar 1998) $160 Europe T/O	667 233 Europe	Asteroids, Quake, Dark Reign, Zark, Pitfall, Mechwarrior	One of the biggest publishers in the eighties nearly liquidated in the nineties.
The company's revival was based on Quake, Quake II and Hexen II. It has acquired German distributors Centresoft and NBG						
Interplay	US	Publisher	$140m (April 1998) $31m Europe	501 47 Europe	MDK, earthworm Jim 3D, Messiah	Underperforming in recent years.
Success limited to Star Trek, Starfleet Academy, Descent and MDK. Searching for new products. Has some new programmers from the Tomb Raider team, who now work for a studio called Confounding Factors. Now part of Titus.						
THQ	US	Publisher			Rugrats, WCW, Small Soldiers	An odd company which supports ageing format. Toy Story on Nintendo and Super Return of the Jedi on Gameboy
The company is not too active in Europe. By sensible choice of games, it has created a 'harvest' position for itself and is quietly profitable.						

Major leisure software companies

Company	Base	Company type	Turnover	Staff	Key products	Key points
Konami	Japan	Developer/Publisher/ Distributor	$308m (Mar 1998)	1,000 50 Europe	FIFA, Road Rash, EA Metal Gear Solid	Konami is the only Japanese publisher with a significant presence in Europe. German base.
The company is also a distributor for companies such as Bandai, Ubisoft, Telstar and TQH. It also publishes Bandai products in the UK, France and Benelux. It suffered in the last part of the 16-bit era with large inventories, but is currently successful with International Soccer Star 64 on Nintendo and Metal Gear Sold						
Take 2 Interactive	US	Developer/Publisher	$100m (1998) £50m Europe T/O	150 60 Europe	Three Lions, Postal	Suddenly in 1997, from nowhere, the company became an important player. They own Gametek, IMSI Alliance and Spidersoft.
Excellent timing sealed the purchase of Gametek. Soon after take-over two successful titles were produced - Postal and Lula The Sexy Empire. Grand Theft Auto						
MicroPose	US	Developer/Publisher	$60m	131 Europe	Civilisation Grand Prix, Star Trek	Very important in the 80s but fortunes fluctuated in the 90s. Now owned by Hasbro.
About two years ago, the company did extremely well with Star Trek, The Next Generation, Civilisation 2 and Grand Prix 2. Since then only the PC version of Worms. They also missed out on the console resurgence. This produced losses of $3.3m in 1998. In 1998 acquired by Hasbro for $70m						
Cendant Software	US	Developer/Publisher	Difficult to separate out	486 Europe	Caesar II, Starcraft, Ultimate Soccer Manager	The software business is part of a huge empire, straddline Avis car rentals and Ramada Hotels, with a combined T/O of $4,000m.
The Company also produces ADI educational software and is the market leader in France and Germany. The Parent company, however is looking to divest the Cendant Software Business						
Microsoft	US	Developer/Publisher	$100m (Leisure software only)		Flight Simulator, Golf, Encarta, Age of Empires	Wants to become a serious player in the Games business. The development however has not been quite right.
The giant has done well on non-games products such as Flight Simulator, Encarta and Autoroute Express. Age of Empires sold 30,000 in the UK and 175,000 in the US						
Virgin Interactive Entertainment	US	Developer/Publisher	$2,423m (1997)	550 150 Europe	Resident Evil, Screamer	VIE has created a very successful budget CD-ROM brand, called the White Label. Third biggest UK publisher in 1997.
The company has applied its marketing expertise to brands such as Command and Conquer, Resident Evil and Star Wars. It was put up for sale in 1996, creating an uncertain environment. It has well established distribution facilities in Spain, France and Germany. It relies heavily on third party developers. In 1998 it lost its long-standing deal with LucasArts						

Source: Acclaim Entertainment, Inc., Screen Digest and ELSPA

3.2 Appendix 2. Market data

(a) World software market

	1994 $'000	1995 $'000	1996 $'000	1997 $'000
Western Europe				
Console total	720,377.60	625,703.30	1,067,199.30	1,936,629.60
PC total	706,373.70	1,600,225.50	1,968,087.00	2,388,142.80
Total market value	1,426,751.30	2,225,928.80	3,035,286.30	4,324,772.40
USA				
Console total	2,115,575.00	1,743,900.00	1,979,650.00	2,987,600.00
PC total	593,335.00	1,292,400.00	1,321,530.00	1,515,800.00
Total market value	2,710,910.00	3,036,300.00	3,301,180.00	4,503,400.00
Japan				
Console total	838,578.00	1,375,004.70	2,311,786.90	3,275,940.30
PC total	86,900.00	325,500.00	562,400.00	712,600.00
Total market value	925,478.00	1,700,504.70	2,874,186.90	3,988,540.30
World				
Console total	3,968,500.00	3,961,200.00	5,494,600.00	8,826,800.00
PC total	1,146,700.00	3,218,700.00	4,335,200.00	5,254,400.00
Total market value	5,115,200.00	7,179,900.00	9,829,800.00	14,081,200.00

(b) Software market values in Europe

	1995 $'000	1996 $'000	1997 $'000	1998 $'000
UK				
Console total	188,516	262,662	549,827	946,084
PC total	215,797	282,040	401,230	601,271
Total market value	404,313	544,702	942,057	1,547,355
Germany				
Console total	132,195	181,311	336,073	622,406
PC total	576,726	841,183	930,159	1,073,672
Total market value	708,721	1,022,494	1,266,232	1,696,078
France				
Console total	161,633	321,790	319,435	443,244
PC total	169,502	189,862	251,984	354,379
Total market value	331,135	511,652	571,419	797,623
Italy				
Console total	38,715	67,568	228,751	523,095
PC total	196,770	157,297	165,917	224,456
Total market value	235,485	224,865	394,668	747,551
Spain/Portugal				
Console total	57,073	93,843	121,694	197,117
PC total	116,868	114,435	134,567	181,232
Total market value	173,941	208,278	256,261	378,349
Scandinavia				
Console total	5,899	41,537	84,758	140,641
PC total	86,362	140,912	224,458	263,809
Total market value	92,261	182,449	309,216	404,450
Benelux				
Console total	32,431	50,486	107,121	213,591
PC total	80,522	113,580	132,945	167,048
Total market value	112,953	164,066	240,066	380,639

(c) **Number of households with hardware installed**

	1995 000's	*1996* 000's	*1997* 000's	*1998* 000's
UK				
Nintendo 64	0	0	640	1,490
Sony PlayStation	125	700	1,930	3,791
Sega Saturn	40	235	365	416
Total PC CD-ROM	1,200	2,270	3,646	4,857
Germany				
Nintendo 64	0	0	540	1,290
Sony PlayStation	63	338	1,175	2,550
Sega Saturn	25	80	95	101
Total PC CD-ROM	3,220	4,513	5,763	7,096
France				
Nintendo 64	0	0	430	1,020
Sony PlayStation	137	510	1,425	2,437
Sega Saturn	40	170	215	233
Total PC CD-ROM	1,080	1,931	2,944	3,878
Italy				
Nintendo 64	0	0	240	420
Sony PlayStation	20	85	445	1,516
Sega Saturn	5	25	40	46
Total PC CD-ROM	1,040	1,474	2,289	2,897
Spain				
Nintendo 64	0	0	137	317
Sony PlayStation	20	100	430	1,063
Sega Saturn	15	105	125	133
Total PC CD-ROM	806	1,194	1,797	2,273
Scandinavia				
Nintendo 64	0	0	125	270
Sony PlayStation	30	99	260	465
Sega Saturn	20	30	35	37
Total PC CD-ROM	605	1,522	2,494	2,731
Benelux				
Nintendo 64	0	0	140	325
Sony PlayStation	15	79	300	728
Sega Saturn	8	20	30	34
Total PC CD-ROM	836	1,678	2,091	2,589

3.3 Appendix 3. Publicity

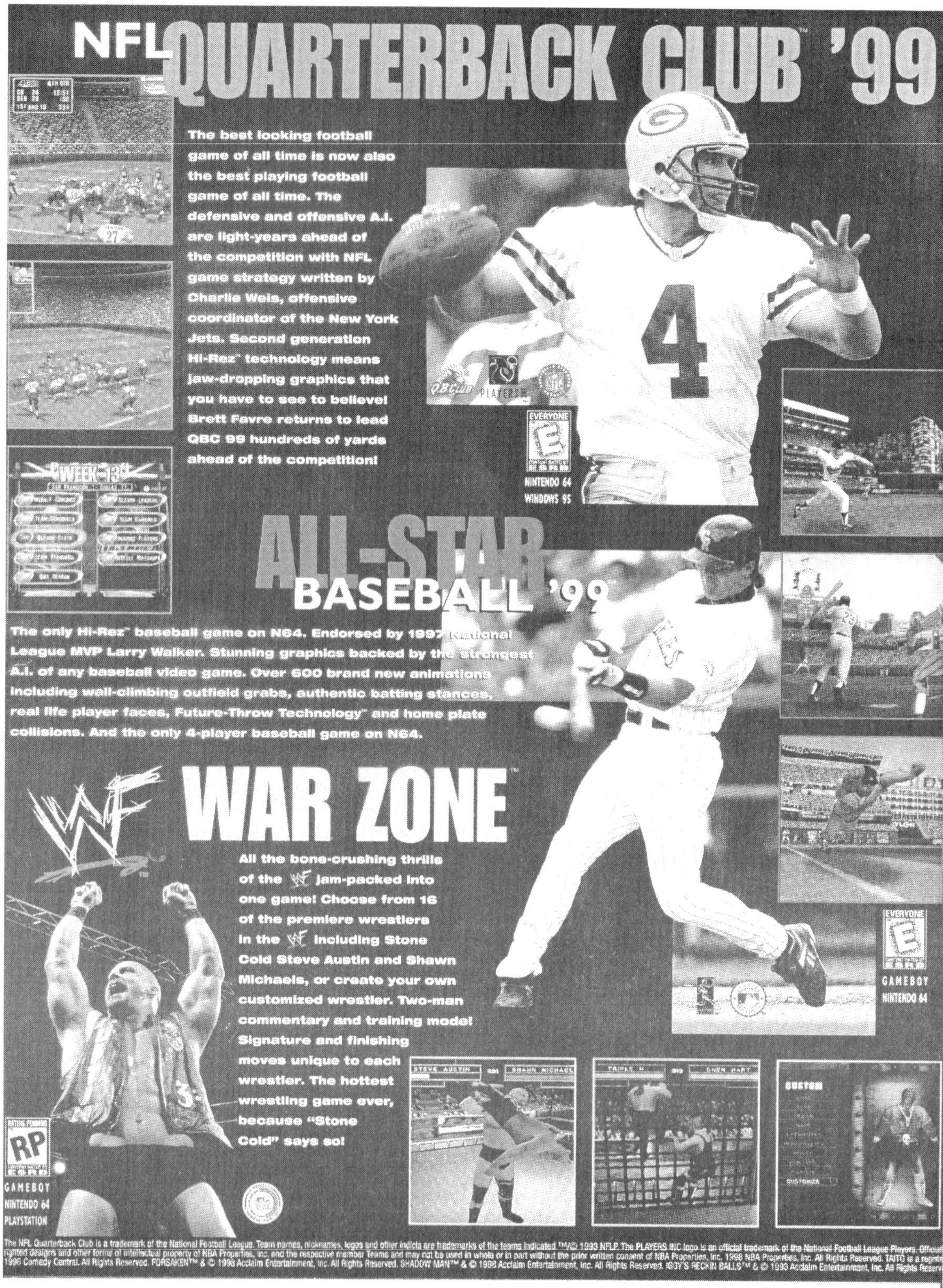

NFL QUARTERBACK CLUB '99
The best looking football game of all time is now also the best playing football game of all time. The defensive and offensive A.I. are light-years ahead of the competition with NFL game strategy written by Charlie Weis, offensive coordinator of the New York Jets. Second generation Hi-Rez™ technology means jaw-dropping graphics that you have to see to believe! Brett Favre returns to lead QBC 99 hundreds of yards ahead of the competition!
EVERYONE
NINTENDO 64
WINDOWS 95
WEEK-13
ALL-STAR BASEBALL '99
The only Hi-Rez™ baseball game on N64. Endorsed by 1997 National League MVP Larry Walker. Stunning graphics backed by the strongest A.I. of any baseball video game. Over 600 brand new animations including wall-climbing outfield grabs, authentic batting stances, real life player faces, Future-Throw Technology™ and home plate collisions. And the only 4-player baseball game on N64.
WWF WAR ZONE
All the bone-crushing thrills of the WWF jam-packed into one game! Choose from 16 of the premiere wrestlers in the WWF including Stone Cold Steve Austin and Shawn Michaels, or create your own customized wrestler. Two-man commentary and training mode! Signature and finishing moves unique to each wrestler. The hottest wrestling game ever, because "Stone Cold" says so!
EVERYONE
GAMEBOY
NINTENDO 64
RP
GAMEBOY
NINTENDO 64
PLAYSTATION
STEVE AUSTIN
SHAWN MICHAEL
TRIPLE H
CUSTOM
The NFL Quarterback Club is a trademark of the National Football League. Team names, nicknames, logos and other indicia are trademarks of the teams indicated. ™/© 1993 NFLP. The PLAYERS INC logo is an official trademark of the National Football League Players. Official
righted designs and other forms of intellectual property of NBA Properties, Inc. and the respective member Teams and may not be used in whole or in part without the prior written consent of NBA Properties, Inc. 1998 NBA Properties, Inc. All Rights Reserved. TAITO is a registe
1998 Comedy Central. All Rights Reserved. FORSAKEN™ & © 1998 Acclaim Entertainment, Inc. All Rights Reserved. SHADOW MAN™ & © 1998 Acclaim Entertainment, Inc. All Rights Reserved. IGGY'S RECKIN BALLS™ & © 1993 Acclaim Entertainment, Inc. All Rights Reserv

JEREMY McGRATH SUPERCROSS '98
NBA JAM '99
It's Showtime! Jump, powerslide, skid and hit the straightaways on mud, sand, water, gravel and ice. Race against the clock or field, and if you win the circuit, take on 8-time champion Jeremy McGrath. But no matter what the terrain, be sure you go all-out, because this is the ultimate supercross racing game.
EVERYONE
PLAYSTATION
NEW JERSEY
44
RE-VOLT
Re-Volt™ takes the racing genre and turns it on it's head! Where you couldn't go before, now there are no limits. Tumble through locations in indestructible vehicles, using whatever tactics necessary to win. Featuring 28 remote control cars, 16 tracks, multi-player capabilities and a wicked track editor! Re-Volt Rocks!
Five on five B-ball comes to the N64 with incredible Hi-Rez™ realism in NBA Jam™ 99. Over 300 true-sized players with real-life faces and authentic team play styles like the Celtics press and Bulls triangle offense. With play-by-play from Kevin Harlan and color commentary from Bill Walton, endorsed by NJ Nets rookie sensation Keith Van Horn, NBA Jam™ 99 provides the most realistic and graphically stunning basketball game on any system.
EVERYONE
GAMEBOY
NINTENDO 64
ACCLAIM®
SPORTS™
SWEAT THE DETAILS
RP
NINTENDO 64
PLAYSTATION
WINDOWS 95
roduct of the NFL Players. All Rights Reserved. Major League Baseball trademarks and copyrights are used with permission of Major League Baseball Properties, Inc. ©MLBPA Officially Licensed By Major League Baseball Players Association. World Wrestling Federation a
rk of TAITO CORPORATION. Bust A Move 2 is a trademark of TAITO CORPORATION. © TAITO CORPORATION 1998. All Rights Reserved. RE-VOLT ™ & © 1998 Acclaim Entertainment, Inc. All Rights Reserved. MACHINES ™ & © 1998 Acclaim Entertainment, Inc. All Rights Reser

IGGY'S RECKIN' BALLS
Swing, bounce, and grapple your way up 100 twisted towers with Iggy and the rest of the 'Reckin' Crew. 5 challenging modes of play including battle mode and fun-packed 4-player racing action. Anything goes in this wild, no-holds barred race to the top. Iggy's 'Reckin' Balls™, the family-friendly gaming sensation!
Iggy's reckin' balls
EVERYONE
E
NINTENDO 64
BUST-A-MOVE 2
BUST-A-MOVE ARCADE 2 EDITION
EVERYONE
E
GAMEBOY
NINTENDO 64
PLAYSTATION
WINDOWS 95
The addictive classic comes to N64! Destroy the bubble-clusters before they destroy you. Don't even think about the muscle-twitching paranoia of 2-player split-screen action. One taste of its maddening challenges and you'll be a bubble-addict forever!
MACHINES
Take control of a silicon-based race of Machines™ on a mission to seed and dominate new worlds. You build them and their environments. Lead them into battle against rival machine forces. Stunning 1st and 3rd person views, unique environmental conditions, campaign mode, five different levels of technologica development. It's the next level in action/strategy.
RATING PENDING
RP
WINDOWS 95
rademarks of Titan Sports, Inc. © 1998 Titan Sports, Inc. All Rights Reserved. Jeremy McGrath SUPERCROSS 98 ™ & © 1997 Acclaim Entertainment, Inc. All Rights Reserved. The NBA and individual NBA Team identifications used on or in this product are trademarks copy-
SEEDS OF EVIL™ © 1998 Acclaim Entertainment, Inc. All Rights Reserved. Extreme-G™ 2 & © 1998 Acclaim Entertainment, Inc. All Rights Reserved. BATMAN, ROBIN and all related characters, names and indicia are trademarks of DC Comics © 1998. South Park ™ & ©

The first one was a monster, the second one's gonna be a mother! Turok 2, the rampaging successor to the best-selling original has broken out! Powered by the ultimate next generation 3D engine, teeming with ferocious creatures, this savage world consists of never-before-seen, graphically unique levels of total non-stop action.
TUROK 2
SEEDS OF EVIL
GAMEBOY
NINTENDO 64
WINDOWS 95
BATMAN & ROBIN
Get in touch with your dark side. A relentless 3 day real-time manhunt through a sprawling 26 square mile Virtual Gotham City. Drive, shoot, explore, fight, and sleuth your way to the frozen Gotham citizens' salvation. Play as Batman, Robin, or Batgirl as you take on the cool, cruel Mr. Freeze and the seductive Poison Ivy.
TEEN
PLAYSTATION
EXTREME-G 2
extreme-G
XG2
NINTENDO 64
WINDOWS 95
Take the maximum vertigo overdrive of the original Extreme-G and multiply it times ten. Then race at velocities beyond human endurance through the fastest, most twisted tracks ever conceived! Over 35 new tracks, an increased arsenal, and 16 all-new hungry vehicles with detailed characters and improved true-to-life physics that takes no prisoners!

FORSAKEN™
FORSAKEN
War over the smoldering corpse of Mother Earth! 360° of absolute control. Advanced particle technology. An arsenal of 25 hi-tech weapons. Furious multi-player combat. And 15 of the universe's most cursed scavengers. With graphics that have left reviewers with "their jaws on the ground", the Future is Forsaken.
MATURE
M
NINTENDO 64
PLAYSTATION
WINDOWS 95
SHADOW MAN™
SHADOWMAN
From the creators of Turok®: Dinosaur Hunter comes the next great Acclaim Comics character: Shadow Man™. Endowed with the mystical powers of a voodoo warrior and armed with black magic weapons, Shadow Man™ walks between worlds to wage war against a legion of other worldly psychos. Huge 3D environments, incredible graveyard graphics, revolutionary character abilities, and genre-busting gaming scenarios make Shadow Man™ the most involving 3D-action/adventure game of all time.
RATING PENDING
RP
NINTENDO 64
WINDOWS 95
SOUTH PARK
Oh my God! They killed Kenny! The Comedy Central smash that's been called "punishingly hilarious," "deliciously deranged" and "devilishly original" is on its way to the hottest video game systems. Kenny, Kyle, Stan, Cartman and the other outrageous characters will twist their way into your hearts and onto your gaming screens this winter.
RATING PENDING
RP
NINTENDO 64
PLAYSTATION
WINDOWS 95
CHEF
COMEDY CENTRAL
SOUTH PARK
TM & © 1998 Comedy Central. All Rights Reserved.
Corporate Headquarters: Acclaim Entertainment, Inc. One Acclaim Plaza Glen Cove, NY 11542 Telephone: (516) 656-5000 Corporate Offices: Acclaim Japan, Ltd.1-6-4, Yurakucho Chiyoda Bldg., 9F Chiyoda-Ku Tokyo, Japan 10
Telephone: 011 81 3 3501 7222 Acclaim Entertainment GmbH Furstenfelder Strasse 9/4 D-80331 Munchen, Germany Telephone: 011-49 89 23 66 24 0 Acclaim Entertainment, Ltd. Moreau House 112-120 Brompton Road Knightsbridge
London SW3 1JJ Telephone: 011 441-71-344-5000 Acclaim Entertainment, SA 12/14 Rond Point des Champs Elysees 75008 Paris, France Telephone: 011 33 1 53831730

3.4 Appendix 4. Financial data

(a) ACCLAIM OPERATIONS AND BALANCE SHEET DATA
FISCAL YEAR END 31 AUGUST

	1998	*1997*	*1996c*	*1995b*	*1994a*
	000's	000's	000's	000's	000's
Statement of operations data					
Net revenues	326,561	165,411	161,945	566,723	480,756
Cost of revenues	148,660	89,818	191,790	291,474	249,902
Gross profit (loss)	177,901	75,593	(29,845)	275,249	230,854
Marketing and sales	61,691	57,266	116,142	125,813	102,035
General and administrative	54,149	68,831	76,625	66,503	46,721
Research and development	37,367	41,689	46,864	12,267	4,628
Goodwill write-down	-	25,200	-	-	-
Litigation settlements	-	23,550	-	-	-
Downsizing charge	-	10,000	5,000	-	-
Earnings (loss) from operations	24,694	(150,943)	(274,476)	70,666	77,470
Other (expense) income, net	(3,240)	(8,117)	5,609	5,608	(475)
Earnings (loss) before income taxes	21,454	(159,060)	(2,68,867)	76,274	76,995
Net earnings (loss)	20,690	(159,228)	(221,368)	44,770	45,055
Basic earnings (loss) per share $	0.4	(3.21)	(4.47)	1.05	1.18
Diluted earnings (loss) per share $	0.37	(3.21)	(4.47)	0.86	1.00

(a) Includes results of operations of Acclaim comics from 29 July 1994.

(b) Includes results of operations of Iguana from 4th January 1995 and of Lazer-tron for the entire year.

(c) Includes results of operations of Acclaim Studies – Salt Lake City, Inc (formerly, Sculptured Software Inc) and Probe Entertainment Ltd ('Probe') for the entire year

31 AUGUST

	1998	*1997*	*1996*	*1995*	*1994*
	000's	000's	000's	000's	000's
Balance sheet data					
Working capital (deficiency)	(19,100)	(64,156)	(10,039)	200,455	131,820
Total assets	160,407	133,175	239,651	442,827	335,878
Current portion of long-term debt	724	1,002	25,527	25,196	1,538
Long term liabilities	56,629	59,472	4,032	461	41,754
Stockholders' (deficiency) equity	(21,773)	(59,046)	93,589	314,707	175,243

(b) **Results of operations**

	Fiscal year ended 31 August		
	1998	*1997*	*1996*
	%	%	%
Domestic revenues	66.4	49.7	58.7
Foreign revenues	33.6	50.3	41.3
Net revenues	100.0%	100.0%	100.0%
Cost of revenues	45.5	54.3	118.4
Gross profit (loss)	54.5	45.7	(18.4)
Marketing and sales	18.9	34.6	71.7
General and administrative	16.6	41.6	47.3
Research and development	11.4	25.2	28.9
Goodwill write-down	-	15.2	-
Litigation settlements	-	14.2	-
Downsizing charge	-	6.1	3.1
Total operating expenses	46.9	137.0	151.1
Earnings (loss) from operations	7.6	(91.3)	(169.5)
Other (expense) income, net	(1.0)	(45.9)	3.5
Earnings (loss) before income taxes	6.6	(96.2)	(166.0)
Net earnings (loss)	6.3	(96.3)	(136.7)

The above table shows statements of consolidated operations data as a percentage of net revenues for the years indicated.

(c) **Net revenues**

The company's gross revenues were derived from the following product categories:

	1998	*1997*	*1996*
	%	%	%
Portable software	1.00	2.00	8.00
160bit software	-	9.00	44.00
32-bit software	30.00	37.00	32.00
64-bit software	57.00	33.00	-
PC software	10.00	15.00	12.00
Other	1.00	4.00	4.00

The numbers in the chart do not show the effect of sales credits and allowances granted by the company in the periods covered, since the company does not track such credits and allowances by product category. Such credits and allowances are material to the company's results of operations in fiscal year 1996. Accordingly the numbers presented may vary materially from those that would be disclosed if the company were able to present such information as a percentage of net revenues.

3.5 Appendix 5. Consolidated balance sheet and geographic financial data

(a) Consolidated balance sheets

(In 000's of $ except per share data)	31st August 1998	1997
Assets		
Current assets		
Cash and cash equivalents	47,273	26,254
Accounts receivable – net	39,177	18,729
Inventories	3,430	3,546
Prepaid expenses	16,571	20,250
Total current assets	106,451	68,779
Other assets		
Fixed assets - net	29,294	34,268
Excess of cost over fair value of net assets acquired – net of accumulated amortisation of $19,218 and $17,104, respectively	21,433	23,547
Other assets	3,229	6,581
Total assets	160,407	133,175
Liabilities and stockholders' deficiency		
Current liabilities		
Trade accounts payable	24,218	17,007
Short-term borrowings	16	643
Accrued expenses	92,207	107,928
Income taxes payable	6,918	4,840
Current portion of long-term debt	724	1,002
Obligation under capital leases – current	1,468	1,515
Total current liabilities	125,551	132,935
Long term liabilities		
Long –term debt	51,931	52,655
Obligation under capital leases – non-current	1,110	2,264
Other long-term liabilities	3,588	4,553
Total liabilities	182,180	192,407
Minority interest	-	(186)
Stockholders' deficiency		
Preferred stock, $0.01 par value; 1,000 shares authorised none issued	-	-
Common stock, £0.02 par value; 100,000 shares authorised; 52,634 and 50,122 share issued, respectively	1,053	1,002
Additional paid in capital	189,645	173,373
Accumulated deficit	(209,180)	(229,870)
Treasury stock, 523 and 474 shares, respectively	(3,103)	(2,904)
Foreign currency translation adjustment	(188)	(647)
Total stockholders' deficiency	(21,773)	(59,046)
Total liabilities and stockholders' deficiency	160,407	133,175

(b) **Operations in geographic areas**

	USA 000's	*Europe* 000's	*Japan* 000's	*Other* 000's	*Eliminations* 000's	*Consolidated* 000's
Year ended 31 August, 1998						
Sales to unaffiliated customers	216,830	107,032	2,699	-	-	326,561
Transfers between geographic areas	6,546	72	-	-	(6,618)	-
Total net revenues	223,376	107,104	2,699	-	(6,618)	326,561
Earnings (loss) from operations	15,852	9,352	(510)	-	-	24,694
Identifiable assets at 31 august 1998	121,945	37,734	728	-	-	160,407
Year ended 31 August 1997						
Sales to unaffiliated customers	82,158	72,401	8,348	2,504	-	165,411
Transfers between geographic areas	4,269	-	-	90	(4,539)	-
Total net revenues	86,427	72,401	8,348	2,594	(4,359)	165,411
Earnings (loss from operations	154,877	4,146	(687)	475	-	(150,943)
Identifiable assets at 31 August 1997	108,132	24,055	859	129	-	133,175
Year ended 31 August 1996						
Sales to unaffiliated customers	57,742	86,043	14,945	3,215	-	161,945
Transfers between geographic areas	6,368	-	-	91	(6,459)	-
Total net revenues	64,110	86,043	14,945	3,215	-	161,945
Earnings (loss) from operations	(281,159)	6,041	1,369	(727)	-	(274,476)
Identifiable assets at 31 august 1998	204,749	23,415	9,442	2,045	-	239,651

Export sales form the USA have insignificant during each of the year sin three year period ended 31 August 1988 (figures in 000's)
Source: for Financial Data – Acclaim Entertainment Inc

3.6 Appendix 6: Newspaper article: DVD

Timid software makers stifle potential of DVD

SOUNDING OFF

This medium has huge potential but too little material is being produced for it, writes **David Hewson**

PRETTY MUCH any mid-range PC worth its salt these days comes with a DVD drive instead of a CD-Rom. By Christmas, I doubt you will find any computers in the shops with just a standard CD drive.

The price of DVD continues to plummet. You can find an industry standard upgrade, such as Creative's excellent Encore 5, complete with a decoder card for playing movies for less than £150. Swap it for your existing CD, feed the audio into a decent surround-sound speaker system and the video output to a standard television set and you have a set-up that can match that of any standard consumer DVD player found on the high street for £400 or more. It will also play standard audio CDs superbly.

Just one thing is missing, and it's an omission that ought to worry the PC industry deeply. DVD is increasingly being seen as the technological successor to today's video cassettes. More and more move titles are coming out on DVD, and finally at reasonable prices that are just a touch higher than VHS tapes. But DVD was never designed to be just a digital medium for movies any more than CDs were supposed to be restricted to audio.

We want some software and frankly, even after a couple of years of DVD drives being on the shelves, it just isn't there. I have been trying for the past few months to assemble a stash of DVD software titles to recommend to you, but with little luck. The shortage shows in the bundled releases you get with most DVD drives. Usually you are lucky to get a single disk with some music videos on them. Creative does at least bundle a couple of games with its drive, both of them a touch long in the tooth and great examples of what not to do with DVD as a games medium.

The difference between DVD and CD is oomph. DVDs store much more data and can dispatch it into the PC at a higher rate. This is why it is possible to play back a full screen, high-quality digital movie from DVD. A CD just doesn't have the space to store the data.

In theory, this offers the software world endless opportunities. Games could have features that were impossible in the past. Software releases that now appear on multiple CDs could be packed into a single DVD disk.

The Creative bundle shows the cheap option. You get the standard CD game but with video inserts added, usually as transitions or trailers that have no interactivity in them whatsoever. Pretty soon, with this type of game, you start to skip the video altogether and play the same game you could get on CD.

The one title I have come across that is designed for DVD from the ground up shows some of the potential of the medium. Dorling Kindersley's World Atlas Deluxe gives you the chance to fly in real time over a 3D landscape of the world, with stunning graphics, plenty of atlas details and a series of MPEG2 videos. I like it because I've never seen anything similar on a PC before, though to be honest it has the ring of gimmickry about it. It's a lot of fun for a while but I suspect it has limited appeal.

The reason DVD software is so sluggish to take off is, of course, cost. It is hideously expensive to fill the desert of gigabytes on a DVD disk. Moving from CD to DVD is like moving from making 30-minute shorts to producing three-hour Titanic blockbusters. Games companies live precarious existences; few can afford to bet the bank on a new medium which, to most users, is primarily a way of watching movies.

Microsoft is in a position to kick-start this market at the budget end as well as the top end. A DVD version of its £30 standard encyclopedia Encarta is mooted to be on the way to join the £80 Encarta Reference Suite recently released on DVD. It would be encouraging to see a company of this size and wealth do something truly creative that puts DVD software on the public agenda.

This is great technology that can make flaky video and low-grade sound a thing of the past. But until more software appears it will best be regarded as a wonderful audio and CD player oddly located inside the belly of your PC.

3.7 Appendix 7: Newspaper article: competition

COMPANIES & MARKETS

 WEDNESDAY APRIL 28 1999 Week 17

Sony forecasts fall in PlayStation sales

Sega's Dreamcast console brings stiff competition

By Paul Abrahams in Tokyo

The meteoric rise of PlayStation, the games console that swept aside established rivals from Sega and Nintendo and re-ignited profits at Sony, is at an end.

Sony Music Entertainment, the music and computer game subsidiary of the Japanese group, yesterday warned that PlayStation sales would fall this year after four years of phenomenal growth.

The warning is a blow for Sony. The parent company is struggling with lacklustre demand for its traditional audio-visual products, and has become used to strong sales growth and operating profits from the computer games business. In just four years, the PlayStation came from nowhere to become the world's top-selling games machine, toppling machines from Sega and Nintendo.

The group is now facing increased competition from Sega's more powerful Dreamcast product, launched last year in Japan and scheduled to be introduced into the US and Europe later this year.

Sony has announced the specifications for the PlayStation 2 to meet the competition from Dreamcast. But it must make the difficult transition to its next generation product without unnecessarily undermining sales of the original. The group said it did not expect PlayStation 2 to make a significant contribution to the current year's results.

Sony, which in January intends to acquire all the shares in Sony Music Entertainment it does not own, will announce full-year results today.

Kazutoshi Shiraishi, executive vice-president at Sony Music Entertainment, said global sales of the PlayStation console in the year to March 2000 would fall from last year's 21.6m units to 17m. He said sales growth had peaked in Japan, down from 4.95m units to 3.75m in the year to March. Sales in Europe, which expanded from 6.9m units to 8.9m units last year, are expected to continue to grow. In the US, they were up from 7.72m units to 8.95m last year.

The strong growth of the PlayStation last year – thanks to software titles such as Crash Bandicoot – offset poor results at Sony Music's traditional recording and music operations.

For the year ending March 31, Sony Music Entertainment's pre-tax profits excluding exceptionals jumped from Y19.54bn to Y35.88bn (£187m) on flat turnover at Y226bn. However, net earnings fell from Y36.26bn to Y31.86bn and operating profits fell from Y18.25bn to just Y246m.

Mr Shiraishi warned that this year the dividend income from Sony Computer Entertainment – its 49.9 per cent affiliate which markets the PlayStation – was likely to fall from Y35.8bn last year to Y30bn in the current year. He predicted pre-tax profits for the whole company of Y42.7bn and net earnings of Y37.2bn on sales of Y222.7bn.

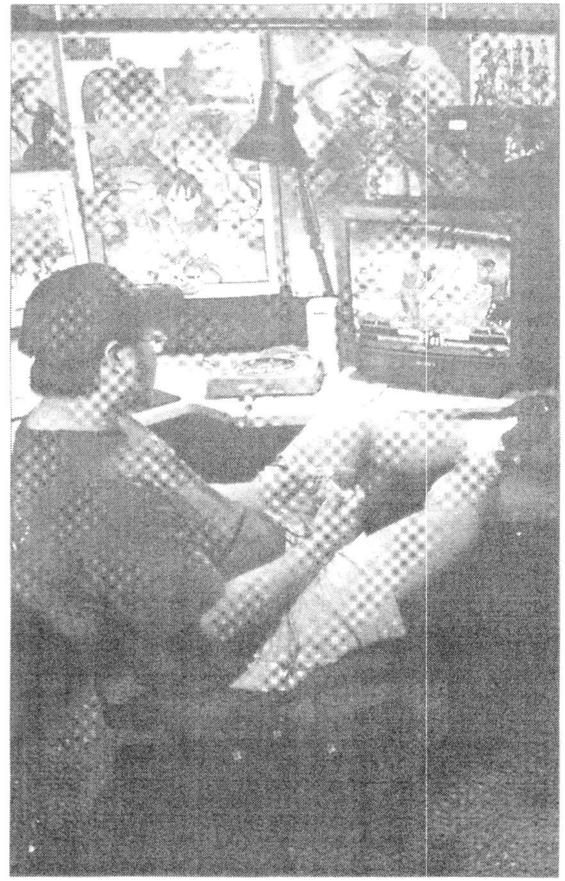

A Sony quality assurance worker puts a PlayStation game through its paces at the company's offices in Foster City, California Picture: AP

13 Acclaim Entertainment Inc: Précis, Marketing Audit, SWOT, Analysis of Appendices

This chapter covers the following topics.

1 INTRODUCTION

1.1 Having now completed your précis you can now compare it with the three specimens which follow.

1.2 *Sample précis 1.* This is minimal in length and content. It is also unstructured. The writer has tended to focus on a single issue, so that by no means can this be considered to be a précis of the case as a whole. It is not very well written and some of the statements made are questionable.

1.3 *Sample précis 2.* This is longer and has some structure. Whilst it is better than sample 1, it does contain some value judgements, rather than being consistently objective and sticking strictly to the facts given in the case.

1.4 *Sample précis 3.* This is the only one of the three which actually gives details of the sort of company Acclaim is. It is also longer and better structured than its predecessors. This précis tends to stick to the facts presented in the case and does not present solutions.

1.5 Well which one of these do you prefer and how does your own compare? Hopefully you will agree that sample précis 3 exhibits more command and would give the reader more confidence in what followed than sample précis 1. You may however, have covered more items in your own précis.

2 SAMPLE PRÉCIS

2.1 *Sample précis 1*

Acclaim finds itself in a very competitive software market where sustainable competitive advantage appears to be very difficult as a number of companies offer very similar levels of value.

Allied to this, the nature of the software development – very high fixed costs and very long development lead times – means the company is now very vulnerable to financial troubles if just one or more of its products fail.

A shake-out of the market already appears to be taking place with the number of players reducing. With this in mind, the future of Acclaim looks bleak unless it can find new ways to sustain long-term competitive advantage.

The choice it faces is simple: it will either go out of business or be taken over by a competitor. New competitive advantage can be found by capitalising on its unique strengths and by exploiting the tremendous new opportunities in the software industry as a result of the Internet and other new technologies.

Acclaim finds itself in what Roach (1981) referred to as the 'V' curve:

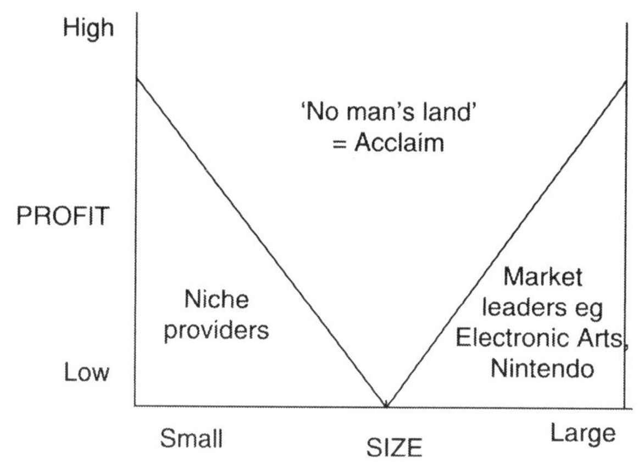

The niche providers ie, the small developers reap high profits just by focusing on development. Medium sized companies such as Acclaim are unable to realise competitive advantage because they have neither the focus of the smaller providers nor the size of the large providers such as 'electronic Arts' which allows them to benefit from economies of scale.

2.2 *Sample précis 2*

Acclaim is a small company competing in a fast moving and highly technical emerging market with a high customer volatility and rapid product obsolescence.

Competition is essentially at a 'title' level and the development of a title is extremely costly. Successful titles are necessary to sustain competitive advantage.

The interactive market is also highly seasonal. Typically, demand soars at Christmas time when competitors invest heavily in promotion.

Market trend

Consumers are becoming better educated, predicating a demand for ever more sophisticated products incorporating special effects, interactive video etc, of greater complexity and cost.

As access to the Internet spreads, online purchase becomes more viable as a new/alternative delivery channel.

Company overview

Product. Acclaim competes on all available platforms and develop software for all the hardware producers (Nintendo = 60% of revenue, Sony = 30%). Research and Development resources are therefore spread. Successful titles have been developed in-house.

Distribution. Acclaim operates internationally, competing for shelf space in USA stores but operating through subsidiaries in other countries. There appears to be a general lack of control of distribution channels, inducing higher costs and lower margins than necessary.

Licensing. Acclaim has to compete to renew all its licences for Nintendo, Sony and Sega, every year.

Promotion. Communications are targeted at the end user using the traditional channels and the Internet.

Competition. Three of the five forces (Porter) are extremely high, namely competitors, threat of substitutes, and the bargaining power of customers. The threat of new entrants is quite low as is the bargaining power of suppliers. Taken together these five forces indicate an extremely tough market. Acclaim must remain on top of technological advance in order to sustain a competitive advantage.

2.3 *Sample précis 3*

The company

Acclaim Entertainment is a worldwide developer, publisher and mass marketer of interactive entertainment software for use with dedicated interactive entertainment hardware platforms and multi-media computer systems. It is one of the earliest multi-platform publishers and one of the largest independent publishers of software for entertainment platforms.

The company now owns a captive development studio – Iguana; Sculptured software, and Acclaim Entertainment Inc Europe based in the UK. It also owns a motion capture studio and technologies for software development. Acclaim invests about 20% of its revenue in product development.

The company has grown rapidly since its establishment but suffered losses in 1996/97 when the industry made the transition from 32-bit to 64-bit platforms. It did, however, return to profit in 1998.

Software distribution is handled by an in-house management team in North America and by subsidiaries of Acclaim Entertainment Inc Europe in the UK, France, Germany Spain, Australia, Japan and Singapore. For other countries, regional distributors are appointed.

The industry

The game industry is driven by the size of the installed base of entertainment platforms such as Nintendo, Sony, Sega and PCs.

Windows of opportunities for PC platforms are typically open for about 18 months and no single interactive entertainment platform has achieved a lasting dominance.

Success in the industry is dependent on the availability of financial resources, since the costs of developing and marketing software are very high. Software development is driven by the hardware platforms.

Rapid technological development in games systems are set to significantly change the shape of the industry and delivery via the internet is becoming more viable.

Competition

This is intense and the number of key players is shrinking. The level of investment and risk entailed acts as a disincentive for new market entrants.

Competition is large based on the number and quality of titles, access to shelf space, sales of the entertainment platforms for which the title is written and the level of marketing support.

The market

Is highly seasonal and typified by inflated sales in the last quarter. The market is growing fast and currently dominated by console sales (67%) by stable and established vendors, but this situation could rapidly change with advances in hardware technology.

The target market is currently mainly male but the trend is towards more female users. The platform segment lies mainly with 15-24 year olds whilst PC games are bought more by the 15-34 year old group. However, customer groups and their age ranges change with increasing sophistication coupled with technological advance.

---

3 MARKETING AUDIT: INFORMATION CHECKLIST

Checklist

3.1 (a) Before doing the audit proper you might like to try the information checklist mentioned in Chapter 8 Paragraph 3.7 and the checklist format in Chapter 1, Paragraphs 2.8 and 2.9.

(b) You should use this checklist to determine the information we have on Acclaim and the information we don't have. You could use a tick to show the information we have and a cross (X) to show the information we don't have (and which might then form the basis of your MkIS/MR recommendations later on in your plan). Further refinements might be to use P for information we have in part only and NA for not applicable. Really organised students might like to note the page numbers on which items ticked or marked P occur.

(c) Having done this operation you might like to compare your results with those of the syndicates which follow noting that there are likely to be some discrepancies, since this exercise is partly judgmental.

Internal

3.2 (a) *Current position*

(i) *Performance*

P Total sales in value and in units
✓ Total gross profit, expenses and net profit
P Percentage of sales for sales expenses, advertising etc
✓ Percentage of sales in each segment
P Value and volume sales by year, month, model size etc
X Sales per thousand consumers, per factory, in segments
P Market share in total market and in segments

(ii) *Buyers/customers*

X Number of actual and potential buyers by area

P Characteristics of consumer buyers, eg income, occupation, education, sex, size of family etc

P Characteristics of industrial buyers, eg primary, secondary, tertiary, manufacturing; type of industry; size etc

P Characteristics of users, if different from buyers

P Location of buyers, users

P When purchases made: time of day, week, month, year; frequency of purchase; size of average purchase or typical purchase

X How purchases made: specification or competition; by sample, inspection, impulse, rotation, system; cash or credit

- P Attitudes, motivation to purchase; influences on buying decision; decision-making unit in organisation

(b) *Products*

(i) *Acclaim*

- P Quality: materials, workmanship, design, method of manufacture, manufacturing cycle, inputs-outputs
- P Technical characteristics, attributes that may be considered as selling points, buying points
- P Models, sizes, styles, ranges, colours etc
- ✓ Essential or non-essential, convenience or speciality
- P Similarities with other company products
- P Relation of product features to user's needs, wants, desires
- P Development of branding and brand image
- P Degree of product differentiation, actual and possible
- X Packaging used, function, promotional
- X Materials, sizes, shapes, construction, closure

(ii) *Competitors*

- P Competitive and competing products
- ✓ Main competitors and leading brands
- P Comparison of design and performance differences with leading competitors
- P Comparison of offerings of competitors, images, value etc

(iii) *Future product development*

- P Likely future product developments in company
- P Likely future, or possible future, developments in industry
- P Future product line or mix contraction, modification or expansion

(c) *Distribution*

(i) *Acclaim*

- P Current company distribution structure
- P Channels and methods used in channels
- X Total number of outlets (consumer or industrial) by type
- X Total number of wholesalers or industrial middlemen, analysed by area and type
- P Percentage of outlets of each type handling product broken down into areas
- X Attitudes of outlets by area, type, size
- X Degree of co-operation, current and possible
- X Multi-brand policy, possible or current
- X Strengths and weaknesses in distribution system, functionally and geographically

X Number and type of warehouses; location

X Transportation and communications

X Stock control; delivery periods; control of information

(ii) *Competitors*

P Competitive distribution structure; strengths and weaknesses
P Market coverage and penetration
X Transportation methods used by competitors
X Delivery of competitors
X Specific competitive selling conditions

(iii) *Future developments*

P Future likely and possible developments in industry as a whole or from one or more competitors

X Probable changes in distribution system of company

P Possibilities of any future fundamental changes in outlets

(d) *Promotion and personal selling*

(i) *Acclaim*

X Size and composition of sales force

X Calls per day, week, month, year by salesmen

X Conversion rate of orders to calls

P Selling cost per value and volume of sales achieved

X Selling cost per customer

P Internal and external sales promotion

X Recruiting, selection, training, control procedures

X Methods of motivation of salesmen

X Remuneration schemes

X Advertising appropriation and media schedule, copy theme

X Cost of trade, technical, professional, consumer media

X Cost of advertising per unit, per value of unit, per customer

X Advertising expenditure per thousand readers, viewers of main and all media used

X Methods and costs of merchandising

P Public and press relation; exhibitions

(ii) *Competitors*

X Competitive selling activities and methods of selling and advertising; strengths and weaknesses

X Review of competitors' promotion, sales contests etc

X Competitors' advertising themes, media used

(iii) P *Future developments* likely in selling, promotional and advertising activities

(e) *Pricing*

(i) *Acclaim*

P Pricing strategy and general methods of price structuring in company

P High or low policies; reasons why

P Prevailing pricing policies in industry

X Current wholesaler, retailer margins in consumer markets or middlemen margins in industrial markets

X Discounts, functional, quantity, cash, reward, incentive

X Pricing objectives, profit objectives financial implications such as breakeven figures, cash budgeting

(ii) *Competitors*

X Prices and price structures of competitors
P Value analysis of own and competitors' products
X Discounts, credit offered by competitors

(iii) *Future developments*

P Future developments in costs likely to affect price structures
X Possibilities of more/less costly raw materials or labour affecting prices
X Possible price attacks by competitors

(f) *Service*

(i) *Acclaim*

P Extent of pre-sales or customer service and after-sales or product service required (by products)

P Survey of customer needs

X Installation, deduction in use, inspection, maintenance, repair, accessories provision

X Guarantees, warranty period

X Methods, procedures for carrying out service

X Returned goods, complaints

(ii) *Competitors*

P Services supplied by competing manufacturers and service organisations
X Types of guarantee, warranty, credit provided

(iii) P Future possible developments that might require revised service policy

External

3.3 *Environmental audit - national and international*

X Social and cultural factors likely to affect the market, in the short and long term

P Legal factors and codes of practice likely to affect the market in the short and long term

X Economic factors likely to affect market demand in the short and long term

X Political changes and military action likely to impact upon national and international markets

✓ Technological changes anticipated and likely to create new opportunities and threats

3.4 *Marketing objectives and strategies*

P Short-term plans and objectives for current year, in light of current political and economic situation

X Construction of standards for measurement of progress towards achieving of objectives; management ratios that can be translated into control procedures

P Breakdown of turnover into periods, areas, segments, outlets, salesmen etc

X Which personnel required to undertake what responsibilities, actions etc when

P Review of competitors' strengths and weaknesses likely competitive reactions and possible company responses that could be made

P Long-term plans, objectives and strategies related to products, price, places of distribution, promotion, personnel selling and service.

3.5 You are now ready to conduct the marketing audit proper, systematically working your way through the environmental audit, to the marketing functions audit and the other functional audits (financial, production and personnel).

CONSULT THE GUIDANCE NOTES FOR THIS STEP IN CHAPTER 8 PARAGRAPH 2.1
STEP 2.1 CONDUCT A MARKETING AUDIT
ALLOW YOURSELF ABOUT THREE HOURS FOR THIS STEP

Have a thoughtful and *critical* look now at the marketing audits submitted in Section 4 below. Although both have some good points, neither are as comprehensive as they should be. Is yours?

(a) The fist audit is quite succinct and somewhat limited. Pie charts have been used to some effect in analysing the computer games market and Acclaim's market performance. The Porter five forces analysis is quite good but the financial overview is very short, although better than nothing. The analysis concludes with a PEST which is adequate Whilst what has been written is fine, there are no marketing operations audits as such.

(b) The second starts creatively with a map of company operations before moving on to the interns/external environments which are not substructured and simply covered by a list of bullet points. The current portfolio is quite well analysed using a Boston matrix and a product life cycle chart.

4 SAMPLE MARKETING AUDIT 1

Current situation

4.1 Key characteristics of computer games market

(a) This is a substantial market (valued at $14 billion 1997) and has huge growth (4,070 in last 3 years).

(b) The technology changes rapidly.

(c) It is very competitive with a number of major players (Sony, Microsoft, Nintendo among others).

(d) Sales of software depend on sales of hardware.

(e) The PC is emerging as global standard for publishers.

(f) Games have a short PLC (1 year).

(g) The average PLC for consoles is 5 years.

(h) 'Hits' have enormous merchandising potential.

(i) Internet and multi-play are significant developments.

(j) No hardware maker is dominant in the console market.

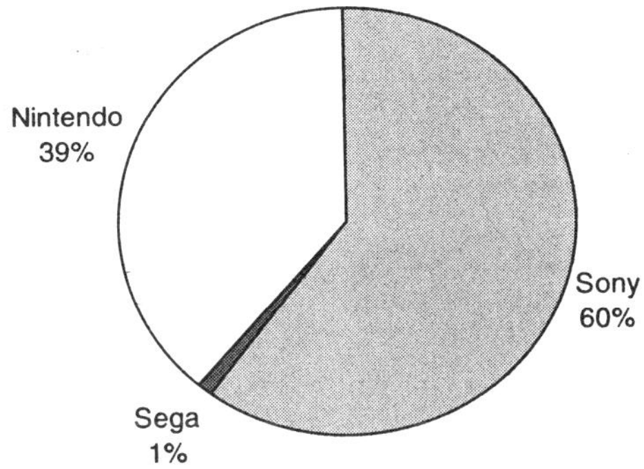

4.2 **AE's (ie Acclaim Entertainment) market performance**

(a) Market share is currently 1.7% although in some formats this is much larger (11% Nintendo, 6% PlayStation).

(b) Majority of sales to Nintendo and Sony.

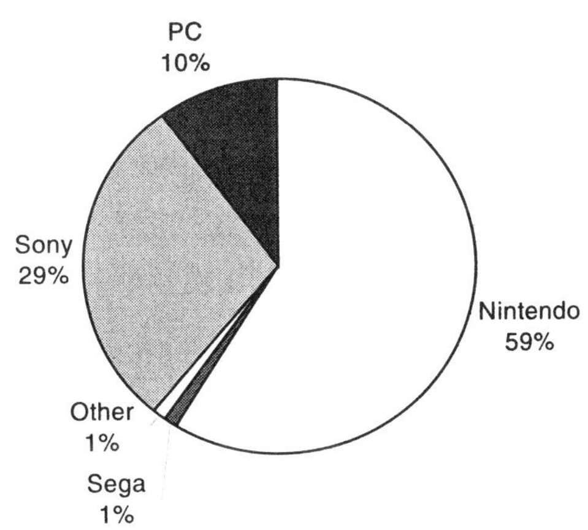

Acclaim's

(c) AE's PC sales are small and shrinking (despite market trends for hardware). Sega's sales are minimal.

(d) AE's international sales account for 34% of turnover, and whilst sales in USA crashed in 1996/97, Europe remained a profitable market throughout.

(e) AE's markets do not reflect the make-up of the world market.

World sales by region 1997

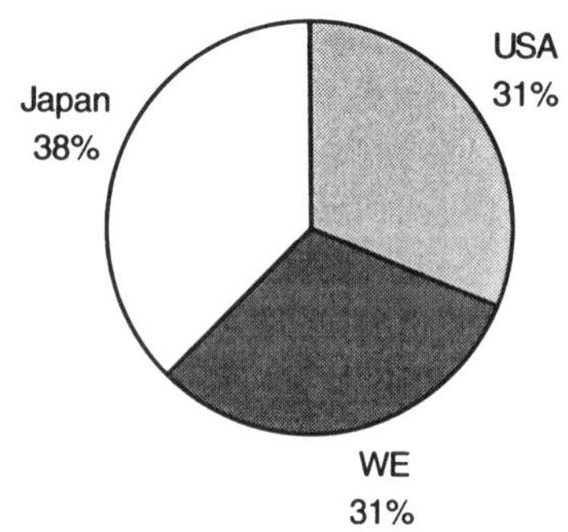

AE sales by region 1997

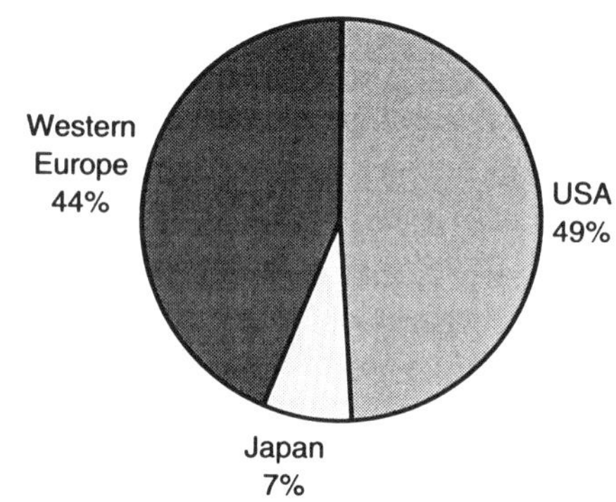

4.3 The competitive position

This is evaluated using Porter's five forces.

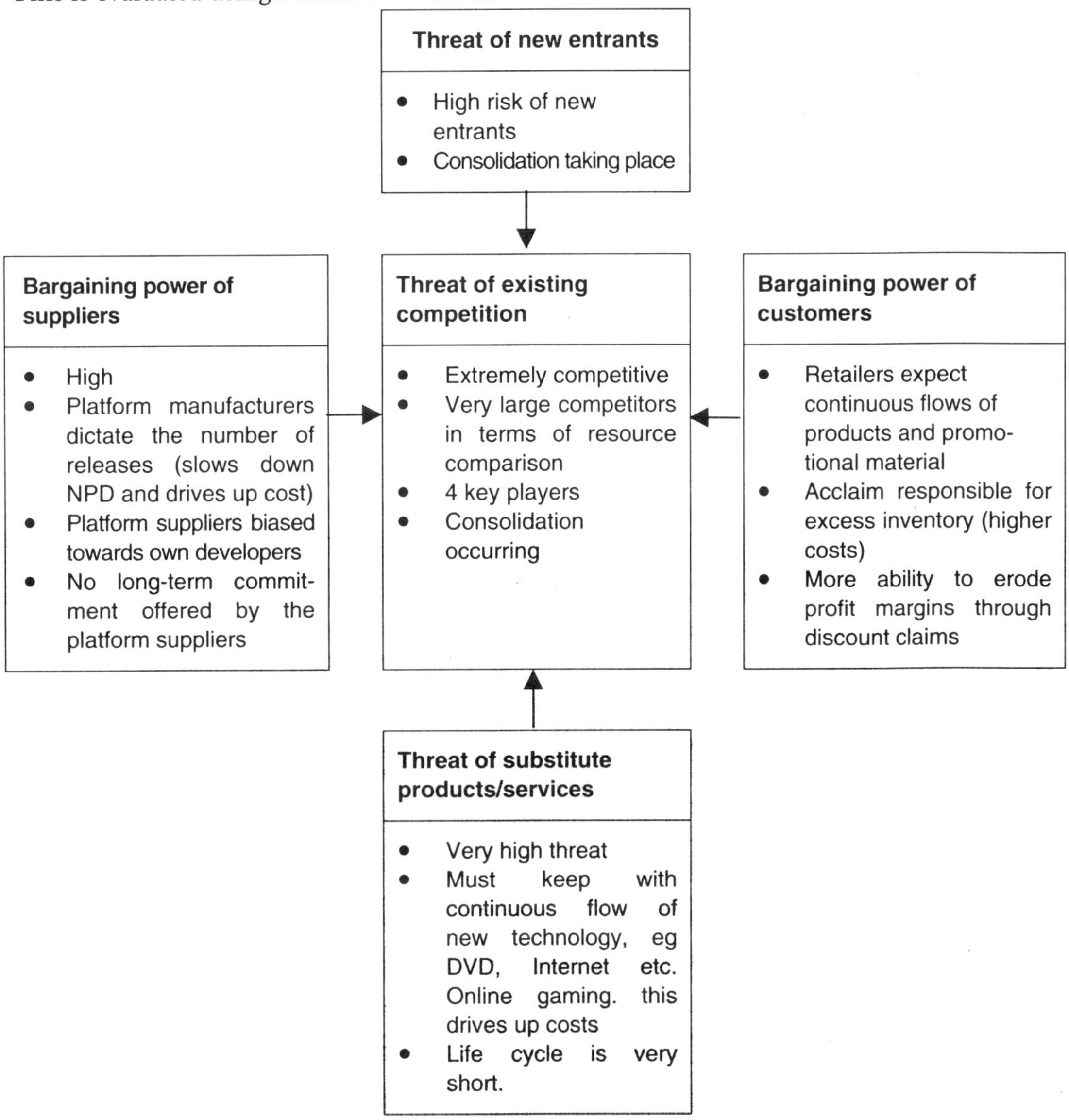

4.4 Financial overview

(a) Working capital for 1998 is negative (due to investment in the development studio).

(b) Earnings per share are increasing over a two year period, ie financial stability is improving.

(c) Gross profit ratio is 1:0.48.

4.5 PEST: Key issues in external environment

(a) **Political**

- Potential legal curbs on advertising to children
- Threat of censorship
- Enquires by European Monopolies and Mergers Commission
- Local legal restrictions and regulatory changes in international markets
- Currency issues
- Tariffs and other economic barriers in international markets

(b) **Economic**

- Rising incomes

- Depression of Japanese economy
- Declining real cost of game equipment and PCs
- Seasonality of market
- Substantial venture capital needed
- Dependency on fluctuating exchange rates
- Volatility of stock price

(c) **Social**

- Increase in leisure time
- Age profile for games is changing
- More women gamers
- Increase in spend on leisure
- Concern over internet addiction
- Usage of technology
- Changes in home entertainment

(d) **Technology**

- Changes quickly
- Times to market are reducing
- Internet becoming ubiquitous
- PCs becoming more widespread
- PCs emerging as global standard for publishers
- DVD becoming standard in PCs
- MP3 setting net standards
- Capabilities becoming increasingly sophisticated
- No single platform dominating

5 SAMPLE MARKETING AUDIT 2

Current situation

5.1 *Map of company operations*

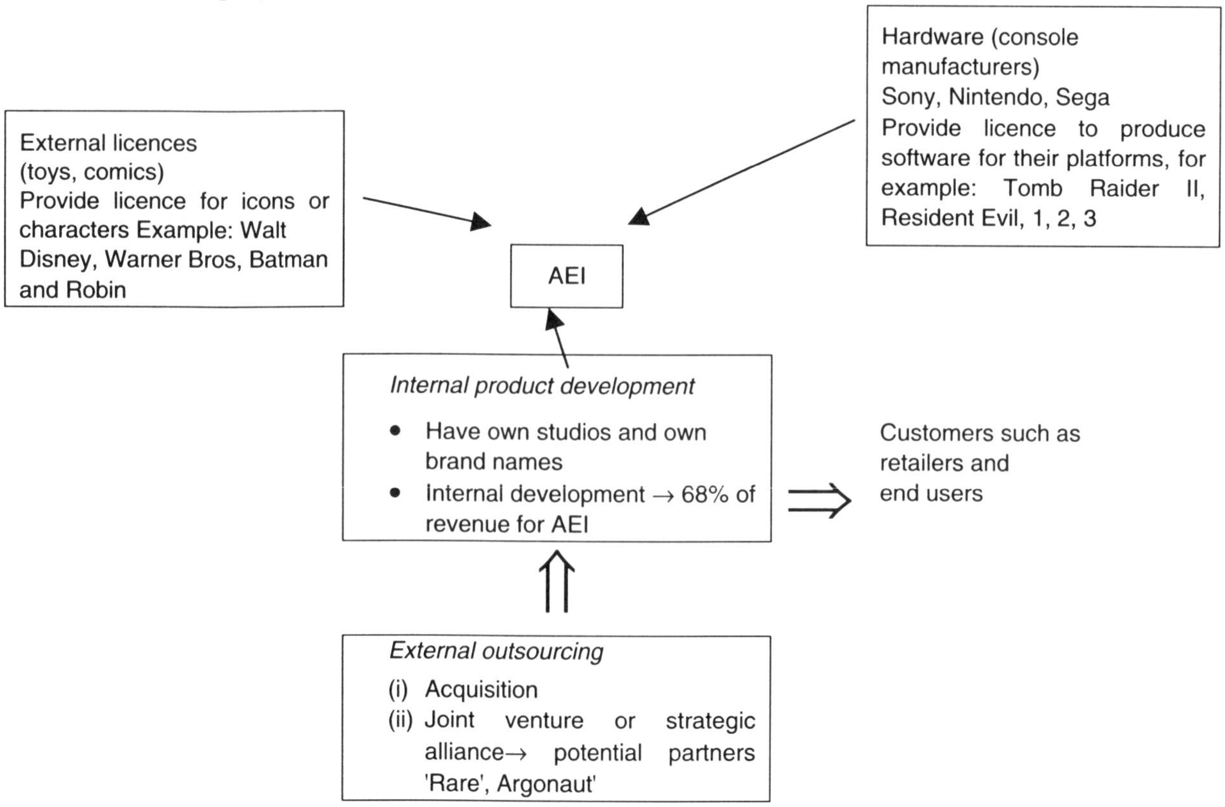

5.2 **Internal environment**

(a) Developers and publishers of software for use by hardware manufacturers – current Nintendo, Sony, Sega, PC's.

(b) Acclaim's primary strengths are in design, technology and quality product offerings.

(c) Acclaim is product-led with little evidence of a planning culture.

(d) The new produce development (NPD) process is too slow and costly for the high tech environment and subsequent speed of the PLC (sales peak at 3 months)

(e) Acclaim is emerging from a period of financial difficulty ie 32-64-bit transition period

(f) To stay competitive, Acclaim requires investment in technology (ie sound digitised speed, music and video)

(g) Reliant on high turnover due to high fixed costs in R&D, marketing , sales and administration

(h) Reliant on key personnel

5.3 **External environment**

(a) Technology is presenting opportunities for competitors: (telecommunications and home appliance makers); and Acclaim (new hardware platforms, DVD, multiplay internet games).

(b) World trade cycles are creating attractive new markets.

(c) Increased leisure time creates more opportunities to play games.

(d) The industry is 'hit' driven.

(e) Games marketers rely on hardware manufacturers.

(f) Software sales in the home market are stable whilst internationally they are declining.

(g) Threats due to the competitive nature of the industry and convergence in technology create opportunities for those outside the games industry.

(h) Competition is squeezing margins on PC games.

5.4 **Market**

(a) The market is influenced by hardware manufacturers creating cycles in software development

(b) Technology is widening the scope for competition and competitive advantage.

5.5 **Market trends**

(a) Hit driven

(b) Rapid technological change – new hardware consoles every 5 years (and 18 months for PC's)

(c) Consolidation as companies globalise

(d) Fierce competition, lower margins

(e) High level of employee mobility

(f) High software development costs

5.6 Current portfolio

(a) Although simplistic in nature, the following portfolio review encourages management to think strategically.

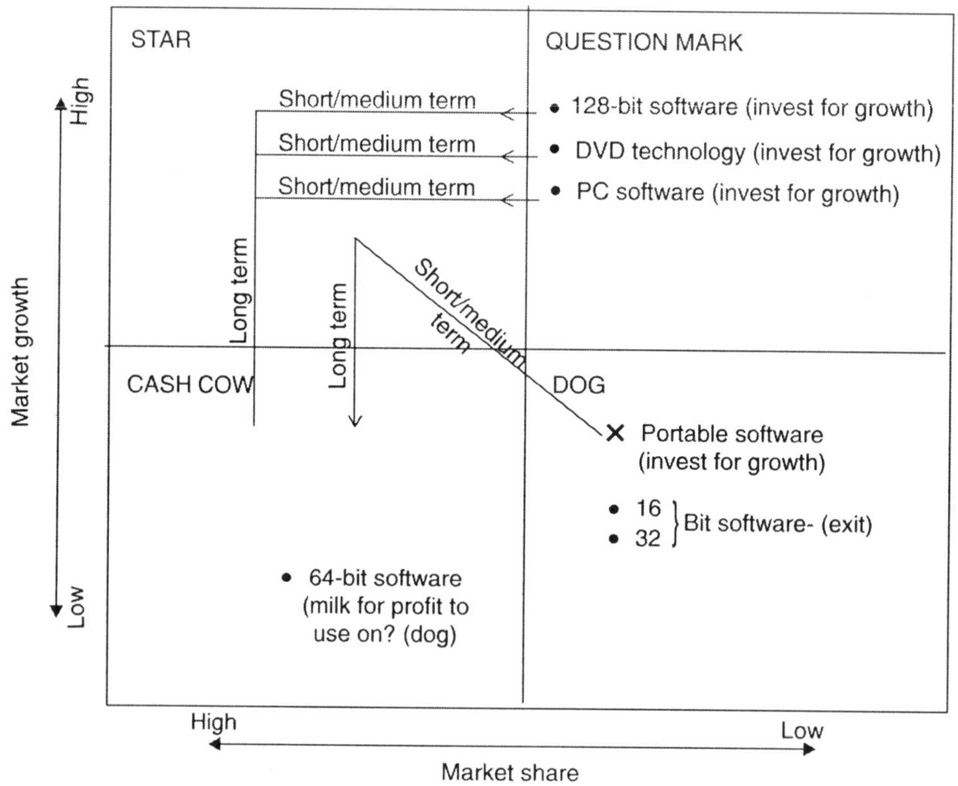

(b) **Future directions of products**

(i) **Assumption.** New Nintendo and Sony hardware will be DVD-driven, 128-bit software.

(ii) Using the information contained in Appendix 4, *Net Revenues*, we can identify the proportion of revenue derived from software sales (and trends over-time).

(iii) Although market share is not known, it is a useful tool, as it highlights the **imbalance in Acclaim's portfolio** as significant investment will be required to fund the question marks and nurture the dogs and turn them into cash cows.

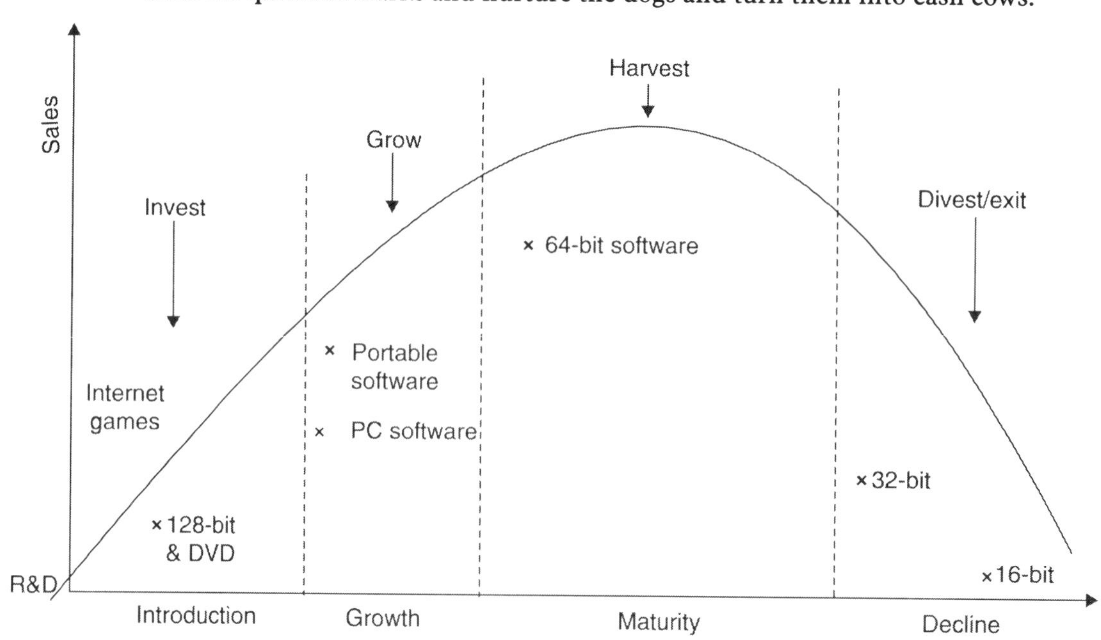

(iv) Acclaim's products are in varying stages of the PLC. In particular the transition period between 64-bit and 128-bit software will need to be managed.

(1) Extending the life cycle of 64-bit games through promotion, cost reductions and differentiation key segments whilst investing in 128-bit software to penetrate the market.

(2) Investment in R&D for games to suit new hardware platforms and new mediums such as Internet games.

6 SWOT ANALYSES

6.1

CONSULT THE GUIDANCE NOTES FOR THIS STEP IN CHAPTER 8 PARAGRAPH 2.2
STEP 2.2 DO A SWOT ANALYSIS
ALLOW BETWEEN 2 AND 3 HOURS FOR THIS STEP

6.2 All three samples which follow are quite good and typical of the norm, give or take differences in the number of items listed. What all three samples **lack is any attempt to categorise the items.**

(a) A strength can be major, middling or minor and of high/medium or low importance. For example, geographical coverage could be rated as a major strength but of low importance, whilst lack of brand awareness could be both a major weakness and of high importance.

(b) Equally, opportunities can be prioritised in terms of high/low attractiveness against the probability of success.

(c) Threats can be ranked on whether the seriousness and the probability of occurrence are **high or low.**

(d) What is certain is that not all the items listed in these SWOTs are of equal weight and importance.

6.3 SWOT analysis: example 1

Strengths	*Weaknesses*
1 The first multiformat published in the industry	1 Over-reliance on outdated platform games
2 A worldwide developer, publisher and mass marketer of interactive entertainment software	2 Poor performance in mid-1990s
3 One of the largest independent publishers of software in US	3 Facing complex task of maintaining old titles as well as promoting new ones
4 Licensing agreement with major hardware suppliers eg Sega, Sony, Nintendo	4 Net revenue decline for international sales in 1998
5 Licensing agreement with toy company	5 In the past, the company experienced significant delays in introduction of certain titles
6 Well developed procedures for testing software by reducing the chance of bugs	

Opportunities	*Threats*
1 Growth in PC market 2 Development of Internet and new channels of distribution 3 Increased demand in software 4 One year technology lag between US and Europe 5 Multiply has become popular 6 Female market	1 Rapid technology change in PC market 2 Globalisation (culture problem) 3 Complexity and increased cost of developing software 4 Unexpected change in environment 5 Entry of new competition 6 Changes in consumer buying behaviour

6.4 SWOT analysis: example 2

Strengths	*Weaknesses*
1 A substantial independent player in the world software games market, with improving results 2 Strong R&D ability. Sophisticated programming of tools and engines for designing and development capability. 68% of revenue comes from internally developed products 3 Proprietary technology and product development capability 68% of revenue comes from internally developed products 4 Management experience and expertise. Better control – the creative process, product quality, release timing of the cost of hardware 5 Extensive and individual promotional campaign for each product 6 Quality product. Well-developed procedures for testing software and eliminating bugs prior to manufacture	1 High development cost 2 Litigation obligation, responsible for any warranty and repair claims 3 Negative equity 4 Restriction from plat from manufacturers – license agreement 5 Too dependent on key personnel
Opportunities	*Threats*
1 Future development of the Internet and PC market 2 Unexplored international markets 3 Licensing of merchandising agreement of its popular characters in interactive entertainment and other media such as movies 4 Cross-merchandising opportunities	1 Unsuccessful licensing negotiation 2 Shortening P/C and increase in the complexity in PC platform 3 Impact from Internet, the change of consumer behaviour 4 High return of goods/claims 5 Unable to anticipate new platforms

6.5 SWOT analysis: example 3

Strengths	*Weaknesses*
• Top ten player • Products for all formats • Vertically integrated in technology • Own intellectual property rights (IPR) on majority of sales • High production standards • Diversified into merchandising and printing • Some strong US product brands • Established distribution in US and Europe (some areas)	• Variable recent financial performance • US-centric • Software bias towards consoles (especially Nintendo 64) • Not presenting hardware markets (vulnerable during platform transactions) • Insufficient market knowledge (long time to market) • Little global or 'umbrella' brand awareness • Japan/ROW present low and falling
Opportunities	*Threats*
• High pace of technology change, allowing improved games, increased data storage, portability and multiplay • Convergence of technologies – games, consoles/DVD film players/audio units/TV • Massive market growth (console growth is phased by region and format) • Broadening age appeal (towards 30-40 group) • New distribution/delivery methods (et via internet, interactive TV) • Merchandising and cross-selling	• Competition intense, increasing number of companies – industry shake-out likely • Constant hardware technology change requires good management of transition periods • Short product life cycles, requiring fast capitalisation • Software piracy preventing profit maximisation • Copyright infringement litigation • Censorship and legal curbs on advertising to children • Mobility of staff and related threat to creative IPR

7 ANALYSIS OF APPENDICES

CONSULT THE GUIDANCE NOTES IN CHAPTER 8 PARAGRAPH 2.3
STEP 2.3 CONDUCT ANALYSES/CROSS ANALYSES OF APPENDICES
ALLOW ABOUT 2 TO 3 HOURS FOR THIS STEP

7.1 The next step is to analyse and cross analyse the appendices. Not all the data will be equally meaningful. Before conducting you analysis be sure to read Chapter 8 Paragraph 2.3 and use the format provided. You will need a clear head and two or three hours to do a reasonable job.

7.2 Remember that the format suggested on Chapter 8 Paragraph 2.3 is a summary document. You will want to underpin this with working papers, perhaps containing graphs, pie-charts and financial analysis.

7.3 Now compare your results with the sample that follows. Do you broadly agree? If you have taken your analysis into more detail then all the better.

7.4 The analysis does not carry out all the calculations it says are possible and this is possibly a weakness. The importance you attach to a given appendix and how far you enter into detailed calculations is a matter of judgement. If an appendix has a considerable bearing on an important strategic decision, it warrants your detailed attention and your analysis can be referred to in the examination to justify your decision.

7.5 Nevertheless, the benefits of undertaking a thorough analysis of the appendices are that it often provides valuation extra insights and also corroborates data contained in the text; you gain more credibility in the examination by referring to support from the appendices.

7.6 To help you refer back to the relevant appendix, the table below gives the paragraph number of each appendix in Chapter 12.

No	*Content*	*Chapter 12 para*
1	Leisure software publishers	3.1
2	Market data	3.2
3	Publishing	3.3
4	Financial data	3.4
5	Consolidated balance sheet and geographic data	3.5
6	Newspaper article – DVD	3.6
7	Newspaper article: competition	3.7

7.7 Sample Analysis of Appendices 1

Appendix number	*What is it essentially saying?*	*How does it help us?*	*What other appendices or text can it be related to? (Ch 12 Para ref)*	*If so, what extra information or insights does this reveal?*
1	Gives details of 26 major leisure software companies - base country, company type, turnover, number of staff, key products, key points and a summary statement	Can be ranked on size ie turnover and number of staff grouped by base country and/or key products and the extent of competitive threat assessed. Also gives details of major platform suppliers/customers and possibilities for future mergers/acquisitions	App 2	Gives us the proportion of the total world software market accounted for by these 26 major companies / groupings
			App 4	Can be compared with acclaim's turnover
			Text pp15/16 (paras 2.33-2.39)	Helps us to position acclaim more accurately against the competition and industry trends
2	P25 (App 2(a)) gives World Software Market in $ for 94-97 split into Consoles and purchase, split into Europe, USA, Japan and (by default) others	We can establish comparative trends and see, for example, that Europe, USA and Japan accounted for c.93% of the world market in 97. Also that the Console market grew by c.60% 97 over 96 to represent c.63% of the total market versus c.37% for PCs. All this helps us to decide which market sectors look most promising for future development	Text pp6,8,19 (paras 2.15-2.18,2.21-2.28)	Corroborates / contradicts data given in the text. Can be used to support our proposals. Illustrates market changes year on year
	p.26 (App 2(b)) splits European market down by country for 1995-98	Tells us for example, that in 98, the UK, Germany, and France accounted for c.68% of the total market for the 8 countries listed	Text p.4 (para 2.11)	UK, Germany and France are the European countries where Acclaim publish and distribute direct
	pp.27/28 (App 2(c),(d))give thenumber of households having hardware installed for Nintendo 64, Sony Playstation and Sega Saturn in 7 European countries 95-98	We can, for example, see that the UK, France and Germany account for c.60% of the total, and establish trends	Text pp.8,9,16,17,19 (para 2.21-2.23,2.40)	Confirms dominance of these 3 platforms, but also illustrates the volatility of the market. Shows future development potentials
3	Not specifically described in the text but assumed to be video front covers and for advertisements for some of acclaim's current range of titles	Adds to the total product knowledge. Gives an impression of the creative platforms being used	Text p15 (para 2.33-2.35)	Illustrates marketing themes and copy platforms
4&5	pp.36/37 (App 4(b), App 5(a) - gives financial data in the form of P&L a/cs and balance sheets for limited periods	Enables financial / ratio analysis to be conducted - see separate example. Gives cause for concern	Text generally. Appendix 2, p.25	Confirms textual data. Adds profitability to the board picture. Indicates that future strategies could be limited by financial/funding difficulties
	p.38 (App 5(b)- adds the financial position for the 3 major trading regions for 96-98	Confirms that the 3 major trading regions account for the vast majority of revenue shows that the USA has moved into profitable operations in 98 following 2 years of losses		
6	Recent article in Sunday Times on DVD	Tells us that there is untapped development potential in DVD	Text generally	Illustrates rapid pace of technological change and potential for future development in this market
7	Recent article in Financial Times forecasting a fall in Sony PlayStation sales	Confirms platform volatility and need for licences from all major players	Text generally Appendix 1	Gives additional revenue and other financial data on Sony

7.8 Example: financial analysis/ratio analysis

(a) *Analysis of Acclaim's current financial performance*

(i) Return on capital employed = $\frac{\text{Profit before tax}}{\text{Total assets} - \text{Total liabilities}}$

Currently negative, so ratio is unhelpful.

(ii) Earnings per share = $\frac{\text{Profit after tax}}{\text{Number of shares issued}} = -3$

Currently negative, which is of concern

(iii) Gearing = $\frac{\text{Long term debt}}{\text{Equity}} = -2:1$

Not covering long-term debt

(b) *Asset utilisation*

(i) Return on assets = $\frac{\text{Sales}}{\text{Fixed assets}} = 11:1$

(ii) Debtor days = $\frac{\text{Debtors}}{\text{Sales}} \times 365 = 44$ days

Debtor days are increasing which is of concern

(iii) Creditor days = $\frac{\text{Creditors}}{\text{Purchases}} \times 365 = 59$ days

Creditor days are decreasing – we are paying our bills more quickly

Stock turn = $\frac{\text{Stock}}{\text{Cost of goods sold}} \times 365 = 8$

Improved from 14, we are turning round our stock faster.

(c) *Profitability*

(i) Gross margin = $\frac{\text{Gross profit}}{\text{Sales}}$ = 54% (Improved from 46% in 1994)

(ii) Healthy gross margin.

(iii) Net profit = $\frac{\text{Net sales}}{\text{Sales}} = 6$

(iv) *Liquidity*

- Current ratio = $\frac{\text{Current assets}}{\text{Current liabilities}} = 0.8:1$
- Quick ratio = $\frac{\text{Current assets - stock}}{\text{Current liabilities}} = 0.8:1$

7.9 General conclusion

Acclaim's financial position is very poor and a cash injection is urgently required to ensure survival.

Sales promotion and cost cutting measures must be employed urgently to improve attractiveness of Acclaim to investors.

14 Acclaim Entertainment Inc: Situational Analysis, Key Issues, Mission Statement, Broad Aims, Major Problems

This chapter covers the following topics.

1 THE STEPS YOU SHOULD TAKE

1.1 In this chapter you will complete your analysis, make judgements and move to decision making mode.

1.2 Firstly you are asked to re-visit your précis, marking audit, SWOT etc and to add further analysis so as to be able to draw up a situation analysis statement summarising all the information, not just the marketing bits.

CONSULT THE GUIDANCE NOTES IN CHAPTER 8 PARAGRAPH 2.4 AND 2.5
STEP 2.4 RECONSIDER YOUR PRÉCIS, MARKETING AUDIT AND SWOT ANALYSIS **STEP 2.5 CONDUCT A SITUATION ANALYSIS**
ALLOW BETWEEN 2 AND 3 HOURS FOR COMPLETING THESE STEPS

1.3 When you have completed your situational analysis statement please compare it with the specimens which follow. The first two are very similar and consist of lists of points. Specimen 3 is actually a severely edited version of the case pages 12 to 16, plus the summary on page 20. Whilst all three specimens are useful and better than nothing, none could be said to cover the entire situation since they exclude quite a lot of the material. Specimen 3 does at least refer to the appendices.

2 SITUATIONAL ANALYSES

2.1 Specimen situational analysis 1

(a) **Internal**

- Acclaim is the fourth largest software company in the world. Poor performance in the 1990s have now been traded out and profit opportunity is better. Still has liquidity problems and negative shareholder equity but underlying gross profits are good for future returns.
- Acclaim has presently enjoyed the growth due to new product introductions and rapid expansion and acquisitions. There is a lack of marketing orientation and customer knowledge, which would provide valuable assistance for future business decisions and survival.
- Acclaim has wide geographical distribution and high level of investment in the US and Europe (studios). However Acclaim her no major market position in any market and falling market share in Japan.
- Acclaim has some established brands – Turok/NFL Quarterback across broad demographic appeal and expertise in software development. Currently 90% of revenues are generated from Nintendo (60%) and Sony (30%) compatible machines.

(b) **External market**

- Software games is a substantial market ($14 billion) with 3 major markets , USA, Western Europe and Japan, making 91% of sales. Growth rates are approximately 40%.
- The market for software is highly dependent upon hardware/platform suppliers and the ability to license software.
- The new technology of providing on-line gaming is a serious threat for Acclaim. This was further endorsed by the **recently announced alliance between Sega and BT for Europe.** Also significant is the growth of interactive TV.
- Successful software titles are highly dependent upon licensing of characters, social mores and brand awareness. This increases the competitive advantage by providing opportunities for cross merchandising.
- Development costs are increasing due to movement to new technology, DVD software, increasing performance expectations.

(c) **External competition**

- Highly competitive with significant amount of sector rivalry
- Substitute technology is evolving rapidly with interactive TV and Internet access to provide on-line gaming.

(d) **Market dynamics**

Clearly there are a number of market forces to consider.

- High dependence on platform suppliers
- Current Acclaim position with Nintendo/Sony 90% of revenue

(i) Factors **driving** the on-line gaming developments

- Increase in Internet access
- Improved channel delivery
- Meeting the need for social interaction
- Potential competitive advantage
- Reach a wider mass market

(ii) Factors **constraining** on-line gaming

- The traditional console base and low costs
- The resolution of Internet images
- Software available/technology

2.2 Specimen situational analysis 2

(a) **Internal**

- Public listed company, traded on Nasdaq
- The first multi-format publisher in the industry
- Markets in USA, European including Germany, UK and France
- Worldwide developer, publisher and mass marketer of interactive entertainment software for use with dedicated interactive entertainment hardware platform (such as Nintendo, Sega, PlayStation) and multimedia computer systems (PCs).
- $^2/3$ of the company's employees are involved in the studio's operations. Sophisticated programming tools and engines help the company to gain competitive advantage in the creation of new and innovative software.
- Responsible for any warranty or repair claims with respect to the software.
- Create its own brands, revenue from licensing and merchandising agreement of its character in interactive entertainment and other media such as motion pictures or television.

Acclaim is a worldwide developer, publisher and mass marketer of interactive entertainment software for use with dedicated interactive entertainment hardware platform and PCs. It acquired companies such as studies to improve its control and develop new and innovative software to USA, European markets. 20% revenue invest on product development.

(b) **Industry**

- The game industry is driven by the size of the installed base of entertainment platforms, such as Nintendo, Sony, Sega and PCs.
- No single entertainment platform or system which has achieved long-term dominance in the interactive entertainment market.
- The life of a **dedicated console** is typically five years. 18 months is the window of opportunity for PC platform.
- Success in entertainment industry depends on the availability of financial resources, as the costs of developing and marketing software are very high.
- Software development is driven by the hardware platforms that are marketed and/or are anticipated to be on the market in future, time and cost of software development for each platform cost of manufacturing software for a platform, possible gross margin for software.

The game software industry is highly dependent on the hardware platform. There are many players but no one platform dominates. Multi-vendors exist but hardware vendors try to maintain preferential relationships to maintain their competitive advantages. PC games follow a trend with

Internet, which gives very low margins for leisure software publishers. The rapid technological advances in games system have significantly changed the look and feel of software and the software development process.

(c) **Competition**

The competition is intense and the number of key players is shrinking. All key competitors have invested heavily in both development and distribution. The whole area of publishing has become more complex and will need to plan for marketing, public relations and development. Globalisation creates cultural problems.

- Acclaim is one of the largest independent publishers of software for entertainment platform. but it has a small share in the more fragmented PC market.
- Competition is based on the quality of the title, access to shelf space, product features sales of the entertainment platforms for which the title is written, the number of titles available for the entertainment platforms and the marketing campaign supporting the title.
- Acclaim's competitive edge is determined by its product quality, marketing and sales ability, proprietary technology and product development capability, capital resources, the strength and depth of its worldwide distribution channels and management experience.

(d) **Product life cycle**

- The development of a game became a skilled task and takes 18 months to complete.
- The initial success of a game is often determined by innovation, write-ups in magazines, and other factors such as recent augmentation of the title through TV or film. The sales pull through of a title often peaks 90-120 days after introduction
- PC software is in the introduction to growth stage of PLC. The overall console market is in growth-to-mature stage.
- The interactive industry is highly seasonal. Typical net revenues are highest during the last quarter of the year.

(e) **Market**

- It is dominated by console sales (63%) by stable established vendors. But it can be seriously affected by new hardware technology. The demand of game software is highly seasonal but it is growing fast.

(f) **Segmentation**

For platform market	aged 15-24
For PC games	aged 15-34

The target market is primarily male but it began to attract a female audience. Customer groups and their age change with technology and are more sophisticated.

2.3 Specimen situational analysis 3

Acclaim Entertainment invests in the creation and development of sophisticated programming tools and engines which are used in the design and development of its software. These particular tools and engines help the company to gain a competitive advantage in the creation of new and innovative software. At present, approximately two-thirds of the company's employees are involved in the studio operations. The company constantly scans the market seeking new sources of brands for use as a base for developing software. The company has well-developed procedures for testing software and eliminating bugs prior to manufacture. The hardware manufacturers also test the software. So far the company's software has not be recalled because of bugs in the system.

Product strategy

The company's intention is to maintain key core product brands in the games industry, and to introduce new products, as potential for a mass market is established. The life cycle of a particular title could range from one to three moths to more than a year. The life cycle is often dependent on the initial success of the title. This initial success is often determined by innovation, write-ups in magazines and other factors such as recent augmentation of the title through TV or film.

Platform licence agreements

The licence agreements with Nintendo, Sony and Sega vary on the rights to develop and distribute software. The company gets non-exclusive rights to utilise the various names (Nintendo, Sega and Sony) on its products. Acclaim Entertainment Inc is responsible for any warranty or repair claims with respect to the software. Fortunately, to date there have been no claims.

Marketing and advertising

In terms of marketing and advertising, the company faces the complex task of maintaining old titles as well a promoting new ones. The target consumers vary from 15-24 for the platform games, and 15-34 for PC games. The target audience is primarily male. Various channels are used for marketing the software such as PR, the Internet, television, radio and magazines. Product sampling is offered through the demonstration software distributed on the Net, as are contests and promotions. The company also undertakes publicity activities, trade shows, co-operative advertising with retailers and in-store advertising.

Production sales and distribution

In order to disseminate its software efficiently, the company tailors its distribution policy to suit each geographic market. Figure 5 shows how distribution is handled in different areas of the world.

Competition

The competition in the interactive entertainment industry is intense. Despite producing software for the major platform manufacturers, the company also faces its most intense competition from them (see Appendix 1). Acclaim Entertainment Inc's size and position in the US market makes it one of the largest independent publishers of software for entertainment platforms (see Table 1). However in the more fragmented PC market it has a small share. Acclaim Entertainment Inc's competitive edges are determined by its product quality, marketing and sales ability (see Appendix 2). The company acquired Acclaim Entertainment Inc Comics in July 1994 and commenced the development and publication of comic book magazines.

Industry trends

The interactive entertainment industry is characterised by rapid technological change. It is clear that there is a never ending battle, with no single entertainment platform achieving long-term dominance (see Appendices 1, 2 and 7). The development of the Internet is likely to create further opportunities and problems for the incumbent software publishers. The interactive industry is highly seasonal typically, net revenues are highest during the last quarter of the year.

Some future developments

The industry is now considering the new generation of console machines. Sega have come out with Dreamcast. They will be able to offer Windows driven software so that the PC platform can be used. DVD technology brings a new dimension to the PC. DVDs store up to 9 times more information than CD-ROMS. Currently very few DVD titles are available, although current PCs now have DVD drives. There is one year lag between the US and Europe. The PCX market is not massive for entertainment software and it is a risky market as the development costs are high with low sales volumes. The life of a dedicated console is typically five years, it is also clear that interactive entertainment is here to stay and the long-term players are likely to be Sony and Nintendo.

The next generation of dedicated consoles will incorporate a portable device such as the Sony Pocketstation, which can receive down-loaded levels of a game for the consumer to carry with them and play, allowing mobility and flexibility.

Gaming has evolved from an isolated experience for a single user to a social environment through the Internet, where on-line gaming connects users across the globe to play against each other. Recently, 'multi'play has become important. This is the need to make games more suitable for many players simultaneously.

Summary

Acclaim Entertainment Inc is a substantial player in the world software games market. As a company it has been very successful, but over reliance on outdated platform games cost it dearly in 1995/96. As it consolidates itself in to a more secure position for the future, numerous problems need to be considered and addressed. These are the growing demand for games on the Internet; the advent on DVD-ROMs with the attendant requirement in design expertise (se Appendix 6), and the continual need for new material and innovative marketing strategies. It enters the millennium with confidence yet with some apprehension as to what the future holds for them.

3 DECIDE KEY ISSUES

CONSULT THE GUIDANCE NOTES FOR THIS STEP IN CHAPTER 8 PARAGRAPH 3.1
STEP 3.1 DECIDE THE KEY ISSUES
ALLOW 1 HOUR TO 1½ HOURS FOR THIS STEP

3.1 You are reminded that the next step is the most important one, since it has the most bearing on the likely examination areas.

3.2 You are also reminded to limit these to a **maximum of six** and that you might like to construct a list of candidate key issues which could then be ranked, as a way of doing this exercise.

3.3 Remember also the technique of parcelling up several minor issues into one major issue as described in Chapter 8 paragraph 3.1.

3.4 Now that you have completed this crucial exercise, please compare your conclusions with those produced by six separate syndicates as given on the next page.

3.5 **Acclaim: Key issues**

Syndicate A2 1 Sales outside the USA 2 Financial performance 3 Dependence upon key personnel 4 The need for licence renewals 5 Legal constraints 6 New product development	*Syndicate B2* 1 Financial performance 2 Sales outside America 3 Dependence on key personnel 4 New product development 5 Licence renewal 6 Legal constraints
Syndicate C2 1 Dependence on key personnel 2 Technological advances 3 Sales outside the USA 4 Legal vulnerabilities 5 Competition 6 Financial performance	*Syndicate D2* 1 Financial performance 2 Dependence on key personnel 3 Competition 4 NPD 5 Licence renewal 6 Dependence on America
Syndicate A1 1 Financial performance 2 Dependence on key staff 3 Legal constraints 4 New product department 5 Sales outside the USA 6 License renewal	*Syndicate B1* 1 Financial performance 2 Competition 3 Dependence on key employees 4 Legal threats 5 NPD 6 Inventory management

3.6 The results of syndicate work in Key Issues indicate quite a strong consensus. Since the Acclaim case study itself (unusually) lists 10 key issues (ie Chapter 11) this is hardly surprising. Do you agree with the consensus? Remember you do not necessarily have to accept the key issues given. What are your best bets with regard to potential exam question areas?

3.7 You are now about to enter the stage when you need to make the big decisions. Hopefully, the standard of your previous analysis will help you to make the right decisions.

4 VISION/MISSION STATEMENT AND BROAD AIMS

CONSULT THE GUIDANCE NOTES IN CHAPTER 8 PARAGRAPHS 3.2 to 3.3
STEP 3.2 DEVELOP A MISSION STATEMENT **STEP 3.3 DECIDE BROAD AIMS**
ALLOW ABOUT AN HOUR FOR EACH OF THESE STEPS

4.1 Remember there should be consistency between your mission statement and your broad aims, also that you should try to limit the latter to four bearing in mind the need to convert these into quantified and time-scaled objectives at a later stage.

4.2 Having completed these two steps you should now compare your results with those of four separate syndicates which follow. Please be critical when looking at these syndicates' work. Since quite a number of companies now precede mission statements with vision statements, some visions have been included.

4.3 **Syndicate C**

Vision statement

AEI will reverse the paradigm of 'hardware sells software' to 'software sells hardware'.

Mission statement

AEI seeks to be a market leader worldwide as a developer, publisher and distributor for major platforms such as Nintendo, Sony and Sega and PC hardware systems. AEI will deliver exciting new multi-layer game formats via the Internet, creating high quality products for a wide variety of audiences.

AEI is focussed on capitalising upon creative and technological competences augmented by marketing and distribution capabilities so as to capture the increasing opportunities in the software and on-line markets.

Broad aims

1 Achieve and sustain growth through sales by continuing penetration worldwide and introducing new quality titles and development of brands

2 To become a category leader by creating benchmark titles

3 To strengthen AEI's position in console games by aligning our product development efforts more closely with our platform customers, and British Telecom or other telecommunication companies

4 To achieve early entrant position in the multi-player, on-line gaming through the Internet, segment

5 To balance the portfolio by increasing the range of titles for the PC market

4.4 Syndicate D

Vision statement

To be recognised as a leading global player in the electronic games market for the delivery of high quality and cutting edge entertainment software

Mission statement

Acclaim Entertainment Inc combines technological expertise and creativity to profitably produce high quality software to fuel customers' imaginations and ensure maximum benefit and enjoyment from leisure time.

Broad aims

1 To further invest in attracting and retaining the top R&D people in the industry

2 To manage relationships with platform manufacturers so as to engender trust and gain long-term contracts

3 To develop markets outside the USA

4 To improve our financial performance

4.5 Syndicate E

Mission statement

To feature in the top five software entertainment providers it the world within the next five years.

Broad aims

1 To achieve a higher level of growth
2 To strengthen our market position
3 To develop more star products
4 To Increase organisational preparedness to deal with industry developments and challenges
5 To continuously innovate and develop eg into the Internet and hardware

4.6 Syndicate F

Vision/Mission statement

To be regarded as the most innovative preferred supplier of interactive entertainment in the markets we serve: This will be characterised by:

- A deep understanding of our customers and delighting them with our product offerings
- Leading edge solutions for creative entertainment
- Partnerships and alliances with our suppliers to develop future innovations
- An exciting and rewarding environment for employees and shareholders
- A continuous programme of marketing research

Broad aims

1 Increase sales organically to improve profit and revenue growth
2 Develop a robust organisational structure, more marketing orientated/customer-facing
3 Anticipate future technological changes
4 Review our information needs

4.7 You were asked to be critical when assessing the work of the above four syndicates. Let us compare notes. If there is woolly thinking at this stage (the initial broad decisions) it is likely to permeate right down through the detail of the ensuing plan. You must ask yourself 'can I convert these broad aims into quantified and time-scaled objectives which will be acceptable to the Board?'

(a) Looking critically at the above - not all aims are consistent with the vision or mission are they? Syndicate C's effort is perhaps a little too wordy and woolly to inspire confidence don't you think? Although the vision statement is quite intriguing, profitability and stakeholder interest are not specifically mentioned in either the mission statement or the broad aims.

Also, some of the broad aims would be quite difficult to convert into SMART objectives eg syndicate E's number 4 and Syndicate F's numbers 3 and 4. Syndicate D's work seems to be the most integrated, although not without its faults.

(b) More often than not syndicates **confuse strategies with objectives** in their minds when drawing up their broad aims. All four syndicates have fallen into this trap to some extent. This leads to the writing of objectives in the examination paper which are really strategies and signals to the examiner that you have not really got your thinking straight at the start.

(c) Too many broad aims = too many objectives and supporting plans. Syndicates C and E has gone beyond the four required. Also, when looking critically at the Mission Statements we should remember that these are intended to be short corporate positioning statements of what business the company is in and its aims for the benefit of target audiences including staff, investors and customers.

4.8 Let us now move on to the next step, that of identifying problems which will get in the way of achieving our mission and broad aims.

5 MAJOR PROBLEMS

CONSULT THE GUIDANCE NOTES GIVEN IN CHAPTER 8 PARAGRAPH 3.4
STEP 3.4 IDENTIFY AND ANALYSE MAJOR PROBLEMS
ALLOW BETWEEN TWO AND THREE HOURS FOR THIS STEP

5.1 Remember to restrict yourself to six major problems in rank order.

5.2 Do not worry if your major problems relate closely with the key issues. This is quite usual.

5.3 Having done this, you can now compare your ranking with those of six syndicates provided below.

5.4 **Acclaim: six major problems ranked by syndicates**

		Rankings					
Problem		A1	B1	C1	D1	A2	B2
1	The financial position, funding for future investment		2	1	2	1	2
2	How to sustain effective new product development	1		3	4	4	3
3	Vulnerability to licence withdrawals and litigation		3	6			
4	Competition		4	5		3	
5	keeping abreast of technological advances	2	5		3		4
6	International expansion into new markets	3	6	2	1	2	1
7	Dependence upon key personnel	4			5		
8	Relationships with platform manufacturers		1	4	6		5
9	Creating and timing of new hits	5				5	6
10	Reduction of risk	6				6	

5.5 It is to be expected that some correlation should emerge between key issues and major problems as well as broad aims. Quite a strong consensus can be seen in the above problems and rankings. This is hardly surprising given the fact that ten key issues have been listed in the case study itself. However, some of the problems are related and can be grouped. Future financial viability is clearly a major concern, together with expansion into new international markets. Other obvious concerns are how to sustain effective new product development, keeping abreast of technological advances and relationships with platform manufacturers.

These are all interrelated – Acclaim can keep abreast of technological advances through closer relationships with the platform manufacturers, thereby developing suitable new products for new international markets, so improving profitable sales and alleviating the currently worrying financial position

5.6 You should now be ready to move forward to your outline plan which hopefully will address these problems.

15 Acclaim Entertainment Inc: Outline Marketing Planning

This chapter contains the following guidance and plans.

1 Introduction: approaching a marketing plan
2 The steps you should follow
3 Outline marketing plan: example 1
4 Outline marketing plan: example 2

1 INTRODUCTION: APPROACHING A MARKETING PLAN

1.1 We are now at the crunch decision stage namely that of drawing up a *complete* marketing plan starting with objectives, progressing through strategy and tactics (including market research) and covering the organisational, financial and human resource aspects. You will also need to schedule, decide review and control mechanisms, and consider contingency action. (All these items are covered in the notes given in Chapter 8, paragraphs 3.5 to 3.6. You will need 15 to 18 hours to do a reasonably thorough job. Relevant examples are given in the next chapter.)

1.2 Remember that you will not be tested on your analysis in itself in the examination room. The purpose of your **complete** plan is to cover and prepare for all potential exam questions.

1.3 Experience shows that syndicates starting on the plan and working against time get bogged down on objectives for far too long, getting mixed up over **corporate objectives** and **marketing objectives**, and then between objectives, strategy and tactics. Tempers can get frayed and confidence lost. A technique we have successfully used to overcome this problem is to get syndicates to blitz through an **outline** plan first, taking a maximum of **one hour** to do this. You can then look at this outline to see that it is reasonably consistent and logical before committing yourself to detail. In this way you see the plan as a whole, whereas if you get straight into the detail you may never see the wood for the trees and never get to the end of your journey. What you are doing is creating a **framework** or a **skeletal plan**.

1.4 A useful **analogy** here is to consider a drawing or a painting. The artist does not normally paint a landscape by immediately painting leaves or blades of grass in great detail. He/she would consider first what proportion of the landscape is to be devoted to sky and what to land; whether the sky is to be cloudy and the land hilly; whether to depict some trees and meadows etc. Having then visualised the painting as a whole and put in the rough parameters, more detail would be added in the sure knowledge that it fitted into the setting. Consider the following two syndicates' work after one hour.

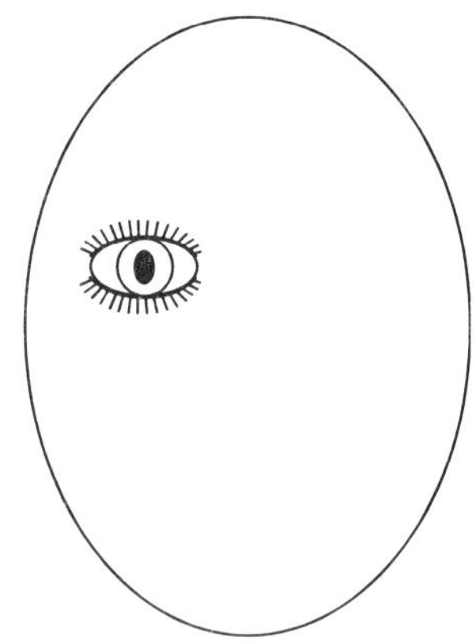

1.5 Syndicate B started with a head and went into great detail on the eye, debating how many eyelashes should be shown, their length, the position of the pupil, the shade of colour etc. They never completed the skeleton.

1.6 Syndicate A visualised their skeleton as a little girl. After one hour they produced a complete skeleton. They then split up to make best use of limited time, one pair to do the detail on the head, another pair the legs, a third pair the arms and a fourth pair the body. After a few more hours, they brought these parts together in the sure knowledge that they would fit.

1.7 If this syndicate had used division of labour without agreeing the skeleton first they might have produced a 'Frankenstein' monster, rather than the perfectly symmetrical little girl they had finished up with.

1.8 Please use this technique now. Produce an outline plan first taking only about one hour. Force it through, do not hover or vacillate over the detail. If it is only rough you can always adjust it later to gain better cohesion and consistency, before doing the detail.

1.9 Having done it, compare it with the very rough outline plans produced by syndicates in about the same time in the pages which follow. These may not be satisfactory but at least the syndicates got there and they all felt a lot better and more in command after the exercise, even though they realised a lot more work needed to be done.

2 THE STEPS YOU SHOULD FOLLOW

2.1 We strongly recommend that you opt to produce an outline plan for Acclaim before developing this into the complete detailed marketing plan required. You are reminded of the steps for the marketing plan proper as follows.

CONSULT THE GUIDANCE NOTES GIVEN IN CHAPTER 8 PARAGRAPHS 3.5 TO 5.2
IN OUTLINE ONLY
STEP 3.5 DEVELOP QUANTIFIED, TIMESCALED OBJECTIVES **STEP 3.6 CONSIDER ALTERNATIVE STRATEGIES. SELECT THOSE MOST APPROPRIATE** **STEP 4.1 DRAW UP DETAILED TACTICAL PLANS COVERING THE MARKETING ORIENTATION** **STEP 4.2 DRAW UP A MARKETING RESEARCH PLAN** **STEP 4.3 CONSIDER ORGANISATIONAL ISSUES, CHANGES AND MARKETING ORIENTATION** **STEP 4.4 CONSIDER ORGANISATIONAL CULTURE AND NEED FOR INTERNAL MARKETING** **STEP 4.5 DETERMINE THE FINANCIAL/HR RESOURCE IMPLICATIONS OF YOUR PLANS** **STEP 4.6 ASSESS COSTS AND DRAW UP INDICATIVE BUDGETS** **STEP 4.7 DRAW UP SCHEDULES GIVING TIMINGS/SEQUENCE OF ACTIONS** **STEP 5.1 SPECIFY REVIEW PROCEDURES AND CONTROL MECHANISMS** **STEP 5.2 DRAW UP OUTLINE CONTINGENCY PLANS** **STEP 5.3 REVIEW YOUR COMPLETE MARKETING PLAN**
YOU WILL NEED ABOUT ONE HOUR TO DO YOUR OUTLINE

Examples of outline marketing plans

2.2 There follows two examples of outline marketing plans drawn up by students, both of which are quite good at this stage and which address some but not all of the problems identified in prior analysis. How does your outline compare?

3 OUTLINE MARKETING PLAN: EXAMPLE 1

Mission statement

3.1 Acclaim Entertainment Inc will continue to maintain its presence in the market, producing customer driven software and establishing strong brands. Through timely product development and strategic partnerships, Acclaim Entertainment Inc will remain focused on emerging technologies and markets.

3.2 Company objectives

Objective	Year 1	Year 2	Rationale
Increase sales from todays level of $326.5m, by:	10%	50%	Sales are predicted to grow in line with the market growth, and effective and efficient marketing activity
Increase gross profit by:	20%	60%	Inline with forecasted sales and efficiency improvements
Increase out market share from current level (estimated to be 24%) by,	2.64%	3.6%	An assumption has been made that the market as a whole is growing at a slower rate than Acclaim, therefore relative market share will increase as sales grow
Increase shareholder values though earnings per share form $0.4	up to $1	$7	Based on strong branding over three years
Reduce NPD time to market from 18 months to,	17 months	12 months	NPD initiative to be instigated to review end-to-end processes and time involvement of strategic partnerships
To become the most recognised non-platform manufacturer software brand (unprompted)	N?A (too short time scale)	Top 3	Stong branding is symbolic of a strong company and lends itself to shareholder value. top 3 over three years is evident after continuous marketing campaign

Corporate strategies

3.3 Corporate strategies

(a) Strategies

(i) The following **assumptions** were used to depict Acclaim against competitors, and Acclaim as objectives are realised.

- The market is growing.
- Acclaim's capability is hindered due to accumulated capital deficit.
- Acclaim's position is compromised by the hardware manufacturers dominance.
- All competitors are in the same market and so are positioned in a vertical plane.
- Appendix 1 was used to determine specific positions/sizes of competitors.

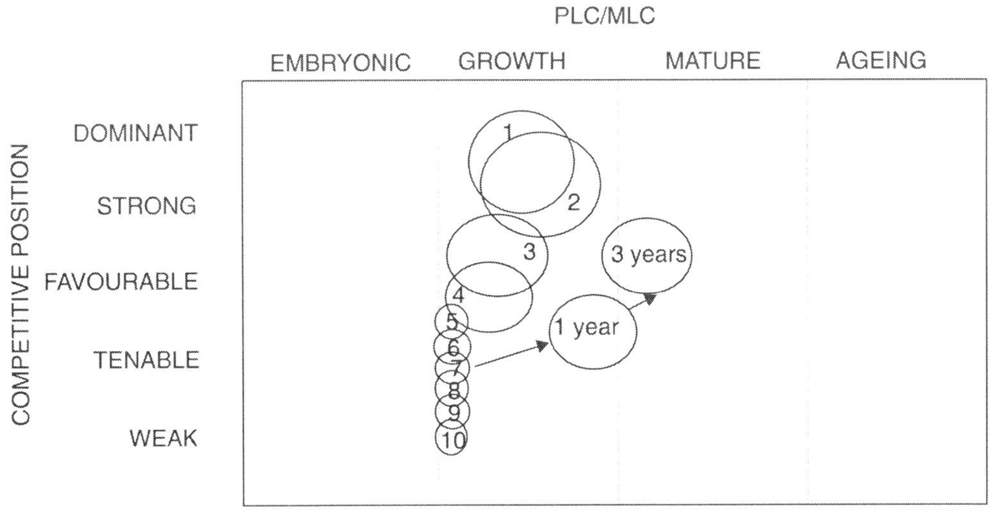

1: Nintendo	2: Sony	3: Virgin	4: Electronic Arts	5: LC
6:Konami	7: Acclaim	8: Activision	9: GT	10: Cedant

→ Represents strategic gap

Shell matrix

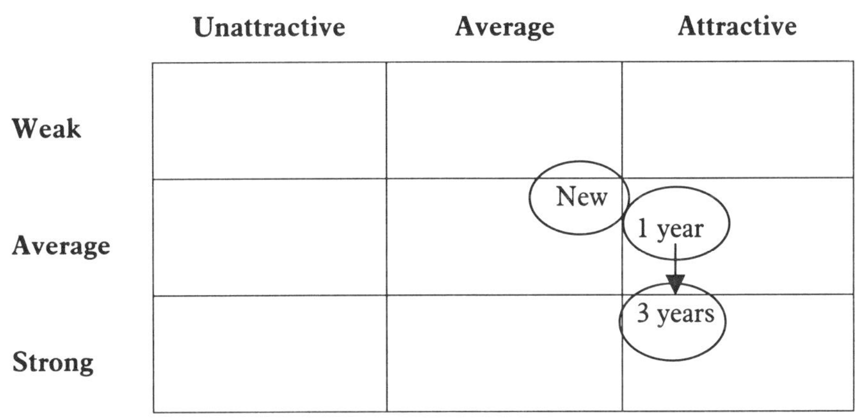

→ Strategic gap

(ii) **Criteria for position**

- Acclaim is in a growing, global market.
- New technological opportunities exist.
- Complex supplier relationships.
- Many competitors.
- Financial constraints.

Shell corroborates the findings of the AD Little matrix and our corporate growth objectives. It must now lead to strategic options to be considered given the above diagnosis and objectives. For this the **Ansoff** matrix will be used.

(b) **Strategic options (Ansoff)**

		PRODUCT	
		Existing	**New**
MARKET/ CUSTOMER SATISFACTION	**Existing**	**Market penetration** • Build brand • Collaborate with suitable partners	**NPD** • DVDs • New film licences • Introduce themed 'pop music' banked into games • Develop new brand's characters internally • Technology partners
	New	**Market development** • Internet • Japan • Other 1st world countries • Over 50s • Females	**Diversification** • Online-only game for internet – no software purchased, just licence

(c) **Strategic options evaluation and justification**

(i) **Market penetration**

In the long term, due to the competitive nature of the market and the perceived likelihood of consolidation, this is an area that must be given high priority. A penetration strategy also supports our corporate objective of increasing market share and brand development.

(ii) **NPD**

This capitalises on technological advances (DVD, telecomms), build brand strength (which reduces the need for external licenses) and ensures long-term sales growth for the company. NPD is fundamental to the survival of Acclaim and should therefore have significant resources allocated to it.

(iii) **Market development**

Encompassing not only geographic legions but also new market segments and delivery channels (Internet) this involves a greater degree of risk as market research information is required to fully evaluate these markets.

(iv) **Diversification**

The most risky option of all, requiring resource commitment and specialist capabilities should be evaluated as an option once the current objectives are fulfilled.

(v) **Recommendation**

It is recommended that Acclaim focus on NPD as its first priority whilst developing market penetration through branding.

(vi) **Implications**

- NPD/Innovation must be instilled in the corporate culture.
- NPD initiative must encompass end-to-end review of current processes and also review/research emerging technologies/trends on order to establisher strategic technology partnership, eg if telecommunication is going to be the

next revolution in this industry, perhaps Acclaim should seek links with the likes of Vodafone Airtouch or the like.

Marketing objectives

3.4 Please refer to corporate objectives for details of marketing objectives.

(a) **Segmentation**

Despite various parameters existing research should be conducted in order to establish segments. The following criteria apply.

- Geography
- Age
- Sex
- Product use/benefit

(b) **Critical marketing strategies**

(i) **Promotion.** Heavy focus on corporate umbrella brand strategy.

(ii) **Product**. NPD/innovation strategy (parallel processing); development of customer focused/driven products (with long, term emphasis on the PC market).

(iii) **Place.** Strategic partnerships; vertical marketing systems (VMS) to be implemented (likely contractual VMS); specific/key growth international markets.

(iv) **Price.** Develop tailored pricing structure to maximise margins, whilst remaining customer focused.

(c) **Timescales and budgets**

Strategy	Time frame (years)	Budget $
Consolidate branding across platforms (corporate branding)	0-3 years	30% of each country's marketing budget
NPD/Innovation initiative	1 year	25% sales
Strategic partnership	1 + continuous	25% 'general and administration budget

(d) **Control targets**

(i) Sales figures (yearly comparison)
(ii) Market share (in comparison to previous years/competitors)
(iii) Profit turnover (net and gross)
(iv) Brand awareness (market research indexing)
(v) Low warranty claims

Review should occur annually, with flexible initiatives implemented as appropriate. Communication through reports/progress meetings.

(e) **Critical success factors**

(i) Revised delivery of NPD initiative
(ii) Maintained presence in consolidating market
(iii) Economic stability of existing markets
(iv) Continuous development of relationships with console manufacturers
(v) Identifying leading edge technology partner to spearhead NPD with

(f) **Contingency**

- Allocate resources as required

- Seek immediate partnership/strategic alliance
- Seek international market entry strategies into untapped markets

4 OUTLINE MARKETING PLAN: EXAMPLE 2

4.1 Corporate objectives

1. To improve earnings from operations to 15% of revenues by 2002 and increase liquidity ratio to 1.
2. To improve shareholder equity from negative to positive by 2001.
3. To minimise risk of negative market forces by developing a market orientated culture by end of 2000.

4.2 Marketing objectives

(a) **Short term 1999 – 2001**

1. To increase revenues to $1,018 billion by end of 2001.
2. To become preferred supplier in the US market for entertainment software increasing market share to 5% by 2001.
3. To establish a credible market share in the Internet gaming sector say 3% by 2001.

(b) **Longer term**

1. Increase market share in PC software from 0.t% in 1998 to 10% by 2002.
2. Develop relative share of domestic/international revenues from 67% to 33% to 50/50 by end of 2002.

4.3 Strategy options – Ansoff

(a)

MARKET PENETRATION	PRODUCT DEVELOPMENT
• US sales focus • Brand strategy • Customer retention • Europe penetration	• Focus on PC titles • DVD software • Internet software • Software for Dreamcast
MARKET DEVELOPMENT	**DIVERSIFICATION**
• Female sector • South East Asia • Japan	• Education • Business software • New forms of entertainment

(b) **Selected strategies**

- Penetration ⇒ Brand building/US focus/loyalty
- Product development ⇒ PCs and Internet compatibility
- Market development ⇒ Europe
- Diversification ⇒ Education

4.4 Justification

(a) Brand development will differentiate and create longer-term competitive advantage and increased profits.

(b) The USA is the largest market and home market for Acclaim with 1% share: culturally compatible; synergies with distribution and product; offers minimal risk.

(c) Loyalty schemes/upgrades will develop closer contact with the consumer/add value to the retailer and increase cross-merchandising.

(d) PCs are the fastest growing sector where traditionally Acclaim are weak. Useful also as a springboard to Internet compatibility (similar demographics).

(e) Internet software as a response to the on-line gaming sector and competitor responses.

(f) Europe is the second largest market and Acclaim has 1% market share. Regarded as market development since only 1% market share. Europe has more cultural compatibility than Japan and Acclaim has higher level of involvement (UK studies).

Competitive position	Unattractive	Average	Attractive
Weak	Divest	Phased withdrawal	Double/quit education
Average	Phased withdrawal	Customer Sega	Try harder • Female (older) • Internet
Strong	Cash generator	Growth • South East Asia • Comics • Sony/Nintendo	Leaders • US focus • Europe penetrate • PCs

Market attractiveness

Note. Whilst Sega's alliance with BT should increase this competitive threat it is highly likely that Sony and Nintendo will respond to this in a forceful way. Acclaim's position with Sony/Nintendo is strong and it is suggested that a modified 'market follower' strategy might be adopted.

4.5 Targeting and positioning

It must be stressed that the absence of qualitative market research in regard to demographics which is challenging and the following is suggested without reverence to detailed data.

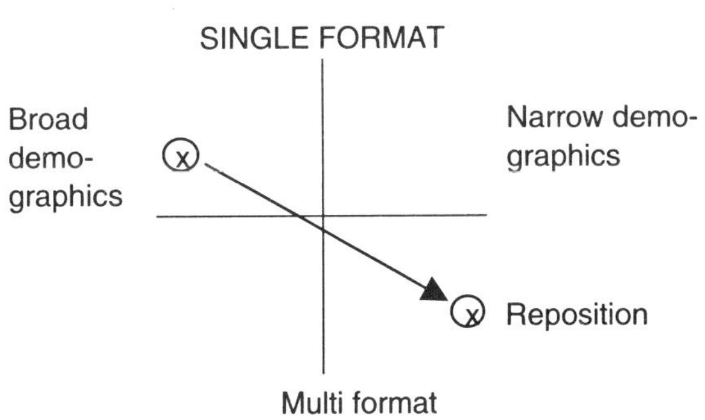

Increase range of formats

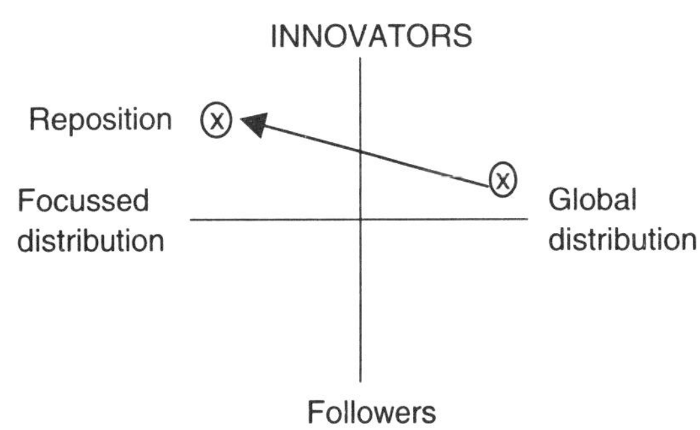

Develop innovative culture

4.6 **Marketing programmes and brand strategy**

(a) **Brand strategy**

(i) Position as creative and imaginative by ensuring success of new products.

(ii) Promote primarily title brands eg Turok, NFE Quarterback with endorsement sub branding 'ACCLAIM'.

(iii) Promote 'ACCLAIM' to trade customers (licences).

(iv) Consider new brand for Internet based games to minimise potential channel conflict eg 'E' bank.

(b) **Implications**

(i) Will require research into current brand offerings.

(ii) Critical success factor is the licensing/success of new games to increase brand recognition, cross merchandising and sequels.

(iii) Targeting of console based games to younger demographic of 15-30; Acha games PC titles and strategy type games to older generation.

(c) **Marketing communications**

(i) Increase brand awareness from current level to 80% in target markets by 2001.

(ii) To develop three new brands each year that will be regarded in the top ten within six months of launch.

(iii) Improve the level of re-purchase of Acclaim products by 50%.

(iv) Improve preferences for Acclaim in the US from 40% to 60% by 2001.

(d) **Marketing mix**

(i) **Product**

- Adapt to meet European demand, particularly sports
- PCs titles to be more strategic
- Console more action orientated
- DVD software to meet all formats

(ii) **Pricing**

- Pricing to support Push/Pull strategy to increase sales in US
- Market orientated

(iii) **Place**

- Consider new distribution channels for PC titles
- Internet sampling
- Management of potential demand
- Conflict with Internet availability and retailers
- Review of effectiveness of US distribution

(iv) **Promotion**

- Push/Pull is US
- Brand building
- Global campaigns for adoption by Europe
- Customer loyalty/upgrade schemes
- New packaging to differentiate on shelves
- Other websites for Internet

16 Acclaim Entertainment Inc: Detailed Marketing Planning

This chapter contains the following plans produced by CIM students in the course of exam preparation

INTRODUCTORY NOTE: THE STEPS YOU SHOULD FOLLOW

Well now, you are almost there save for the finishing touches. Just how much work you need to do depends upon the amount of detail in your outline plan but we suggest you make one last big effort to ensure your plan makes the grade for this important examination.

At this point we need to advise that whereas a complete marketing plan is intended to cover you for all eventualities, it cannot of course provide all the detail that might be needed for a specific examination question. You will therefore have to **add detail as required in the examination itself**. Moreover, the CIM reserves the right to introduce additional material to you in the examination hall.

However, in anticipation of examination questions signalled in the case study some syndicates will prepare extra materials on, say, branding or market segmentation or marketing research.

CONSULT THE GUIDANCE NOTES GIVEN IN CHAPTER 8 PARAGRAPHS 3.5 TO 5.2
STEP 3.5 DEVELOP QUANTIFIED, TIMESCALED OBJECTIVES **STEP 3.6 CONSIDER ALTERNATIVE STRATEGIES. SELECT THOSE MOST APPROPRIATE** **STEP 4.1 DRAW UP DETAILED TACTICAL PLANS COVERING THE MARKETING MIX** **STEP 4.2 DRAW UP A MARKETING RESEARCH PLAN AND MKIS** **STEP 4.3 CONSIDER ORGANISATIONAL ISSUES, CHANGES AND MARKETING ORIENTATION** **STEP 4.4 CONSIDER ORGANISATIONAL CULTURE AND NEED FOR INTERNAL MARKETING** **STEP 4.5 DETERMINE THE FINANCIAL/HR RESOURCE IMPLICATIONS OF YOUR PLANS** **STEP 4.6 ASSESS COSTS AND DRAW UP INDICATIVE BUDGETS** **STEP 4.7 DRAW UP SCHEDULES GIVING TIMINGS/SEQUENCE OF ACTIONS** **STEP 5.1 SPECIFY REVIEW PROCEDURES AND CONTROL MECHANISMS** **STEP 5.2 DRAW UP OUTLINE CONTINGENCY PLANS** **STEP 5.3 REVIEW YOUR COMPLETE MARKETING PLAN**
YOU WILL NEED BETWEEN 15 AND 18 HOURS TO DO THIS MAJOR TASK

Having made your last one big effort how does your plan compare with the examples which follow each of which has its own strengths and weaknesses.

Example 1 This is somewhat run of the mill and quite sketchy in parts. There are too many bullet points and lists, especially on the all-important strategic aspects. Note that some of the objectives are actually strategies. Budgets are shown as percentages rather than figures and the control aspects have been largely omitted

Example 2 This has been included to illustrate the importance placed on segmentation which is explored in some detail. The analysis includes a PEST but excludes a format SWOT. The marketing mix is covered in greater depth than Example 1 and budgets are expressed in figures. However, again, the control aspects have been overlooked

Example 3 This is an example of quite a well thought-out strategy which has been developed in some depth. There is a SWOT but no PEST. The international strategy based on the Internet is quite good. Otherwise coverage of the marketing mix is cursory in the extreme

Hopefully, your own detailed plan will combine the strengths of these three examples and add some of your own.

1 DETAILED MARKETING PLAN: EXAMPLE 1

Situation analysis

1.1 Internal strengths

- Strong sales in Europe
- Significant market share of software sales for N64 and Playstation
- Network of relationships with third party publishers and developers
- Key staff with relevant experience
- Skilled staff
- Can produce games in house
- Own source of games
- Good at spotting new trends
- Reputation for quality

1.2 Internal weaknesses

- Weak financial position (insolvent by some measures)
- Evidence of poor inventory management
- Need to develop relationships with other hardware manufacturers than Nintendo
- Poor past management and dependency on staff
- Lack of detailed market knowledge so cannot predict and manage both threats and opportunities
- Unbalanced portfolio

1.3 External opportunities

- Substantial and growing market
- Scope for new scope and new products
- Merchandising
- Other uses for skills and technology
- Mass market potential if right segmentation used

1.4 External threats

- Changes in technology (eg Internet access for consoles)
- Difficult relationships to manage (eg hardware manufacturers by competitor)
- Changes in international markets
- Seasonal nature of sales
- Litigation
- Employee mobility and risk of poaching

1.5 Sources of competitive advantage

- Ability to produce own games
- Speed to market
- Proprietary knowledge
- Marketing intelligence
- Ownership of source of licences
- Financial back
- Relationships with hardware manufacturers
- Distribution systems
- Staff

- Differentiated position
- Strategies to maximise potential of 'hits'
- Strategies to exploit interest
- Strategic relationships with other software companies for distribution

1.6 **AE's core competences**

- Reputation for good quality and exciting products
- Ability to produce games so not dependent on external producers
- Proprietary knowledge
- Established distribution network in some countries
- Skilled staff
- Ownership of licences

Strategic direction for AE

1.7 **Strategic business objectives**

Main objective - to achieve stable and protectable growth with a long-term aim of rebuilding company's position to 9% market share it held in 1999. AE must focus on the business it is in, their customers and their shareholders.

Assumption: that market continues to grow at 40% per year.

1.8 **Key objectives**

1	Achieve turnover of $2bn by 2001 (50% growth year on year)
2	Achieve pre-tax earnings of 165% by 2001
3	Create a market oriented company

(a) **Vision**: to become one of top five companies in global entertainment software market.

(b) **Mission:** AE is committed to:

- Developing and distributing unique and exciting games for all major formats
- Using technological advantages and skills to create best selling games
- Providing first class customer service

1.9 **Marketing objectives**

- Restore ROS (return on sales) to 1994 level of 16%
- Achieve market share of 2% by 2001
- Position each game in top ten list for format published in
- Establish each game as unique brand
- Build balanced portfolio of titles
- Enter new geographical markets
- Establish internet strategy for distribution, promotion and multi-gaming

1.10 Strategic direction

Marketing strategies proposed

1	Differentiate AE products from each other and competition, and seek to establish them as unique brands
2	Differentiate AE by distribution (internet) and customer relations
3	Develop and launch new products, as well as rejuvenate existing products, to create balanced portfolio
4	Exploit full potential of products by extending product life cycle with game extensions and sequels
5	Develop additional game segments in terms of geography and end user
6	Sell licences to eternal developers to exploit merchandising opportunities of AE's own games

1.11 Use of theory to justify strategies

(a) Porter's generic strategies

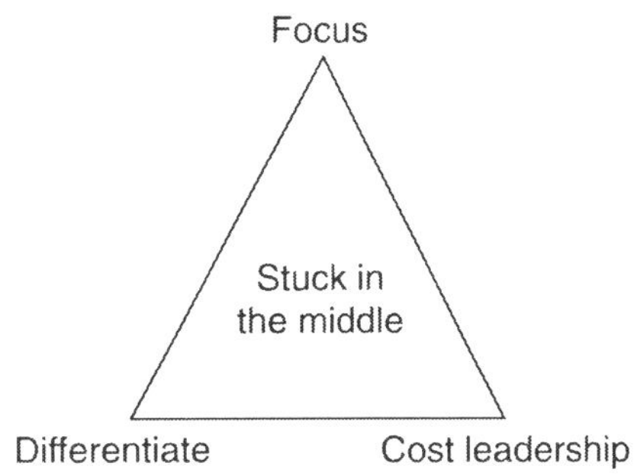

Differentiation is the obvious course of action

- Creates recognition in market
- Allows powerful promotional messages
- Customers assume different means better
- Establishes barriers to entry
- Leads to higher returns

(b) Ansoff Matrix

	Existing products	New products
Existing markets	Market penetration strategy - more purchasing and usage from existing customers - clear branding strategy - build relationships with customers 1	Product development strategy - develop new games - extend existing games with new levels 2
New markets	Market development strategy - enter new segments, eg - exploit new distribution channels, eg internet - establish new geographical markets 3	Diversification strategy - sell licences to external developers - use technology in vertical markets, eg health - explore alternative revenue streams, eg rent studio 4

Risk level: Low = 1, High = 4

Three Ansoff strategies fill planning gap.

(i) **Market development (new countries and new segments)**

This will expand overall market, recapture market share and establish AE further as international player.

(ii) **NPD**

This will replace mature products, provide stable sales, ensure full potential exploited from each product, show innovation.

(iii) **Market penetration** (branding, positioning, relationship marketing)

This will provide differentiation from competitors, facilitate rebuy and promote loyalty.

(c) **Product life cycle**

(i) This is particularly relevant as the PLC is so short with transition phases between each (see illustration 3).

(ii) Accurate knowledge of market and relative position on plc of hardware paramount (see MKIS).

(iii) Can use PLC to arrest decline.

PLC

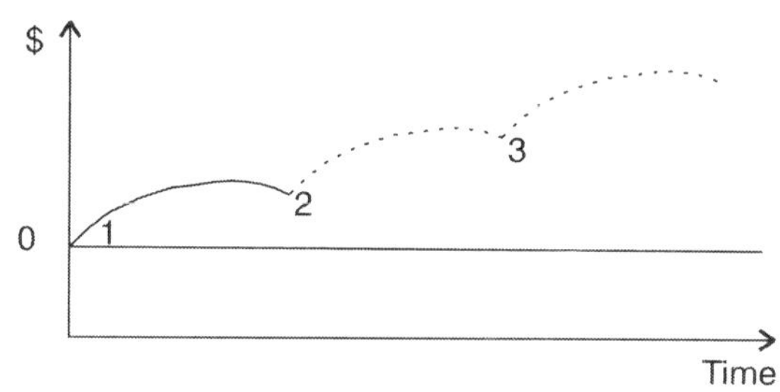

(iv) Consideration of buyer behaviour relevant particularly adoption process. AE's knowledge of innovators and early adopters must be extensive to target them accurately.

(v) **Innovation diffusion**

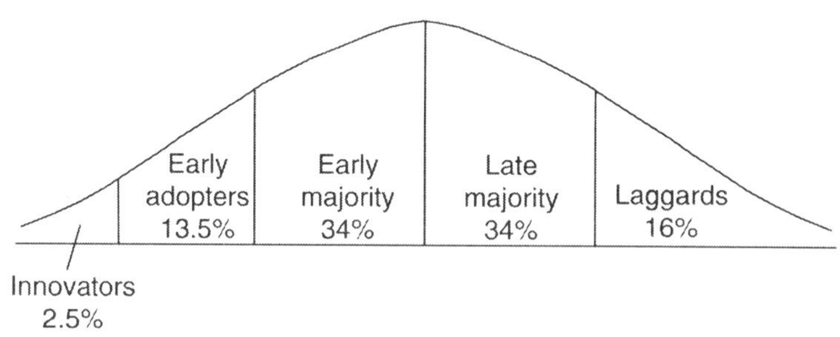

Combined PLC/Diffusion

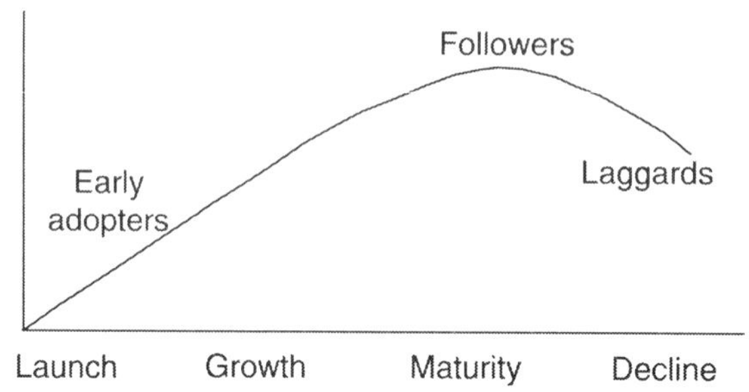

(vi) Relevant for accurate targeting are PLC of product

Segmentation, targeting and positioning

1.12 Segmentation

(a) AE needs to categorise buyers on basis of their characteristics and product needs

(b) AE can use knowledge to build mass market for products by targeting relevant segments for each product

1.13 Targeting

Likely targets for AE will include:

- Girls
- Parents with PCs at home
- New geographical markets
- Older customers

1.14 Positioning

(a) The **current approach** is to brand on basis of title, type of product and company name
(b) Propose a new philosophy as follows.

Each game is a business

Taking the **film industry** as a model, AE should create **each game as a unique brand** and then take a selective marketing approach by appealing to specific segments of audience with specific messages in specific media parts.

This will differentiate AE's products from their competitors. Acclaim itself as a brand has no relevance to these customers.

Treating each as a business means that aim to maximise PLC and exploit potential as long as possible.

Action plan

1.15 Branding: Key issues

- Establish emotional and functional brand values
- Identify relevant segments
- Use brand values to develop sequels, add on etc
- Exploit the full potential of brands
- Reflect brand in all elements of mix

1.16 Product key issues

- Balance portfolio
- Reduce speed to market
- Maintain product quality
- Extend the product life cycle of hits so full potential exploited
- Consider issues of adaptation and standardisation

This will require investment in R&D (re-establish to 2% of turnover), motivated staff, MKIS, Playstation expertise and DVD (may need to recruit specialists).

Note AE's portfolio is key to success. Must support all formats and never again be unprepared for transition phases.

1.17 **Promotion: key issues**

- Integrated campaigns
- Relationships with retailers and customers
- Restore budget to 22% of turnover as in 1994
- Internet strategies for promotion, information, building relations

1.18 **Place: key issues** (see next section)

- Increase penetration
- Push more to sales reps in USA

1.19 **Price: key issue**

- Maintain premium pricing for branded titles. Will require info from MKIS.

1.20 **People: key issues**

- Staff and skills critical
- Establish strategies to develop, motivate, improve loyalty
- Employ senior marketing person

1.21 **Processes: key issue**

Emphasis on quality and customer care

1.22 **Physical evidence: key issues**

Provide a good quality environment for staff

1.23 **MKIS**. It is clear that AE does not have a good MKIS in place. As this is crucial for success, it should be actioned immediately.

1.24 **Internet strategy**

(a) Functions

- Information on products
- E-commerce services
- Platform for on-line gaming
- Customer contract/building relationships

(b) Objective

- Achieve one million visitors per month
- Differentiate AE by distribution
- Differentiate AE by quality of customer contact

(c) Tactics

- Part of integrated communication strategy for each brand
- Employ a specialist to deal with this

1.25 **Creating a marketing orientation**

(a) **Relationship marketing**

Build relationships with:

- Customers
- Staff

- Manufacturers
- Hardware companies
- Shareholders

(b) **Internal marketing**

- Contributes to performance

(c) **Contingencies**

- AE must prepare for unexpected

(d) **Timescales and budgets**

- M&S budget should be at least 20% of turnover. Breakdown of budget is as follows.

	%
Advertising	25
Distribution	20
Sales promotion	15
Direct mail	10
Internet	15
Research	10
Contingency	5
	100

MKIS should be budgeted for separately.

2 DETAILED MARKETING PLAN: EXAMPLE 2

Strategic marketing plan for Acclaim Entertainment - 2000-2002

Introduction

2.1 Acclaim Entertainment is a worldwide developer, publisher and mass marketer of interactive entertainment software for use with dedicated interactive entertainment hardware platform and multi-media computer systems. It is among the earliest multi-platform publisher. Its size and position in the US market makes it one of the largest independent publishers of software for entertainment platforms.

2.2 The company is now owning a captive development studio Iguana, Sculptured Software, and Acclaim Entertainment Inc Europe based in UK. Also it is owning a motion capture studio which assists its Internal Advanced Technology Group in creating software tools, technologies and development engines for software development. The company has invested about 20% of its revenue in product development.

The company had grown rapidly since its establishment. However, it had suffered losses during 1996-97 period due to the industry transition from 32 bit to 64 bit platforms.

2.3 Now the company's net worth is $-21.7m, due to an accumulated deficit from past year. Nevertheless the company had come into profit in 1998.

2.4 Software distribution is handled by in-house management team in N America, and by subsidiaries of Acclaim Entertainment Inc Europe in UK, France, Germany, Spain, Australia, Japan and Singapore. For other markets, regional distributors are appointed.

Macro environmental audit studies

2.5 **Political** environment: Main trends perceivable include the following.

(a) The opening of the market in the telecommunication industry will lead to intensified competition amongst telecom companies, each striving to provide more service and develop a new market to the end users.

(b) China's entrance into the World Trading Organisation will be realised in the near future. This will boost further regional growth, and also open a new market for telecommunication and interactive entertainment business. Flows of goods, capital and people will be facilitated.

(c) Traditional trade barriers will be further by-passed by the development of the internet which offers a new frictionless distribution channel for software producers.

(d) Under the current practice, the software producers and not the platform manufacturers will be responsible for any claims and litigation settlement. This has direct profit implications. For instance, in 1997, Acclaim had allowed for $23.6m for claims of this kind.

2.6 **Economic factors**

(a) World economy is recovering steadily from the depression in mid 90s.

(b) There is growth in USA, Europe and Japan.

(c) China is growing into a major economic power.

(d) As Japan picks up again, it may make up a larger share of world market.

2.7 **Social factors**

(a) As people become more affluent in the developing nations such as China, South East Asia, South America, demand for entertainment software, communication, information technology product is growing.

(b) The demographic range of the market is expanding to different age groups and women.

(c) Globalisation is creating a world culture.

(d) Gaming is developing from 'single player' to 'multiplayer activities' over the internet. It is assuming an expanded role, becoming more than just a pastime and developing into a social activity.

2.8 **Technological factors**

(a) Development of higher capacity processors, multimedia features has made the PC an increasingly important medium for entertainment software. Also the PC's price is falling rapidly.

(b) New technology like DVD driver has provided new opportunities for developing more sophisticated software that simulate the virtual environment.

(c) As a result of above the development cost of software for entertainment has increased dramatically up to £1.5m (around US$2.5m).

(d) The development cycle for entertainment software now takes around 18 months to complete. However, the PC technology can advance dramatically within 12 months. There is a need for effective market intelligence to predict the technological trend. To a lesser extent, this is also time for the console machine, wrong investment in obsolete technology would render the software in an inappropriate format when it is sold in the market.

Corporate objectives and mission statement

2.9 In view of the tendency for product orientation of the company, it is suggested that a new mission of statement be devised.

> 'Acclaim Entertainment Inc engage in the entertainment business software over various platforms and technologies to satisfy people's different recreational, social, and educational needs. The company aims for success through superior customer knowledge, advances in new product development capability, effective market strategy as well as personnel policy, and a comprehensive market intelligence system. Creativity and entrepreneurial endeavour in discovering new .... or ways to satisfy these needs is the key to success for the company.'

Target market

2.10 The market can be segmenting by one of the methods below or a combination of them.

(a) **Type of hardware platform**

- Console
- Portable form
- PC
- Over the internet: games networks

(b) **Hardware**

- Nintendo compatible product
- Sega compatible product
- Sony compatible product
- PC compatible

(c) **Technology employed**

CD 32 bit: Saturn, Playstation
64 Cartridge: N64
64 bit CD: Playstation, N64
128GD/DVD: Dreamcasts/Playstations (128)/Dolphin (128)
PC and internet game

(d) **Geographical segment**

(i) USA: which is becoming more and more important to the company, making up 68% of the company's revenue, the total value of US market is also increasing, even though the share in world market is slightly decreasing.

(ii) Europe: a stable market. The income contribution of the market is decreasing from 53% in 1996 to 33% in 1996.

(iii) Japan: total value and share of Japan in world market is increasing from 18% in 1994 to 28% in 1998. Income contribution to Acclaim has decreased from 9% in 1996 to only 1% in 1998.

(iv) Others: total share in world market of the other countries has increased from 1% in 1994 to 9% in 1998.

Acclaim has limited presence in this market.

(e) **Needs of the end users**

(i) Family entertainment: which is relatively healthy and clean. Should have educational advantage and help nourish creativity.

(ii) Adults' entertainment (18-30 age group): Games like sports, characters and theme from TV, films, comics: Demand great details in replicating the virtual environment; pay more attention to the logics and elements like: humour, creativity etc. Required more emotional involvement from the player.

(iii) **Teenage entertainment** (12-18 age groups): games similar to adult entertainment but demand less in graphical details and more in impulsive stimulation, eg fun, speed, excitement.

It is likely that for (i) and (iii), the console platform will be adopted, whereas there will be higher PC population among (ii).

(f) **Segmentation conclusions**

Even though it may seem very convenient to segment the market by type of platform, it would not enable market oriented approach to create software that will be attractive to the end user.

It is suggested that the market will be segmented by the needs of the end user and then by the characteristic of the platform as subsegments.

Referring to Table 1, there will be different brands for T, A, F. The relative importance of (i), (ii), (iii), (iv) and (v) will be different for group (T), (A), (F) and thus given different emphasis in new product development (NPD).

Market segment (Table 1)

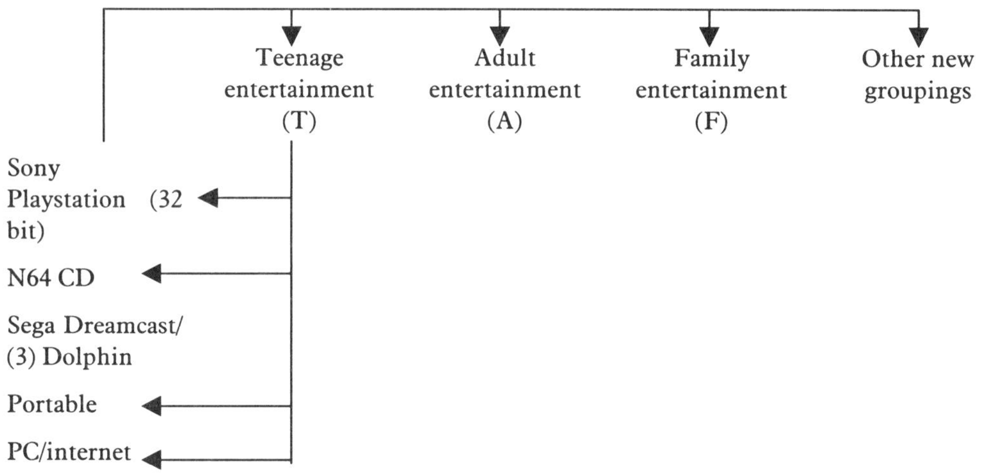

(g) **International issues**

(i) To cope with different cultural and regulation needs in different countries, there may be a need to adapt products if they are sold overseas.

(ii) As global culture is generally prevalent among interactive entertainment business, this adaptation is manageable within the above segmentation groupings. In fact, different games could also be developed for an overseas market if the market, potential is large enough. Market research would be requited on the local culture to study the market potential before NPD process is undertaken.

(iii) It is suggested that a full scale customer analysis be undertaken to establish major characteristics of different segments.

2.11 **Marketing objectives**

(a) To make a comprehensive study on the end users, so that more appropriate segment can be established

(b) To increase overall market share from 1% to 5% in next three years

(c) To increase the presence in the PC platform segment from negligence to 5% over the next three years

(d) To increase share in Japanese market from negligible to 5% in the next three years

(e) Alliance with platform producer in NPD and distribution

(f) To discover new genres that would satisfy needs where market potential is evident in the long run

Targeting and positioning

2.12 The market attractiveness and positioning of the company is summarised below.

GE matrix

Market attractiveness \ Business strength	Strong	Medium	Weak
High	Teenage (ii) A(iv) A(ii)	T(iv) A(iii) A(i)	
Medium		T(i) F(i) (ii) (iii)	A(v) T(iii)
Low			T(v) F(iv) A(iv) F(v)

T - teenage entertainment; A - adult entertainment; F - family entertainment

(i) - Playstation; (ii) - N64; (iii) - Dreamcast/Playstation (128)/Dolphin; (iv) - Portable; (v) - PC.

(a) **Market attractiveness** depends on current revenue, size, potential income, growth rate, NPD complexity/cost, life cycle length and compatibility with NPD time.

(b) **Market strengths**: share, appropriate technology, NPD capability, distribution capacity, management experience.

(c) Major emphasis will be given in targeting markets T(ii) A(ii). A(i) show great potential and investment will be needed to move it to the left of the chart, ie the prime position. A(v) needs more investment to cope with future growth in PC platform.

(d) A(iii) needs be strengthen to replace A(ii) in the future.

(e) T(iv) may be maintained for cash income as it required less advance technology.

(f) F(iv) and A(iv) can be discarded. F(i) (ii) (iii) may be studied for market potential.

(g) More investment in T(iii) and (v) may be required for future growth.

Market strategy

2.13 The Ansoff Matrix can be utilised in developing the market strategy.

		Market: Existing	Market: New
Products	Existing	*Market penetration* T(ii) (iv) (i) A(ii) A(iii)	*Market development* F T(iii) T(v)
	New	*Product development* Education for T Movie, new G for A over internet	*Diversification* - As Ts - Cultural genre - research simulation software - female recreational software etc

2.14 The generic market strategy is multi segment market specialisation: different software brands and titles offered to different segment.

2.15 Differentiation market strategy is adopted to generate higher return by offering superior products. The differentiation effort will include better product quality and service, superior market knowledge, convenience for customer, creativity, supported by an effective personnel policy and NPD organisation and distribution system.

Marketing mix

2.16 **Product**

(a) Service and warranty to suit customer needs.

(b) New products to cater for customers' needs.

(c) Shortened NPD process through outsourcing part of the process.

(d) A family branding policy be adopted to create various main brands for each segment. (Some brands can be shared among different segments by altering the pricing, affordability, complexity, 3D effect for different groupings.)

Titles will be created in serial for each brand.

Some brands for adults can be made available in a junior version for the teenage segment and be written at a platform affordable to the teenager.

This will help reducing NPD cost.

(e) The comics business may provide a source for deriving new brands for the software business.

(f) The brands can provide merchandising and licensing income for the company in areas like movies, clothing etc. This would even help the promotion of the software business.

(g) Great emphasis will be given in developing products that will be run in the internet and PC systems.

2.17 Promotion

(a) Personal selling would be given greater emphasis.

Training programme is needed to reorient the technical sales person towards needs of the customers.

(b) Advertising will be administered to promote the brands through differentiation to reach the target customers, eg TV and movie for (F) and (T), magazine for (A).

(c) Trade fairs will be attended to promote the product to platform manufacturers.

(d) Free sample will be available in time-limit format to end users.

(e) Joint effort with platform supplier in market testing.

(f) Direct marketing attempt through internet starting third quarter of 2000.

2.18 Place

Emphasis will be placed on developing distribution through the internet.

2.19 Pricing

Premium pricing will be adopted for skimming the market for (A) grouping. Whilst the price for (T), grouping and for product at the end of its technological cycle will be set low for market penetration and share maintenance and cash harvesting.

2.20 Implementation and budget

	Y_1	Y_2	Y_3	Y_4
	$	$	$	$
Promotion of brands				
- trade fair	500,000	500,000	500,000	1,500,000
- advertising	1,000,000	1,500,000	1,000,000	3,500,000
- personnel training	1,000,000	500,000	500,000	2,000,000
NPD for adapting to PC format	100,000,000	100,000,000	120,000,000	320,000,000
Distribution				
- incentives to channels	4,000,000	2,000,000	2,000,000	8,000,000
Total expenditure				335m
Revenue from				
Titles for (A) (T) (F) and others	$549m	$951m	$1,546m	
Market share	3%	4%	5%	
World market	$18,305m	$23,796m	$30,935m	

3 DETAILED MARKETING PLAN: EXAMPLE 3

Strategic marketing plan

3.1 Mission statement

To become a leading force in the provision of home entertainment through the distribution of entertainment software.

3.2 Corporate objectives

1. Create shareholder value by developing innovative entertainment solutions in the home entertainment market
2. Lessen the risk faced by the company currently, in the home entertainment market.
3. Develop incremental and additional sources of revenue over the coming financial year

3.3 **SWOT analysis**

Strengths	Weaknesses
• Ability to provide one-stop service: development/publishing/distribution • Strength of quality software • Sales and marketing ability • Proprietary technology • Product distribution channels • Management experience	• Many other companies seem to be thriving without one-stop service • Over-reliance on a few successful games for profitability • Limited in number of games Acclaim is allowed to release • Lacks size and market share of larger competitors • Weakened financially and now has limited reserves. It would struggle to cope with further financial problems.
Opportunities	**Threats**
• Technological convergence of internet, telecoms and games hardware, eg Sega. Sony leads to new product and distribution possibilities • Internet provides opportunities for Acclaim to appeal directly to the consumer rather than via retail outlet. This could create greater profitability • Voice, data and video convergence via Internet Protocol (IP) will allow explosion in new hardware applications and software, eg video-conferencing; films via telephone-lines	• 'Boom or bust' nature of industry due to: (i) high games development costs; (ii) constant technological progress of games consoles. This makes Acclaim vulnerable. • Strategic alliances between hardware vendors and PC software/hardware providers could lead to impenetrable markets (ie defensive strategies employed by Acclaim's suppliers). • Acclaim is at mercy of games suppliers to renew licences. • The suppliers, eg Sony, Sega have strategic objectives for their own software development units.

3.4 **SWOT summary**

(a) Acclaim finds itself in a very competitive software market where sustainable competitive advantage appears to be very difficult as a number of companies offer very similar levels of value.

(b) Allied to this, the nature of the software development business - very high fixed costs and long development lead times - means the company is now very vulnerable to financial troubles if just one or more of its products fail.

(c) A shake-out of the market already appears to be taking place with the number of players reducing. With this in mind, the future of Acclaim looks bleak unless it can find new ways to sustain long-term competitive advantages.

(d) The choice it faces is simply: it will either go out of business or be taken over by a competitor. New competitive advantage can be found by capitalising on its unique strengths and by exploiting the tremendous new opportunities in the software industry as a result of the internet and other new technologies.

Acclaim's position within the games industry

3.5 Acclaim finds itself in what Roach (1981) referred to as the 'V' curve.

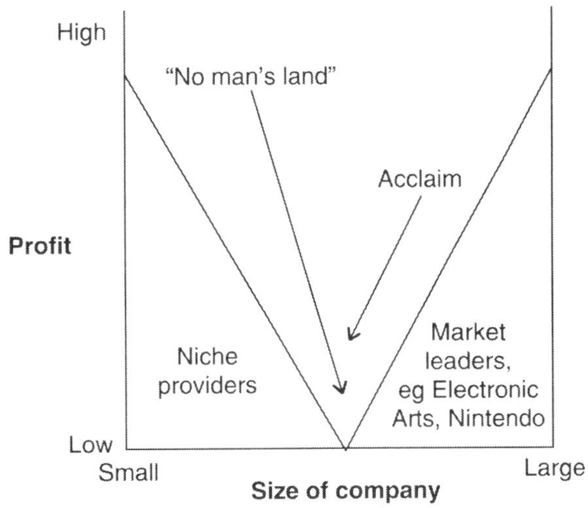

The niche providers, ie the small developers, reap high profits by focusing just on development. Medium-sized companies such as Acclaim are unable to realise competitive advantage because they have neither the focus of the smaller providers nor the size of the larger providers such as "Electronic Arts" which allows them to benefit from economies of scale.

3.6 **Formulation of strategy**

Given this analysis, Acclaim needs to get out of "no man's land".

There are two options available.

(a) It could **continue its strategic direction** of the early 1990s and adopt a strategy of building **market share by upstream integration,** ie buying software studios and developing "one-stop shop" capability. Continuing this acquisition strategy could lead to sizeable market share and a movement up the 'V' curve.

(b) It could adopt a '**focus**' **strategy**, by pulling out of one or more of the three core activities it currently undertakes: software development, publishing, distribution and concentrating on one activity with a view to achieving competitive advantage.

3.7 **Factors that militate against continuing broadly on the same lines**

The company has **few obvious** distinct, unique, competitive, sustainable **advantages**. Many of Acclaim's larger competitors are also in a dire state, which backs up the idea that size will not bring competitive advantage. Due to the high underlying fixed costs of the business, ie development costs, plus the very high risks of the games industry in general, it seems likely that the following will occur.

(a) Few economies of scale would be achieved through acquisitions/mergers of similar businesses, therefore the underlying health of the business would remain poor.

(b) There is considerable evidence to suggest that corporate mergers rarely add shareholder value - a key corporate objective of Acclaim.

(c) The 'one-stop shop' capability resulting from Acclaim's previous expansionist strategy appears of dubious benefit, as many other companies without it appear to prosper. By definition, therefore, there is clearly a market for third party publishing and distribution.

(d) It no longer has the financial muscle to follow aforementioned strategy.

Given the summary above, Acclaim's broad marketing strategy must therefore be to focus on one or two activities and develop competitive advantage.

Acclaim's new strategic focus

3.8 Acclaim now has a choice of focusing of one or more activity. Its current activities are these:

(a) Development of software engines and tools for software

(b) The purchasing of licences for games and the development of relationships with licensors

(c) The publishing of games (and comics)

(d) Software development

(e) The distribution of games (Acclaim games and third party games)

3.9 Game software development, in the long-term should be dropped as a core capability for the following reasons.

(a) The market for development is so competitive. Analysis by Michael Porter (five forces) shows considerable supplier power (who are also concurrently competitors), considerable scope for new entrants and for product substitutes (eg Dreamcast).

(b) The development area forms a high proportion of fixed costs. It is risky due to changeable nature of the hardware market, the fickle nature of consumers.

(c) The product titles, eg South Park, do not appear to offer a significant competitive advantage, as there appears to be a limitless supply of potential popular genres.

Acclaim's new strategy

3.10 **Publishing and distribution**

There is already evidence that Acclaim is developing this side of the business. Indeed, 9% of revenues come from servicing just one other software developer. Furthermore, the market is full of companies with development but no in-house publishing or distribution expertise. Acclaim should therefore focus on this **core capability of bringing games to market through third party distribution capabilities**, with a view to diluting the company's reliance on games software development in terms of revenue with the technological convergence between the computer games industry, the internet and the PC industry, through various strategic alliances. Acclaim should also be looking to develop its core competence for distribution to include the Internet, both to games consumers and via existing business-to-business channels that it operates.

Marketing objectives

3.11 **Objective One**

Reduce reliance on small number of internally developed software titles from 68% to 50% in forthcoming financial year, with a view to reducing still further to 30% in year 2. Reduce % of workforce involved in studio development from current 66% to 45% in forthcoming financial years with a further reduction to 30% in year 2.

3.12 **Objective Two**

Increase revenues from publishing and distribution activities by 50% in forthcoming financial year.

Marketing strategies

3.13 Product

(a) A **harvest strategy** should be developed for existing popular titles. The brands could be sold off to other developers.

(b) New publishing and distribution packages need to be developed for the independent software business.

3.14 Price

- Pricing strategies need to be developed for harvest strategy of existing titles.
- Work needs to be undertaken to identify pricing strategies for a structure of charges for distribution and publishing capabilities to be offered to third party developers.

3.15 Place

In terms of the future marketing mix, this is perhaps the most key area. With the technological revolution of the internet, many new channel opportunities will become available.

3.16 Promotion

The internet will also have considerable implications for the future promotional mix to be employed by Acclaim in developing its publishing and distribution markets.

3.17 Distribution via the internet

The internet must be the key source of distribution for Acclaim over the next few years. It has clear strategic advantages for Acclaim.

(a) It ties Acclaim into current environmental (technological) changes which will see the Internet take a prominent role in the games and television industry, through digital television.

(b) Intrinsically, the internet as a distribution channel offers a number of advantages.

(i) It is truly global and can reach a large number of potential consumers.

(ii) Potentially it cuts out distributors and retailers and can therefore provide increased profitability.

(iii) It can provide a 'frictionless' purchase process whereby games players can 'try before they buy'.

(iv) It can offer savings in terms of operations and logistics, eg shelf-space, distribution to retail outlets.

3.18 There are however a number of problems with the internet today which means that Acclaim should also maintain its existing distribution channels and build on them.

(a) Age of many consumers (ie 12-16 years old) will mean that they will not be able to buy games over the Internet as they will not possess credit card facilities.

(b) Current download speeds via the internet are very slow and expensive. It will be a number of years before unfettered local calling and Asymmetrical Digital Subscriber Line (ADSL) technology will allow users to economise and high speed download speeds over existing copper wire.

(c) There is some evidence that Amazon, the standard bearer for on-line trading is now experiencing a plateau in book sales over the internet: in the USA, only 2-2.5% of sales are over the internet and this is not increasingly significantly.

Given the advantages of the Internet, however, Acclaim should not invest large amounts of money in building Acclaim operations in other countries of the coming years, but instead focus on lower cost entry modes such as agent and franchising networks.

Markets

3.19 (a) Acclaim should clearly target its existing international markets as it will already have strong 'non-internet' distribution and publishing capabilities set up.

(b) Subsequent entry into other markets should take account of legal, cultural, economic conditions in new markets. This will clearly suggest that Acclaim should be seeking to develop its international distribution network, ideally where:

(i) Games consoles have already been introduced

(ii) The internet is gaining hold

(iii) Cultures are not too dissimilar to its existing core market: USA. (This would suggest entering the existing English speaking world - UK, Australia, South Africa, New Zealand.)

International branding strategy

3.20 If Acclaim is to succeed in developing its publishing and distribution capabilities over the internet, it is clear that it needs to develop a clear idea of where it is taking its brand.

3.21 This is because the Internet will also allow its potential customers, ie other software developers, to develop direct distribution strategies that could also potentially cut out Acclaim.

3.22 **Acclaim must therefore develop a very strong brand both to its potential customers**, ie the **developers** who wish to use Acclaim's distribution capabilities but also to **consumers**, ie the games players who need to be drawn to Acclaim's website to buy games.

Acclaim should develop a 'portal' strategy, whereby Acclaim's website is the automatic site to visit for anything to do with games. In the future, it is believed that those companies which control 'portals' or entry points on the internet will also be those companies that benefit most from on-line e-commerce.

Acclaim must therefore develop a branding strategy that appeals to all its various markets and pushes its website address as the place to find out about and buy games. It is only through this brand development that Acclaim can potentially defeat other games companies in their attempts to go 'direct' themselves.

Budgets

3.23 Website development with all the relevant software for on-line credit card validation, game trials etc will cost in the region of £1-1½ million.

3.24 In addition, a global branding campaign reaching core markets of US and western Europe will cost conservatively £8-10 million. It is anticipated that promotional budgets will be considerable over the forthcoming 2-5 years in order to build the Acclaim brand to the consumer market.

Change management implications: people

3.25 Although it will be ultimately for the board to decide how to withdraw from software development over the longer term, it will clearly have far-reaching implications for Acclaim's workforce, a majority of which are currently involved in software development. Considerable care will have to be taken to communicate the new strategic focus to existing staff, so that a continuum can be maintained in the short term to medium term while existing and games currently in development are brought to the market.

It is suggested that considerable care be taken to keep all employees informed and aware of the developments as they happen and the rationale for them.

4 THE EXAMINATION

4.1 You must now get your preparations finalised for your first mock exam before turning to the exam paper which follows in the next chapter.

4.2 You need to conduct two final steps in the recommended methodology.

4.3

CONSULT CHAPTERS 8 AND 10 FOR GUIDANCE NOTES.
STEP 6.1 DRAW UP YOUR EXAMINATION PLAN **STEP 6.2 PRACTISE WRITING IN TRUE REPORT STYLE**
ALLOW AS LONG AS NECESSARY FOR THESE LAST TWO STEPS

4.4 Good luck in your first practice exam!

17 Acclaim Entertainment Inc: The Examination Paper, Answers and Examiner's Comments

ACCLAIM ENTERTAINMENT INC

THE EXAM QUESTIONS ARE ON THE NEXT PAGE

DO NOT LOOK UNTIL YOU ARE READY TO SPEND THREE HOURS ON DOING THESE AS A MOCK EXAM

1 THE EXAMINATION PAPER

New information on the day of the examination

British Telecom's deal with Sega is soon to be on stream, offering free internet access to Dreamcast owners in Europe. There are rumours that the new Sony and Nintendo machines may be equipped with modems, possibly with the power to download and play films. Many of the hardware manufacturers see the market expanding to encompass telecommunications companies and home appliance makers. The race is already on between software companies, telecommunications firms and home appliance makers to decide which will set the format for the digital network age. These dramatic changes in the industry with possible distribution and delivery implications for Acclaim are now being actively considered by the company's management team.

Question 1

Produce a strategic marketing plan for Acclaim Entertainment Inc for the next three years, taking into account any branding decisions that may be necessary. Justify your recommendations.

Question 2

Acclaim sells a range of products into diverse geographical markets. Given the nature of the technological (both hardware and the internet) changes, outline the best international marketing strategy for the company to follow.

Question 3

Assessing marketing performance (marketing metrics) is often a difficult problem for many companies. Outline the key indicators that you would use to assess Acclaim's market performance, currently and in the future, justifying your choices.

2 SENIOR EXAMINER'S OVERVIEW OF THE ISSUES THAT SHOULD BE COVERED

The case

2.1 The case study has been based on a real organisation. The case poses a real problem and takes into account the difficulties a good-sized, technologically-led company has in developing a coherent marketing strategy in a fast growth, ever changing market. This case has no personalised comments, is factual and contains no red herrings. Nonetheless, as usual, there is the usual problem of an extensive range of detailed information. There is a need to develop clear and concise insights into the key issues involved in developing a strategy.

2.2 **Key issues**

(a) The unsettled nature of the market

(b) The need continually to update or produce 'hits'

(c) Develop and sustain many and differing brands

(d) The industry sector is going through a phase of consolidation

(e) Games producers such as Acclaim are heavily dependent on the hardware manufacturers

(f) The difficulty of creating a 'balance' between the creation of 'own' brands such as Turok and brands that 'belong' to the hardware manufacturers

(g) The low revenues from developing PC games

(h) The growth of 'on-line' usage and the development of games suited to this medium

(i) The cultural differences in the various European and international markets

(j) The advent of DVD technology and its impact on games production

(k) The complex nature of the development process

(l) The need to help key talent in software development

(m) The ever present possibility of a software failure

(n) The need to recoup the heavy losses sustained in 1996/97 and to continue the recovery strategy

(o) Stockholders need to be convinced of the recovery of their equity is losing value

(p) The asset/liability ratio needs addressing over the next few years

(q) US revenues are growing faster than the rest of the world

(r) The company is big enough to acquire some smaller players, but could itself be the target of a takeover bid as it is five times smaller than Electronic Arts

(s) The company needs to back the 'right horse' in the new interconnected arena. Will this be Nintendo, Sega or Sony?

(t) The UK, Germany and Italy show the greatest volume growth in the sales of consoles outside the USA. Given the potential number of households in Europe, the penetration is still small, offering Acclaim opportunities for greater sales

(u) Sony is clearly the market leader in the console market

(v) Acclaim appears to have around 15% of the European market for games software. It has 6% of the total world market in software

(w) The potential threat from the Dreamcast linkup with Microsoft

(x) The best way to use the internet for selling/distribution

2.3 **The Answers**

This case is reasonably straightforward and does not contain many surprises. It is important, therefore that the following issues are considered.

1	The application of theory
2	The amount of international marketing theory/application that the students can apply to the case. The amount of communication theory that they can also apply
3	The candidates should be thinking strategically not tactically
4	The answers given must be realistic and practical
5	A degree of innovation and lateral thinking should be rewarded
6	It is important that the questions are answered within the given context
7	The additional information is quite important in making a clearer assessment of the company's strategy. The information alludes to the way the market is moving with a potentially great impact for the marketing strategies developed by Acclaim

Question 1 Produce a strategic marketing plan for Acclaim Entertainment Inc for the next three years, taking into account any branding decisions that may be necessary. Justify your recommendations.

2.4 This question requires students to use many of the strategic planning models used by marketers. These are McDonald, Andrews, Doyle etc. Candidates will then need to consider the following.

(a) Consider the **objectives** that they wish to set for Acclaim for the long and the short term. In the short term some marketing contingencies such as the way they intend to improve their future marketing stance so that the profitability stays on an upward path. In the longer term they need to consider their key alliance partners.

(b) Take into account the rate of technological changes and consider the degree of flexibility allowed by the plan.

(c) Take into account the fragmented nature of the products and the markets and map out the key growth areas.

(d) The possibility of **expanding** in the European market.

(e) The **strategic** vision should be based on commissioning market research in order to improve the way they direct their energies.

(f) The strategy should take into account the financial status of the company. Any well developed strategy will require sound financing. Currently, although the company is profitable, it does not have enough financial clout to go for a major acquisition.

(g) What market positioning strategies should the company adopt vis a vis the different markets? Appendix 1, 2 and 3 are quite important.

(h) The company has some good titles such as Turok and South Park.

(i) The company's key strengths need to be in creativity and branding.

(j) How are the different products/services to be positioned in the markets?

(k) What are realistic market share objectives for the company in each of the geographic markets and the overall world market?

(l) The company has to take risks with the hardware manufacturers it works with as the development time is so long.

(m) Models such as Porter, Ansoff, BCG, GEC, Shell Directional and GAP could be used in the analysis of the case.

(n) What are the constraints to the given strategy? How can the company follow a market led strategy? What would be a realistic marketing budget?

(o) Which markets are the key priorities and why?

(p) As no organisation chart is provided, how should the company execute its marketing strategies?

(q) How much of the company's money should be directed towards developing an internet strategy?

(r) The fast growing markets can create too many cash hungry stars as opposed to revenue earning cash cows.

(s) The company needs to consider possible alliances, though this type of market is usually quite secretive.

(t) Should the company consider JVs or link up with major internet companies in order to distribute its products?

(u) The problems of supporting multiple brands and the consideration of the possibility of developing an effective umbrella strategy for its products.

2.5 **Points in a strategic plan**

1	Set corporate objectives
2	Identify target markets
3	Set marketing objectives
4	Develop marketing strategy and tactics
5	Organise control systems

2.6 **Given the points above, the best answers should have shown a clear grasp of the following.**

1	A good analysis of the current position
2	The development of a strategic plan with fully developed implementation strategies
3	A good justification of the strategies to be adopted

Question 2 Acclaim sells a range of products into diverse geographical markets. Given the nature of the technological (both hardware and the internet) changes, outline the best international marketing strategy for the company to follow.

2.7 This is not an easy question to answer. Acclaim are at the juxtaposition of selling physical products such as CD ROMs, DVDs and the possibilities of a 'seamless' software distribution through the internet.

2.8 Given the possibilities of 'instant' global communications through the internet, the normal international strategies of exporting physical goods will gradually be overtaken by sales and distribution through the internet. The company, therefore, before embarking on an international strategy needs to consider the following.

- Infrastructure development in different countries and the strength of network servers (host computers)
- The size of the internet economy in different countries
- The types of individuals using the internet
- The extent and nature of consumer acceptance
- Using their own site for market research
- The nature and type of 'cultural' blockages that may occur in each country, ie the legal restrictions on the use of sex and violence

Strategies for developing the international marketing strategies for Acclaim

Use of the internet	Good	Poor
High	Expand distribution of games through the internet and set up rigid country protocols for e-commerce *Continue physical distribution strategies, lower emphasis on them*	Go fully operational on the internet.
Low	Continue placing emphasis on distribution with expansion of marketing activities directed at the innovators	Emphasis will depend on market potential. The company will need to market actively to the innovators.

Physical distribution networks

In each case, the company will need to work actively with the hardware developers such as Sony and Nintendo. Sega are already offering internet enabled games playing. The company therefore needs to have in place a well developed e-commerce strategy to cater for the needs of the innovators, having data encryption codes in place.

2.9 As the use of the internet grows, the company will need to provide websites which offer the concept of a 'virtual community' where active games players can discuss and argue about strategies for games and offer the company insights into what works when designing games for an international market.

2.10 Even when **CD-ROMs are sold** they should contain hyper-links to websites. In addition to the above strategies, the company could also, at the website have the following.

- New product announcements
- E-mail and user group facilities
- The ability to learn first hand about new software and hardware by logging on and actually 'test driving' new systems
- Product brochures and specifications
- Interactive catalogues detailing all the products and where they could be obtained
- Links to related information to clarify new concepts and themes
- Audio and video multimedia linkages
- Interactive features engaging the consumers in a dialogue about product requirements or usage ideas
- Customer feedback mechanisms

2.11 Also when developing all these ideas, the candidates should utilise the wealth of data contained in the case and look for anomalies such as the greater use of PCs in Scandinavia (the most wired set of countries in Europe).

2.12 **A good answer should have taken the following into account.**

1	Analysis of the key issues
2	Development of an international strategy
3	Links with the overall strategy

Question 3 Assessing marketing performance (marketing metrics) is often a difficult problem for many companies. Outline the key indicators that you would use to assess Acclaim's market performance, currently and in the future, justifying your choices.

2.13 This particular question should have come as no surprise as the opening introduction to the case already contains a statement concerning market performance. Therefore, given the wealth of data, candidates could have considered the following.

(a) The types of performance measures that should be adopted and why.

(b) That performance measures can be used to measure both 'soft' and 'hard' statistics.

(c) The use of measures should encompass financial and marketing measures with each augmenting the other.

(d) Justify their choice of measures in the light of the strategies adopted.

2.14 **Types of measures that could be adopted**

(a) X% increase in revenue. Probably between 10-25%.

(b) Increase in revenues per platform.

(c) Release of new products.

(d) Growth in sales of well known brands such as NBC and Turok. Establish South Park as a big selling title.

(e) Targets for in-house production to rise to 90%.

(f) To improve the acid ratio and the liquidity ratios within the normal ranges.

(g) Increase profitability.

(h) Increase market share per region.

(i) Consider market share objectives using a Boston type matrix for each of the brands.

(j) Set targets for interactive users.

(k) Monitor the number of 'hits' at different brand sites.

(l) Worldwide increase in software sales from 6% to 7%?

(m) Targets for how much market share has to be gained on the new platforms.

(n) To improve debtor turnover.

(o) Manage the declining format titles with market share objectives.

2.15 Candidates should have been aware of the debates surrounding marketing performance measures. There is a great deal of complexity in the games industry and good candidates should have been able to reflect on this complexity and choose appropriate measures. Above all they should have been able to **justify** their choices.

Analysis of current performance: choice and justification of measures

2.16 As usual, the triangle for formulating answers should be carefully considered by candidates.

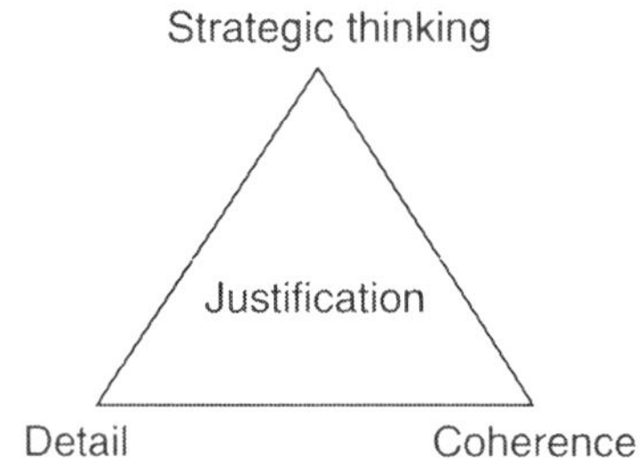

The following two answers were chosen from the December 1999 sitting of the case study as illustrative of good answers within the given time constraints.

3 SPECIMEN ANSWERS WITH EXAMINER'S COMMENTS: SCRIPT 1

REPORT

From: Sam Lee
To: Acclaim Directors
Date: 10/12/99

Contents **Section**

Three year strategic marketing plan

1.0 **Overview**

Acclaim operates in a new and growing market. It is in an extremely competitive, fast changing, unpredictable technological environment. The information I have received today confirms that there will be major changes in the whole gaming and home entertainment industry.

Although eighth in the market place (Appx 1 of information provided to me), Acclaim nevertheless has a relatively small share of the market, at around 5%. Their position can be clearly illustrated in the BCG growth matrix (see below figure 1).

The market is still in growth stage and it is difficult to predict when growth will slow. The information I have received today, suggests that an industry shake-out will occur in the near future. This will be a major threat to Acclaim, in its current weak position.

Figure 1 - BCG Growth Matrix

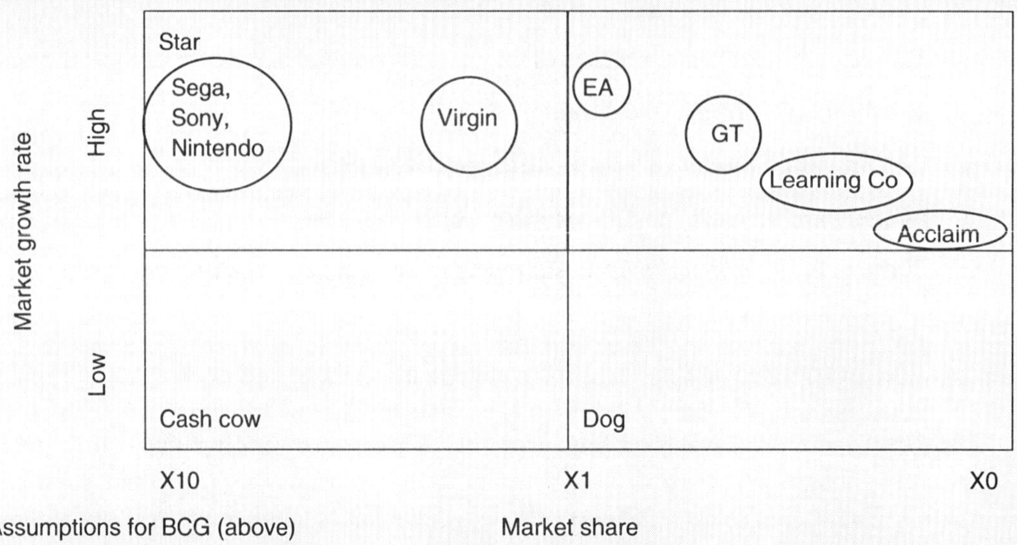

Assumptions for BCG (above)

1 Sega, Sony, Nintendo combined have largest market share
2 Market growth rate was 43% in 1998 (Appx 2)
3 Turnover figures remain static for those reported in 1996 and 1997.

The growing industry is changing fast and from the information I have received today, the market forces are shifting.

1.1 **Porter's five forces illustrates the nature of the market**

Threat of new entrants

- Increasing number of new distribution channels for games software: Digital TV, internet, telecommunications companies.
- Limited loyalty to software companies amongst end-users.
- Massive growth and convergence of technologies.
- Barriers to entry are extremely low.

Threat of substitute products

- Any other leisure activity, eg music, TV.

Bargaining power of suppliers

- Manufacturing of games is outsourced - threat of price increases.
- Reliance of brand suppliers (licensers).

The bargaining power of customers

- Customers are varied, from retailers to console manufacturers, and hardware, home appliance manufacturers. The bargaining power of these all is quite high, as they demand strict compliance with their product.
- Retailer power is also very high, due to lack of end-user loyalty and pressure from them for margin.

Industry rivalry

- From the information received today it is obvious that this will only intensify further. The race for the preferred format will soon be won and there will be a massive industry shakeout.
- Building on this overview, I will now use the TOWS matrix to show the specific application of Acclaim's strengths and how Acclaim needs to overcome its weaknesses, to survive and grow in this environment.

1.2 SWOT analysis/TOWS matrix

Internal elements / External elements	Organisational strengths	Organisational weaknesses
Environmental opportunities and risks	SO 1 Use R&D skills to produce games for widening audience 2 Use R&D skills to produce games to sell over the internet 3 Use strong brands for brand extension 4 Use R&D skills to keep up with changes in technology	WO 1 Overcome weak position and take advantage of new channels by developing strong partnerships 2 Strengthen relationship with console manufacturers to take advantage of new technologies 3 Strengthen brand to appeal to wider audience 4 Through effective segmentation, targeting and positioning satisfy sectors currently not well served
Environmental threats	ST 1 Use technical staff to shorten R&D timescales to respond to changing environment 2 Ability to use high quality niche products to strengthen Acclaim in fragmented market 3 Look for partners to combat shakeout 4 Use strength as distributor of third party games to increase profit	WT 1 Strengthen Acclaim brand to reduce bargaining power of buyers 2 Improve internal communications to engender staff loyalty 3 Adopt marketing orientation to become customer focused 4 Develop relations within industry to lobby against monopolistic practices

1.3 Critical issues for success

1. Define Acclaim's business to provide strategic focus and vision.
2. Seek partnerships to survive as convergence forces out weaker players (from the information received today, this is very important).
3. Withdraw from unprofitable markets, eg Japan.
4. Become more responsive to changing market conditions.

1.4 Corporate objectives and mission

Mission

I propose this mission statement to you so that I have a guide for my subsequent advice.

Mission statement for Acclaim

To grow profitability through the satisfaction of our customers' gaming and entertainment needs, through the development of innovative, high quality products and delivery methods, which harness the power of new technologies.

Corporate objectives

- Reduce reliance on console manufacturers to achieve 30% of Acclaim's own title revenue from the sale of non-console software.
- Rationale: from the information received today it is clear Acclaim must produce software for a number of different manufacturers and service providers.

Revenue and market share objectives

Expected market	Year 1 (end)	Year 3 (end)
	$11.8bn	$23bn
Growth rate		
Acclaim revenue	$570m	$1.04bn
Rev. growth rate	25%	35%
Profit for Acclaim	$45.6m	$124.8m
Profit %	8%	12%
Resulting market share	5%	5%

Although Acclaim have question marks on the BCG growth matrix, which involve a high spend strategy, cost control and market skimming will apply.

1.5 **Corporate strategy**

According to the AD Little model, Acclaim currently occupy a **Tenable: Growth** position.

The recommendation is that Acclaim grows through a niche strategy to achieve a favourable: Growth/Mature position.

This approach will help Acclaim achieve revenue/project/market share objectives.

Implementation

1 Build awareness of Acclaim umbrella and title brands.

2 Seek strategic partnerships to achieve a favourable position.

3 Target clearly defined market segments with a differentiated offer, providing superior value to competition.

(International considerations will be referred to later).

Looking at Porter's Generic Strategies, we can see Acclaim does not occupy a clear position.

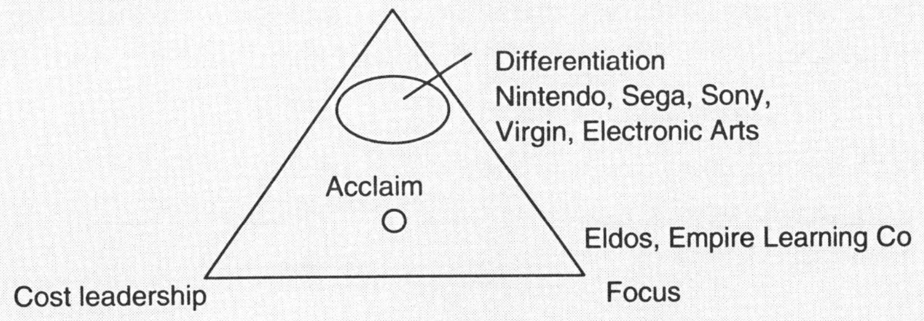

Our findings reinforce those of the ADL model. Acclaim should adopt a focus strategy to enable a more detailed understanding of chosen segments. Acclaim can aim to be the technology leader in its chosen market segments and adopt a challenge mentality.

Conclusion of strategy formulation

Flanking attack

- Target segments not currently satisfied by competitor products
- Tailor Acclaim's proposition and deliver in terms of product performance and new platforms

This will enable Acclaim to build a position of strength, whilst avoiding retaliation from major players.

Acclaim should pursue a differentiation focus strategy in the short term. Longer term seek to adopt a broad based approach.

Acclaim's core capabilities will be exploited to develop competitive advantage based on:

- Superior product and service (in eyes of customer)
- Perceived advantage through brand
- Super relationships and total value chain management with new partners such as AOL, Microsoft etc

In order to achieve the above, Acclaim must implement an effective **internal marketing programme** and review its New Product Development process.

1.6 **Segmenting targeting and positioning**

Customer type, primary criteria	
End users	**Lifestyle**
Hardware manufacturers	Technology format, eg DVD, TV, Internet
Media	Profile of readership
Shareholders	External and internal
Employee's Retail Outlets	

End user lifestyle segments	Primary segmentation criteria (not geographically significant)
Techies	Male - 25-35, professional. PC to chat, shop and game. Want high graphics and long playability games.
Homeboys	Young males. C1, C2, D1. Pocket money, and part-time.
Clubbers	Male and female. Generation X.
Mind benders	C1-Ds all ages, puzzles.
Kids fun	8-16 yrs. Character based games.
Sporties	16-45, males, 'real-life' sports games.

Appeal of current games to proposed segments

Game	**Segment**
USA sports games	Sporties USA
Recking Balls	Kids fun
Bust A Move	Mind benders
Machines	Techies
Turok 2	Techies
Batman & Robin	Action Man

Following a market segment evaluation, Acclaim should specialise in two segments of the market that provide a fit with our objectives and resources, and are attractive in terms of profit potential.

I have identified that 'technies' and 'sporties' fit these criteria and should therefore be selected.

1.7 Marketing objectives

		Year 1	Year 3
1	Increase sales of current products to chosen segments	$342m	
2	Further increase sales to chosen segments with new products and divest non-core titles		$624m
3	For Acclaim titles, increase revenue derived from non-console software sales and via new routes to market	5%	15%
4	Increase awareness of Acclaim umbrella and title brands amongst chosen segments	40%	70%
5	Build loyalty to Acclaim brand	10%	15%

1.8 Marketing strategy

Recommended growth strategies

Products / **Markets**	**Existing**	**Related**	**New**
Existing	Increase purchase from existing customers - Yr 1	Improved versions of current products - Yr 2-3	Broader range of games - Yr 2-3
Related	Convert non-game players - Yr 2-3		
New		New distribution channels, eg WWW, telephones - Yr 2-3	

From the Ansoff growth strategies above, I recommend that in the short-term Acclaim pursues a market penetration strategy and then moves to a new product and new market development strategy.

The market penetration strategy is low risk, speedy to implement and offers fast payback.

New product development will ensure Acclaim maintains a competitive advantage through innovation and along with market development, ensures they respond to the changing environment.

1.9 Internal marketing programme

Acclaim will need to sell the plan internally to gain commitment from staff for the required changes.

This will require the implementation of an internal marketing plan, which I will be happy to advise you on.

1.10 Global branding

- Acclaim are not using their Umbrella and the brands to full effect
- Acclaim has no clear differentiator
- There appears to be no brand loyalty to Acclaim

A future brand strategy needs to address the following critical issues.

- Establish a brand differentiator and personality
- Communicate strengths (innovation, creativity) to target evidence
- Develop favourable image of Acclaim

Brand objectives

- Develop a brand position for Acclaim
- Achieve 70% spontaneous awareness amongst target segments of 'Etches' and 'Sports' by Year 3

Target markets	Need
Consumers	Superior value, excitement
Retailers	Profit margin, football
Press	New news
Shareholders	Security, performance
Employees	Security, motivation
Platform suppliers	End user pull
Third parties	Security, profit

Brand strategy

Brand name	Acclaim and Title
Market description	Leisure software
Brand discriminator	Challenging, innovative
Proposition	High quality, affordable
Personality	Innovative, progressive

Media

See promotions section in 1.11.

Acclaim will need to provide brand usage guidelines and ensure branding is protected legally.

Budget, timescale and control

See Marcomms plan.

1.11 **Marketing mix proposals**

Technies

(a) **Product**

- Develop and publish high quality, multi-play internet based strategy games
- In order to achieve this Acclaim needs to review its NPD process and reduce development time to nine months, to take advantage of technological changes
- It will also need to work together with partners owning emerging technologies, eg AOL, Microsoft etc

(b) **Pricing policy**

Operate across US and Europe therefore need to minimise grey imports. Market skimming to achieve required profit levels

(c) **Distribution**

- Acclaim must look at total value chain management and the emerging opportunities
- Acclaim cannot afford to ignore the internet as a new distribution channel

Sporties (USA only)

(a) **Product**

- New sports games with USA scheme
- NPD times must also be reduced for this segment

(b) **Pricing**

Adopt a mass market approach in US only. Competitive priority - R&D recouped through high volume unit sales

(c) **Distribution**

As above for 'Technies'

Promotions for both segments

Advertising — Digital TV: cost effective
PC Press: highly targeted (Objectives 1, 2, 3, 4, 5)

Sales promotion

Internet challenges (Objectives 1, 2, 3)
Multi-packs for sporties (Objectives 1, 2)

Personal selling

Store commission incentives, to develop retailer relationship (Objectives 1, 2)

PR

Review of games to build reputation as specialist (niche strategy) (Objectives 1, 2, 4). Sponsor Little League events in USA.

Communications and budget schedule

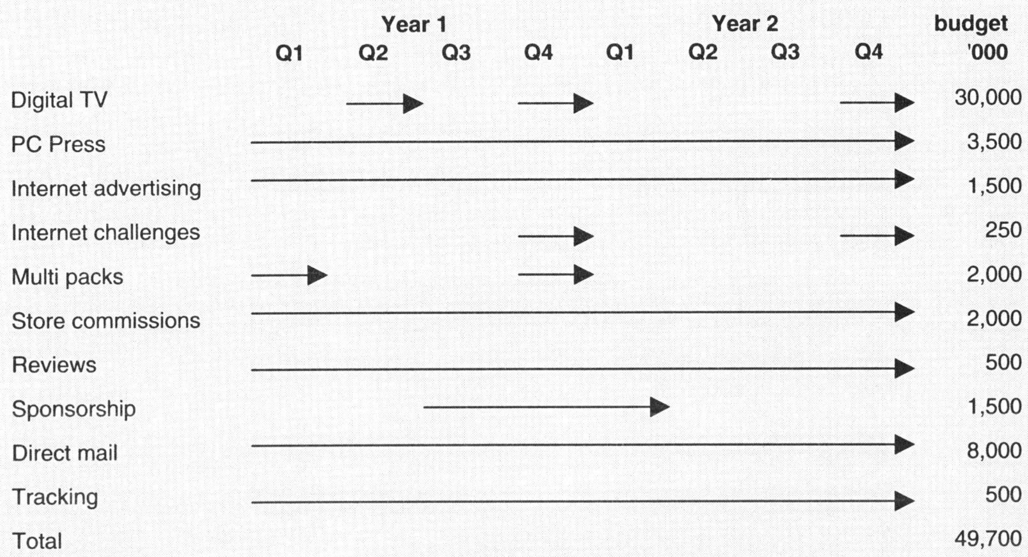

Year 1
Year 2
budget
'000
Q1
Q2
Q3
Q4
Q1
Q2
Q3
Q4
Digital TV
30,000
PC Press
3,500
Internet advertising
1,500
Internet challenges
250
Multi packs
2,000
Store commissions
2,000
Reviews
500
Sponsorship
1,500
Direct mail
8,000
Tracking
500
Total
49,700

Strategy implementation

The implementation of this plan requires Acclaim to make three key changes.

- Adoption of a marketing orientation
- Overhaul of NPD process
- Improvement of relationships between Acclaim and console manufacturers and new and current partners through total value chain

Control and measurement

Implementation of a control system is vital to regulate the activities and achieve the required objectives.

Examiner's comments

This answer is good on analysis. The decisions made are also reasonable if a little overoptimistic in terms of the teaching a $1bn turnover fairly quickly. Nonetheless, erratic and high growth rates are symptomatic of a relatively new industry sector. The candidate could have dealt a little more with the advent of the internet and the possibilities afforded by e-commerce. Given the time constraints this is a good answer. A little more on the control measures and cross-relating them to question 3 would have been useful. It would also have been useful to point out that both umbrella and branding concerned with the individual identifies of the products would have been useful. Games are often sold on the strength of the name such as South Park. In some way, the umbrella brand needs to play an equally strong role in the promotion of these games.

3.2 Answer to question 2

International strategic plan

Situation

- Acclaim operates in diverse markets
- The BCG growth/gain matrix indicates Acclaim should review their presence in Japan, as Acclaim sales are falling, whilst the Japanese market is growing

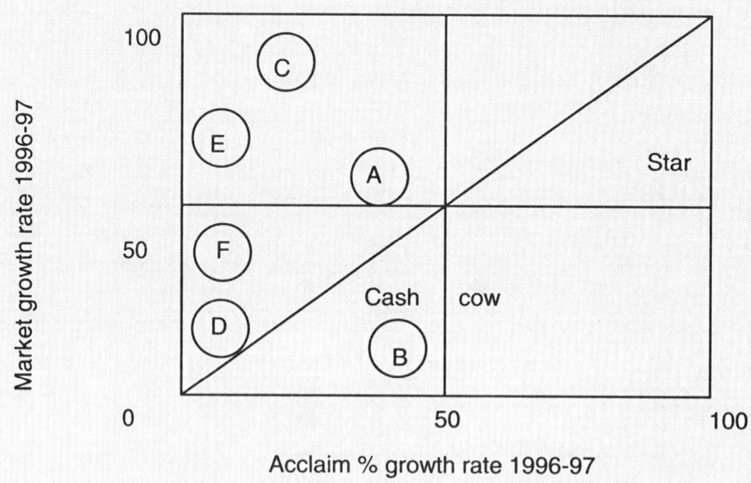

A = USA Console software
B = USA PC software
C = Europe Console software
D = Europe PC software
E = Japan Console software
F = Japan PC software

Acclaim has established distribution channels in Europe, Japan and USA but these are set to change with the new technological changes taking place in the market.

- Cultural issues are shown to affect product acceptance
- European distribution through subsidiaries has allowed Acclaim to benefit from their knowledge of local conditions

What areas should Acclaim operate in? Business portfolio matrix (Harrell & Kiefer)

		High	**Medium**	**Low**
Acclaim comparability country	High	USA, Fr, DE, UK	Spain, Italy	
	Medium		Eastern Europe	Japan
	Low		Asia	

- Clearly the USA, France, Germany and UK are primary opportunities for Acclaim and the most attractive.

Target audience

See Segmentation, Targeting, Positioning tables earlier. These transnational segments have similar characteristics and interests across geographic boundaries.

Strategy

Current strategy is based on indirect export via subsidiaries, which may be cost effective but can lead to loss of control.

There are a number of market entry options open to Acclaim.

Indirect exporting

- UK buying offices
- Export house
- Trade missions
- Piggy backing

Direct exporting

- Overseas agents
- Overseas distributors
- Overseas sales offices

Overseas production

- Licensing
- Franchising
- Contract manufacturing
- Joint venture

Control	Higher	Lower
Higher	• Wholly owned subsidiary	• Joint venture • Franchise • Licensing
Lower		• Piggy backing • Agents and distributors

Of the traditional routes to market the preferred options would be direct export via distributors. Distributors take title for the goods, therefore giving more commitment to the sales.

This would be a quick and effective mode of entry.

However, the **internet** means that the whole world can now be reached much more easily. Acclaim may be able to sell games directly over the Internet, with the customer downloading the game to his/her hardware from Acclaim's site.

- This would offer excellent opportunities for Acclaim through reduced costs, administration and manufacture of games onto CD or DVD.
- It would also offer Acclaim a direct relationship with its customers.
- I strongly advise further investigation of this strategy.

Acclaim will also need to talk with the emerging hardware manufacturers. There may be opportunities to piggyback using their distribution systems.

International pricing

In line with the proposed marketing plan, I recommend Acclaim adopts a market skimming policy on the launch of new products aimed at the 'Technies' segment, across all markets.

In Europe, pricing should be transparent to minimise grey importing.

Examiner's comments

The international analysis is particularly good on this answer and shows that the candidate has at least attempted to make use of the country data given. In this answer in particular, the extra information supplied should have been taken into account. This extra information signals the way in which the internet is going to play an increasing role in both the marketing and the distribution of the games. The Sega linkup means that as a supplier, Acclaim needs to 'build in' specific software to ease on-line sales. There could also be an opportunity to sell to PC active audiences, compared tot he ones still relying on dedicated consoles.

3.3 Answer to Question 3

Assessing Acclaim's market performance

There are a number of ways to assess Acclaim's market performance. These fall into two categories: internal factors and external factors. I shall look at each in turn.

Internal factors

The marketing plan which I propose suggests a number of objectives at a corporate and marketing level. Some of these objectives refer to internal requirements such as improvements in NPD processing (reduce time to nine months).

The measurement of how well the company responds internally to external threats and opportunities is a good indicator of the company's market performance.

Some measurement criteria and reasons for them are as follows.

Staff turnover

Acclaim should aim to benchmark this against industry standards and improve upon it. Staff loyalty is key to effective performance.

NPD success rate

New product development is extremely important in the game and entertainment industry, especially with the new technological changes which are happening.

Acclaim needs to measure how well it is responding to the changes in the environment. NPD success/failure rates, and time taken to develop a new game from idea generation to commercialisation are two important indicators of success.

Total value chain management

Acclaim needs to ensure that it improves relationships with all of those involved in the current and emerging value chain of which it is a part.

The measurement of this will be through satisfaction of its customers in the chain and the perception of both suppliers and customers of Acclaim.

External factors

These factors relate to outputs, such as revenue, market share, profitability.

Market share

The PIMS study, and the Boston Consulting Group growth matrix both imply that market share is a good measure of success.

The PIMS study states that a 10% increase in market share equates to a 5% increase in profit before tax.

Acclaim should not however measure its success through market share. As I recommend a focus differentiation strategy for Acclaim, market share is not a suitable measure of success. Profitability does not equate to market share in every case and a niche strategy does not aim for market share.

Profitability would be a better measure of Acclaim's success (at least until Acclaim move to a broad-differentiator strategy). Currently, Acclaim needs to increase its profitability to attain a more stable position from which to grow.

In the marketing plan, I suggest an objective of 12% profit as a percentage of revenue by year three. This cannot be achieved by internal cost reduction alone, but through the production and marketing of games which have strong appeal to the target market. This requires Acclaim to understand its segments' needs and respond with the right product, in the right place, at the right time at the right price. It is therefore a good indicator of Acclaim's market performance.

Acclaim should attempt to benchmark its profitability against similar size companies following similar strategies (The Learning Co) now and in the future.

Another important indicator now and in the future is **share price and P/E ratio**. Shareholders will constantly be assessing Acclaim's market performance, as they see it. Potential investors also affect the share price, as demand for shares increase the price.

The stock market will judge Acclaim's performance and the share price will reflect their view. Equally, Acclaim's dividend payment will reflect its success.

The stock market looks not only at current and past performance but also of course at future performance. This is particularly true in the hi-technology industries. Internet companies have seen an amazing interest from the stockmarket, and prices have soared following flotation, on the basis of future potential, not current value.

Examiner's comments

This answer was deliberately kept fairly open to see whether candidates could think beyond the basic financially based performance measures. This answer varies in its suggestions. The main weakness is the lack of actual figures linked to the case. There is much in the case on geographical growth, competitors, market growth rates and market share. Also there is enough data on financial ratios and performance trends. Again, the answer is good in that a large range of possible measures are chosen, with enough justification as to why they were used.

4 SPECIMEN ANSWERS WITH EXAMINER'S COMMENTS: SCRIPT 2

4.1 Answer to Question 1

To: Directors, Acclaim Entertainment
From: Sam Lee, Marketing Consultant
Date: 10 December 1999

Contents

- Strategic marketing plan
- International marketing strategy
- Assessment of Acclaim's market performance, current and future indicants to use

A Strategic Marketing Plan for Acclaim Entertainment Inc for 1999-2000

- Using the information available to me, I am writing this report to recommend a strategic marketing plan for AEI.
- Having analysed the market there is still a vast amount of information required for accurate and effective decision making.
- However, in the absence of actual information certain assumptions have been made from my own experience in the audio and electronics market and these have been noted.
- The expert will outline a strategic marketing plan covering the following topics.
    - Current situation analysis
    - Vision, brand values, mission statement
    - Objectives
    - Strategies
    - Marketing mix

- Implementation
- Evaluation and controls

1 **Current situation analysis summary**

1.1 **Internal**

- Lack of clear direction and strategy, with no evidence of planning and control culture
- Current liquidity problem leaves Acclaim vulnerable and dependent on high turnover to cover fixed costs
- Over reliance on two funders of company and lack of evidence of key management structure
- Dependence on renewal of licenses from third party organisations
- Low margins on PC title sales
- History of relationship with hardware manufacturers, eg Microsoft
- Strong R&D focus

1.2 **External**

- Strategic alliances - major trend within industry
- Rapid changes in technology stimulates growth and opportunity but increases competitiveness of market
- Under performance in European market in relation to overall market growth
- Increasing exposure to copyright and litigation issues
- Increasing leisure time of consumers

1.3 **Market**

- Based on information available AEI is fifth largest software company in its sector by turnover
- AEI currently sells direct in USA, Japan, UK, France, Germany, Australia and Singapore and operates through regional distributors in other markets
- The crucial issue currently affecting demand for AEI's products is the size of the installed base of entertainment platforms
- However the recent deal between British Telecom and Sega and the expansion of the market to encompass telecommunications companies creates a great area of opportunity for AEI

1.4 **Current portfolio analysis**

- I recommend that AEI should carry out a portfolio analysis of its products using the BCG matrix
- This matrix will help AEI to see current position of company products in relation to market share and market growth
- It will also help to formulate product strategy
- However more information is required by AEI in order to carry this out, eg sales of each title, market size by country market share

		High	Low
Relative market growth	High	Stars	Question mark
	Low	Cash cow	Dog

Relative market share

1.5 **Product life cycle by platform**

- AEI's products are in various stages of the plc, which has an effect on the financial position of the company
- As the industry is dynamic this model is useful as a starting point to enable AEI to identify relevant strategies in relation to each product segment

- As AEI's sales are driven by the size of the installed base the analysis below can be used to identify platform hardware with the greatest potential for growth and long term profit

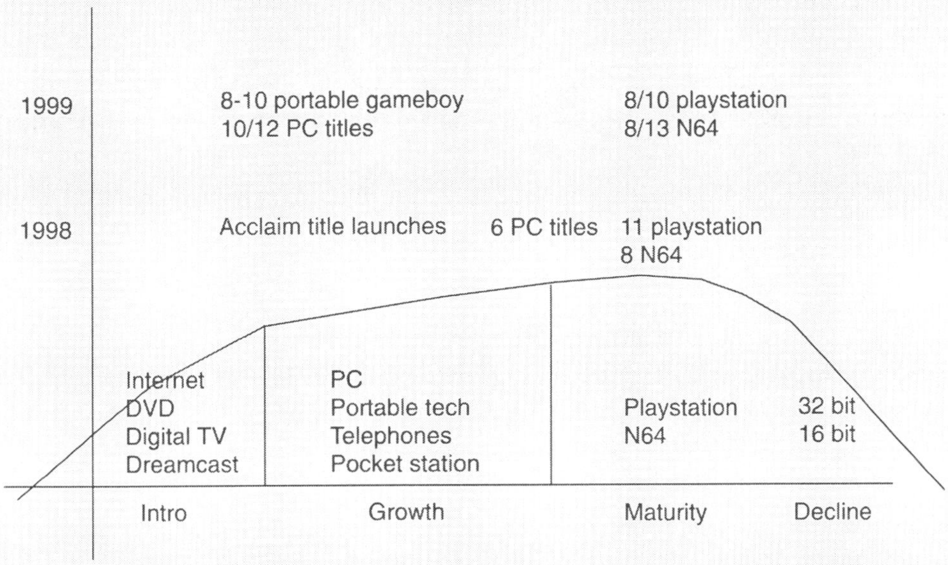

1.6 **Current position**

AEI can be identified currently as being a regiocentric organisation with a product focus.

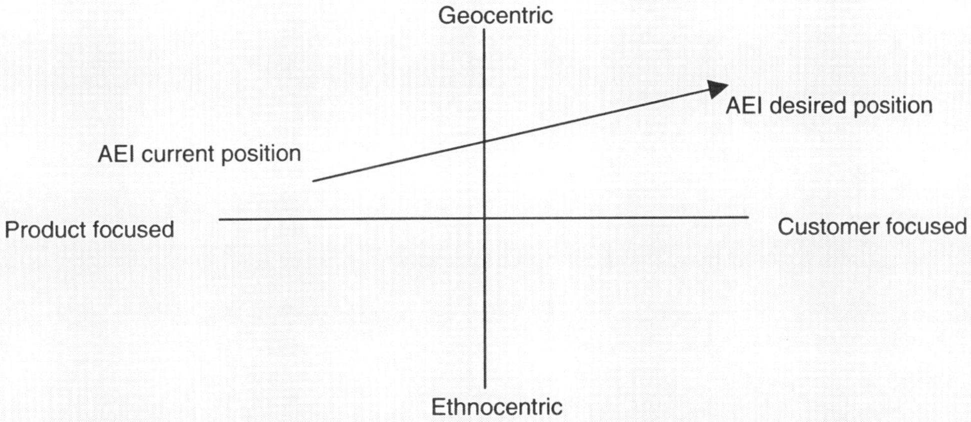

I recommend that over time AEI may wish to move their position in order to become a geocentric organisation with a customer focus.

1.7 **Current strategies**

- Penetration - Little evidence of this due to lack of strategy
- Market Development - again, this is limited to due lack of strategy
- Product Development - strong focus on new product development reflect product orientation
- Diversification - limited diversification via licensing into toys and books

1.8 **Market trends**

As identified in the additional information, the market is characterised by strategic alliances and the emergence of new players such as telecommunication firms and home appliance manufacturers.

1.9 **Competitive position**

It is useful to use Porter's five forces to analyse the competitive nature of the market.

New entrants

1 High R&D costs
2 Rapid changes in market provide opportunities

Bargaining power of suppliers

1 High power through licensing

Existing market

1 Intense competition
2 Consolidation
3 Hits drive market

Bargaining power of buyers

1 Brand loyal customer if like product
2 Retailers - power, eg Toys R Us

Threat of substitutes

1 Piracy and copyright major issue
2 Software market strong

This diagram highlights the dynamic market that AEI are in.

AEI need to monitor each of five forces as they can all provide change in the profit margin of the sector.

1.10 **Key problems**

- No clear corporate marketing planning structure
- Poor penetration of existing markets
- High level of control exerted by hardware manufacturers
- No definitive trend architecture
- Product focused

2 VISION, MISSION, VALUES

2.1 **Vision**

AEI will become the leading world-wide developer, publisher and mass market of software for interactive entertainment industry.

2.2 **Mission statement**

In the absence of a current mission statement I suggest the following:

> "Acclaim Entertainment Inc will strive to be the leading global provider of innovative, quality customer focused solutions for the interactive media industry."

2.3 **Brand values**

- The current values of AEI are based on high quality innovative products
- In future these values should be joined by strong branding, high quality products and target marketing to back up AEI's position as world class player in interactive entertainment industry

2.4 **Objectives and planning gap**

In order for AEI to maintain and improve its position in the market it is vital to stabilise the current financial position. Increase profitability and satisfy internal and external customers.

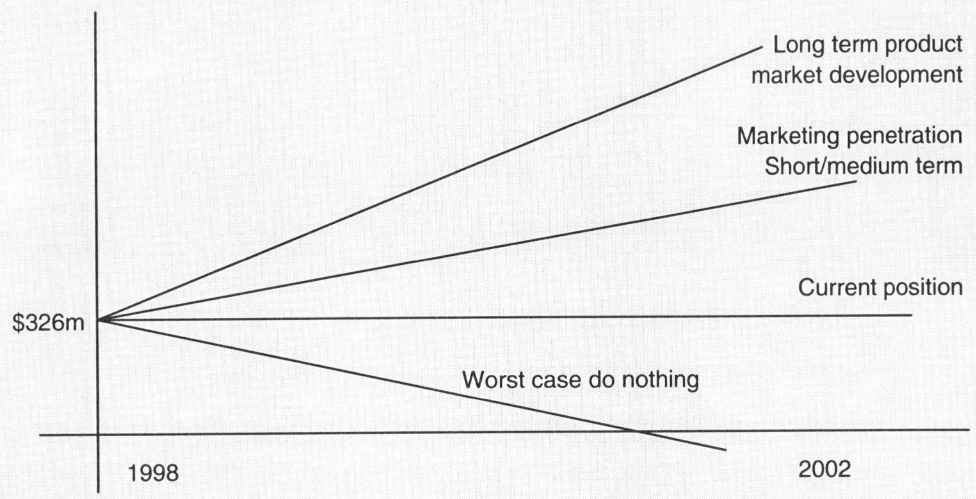

3 CORPORATE OBJECTIVES

In the absence of any current corporate objectives I recommend the following.

3.1 Profitability

To stabilise net profit margin in short term and grow in medium term to minimum of 15% by 2003.

3.2 Growth

Aim to grow and stabilise share of interactive software market from 0.4% in 1997 to 5% by 2002.

3.3 Culture

To become a marketing orientated organisation.

Corporate strategy is vital to the marketing planning process as highlighted in diagram by Kotler below.

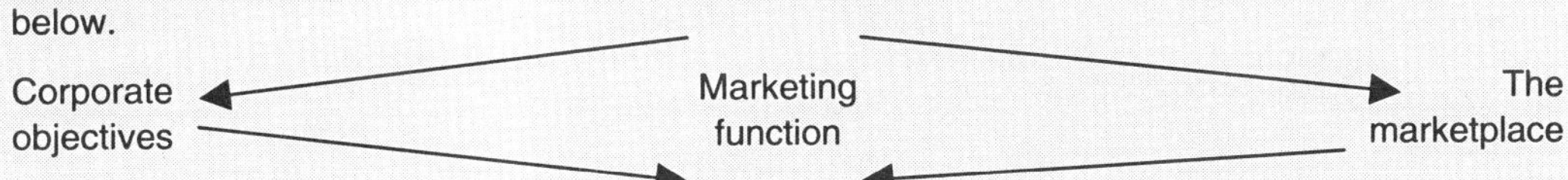

Kotler

4 MARKETING OBJECTIVES

- Implement a comprehensive MKIS by end of 2000.
- Increase sales via internet by 10% by end of 2000.
- Establish strategy to increase revenues from non-console based software to 20% of total revenue by 2002.

  (This will be monitored quarterly as internet usage is doubling every 100 days.)
- To increase turnover from $236m in 1998 to $795m by 2002.

5 STRATEGIES

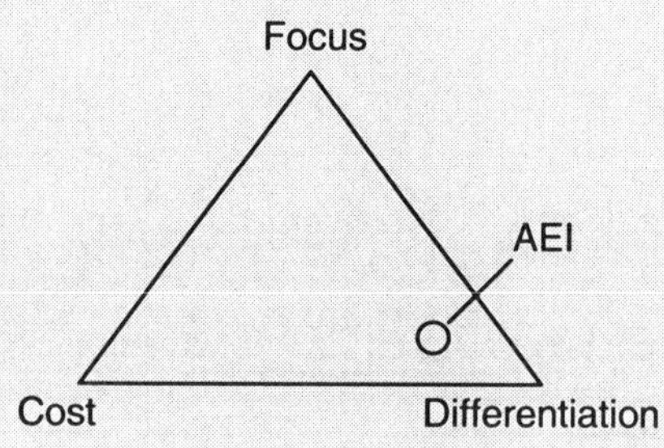

5.1

- Using Porter's model there are three alternative strategies open to AEI.
- However the strategy which makes sense to follow is differentiation.
- This strategy will allow AEI to use its strengths such as technical innovation and high quality products to differentiate it from competitors.
- Cost leadership strategy is rejected due to the high development costs involved.

5.2 **GEC multifactor portfolio**

Market attractiveness / Business strengths	Strong	Medium	Weak
High	Internet Nintendo Playstation	PC Digital TV	
	Portable consoles Dreamcast		
Low	32 bit platforms		

From this model it is clear that AEI should:

- Invest for growth in games for internet, N64, Playstation
- Explore DVD, Digital TV market
- Develop products for PC market

However, it is important to note that AEI need to monitor the industry closely due to continuing change.

5.3 **Ansoff's matrix**

		Product: Current	Product: New
Market	Current	Penetration	Product development
	New	Market development	Diversification

Market

AEI should pursue the following strategies identified by Ansoff's matrix.

1 Penetration

relationship marketing
view distribution methods

2 Market development

Broaden age range of target customers
Target new users - females
Use internet to broaden market

3 Product development

Important to develop games for emerging formats - DVD, digital on-line gaming - as highlighted in additional information

4 Diversification

- AEI may wish to pursue this strategy at a later date.
- Due to high risks and costs involved it is not recommended at present.

5.4 **Segmentation**

- I recommend that AEI segment market by hardware platform and by user.
- More detail will be given on this later in international strategy recommendation.

5.5 **Positioning**

- More information is required from the market to develop a positioning strategy for AEI.
- However it is important for AEI to position itself carefully in order to maximise growth and potential.

6 MARKETING MIX

Marketing mix is an important area. At this stage I will give outline recommendations.

6.1 **Product**

- NPD very important as market changes rapidly
- Develop branded products
- Assess customer expectations via MKIS to deliver augmented product

6.2 **Price**

- At present there is little information on pricing available.
- Therefore I recommend that AEI should adopt a pricing strategy that is in line with the differentiation strategy adopted.

6.3 **Promotion**

- Support for products in all channels of distribution
- Implementation of push and pull strategies

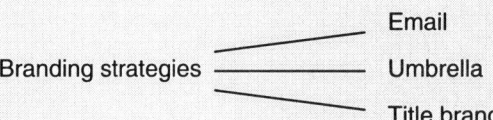

Branding strategies — Email / Umbrella / Title brand

6.4 **Place**

- Investigate new channels, eg internet
- Re-assess current distribution methods
- Devise web-site with regional pages

7 TIMESCALES, EVALUATION AND CONTROLS

- In order to measure effectiveness of this plan measurement should be against objectives set
- The process should be regularly monitored against short term targets and tactics modified where necessary to achieve goals
- Control will be required with regard to finances, human resources and marketing
- Any change of plan requires investment in marketing and skills and an MKIS system. There may be requirement for changes in structure, culture and attitude to become more customer focused and profitable

Timescale

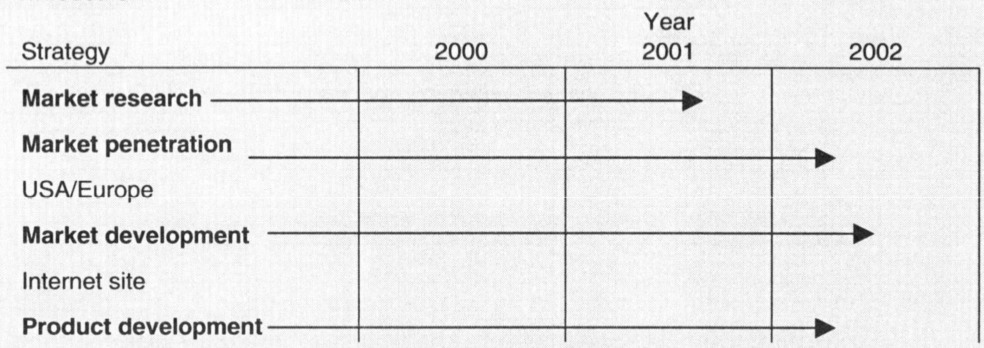

Internet launch schedule will need to be re-assessed monthly.

Examiner's comments

This question, although well handled, needs to make more of the extensive detail contained in the case. Some analyses of country trends and key segments within them would have helped. In general though, most of the key issues have been addressed and issues surrounding the internet have been addressed. I would have also expected more justifications for the strategies proposed.

4.2 Answer to Question 2

1 SITUATION ANALYSIS

I would like to recommend the best international market strategy for Acclaim Entertainment Inc.

- AEI has offices in USA, UK and sales offices in Japan, Germany, France
- It sells directly in these markets and operates via regional distributors in others
- Clearly it has experience in international market place

1.1 **Environmental analysis**

- International market dynamic shows the demand for games is growing world-wide
- Globalisation of games market
- Piracy and copyright

1.2 Competitive situation

- All major competitors to AEI operate globally
- In order to compete AEI need to be global also

1.3 Critical success factors

- Relationship building with retailers and consumers
- Market knowledge
- Consumer awareness of Acclaim brand

1.4 Opportunities

Europe

- Alliance with BT and Sega Dreamcast
- May provide AEI with opportunity to become key game developer
- Use of internet as means of entry into markets where AEI currently have no presence

World-wide

- Alliance with BT and Sega will have world-wide implications
- Other strategic alliances with manufacturers of DVD/Digital TV technology
- Develop use of internet as global distribution channel

1.5 Objectives

- Increase sales via internet by 10% by end of 2000
- Establish strategy to increase revenues from non-console based software to 20% of turnover, by 2002
- Establish brand awareness of 50%
- Long term: grow non-domestic sales to account for 50% of total turnover by 2005
- Short term: initiate a comprehensive marketing information system by 2002

2 STRATEGIES

- Market development with a differentiated focus (as explained in strategic plan for AEI)
- Products will be standardised where possible but adapted where necessary to meet the needs of the market

3 METHOD OF ENTRY

Market attractiveness	Strong	Medium	Weak
High	Internet Retailer direct sales	Piggy backing	Agents
Medium	Exclusive distributors		
Low			Subsidiary

AEI strengths

It is clear that the ideal methods of entry for AEI into international markets are:

(1) Internet - as distribution
(2) Via established retailers
(3) Using direct sales force

Having used this model it is clear that AEI should pursue international market strategy via internet as a global means of distribution.

4 **SEGMENTATION**

AEI should segment their international markets by platform used and by the demographics of the consumer.

5 **TARGETING**

Concentrated strategy all 15-34 year old game players

6 **POSITIONING: High quality, innovative product**

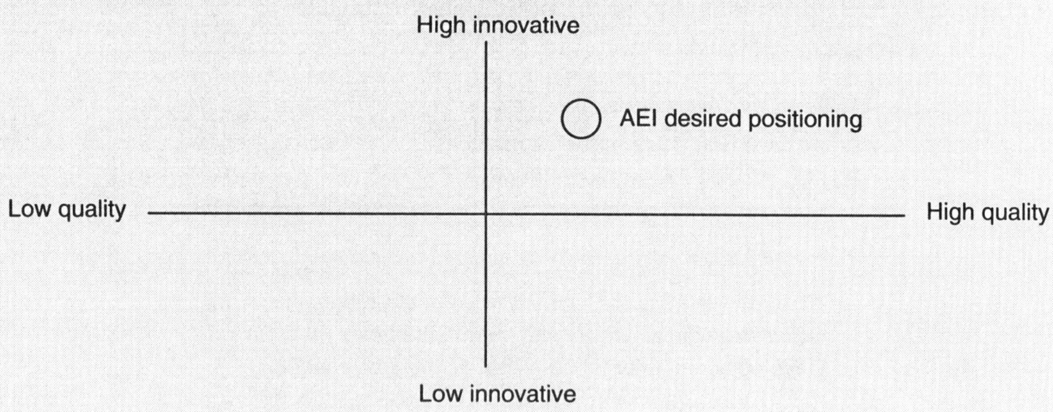

7 **MARKETING MIX**

Product

- Adaptation of games/software content for certain markets where violence is not acceptable
- Brand - build brand awareness via use of Acclaim and logo on all packaging

Place

- Review market entry methods, ie salesforce/internet
- Local market knowledge is useful
- Develop internet site with dedicated regional pages for different markets
- Recent research showed that 80% of all who purchase on internet buy within their own country - need to reassure customers

Price

- Pricing strategy will need to be in line with differentiation strategy

Promotion

- In-store demos
- Push/pull strategies vital

People

- Appoint key account managers
- Appoint individual responsible for internet sales
- Training in cultural differences

8 **IMPLICATIONS**

Marketing

- International marketing information system required
- Appointment of key marketing personnel

Organisation

- Change in culture will be required from marketing to product focus

Operational

- Distribution depots may need to be set up in order to service the sales from the internet site
- Distribution may need to be located in different countries

Financial

- Finances will be required to develop internet site
- Budget will be needed for support of internet site

9 **EVALUATION AND CONTROL**

- Measure number of hits on websites against orders placed
- Measure market share and margins

10 **RECOMMEND**

- In the short term, AEI should continue with market penetration strategy in existing markets
- Focus on establishment of internet site as key to international marketing strategy in long term - but AEI should start this now

Examiner's comments

There are some good points made here with some good international positioning analyses. It is good that the candidate has considered the impact of the internet and how the distribution strategies may need to change in the longer run.

4.3 Answer to Question 3

Key indicators to assess AEI's performance, current and future

1.0 **Introduction**

The key indicators which are useful to assess AEI's performance can be divided into:

(1) Financial indicators
(2) Marketing indicators/customer analysis

1.1 **Financial indicators**

The following are a few of the financial indicators used to assess company performance

- Gross margin
- Net margin
- Research and development expenditure
- Liquidity ratios
- Turnover
- Domestic revenue
- Foreign revenue
- Internet states revenue
- Revenue by product category/profitability
- Performance against budget

1.2 **Justification**

The financial indicators above are important as they show AEI's management:

- How AEI are performing year on year
- How AEI are performing in comparison to competition
- By comparing gross margin and net margin AEI can begin to examine the nature of its fixed costs and identify areas of high expenditure
- The amount of revenue from domestic market vs foreign markets vs internet sales can be used by AEI to establish how much growth has been achieved in the target markets
- The indicator of revenue/profitability by product category is also vital as it can indicate which products are contributing to profit and which either need more development or withdraw from the market

1.3 **Financial indicators - key points**

It is important that AEI look at these indicators in the context of their operating market.

- Ideally AEI should compare their financial indicators against those of others in the industry
- This is important as it allows AEI to position itself against the competition and identify those players who are weak and may be available for take-over or merger
- I have not identified share price as an indicator as it is volatile in a market of this nature
- Generally firms in this industry suffer from an over-valued share price

2.0 **Marketing indicators**

The following are market indicators useful to assess performance

- Brand awareness
- Market share
- BCG matrix
- Customer surveys
- Sales per title

Justification

2.1 **Brand awareness**

- AEI should measure brand awareness as it indicates the effectiveness of its brand strategy
- This is normally assessed by a survey of customers
- It is a helpful device as it can help to evaluate the effectiveness of AEI's marketing communications strategy

2.2 **Market share**

- The measurement of market share by platform, by country is useful as it allows AEI to place itself in the context of the market
- It also helps to asses whether AEI are market-leaders, followers or challengers

2.3 **BCG matrix**

- This matrix outlined earlier in the report is a useful indicator of the balance of the portfolio of products
- To be of use to AEI, it should be carried out by country and by platform
- This will help formulate product strategy

2.4 **Customer surveys, competition surveys/audits**

Surveys of customers and competition via marketing audits can help AEI to:

(1) Establish clear view of how customers see their positioning
(2) Identify customer needs
(3) Assess competition and strategies

These are vital indicators as they help formulate future strategy for AEI.

3.0 **Conclusion**

- Evaluation and control is a constant process and should become part of company culture
- AEI need to evaluate performance against objectives both corporate and marketing

Examiner's comments

There is much detail here on the necessary performance indicators for Acclaim. This is a good answer from that point of view. The answer could have been enhanced by the use of some of the data that is already available and utilising it to show how the performance indicators would be evaluated.

Overall summary by examiner

This paper was fair and had a considerable amount of data. It was therefore important for candidates to analyse this data in order to reach sensible decisions. Good answers need both good analytical skills and decision making skills. Decisions reached also have to be executable. In that sense there are no right or wrong answers, only sensible and realistic solutions to the problems. The above two specimen answers show the extent to which each candidate has addressed the questions effectively by analysing the data given.

5 A FINAL WORD

5.1 So how did you do? Did your answers shape up to the specimens supplied?

5.2 See how you do in the next case.

18 Clerical Medical Investment Group Ltd: Case Study Documentation

This chapter includes the case study information sent to candidates.
1 Candidate's brief
2 Clerical Medical Investment Group Ltd: text
3 Appendices to Clerical Medical Investment Group Ltd

CONSULT THE GUIDANCE NOTES FOR STAGE 1 IN CHAPTER 8 SECTION 1
STEP 1.1 READ THE CASE **STEP 1.2 AFTER AN INTERVAL, RE-READ THE CASE** **STEP 1.3 REFLECT ON THE INSTRUCTIONS AND CANDIDATES' BRIEF** **STEP 1.4 THINK YOURSELF INTO THE ROLE AND THE SITUATION** **STEP 1.5 RE-READ THE CASE AND WRITE A PRÉCIS - IN NOT MORE THAN TWO A4 SIDES**
ALLOW YOURSELF BETWEEN 3 AND 6 HOURS FOR THESE STEPS

INTRODUCTORY NOTE

The second practice case is Clerical Medical Investment Group Ltd - a medium-sized mutual dealing in life assurance, pensions and investment products. It is about a quarter of the size of the Pru and 10% that of NatWest. Clerical Medical was formed in 1824 to insure the lives of doctors and clergymen. It has traditionally sold through independent brokers and had a low public profile. Like most of its competitors it has only recently developed full-service marketing activities and adopted a strategic approach to marketing planning. The market is increasingly intensively competitive and the government being generally unhappy with the industry has become more interventionist and regulatory in recent years.

1 CANDIDATE'S BRIEF

1.1 You are **Mr Don Sherwood** a Marketing Consultant who has had considerable experience in analysing different industry sectors for a number of companies with a view to helping them to perform competitively. For this assignment, the Clerical Medical Investment Group Limited has invited you to undertake an internal and external analysis of their current situation.

1.2 You have consulted widely within the industry and within the group. The insurance and pensions industry is quite complex, yet you have managed to find some useful information on consumer profiles and the competitive positions of the various players in the sector.

1.3 As a result of your efforts you have built up an interesting profile of the industry and Clerical Medical's position within it. At a future meeting to be set on the 16 June 2000, you are to present your findings to the Marketing Director, Mr James Broadbent, in order to help him to develop future plans for the organisation.

2 CLERICAL MEDICAL INVESTMENT GROUP LTD: TEXT

2.1 Clerical Medical was formed in 1824 in a public house called 'The Freemason's Tavern', in Great Queen Street, London. A small group of men, led by Dr George Pinckard, met to form a life assurance society. The society was formed to insure the lives of doctors and clergymen, hence the original name Clerical, Medical and General Life Assurance Society. Between 1833 and 1840, the competition in the life assurance market was fierce, with 47 companies being formed. Companies ensured survival by specialising in a particular group of customers. Clerical Medical managed to succeed against opposition as it had two specialist market clientele, namely doctors and clergymen, offering exclusivity to them. It offered to assure 'persons subject to such deviations from the common standard of health as do not essentially tend to shorten life.' Basically this meant that the company assured people who had certain ailments or diseases that other insurance companies would not envisage offering a service to.

2.2 In the 1890s some notable policy holders included Queen Victoria, Benjamin Disraeli and Thomas Addison. Acquired by the Employer's Liability Assurance Corporation Ltd, Clerical Medical continued to operate as an autonomous subsidiary. The company began to attract European clientele, though in 1923 Benito Mussolini was declined a policy as his situation was regarded as offering an unacceptable risk.

2.3 In 1956, St James's Square, London, became Clerical Medical's first true Head Office. Before that it operated out of four separate buildings in the Bloomsbury Road area of London. In 1950 Clerical Medical became independent again when the Employer's merged with the Northern Assurance Company. In 1961 Clerical Medical became a mutual[1] office by an Act of Parliament. The mutuality meant that the company did not have to pay any shareholders and that it was solely owned by the policy holders. In 1975 the Bristol Head Office was opened.

[1] Mutual companies are generally 'owned' by policy holders and are not part of banks or listed on the stock market.

2.4 In 1981 Clerical Medical Management Funds Ltd was formed. Its principal activity is the transaction of long-term insurance business, written as 'managed funds' arrangements for approved pension schemes. The company offers specialist administration and technical services to pension fund trustees. In 1984 Clerical Medical Unit Trust Managers Ltd was formed (CMUTM). This company markets and manages a comprehensive range of unit trusts and acts as an ISA[2] manager. Later in 1987, the company established its first international operation, Clerical Medical International (CMI), which now produces more than a quarter of the group's new business. It is recognised as a leading name in the field of international financial services. A second administration centre was opened in Clevedon near Bristol in 1992. The year 1996 marked a great change for the company when it offered itself for sale, with the aim of being acquired by a large and powerful parent company. As a result of this, on 1 January 1997, Halifax acquired Clerical, Medical and General Life Assurance Society at a cost of around £800 million. It demutualised and became the Clerical Medical Investment Group Limited, a wholly owned subsidiary of the Halifax Group. Halifax is now a large bank. It was originally a building society.

[2] Individual Savings Accounts which are often linked to investment funds or companies.

This move was necessary as Clerical Medical was only a medium sized player in the field and needed the shelter of a larger organisation. The acquisition also gave Halifax a larger share of the insurance industry. A special bonus, called the Halifax Special Bonus, was paid to Clerical Medical's with-profit policy holders, in return for allowing the acquisition to take place.

The insurance industry environment

2.5 The life assurance industry in the UK is quite a significant sector of business. The total sum invested at the end of 1998 was over £18.6 billion (see Table 1). The net premium is about 7 per cent of the Gross Domestic Product (GDP). The original purpose of the industry was to provide protection against misfortune. This role has now expanded to cover pensions, longer-term savings and the investments of individuals. There are many links between the UK industry and the life assurance industries in Europe and the rest of the world. However, the assurance industry is still not global. Certain national characteristics such as taxation, legislation, regulation and consumer preferences, mean that there is only a limited amount of business selling across national boundaries, in spite of the borders being removed within the European Union (see Appendix 2).

2.6 The industry underwent rapid expansion in the 1980s and 1990s, although there have been short periods of slow growth. However, the advent of electronic commerce could herald another growth spurt. So could the development of Stakeholder Pensions, which are designed to widen the penetration of pensions throughout the UK. The earlier boom in selling was largely due to the selling of endowment policies to individuals taking out mortgages as part of the housing boom and the introduction of personal pensions in the late 1980s.

Table 1

	1985 £bn	*1995* £bn	*1998* £bn	*1999 (Q1 - Q3)* £bn
Individual life (AP + SP)[3] Total Premiums	4.1	9.9	19.4	18.6
Individual pensions (AP + SP) Total Premiums	0.9	4.3	6.1	4.6
Total long-term business funds	142.6	554.8	827	Not available
Total policies in force	100.2m	100.7m	97.9m	Not available

Source: ABI

[3] AP: This represents products where customers make monthly payments
SP: These are products where customers make one single payment only

Demand analysis

2.7 The rapid growth slowed in the 1990s. This happened for the following reasons.

(a) **Decline of mortgage related business.** The selling of endowment policies has fallen significantly and has been largely discredited, many consumer chose PEPs[4] or repayment mortgages and more recently, ISAs to support the repayment of their mortgages.

(b) **Competition from new tax efficient products.** PEPs, TESSAs[5] and ISAs have the benefit of tax relief. These savings are free of capital gains and income taxes, compared to some life policies which are less flexible and can attract capital gains tax.

(c) **Depressed savings market.** Consumers are often enticed to repay debt rather than saving. However, the pendulum may be swinging the other way as a result of increasing interest rates.

(d) **Mature market.** The life assurance market is essentially at a mature stage in the UK, with the market size higher than anywhere else in the world, at 7.3% of GNP. In France and Germany the respective GNP percentages are 3.77 and 2.63.

(e) **Value for money.** The disclosure of expenses has shown the high costs associated with selling and servicing. Companies have responded to this by lowering costs. However, it is increasingly difficult for companies to absorb the reductions as yields are getting lower.

(f) **Pensions mis-selling.** This has had a high profile in the press (see Appendix 2) and it is likely to cost the industry up to £4 billion in compensation.

(g) **Consumer mistrust of product providers.** Public scandals have contributed to the creation of a poor image of the industry. The bad selling policies of some of the companies have tarnished the whole sector.

(h) **Regulation.** This has added to the costs of the industry. This has constrained the industry and reduced the number of distributors of life and pension products. The direct sales forces have dwindled from 100,000 in 1990 to less than 30,000 now, although the number of Independent Financial Advisers (IFAs) has stood at around 21,000 for the last 10 years.

[4] Personal Equity Plans which attracted tax relief and were usually individual funds invested in companies.

[5] Tax Exempt Shares and Savings Account.

2.8 In spite of problems, business has picked up in the last two to three years, owing to more buoyancy in the economy and reasonable growth in the business that is already in force. An industry that has a long-term basis, where premiums can be paid over 25 years, can be reasonably resilient to changing economic circumstances.

New entrants

2.9 The industry faces a glut of suppliers. Although there has been a spate of mergers and acquisitions, many new entrants with strong brand identifies have also entered the market. These are:

- Ten new bancassurers (including building society subsidiaries).
- Medical insurers offering life assurance with protection products.

- Providers of consumer products, such as Marks and Spencer, Virgin and Direct Line among others.

2.10 Banks have entered the market as a result of the housing boom and saw the opportunity to make money from selling endowment policies to existing mortgage holders. The opportunity for long-term profits from a relatively secure customer base was very attractive. Each entrant has a good brand image although, despite public perceptions, their products are no better than the best of the existing players. The companies that have withdrawn from the market were smaller providers, with less than one per cent market share, a limited customer base and limited availability of capital. The environment is very competitive with an over supply which outstrips the growth in demand. It is more difficult to make a profit on new business. In the long run, especially in the light of the introduction of the Euro, the single market and Stakeholder Pensions (with capped charges and profits), it is certain that there will be more cost reduction and rationalisation within the sector.

2.11 The industry is still fairly fragmented with over 200 authorised life assurers within the industry. There are 60 'large' providers, with no company having more than a ten per cent market share. The top ten life and pension providers have 46 per cent market share and 52 per cent of the assets.

2.12 For instance, the top ten banks or building societies have over 90 per cent market share of the deposit markets. The top ten car manufacturers have 80 per cent market share of new car registrations.

2.13 As the sector is fragmented, the costs of remaining in business are high. In spite of this, most companies have a wide range of products and customer focus is not very clear. Distribution takes place through numerous channels and each company has its own customer administration, computer operations, human resources, finance and actuarial sections. In spite of brand building and advertising, the brands of the old established players, such as Clerical Medical, are less well known than the banks, supermarkets or companies such as Virgin. In the end, it remains to be seen whether the consumers will gravitate towards a particular type of provider, helping to create a large market share of around ten to fifteen per cent.

Other issues

2.14 Many companies have to contend with the following issues.

(a) Expensive 'legacy' computer systems which are not very effective at providing good customer service. (See section on IT, para 2.25.)

(b) Poor customer segmentation and an inability to offer specific products to specific customers.

(c) High base costs, so that about 20 per cent of the premiums are required to cover expenses.

(d) A generally poor reputation for customer service. Only about five of the top companies obtained a 5-star rating for service in 1999. (See Appendix 3.)

(e) An eroding capital base as a result of rising costs and payment of policy holder bonuses which are grater than investment returns would justify, in order that the companies can position themselves competitively.

(f) Losses on new business, with few companies adding value to shareholders. Many companies are forecasting lower returns for customers holding with-profits policies, although this is mainly driven by falling long-term interest rates.

(g) Marketing strategies are often not clear. Companies have a variety of products, and they spread their management, marketing and financial resources too thinly over a range of channels and consumers.

(h) The company management structures often consist of individuals who have been 'promoted from within'. There is a general lack of entrepreneurial behaviour and relatively few graduates are recruited.

2.15 An important piece of legislation, the Financial Services Act, was passed in 1986. As a result, any individual selling life and pensions products had to either be tied to one company or become an Independent Financial Adviser (IFA). Tied agents can only advise on the products of their host company, while IFAs must select the best product for their clients from across the market. In order to ensure that standards improved, all distributors have been required to increase the resources devoted to training and compliance with these regulations. The Personal Investment Authority, and now the Financial Services Authority (FSA) conduct rigorous checks and reviews of tied agents and IFAs to ensure that standards are being maintained. The FSA has and uses powers to fine companies and force them to close for a period until they have dealt with their processes and problems.

2.16 As a result of this, a large number of advisers, particularly tied direct salespeople, have left the industry and the quality of advice has improved significantly. However, the cost of implementing this has been substantial, affecting the productivity and running costs of all distributors. Many small IFA businesses have left the sector and even some small providers have closed themselves to new business.

2.17 A further impact of the 1986 Act was that the banks decided to set up their own in-house life assurance companies. This is because they considered the tied route to be cheaper to operate and they experienced the relative profitability of life assurance to be better than traditional current account banking and related services. The outcome of this is that a majority of the high street banks and building societies have their own life companies, this is referred to as 'bancassurance'. However, despite the fact that banks have a wealth of customer data and regular customer contact, they have been unable to fully develop their life companies. This may be because life assurance operates a relatively long time horizon (many policies are designed to run at least 25 years), whereas decision taking in banks will be heavily influenced by the much shorter-term pressures related to shareholder value. In such circumstances, longer-term investments may not be allowed sufficient time to deliver profit and value. As a result, banks only have around 15 per cent of the life and pensions market, with the IFA channel denominating the market with a 60 per cent share. The rest of the share is accounted for by tied agents and the direct sales staff of the life companies. Interestingly, despite the fact that the IFA channel contains many small businesses, its share has doubled over the past 5 years.

2.18 There is a clear trend of consolidation in the market as the major businesses move into each others' territory. For example, life assurers such as Prudential and Standard Life also offer banking products, and banks such as Lloyds-TSB, Halifax and Abbey National have acquired life companies. However, while this secures several economies of scale, the current trend is to retain bands for particular product markets and customer types. As a result, Halifax is targeted broadly at all adults with a wide range of products, whereas Clerical Medical, its subsidiary, targets higher net worth individuals through IFAs with a more specialist range of products.

2.19 The structure of the broad financial services sector is shown in Figure 1, the structure of the life insurance industry is shown in Figure 2 and Figure 3 highlights the key groupings within the life industry. The diagrams illustrate the changing nature of the industry, with the bigger banks trying to play a more important role in the whole sector. The environment is getting more complex and pressures for increased size are growing, as well as pressures for systems integration via the use of technology and considerable reductions in the cost base.

Figure 1

Structure of the financial services sector

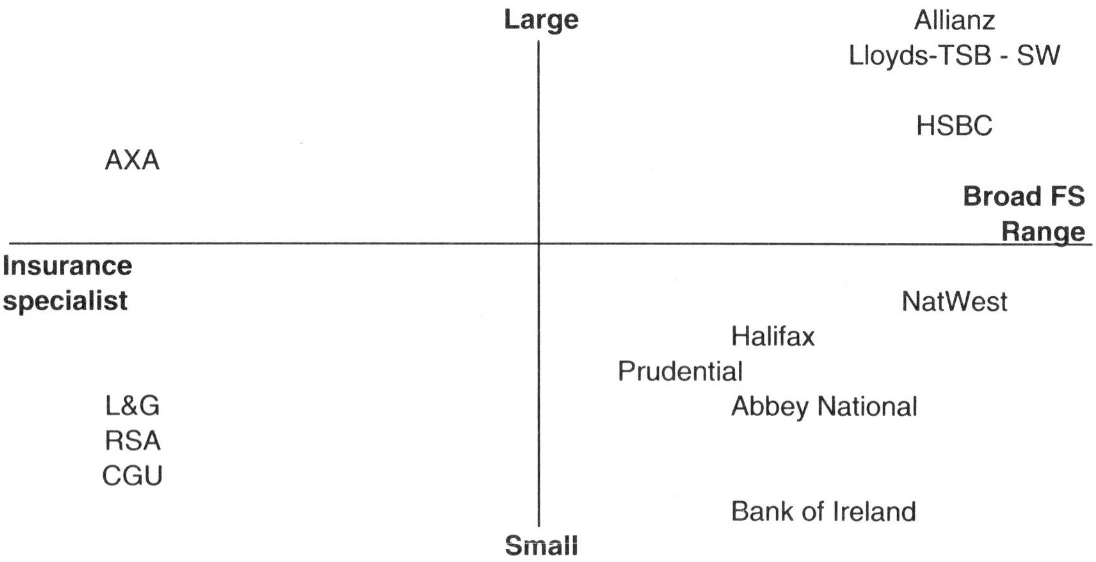

Figure 2

Structure of the life industry

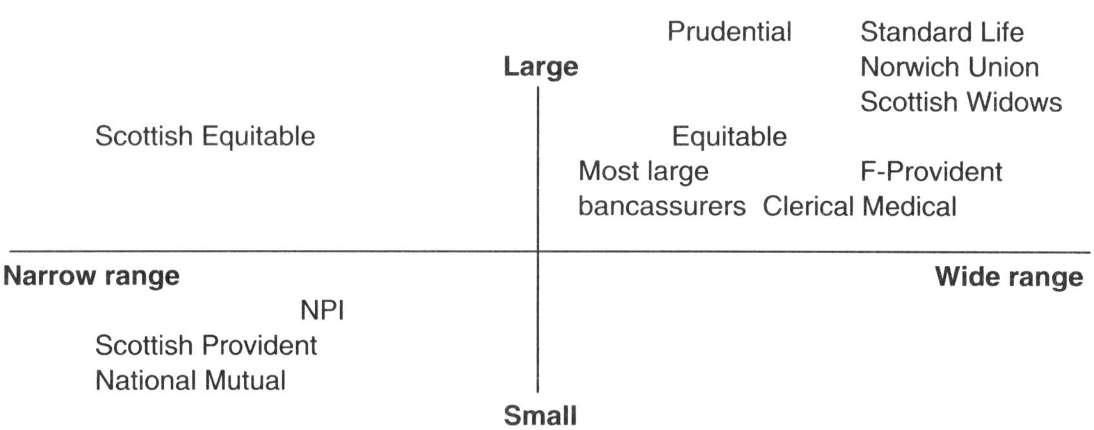

Figure 3

Structure of the life industry

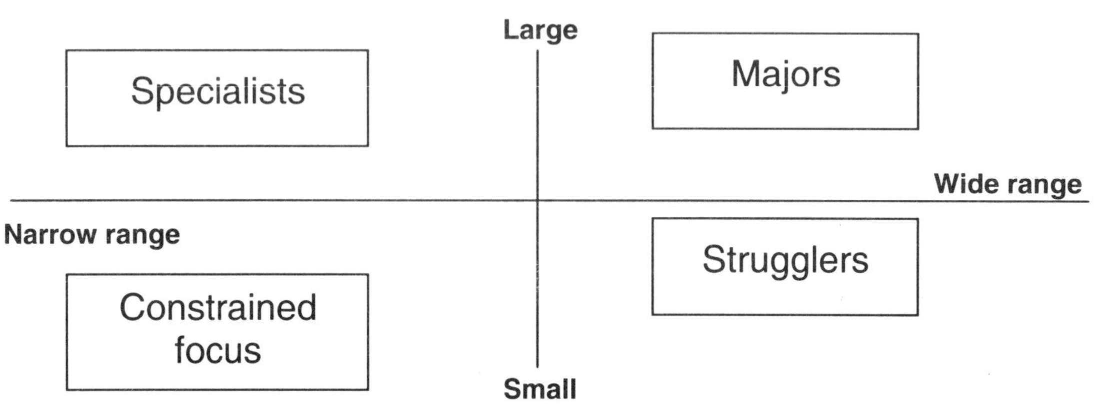

The role of the government

2.20 The UK Government feels that the industry in general fails to take responsibility for its actions and often fails to clean up its problems. It feels that the consumers are often short changed when policies are sold, as the 'up front' costs can be considerable. The Government also judged that there was mis-selling of pensions. Many individuals were enticed out of company pension schemes into private pension arrangements that have not proved to be good purchases. The Government review began in 1994 as there were so many cases. Companies were asked to deal with priority cases, for example, people who had retired or who were close to retirement. The Financial Services Authority also advertised on TV, radio and in the newspapers, reminding people to take action if they wanted their cases checked. This pressure from the Government has meant that many companies have had to set aside considerable funds for compensation. The FSA now requires investment companies to show integrity, skill, care and diligence. They have to be considerate to the customers and have good relations with the regulators. In order to do this, investment companies and advisers have to have well-training personnel at their disposal.

2.21 The Government also feels that Independent Financial Advisers (IFAs) are mainly for the rich and that they lack professionalism. They are also perceived as expensive and may not be truly 'independent'. For the future, the Government wishes to encourage cheap, simple and flexible products, in the hope that there is a reduced need for advice. The products will have to be designed to certain standards, in terms of charges and other features. In time, this is likely to cover a wide range of savings, pensions, ISAs and in the future, through the introduction of stakeholder pensions, the Government is trying to encourage individuals to take long-term responsibility for their retirement and old age. The key features of such a pension are outlined below.

2.22 **Stakeholder pensions**

(a) When the plan it set up, the investor may choose to **allocate contributions** to one or more of four products; the investment return within the fund will be tax free.

   (i) A broad based equity product which can be expected to increase in-line with share prices generally.

   (ii) A managed fund product where there is a mixture of equities, fixed interest, property and cash.

   (iii) A with-profits product which in the long-term will perform in a similar way to the equity fund but where investment returns are smoothed.

   (iv) A fixed interest product which will produce an investment return based on the rate of return on Government securities and corporate bonds.

(b) **Transfer options**

   (i) Money can be switched between the four 'products' without cost once a year.

   (ii) The funds can be transferred to another stakeholder pension provider without penalty at any time.

(c) **Charges**

   (i) There is no charge for setting up the plan.

   (ii) There will be an annual fixed charge for the funds under management, or the equivalent for a with-profits product.

   (iii) There will be no other charges.

(d) **Information**

An annual statement as at 5 April each year will be provided not later than 15 May showing:

(i) Fund value at the beginning of the year
(ii) Contributions during the year
(iii) Charges
(iv) Investment return
(v) Fund value at the end of the year
(vi) Projected fund value at age 60
(vii) Projected pension
(viii) A statement of the value of the fund may be obtained at any time on request

As can be seen, the stakeholder concept is for general provision for the populace, without any hidden costs involved. In order to provide such a service, companies and advisers are going to need a very efficient cost base, which is substantially lower than that at present. It is likely that the new Stakeholder Pensions will allow for more growth in the industry, but economies of scale will become important. Marketing will also take on a greater significance as companies will be vying for business with standard designed, rather than individually designed products. The changes are therefore likely to favour large players.

Distribution

2.23 The major and growing distributors of business, since the inception of the Financial Services Act have been the Independent Financial Advisers (IFAs). Their growth is shown in Appendix 1. The main distributors of financial products are as follows.

(a) **Banks**

The general distribution of financial services by banks is termed 'bancassurance'. The success of this channel is patchy and as yet it is not clear that all the opportunities available to the sector have been fully grasped.

(b) **Tied agencies**

These are agencies which are tied to particular assurance companies. Usually they are expensive and difficult to manage by the host, and often offer limited choice, flexibility and quality.

(c) **Traditional direct sales**

This group which flourished before the nineties, are now too expensive to manage for providers. For the consumer, it represents an expensive method of purchasing financial products, as a large proportion of the early payments are taken as commission. This channel has become almost unviable as its productivity is low and the cost base has been rising.

(d) **Direct writers**

These are companies that are selling directly to the public mainly by telephone. As yet they have not made a huge impact on the market share. However, such providers are forcing the pace of change within the sector and are seen to be attractive to politicians because they appear to offer a simple proposition.

The above discussion shows the fundamental weaknesses in the channels. These weaknesses provided the IFAs with a relatively clear run in the 1990s.

If the IFAs are to retain their dominant position, they will need to react quickly to the changes and pressures in the market. For instance IFAs will need to:

- Be first choice for their clients
- Retain and source new clients
- Shift to professional status
- Move from commissions towards fees for remuneration
- Exploit the opportunities offered by electronic commerce
- Build corporate business. (Advise on stakeholder pensions to be provided via companies, then offer additional advice to pension scheme members.)
- Cut costs and raise productivity

Consumers

2.24 The consumer profile for the purchase of Financial Services is changing. The population is ageing, with a larger proportion expected to be over 60 in the future in all major developed countries. With the patterns of employment predicted to change in the future, it is likely that fewer will be in full-time employment by 2010. More and more people are expected to be self-employed and will therefore need more flexible products and regular reviews of their financial plans. The employment structure is shifting towards more 'ABC1' type jobs. (For a full analysis of potential market segments see Appendix 1.)

2.25 **Consumer typologies in the life and pensions sector**

(a) **Passive brand loyal**

These are consumers who are comfortable with the purchase of products from existing banks, insurers and other providers. They mainly buy mortgages, pension and savings with few 'risk' investment products. They implicitly trust well-known brands and feel obliged to stick with existing providers.

(b) **Suspicious and confused**

This group of consumers do not trust advisers and are often suspicious of traditional players. They require product information and not necessarily recommendation. This group is less likely to buy 'risk' products, and ideally would like to buy direct and select products based on their own assessments.

(c) **Active, seeking personalised solutions**

This group tends to trust and respect advisors but personal recommendations is important to them. They tend to be long-term planners who will buy across the range of products available.

An important sub-segment of the broad ABC1 group is professional people.
These include:

(i) The self-employed who grow their companies into mature businesses. This group is an important area for consideration, as more and more individuals are likely to be self-employed in the future.

(ii) The professionals who tend to study for a long period before qualifying. Many aspire to become partners in their own practice.

(iii) Managers or Directors who are highly mobile with good transferable skill. In many cases they may also be specialists in particular market sectors.

(iv) Professional women who are a large and growing sector. This category includes singles, married, divorced, etc.

(v) Career professionals such as teachers, policemen, nurses, librarians, etc. There is often a clear defined path within these professions. Often there is bias towards the public sector, though the earning power is lower than some other groups.

(vi) The final group comprises of student professionals who are studying for courses which lead to a profession.

Clerical Medical generally focuses on the high earning consumers.

The Role of IT

2.26 The role of IT in the life and pensions industry is extremely complicated. Over the last thirty years or more, a wide range of different products with different features has been introduced. Typically, traditional life companies have installed new systems for each new product that they have introduced. Each system has to keep track off each clients product performance over a number of years. These systems are known as 'legacy' systems. In general, the various systems have differing protocols and do not 'talk' to each other. Each system has its own way of collecting direct debits and tracking policies. The systems were also set-up by software engineers at different times, under different conditions, with different technologies. In essence the decision making was not market driven but IT driven. However, some of the 1960s systems are still performing well. With the range of 'legacy' systems it is difficult to build customer based systems. As the systems are policy based, there is immense difficulty in acquiring customer profiles. Overall expenditure on IT is often the single biggest investment. New legislative requirements have to be incorporated quickly into existing systems. With the demand for the new stakeholder systems likely to be driven by the Governments new and better IT platforms will be required, but major investment will be required by the life and pensions industry to provide them. There is no time to 'stop the clock' and improve the old systems, as there are systems constraints within the design that have to be managed differently.

2.27 Given this structural problem which besets the more established players in the industry, newer, agile players, armed with the latest technology, could exploit 'greenfield' opportunities. The advent of the Internet allows not only new players to enter the business, but it also poses a question for the current providers and the IFAs. There is tension between the 'old' and the new. The new information age allows for more customer data to be held in order to create profiles, but also needs more creative and innovative people to manage the systems, in order to take advantage of the newer technology interface.

Competitiveness

2.28 The industry grew substantially in the 1980s with high investment returns. Life was generally easier for the companies. The 1990s presented an altogether more difficult environment, with poorer returns and bad publicity. Some insurance companies were also forced to retract earlier projections made on returns on endowment policies. As we enter the next millennium there are even tougher demands on management. In spite of a booming stock market, there is still considerable pressure for cost reduction and product rationalisation. It is interesting to note the top fifteen performers over the last decade in order of long-term investments. Table 2 shows the league tables for both the companies that deal in life assurance per se and also the larger, combined companies resulting from mergers and acquisitions.

2.29 Some of the bases that can be considered for benchmarking competitive performance are shown in the table in Appendix 3. In 1999, Money Marketing focused on a range of measures based on the returns to the Department of Trade and Industry. One measure of effectiveness is the table showing the expense ratios in 1998 (see Appendix 3). This table shows the trends over 8 years: in essence, the lower the percentage, the more cost-effective a company is.

Table 2

	Total new business *1998* £m (AP + 10% SP)	*Funds under management* *1998* £bn
1 Prudential, Scot Am & M&G	617.7	87.34
2 Equitable Life	601.4	27.34
3 Standard Life	457.9	54.5
4 AXA Sun Life	369.7	38.8
5 CGU	349.8	31.5
6 Legal & General	341.6	34
7 Scottish Equitable	327.2	19
8 AIG	266	3.83
9 Allied Dunbar	249.7	21
10 Scottish Widows	228	31.52
11 Norwich Union	209.4	N/S
12 Scottish Mutual	182.3	8.4
13 Friends Provident	179.3	30
14 Royal & Sun Alliance	178.9	28.84
15 Skandia	176.7	7.18
16 Clerical Medical	140	20.54

Source: Money Management June 1999
Total Individual and Group Pensions

Figure 4

Increase or decrease in free asset ratios in 1998 of the companies participating in the financial strength survey

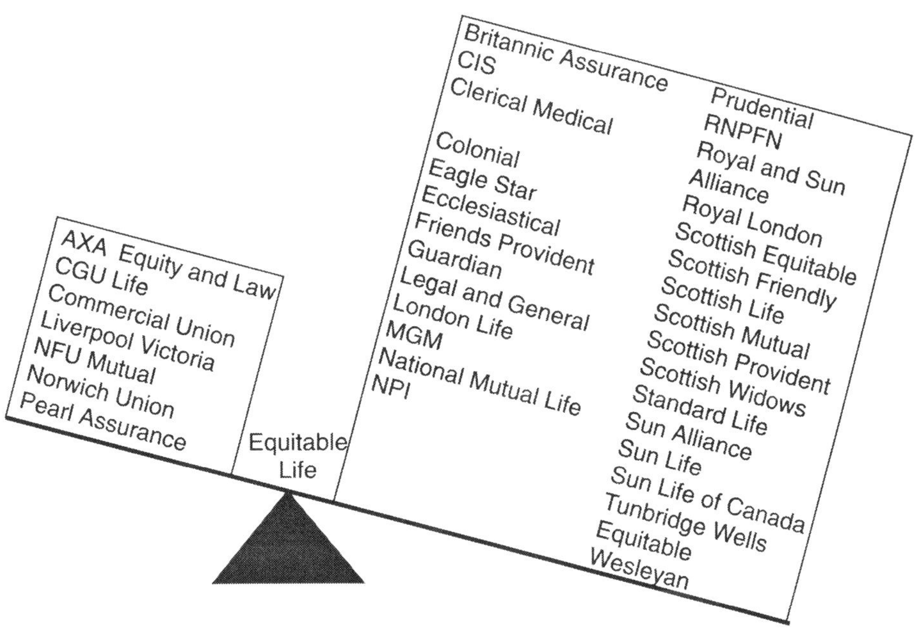

2.30 Another possible measure of financial strength is the free asset ratio which is arrived at through complex calculations for each company. Figures are arrived at in different ways and have therefore not been shown here. However, Figure 4 shows the increase and decrease in free asset ratios in 1998, with the companies on the left in a stronger position than the ones on the right. With a company like Clerical Medical, these ratios may have less meaning, as it has the cash backing of Halifax. Currently there is considerable debate as to whether the issue of financial strength, incorporating expense ratios and free asset ratios, should be made clear to consumers. Some measures of financial strength could be useful to consumers in making an informed choice for choosing policies.

Appendix 3 shows the Standard and Poor's Insurance ratings in a comparative fashion, taking many factors into account. These ratings reflect the way the companies are performing and their financial strength. Clerical Medical overall seems to be performing satisfactorily.

Clerical Medical's markets

2.31 Clerical Medical offers a wide range of life assurance, pensions and investment products. In 1999 the mix of business in the UK retail market was as follows.

- Personal pensions – 19%
- Group (company) pensions – 15%
- Investments – 38%
- Offshore investments – 28%

In 1999 the total value of this business was over £2.5 billion and it was sold entirely through independent financial advisers. This means that Clerical Medical products have to be recommended by the IFA as the best product to suit their client's requirements.

2.32 Personal pensions are exactly as their name suggests, pensions held by individual people who are not part of a company pension scheme. People can make monthly contributions to these or single one-off payments. Group pensions are company schemes and membership ranges from around 20 employees up to several thousand. The investment range comprises products such as With-Profits Bonds (which are a relatively low risk form of investment, which is designed to grow the value of the initial investment) and Distribution Bonds which produced the investor with income. These products are normally taken up by people in retirement, as they help provide income in addition to pensions.

2.33 Offshore products are typically single premium (one-off) investments in products held overseas, to which different tax rules apply. Holders of these products only pay tax on the proceeds when they terminate their investment and bring their money back into the UK. The main benefit of these products is tax efficiency and growth of the initial investment. Better-off people tend to use these products and the age range of buyers is wider than other investment products: from mid-30s to retirement.

2.34 In addition to the above, Clerical Medical also conducts business in the wholesale market. This relates to the direct management of funds for major pension schemes and was valued at £0.5 billion in 1999. This type of business is sold through specialist advisers to pension fund trustees and is very competitive, particularly with regard to the investment performance of the funds.

2.35 Finally, Clerical Medical sells investment products in international markets to UK citizens who live and work abroad, as well as foreign nationals. This is sold through 'Master Distributors', who can also carry the products of other companies.

2.36 In 1999 overall business was dominated by the UK retail market, the geographic split was:

- UK – 79%
- Europe – 14%
- Other countries – 7%

E-commerce

2.37 The financial sector is one of the important sectors that have been identified for growth on the internet. Direct customer links could more than halve the present transaction costs allied to policy selling and maintenance. However, the development of direct communication and transaction strategies for companies like Clerical Medical will need well-thought-through plans with a clear indication of the rationale for how they will benefit the consumer. The networked economy needs more dynamic strategies and shorter planning cycles.

Summary

2.38 As Clerical Medical moves into the next millennium, it appears to be in good shape, with a growing international aspect to its business. Since 1996 its market share has doubled to over 3 per cent, and it has moved up the new business rankings into the top ten. However, insurance companies are in the spotlight and hardly a day goes by without some comment about performance or the general perceived lack of customer service in the newspapers. The channels of distribution will probably change and the role of intermediaries is likely to change. The challenge for Clerical Medical is the effective adoption of customer relationship management (CRM). CRM is likely to be increasingly important in relation to the IFAs. In turn, the IFAs will need good CRM with regard to the end client, becoming specialised in professional relationships. New entrants may benefit from the use of technology. The competition is likely to get more intense in a global market. However, historical and cultural barriers may still endure for some time. It is likely to take some time to dismantle these. The future presents both opportunities and threats. The company needs to develop strategies to take advantage of the opportunities and minimise the impact of the threats.

3 CLERICAL MEDICAL: APPENDICES

3.1 Appendix 1: Consumer data and distribution channels

Life Assurance and Pension Schemes

(a) **Savings, investments and life assurance cross holdings, 1997**

Percent of population

	Endowment		Investment	
	Unit linked	**With-profit**	**bond**	**PPP**
All adults	(2)	(10)	(4)	(8)
Adults with:				
Traditional bank savings accounts	3	13	6	10
Converted building society accounts	3	13	6	10
Mutual building society accounts	3	15	9	11
TESSAs	4	16	15	10
National Savings	3	14	10	10
Stocks and shares	4	16	10	13
Unit trusts or PEPs	6	19	17	15

Base: All adults (18%)

Note: For example, 16% of adults (18+) hold both a TESSA account and a 'with-profits' endowment policy

Source: NOP/FRS

(b) **Profiles of protection and savings products, 1997**

Percent

	Any life assuarnce[1]	Any protection	Any savings
Market Penetration	37	29	12
Gender			
Male	51	50	55
Female	49	50	45
Social class			
AB	17	17	22
C1	28	28	31
C2	25	25	26
DE	29	30	21
Age			
18-20	1	1	1
21-24	2	2	3
25-34	17	16	18
35-44	20	19	22
45-54	21	20	26
55-64	18	17	20
65+	22	25	10
How long policy held			
Less than 1 year	6	6	6
Longer	90	90	93
Don't know/refused	1	1	1

Base: All adults (18%)
Note: [1] 'Any life assurance' is any protection or any (non-mortgage) saving based endowment
Source: NOP/FRS

(c) **Profile of (non-mortgage) life assurance: Premium payers, 1997**

Percent of total

	Existing policies	New in last 12 months
Age		
18-20	1	3
21-24	2	5
25-34	17	36
35-44	20	23
45-54	21	16
55-64	18	11
65+	22	5
Social class		
AB	17	16
C1	28	32
C2	25	27
DE	29	25
Region		
London	8	10
South, excluding London	33	30
Midlands and Wales	22	23
North	27	27
Scotland	10	11

Base: All adults (18%) covered by (non-mortgage) life assurance who personally pay the premium.

Source: NOP/FRS

(d) **Profile of new (non-mortgage) life policy holders, 1997**

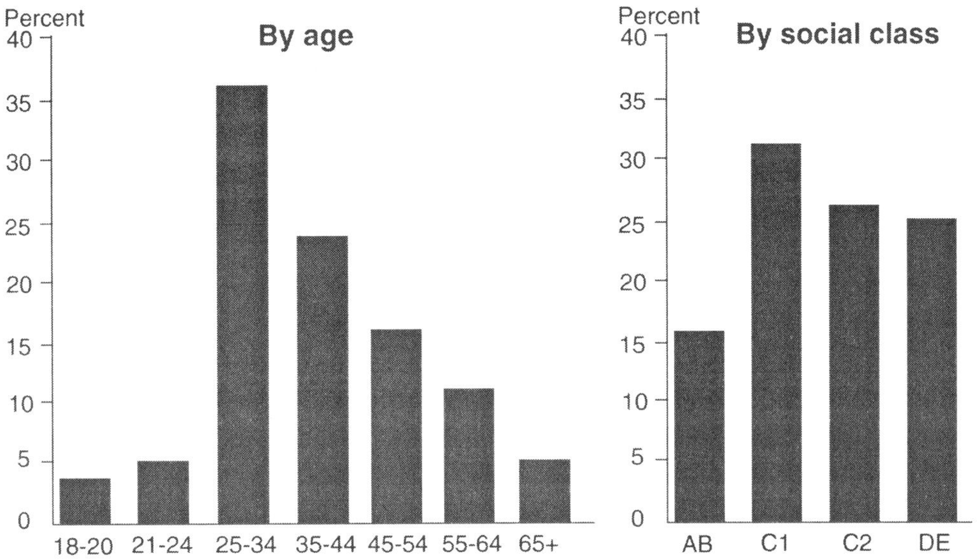

Base: All adults (18%) covered by (non-mortgage) life assurance who personally pay the premium.

Source: NOP/FRS

(e) **Total new individual life assurance, pension and annuity business in the UK**

	1985	1993	1994	1995	1996	1997
New yearly premiums	£m	£m	£m	£m	£m	£m
Ordinary life (Total)	886	1,510	1,339	1,131	1,186	1,354
Non-linked	598	866	766	686	737	882
Linked	288	644	573	445	449	472
Industrial life	232	152	129	92	83	65
Pensions (total)[1]	451	936	897	832	973	1,192
Non-linked	242	452	377	364	391	424
Linked	209	484	520	467	582	768
FSAVCs (total)	-	161	140	110	107	106
Non-linked	-	65	51	45	39	30
Linked	-	96	89	65	68	76
PHI	-	49	47	43	54	64
Total	**1,568**	**2,810**	**2,553**	**2,208**	**2,454**	**2,821**
New single premiums						
Ordinary life (total)	2,576	10,031	9,393	9,206	12,489	13,930
Non-linked	196	3,443	2,769	4,963	6,427	8,441
Linked	2,380	6,588	6,624	4,243	6,062	5,489
Annuities (total)	379	860	458	316	806	399
Deferred	46	22	22	17	10	1
Immediate	333	838	436	299	796	398
Pensions (total)[1]	563	5,301	4,100	3,390	4,129	5,209
Non-linked	398	2,592	1,844	1,598	1,865	2,127
Linked	165	2,363	2,045	1,638	2,162	2,915
DSS rebates	-	346	211	154	102	167
FSAVCs (total)	-	64	66	63	72	89
Non-linked	-	34	29	30	33	38
Linked	-	30	37	33	39	51
PHI	-	6	7	9	19	27
Total	**3,518**	**16,263**	**14,023**	**12,985**	**17,515**	**19,652**
Total new premiums	**5,086**	**19,073**	**16,576**	**15,193**	**19,969**	**22,473**
Number of new policies	'000	'000	'000	'000	'000	'000
Yearly	-	6,043	5,185	4,266	4,470	4,687
Single	-	1,934	1,648	1,212	1,266	1,418
Total	**9,467**	**7,977**	**6,832**	**5,479**	**5,736**	**6,105**
Average payment into new policy	£	£	£	£	£	£
Yearly	-	465	492	518	549	602
Single	-	8,409	8,509	10,714	13,835	13,859
Total	**537**	**2,391**	**2,426**	**2,773**	**3,481**	**3,681**

Note: [1]Excluding pension annuities

Source: Association of British Insurers (ABI); NTC

(f) **Payments made to UK policy holders**

	1985	1993	1994	1995	1996	1997
Benefits paid on UK contracts	£m	£m	£m	£m	£m	£m
Ordinary branch policy holders[1]						
Life insurance (total)	**4,064**	**12,877**	**13,090**	**13,848**	**16,398**	**18,444**
Death claims	638	1,683	1,889	2,060	2,285	2,518
Maturities	1,216	6,000	5,479	5,399	7,002	8,130
Surrenders/refunds	2,210	5,193	5,722	6,388	7,111	7,796
Annuities (total)	**580**	**1,172**	**1,163**	**1,106**	**1,061**	**1,011**
Death claims	14	23	34	20	21	18
Maturities	44	70	39	41	43	40
Periodical payments	479	1,014	1,035	993	947	897
Surrenders/refunds	43	65	55	52	50	56
Pensions[2] **(total)**	**4,296**	**14,240**	**14,359**	**15,797**	**20,485**	**25,520**
Death claims	306	593	667	675	754	858
Maturities	649	2,850	2,967	3,799	4,659	5,468
Periodical payments	716	2,718	2,970	3,643	4,205	4,689
Surrenders/refunds	2,625	8,079	7,755	7,679	10,867	14,505
PHI	**69**	**243**	**268**	**318**	**357**	**462**
Total	**9,009**	**28,531**	**28,880**	**31,069**	**38,302**	**45,437**
Industrial branch policy holders[1]						
Death claims	219	431	428	442	455	488
Maturities	509	1,363	1,382	1,443	1,415	1,491
Surrenders/refunds	343	375	358	320	297	258
Total	**1,071**	**2,169**	**2,169**	**2,194**	**2,168**	**2,237**
UK total	**10,080**	**30,700**	**31,049**	**33,263**	**40,469**	**47,674**
Benefits paid on overseas contracts						
Death claims	238	711	813	1,063	1,059	1,188
Maturities	171	625	717	886	1,309	1,425
Periodical payments	309	1,702	2,214	2,449	2,493	2,677
Surrenders/refunds	681	2,547	3,336	3,974	4,096	4,753
Overseas total	**1,399**	5,585	7,079	8,373	8,957	10,042
Total payments						
Current prices	**11,479**	**36,285**	**38,128**	**41,636**	**49,426**	**57,716**
Constant '97 prices[3]	**19,113**	**40,627**	**41,659**	**43,992**	**50,974**	**57,716**
of which percentage:						
Death claims	12.3	9.5	10.0	10.2	9.3	8.8
Maturities	22.6	30.1	27.8	27.8	29.2	28.7
Periodical payments	13.1	15.0	16.3	17.0	15.5	14.3
PHI	0.6	0.7	0.7	0.8	0.7	0.8
Refunds	22.9	22.3	20.3	18.4	22.0	25.1
Surrenders	28.5	22.5	24.8	25.8	23.4	22.3

Notes: [1]An ordinary branch policy is a policy sold through brokers etc. An industrial branch policy is a policy sold through direct agents etc.

[2]Includes benefits paid on both individual and group pensions.

[3]Deflated by the Retail Prices Index (1997 = 100).

Sources: Association of British Insurers (ABI); NTC

(g) **Pensions business**

	1993	1994	1995	1996	1997
Personal pensions business					
Number of policies	Million	Million	Million	Million	Million
In force at year end	18.11	18.91	19.92	20.05	20.93
of which					
Free-standing AVCs*	0.66	0.78	0.82	0.91	0.96
New policies	1.84	1.33	1.08	1.16	1.36
Premium income	£m	£m	£m	£m	£m
In force at year end					
Linked	2,393	2,543	2,765	2,822	3,247
Non-linked	2,641	2,596	2,676	2,787	2,878
Total	**5,034**	**5,138**	**5,441**	**5,609**	**6,125**
New business					
Yearly (total)	937	898	832	973	1,192
Linked	484	520	467	582	768
Non-linked	452	377	365	391	424
Single (total)	4,955	3,889	3,236	4,027	5,042
Linked	2,363	2,045	1,638	2,162	2,915
Non-linked	2,592	1,844	1,598	1,865	2,127
DSS rebates (total)	346	211	124	102	166
Linked	207	131	101	68	120
Non-linked	139	80	53	34	46
Total	**6,238**	**4,998**	**4,222**	**5,102**	**6,400**
Pension annuities					
Pension annuities in payment					
Personal pensions	846	870	1,043	1,280	1,709
Occupational pensions	1,878	2,104	2,309	2,599	2,747
Total	**2,724**	**2,974**	**3,352**	**3,879**	**4,456**
	Million	Million	Million	Million	Million
Number of people in receipt of occupational pensions	1.35	1.36	1.39	1.56	1.49
Occupational pensions business					
Premium income	£m	£m	£m	£m	£m
In force at year end					
Insurer administered	5,313	5,476	5,319	6,060	7,351
Managed fund	3,690	2,968	3,690	6,200	10,358
Total	**9,003**	**8,444**	**9,009**	**12,260**	**17,709**

Source: Association of British Insurers (ABI)

* Additional Voluntary Contributions

(h) Consumer profile of pension schemes by main types, 1997

Percent of population

	Any pension	PPP	Non-contributory	Contributory	Any AVCs
Market Penetration[1]	(56)	(15)	(7)	(35)	(8)
Gender					
Male	64	74	61	61	68
Female	36	26	39	39	32
Social class					
AB	25	23	29	26	33
C1	36	33	42	36	32
C2	27	32	21	25	23
DE	13	13	8	13	11
Age					
18-20	1	1	1	1	-
21-24	4	3	4	4	2
25-34	31	31	31	30	22
35-44	29	29	30	29	31
45-54	26	26	26	26	32
55-64	9	11	8	9	12
65+	-	-	-	-	-

Base: All adults (18+) in employment (22.3m).
Note: [1]Percentage of adults (18+) in employment holding such pensions schemes.
Source: NOP/FRS

(i) Contributions to pension schemes, 1997

	Percent of population
Any pension	**56**
Personal pension plan	15
Non-contributory company schemes (total)	7
AVCs to company scheme	1
Free-standing AVCs	-
No AVCs	5
Contributory company schemes (total)	35
AVCs to company	5
Free-standing AVCs	2
No AVCs	28
Any AVCs	8
of which	
Free-standing AVCs	2
None arranged	42
Don't know/refused to answer	-

Base: All adults (18+) in employment (22.3m).
Source: NOP/FRS

Consumers expenditure

(j) TGI financial product profiles by ACORN Group

This table shows the ACORN Group with highest penetration across financial products by TGI product type. For example, 36.2% of adults in ACORN Group C06 have a bank account, whereas only 27.4% of all adults in Great Britain have this type of account.

TGI Product	ACORN Group with highest penetration		Penetration (%) by ACORN	Penetration (%) by GB
Household income levels	(Pay check data[1])		**Households**	
Up to £4,999	F16	Council estate res, greatest hardship	23.9	10.9
£5,000 - £9,999	F16	Council estate res, greatest hardship	29.2	16.3
£10,000-£14,999	F16	Council estate res, greatest hardship	22.9	18.2
£15,000-£19,999	B05	Well-off workers, family areas	17.7	15.7
£20,000-£24,999	B04	Affluent executives, family areas	15.5	12.0
£25,000-£29,999	B04	Affluent executives, family areas	13.0	8.5
£30,000-£39,999	B04	Affluent executives, family areas	17.3	9.8
£40,000-£49,999	A01	Wealthy achievers, suburban areas	8.6	4.5
£50,000+	C07	Prosperous professionals, metro areas	10.8	4.2
Current accounts			**Adults**	
Bank account with interest	B04	Affluent executives, family areas	72.8	62.8
Building society account with interest	C06	Affluent urbanites, town and city areas	30.0	26.8
Bank account without interest	A03	Prosperous pensioners, retirement areas	39.2	34.7
Bank account opened in last 6 months	B04	Affluent executives, family areas	4.4	2.6
Deposit or savings account			**Adults**	
Bank account	C06	Affluent urbanites, town and city areas	36.2	27.4
Building society account	A01	Wealthy achievers, suburban areas	62.2	51.4
Opened in last year	B05	Well-off workers, family areas	1.1	0.5
Opened first account in last year	B04	Affluent executives, family areas	2.6	1.8
Other investments			**Adults**	
National Savings Certs	A01	Wealthy achievers, suburban areas	6.0	3.2
National Savings/PO Bank	A02	Affluent greys, rural communities	13.7	9.8
Premium bonds	A01	Wealthy achievers, suburban areas	33.9	23.7
Stocks and shares	A01	Wealthy achievers, suburban areas	31.8	20.3
TESSAs	A01	Wealthy achievers, suburban areas	13.7	8.0
Unit trusts	A01	Wealthy achievers, suburban areas	12.6	6.8
Pensions/life assurance schemes			**Adults**	
Company pension	B05	Well-off workers, family areas	45.6	36.6
Life assurance	B05	Well-off workers, family areas	62.6	56.9
Personal pension plan	A02	Affluent greys, rural communities	16.4	13.0
State pension only	A02	Affluent greys, rural communities	50.0	41.2
Insurance			**Adults**	
Building insurance	B05	Well-off workers, family areas	74.9	60.9
Home contents insurance	B05	Well-off workers, family areas	75.3	64.6
Mortgage (by source)			**Adults**	
Building society	B05	Well-off workers, family areas	41.6	29.2
Other source	B05	Well-off workers, family areas	18.4	12.8
Plastic and credit card ownership			**Adults**	
MasterCard	A01	Wealthy achievers, suburban areas	37.2	24.8
Visa	C07	Prosperous professionals, metro areas	48.2	35.3
Other credit cards	C07	Prosperous professionals, metro areas	9.3	3.8
Debit cards2	B04	Affluent executives, family areas	53.7	42.4
Store card	A01	Wealthy achievers, suburban areas	40.8	28.2

Notes: [1]See page 21 of CACI's PayCheck classification
[2]For example, Switch, Connect etc

Source: TGI, © BMRB International Limited, 1997. Buying potential info modelled using data from TGI 4/96-3/97.

(k) **Savings[1]: Per household (holdings at 31 December, constant 1997 prices)**

£ per household

	1985	1993	1994	1995	1996	1997
National Savings (total)	**2,349**	**2,230**	**2,367**	**2,408**	**2,625**	**2,582**
Certificates (total)	1,329	847	841	854	878	826
Index-linked	336	378	374	376	390	411
Other issues	993	469	467	478	488	415
SAYE (total)	53	43	37	35	26	16
Index-linked	38	5	-	-	-	-
Yearly plan and other	14	38	37	35	26	16
Bonds etc (total)	420	837	994	1,045	1,255	1,295
Premium saving	140	144	217	261	334	395
Income	254	507	508	469	441	415
Deposit	26	33	32	27	26	25
Capital	-	100	102	106	107	82
Other bonds etc[2]	-	-	134	182	347	378
National Savings Bank (total)	547	507	495	474	467	436
Ordinary account deposits	131	67	65	62	60	58
Investment account deposits	416	440	430	412	407	378
Bank deposits (total)	**4,929**	**8,125**	**7,900**	**8,770**	**9,403**	**14,959**
Sterling accounts	4,757	7,933	7,711	8,588	9,184	14,696
Sterling money market instruments	-	24	28	22	43	62
Foreign currency[3]	171	167	162	159	176	201
Building society deposits (total)	**8,045**	**9,474**	**9,606**	**9,221**	**8,991**	**4,071**
Sterling accounts	8,045	9,469	9,597	9,212	8,979	4,067
Sterling money market instruments	-	5	9	9	13	4
Foreign currency[3]	-	-	-	-	-	-
Other savings	**30**	**19**	**14**	**13**	**12**	
Total savings[1]	**15,353**	**19,848**	**19,887**	**20,413**	**21,032**	**21,624**

Notes: [1]Amounts held in bank, building society and National Savings accounts on 31 December of each year.
[2]Including stamps and gift tokens. From and including 1994 Pensioners' Guaranteed Income Bonds
[3]Princpally foreign currency money market instruments, but also includes foreign currency holdings
Please note that the 'savings' and 'investments' pages are guides and in no way represent how an individual or a financial institution might view these assets. In generally, assets held in financial institutions, such as banks or building societies, have been called savings, while assets held as stocks and shares have been called investments.

Sources: Office of National Statistics, NTC.

(1) **Savings[1]: Per household (change in savings per year, constant 1997 prices)**

					£ per household	
	1985	1993	1994	1995	1996	1997
National Savings (total)	**32**	**96**	**137**	**41**	**216**	**–42**
Certificates (total)	–23	38	–6	13	12	–51
Index-linked	–45	15	–4	2	13	22
Other issues	22	23	–2	11	10	–73
SAYE (total)	–2	4	–6	–2	–10	–9
Index-linked	–12	-	–5	-	-	-
Yearly plan and other	9	4	–1	–2	–10	–9
Bonds etc (total)	54	62	157	51	210	41
Premium saving	–5	16	74	44	73	61
Income	54	22	1	–39	–28	–26
Deposit	9	–1	–1	–6	–1	–1
Capital	-	22	1	5	1	–25
Other bonds etc[2]	–4	-	134	47	165	31
National Savings						
Bank (total)	3	2	–13	–21	–7	–31
Ordinary account deposits	–13	–2	–2	–3	–2	–2
Investment account deposits	17	4	–10	–18	–5	–28
Bank deposits (total)	**30**	**–100**	**–225**	**870**	**633**	**5,556**
Sterling accounts	57	–95	–223	878	596	5,512
Sterling money market instruments	-	9	4	–6	21	19
Foreign currency[3]	–26	–14	–6	–2	16	26
Building society deposits (total)	**512**	**234**	**132**	**–385**	**–230**	**–4,921**
Sterling accounts	512	239	127	–384	–234	–4,912
Sterling money market instruments	-	5	9	9	13	4
Foreign currency[3]	-	-	-	-	-	-
Other savings	**–6**	**-**	**–5**	**–1**	**-**	**–1**
Total savings[1]	**568**	**229**	**39**	**526**	**619**	**593**

Notes: [1]Changes in the amounts held in bank, building society and National Savings accounts each year.

[2]Including stamps and gift tokens. From and including 1994 Pensioners' Guaranteed Income Bonds

[3]Princpally foreign currency money market instruments, but also includes foreign currency holdings

Please note that the 'savings' and 'investments' pages are guides and in no way represent how an individual or a financial institution might view these assets. In generally, assets held in financial institutions, such as banks or building societies, have been called savings, while assets held as stocks and shares have been called investments.

Sources: Office of National Statistics, NTC.

Personal investments

(m) Personal investments: total (holdings at 31 December)

	1985	1993	1994	1995	1996	1997
	£bn	£bn	£bn	£bn	£bn	£bn
UK company stocks and shares (total)	**75.1**	**326.6**	**322.8**	**374.4**	**409.4**	**569.6**
Unit trust units	10.0	39.4	43.5	56.0	60.6	69.9
UK company securities	65.1	287.2	279.3	318.4	348.8	499.7
Government gilts and securities (total)	**17.1**	**21.0**	**13.6**	**16.2**	**16.7**	**10.3**
British government securities	15.7	20.8	13.3	16.0	16.3	10.1
Northern Ireland central government debt	0.3	0.1	0.1	0.1	0.1	0.1
Local authority debt (total)	1.0	0.1	0.2	0.1	0.3	0.1
Sterling securities	0.1	-	0.1	-	0.2	-
Other sterling debt	0.9	0.1	0.1	0.1	0.1	0.1
Public corporations sterling debt	0.2	-	-	-	-	-
Life assurance and pension funds (total)[1]	**290.8**	**882.8**	**832.3**	**974.8**	**1,059.5**	**1,278.3**
Self-administered pension funds	175.7	480.6	443.5	508.6	543.9	644.0
Life assurance funds	115.2	402.2	388.8	466.2	515.6	634.3
Identified domestic trade credit	**25.3**	**51.7**	**53.0**	**52.1**	**51.8**	**52.1**
Overseas investments (total)	**8.5**	**17.0**	**17.4**	**19.8**	**14.2**	**15.5**
Overseas company securities	8.1	16.4	16.8	19.1	13.5	14.9
Direct and other investment abroad[2]	0.4	0.6	0.6	0.7	0.7	0.6
Other investments	**17.3**	**48.3**	**50.6**	**56.7**	**70.0**	**71.8**
Total investments	**434.2**	**1,347.5**	**1,289.7**	**1,494.0**	**1,621.6**	**1,997.6**

Notes: [1]Includes contributions paid into funds by employers. Please also note that 'self-administered pension funds' includes notionally funded schemes, while 'life assurance funds' includes pension funds administered by insurance companies.

[2]For example, UK residents buying property abroad. Please note that the 'investments' and 'savings' pages are guides and in no way represent how an individual or a financial institution might view these assets. In generally, assets held in financial institutions, such as banks or building societies, have been called savings, while assets held as stocks and shares have been called investments.

Sources: Office of National Statistics, NTC.

(n) **Investments: per household (holdings at 31 December, constant 1997 prices)**

	1985	1993	1994	1995	1996	1997
	£bn	£bn	£bn	£bn	£bn	£bn
UK company stocks and shares (total)	**5,813**	**15,628**	**14,922**	**16,574**	**17,529**	**23,421**
Unit trust units	777	1,885	2,011	2,479	2,595	2,874
UK company securities	5,036	13,742	12,911	14,095	14,934	20,547
Government gilts and securities (total)	**1,324**	**1,006**	**630**	**718**	**715**	**424**
British government securities	1,214	995	615	708	698	415
Northern Ireland central government debt	21	5	5	4	4	4
Local authority debt (total)	74	5	9	4	13	4
Sterling securities	6	-	5	-	9	-
Other sterling debt	67	5	5	4	4	4
Public corporations sterling debt	15	1	1	1	-	-
Life assurance and pension funds (total)[1]	**22,495**	**42,241**	**38,475**	**43,154**	**45,364**	**52,562**
Self-administered pension funds	13,588	22,996	20,502	22,515	23,288	26,480
Life assurance funds	8,909	19,245	17,973	20,638	22,076	26,081
Identified domestic trade credit	**1,954**	**2,474**	**2,450**	**2,306**	**2,218**	**2,142**
Overseas investments (total)	**661**	**813**	**804**	**877**	**608**	**637**
Overseas company securities	630	785	777	846	578	613
Direct and other investment abroad[2]	31	29	28	31	30	25
Other investments	**1,340**	**2,316**	**2,339**	**2,510**	**2,997**	**2,952**
Total investments	**33,586**	**64,478**	**59,620**	**66,140**	**69,431**	**82,138**

Notes: [1]Includes contributions paid into funds by employers. Please also note that 'self-administered pension funds' includes notionally funded schemes, while 'life assurance funds' includes pension funds administered by insurance companies.

[2]For example, UK residents buying property abroad. Please note that the 'investments' and 'savings' pages are guides and in no way represent how an individual or a financial institution might view these assets. In generally, assets held in financial institutions, such as banks or building societies, have been called savings, while assets held as stocks and shares have been called investments.

Sources: Office of National Statistics, NTC.

(o) **Investments: per household (change in investments per year, constant 1997 prices)**

	1985	1993	1994	1995	1996	1997
	£bn	£bn	£bn	£bn	£bn	£bn
UK company stocks and shares (total)	**159**	**3,680**	**–706**	**1,652**	**955**	**5,892**
Unit trust units	131	723	126	468	116	279
UK company securities	28	2,957	–831	1,184	839	5,612
Government gilts and securities (total)	**–342**	**53**	**–376**	**88**	**–3**	**–292**
British government securities	–310	58	–380	93	–10	–283
Northern Ireland central government debt	–1	-	-	-	-	-
Local authority debt (total)	–31	–5	4	–5	8	–9
Sterling securities	–7	–5	5	–5	8	–9
Other sterling debt	–25	-	-	-	-	-
Public corporations sterling debt	-	-	-	-	-	-
Life assurance and pension funds (total)[1]	**2,049**	**8,164**	**–3,767**	**4,679**	**2,210**	**7,197**
Self-administered pension funds	1,434	4,261	–2,495	2,014	773	3,192
Life assurance funds	615	3,903	–1,272	2,665	1,438	4,005
Identified domestic trade credit	**-**	**61**	**–24**	**–144**	**–89**	**–76**
Overseas investments (total)	**–51**	**78**	**–9**	**72**	**–269**	**29**
Overseas company securities	–44	88	–8	69	–268	35
Direct and other investment abroad[2]	–7	–11	–1	3	–1	–5
Other investments	**95**	**–43**	**23**	**171**	**487**	**–45**
Total investments	**1,911**	**11,992**	**–4,858**	**6,520**	**3,292**	**12,707**

Notes: [1]Includes contributions paid into funds by employers. Please also note that 'self-administered pension funds' includes notionally funded schemes, while 'life assurance funds' includes pension funds administered by insurance companies.

[2]For example, UK residents buying property abroad. Please note that the 'investments' and 'savings' pages are guides and in no way represent how an individual or a financial institution might view these assets. In generally, assets held in financial institutions, such as banks or building societies, have been called savings, while assets held as stocks and shares have been called investments.

Sources: Office of National Statistics, NTC.

NB Please note that all the figures in the tables are as given by the sources quoted and there may be some discrepancies.

(p) **Relative consumer profiles of current personal pension plan (PPP) contributors, 1997**

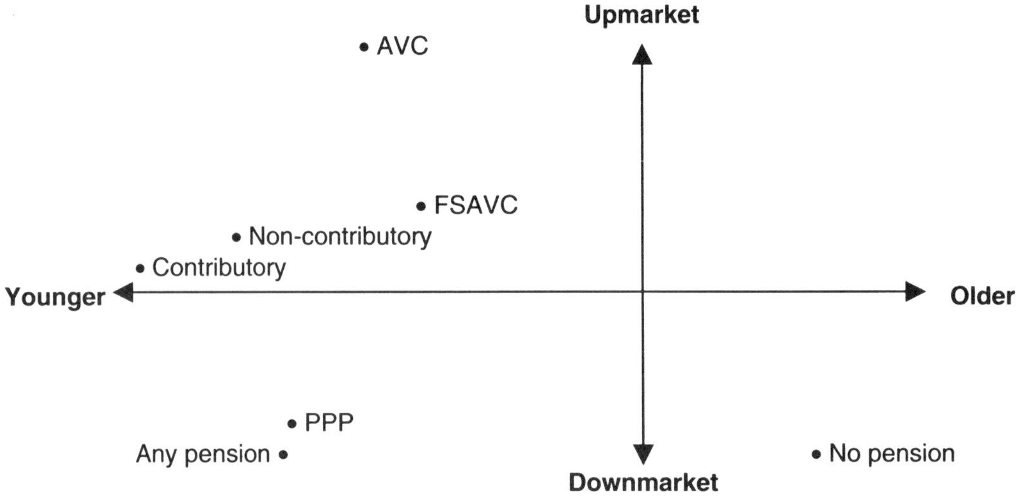

Base: All adults (18+).

Notes: AVC: Additional voluntary contribution scheme
FSAVC: Free-standing additional contribution scheme
PPP: Personal pension plan

Source: NOP/FRS

(q) **IFA market share - 1993-1999 (percentages)**

Individual life and pensions

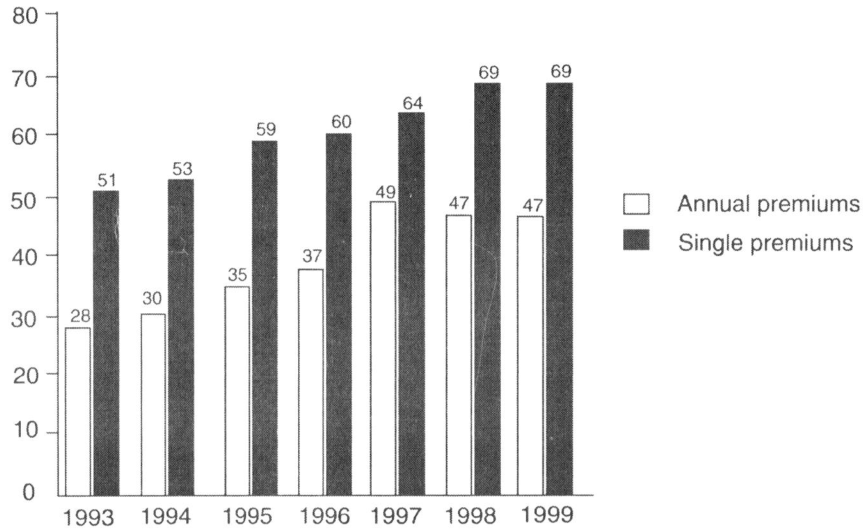

Source: ABI

(r) **Structure of IFA channel 1998-2005**

	Value - %	
	1998	**2005**
Nationals	30	35
Networks	15	20
Regionals	45	40
Small	10	5

- Consolidation will build nationals' share
- Small will move to networks/tied
- Regionals will consolidate to no less than 40%

(s) **Employment structure drives pattern of demand**

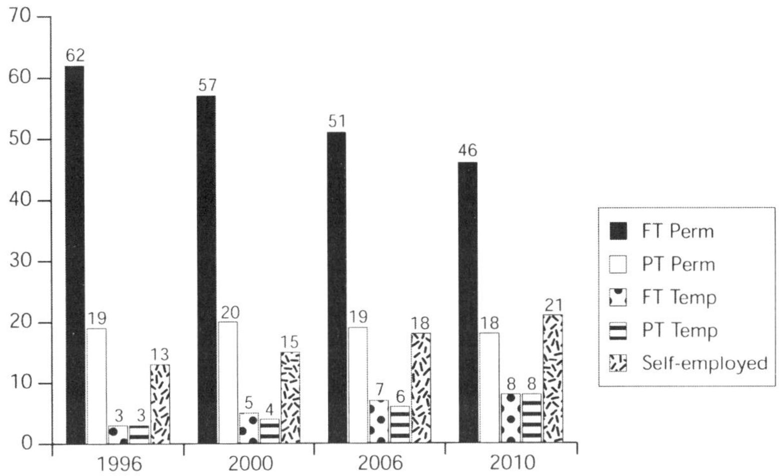

Source: Henley Centre

(t) **Percentage of population - 60 and over - 1990 and 2030**

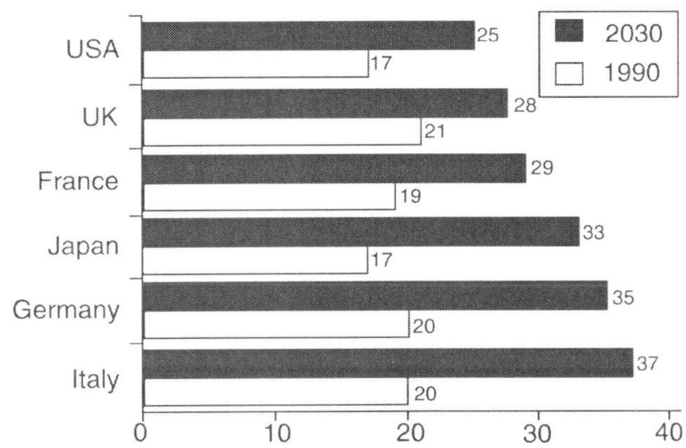

Long-term trends are well known - they drive shape of personal financial planning and privatisation of welfare

(u) **Consumers have more choice - and less time. They are less confident in product/ provider section**

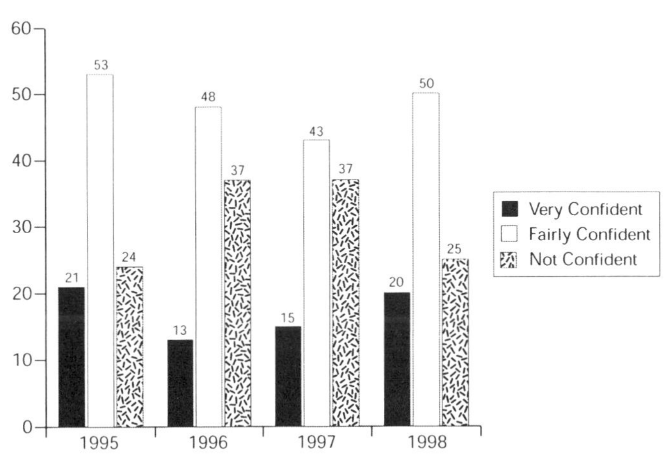

Scandals and Confusion Cut Confidence – Trust is the Issue

Source: Henley Centre

(v) **How knowledgeable are you about financial matters?**

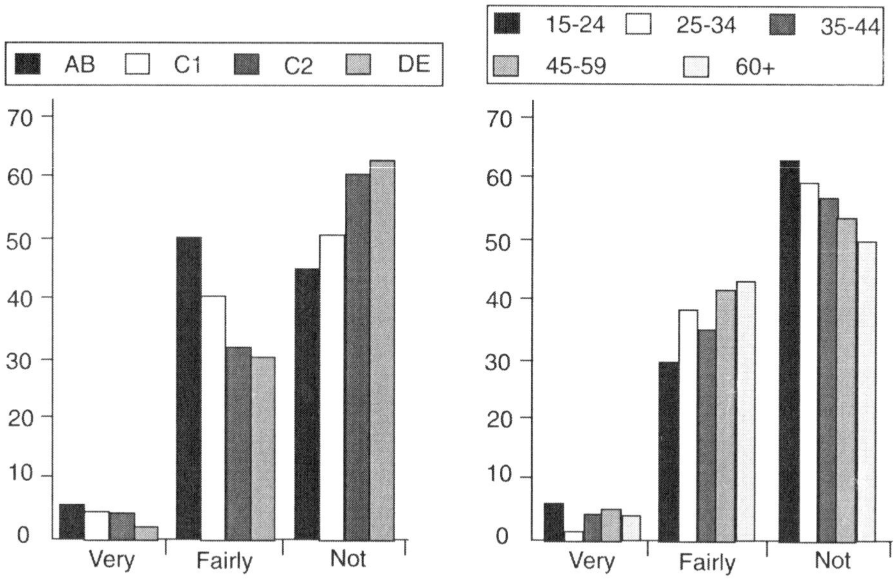

Source: Henley Centre

(w) **Brand triangle - 1998**

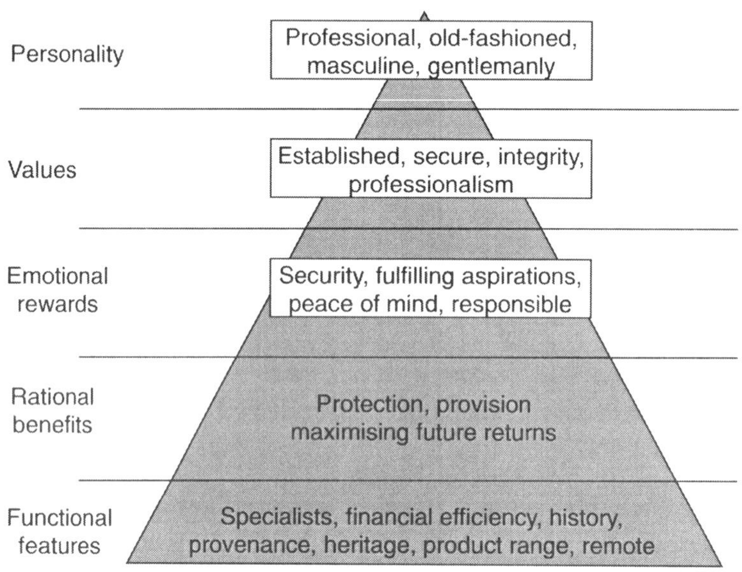

Brand triangle for Clerical Medical 1998

3.2 Appendix 2

Legal issues and selected news items

(a) European laws

The Treaty of Rome

The Treaty of Rome, signed in 1957, in article 8, calls for the Common Market to be 'progressively established during a transitional period of 12 years'. The two principal methods of achieving this are set out in the following articles.

Article 3(c) of the Treaty provides for:

'*The abolition, as between Member States, of obstacles to freedom of movement for persons, services and capital.*'

In financial services, this means the right of insurers to set up business either through a company or a branch, in any Member State (Freedom of Establishment). In addition, it means the right to provide services in Member States without being established there (freedom to provide services).

Article 3(h) provides for:

'*The approximation of laws of Member States to the extent required for the proper functioning of the Common Market.*'

Article 8(a) of the Treaty defines the internal market as:

'*An area without frontiers in which the free movement of goods, persons, services and capital is ensured in accordance with the provisions of this Treaty.*'

In introducing the Non-life Framework Directive and the Life Framework Directive, the Commission defined the goals of the single market in insurance as:

(a) The freedom for consumers to choose any insurance policy from any insurer authorised in any Member State.

(b) The freedom for insurers authorised in any one Member State to market policies throughout the EC under the principles of freedom of establishment and freedom to provide services.

(c) The freedom for insurers to compete equally on price, product and service; all unnecessary barriers to competition being removed.

In 1986 further directives were introduced to ease the cross-border sales of insurance services. The Third Non-life Insurance Directive and the Third Life Insurance Directive (known as the Framework Directives) are the culmination of the creation of the single community market in insurance. These became effective from 1 July 1994 in all Member States, subject to certain transitional provisions for Spain, Portugal and Greece.

Insurance companies are free to provide cross-border services. They are also obliged to give potential customers information about themselves, and also information about certain essential features of their policies - including surrender and paid up values, profit sharing arrangements and cancellation clauses - and to continue to keep policy holders informed of any changes to these features. The information on the commitment has to be provided in writing, in the language of the Member State.

Liberalisation of advertising rules

As in the case of the Non-life Framework Directive, the Directive enables life insurance companies to advertise throughout the EC on the basis of their home country rules, provided these rules do not conflict with the rules for the protection of policy holders in the Member State in which the risk is situated. It is necessary for insurers to be familiar with local marketing rules.

(b) **Guardian article**

The Guardian Saturday January 15 2000

Pensions

Small firms escape stakeholder rules

Hundreds of thousands of workers may now miss out on the chance to provide for their old age, writes Rupert Jones

The government has been accused of watering down its plans for low-cost "stakeholder" pensions by effectively excluding hundreds of thousands of workers in small companies.

Ministers have dropped their original proposal that all firms would have to offer employees a company pension scheme or give them access to the new breed of personal pension. Small companies have now been let off the hook.

Labour has been banging on about the stakeholder pension since it was in opposition but it is only now that all the pieces of the jigsaw are finally falling into place.

Stakeholder pensions will be available from April 2001 and the government promises they will be good value and user-friendly. The aim is that they will encourage millions more people to put money aside for their old age.

Anyone will be able to take one out, but their target market is the millions of low to middle-income earners with no private pension provision.

Social security secretary Alistair Darling this week announced that firms with fewer than five staff – around two-thirds of all Britain's employers – will not have to make stakeholder pensions available to their workers. He made this change after small firms claimed they were already buckling under the weight of a raft of new legislation, from the working time directive to the minimum wage, and having to give workers access to these new schemes was an administrative headache they could well do without.

People who work for small companies will still be able to obtain stakeholder pensions, but they will have to buy them direct from pension companies. However, the Consumers' Association suspects that, faced with sorting things out themselves, many of these people are likely to simply do nothing. Under the original plans, the boss of a small firm with no pension scheme would have had to select a stakeholder plan for staff to pay into if they wished, and arrange for pension contributions to be deducted from their earnings if requested.

The GMB union blasted the decision, saying that by "excluding" hundreds of thousands of workers in this way, the government was "undermining the whole basis of stakeholding". The change seriously affects the accessibility of the new pensions, and makes their success far less likely, says GMB national pension officer Bill Day.

Companies operating group personal pension schemes will also be exempt from the requirement to make stakeholder plans available, provided employers contribute the equivalent of at least 3% of employees' earnings to the GPP scheme.

In addition, the government has announced it is raising the minimum contribution that someone can make to a stakeholder pension. Previously it said people would be able to open one for as little as £10 but this has now been doubled to £20 – a change which the CA warns is not going to help when it comes to trying to encourage low earners to take the pension plunge. "It's disappointing," says Philip Telford, senior policy adviser at the CA. "We would favour it being as low as possible."

However, pension companies insist it is simply not realistic for people to think they can end up with a decent-sized pension on contributions of £10 a month.

"If you paid £10 a month for your entire working life you'd get a pension in real terms that would be about half the value of the basic state pension. That's not much of a top-up," says Adrian Boulding at insurer Legal & General. He adds that £20 is "a more realistic starting level".

In order to call themselves stakeholder pensions, schemes will have to meet a range of minimum standards. The main one is that the maximum a company can charge for managing the fund is 1% a year. This figure was finally confirmed this week after months of umm-ing and ahh-ing by ministers, and has been hailed as good news for the consumer. However, this 1% charge will cover only the cost of receiving basic financial advice – those people wanting more detailed advice tailored to their particular circumstances may have to pay an extra fee which could amount to several hundred pounds.

Stakeholder pensions will be offered by all the usual providers – insurers, banks, investment houses and financial advisers – but will also be available from organisations such as trade unions.

They may not go on sale for another 15 months but there are already some pension plans available offering stakeholder-style low charges and flexibility. Wolverhampton-based independent broker Torquil Clark (0800 0561836) has linked up with insurer Friends Provident on a personal pension with an all-in annual management charge of 0.95% with no minimum contribution level.

Those keen to find out more about the stakeholder concept can now log on to a new website specifically dedicated to the subject. The site has been launched this week by Interactive Investor International (iii), an online personal finance service, and can be found at www.iii.co.uk/stakeholder

Social security secretary Alistair Darling: Exempts small employers

(c) **FT article (1)**

FINANCIAL TIMES TUESDAY DECEMBER 14 1999

BANKS INITIAL STAFF ESTIMATES FOR STAND-ALONE GREENFIELD.CO OPERATION DOUBLED TO 1,100

Halifax steps up plans for the internet

By Mark Nicholson, Scotland Correspondent

Halifax has announced a "significant" increase in the size and potential scope of its planned stand-alone internet banking operation in Scotland. It has more than doubled initial staff estimates for the business, code-named Greenfield.co, to more than 1,100.

Jim Spowart, chief executive of Greenfield.co, declined to give details of the product beyond saying that the proposed venture would begin by offering online banking, but eventually "go well beyond one product".

"We're moving quickly to build the leading internet-led financial services business in the UK," he said.

The expansion follows what Mr Spowart called a "complete review" of the venture, whose launch was announced eight weeks ago.

He said the venture had already bought a second site in Livingston to house an expansion, which he said was within the initially announced investment of £100m.

An additional 600 staff would be recruited for the 200,000 sq ft facility bought for £4m on the high-technology Kirkston campus in Livingston.

The new facility would in part supply training and support services for Greenfield.co's Edinburgh Park offices, where some 80 of an eventual 500 staff are in place.

However, Mr Spowart indicated that the early expansion into new premises signalled that Halifax has upgraded its internet ambitions. "We think it will be big. It's going to be extremely ambitious, offering a range of products to fit the internet," he said.

Mr Spowart, who set up both Direct Line, the insurer, and Standard Life Bank, which itself now employs more than 1,000, described Greenfield.co as "the biggest scale project" he had worked on.

It is expected to begin offering online banking services by late April or early May, Mr Spowart said.

He said the venture was expected to return losses for the first two years of operation, becoming profitable in years three and four.

(d) **FT article (2)**

Wednesday January 12 2000

BANKS, LIFE COMPANIES AND RETAILERS TO OFFER STAKEHOLDER DEALS DESPITE INDUSTRY CRITICISM OF SCHEME

Top groups to sell new pension

By Nicholas Timmins and Andrew Bolger

Nine of the UK's top 10 life companies and some key retail banks have decided to offer stakeholder pensions in spite of strong industry criticism of the scheme.

In addition, retailers such as Marks and Spencer and Tesco and direct sellers such as Virgin and Direct Line said they would enter the market.

The low-cost money purchase products will come on the market next year.

The mass move into stakeholder pensions comes in the face of protests from parts of the pensions industry that the maximum 1 per cent annual charge for running stakeholders – insisted on by the government – was too low.

While the figures look encouraging for Alistair Darling, social security secretary, significant providers such as Standard Life, Europe's largest mutual group, National Westminster and Barclays all said they had yet to make a decision, pleading the need for more details and discussion.

The new pension is key to the government's plan to ensure that those on low-to-middle incomes have adequate income in retirement and to reverse the present balance of public and private provision, so that 60 per cent of pensions are privately funded. There were also doubts in the industry over how many will market the new pensions to the full range of the government's target group – the 5m earning £9,000 to £18,000 a year who lack a private pension.

Some, analysts believe, will concentrate on higher earners, many of whom already have some private provision. Many smaller providers may enter the market only defensively, chiefly making them available to existing customers who want a transfer.

Philip Scott, chief executive of Norwich Union Long Term Savings, said his company intended to market the new pension vigorously, but warned that stakeholders would only be "part of the continuum" of money purchase products that include group personal and executive pensions. "It will be the bottom-end product, not the dominant product," he said.

Stephen Cameron of Scottish Equitable said his company would offer them but that "it may be that only the biggest, strongest, most committed life offices" would sell them vigorously.

Peter Thomson of William Mercer, the employee benefits consultancy, said the economics of stakeholders were such that those that merely offered them defensively "won't be there in a few years".

Prudential, expected to invest heavily in the new pension, reflected doubts among big providers about whether they would sell stakeholders to individuals as opposed to groups through employers and affinity groupings.

That could leave the self-employed and those in small companies with little or no choice of providers. The GMB union warned that excluding small businesses from the requirement to make them available undermined "the whole basis of stakeholding".

Big insurers that said yesterday they intended to enter the market included Legal and General, CGU, Axa Sun Life, Zurich Financial Services and Friends Provident.

3.3 Appendix 3

(a) Company ratings and Clerical Medical financial data

FOCUS UPDATE: FINANCIAL STRENGTH

TABLE: EXPENSE RATIOS 1998

Acquisition

Company	1998 Values (A) £m	(B) £m	(C) (1998)	Previous Values of (C) (C) (1997)	(C) (1996)	(C) (1995)	(C) (1994)	(C) (1993)	(C) (1992)	(C) (1991)	(C) (1990)
AXA Equity & Law	113	464	24%	(116%)	(128%)	(113%)	(119%)	(117%)	(117%)	(118%)	(118%)
Britannic (1)	39	47	82%	(62%)	(64%)	(85%)	(72%)	(74%)	(84%)	(81%)	(85%)
CGU Life (9)	233	229	102%	(110%)	(94%)	(96%)	(113%)	(133%)	(118%)	(150%)	(155%)
CIS (1)	51	96	53%	(65%)	(62%)	(71%)	(69%)	(61%)	(57%)	(59%)	(63%)
Clerical Medical	110	221	49%	(42%)	(59%)	(107%)	(108%)	(93%)	(91%)	(94%)	(101%)
Colonial (2)	19	21	91%	(57%)	(277%)	(315%)	(227%)	(176%)	(197%)	–	–
Commerical Union	107	110	98%	(106%)	(106%)	(127%)	(148%)	(125%)	(114%)	(186%)	(173%)
Eagle Star	87	81	107%	(146%)	(152%)	(189%)	(187%)	(161%)	(134%)	(116%)	(92%)
Ecclesiastical (2) (5)	1	1	100%	(90%)	(103%)	(132%)	–	–	–	–	–
Equitable Life	107	637	17%	(14%)	(15%)	(17%)	(18%)	(24%)	(24%)	(26%)	(24%)
Friends Provident	186	227	82%	(90%)	(97%)	(132%)	(122%)	(107%)	(102%)	(98%)	(111%)
Guardian	30	29	101%	(100%)	(151%)	(270%)	(177%)	(205%)	(149%)	(154%)	(168%)
Legal & General	250	326	77%	(73%)	(73%)	(89%)	(106%)	(98%)	(107%)	(128%)	(108%)
Liverpool Victoria (1) (2) (5) (6)	19	2	899%	(192%)	(263%)	–	–	–	–	–	–
London Life (2) (5) (7)	<1	12	3%	(5%)	(5%)	(91%)	–	–	–	–	–
MGM	22	17	126%	(133%)	(121%)	(130%)	(118%)	(140%)	(167%)	(167%)	(118%)
National Mutual Life	43	63	69%	(65%)	(64%)	(72%)	(70%)	(75%)	(89%)	(95%)	(100%)
NFU (2)	12	28	43%	(65%)	(68%)	(108%)	(110%)	–	–	–	–
Norwich Union	157	262	60%	(69%)	(89%)	(97%)	(112%)	(162%)	(154%)	(108%)	(115%)
NPI	114	151	76%	(73%)	(78%)	(94%)	(81%)	(92%)	(92%)	(100%)	(98%)
Pearl	107	106	100%	(128%)	(128%)	(109%)	(104%)	(90%)	(77%)	(77%)	(63%)
Prudential (1)	503	608	83%	(72%)	(70%)	(86%)	(68%)	(77%)	(76%)	(64%)	(68%)
RNPFN	8	23	36%	(35%)	(40%)	(45%)	(46%)	(46%)	(61%)	(39%)	(34%)
Royal & Sun Alliance Life (8)	104	80	130%	(161%)	(134%)	(149%)	(119%)	(91%)	(121%)	(174%)	(170%)
Royal London (1)	41	47	88%	(79%)	(64%)	(93%)	(88%)	(79%)	(59%)	(55%)	(47%)
Scottish Amicable	124	163	76%	(95%)	(92%)	(100%)	(90%)	(90%)	(84%)	(86%)	(90%)
Scottish Equitable	190	367	52%	(59%)	(52%)	(55%)	(54%)	(59%)	(60%)	(57%)	(59%)
Scottish Friendly (1) (2) (5) (6)	5	9	57%	(68%)	(60%)	–	–	–	–	–	–
Scottish Life	63	107	59%	(60%)	(67%)	(81%)	(71%)	(69%)	(68%)	(86%)	(88%)
Scottish Mutual	98	162	60%	(64%)	(67%)	(82%)	(89%)	(96%)	(114%)	(130%)	(116%)
Scottish Provident	134	108	124%	(126%)	(129%)	(135%)	(124%)	(114%)	(100%)	(104%)	(107%)
Scottish Widows	168	268	62%	(60%)	(63%)	(94%)	(93%)	(86%)	(84%)	(86%)	(87%)
Standard Life (4)	345	638	54%	(53%)	(57%)	(66%)	(72%)	(56%)	(55%)	(62%)	(57%)
Sun Alliance	111	106	104%	(132%)	(168%)	(230%)	(190%)	(159%)	(107%)	(142%)	(149%)
Sun Life	107	293	36%	(53%)	(59%)	(88%)	(75%)	(79%)	(86%)	(81%)	(101%)
Sun Life of Canada (2) (3)	29	29	99%	(90%)	(145%)	(62%)	(147%)	–	–	–	–
Tunbridge Wells (5) (6)	8	7	124%	(101%)	(86%)	(77%)	(71%)	(74%)	(68%)	(93%)	(91%)
Wesleyan (1)	50	29	173%	(196%)	(145%)	(250%)	(190%)	(143%)	(118%)	(66%)	(85%)
Average Ratios (10)			78%	(84%)	(93%)	(115%)	(107%)	(102%)	(98%)	(99%)	(98%)

Other

Company	1998 Values (D) £m	(E) £m	(F) (1998)	Previous Values of (F) (F) (1997)	(F) (1996)	(F) (1995)	(F) (1994)	(F) (1993)	(F) (1992)	(F) (1991)	(F) (1990)
AXA Equity & Law	52	992	5%	(4%)	(4%)	(5%)	(5%)	(4%)	(5%)	(6%)	(9%)
Britannic (1)	86	311	28%	(16%)	(13%)	(8%)	(7%)	(5%)	(5%)	(5%)	(6%)
CGU Life (9)	53	1,890	3%	(2%)	(4%)	(2%)	(3%)	(4%)	(4%)	(5%)	(8%)
CIS (1)	101	927	11%	(14%)	(13%)	(7%)	(6%)	(4%)	(5%)	(5%)	(6%)
Clerical Medical	57	2,184	3%	(3%)	(6%)	(6%)	(6%)	(5%)	(5%)	(4%)	(5%)
Colonial (2)	26	225	12%	(6%)	(16%)	(17%)	(8%)	(12%)	(19%)	–	–
Commerical Union	68	815	8%	(6%)	(6%)	(5%)	(7%)	(6%)	(5%)	(8%)	(11%)
Eagle Star	55	724	8%	(11%)	(12%)	(21%)	(21%)	(15%)	(15%)	(13%)	(11%)
Ecclesiastical (2) (5)	2	13	14%	(8%)	(6%)	(5%)	(5%)	–	–	–	–
Equitable Life	41	3,733	1%	(1%)	(1%)	(1%)	(2%)	(2%)	(2%)	(3%)	(3%)
Friends Provident	76	1,898	4%	(4%)	(4%)	(7%)	(4%)	(5%)	(5%)	(6%)	(8%)
Guardian	43	353	12%	(11%)	(13%)	(15%)	(13%)	(14%)	(9%)	(13%)	(13%)
Legal & General	277	2,591	11%	(9%)	(6%)	(9%)	(8%)	(6%)	(6%)	(5%)	(8%)
Liverpool Victoria (1) (2) (5) (6)	44	68	64%	(7%)	(8%)	–	–	–	–	–	–
London Life (2) (5) (7)	15	160	9%	(4%)	(12%)	(12%)	(9%)	(8%)	(8%)	(7%)	(6%)
MGM	8	99	8%	(8%)	(8%)	(7%)	(6%)	(7%)	(7%)	(9%)	(8%)
National Mutual Life	22	471	5%	(3%)	(3%)	(3%)	(3%)	(2%)	(4%)	(4%)	(8%)
NFU (2)	7	291	2%	(5%)	(3%)	(4%)	(4%)	–	–	–	–
Norwich Union	147	2,711	5%	(5%)	(5%)	(6%)	(7%)	(7%)	(9%)	(6%)	(7%)
NPI	88	1,365	6%	(5%)	(5%)	(5%)	(6%)	(5%)	(4%)	(7%)	(8%)
Pearl	96	708	13%	(16%)	(23%)	(31%)	(23%)	(17%)	(12%)	(11%)	(12%)
Prudential (1)	583	5,769	10%	(5%)	(4%)	(5%)	(6%)	(5%)	(7%)	(7%)	(8%)
RNPFN	6	172	3%	(3%)	(3%)	(4%)	(4%)	(5%)	(5%)	(6%)	(7%)
Royal & Sun Alliance Life (8)	34	834	4%	(7%)	(8%)	(4%)	(5%)	(3%)	(5%)	(11%)	(8%)
Royal London (1)	63	362	17%	(20%)	(21%)	(11%)	(9%)	(9%)	(9%)	(10%)	(11%)
Scottish Amicable	3	696	<1%	–	(6%)	(7%)	(6%)	(5%)	(5%)	(5%)	(5%)
Scottish Equitable	76	2,424	3%	(3%)	(4%)	(4%)	(4%)	(4%)	(4%)	(6%)	(6%)
Scottish Friendly (1) (2) (5) (6)	7	25	27%	(20%)	(14%)	–	–	–	–	–	–
Scottish Life	34	693	5%	(7%)	(8%)	(9%)	(9%)	(8%)	(8%)	(9%)	(12%)
Scottish Mutual	37	1,400	3%	(3%)	(3%)	(3%)	(4%)	(4%)	(7%)	(7%)	(8%)
Scottish Provident	63	637	10%	(11%)	(10%)	(10%)	(10%)	(7%)	(3%)	(6%)	(7%)
Scottish Widows	96	2,094	5%	(4%)	(7%)	(6%)	(8%)	(7%)	(5%)	(6%)	(8%)
Standard Life (4)	216	4,860	4%	(5%)	(4%)	(5%)	(4%)	(3%)	(4%)	(4%)	(4%)
Sun Alliance	38	1,026	4%	(5%)	(8%)	(10%)	(9%)	(9%)	(8%)	(8%)	(11%)
Sun Life	61	2,392	3%	(4%)	(5%)	(4%)	(3%)	(3%)	(5%)	(4%)	(6%)
Sun Life of Canada (2) (3)	42	303	14%	(11%)	(8%)	(13%)	(19%)	–	–	–	–
Tunbridge Wells (5) (6)	8	64	12%	(11%)	(11%)	(10%)	(9%)	(8%)	(9%)	(10%)	(13%)
Wesleyan (1)	28	226	12%	(16%)	(17%)	(14%)	(9%)	(6%)	(7%)	(10%)	(8%)
Average Ratios (10)			8%	(8%)	(8%)	(8%)	(8%)	(6%)	(7%)	(7%)	(8%)

Footnotes: (A) = Acquisition Expenses (Form 41, Lines 41 + 43 gross). **(B)** = Total New Annual Premiums plus 10% of New Single Premiums (Form 47). **(C)** = Acquisition Expense Ratio: [(A)(B)] x 100%. **(D)** = Expenses (Form 41, Lines 42 + 44 45 gross). **(E)** = Total Premiums Receivable (Form 41, Lines 19 + 29 gross). **(F)** = Other Expense Ratio: [(D)(E)] x 100%. See glossary on page 4 for full definitions of the above items. **(1)** Figures are for Ordinary Business – Industrial Business excluded. **(2)** Full history of expense ratios unavailable. **(3)** Figures relate to UK branch. **(4)** Figures are for year to November 15, 1998. **(5)** Ratios calculated using unrounded values as values are small. **(6)** Friendly society. **(7)** Figures are for London Life Ltd, which now incorporates the entire former AMP (UK) branch (including the London Life Subfund), and the former London Managed Funds. **(8)** Formerly Royal Life. **(9)** Formerly General Accident Life. **(10)** Average Acquisition Expense Ratios for 1996-98 and Other Expense Ratio for 1998 exclude the Liverpool Victoria figures. Caveats: Figures relate to all business as opposed to being specific to with-profits business. Expense ratio comparisons between office should be treated with caution as ratios can be distorted by various factors. Trends in an office's ratio are more relevant. In general for 1995 and prior acquisition ratios, it was usually possible to include increment business in the denominator as the relevant information was not available. However, where information on increment business was provided voluntarily it was included. From 1996, increment business is included in Form 47.

Glossary for table

Acquisition expenses ratio

An indication of the proportion of new business premiums that are spent on acquiring the business. Makes use of equivalent annual premiums as the denominator.

Equivalent annual premiums

A way of converting single premiums and regular premiums into a single measure that is comparable with annual premiums. Ten per cent of single premiums are added to the regular premium amount. The rationale behind this is that regular premium business is normally more profitable/valuable than single premium business, due to its recurrent nature and that a ratio of 10:1 is broadly appropriate.

Other expense ratio

An indication of the proportion of total premium income that is spent on expenses, other than acquisition expenses. Such other expenses include regular ongoing maintenance expenses, together with any one-off or exceptional expenses which have been incurred.

(b) **Investment ratings summary**

PAGE 10 2 December 1999 ■ Financial Adviser

INVESTMENT PROVIDER RATINGS

Five star providers

★★★★★

Excellent service

NORWICH UNION
STANDARD LIFE
SCOTTISH WIDOWS
SCOTTISH AMICABLE
CLERICAL MEDICAL

Dead heats for the high scorers as insurers reign supreme

THIS category has the interesting phenomenon of joint winners.

Norwich Union and Standard Life have both scored an average of 7.13 to tie for top place. Norwich Union excelled in the personal contact criteria and Standard Life had particularly high scores in the business processing and the commission and service criteria.

This was Standard Life's third successive year as the highest rated company in the Financial Adviser/AIFA Service Awards in the life and pensions and investment categories.

The marks this year were particularly high, ranging from 6.81 to 7.13. Both the winners and those in second place scored over seven out of 10. Both had only one score of less than seven.

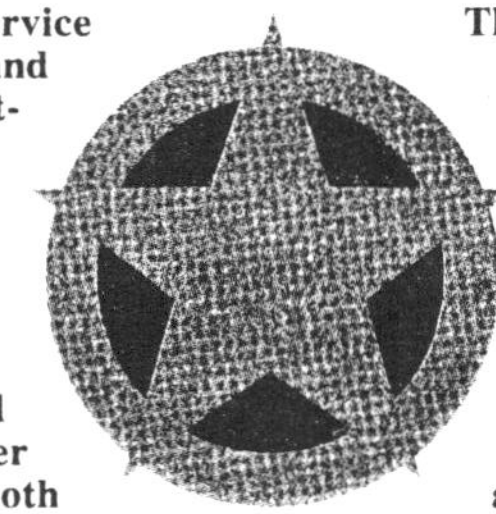

The second place was also taken by two companies, Scottish Widows and Scottish Amicable, who both scored 7.03. This is Scottish Widows' third five-star rating. Scottish Amicable has achieved its first five-star rating. It has held a four star ranking for the past two years. In 1996's unit trust category it only picked up one star.

Clerical Medical has moved upwards, from three stars in 1997, four last year and this year finally it has hit the winning spot.

Two years ago unit trusts and investment trust companies were merged into the same investment category.

The big winners this year were insurers again. This feature has remained throughout 1998 and 1999.

(c) **Investment ratings detail**

Investment providers and packagers: ratings

All scores are out of 10

Name of company	New business processing	Product support	Personal contact	Central processing	Commission service	Overall average
*****Excellent service						
Norwich Union	7.24	7.19	7.09	6.93	7.19	7.13 (tie)
Standard Life	7.37	7.15	6.94	7	7.2	7.13 (tie)
Scottish Widows	7.43	6.93	6.22	7.13	7.45	7.03
Scottish Amicable	7.21	7.09	6.64	6.98	7.25	7.03
Clerical Medical	6.95	6.9	6.35	6.82	7.02	6.81
****Good service						
Skandia	7.16	7.25	6.08	6.5	6.65	6.73
Sun Life	7.12	6.84	6.44	6.57	6.61	6.72
Threadneedle	7.15	6.65	6.47	6.48	6.63	6.68
Perpetual	7.55	7.23	4.27	7.12	7.1	6.65
Allied Dunbar (Zifa)	6.81	6.49	6.59	6.8	6.53	6.64
Exeter Asset Mgt	7.18	6.77	5.56	6.77	6.68	6.59
Friends Provident	6.65	6.61	6.04	6.36	6.78	6.49
Fidelity	7.27	7.1	4.31	6.88	6.8	6.47
Scottish Mutual	6.75	6.51	6.16	6.18	6.69	6.46

(d) **Life and pensions ratings summary**

PAGE 6 2 December 1999 ■ **Financial Adviser**

LIFE AND PENSIONS PROVIDER RATINGS

Five star providers

★★★★★

Excellent service

STANDARD LIFE
SCOTTISH WIDOWS
NORWICH UNION
SCOTTISH PROVIDENT
SCOTTISH AMICABLE
CLERICAL MEDICAL
SKANDIA LIFE

Standard sets the pace as newcomers rise to challenge

SCOTTISH Provident and Clerical Medical have both taken a step up from the four star category this year.

Clerical Medical has made a steady climb, from a low of two stars in 1996, as has Scottish Provident. This year Scottish Provident scored exceptionally well in the category of business processing. It was given 7.09 out of 10, the second highest mark of any of the life and pension providers.

All other five-star winners are still holding on to the five star rating they were awarded last year. Standard Life is clear winner in the life and pensions category, holding on to the top spot it won first in 1997 and again in 1998. This year it collects its fourth successive five star rating. It was the only company this year to score an average of over seven out of 10.

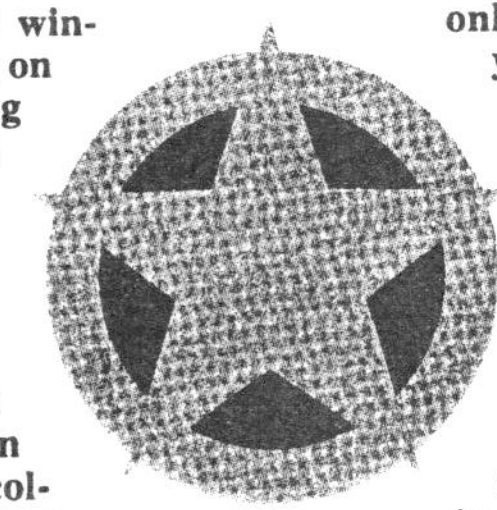

Only five years ago the company was considered worthy of no more than two stars. Standard Life and Standard Life Bank are five star winners in all the categories this year.

Scottish Widows was the second five star rated company in this year's awards – its fourth five star rating in as many years. In 1995 the company scored only three stars, then moved up to its five star position in 1996.

Scottish Amicable scored five stars last year after two years in the four star category.

Skandia Life has managed to hold onto the five star rating it regained last year. Norwich Union also scored five stars last year.

(e) **Life and pensions ratings: detail**

Life and pensions providers and packagers: ratings

All scores are out of 10

Name of company	New business processing	Product support	Personal contact	Central processing	Commission service	Overall average
*****Excellent service						
Standard Life	7.4	7.28	6.79	6.98	7.34	7.16
Scottish Widows	7.4	6.79	6.16	7.09	7.4	6.97
Norwich Union	6.65	6.93	6.48	6.43	6.76	6.65
Scottish Provident	7.09	6.77	5.72	6.59	6.94	6.62
Scottish Amicable	6.8	6.67	6.09	6.42	6.78	6.55
Clerical Medical	6.78	6.68	6.12	6.27	6.83	6.53
Skandia	6.82	6.88	5.92	6.39	6.64	6.53
****Good service						
National Mutual	6.44	6.46	6.1	6.02	6.48	6.3
CGU	6.51	6.55	5.85	6.04	6.45	6.28
AIG	6.8	6.19	5.25	6.39	6.71	6.27
Zurich Life (Zifa)	6.67	6.39	5.43	6.41	6.43	6.27
NPI	6.28	6.67	6.05	5.98	6.33	6.26
Scottish Life	6.44	6.47	6.03	5.98	6.23	6.23
Sun Life	6.54	6.34	5.82	6.03	6.35	6.22
Stalwart	7.24	6.27	3.43	6.89	7.17	6.2
Friends Provident	6.36	6.36	5.72	5.92	6.43	6.16
Scottish Mutual	6.24	6.41	5.86	5.72	6.44	6.14
SMA Pegasus	6.33	6.57	5.48	5.94	6.33	6.13
***Average service						
Scottish Equitable	5.95	6.25	6.24	5.64	6.25	6.07
Tunbridge Wells	6.7	6.27	4.37	6.45	6.41	6.04
Unum	6.71	6.07	4.97	6.04	6.14	5.99
Allied Dunbar (Zifa)	6.31	6.15	5.69	4.76	5.84	5.95
Family Assurance	6.67	6.16	3.83	6.29	6.27	5.84
M&G	6.22	6.06	4.09	5.86	6.34	5.71
Eagle Star (Zifa)	5.69	5.51	5.74	5.33	5.73	5.6
**Poor service						
Permanent	6.41	5.37	3.98	5.98	6.02	5.55
Swiss Life	5.98	5.56	4.18	5.83	6	5.51
Prudential	5.87	5.79	4.1	5.43	6.14	5.47
Royal & Sun Alliance	5.56	5.81	5.03	5.07	5.55	5.4
Legal & General	5.18	5.67	5.14	4.85	5.71	5.31
Canada Life	5.7	5.41	4.63	5.07	5.75	5.31
Guardian	5.98	4.9	3.7	5.22	5.81	5.12
*Very poor service						
Abbey Life	3.21	2.94	2.34	3.09	3.71	3.06

(f) Ratings analysis

FOCUS UPDATE: FINANCIAL STRENGTH

Assessing the ratings

Martin Lees, director at Standard & Poor's Insurance Ratings, provides a guide to the S&P analytical process and definitions of its security ratings

The Standard & Poor's analysis is a comprehensive process that considers the following eight factors before assigning a rating to an insurer. These major factors are scored by Standard & Poor's analysts. However, the weighting of these factors is subject to analytical judgement.

1 Industry risk
Analyses the competition and the inherent risk of the marketplace dynamics and considers:
- lines of business
- geographic profile
- regulatory, legal and accounting framework.

2 Business review
Analyses the overall health and standing of the company in the areas of:
- competitive strengths/weaknesses
- organisation structure
- diversification
- growth rates
- market share
- distribution channels
- products offered in relation to market demand.

3 Management and corporate strategy
The effect of past, present and future strategies involving:
- strategic positioning
- operational skill
- financial risk tolerance.

4 Operating performance
A look at the bottom line including:
- risk-adjusted earnings adequacy
- underwriting performance
- earning yield
- expense efficiency.

5 Investments
Examines asset management and its relationship to the following:
- asset allocation
- portfolio diversification
- asset credit quality
- interest rate risk management
- liquidity
- market risk.

6 Capitalisation
Examines the management of capital and considers a risk-adjusted analysis of how it relates to:
- asset risks
- reinsurance protection/quality
- liability risks (mortality/morbidity/underwriting)
- interest rate risks
- pricing risks
- general business risks
- financial leverage/interest coverage.

7 Liquidity
The interrelationship of an insurer's assets to its liabilities including:
- sources of liquid assets
- cash demands and liabilities
- large contractual maturities
- underwriting/operating cash flows.

> 'The Standard & Poor's analysis is a comprehensive process that considers eight factors'

8 Financial flexibility
Alternative sources such as:
- External sources of capital or liquidity.

UK LIFE FINANCIAL STRENGTH RATINGS LIST

Company name	Security circle	Rating as at 26/08/99	Rating as at 26/08/98	1997 New business breakdown (%) Linked	With-profit	Non-profit	Industrial Branch	Linked assets/ total policyholder assets (%) (1)
American Life UK Branch*	◉	AAA	AAA	54.5	0.0	45.5	0.0	47.5
Legal & General	◉	AAA	AAA	39.3	39.4	21.3	0.0	18.1
Pearl	◉	AAA	AAA	0.0	93.9	4.7	1.3	0.4
Prudential	◉	AAA	AAA_{pi}	10.2	79.1	10.7	0.0	4.7
Scottish Amicable Life	◉	AAA	NR	54.2	45.8	0.0	0.0	97.6
Scottish Equitable	◉	AAA	AAA	79.0	20.0	0.9	0.0	0.6
Standard Life	◉	AAA	AAA	44.5	32.8	22.6	0.0	5.7
Canada Life*	◉	AA+	AA+	57.5	1.8	40.7	0.0	57.2
Sun Life of Canada*	◉	AA+	AAA	46.4	26.8	26.8	0.0	35.6
Abbey National	◉	AA	AA	59.5	39.4	1.1	0.0	85.7
CGU Life	◉	AA	AA	71.4	15.0	13.7	0.0	5.3
CGU Linked Life	◉	AA	AA	86.2	9.2	4.6	0.0	47.2
Clerical Medical	◉	AA	AA	14.0	67.7	18.3	0.0	8.2
Norwich Union	◉	AA	AA	17.5	43.3	39.3	0.0	0.2
Scottish Mutual	◉	AA	AA	62.9	35.6	1.5	0.0	31.6
Britannic		AA_{pi}	NR	48.4	19.8	5.4	26.5	0.0
Commercial Union		AA_{pi}	AA_{pi}	24.7	68.9	6.4	0.0	0.6
Royal London		AA_{pi}	AA_{pi}	0.8	62.3	4.6	32.4	0.4
Scottish Widows		AA_{pi}	AA_{pi}	22.4	60.6	17.0	0.0	17.8
Eagle Star	◉	A+	A+	25.5	40.8	33.6	0.0	13.4
Equitable Life	◉	A+	AA	17.8	79.5	2.8	0.0	10.2
Friends Provident	◉	A+	A+	27.5	61.2	11.2	0.0	2.2
Scottish Life	◉	A+	A+	50.9	45.5	3.6	0.0	18.8
Scottish Provident	◉	A+	A+	22.4	46.3	31.2	0.0	20.6
National Provident	◉	A	A	32.5	60.8	6.7	0.0	20.3
Co-operative Insurance Society		A_{pi}	A_{pi}	0.0	85.3	3.1	11.6	0.0
Midland Life		A_{pi}	A_{pi}	68.8	0.0	31.2	0.0	86.2
National Mutual		A_{pi}	A_{pi}	72.2	27.4	0.3	0.0	36.6
National Westminster		A_{pi}	A_{pi}	88.2	0.0	11.8	0.0	79.1
Royal & Sun Alliance		A_{pi}	A_{pi}	14.5	51.6	33.9	0.0	2.3
Skandia Life		A_{pi}	A_{pi}	100.0	0.0	0.0	0.0	95.1
J Rothschild	◉	BBB+	BBB_{pi}	96.2	0.0	3.8	0.0	95.7
Lincoln	◉	BBB	A	96.9	0.0	3.1	0.0	81.9
Allied Dunbar Assurance		BBB_{pi}	A_{pi}	99.9	0.0	0.1	0.0	94.0
Barclays		BBB_{pi}	BBB_{pi}	66.7	0.0	33.3	0.0	89.0
Black Horse		BBB_{pi}	BBB_{pi}	78.4	0.0	21.6	0.0	85.0
GE Financial		BBB_{pi}	NR	30.9	0.0	69.1	0.0	48.9
M & G		BBB_{pi}	NR	96.2	0.0	3.8	0.0	95.9
Royal Scottish		BBB_{pi}	NR	93.7	0.0	6.3	0.0	86.1
United		BBB_{pi}	NR	17.3	49.5	3.3	30.0	8.1
Winterthur Life		BBB_{pi}	NR	98.3	0.2	1.5	0.0	66.9
Abbey Life		B_{pi}	BB_{pi}	89.4	0.0	10.6	0.0	85.1
Britannia		B_{pi}	BB_{pi}	91.1	2.0	6.9	0.0	42.3
AXA Sun Life		NR	NR	54.9	37.4	7.6	0.0	18.1
Guardian Assurance		NR	BBB–	42.2	12.5	45.3	0.0	24.1
Halifax Life		NR	NR	87.2	0.5	12.3	0.0	91.1
London & Manchester		NR	BBB_{pi}	66.3	6.7	18.8	8.2	40.4
PPP Lifetime Care		NR	NR	10.7	0.0	89.3	0.0	21.6

Footnotes: ◉ Identifies insurers which have voluntarily undergone Standard & Poor's comprehensive rating process. The subscript "pi" denotes ratings are based on information available in the public domain (see text on the right for a fuller explanation). Pi ratings are reviewed annually based mainly on each new year's Financial Services Authority returns (previously HM Treasury returns and DTI returns) as they become available. The ratings shown under 1999 above are based on 1997 year end returns (1998 are based on 1996 year end returns). Interactive (Security circle) ratings are constantly under review. (1) Linked assets/total policyholder assets (%): This gives an indication of the extent to which the company's asset base relates to unit-linked rather than with-profit and non-profit business. *Rating applies to UK branch only.

Standard & Poor's Insurer Financial Security Rating Definitions

An insurer rated BBB or higher is regarded as having financial security characteristics that outweigh any vulnerabilities, and is highly likely to have the ability to meet financial commitments.

AAA
An insurer rated AAA has "extremely strong" financial security characteristics. AAA is the highest Insurer Financial Strength Rating assigned by Standard & Poor's.

AA
An insurer rated AA has "very strong" financial security characteristics, differing only slightly from those rated higher.

A
An insurer rated A has "strong" financial security characteristics, but is somewhat more likely to be affected by adverse business conditions than are insurers with higher ratings.

BBB
An insurer rated BBB has "good" financial security characteristics, but is more likely to be affected by adverse business conditions than are higher rated insurers.

An insurer rated BB or lower is regarded as having vulnerable characteristics that may outweigh its strengths. BB indicates the least degree of vulnerability in the range, CC the highest.

BB
An insurer rated BB has "marginal" financial security characteristics. Positive attributes exist, but adverse business conditions could lead to insufficient ability to meet financial commitments.

B
An insurer rated B has "weak" financial security characteristics. Adverse business conditions will likely impair its ability to meet financial commitments.

CCC
An insurer rated CCC has "very weak" financial security characteristics, and is dependent on favourable business conditions to meet financial commitments.

CC
An insurer rated CC has "extremely weak" financial security characteristics and is likely not to meet some of its financial commitments.

R
An insurer rated R has experienced a "regulatory action" regarding solvency. The rating does not apply to insurers subject only to non-financial actions such as market conduct violations.

NR
An insurer designated NR is "not rated", which implies no opinion about the insurer's financial security.

Plus (+) or minus (–) signs following ratings from AA to CCC show relative standing within the major rating categories.

Pi ratings
Pi ratings, denoted with a pi subscript, are insurer financial strength ratings based on an analysis of published financial information and additional information in the public domain. They do not reflect in-depth meetings with an insurer's management and are therefore based on less comprehensive information than ratings without a pi subscript. Pi ratings are reviewed annually based on a new year's financial statements, but may be reviewed on an interim basis if a major event that may affect an insurer's financial security occurs. Pi ratings are not subject to potential CreditWatch listings.

SEPTEMBER 23, 1999 **FOCUS UPDATE** 11

(g) **CM business mix**

1998

Full year - business mix

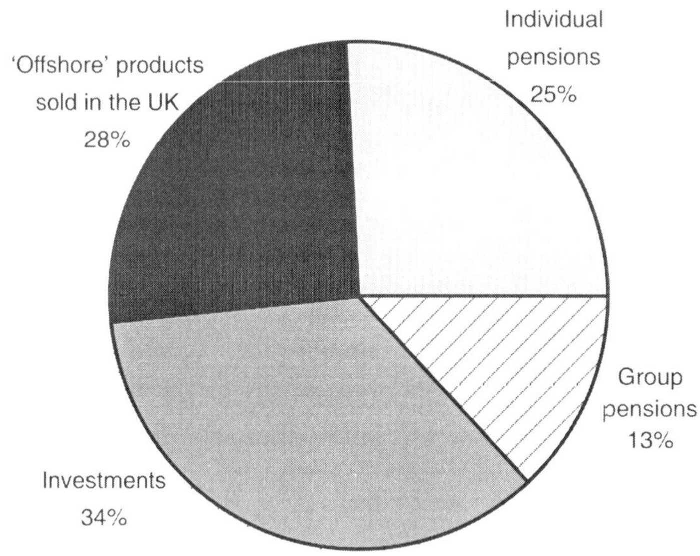

(September) 1999

Year-to-date - business mix

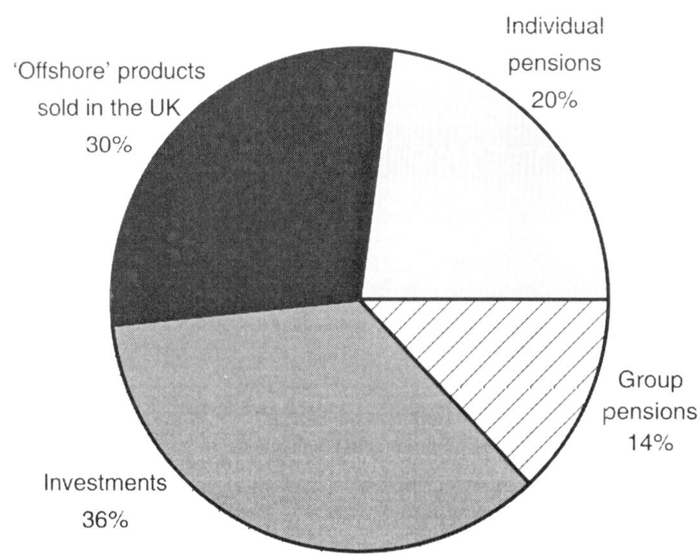

Clerical Medical Business Mix
Sales Figures September

1999 Annual report and accounts

(h) Balance sheets

	Group 1999 £m	Group 1998 £m	Company 1999 £m	Company 1998 £m
As at 31 December 1999				
Assets				
Investments				
Land and buildings	1,436.8	1,113.2	-	-
Investment in group undertaking and participating interests	219.0	185.0	1,351.2	851.0
Other financial investments	15,688.8	11,797.6	-	-
Other - present value of in-force business	699.7	630.1	-	-
	18,044.3	13,725.9	1,351.2	851.0
Assets hold to cover linked liabilities	6,316.9	5,088.9		
Reinsurers' share of technical provisions				
Long term business provision	8.2	8.3	-	-
Claims outstanding	1.4	-	-	-
	9.6	8.3	-	-
Debtors				
Debtors arising out of direct insurance operations	8.0	18.3	-	-
Other debtors	125.8	104.3	0.2	-
	133.8	122.6	0.2	-
Other assets				
Tangible assets	17.8	10.5	-	-
Cash at bank and in hand	215.8	83.6	-	-
	233.6	94.1	-	-
Prepayment and accrued income				
Accrued interest and rent	19.3	15.1	-	-
Deferred acquisition costs	84.2	169.8	-	-
Other prepayments and accrued income	8.0	14.2	-	-
	111.5	199.1	-	-
Total assets	**24,849.7**	**19,238.9**	**1,351.4**	**851.0**

(i) **Balance sheets**

	Group		*Company*	
	1999	*1998*	*1999*	*1998*
	£m	£m	£m	£m
As at 31 December 1999				
Liabilities				
Capital and reserves				
Called up share capital	1,351.2	851.0	1,351.2	851.0
Revaluation reserve	91.7	41.8	-	-
Profit and loss account	(129.5)	(111.4)	-	-
Other reserves	(2.6)	(2.6)	-	-
	1,310.8	778.8	1,351.2	851.0
Subordinated liabilities	147.3	-	-	-
Fund for future appropriations	4,591.5	2,934.4	-	-
Technical provisions	8.2	8.3	-	-
Long term business provision	11,963.7	10,029.0	-	-
Claims outstanding	29.4	17.9	-	-
	11,993.1	10,046.9	-	-
Technical provisions for linked liabilities	6,316.9	5,088.9	-	-
Provisions for other risks and charges	59.9	42.9	-	-
Creditors				
Creditors arising out of direct insurance operations	63.1	29.4	-	-
Other creditors including tax and social security	332.8	296.2	0.2	-
	395.9	325.6	0.2	-
Accruals and deferred income	34.3	21.4	-	-
Total liabilities	**24,849.7**	**19,238.9**	**1,351.4**	**851.0**

(j) **Group profit and loss account**
Technical account - long term business

	1999		1998	
	£m		£m	
Year ended 31 December 1999				
Income				
Earned premiums				
Premiums written				
- gross amount	3,283.1		2,566.1	
- outward reinsurance	(13.7)		(4.8)	
- net of reinsurance		3,269.4		2,561.3
Investment income		1,497.5		1,046.9
Unrealised gains on investments		2,129.1		1,127.9
Other technical income, net of reinsurance		52.7		36.8
Total income		**6,948.7**		**4,772.9**
Expenditure				
Claims incurred				
Claims paid				
- gross amount	1,569.5		1,559.4	
- reinsurers' share	-		(1.0)	
- net of reinsurance		1,569.5		1,558.4
Change in provisions for claims				
- gross amount	12.9		3.4	
- reinsurers' share	(1.4)		-	
- net of reinsurance		11.5		(3.4)
Claims incurred, net of reinsurance		1,581.0		1,555.0
Change in other technical provisions				
Long term business provision				
- gross amount	1,934.7		1,848.4	
- reinsurers' share	0.1		11.7	
- net of reinsurance		1,934.8		1,860.1
Net technical provision for linked liabilities		1,228.0		666.2
Net operating expenses		364.8		199.2
Investment expenses and charges		85.0		79.7
Tax attributable to the long term business		116.1		65.8
Transfers to the fund for future appropriations		1,657.1		326.5
Total expenditure		**6,966.8**		**4,752.5**
Balance on the technical account		**(18.1)**		**20.4**

(k) **Group profit and loss account**
Non technical account

Year ended 31 December	*1999*	*1998*
	£m	£m
Balance on the technical account - long term business	**(18.1)**	**20.4**
Tax attributable to the balance on the technical account	7.6	6.1
Shareholders' pre-tax profit arising from long term insurance business	**(10.5)**	**26.5**
Investment income	-	-
Operating profit	(10.5)	26.5
Other charges, including value adjustments	-	-
Profit on ordinary activities before taxation	**(10.5)**	**26.5**
Tax on profit on ordinary activities	(7.6)	(6.1)
Profit for the financial year	**(18.1)**	**20.4**
Dividends	-	-
Retained profit for the financial year transferred to reserves	**(18.1)**	**20.4**

All of the above amounts are in respect of continuing operations

The notes on pages ?? and ?? explain part of these accounts.

Of the profits dealt with in the group profit and loss account above, £nil relates to the company.

(l) **Group statement of total recognised gains and losses**

Year ended 31 December	*1999*	*1998*
Profit for the financial year	(18.1)	20.4
Other changes in value of long term business	49.9	11.1
Total recognised gains and losses relating to the year	**31.8**	**31.5**

(m) **Reconciliation of shareholders' funds**

Year ended 31 December	*1999*	*1998*
Total recognised gains and losses	31.8	31.5
Issue of share capital	500.2	-
Shareholders' funds at 1 January	778.8	747.3
Shareholders' funds at 31 December	**1,310.8**	**778.8**

(n) **Notes to the accounts**

1 **Accounting policies**

The following accounting policies have been applied consistently in dealing with items which are considered material in relation to the accounts.

Basis of preparation

The accounts have been prepared in accordance with ss 255 and 255A of, and Schedule 9A to, the Companies Act 1985. The accounts have also been prepared in accordance with applicable accounting standings and have been drawn up under the historical cost convention, modified to include the revaluation of investments, and comply with the revised Statement of Recommended Practice issued by the Association of British Insurers. The Group has adopted the modified statutory solvency basis for determining technical provisions.

The financial statements have been prepared in accordance with the requirements of three new Financial Reporting Standards (12, 15 and 16). There have been no changes to reported figures as a result of adopting the new standards.

The Group accounts comprise the accounts of Clerical Medical Investment Group (Holdings) Limited and its subsidiary undertakings. As the year ends of the Luxembourg subsidiaries named in Note 16 are different from that of the Company (Universe, the CMI Global Network Funds and The CM Institutional Fund have accounting dates of 30 September), the company's interim financial statements were used for consolidation purposes. These subsidiaries have different accounting dates from that of Clerical Medical Investment Group (Holdings) Limited for administrative reasons. The underlying nature of the two companies is that of vehicles for pooling interests in investments rather than controlled subsidiaries. As such, full consolidation, with identification of the funds not owned by the group as a minority interest, is not considered to be appropriate. Accordingly, the directors have exercised a true and fair override in performing a proportional consolidation of the fund.

As permitted by s 230 of the Companies Act 1985, the parent company's profit and loss account has not been included in these accounts.

Foreign currencies

Assets and liabilities denominated in foreign currencies are expressed in sterling at the rates of exchange ruling at the balance sheet date. Revenue transactions and those relating to the acquisition and realisation of investments are converted at rates of exchange ruling at the time of the respective transactions with the exception of transactions in some subsidiary undertakings where average rates are used.

Premiums

Premium income is accounted for on a cash basis in respect of single premium business and pensions business not subject to contractual regular premiums. For all other classes of business, premium income is accounted for in the year in which it is due for payment. Outward reinsurance premiums are accounted for when related premium income is recognised.

Investment income

All income from listed stocks and shares is included in the accounts when the security becomes ex-dividend, with the exceptions of some overseas subsidiary undertakings where investment income is included on a cash received basis. Other investment income, including rents, is accrued up to the balance sheet date. Realised gains and losses on investments are calculated as the difference between net sales proceeds and the original cost.

In accordance with the ABI Statement of Recommended Practice, the investment return arising during the accounting period in relation to investments held within the shareholders' fund has been included in the long term business technical account.

Unrealised gains and losses on investments

Unrealised gains and losses on investments represent the difference between the valuation of investments at the balance sheet date and their purchase price or, if they have previously been revalued, their valuation at the last balance sheet date.

19 Clerical Medical Investment Group Ltd: Précis, Marketing Audit, SWOT, Analysis of Appendices

This chapter covers the following topics.

1 INTRODUCTION

1.1 Having now completed your précis you can now compare it with the specimens which follow.

1.2 **Sample précis 1** is quite comprehensive and has the benefit of structure. It is however a little staccato with its bullet points and lists. You may challenge the advocacy of including the fact that Queen Victoria and Benjamin Disraeli featured among Clerical Medical's former clients.

1.3 **Sample précis 2** certainly has plenty of facts and figures but it is unstructured and you might not find it summarises the case as a whole particularly well.

1.4 **Sample précis 3** is in essay format but it reads well and covers quite a lot of ground in very little space. It does provide a good grasp of the basics of the case and its appendices but you may prefer a more structured approach. This précis, like the previous two, has the merit of refraining from value judgements and recommendations, thereby sticking strictly to the facts.

2 SAMPLE PRÉCIS

2.1 Sample précis 1

The role of Mr Don Sherwood is to undertake an internal and external analysis of the current situation.

Clerical Medical was formed in 1824 and insured the lives of doctors and clergymen. It fought tough competition between 1833 and 1840 because it concentrated on the doctors and clergymen and people who had certain ailments and diseases that other insurance companies would not insure.

They had some notable clients including Queen Victoria, Benjamin Disraeli etc.

In 1981 Clerical Medical Management Funds Ltd was formed with the principal activity being the transaction of long-term insurance business, written as 'managed fund arrangements for approved pension schemes'. The company offers specialist administration and technical services to pension fund trustees.

1984 - Clerical Medical Unit Trust Managers Ltd was formed (CMUTM) - the company manages unit trusts and acts as an ISA manager.

1987 - The company established its first international operation, Clerical Medical International (CMI) which now produces more than a quarter of the group's new business. It is recognised as a leading field in international financial services.

1997 - Halifax acquired Clerical, Medical and General Life Assurance Society at the cost of £800 million.

The life assurance industry

Worth £18.6 billion at the end of 1998. The net sum invested is about 7% of the GDP. The original purpose of the industry is to provide protection against misfortune. The role has been to expand into insurances etc.

Two possible growth spurts - the advent of electronic commerce and the development of stakeholder pensions, which are designed to widen the penetration of pensions throughout the UK.

New entrants

- Ten new bancassurers
- Medical insurers offering life assurance with protection products
- Providers of consumer products such as M&S, Virgin and Direct Line.

Very competitive market, with an over supply that outstrips demand.

The industry is very fragmented with over 200 authorised life assurers within the industry. There are 60 top ten providers, with no company having more than a 10% market share. The top ten life and pensions providers have 46% market share and 52% of the assets.

Banks have only about 15% of the life and pensions market, with the IFA channel dominating the market with a 60% share. Despite the fact that the IFA channel contains many small businesses, its share has doubled over the past 5 years.

In order to provide a service for the stakeholder pensions, companies are going to have to have a very efficient cost base, and economies of scale are important.

Distribution

The distribution of financial products are by:

- IFAs (they had a direct run in the challenge of competition)
- Banks
- Tied agencies
- Traditional direct saes
- Direct writers

Consumers

Ageing population
Fewer in full time employment and more self employed
Employment structure moving into ABC1 types

Passive brand loyal
Suspicious and confused
Active seeking personalised solutions

The role of IT

Poor IT systems are in place and there are needed to be more IT development.

Clerical Medical's markets

Persona pensions - 19%
Group (company) pensions - 15%
Investments - 38%
Offshore investments - 28%

In 1999, the total value of this business was over £2.5 billion and it was sold entirely through financial advisors. So the products have to be recommended through IFA.

They also operate in the wholesale market which relates to the direct management of the funds for major pension schemes and was valued at £0.5 billion in 1999.

In 1999 overall business was dominated by the UK retail market, the geographic split was

- UK - 79%
- Europe - 14%
- Other countries - 7%

2.2 Sample précis 2

Clerical Medical Investment Group Limited (CMIGL) was acquired by the Halifax Bank (formerly a building society) in 1997 at a cost of £800m. CMIGL was originally formed in 1824 offering doctors and clergymen health insurance against particular ailments that other companies excluded.

In 1950 CMIGL merged with the Northern Assurance Co and became a mutual in 1961.

In 1981 Clerical Medical Management Funds was formed to offer specialist administration and technical services to pension fund trustees.

In 1984 Clerical Medical Unit Trust Managers Ltd was formed to market and manage a comprehensive range of unit trusts and acts as an ISA manager.

The life assurance market is sized at c£19 billion total sum invested at end 1998 following a period of rapid growth in the 1980s which slowed in the 1990s. The market could return to more rapid growth spurred by e-commerce and the pending introduction of government-backed stakeholder pensions.

The industry is still fragmented with over 200 authorised life assurers. There are 60 large providers but none with more than 10% market share. The top ten have 46% market share and 52% of the assets.

There is a clear trend of consolidation in the market as the major businesses move into each other's territory. For example life assurers such as Prudential and Standard Life also offer banking products whilst banks such as Lloyds-TSB, Halifax and Abbey National have acquired life companies. Whilst this secures economies of scale, the current trend is to maintain brands for particular product-markets and customer types. Thus Halifax is targeted broadly at all adults with a wide range of products whereas CMIGL targets high net worth individuals through IFAs with a more specialist range of products.

The Financial Services Act was passed in 1986 following increasing public dissatisfaction with the self-regulated industry. Anyone now selling life and pensions products has either to be tired to one company or to be an Independent Financial Adviser (IFA). Rigorous checks are made to ensure standards.

A government review began in 1994 into alleged mis-selling of pensions and pressured miscreants into providing compensation. The government also feels that IFAs are mainly for the rich, lack professionalism and may not be truly independent. The government-induced stakeholder pensions will not impose any setting-up charges and are designed to be cheap, simple and flexible - so as to reduce the need for advice.

In 1999 CMIG's life assurance, pensions and investment products business in the UK was valued at £2.5 billion, split 38% investments, 28% offshore investments, 19% personal pensions and 15% group (company) pensions. All this business was conducted through IFAs. As far as can be ascertained this represents a UK market share in the order of 3% and CMIG do not feature in the top ten in terms of total business. A further £0.5 billion in 1999 was raised in the wholesale market from the direct management of funds for major pension schemes.

Also in 1999, overall business was dominated by the UK retail market, to the extent of 79%, with 14% from Europe and 7% other countries.

2.3 Sample précis 3

CM became a wholly owned subsidiary of the Halifax bank in 97. This was symptomatic of a general consolidation in the financial services industry where large assurance companies now offer banking services and banks also market assurance.

The business of CM is life assurance, pensions and investments, largely in the UK. This is set to continue flourishing due to factors such as population ageing, the advent of the internet and the forthcoming stakeholder pensions - simpler, cheaper products, sponsored by the government. CM's income rose by 45%, 99 over 98, to nearly £7bn, despite which a loss of some £18m was sustained, due almost entirely to large increases in provisions for future liabilities and appropriations. Nevertheless CM is a relatively small player with a share of some 3% in a fragmented market of over 200 life assurers where no one provider has more than 10%.

CM's current target market is peop0le of higher than average net worth, seeking specialised products. All CM's UK business - almost 80% of its total, is conducted through IFAs.

Ratings which reflect company performance and financial strength show that CM overall is performing satisfactorily and it occupies 5th position in the league for excellent service having made significant improvements since 97.

Competition is set to further intensify with pressures for cost reduction and product rationalisation. Bases for benchmarking against competitors are available in the market data. The financial services sector suffers from a bad press and general consumer mistrust, not helped by the pensions mis-selling scandal for which compensation must now be paid. The forthcoming stakeholder pensions have been stimulated by a government which mistrusts IFAs and wants to encourage more younger people to make more provision for old age and retirement. The CM brand is relatively little known compared with the Pru or Scottish Widows.

Typically, assurers have installed tailor-made IT systems for each new product introduced which have to keep track of each client's product performance over a number of years. These systems mostly have different protocols and do not 'talk' to each other.

New entrants armed with the latest technology and trading on the internet could exploit 'greenfield' opportunities such as stakeholder pensions, where the intention is that funds can be transferred to another provider without penalty at any time.

---

3 MARKETING AUDIT CHECKLIST

3.1 Before doing the audit proper you might like to try the information checklist mentioned in Chapter 8 Paragraph 3.7 and the checklist format in Chapter 1, Paragraphs 2.8 and 2.9. You should use this checklist to determine the information we have on Clerical Medical and the information we do not have. You could use a tick to show the information we have and a cross(X) to show the information we do not have (and which might then form the basis of your MkIS/MR recommendations later on in your plan). Further refinements might be to use P for information we have in part only and NA for **not applicable**. Really organised students might like to note the page numbers on which items ticked or marked P occur. It is easy for people to panic when they realise how little information the case study gives them. However, in real life we often take decisions based on inadequate information: the important thing is to recognise this and make reasonable assumptions. Having done this operation you might like to compare your results with those of the syndicate which follows, noting that there are likely to be some discrepancies, since this exercise is partly judgmental.

Internal

3.2 (a) **Current position**

(i) **Performance**

- ✓ Total sales in value and in units
- ✓ Total gross profit, expenses and net profit
- X Percentage of sales for sales expenses, advertising etc
- ✓ Percentage of sales in each segment
- NA Value and volume sales by year, month, model size etc
- NA Sales per thousand consumers, per factory, in segments
- ✓ Market share in total market and in segments

(ii) **Buyers**

- P Number of actual and potential buyers by area
- ✓ Characteristics of consumer buyers, eg income, occupation, education, sex, size of family etc
- P Characteristics of industrial buyers, eg primary, secondary, tertiary, manufacturing; type of industry; size etc
- NA Characteristics of users, if different from buyers
- P Location of buyers, users
- X When purchases made: time of day, week, month, year; frequency of purchase; size of average purchase or typical purchase
- P How purchases made: specification or competition; by sample, inspection, impulse, rotation, system; cash or credit
- P Attitudes, motivation to purchase; influences on buying decision; decision making unit in organisation

(b) **Products**

(i) **Clerical Medical**

- P Quality: materials, workmanship, design, method of manufacture, manufacturing cycle, inputs-outputs
- P Technical characteristics, attributes that may be considered as selling points, buying points
- ✓ Models, sizes, styles, ranges, colours etc
- P Essential or non-essential, convenience or speciality
- P Similarities with other company products
- P Relation of product features to user's needs, wants, desires
- P Development of branding and brand image
- P Degree of product differentiation, actual and possible

NA Packaging used, function, promotional

NA Materials, sizes, shapes, construction, closure

(ii) **Competitors**

✓ Competitive and competing products

✓ Main competitors and leading brands

P Comparison of design and performance differences with leading competitors

P Comparison of offerings of competitors, images, value etc

(iii) **Future product development**

P Likely future product developments in company
✓ Likely future, or possible future, developments in industry
P Future product line or mix contraction, modification or expansion

(c) **Distribution**

(i) **Clerical Medical**

✓ Current company distribution structure

✓ Channels and methods used in channels

P Total number of outlets (consumer or industrial) by type

P Total number of wholesalers or industrial middlemen, analysed by area and type

P Percentage of outlets of each type handling product broken down into areas

X Attitudes of outlets by area, type, size

P Degree of co-operation, current and possible

P Multi-brand policy, possible or current

P Strengths and weaknesses in distribution system, functionally and geographically

NA Number and type of warehouses; location

NA Transportation and communications

NA Stock control; delivery periods; control of information

(ii) **Competitors**

P Competitive distribution structure; strengths and weaknesses

✓ Market coverage and penetration

NA Transportation methods used by competitors

NA Delivery of competitors

P Specific competitive selling conditions

(iii) **Future developments**

P Future likely and possible developments in industry as a whole or from one or more competitors

P Probable changes in distribution system of company

P Possibilities of any future fundamental changes in outlets

(d) **Promotional and personal selling**

(i) **Clerical Medical**

P Size and composition of sales force

X Calls per day, week, month, year by salesmen

X Conversion rate of orders to calls

X Selling cost per value and volume of sales achieved

X Selling cost per customer

P Internal and external sales promotion

X Recruiting, selection, training, control procedures

P Methods of motivation of salesmen

P Remuneration schemes

X Advertising appropriation and media schedule, copy theme

X Cost of trade, technical, professional, consumer media

X Cost of advertising per unit, per value of unit, per customer

X Advertising expenditure per thousand readers, viewers of main and all media used

X Methods and costs of merchandising

P Public and press relations; exhibitions

(ii) **Competitors**

X Competitive selling activities and methods of selling and advertising; strengths and weaknesses

X Review of competitors' promotion, sales contests etc

X Competitors' advertising themes, media used

(iii) P **Future developments** likely in selling, promotional and advertising activities

(e) **Pricing**

(i) **Clerical Medical**

P Pricing strategy and general methods of price structuring in company

P High or low policies; reasons why

P Prevailing pricing policies in industry

P Current wholesaler, retailer margins in consumer markets or middlemen margins in industrial markets

P Discounts, functional, quantity, cash, reward, incentive

X Pricing objectives, profit objectives financial implications such as breakeven figures, cash budgeting

(ii) **Competitors**

P Prices and price structures of competitors

P Value analysis of own and competitors' products

X Discounts, credit offered by competitors

(iii) **Future developments**

P Future developments in costs likely to affect price structures
NA Possibilities of more/less costly raw materials or labour affecting prices
P Possible price attacks by competitors

(f) **Service**

(i) **Clerical Medical**

P Extent of pre-sales or customer service and after-sales or product service required (by products)

P Survey of customer needs

NA Installation, deduction in use, inspection, maintenance, repair, accessories provision

P Guarantees, warranty period

P Methods, procedures for carrying out service

P Returned goods, complaints

(ii) **Competitors**

P Services supplied by competing manufacturers and service organisations

P Types of guarantee, warranty, credit provided

(iii) P Future possible developments that might require revised service policy

External

3.3 (a) **Environmental audit - national and international**

P Social and cultural factors likely to affect the market, in the short and long term

P Legal factors and codes of practice likely to affect the market in the short and long term

P Economic factors likely to affect market demand in the short and long term

P Political changes and military action likely to impact upon national and international markets

P Technological changes anticipated and likely to create new opportunities and threats

(b) **Marketing objectives and strategies**

P Short-term plans and objectives for current year, in light of current political and economic situation

X Construction of standards for measurement of progress towards achieving of objectives; management ratios that can be translated into control procedures

P Breakdown of turnover into periods, areas, segments, outlets, salesmen etc

X Which personnel required to undertake what responsibilities, actions etc when

P Review of competitors strengths and weaknesses likely competitive reactions and possible company responses that could be made

P Long-term plans, objectives and strategies related to products, price, places of distribution, promotion, personnel selling and service.

3.4 You are now ready to conduct the marketing audit proper, systematically working your way through the environmental audit, to the marketing functions audit and the other functional audits (financial, production and personnel).

CONSULT THE GUIDANCE NOTES IN CHAPTER 8 PARAGRAPH 2.1
STEP 2.1 CONDUCT A MARKETING AUDIT
ALLOW YOURSELF ABOUT THREE HOURS FOR THIS STEP

3.5 Have a thoughtful and **critical** look now at the marketing audits submitted below by different syndicates. All three audits are quite good in their different ways, although not all quite as complete as they should be. Is yours?

4 EXAMPLE MARKETING AUDIT 1

Clerical Medical Investment Group Limited

4.1 **Company**

- **(1981) Clerical Medical Management Funds Ltd**

  Transaction of long term insurance business, written as 'managed fund' arrangements for approved pension schemes

  Offers specialist administration/technical services to pension fund trustees

- **(1984) Clerical Medical Unit Trust Managers Ltd**

  Markets/manages comprehensive range of unit trusts and acts as ISA manager

- **(1987) Clerical Medical International**

  Produces more than a quarter of the company's new business

  Recognised as leading name in field of international financial services

- **1997 Clerical Medical Investment Group Ltd - a wholly owned subsidiary of the Halifax Group**

4.2 **Products**

- Offers wide range of life assurance, pensions and investment products
- 1999 - Personal pensions 19%, Group (company) pensions 15%, Investments 38%, Offshore investments 28%
- Business worth over 2.5 billion
- Sold entirely through Independent Financial Advisors (IFAs)

4.3 **Market**

- Wholesale market - direct management of funds for major pension schemes
- Valued at £0.5 billion in 1999
- Sold entirely through specialist advisors to pension fund trustees
- Very competitive with regard to investment performance of funds

- International market - investment products to UK citizens living/working abroad and foreign nationals
- Sold through 'master distributors' who also carry products of other companies
- 1999 geographic split of markets

  UK - 79%
  Europe - 14%
  Other countries - 7%

4.4 **Key issues**

- Environment very competitive; supply outstrips demand
- Industry still not global - due to national characteristics, taxation, legislation, regulation, consumer preferences
- Industry has a lot of suppliers/fragmented - cost of remaining in business high
- 60 large providers - no company has more than 10% market share
- Companies have large number of products; not customer focused
- Despite attempts at brand building older companies such as Clerical Medical are not well known as banks, supermarkets etc
- Bad press - pensions mis-selling
- Financial Services Act created tied agents and IFAs. Rigorous FSA checks to make sure correct advice is given, penalties are implied to companies who fail checks
- Trend for consolidation within market

Market sectors/size/trends

4.5 **Pensions**

(a) **Market size**

- 1998 - individual pensions 25%
- Group pensions 13%
- 1999 - individual pensions 20%
- Group pensions 14%
- Personal pensions: 19% of company's activities
- Group/company pensions: 15% of company's activities
- Market saturation 56%
- PPP 15%/35% co pensions
- 36% female/64% male

(b) **Trend**

- Young: contributory, non-contributory, PPP
- Middle: free-standing additional contribution scheme, voluntary contribution scheme
- Older: no pension
- Cl group, age 25-34
- 1% group pensions demand
- 5% decrease demand for individual pension

- Acorn groups: company pensions B05 (comfortable workers, family areas)
- PPP A02 (affluent greys, rural communities)
- State pensions A02

4.6 **Assurance**

(a) **Market size**

- 37% saturated market, 51% male, 49% female

(b) **Trend**

- Social class group DE
- Age 65+
- Policies held longer than a year in 90% of policies
- Acorn group B05 (comfortable workers, family areas)
- New policies in last year - 25-34 age group, social class C1, south region (exc London)

4.7 **Investments**

(a) **Market size**

- 1998: Investments 34%/Offshore 28%
- 1999: Investments 36%/Offshore 30%
- Investments: 38% of companies activities
- Offshore investments - 28% of companies activities

(b) **Trend**

- Acorn group A01 (wealthy achievers)
- Favour premium bonds
- UK company stocks increase by 39%
- 78% increase in bank deposits
- 27% increase in life assurance and pension funds

4.6 PEST analysis

Political	Economical
• **Financial Services Act** Advertisements by the government have meant that consumers are more weary, seek more information Companies have rigorous checks, have been forced to become more responsible Investment companies and advisers need more well trained personnel • **Foreign trade barriers** EU policy National characteristics, taxation, legislation, regulations, consumer preferences • **Stakeholder pensions**	• Interest rates • Increasing choice (PEPs, ISAs etc) • Unemployment • Stock market Potential losses, threat to providers and suppliers
Social	**Technological**
• **Education** More people going to university and subsequently more semi/professionals generated • **Perception of industry by the consumer** Negative media reports, pension mis-selling • **Ageing population, employment pattern changes** Less people predicated to be in full time employment, shorter employment contracts, more self employed; greater product flexibility required to meet these needs • **Cost of living increase** People have less disposable income	• **Internet** Making it easier for new players to enter market Future of IFAs as people become more knowledgeable through simpler on-line education policies etc • **Advances in medicine** Longer life spans; people leaving it later to think about pensions • **Improved IT platforms: direct debits, collecting policies, policy information, client information** Enable companies to become more sophisticated and enable policies to be accurate to customer need/life styles/ capabilities • **Customer relationship management**

5 EXAMPLE MARKETING AUDIT 2

Key factors for success

5.1 Clerical Medical

- A subsidiary of the Halifax Bank, with the security of their financial backing
- Well established
- Have a specialist product portfolio
- Target higher net worth individuals through Independent Financial Advisors (IFAs)
- Lack a marketing strategy/marketing focus

Marketing environment audit

5.2 The environment

Political/legal	Economic
• Increasing regulation imposed by government • Increasing level of involvement by government, ie making recommendations about pensions • Introduction of stakeholder pensions in UK will limit profitability • Single community market for insurance from July 1994 introduced international competition	• Varying interest rates across Europe deliver varying returns on investment • Stages in economic cycle, ie recession • Level of disposable income affects willingness to invest • FTSE Share Index affect on returns of endowment policies • Pressure to reduce cost base
Social	**Technological**
• Ageing population so increased pressure on government to support them • Public perception of industry (see as complicated and not to be trusted) • Changing profile of workforce - more part time and self employed workers	• Legacy system is slow and inflexible • Development of e-commerce channels • Other financial services use telesales/call centres

(a) To improve their customer focus, targeting and reduce current transaction costs, Clerical Medical need to look at replacement of their currency legacy computer system and implement a new system that is both flexible and e-commerce enabled.

(b) Clerical Medical also need to assess the stakeholder pension and decide if it is a product that will enhance their portfolio. Stakeholder pensions could be used to help change people's perceptions of pensions as they are seen to be government approved and much less complicated than previous pensions.

5.3 The market

- International but not global
- Highly fragmented
- Poor customer segmentation
- Intangible as it is a service
- Very competitive
- It is in a mature phase with slow growth
- The life assurance market consists of: investments, life assurance, individual pensions and group pensions
- Increased money in investment at the expense of pension schemes which are in decline
- High amounts of capital and large customer base are required

Clerical Medical needs to investigate how to improve customer segmentation and customer focus. They also need to work to reinforce the tangible benefits of their investments.

5.4 Competition

- Sixty major players, the top ten of who only have a total of 46% market share. No one company has more than 10% market share
- Smaller companies are consolidating and being acquired by larger organisations

- Strong new entrants include banks and consumer brands, eg Virgin and strong brands are becoming more important in influencing customer choice
- Tax efficient products such as ISAs are taking market share away from traditional products

Clerical Medical are in a highly competitive market place and need to work on branding to increase awareness and position themselves to minimise the impact from new entrants.

5.5 Distribution

Five types of distributors

(a) Banks

(b) Tied agencies

(c) Traditional direct sales

(d) Direct writers

(e) IFAs - major distributors and growing:

- split into nationals 30%, networks 15%, regionals 45% and small 10% (1998)
- estimated split by 2005 nationals 35%, networks 20%, regionals 40%, small 5%

IFAs are the main type of distribution, however the government has stated that they are perceived as being for the rich and lacking in professionalism. Clerical Medical needs to look into working with the IFAs to improve the way they are perceived as well as investigating other possible channels for distribution.

5.6 Porter's five force analysis - current and ten year forecast

	Current	10 year forecast
Existing market	• Low growth rate • Highly fragmented • Large • Mature	• Slightly higher growth rate • Less but larger competition • Less fragmented • Larger market • Moving from maturity to re-growth
Barriers to entry	• Complex regulations • Need for proven track record • Market supply surpasses demand	• Regulation become less complex • Proven track record of brand important • Market supply more in-line with demand
Supplier power	• Supplier power is low	• Supplier power is still low
Buyer power	• Lots of choice • Freedom of choice (eg international) • Complex purchase - can take time	• Increase in choice • More freedom of choice • Complex purchase - can take time
Substitutes	• Direct substitutes (eg ISAs) • Indirect substitutes (spend not save)	• Direct substitutes increased • Indirect substitutes same

(a) In ten years, the market will still be entering another growth phase. The introduction of stakeholder pensions and the restrictions they have put on charges will lead to the smaller suppliers either leaving the market altogether or being acquired by larger (possibly global) players. There will be fewer competitors; however, such organisations will be larger.

(b) The ageing population will have stretched the government to its limit and people will realise that they need to invest for their future. Even though the market size is higher than that of France or Germany, at 7.3% of GDP this sudden investment will start another growth phase in the product life cycle. The market will become less fragmented with more generic investment options such as the **stakeholder pension**. Supplier power will be slightly stronger as supply will be more in-line with demand, however buyers will still have lots of choice.

Internal marketing audit

5.7 **Strategy**

- Not customer focused
- Unclear marketing strategy
- Inherited from history (eg target clerics and medics)

5.8 **Systems**

- Poor marketing information systems (MkIS)
- IT systems are inflexible

5.9 **Organisation**

- Traditional and well established
- Subsidiary of large well known bank

5.10 **Promotion**

- Recommendation by IFAs (unclear what promotion there is aimed at IFAs other than area on Clerical Medical website)
- Direct mail
- Advertising
- Word of mouth

5.11 **Product**

- Wide range of specialist investment and pensions
- Intangible
- Complex
- Personal pensions 19%, group pensions 15%, investments 38%, offshore investments 28% (£2.5bn in 1999)

5.12 **Distribution**

- All UK business in 1999 through IFAs (79%)
- International investment products sold through 'master distributors' who carry other organisations' products (Europe 14%, other countries 7%)

5.13 **Price**

- Further investigation into market required to establish position in relation to competition in terms of return on investment
- Acquisition expense ratio for 1998 (49%) ranked Clerical Medical 7th out of 39 investment companies

5.14 **Physical evidence**

- Awards won - 5 star award in 1999 (investment provider ratings and life and pensions provider ratings)
- Ranked 16th in 1998 table of top performers based on new business. Ranked 11th in terms of funds under management

5.15 **Process**

- Good customer service to existing customers
- For new customers contact with Clerical Medical is through IFAs or master distributors

5.16 **People**

Needs further investigation, however from initial findings:

- Insufficient up-to-date training
- Stale recruitment process

5.17 **Conclusion**

Clerical Medical need to create a marketing orientation within the organisation and ensure they have clear strategies that all stakeholders are aware of. Work needs to be undertaken on the IT systems which will be needed to support the development of a MkIS. They need to look at varying methods of promotion as well as new channels of distribution. The staff at Clerical Medical need to have a training schedule drawn up for them and the recruitment process needs overhauling.

6 EXAMPLE MARKETING AUDIT 3

Marketing environment audit (macro)

6.1 **Social**

(a) Current forecast estimate: more people will be part time/self employed by 2010. These people will need their own personal pensions, which will need to be more specialist, flexible products with advice.

(b) Employment structure is shifting towards more ABC1 type jobs.

(c) An ageing population, with a larger proportion expected to be over 60 in the future, in all major developing countries.

(d) UK consumers mistrust pension/financial industry. CM must distance themselves from bad practices and reflect this in their brand values.

6.2 **Legal**

(a) Funds have been set aside for pension mis-selling and compensation. Not clear of CM impact but there are provisions set aside in the 1999 P&L account.

(b) Opportunities in Europe and further afield must be weighed up against regulations (tax, consumer preferences etc).

(c) UK is becoming increasingly regulated which will continue to depress profits and increase costs. This is a threat for firms with poor economies of scale and high cost base.

6.3 **Economic**

(a) UK economy is currently in good shape, offering potential for growth in the market.

(b) Life assurance industry operates with a long payback period (repayments over 25 years). This practice weathers economic highs and lows.

(c) If the increase in interest rates continues, this could correlate to an increase in consumer savings. Possible opportunities for CM. However, low interest rates make investment in stocks and shares attractive.

6.4 **Political**

(a) The government wants a mass market product on the market, with reduced need for advice. This will satisfy low value standard products, CM are not currently in this market.

(b) Pressure from government for financial services sector to be more accountable and professional. CM may have some training/changes in practices but limited as they have no direct customer contact, currently.

(c) Government feels that Independent Financial Advisors (IFAs) are mainly for well off clients. As this is CM's only distribution channel, they will need to monitor any implications that may arise from this.

(d) Government wants to increase ownership of privately financed pensions from 40% to 60%. This will be a strong growth area, CM needs to consider.

6.5 **Technological**

(a) New technology gives new entrants a competitive advantage, selling direct, with how distribution costs.

(b) The financial services industry is recognised as one of the main industries influenced by e-technology. CM must grasp this.

Marketing environment audit (Micro)

6.6 **Competition**

(a) Competition comes in four forms.

(i) Banks (bancassurance)
(ii) Life assurance companies
(iii) New entrants, eg BUPA expanding from just medical insurance
(iv) Consumer product provider, eg M&S and Virgin

(b) Most firms are product-led and have a wide range of products. CM needs to evaluate this and decide whether they can compete with the larger players on this. (I don't think they can.)

(c) The industry is fragmented, with over 200 firms operating in the UK.

(d) New regulation will continue to depress industry profits and require firms to become more adaptable to change or risk failure.

(e) Tradition distribution channels are inefficient and carry a high cost of doing business. CM needs to reduce this cost.

(f) Oversupply gives a very competitive environment (likely to continue). CM needs to differentiate.

Markets

6.7 Who buys what product?

- 37% UK population have life assurance
- 30% have some form of protection
- 12% have savings

6.8 Increased trend towards part time/self employed. CM need to meet the needs of these people.

6.9 Government trend towards promoting management of own financial security. CM needs to consider delivery channels which are currently only through IFAs.

6.10 25% of people are not confident and 50% people know very little of product/provider selection. CM communications and branding will need to address this.

Customers

6.11 We can broadly look at three types of customers (end users).

(a) Passive brand loyals
(b) Suspicious/confused
(c) Active seeking professionals

CM needs to choose which type of customer it wants to attract and then identifying them and satisfy their needs.

6.12 **How do they buy?**

There are three main distribution channels, however, CM's customer can only buy through IFAs. CM are in danger of putting 'all their eggs in one basket'.

6.13 **When do they buy?**

The number of policies sold to 25-34 age group has doubled in the last 12 months. These people would be newly-weds or bachelor or fist born type lifestyles.

6.14 **Why do they buy?**

Need to continue their lifestyle when they retire - pressure of future.

6.15 **What do they buy?**

- Security
- Peace of mind
- A future

Marketing environmental audit (internal)

6.16 **Marketing strategy audit**

There is no clearly defined marketing strategy. This stems from the fact that CM have not clearly segmented their market.

Marketing organisational audit

6.17 Product/process driven company. Outdated structures and stuffy image.

6.18 Promotion stem from within. Lack of progressive technically minded skills.

6.19 **Marketing systems audit**

(a) Legacy systems, product drive not customer focussed.
(b) No meaningful customer data.
(c) Apparent lack of MkIS.

Marketing functions audit

6.20 **Four main products**

(a) Personal pensions

(b) Group pensions

(c) Investment pensions

(d) Overseas investments

Price - companies competing on price. CM need to continue to differentiate and reduce costs.

100% distribution through IFAs. CM needs to address this as new business is diminishing.

There is a lack of new skill/technically minded staff.

6.21 Little, visible on-going promotional activity (complacency). There is low brand awareness compared with new entrants, eg Virgin.

7 SWOT ANALYSES

7.1

CONSULT THE GUIDANCE NOTES IN CHAPTER 8 PARAGRAPH 2.2
STEP 2.2 DO A SWOT ANALYSIS
ALLOW YOURSELF ABOUT THREE HOURS FOR THIS STEP

7.2 Look now at the four SWOT analyses conducted by students/syndicates which follow and see how these compare with yours.

7.3 None of the samples are scored or referenced. Sample 1 is average and somewhat minimal. Sample 2 is even more minimal but ranked, although it doesn't say on what basis. Sample 3 contains quite a lot of items. Sample 4 is interesting in that it is in fact an audit of the marketing planning framework split into strengths and weaknesses, ie the strengths and weaknesses have been categorised. However it is incomplete.

7.4 How did your SWOT compare? Did it include the ingredients of categorisation, referencing, scores and degrees of importance? If so - go to the top of the class.

Sample SWOT 1

7.5 SWOT analysis

Strengths	Weaknesses
1.1 Excellent service provider, CMIG has been awarded 5 stars by the life and pension providers ratings. 1.2 Backed by strong banking group, ie Halifax. 1.3 Long established company since 1824. 1.4 Established market share, ie 3% of the fragmented market. 1.5 Good expense ratio. 1.6 Good reputation in home market.	2.1 Out of date standalone legacy system. 2.2 No clear mission and objectives. 2.3 Limited international experience and poor penetration of international market. 2.4 Poor profitability status. 2.5 Lack of research and information on Europe and other international market. 2.6 Lack of strategic planning, no clear evidence of international marketing strategy. 2.7 Lack of customer focus. 2.8 Product orientated. 2.9 No clear MIS and MkIS strategy. 2.10 Weak ROCE ratio. 2.11 Weak liquidity ratio.
Opportunities	**Threats**
3.1 E-business - internet transaction. 3.2 Favourable government legislation (IFA). 3.3 Globalisation of the international market. 3.4 CRM – customer relationship management. 3.5 Increase in individual disposable income. 3.6 Increase in professional and career women.	4.1 New entrants - stronger competition from other company, ie Tesco, Marks & Spencer, Sainsbury, banks and so on 4.2 Changes in fiscal policy, ie changes in interest rates. New legislation from UK and the European Union.

Sample SWOT 2

7.6 SWOT analysis

Strengths	Weaknesses
1 Positive customer perception 2 Strong financial backing from Halifax 3 Halifax provides alternative routes to market 4 Recognised company 5 Well established and seen to provide reassurance and experience	1 Poor IT system preventing customer relationship management 2 Lack of marketing focus 3 No strong brand identity 4 Lack of innovation and entrepreneurial approach 5 Limited product portfolio (specialist investments and pensions only)
Opportunities	**Threats**
1 Development of e-commerce as a new channel of distribution 2 Introduction of stakeholder pensions 3 New growth markets overseas 4 New target market of young professional 5 Expansion via strategic alliances and mergers	1 Strongly branded new entrants 2 Increasing regulation and economic changes 3 Heavy reliance on intermediaries (IFAs) 4 Threat of scandal (mis-selling of pensions) 5 Hostile takeover/being sold by Halifax

Sample SWOT 3

7.7 SWOT analysis

Strengths	**Weaknesses**
• Owned by Halifax • Long trading history • Not short-term driven (like banks) • Wide range of financial products • Ranked as large player (in top 10), 3% market share • Growing international business • Potentially good brand image, established for over 175 years • 5 star service award • Recognition that they need help from outside marketing	• Brand image - old fashioned stuffy • Brand is not widely recognised • Legacy IT systems - policy driven, not customer driven • Poor segmentation • High base costs • Lack of entrepreneur culture • Most sales through IFAs • Lack of consumer profiles
Opportunities	**Threats**
• Halifax developing e-banking service • Limited amount of selling abroad • Barriers to trade abroad are being removed could be a threat to domestic UK market? • Business growth through acquisition of local companies • Different stages of product life cycle in different countries • E-commerce could herald growth with transaction costs halving • New channels • Reduced cost base • Stakeholder pensions • Direct sales • IFAs must move from commission to fees • Market for flexible • Network of high street banks (Halifax) • Customer relationship marketing	• History of pension mis-selling in industry • Regulations concerning stakeholder pensions • Mature market for life assurance in UK • Competition from other products • Glut of suppliers • New suppliers, with well known, respected image; bancassurers, medical, new image players (M&S, Virgin) • Difficult to make profit • Government not keen on IFAs • General election within 2 years

7.8 Sample SWOT 4

STRENGTHS ◄——————► **WEAKNESSES**

Purpose

Have been 'specialised'

Do not seem to have a vision or mission

Structure

Appears to be structured around products

(P5) (ea Co. - CM too?) Customer admin, computer operations, HR, finance, actuarial sections

Culture

Professionalism, integrity, secure	Old fashioned, gentlemanly, masculine

Profitability

£3.2bn T/O P.16			% of £4bn compensation (P4)
1999 overall business dominated by UK retail market			
UK	- 79% £2.528bn		
Europe	- 14% £448m	investment products	
Other countries	- 7% £224m	investment products	
Market value £107m			

People - management

We do not know - no information

Processes - business operations

We do not know - no information

Technology/task

Legacy computer systems

Influence/image of marketing in firm

Little evidence to support strategic marketing understood

Planning and control processes

Likely to be financial driven - budget planning
Financial controls - little other
Tactical

Current marketing strategy

Have specialised	Segmentation crude and based on what company can do not customer needs
No evidence strategic effort to position	

Brand and values

Strengths:

- Professional, established, secure, integrity
- Security, fulfilling aspiration, peace of mind, responsible
- Protection, provision, maximising future returns
- Specialists, financial efficiency, history
- Provenance, heritage

Weaknesses:

- CM less well known than new entrants
- Gentlemanly, old fashioned, masculine, remote?

Little concerned about who's perceptions these are!

MKIS and marketing research

Very broad, general and mainly secondary (old).
Almost no primary - apparently no database management providing customer information

STRENGTHS **WEAKNESSES**

Product

P 16 Wide range life assurance, pensions, investments

UK retail market	1999	£	1998
Personal pensions 19%	475m	475	25%
Company pensions 15%	375m	247	13%
Investments 38%	950m	646	34%
Offshore investments 28%	700m	532	28%
Total	2.5bn	1.9bn	
Wholesale	0.5bn	0.5bn	
International	186m	0.2bn	
(Europe £124m Other £62m)			

NOTE: We do not know if these are a strength or weakness

Price

Premiums paid either yearly or single payment
Average premium £602 (new policy) P20

NOTE: We do not know if these are a strength or weakness

Place

P7 P16 IFAs (£20.5bn?) retail market to consumers
P17 Specialist advisers (£0.5bn) whole market pension fund trustees (major pension schemes)
P17 Master distributors sell investment products inter'l (ex pats) markets (£0.2bn)

NOTE: We do not know if these are a strength or weakness

Promotion

We do not know

People

Can only assume good because of 5* rating but no real information

Processes

Can only assume good because of 5* rating BUT variety unconnected computer systems P6

Physical evidence

We do not know

8 ANALYSIS OF APPENDICES

8.1 The next step is normally to analyse and cross analyse the appendices following the format suggested in Chapter 8 Paragraph 2.3.

8.2 However, there are over 30 tables and charts in the appendices, not separately numbered. It does therefore make sense to list these in order of appearance and endeavour to categorise these into groups for subsequent further analysis.

8.3 You may then wish to analyse the appendices in groups rather than individually. Either way please do this **before** comparing your efforts with those that follow.

8.4 LIST OF APPENDICES (in order of appearance)

			Category
1	1	Consumer savings & Investments and Life Ass Cross Holdings, 97	Market segmentation
	2	Consumer Profiles of protection and savings products, 97	Market segmentation
	3	Consumer Profiles of Life Assurance (non mortgage), 97	Market segmentation
	4	Consumer Profiles of New Life Policy Holders, 97	Market segmentation
	5	Total New life, pension & annuity business UK 1985-97	Market size/trends by segment
	6	Payments made to life & pension policy holders 1985-97	Market size/trends by segment
	7	Life Assurance and Pension schemes - premium incomes 1993-97	Market size/trends by segment
	8	Consumer Profiles of pension schemes by main types, 97	Market-product segmentation
	9	Contributions to pension schemes - percentage of population 97	Product segmentation
	10	Acorn group product profiles	Product/household segmentation & trends
	11	Savings per household by type 1985-97	Product/household segmentation & trends
	12	Savings per household by type 1985-97 Annual changes	Product/household segmentation & trends
	13	Personal investments, total holdings by type 1985-97	Market/segment sizes and trends
	14	Investments per household, holdings by type 1985-97	Market/segment sizes and trends
	15	Investments per household, holdings by type 1985-97 Annual changes	Market/segment sizes and trends
	16	Relative consumer profiles of personal pension plans 1997 by type	Product positioning
	17	IFA Market Shares 1993-99 by premium type	Distribution trends
	18	Structure of IFA Channel 1998-2005 by IFA type	Distribution trends
	19	Employment structure forecasts 1996-2010	Demand drivers
	20	Population % over 60 by country 1990 and 2030	Personal financial planning drivers
	21	Consumer confidence estimates 95-98	Consumer buying behaviour
	22	Consumer financial knowledge, undated, by social class & age	Segmentation/ communications
	23	Brand triangle for Clerical Medical 1998	Branding/communications strategy
2	24	Legal issues & selected news items	Legal constraints/liberalisation
	25	Stakeholder pension rules - changes	New Product Development
	26	Halifax plans for the Internet	Distribution/communication channels
	27	Top groups to sell new stakeholder pensions	Competition

			Category
3	28	Company expense ratios 98	Competitor values & financial strengths
	29	Service quality awards 1999 - Investment, Life & Pension	Positioning re main competitors
	30	Financial strength ratings 99	Competitive positioning
	31	Clerical Medical Business Mix 98 and year to date Sept 99	Product Portfolio Analysis
	32	Annual Reports - Balance Sheet & P&L Account 99	Current financial situation

8.5 **Summary of appendices in groups**

(a) Appendix 1 contains various sub-groups which are mainly useful for establishing the segmentation variables, the segment sizes and their trends.

(b) However Appendix 1 contains other exhibits which can contribute to marketing strategy development in the following areas:

- Branding/communications
- Distribution
- Product positioning
- Consumer buying behaviour

(c) Appendix 3 contains data enabling Clerical Medical to benchmark itself against competitors on a variety of attributes.

(d) Appendix 3 exhibits include the accounts for 1999 and 1998 but two sets of figures is said to be insufficient to draw any meaningful conclusions.

(e) Appendix 2 is generally useful for NPD.

(f) All appendices corroborate and extend the data in the text and there are few if any, major anomalies.

8.6 Despite the difficulties, one group did, to their credit, make an attempt to analyse the appendices in a structured way, close to the format recommended. The group's effort follows - if you did as well, you can give yourself a pat on the back.

Appendix analysis

KEY ISSUES	APPENDICES (Chapter 18)	TEXT TO WHICH IT RELATES (Chapter 18)	POSSIBLE STRATEGIC OPTIONS
The insurance industry/ environment	Appendix 1 - p20-p21	(2.5/2.6) - The insurance industry/environment (2.7) - Demand analysis (2.20-2.21) - The role of the government	- Individual life insurance and pensions are increasingly yearly up until 1997. But payments have been increasing in respect of this.
Consumer profiles	Appendix 1 – TGI financial product profiles by ACORN Group 3.1 (a)-(c),(h),(i)	(2.23-2.24) Consumers + consumer typologies in the life of the pensions sector.	(64%) are males. In class C1, aged 25-34 with a non-contributory pension. Most people have had their policy for longer than one year. 56% of the population have any pension. The population of over 60 is growing and will move to 28% in the year 2030. The European populations are increasing in age 60+ as well. People are less confident about the plans that they are getting. Most people are not knowledgeable about what they are getting for their financial products.
Patterns of saving	Appendix 1 – p25-p26		Savings are up from 1985-1997 by £6,271 (71%).
Competition	Appendix 1 - p31	(2.9-2.13) - New entrants (2.26-2.28) - Competitiveness	IFA have a 69% share of the market and with annual premiums and 47% single premium share. Regional IFAs are going to be more popular although they will see a decline in market share from 45% to 40%.
	Appendix 3, (a) (b)		Norwich Union and Standard Life, have excellent service awards. Clerical Medical has moved up from three stars and hit the spot for a five star provider of customer service.
Clerical Medical - The brand	Appendix 1 Appendix 2 (c)-(f)		Values of the brand. Excellent customer service awards.
Legal issues	Appendix 2 (a)		Obstacles have been removed to trading in other European countries.
Corporate culture	Appendix 2, (c)	Other issues (2.25) - The role of IT (2.28-2.32) - Clerical Medical's markets	
Clerical Medical products/markets	Appendix 3 (g)		Investments from the majority of 34% in 1998 and in September 1999, 36% of products are investments.
Financial data	Appendix 3, (h)		Balance sheets show that total assets have increased to £24,849.70

20 Clerical Medical: Situational Analysis, Key Issues, Mission Statement, Broad Aims, Major Problems

1 THE STEPS YOU SHOULD TAKE

1.1 It is now time to move on to the next two steps.

CONSULT THE GUIDANCE NOTES IN CHAPTER 8 PARAGRAPHS 2.4-2.5
STEP 2.4 RECONSIDER YOUR PRÉCIS, MARKETING AUDIT AND SWOT ANALYSIS STEP 2.5 CONDUCT A SITUATIONAL ANALYSIS
ALLOW BETWEEN 2 AND 3 HOURS FOR COMPLETING THESE STEPS

1.2 When you have completed your situational analysis please compare it with the three specimens which follow.

2 SITUATIONAL ANALYSES

2.1 Situational analysis 1

I am Don Sherwood, a marketing consultant with considerable experience in industry sector analysis for a number of companies, retained by Clerical Medical to undertake an internal and external analysis for the Marketing Director James Broadbent. These analyses are intended to help Mr Broadbent develop future marketing plans.

I have located a variety of useful information on consumer profiles and the competitive positions of the various players in the sector to add to data gathered from consulting widely within the industry and within the Group.

Clerical Medical's (CM) situation is that of a medium sized player in life assurance, pensions and investments, which has very recently become a wholly owned subsidiary of the Halifax Group. Clearly Halifax will be looking for a return on their investment of £800m in the medium term.

CM's situation is really quite rosy. It operates in a market which has enjoyed considerable growth in the past, which appears set to continue into the medium-term future, albeit in a more intensively competitive environment. CM has reported a spectacular increase in income 99 over 98 to some £7 billion. The relatively small loss of £18m appears due to very large increases for future liabilities and appropriations.

CM have an excellent reputation for service through independent financial advisors and particularly target higher than average income people with specialised products. Since Halifax focus on a wider target market with a broader range there would seem some potential for synergy and cross-selling and CM could use Halifax for both market and product expansion at very little cost.

Decisions are needed with regard to marketing the new stakeholder pensions due to be launched under government pressure shortly and also how to modernise the IT systems and how to utilise the internet.

2.2 Situational analysis 2

The company is a professional and well established business which is under the protection of the larger Halifax group. Profits for both group and the company are down and the company, Group is making a loss of –18.1

The main products have not changed over the last year but they have changed in the percentages that they contribute:

'Offshore' products - increased by 2%
Individual pensions - increased by 5%
Group pensions - increased by 1%
Investments - increased by 2%

The biggest increase is in the amount of 'offshore' products and investments that are being sold - they account for most of the business.

The economic environment is facing a depressed savings market (so we are told, but we have not seen the figures for this), and a housing boom. Possible growth spurts that we need to think about are the introduction by the government of stakeholder pensions and the need to make insurance simpler and more understandable. In order to provide stakeholder pensions, insurance companies are going to have to become more cost-efficient, and economies of scale are becoming more important. Also the provision of a customer relationship management system that will offer us a competitive advantage over other insurance providers. The market environment is changing and we need to think about what we are going to offer for more self-employed people (flexible policies) and for the over 60s as the ageing population increases. We need to consider that more people are going to use independent financial advisors. We also need to consider the technological side of developments and need to become more system integrated and develop our e-commerce capabilities. We need to provide a service to IFAs if we are to sell to them - we need to treat them as our customers.

The key issues that we need to develop are:

1 Customer service to the IFAs as distribution channels are changing

2 Need to become more system integrated with e-commerce capabilities

3 Feed off the Halifax group and their customers

4 Consider our policies and a CRM for our customers - particularly the self employed and the over 60s. We need to sell them more policies

5 We must provide the stakeholder pension and explain our policies more/make them simpler

6 Target a specific range of clientele selling on our brand benefits and points

7 Make the business more cost-effective

8 Competitor information

2.3 Situational analysis 3

---

1 Clerical Medical (CM) faces many problems due to strategic wearout. Its marketing strategy is not suitable for today's competitive environment.

2 During the study a number of issues and points were raised to support this assertion.

3 CM is a traditional product-orientated organisation that has been in existence for 176 years.

4 CM is owned by the Halifax a key strength for both business expansion and financing.

5 The insurance market is mature and competitive and likely to follow the pattern of banking and car manufacture where the top 10% of companies have been them a 80-90% market share.

6 This means CM must grow from 3% to at least a 10% market share. CM is currently ranked 16th in terms of new business.

7 Reaching this higher market share will mean redefining its market.

8 CM is rated 5th on service by its customers, the IFAs. By dealing with end users via IFAs CM has lost direct contact with the consumer.

9 Insurance companies are currently seeking answers to four problems:

(1) Poor customer relationships with end users

(2) Cost savings to support profitable growth, lack of systems to do this

(3) New entrants in the form of brand extenders (Tescos) and bancassurers, possible mergers and acquisition

(4) Legal systems that do not support required business processes and new product development (stakeholder pensions as an example)

10 The future trend will be more involvement from the government due to the burden on welfare and state pension schemes.

11 This burden has been increased by an ageing population and less employer managed schemes.

12 As has been revealed by the additional information the industry regulator spurred by the government will be rigorous about ensuring new products such as stakeholder pensions meet all requirements criteria.

13 The current brand image is masculine and traditional. This brand needs to be developed to appeal to the newly affluent women pensioners and ABC1 households (Europe and UK).

The brand should be also targeted at IFAs and brand extenders. Brand extenders for wholesale products. The rationale is that this market will grow as Energis's did for internet source providers so we should service this market.

14 Using psychodemographics the brand should be positioning to be one of trust and security in the mind of the customer at all stages of the life cycle.

2.4 All three situational analyses demonstrate some overall grasp of the situation although there is not a great deal of consistency as regards the major issues. They also exhibit a degree of confidence in the sort of decisions that need to be taken. This is probably because the case is comparatively clear with few anomalies.

2.5 So how does your situational analysis compare with these examples? Were you able to confine yours to no more than a page of text?

3 DECIDE KEY ISSUES

READ THE GUIDANCE NOTES IN CHAPTER 8 PARAGRAPH 3.1
STEP 3.1 DECIDE THE KEY ISSUES
ALLOW 1 HOUR TO 1½ HOURS FOR THIS STEP

3.1 You are reminded that the next step is the most important one, since it has the most bearing on the likely examination areas.

3.2 You are also reminded to limit these to a **maximum of six** and that you might like to construct a list of candidate key issues which could then be ranked, as a way of doing this exercise.

3.3 Remember also the technique of parcelling up several minor issues into one major issue as described in Chapter 8 paragraph 3.1.

3.4 Now that you have completed this crucial exercise, please compare your conclusions with those produced by four separate sources as given on the next page.

3.5 You will note quite a reassuring degree of unanimity in these four separate sources as regards the issues themselves, although the rank orders differ.

3.6 **Clerical Medical: key issues**

Syndicate A1 1 No clear segmentation strategy 2 Outdated legacy systems - IT overhaul 3 Conflict - Internet and IFAs 4 Brand re-positioning 5 Customer relationship management 6 Achieving synergy with Halifax	*Syndicate B1* 1 Whether/how to launch stakeholder pensions 2 Target market expansion 3 Re-positioning 4 Future distribution strategy 5 Relationship marketing 6 Marketing research
Syndicate A2 1 Future competition - new entrants using the internet and from European Union 2 Low awareness of CM and its values among consumers 3 What to do about stakeholder pensions 4 Lack of information/marketing research 5 No clear marketing strategy 6 Feeding off Halifax	*Syndicate B2* 1 Lack of clear marketing strategy 2 Relatively high cost base versus competitors 3 New product development 4 Public relations - lack of awareness of brand 5 Positioning 6 Future synergies with Halifax

4 MISSION STATEMENT AND BROAD AIMS

CONSULT THE GUIDANCE NOTES IN CHAPTER 8 PARAGRAPHS 3.2 TO 3.3
STEP 3.2 DEVELOP A MISSION STATEMENT **STEP 3.3 DECIDE BROAD AIMS**
ALLOW ABOUT AN HOUR FOR EACH OF THESE STEPS

4.1 Remember that there should be consistency between your mission statement and your **broad aims**. Also try to limit the latter for **four** bearing in mind the need to convert these into quantified and time-scaled objectives at a later stage.

4.2 Having completed these two steps, you can now compare your results with those of the syndicates which follow.

4.3 **Syndicates' vision/mission statements**

Syndicate A	Our mission is to provide independent advisors with expertise, products and services which enable them to develop profitable relationships with their clients to satisfy their long-term financial ambitions.
Syndicate B	To continue to provide financial peace of mind to our chosen customers by providing the highest quality investment solutions, thereby creating stakeholder value.
Syndicate B1	To continue to be one of the longest established and financially strongest providers of pension, investment and life assurance to our distributors and end-customers within the UK and internationally, by building profitable lifelong relationships through excellent customer service and investment returns.
Syndicate D	Together with the Halifax, to be the market leader in the provision of customer-focused financial services, providing life-long financial security, peace of mind and return on investment to all customers through innovation, customer service and financial expertise.
Syndicate E	To build on our heritage of professional integrity, trust and technical outlook in an innovative way using the latest proven techniques. To maintain our commitment to customer and stakeholder needs and endeavour to become the most respected niche provider in the global investment industry.

4.4 (a) **Reminder of contents.** A mission statement should:

(i) Offer a statement of the organisation's purpose

(ii) State what the organisation wants to accomplish in the larger environment

(iii) Indicate the particular customer groups to be served, their needs and the technologies to be utilised

(b) **A clear mission statement:**

(i) Guides people in the organisation so they can work independently and yet collectively

(ii) Should not be too narrow or too broad

(iii) Should be specific, realistic and motivating

4.5 Other mission statement assessment criteria might be listed as follows.

- Generality versus limited focus (ie balance)
- Longevity
- Purpose
- Audiences - stakeholders
- Clarity - what business are we in? Boundaries (geographical, product areas)
- Brevity
- Ease of memorisation
- Credibility
- Consistency - with broad aims

Broad aims

4.6 The above five syndicates' broad aims are given below and are quite good in their relationship to the mission/vision statements made. **Not all the aims stated can be easily converted into SMART marketing objectives** and this is perhaps a weakness.

Syndicate A

1 To increase our market shares in our existing markets but also reach the mass market through the Halifax and its internet links
2 To further reduce our cost base
3 To improve the management of our relationships with IFAs and end-customers by integrating information flows allowing us to better understand the market and tailor products to changing needs
4 To re-position the brand as a forward thinking organisation that puts customer needs first

Syndicate B

1 To develop a more innovative, customer-orientated culture in terms of marketing style, CRM and integrated IT
2 To increase market shares by product differentiation and NPD
3 To maximise existing distribution channel and examine feasibility of direct marketing
4 To look for trading up opportunities with the Halifax customer base

Syndicate B1

1 To develop CRM through opportunities available, significantly the internet
2 To develop an integrated communications strategy which re-positions the brand
3 To increase international business by building on existing presence in higher growth markets
4 To exploit the opportunity of moving into the mass market of stakeholder pensions - with Halifax

Syndicate D

1 To develop internet technology so as to provide a better service whilst lowering costs
2 To use IT to develop better understanding of customers and improve relationships
3 To increase market share by market development
4 To create a clearer, better-known brand

Syndicate E

1 To achieve synergy through distribution channels - staff, IFAs and the internet - and the Halifax
2 To build upon existing brand values to achieve greater differentiation and communicate the brand more effectively
3 To move into stakeholder pensions - in co-operation with Halifax
4 To improve information systems

---

5 MAJOR PROBLEMS

CONSULT THE GUIDANCE NOTES IN CHAPTER 8 PARAGRAPH 3.4
STEP 3.4 IDENTIFY AND ANALYSE MAJOR PROBLEMS
ALLOW BETWEEN 2 AND 3 HOURS FOR THIS STEP

5.1 Remember to restrict yourself to six major problems in rank order.

5.2 Do not worry if your major problems relate closely with the key issues. This is quite usual.

5.3 Having done this, you can now compare your items/rankings with those of eight syndicates provided below.

5.4 **Clerical Medical: major problems**

				Rankings				
Item	*A1*	*B1*	*C1*	*D1*	*A2*	*B2*	*C2*	*D2*
1 How to harness the Halifax brand and customer base	2							5
2 Repositioning the CM and communicating its values/image		1	3		4	4	6	
3 Increasing market share against growing competition	1	6		4	3	2	1	
4 Whether to offer stakeholder pensions		5	1					4
5 How to exploit IT and the internet		2			6		5	
6 Whether to market direct as well as through IFAs				1	5	5		3
7 Customer relationship management	4	3	5			3	3	2
8 Insufficient marketing research						6		
9 Competition from new entrants, eg Virgin			6					
10 Negative PR								6
11 Increased regulation - UK and Europe	6			2				
12 International expansion				6	2			
13 How to maintain *profitable* growth	3		4	3	1		2	1
14 Market segmentation	5	4	2	5		1	4	

(a) Problems 13 and 3 are related and concern the setting and achievement of objectives so that it is understandable that they received high rankings.

(b) Problems 5, 6 and 7 are also related and rankings reflect concern over the future of IFAs as the sole distribution channel and how to retain their goodwill.

(c) Segmentation and brand re-positioning are then seen as further strategic problem priorities.

(d) Problems 1, 12 and 14 could be said to relate to market development.

5.5 It is wise to have a really good think here before finally making up your mind on what problems you plan will address and in what order.

5.6 You can also distinguish between problems in terms of overall objectives, overall strategies and the marketing mix.

5.7 Please remember that whatever you have listed on your own problem sheet should be addressed in your marketing plan.

21 *Clerical Medical Investment Group Ltd: Outline Marketing Planning*

This chapter contains the following guidance and plans.

1 INTRODUCTION: APPROACHING A MARKETING PLAN

1.1 You will, we hope, remember at least some of the rationale for producing an *outline* marketing plan prior to a detailed plan which is the final stage. If not then please consult the previous case **Acclaim** ie the start of Chapter 15. For your convenience we have repeated the basic notes below.

1.2 Experience shows that syndicates starting on the plan and working against time get bogged down on objectives for far too long, getting mixed up over **corporate objectives** and **marketing objectives**, and then between objectives, strategy and tactics. Tempers can get frayed and confidence lost. A technique we have successfully used to overcome this problem is to get syndicates to blitz through an **outline** plan first, taking a maximum of **one hour** to do this. You can then look at this outline to see that it is reasonably consistent and logical before committing yourself to detail. In this way you see the plan as a whole, whereas if you get straight into the detail you may never see the wood for the trees and never get to the end of your journey. What you are doing is creating a **framework** or a **skeletal plan**.

2 THE STEPS YOU SHOULD FOLLOW

2.1 These are of course the same as for the detailed marketing plan and are given below for your convenience.

CONSULT THE GUIDANCE NOTES GIVEN IN CHAPTER 8 PARAGRAPHS 3.5 TO 5.2
IN OUTLINE ONLY
STEP 3.5 DEVELOP QUANTIFIED, TIMESCALED OBJECTIVES **STEP 3.6 CONSIDER ALTERNATIVE STRATEGIES. SELECT THOSE MOST APPROPRIATE** **STEP 4.1 DRAW UP DETAILED TACTICAL PLANS COVERING THE MARKETING ORIENTATION** **STEP 4.2 DRAW UP A MARKETING RESEARCH PLAN** **STEP 4.3 CONSIDER ORGANISATIONAL ISSUES, CHANGES AND MARKETING ORIENTATION** **STEP 4.4 CONSIDER ORGANISATIONAL CULTURE AND NEED FOR INTERNAL MARKETING** **STEP 4.5 DETERMINE THE FINANCIAL/HR RESOURCE IMPLICATIONS OF YOUR PLANS** **STEP 4.6 ASSESS COSTS AND DRAW UP INDICATIVE BUDGETS** **STEP 4.7 DRAW UP SCHEDULES GIVING TIMINGS/SEQUENCE OF ACTIONS** **STEP 5.1 SPECIFY REVIEW PROCEDURES AND CONTROL MECHANISMS** **STEP 5.2 DRAW UP OUTLINE CONTINGENCY PLANS** **STEP 5.3 REVIEW YOUR COMPLETE MARKETING PLAN**
YOU WILL NEED ABOUT ONE HOUR TO DO YOUR OUTLINE

2.2 The outline plans were all drawn up by individual students and they each have their own strengths and weaknesses.

Example 1 covers a lot of ground and puts forward different marketing mixes for different strategies. This student has prepared a separate marcoms plan which is not shown. Many students/syndicates prepare separate special plans in anticipation of particular questions and you will find some examples of these in the next chapter.

Example 2 is a little more staccato and sketchy than the first example but is all right as an outline.

Example 3 is rather too generalised and over-wordy in parts but it does try hard on justification of strategic recommendations which is an important strength.

2.3 Hopefully your own outline will have combined the strengths of these three examples.

3 OUTLINE MARKETING PLAN: EXAMPLE 1

Mission and goals

3.1 **Mission**

To be a leading, specialist provider of financial security to our customers and long term value to our shareholders achieve by:

- A range of compliant and customer focused products
- Excellent relationships with our stakeholders

- Financial efficiency through the effective use of leading edge technology

3.2 **Corporate objectives**

1. To grow new business by 20% for each of the next three years
2. To increase the skills base by 10% within 2 years
3. To ensure that 90% of business continues to its full contract term
4. To maintain our 5* rating for customer service year on year

3.3 **Marketing objectives**

1. To obtain 50% of new business target from sale of stakeholder pensions in year 1
2. To achieve 15% of market share of corporate stakeholder pensions within 3 years
3. To improve and maintain two way communication flows between CM and IFAs over the next 3 years
4. To invest £25,000 on conducting a CRM audit in the next 12 months
5. To increase the average investment per individual by 5% in the next 3 years
6. To increase market share of the individual investment segment by 10% over the next 3 years by active targeting of the 'trust activist' sector

Segmentation

3.4 **Outline segmentation bases**

CM need to segment customers according to their financial objectives.

(a) Retirement planning (pensions)
(b) Wealth generation (investment)

3.5 **Retirement planning**

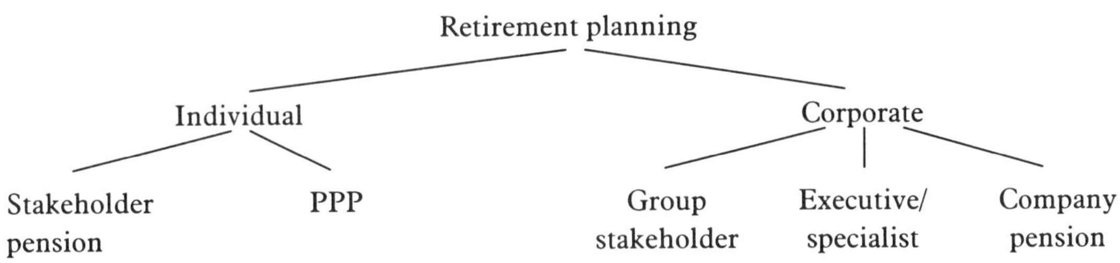

CM is already active in all but the stakeholder pension groups.

3.6 **Wealth generation**

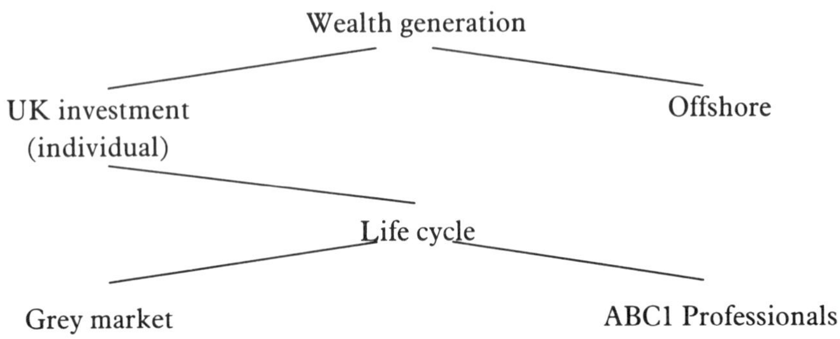

(a) Grey market characteristics

- +50 years
- 'Empty nesters'
- Financially secure
- Pension and disability needs already catered for

(b) ABC1 segment can be segmented further according to current macro environmental factors.

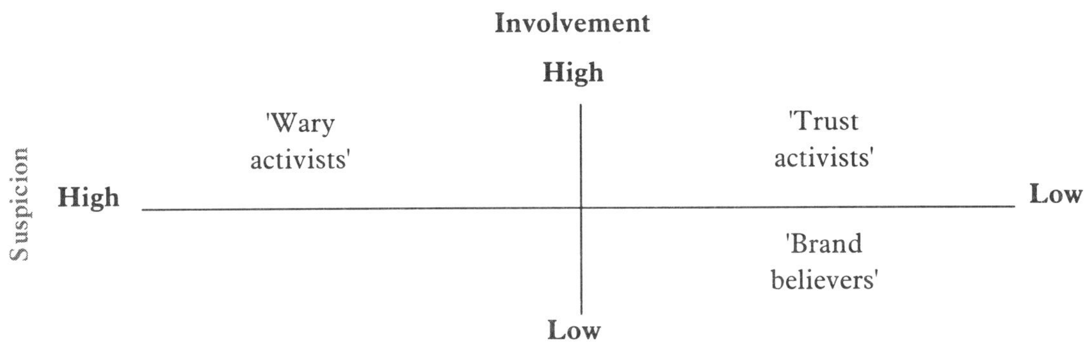

(i) Brand believers - Halifax customers

(ii) Wary activists - suspicious of IFAs and financial organisations

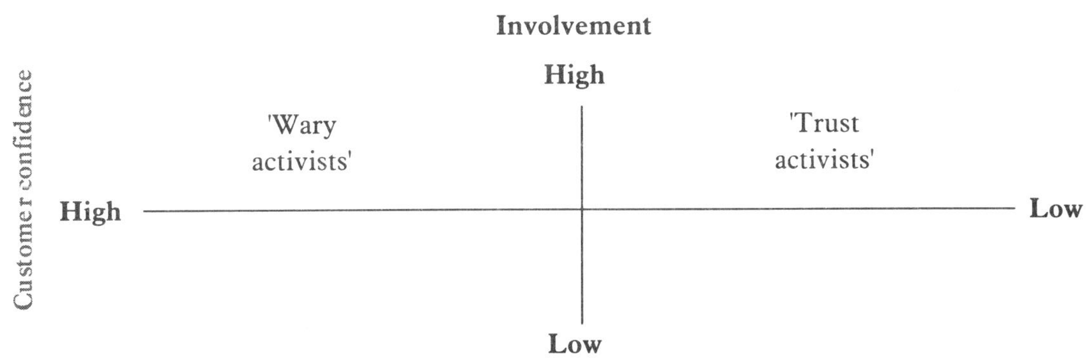

(iii) **Characteristics of trust activist - attractive to CM**

- Fastest growing segment
- Low suspicion of IFAs, low confidence due to purchasing complexities, high desired involvement - CM's flexible portfolio
- ABC1, professional, high net worth
- Active, seeking personalised solutions
- Want relationship with IFAs - CM's distribution channel

CM: have existing relationships with IFAs and are assessing benefits of implementing a CRM programme to enhance relationship building.

Strategy decisions

3.7 Strategy models

(a) Directional policy matrix

Market attractiveness	Degree of competition: Strong	Medium	Low
High			
Medium			
Low	Protect and refocus		

Therefore:

- Concentrate on attractive segments
- Defend strength
- Manage for current earnings

(b) Arthur D Little matrix

Competitive position	Embryonic	Growth	Maturity	Decline
Dominant				
Strong				
Favourable			X	
Tenable				
Weak				

Stages of industry growth

X Focus
Differentiate
Hit smaller firms

(c) Porter's strategic options

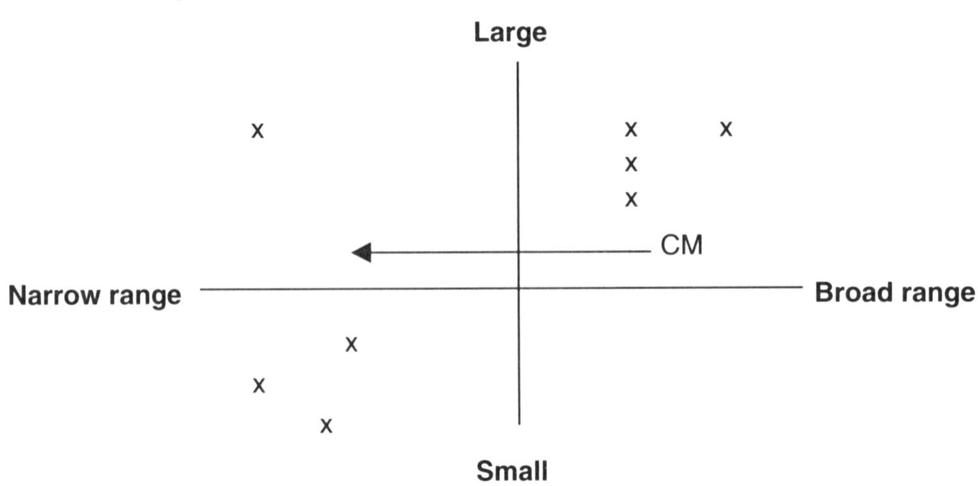

CM is smallest of players with large product range - difficult to compete in high fixed cost industry.

(d) **Direction of growth**

Ansoff's growth matrix

		Product: Existing	Product: New
Market	Existing	UK • Managed pension funds • UK Inv bonds • Life assurance • Pensions	Stakeholder Pension Unit linked bonds Career break bonds
	New	• Int'l expansion • E-commerce	• Sell admin + IT functions • Property investment + joint ventures

3.8 **Summary of proposed strategies**

Strategy	(2a) 9m - 1 yr	(1) 0-1 y (2b) 9-18m
	(3) 18-3yr (4) 2-3yr	5

(a) **Strategy 1**

- Sell corporate stakeholder pensions via IFAs
- Minimise threat of losing customers who want to switch
- Defensive, short term strategy
- Co-operation with Halifax over fund mgmt

(b) **Strategy 2a + b**

Target specific trust activist market segment with existing product portfolio via IFAs short-to-medium term.

(c) Introduce new product (eg career break bonds) and new unit-linked bonds for above segment.

Marketing mix for Strategy 1

3.9 **Product development**

(a) **Justification**

(i) **Reactive strategy**

By offering a stakeholder pension, we can also offer existing customers this product without need to switch providers (see corporate objective 3).

(ii) **Co-operative strategy**

Charges will be fixed so efficiency of operations is essential. No conflict with Halifax, who will be targeting individuals, therefore co-operation with them regarding portfolio and fund management will be desirable.

(b) **Product**

- Standardised product and advice and post sales support
- 5 star customer service
- Set regulations and minimum contributions as stipulated by the government
- Aimed at C2DE workforce via ABC1 employees

(c) **Price**

- Ceiling imposed by government
- No price competition after April 2001
- Before April 2001, market penetration pricing advised - important to gain volume in first few months as it is predicted that there will be low switching rate

(d) **Promotion**

(see separate MARCOMS plan)

(e) **Place**

- Sell via IFAs
- Account managers will maintain contact and provide contact point. Website will be used as an information source and can provide access to info such as investment return, fund value and projected pension etc.

(f) **Processes**

- CRM database/management (section 3).
- Combined fund management to ensure managed fund efficiency, annual fixed charge admin and ease of transfer between the 4 products for end users. This will also reduce the pressure of with profits bonds on CM.

3.10 **Marketing mix**

Strategies 2a and 2b

(a) **Product**

- Specialist product portfolio
  Flexible products offering personalised solutions
- New product development to complement existing range
- Possible reassessment of portfolio needed and in medium term product rationalisation may be required
- Advice and 5 star service

(b) **Price**

- Structure and delivery
- Premium price
- Paying for features
- Give customers choice how to pay fees and commission
- Be transparent - it is a sign of trust!

(c) **Promotion**

(See separate MARCOMS plan.)

(d) **Place**

- 100% IFA distribution
- Trust activists - respect and seek advice
- Marketing material available on the website

(e) **Processes**

- Website can be used as medium for on line access to product performance
- CRM (section 3)

(f) **Physical evidence**

- Website
- Literature
- Direct mail
- Statements
- Newsletters

(g) **People**

- Senior management - support needed for CRM and e-commerce development
- Employees - level of corporate, cultural adaptations
- Database analysts
- IFAs - high quality core team
- Account managers - for relationship building with IFAs

3.11 **Budgets**

(a) **Outline**

	£
Product design and profit testing	40,000
IT build and testing	495,000
Website design and build	515,000
Literature design, production and distribution	250,000
Recruitment	100,000
Training	250,000
Devise contact strategy	20,000
Launch advertising	240,000
Review and control contingencies 10%	190,000
	2,100,000

(b) The budgeted figure for strategies 1 and 2a + b outlined above is £2,100,000.

This takes into account the effort expected to be expended by CM's own staff as well as costs associated with hiring and outsourcing. Some savings may be possible using the know how or business relations already established by Halifax but this is unknown at present and so no allowances have been made.

(i) 1998 (most recent figures available) total value of new business was £140m equating to a market share of 2.9%.

(ii) Objective is to grow new business by 20% each year so expected increase over 3 year period is £102m.

(iii) The budgeted figure of £2,100,000 amounts to 2% approximately of the increase. This represents only a small addition to CM's acquisition expenses over the 3 years and will have minimal effect on CM's expense ratio.

3.12 Implementation

Gantt chart

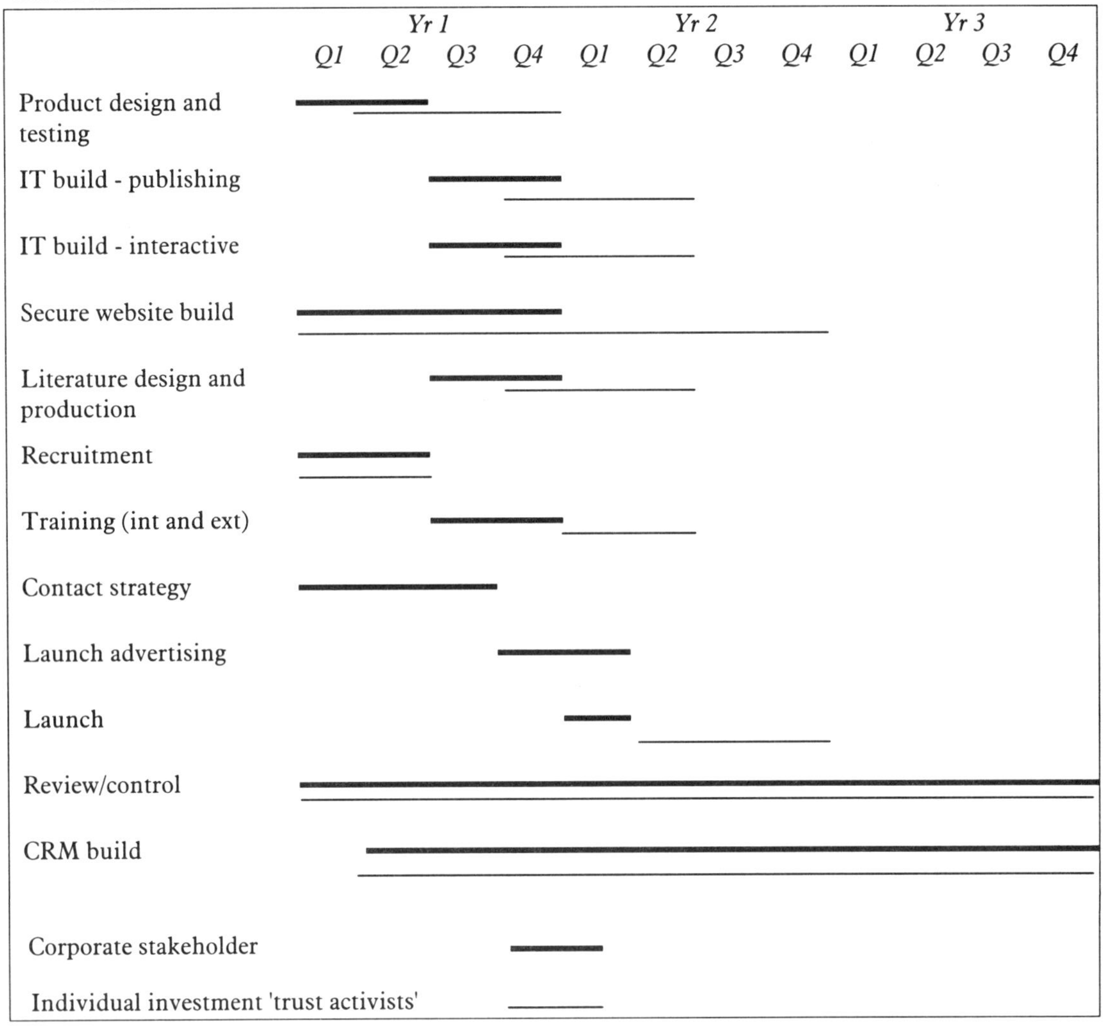

3.13 Control and contingencies

(a) Financial analysis of each business function will form the basis of measuring the success of CM.

(b) Success is measured against the initial objectives to control implementation of the plan, correcting deviations where necessary.

(c) Sales and market share objectives must be broken down and translated into sales targets for each account manager.

(d) CM's MIS must enhance accurate and timely information on the following key performance indicators.

 (i) Sales against targets weekly
 (ii) Business mix on a monthly basis, ie numbers of each contract type sold
 (iii) Persistency figures to monitor early transfers

(e) To highlight successes and under achievers, it should be possible to interrogate the system to provide a breakdown by account manager or region.

 (i) Proprietary research systems such as 'Touchstone' should be employed to measure support that CM receives from major IFAs compared to competition.

 (ii) To monitor competitors' activities in the macro environment, full product and market audits should be completed every 6 months.

3.14 Outline contingency plans are needed including

(a) Responding to competitor innovations careful analysis of competitor offerings
(b) Under-performance against sales targets
(c) Poor investment performance - changes to investment strategy or investment team

4 OUTLINE MARKETING PLAN: EXAMPLE 2

4.1 Vision

(a) CM should become a specialist in personal **wealth management.**

(b) **Rationale**

The market is crowded. CM's strengths are its ability to manage money, its established award winning reputation, its targeting of affluent and potentially affluent customers, **whilst practising a 'social conscience' in specific dealings with customers and various stakeholders.**

4.2 Broad aims

1	Increase market share
2	Become market led
3	Increase average lifetime value of customers
4	Make effective use of new technologies
5	Develop a brand strategy

4.3 Corporate objectives

1	To increase net profits by 5% by 2003
2	10% income to come from new products (which are less than 2 year old) by 2003
3	To withdraw from the mass market to minimise threat of new entrants and existing competition by 2002
4	*To work with the regulators to set new industry standards in terms of Code of Ethics by 2003*

4.4 Corporate strategy

(a) To move from the present cost-focus generic strategy (Porter) to a differentiation-focus strategy (multi-nicheing)

Positioning map

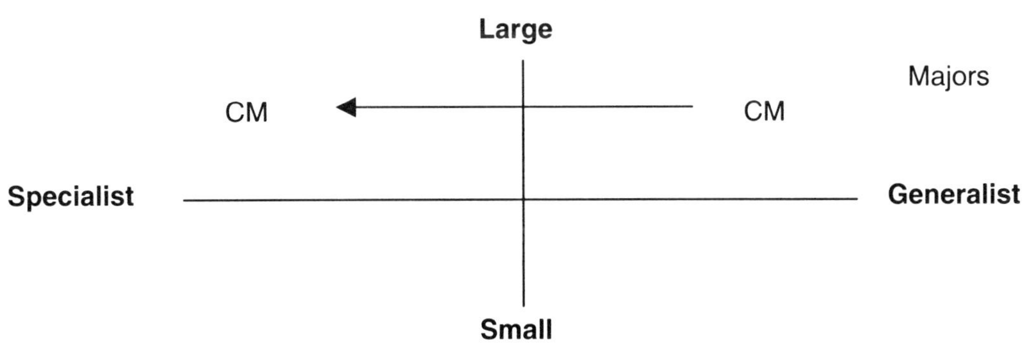

According to the directional policy matrix, Long Range Planning 1978, CM should 'try harder' given the company's strength.

(b) **UK market development**

CM should target customers with specialist needs (self-employed, professional women etc).

(c) **International market development**

Research overseas markets which match CM competencies/strength, by looking at market potential, accessibility and similarity.

(d) **Resources**

IT, CRM, HR and finance, the Halifax.

4.5 Marketing objectives

1. To reposition the brand and increase brand awareness to 40% by 2003
2. To increase sales by 15% by 2003
3. To increase market share to 5% by 2003
4. To improve customer retention by 2% by 2003.

4.6 Positioning

CM as a high service provider of tax-efficient and wealth-generating products *whilst having a 'social conscience'*.

4.7 Marketing strategy (using Ansoff)

Penetration years 1-4 by **organic growth** • Package products, eg pensions to include life insurance • Incentivise single premium payers to make regular payments • Gain customers from competition. Pay switching costs • Convert non-users 'doers' to become planners (see section 2).	**Product development** years 2-3 by **organic growth** • Improve product - make existing products more *flexible/transparent* • Competitive product, stakeholder 2002 (late to market advantage) • Breakthrough product life-time solutions (through superior relations CRM)
Market development years 2-3 by strategic alliances/shareholdings • EU • Internet (only for information) • Communication • Expatriates in other parts of the world	**Diversification** year 4 by strategic alliances To be investigated • Income protection • Health insurance • Consultants for Eastern Europe

4.8 **Porter: differentiation-focus** recommended

Justifications

- Size of CM
- Ability to sustain competitive advantage
- No compromise to CM's reputation
- Complements premium price policy
- Cost-focus does not suit CM's size, existing brand or existing distribution structure.

4.9 **Competitive strategy** (Kotler and Singh)

Recommend: Flank attack

In this way we will be engaging competitors in those products/segments where they are weak, ie segmentation flanking.

4.10 **Ethics**

By continuous improvements to transparency and ethics this can be a source of competitive advantage.

4.11 **Segmentation**

Current situation: by social class, target ABC1. This is unsophisticated, and does not demonstrate consideration of buyer behaviour, consumer goals and time horizons.

4.12 **Methods of segmentation**

(a) **Psychographic**

- Passive brand loyal
- Suspicious and confused
- Active seeking

(b) **Socio demographic**

- Dinky (dual income, no kids yet)
- Sitcom (single income, two children, oppressive mortgage)
- Pepsi (post-ecstacy, pre-senility)
- Snoppy (sensible older person with pension and insurance)
- SWEL (senior citizen with energetic lifestyle)

The family life cycle is a method of market segmentation (however sometimes it is difficult to decide which categories families belong to).

4.13 **Segmentation recommendation**

(a) **Time preference**

- Receive a certain amount of money immediately: 'doer'
- Receive a larger amount later: 'planner'

(b) **Current wealth** (socio-demographic data and family life cycle indicate the levels of disposable income).

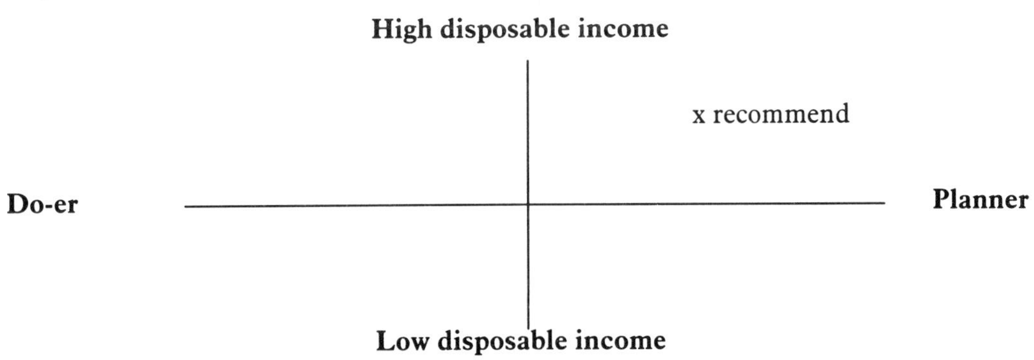

(c) Need to research life-time value of these segments, extensive levels of customer service required, source of competitive advantage, supports brand image.

(d) **Implications**

(i) Internal marketing programme and training

(ii) Management of IFA

(iii) Develop effective branding

(iv) Target segments - differentiated targeting strategy

- Go getting career women
- Go getting professionals (trainees)
- Entrepreneurial self employed

4.14 **Marketing mix**

(a) **Place**

Route to market for UK consumers: independent financial advisers (IFAs)

(b) **Product**

	Year
• Add value through promoting advice service to IFA (extranet)	1-2
• Extend maturity stage of complex products by making them more flexible	1-2
• Adapt products for overseas markets	2-3

(c) **Price**

	Year
• Premium - as initial stage of PLC for lifetime solutions of other products	2-3
• Competitive - stakeholder pensions (but consider Halifax's view)	2-3
• Increase commission to IFA for penetration strategy	1-2
• Adapt price for o/s market	2-3

Promotion (see separate plan, communication strategy)

(d) **People**

	Year
• Internal marketing	1-3
• Poach staff from competitors	0-2
• Training IFA/staff on new products	

4.15 **Recommendations**

CM should monitor the situation. **Further to a new pensions survey recently published, on stakeholder friendly pensions there may be a 'late to market advantage' as CM should consider benchmarking themselves against the '5' successful companies who measure up to the criteria.**

4.16 Schedules and budgets

	Yr 1	Yr 2	Yr 3	% of annual budget
Activity				
Market research	✓			15
Training and development	✓	✓		10
IFA training and development		✓	✓	10
Internet	✓	✓	✓	2
Internal marketing	✓	✓	✓	1
IFA CRM		✓	✓	10
IFA extranet	✓	✓	✓	5
Consumer CRM		✓	✓	10
Internet consumer info		✓	✓	10
IFA management system to form MIS		✓	✓	10
Brand re-positioning and development	✓	✓	✓	10
Contingency				10
				112%
MkIS (separate IT budget)				20

Note additional funding may be required from Halifax.

4.17 Controls

To be reviewed on an on-going monthly basis.

- Consumer awareness
- Customer satisfaction survey
- IFA satisfaction
- *Independent ethics review '6 monthly'*
- Benchmarking (6 monthly)
- Sales
- PIMS
- Expense ratio

5 OUTLINE MARKETING PLAN: EXAMPLE 3

5.1 Mission statement

To become the leading provider of pensions and life assurance in our chosen markets, providing a high quality in all our products and services, making Clerical Medical the choice of the professional.

5.2 Marketing aims

1. Actively encourage employee participation in the achievement of the company's goals
2. Build stronger relationships with all of our customers to develop trust and loyalty
3. Strengthen Clerical Medical's brand image and reposition the brand from its current image ('old-fashioned, masculine, gentlemanly') in order to appeal to different segments
4. Maintain existing distribution channels and work with them to maximise revenue. Develop new channels in an effort to be more accessible to the end customer

Objectives and issues

5.3 Corporate objectives

1. Increase operating profit by 10% per annum
2. Reduce operating costs as % of profit to 14% by 2003
3. Increase operating profit as % of premiums by 2% per annum

5.4 Marketing objectives

1. To increase sales revenue by 30% by the end of the three year period
2. To develop chosen segments in order to increase new business and to increase market share by 3% at the end of year 3
3. To develop methods of direct distribution that will complement our existing channels and provide at least 15% of the company's sales revenue by the end of the 3 year planning period

5.5 Statistical overview of corporate objectives

	1998	1999	2000	2001	2002	2003
Operating profit (£m)	492.4	1,840.1	2,024	2,226	2,449	2,694
Operating expenses as % profit	40.4	19.8	18	17	16	14
Operating profit as % of premiums	19.2	56	58	60	62	64
Premiums (£m)	2,566.1	3,283.1	2,490	3,710	3,950	4,209

5.6 Key issues

- E-commerce potential
- Distribution strategy and relationship with intermediaries
- Stakeholder pension; should we provide it?, who do we target? and how do we position it?
- Potential for geographic expansion
- Special segmentation, targeting and positioning
- Branding
- Need for investment in customer focused IT systems
- Development of CRM

Strategies

5.7 Porter's 3 generic strategies

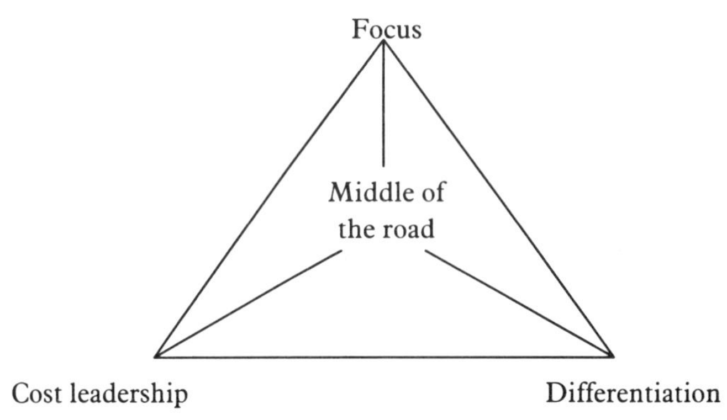

5.8 Clerical Medical's generic strategy

(a) From the information gathered so far, it would appear that the best strategy for Clerical Medical is one of focused differentiation.

(b) This means that the company will concentrate its efforts on one or a small number of segments and will create a strong and specialist reputation.

5.9 Why should CMIG pursue this strategy?

(a) CM Already has history of targeting higher net worth individuals with a more specialist product range; therefore knowledge of the market should be good.

(b) Will enable company to concentrate its efforts and therefore face less expenditure than if it pursued the other options.

Given the clear needs that the business has currently for an improved IT system, greater brand promotion and better CRM a less costly strategy is recommended so that the company can build on these basic needs and put itself in a position of strength from which it can attack wider segment in the future should it wish to do so.

(c) The company's size and financial strength would not support a cost leadership or broad differentiator approach.

(d) CMIG can build its brand and reputation for being specialists.

(e) Being a 'nicher' can enable it to differentiate itself from its closest competitors and create barriers to entry.

5.10 Product-market strategies

The tool used for deciding on CMIG's product market strategy is the Ansoff matrix. Please see overleaf for a more detailed outlook.

Products

Existing markets	**Market penetration** • More purchasing and usage from existing customers → cross selling • Gain customers from competitors • Convert non customers in the same segments into customers • Improve personal contact • Reduce surrender/switching	**Product development** • Financial consultancy B2B consumer • University funds and school funds management • Non financial premium investments (works of art, antiques)
New markets	**Market development** • Broaden distribution channel • New segments - young people high disposable income - professional women • Global expansion • B2B stakeholder pensions • Self employed (high income)	**Diversification** • Mass market stakeholder pensions • Reinsurance • Consultancy • Mortgages loans • Banking services

(a) At this stage Clerical Medical should pursue the market penetration and market development strategies. A diversification strategy would prove too costly and product development although not as costly would require higher financial investment in the short term than is advisable.

(b) Market penetration and market development strategies will allow the company to consolidate and focus on its existing markets and key competence. In the short term this is costly and involves less risks.

5.11 Stakeholder pensions

(a) Stakeholder pensions will have a huge impact on the life and pensions market.

(b) In CMIG's case it is something the company should steer clear of in the short to medium term in terms of a mass market approach that could provide on a B2B basis. This is for the following reasons.

(i) Financial strength not strong enough to support mass market approach

(ii) Systems are not in place to enable it to do MkIS

(iii) Brand needs building in short term and CRM and intermediary relationship needs to be addressed

(iv) All the above will be fairly costly and stakeholder pension may add too much pressure on company cash flows

(v) Business-to-business option enables CMIG to gather information and learn about product

(vi) Segment is smaller and therefore costs and effort to reach it is less

Segmentation

5.12 Segmentation matrix

Segment name	Benefit sought	Demographic strength	Behavioural characteristic	Personality	Lifestyle
Professional women	Personal and family security	Aged 30-55	Seek security of well known brands	Independent career	Conservative
Self employed, high income	Flexibility, family coverage	35-55	Flexible, tailored product ROI	Independent	Conservative
IFAs	Quality, flexibility	Dominant, powerful	Information seeks, value/ benefit	Objective	Sociable
Master distributors	Quality, flexibility, relevance	Specialist. Good market knowledge	Value/benefit	Objective	Sociable
Medium sized companies	Employee protection and satisfaction	50 plus employees	Driven by government regulation	Reluctant purchasers	Price and benefit-driven
Young upwardly mobile	Potential to increase wealth	25-40	Risk takers	Single, high self involvement	Active

5.13 GE matrix

300	200	100	
	High * women Self employed	Medium * young upwardly mobile	Low
200		* Medium sized company	
100			

(BPP Note: In this example the candidate has not marked up the matrix, and so it is, on the surface, meaningless.)

5.14 **Perceptual map for CMIG**

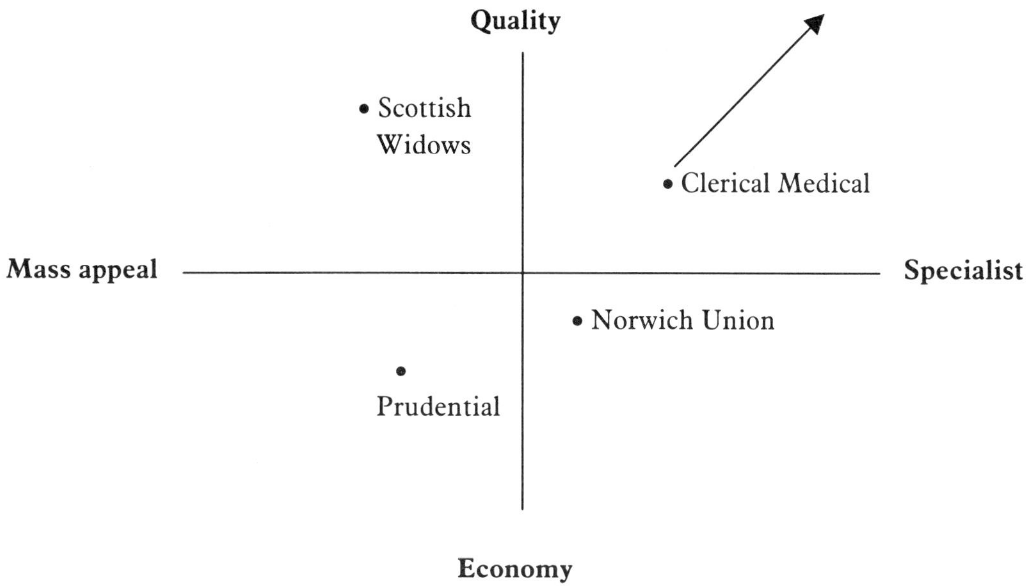

5.15 **Processes and systems**

(a) Up to date and improved MkIS should be developed to deal with the need for better customer profiling and for greater market research

(b) CMIG must ensure data is accurate and adequate for all segments

(c) Development of a promotional campaign to be implemented across all markets

5.16 **Controls**

(a) Intermediate goals and individual targets

(b) Quarterly reviews of performance with awards for the best performer who has lived up to CMIG's values and produced the most revenue

(c) Standards set from the start to measure performance

(d) Continuous assessment of the plan and its performance to discover any deviations which should be corrected

(e) Regular staff and customer feedback through surveys and focus groups

(f) Monitor competitor performance against success and performance of CMIG plan to see what steps might be needed to protect the company and plan from competitor attack

22 Clerical Medical Investment Group Ltd: Detailed Marketing Planning

This chapter contains the following plans, produced by CIM students in the course of their exam preparation

1 Introductory note: the steps you should follow.

2 Detailed marketing plan: example 1

3 Detailed marketing plan: example 2

4 Stakeholder pensions: launch plan

5 e-commerce plan

6 customer relationship management plan (1)

7 customer relationship management plan (2)

1 INTRODUCTORY NOTE : THE STEPS YOU SHOULD FOLLOW

1.1 At this point we need to advise that whereas a complete marketing plan is intended to cover you for all eventualities, it cannot of course provide all the detail that might be needed for a specific examination question. You will therefore have to add detail as required in the examination itself. Moreover, the CIM reserves the right to introduce additional material to you in the examination hall and normally will do so.

1.2 However, in anticipation of examination questions signalled in the case study, some syndicates will prepare extra material on, say, organisations or financial implications or marketing research. You have already been introduced to this idea in previous chapters. Examples of such extra material have been included in this chapter in the form of subsidiary plans.

1.3 Two detailed marketing plans have been included as quite good efforts to develop creative and convincing marketing plans, although ideally there should be **more justification** for the recommendations made and more on marketing research.

1.4 Hopefully, these two detailed plans and subsidiary plans combined with the three example outline plans already reviewed will stimulate your own ideas and confidence in tackling your second **mock exam** coming up in the next chapter.

CONSULT THE GUIDANCE NOTES GIVEN IN CHAPTER 8 PARAGRAPHS 3.5 TO 5.2
STEP 3.5 DEVELOP QUANTIFIED, TIMESCALED OBJECTIVES **STEP 3.6 CONSIDER ALTERNATIVE STRATEGIES. SELECT THOSE MOST APPROPRIATE** **STEP 4.1 DRAW UP DETAILED TACTICAL PLANS COVERING THE MARKETING MIX** **STEP 4.2 DRAW UP A MARKETING RESEARCH PLAN AND MKIS** **STEP 4.3 CONSIDER ORGANISATIONAL ISSUES, CHANGES AND MARKETING ORIENTATION** **STEP 4.4 CONSIDER ORGANISATIONAL CULTURE AND NEED FOR INTERNAL MARKETING** **STEP 4.5 DETERMINE THE FINANCIAL/HR RESOURCE IMPLICATIONS OF YOUR PLANS** **STEP 4.6 ASSESS COSTS AND DRAW UP INDICATIVE BUDGETS** **STEP 4.7 DRAW UP SCHEDULES GIVING TIMINGS/SEQUENCE OF ACTIONS** **STEP 5.1 SPECIFY REVIEW PROCEDURES AND CONTROL MECHANISMS** **STEP 5.2 DRAW UP OUTLINE CONTINGENCY PLANS** **STEP 5.3 REVIEW YOUR COMPLETE MARKETING PLAN**
YOU WILL NEED BETWEEN 15 AND 18 HOURS TO DO THIS MAJOR TASK

2 DETAILED MARKETING PLAN: EXAMPLE 1

Marketing audit - macro

2.1 PEST analysis

Political • Government is encouraging private stakeholder pensions • Pension mis-selling - high profile • European Union: freedom of movement. Will we join the Euro? • Taxation, legislation, regulation - FSA and PIA • Rising costs, due to more provisions for compensation	**Economic** • Euro, single currency and stakeholder pensions → more cost reduction and rationalisation • Mature life assurance market within the UK - trend towards consolidation • Stock market volatility/strong pound • Long term products - resilient to changing economic circumstances • PEPs/ISAs/tax free products • High costs of training and compliance
Social • Demographics - ageing population • Flexible working practices • Changing attitudes to responsibility • Repay debt rather than savings • Poor understanding of financial products especially with the lower classes and younger people • Poor perception of the investment industry	**Technology** • Internet development • Databases allow profiling of target markets • High IT investment required • Simple, direct methods attractive to politicians and customers • E-business, e-CRM, integrated customer relationship management

Marketing audit - micro

2.1 The market

- Pensions, long-term savings and investments for individuals
- Links with Europe and rest of world (but not global)
- £18.6 billion invested in life assurance in the UK at end of 1998. Net premiums = 7% GDP
- Still no level playing field in EU regarding taxation, legislation and regulation
- Trend towards consolidation

2.2 Competitor profile

- Fragmented, 200 authorised life assurers - no company has over 10% market share
- Includes 60 'large' providers
- Top ten (including CMI) have 46% market share, 52% assets
- New entrants: 10 new bancassurers (15% of life and pensions market), medical insurers offering life assurance and protection products, providers of consumer products such as M&S, Virgin, Direct Line
- Competitive environment - oversupply outstrips growth in demand
- New and agile competitors can exploit opportunities
- Clear trend of consolidation, but brands are retained for particular product markets and customer types
- In spite of brand building etc, companies like CMI are less well known than new entrants such as Virgin
- CMI doubled its market share to over 3% since 1996

2.3 Consumer typologies

- **Passive, brand loyal** - implicitly trust well-known brands
- **Suspicious and confused** - do not trust advisers. Prefer to buy direct and select products based on their own assessments
- **Active, seeking personalised solutions.** This is important sub-segment of the broad ABC1 category: professional people, self employed professionals, managers or directors, professional women, career professionals such as teachers, policemen, nurses, librarians, student professionals

2.4 Micro environment Porter - now

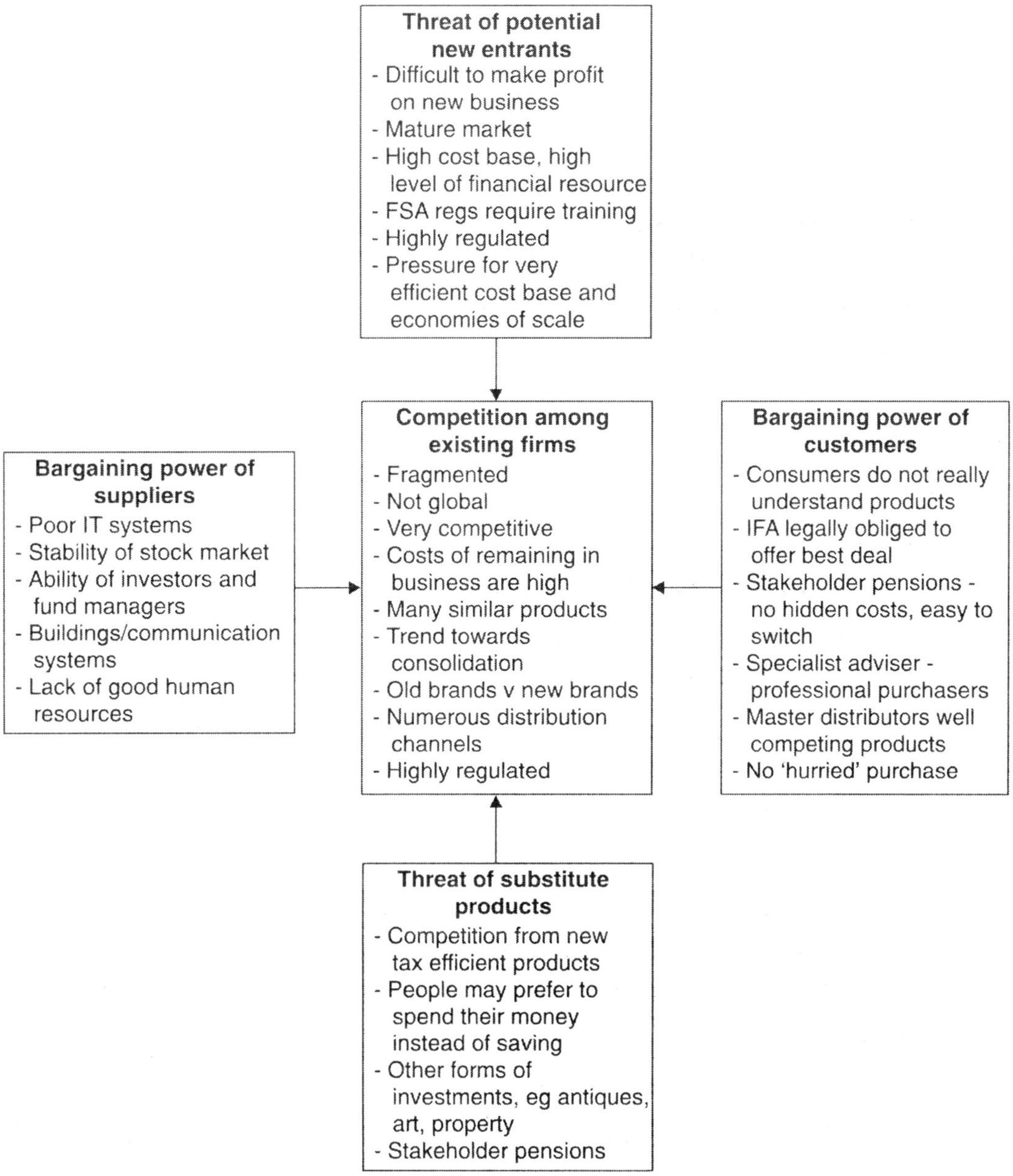

Threat of potential new entrants
- Difficult to make profit on new business
- Mature market
- High cost base, high level of financial resource
- FSA regs require training
- Highly regulated
- Pressure for very efficient cost base and economies of scale
Bargaining power of suppliers
- Poor IT systems
- Stability of stock market
- Ability of investors and fund managers
- Buildings/communication systems
- Lack of good human resources
Competition among existing firms
- Fragmented
- Not global
- Very competitive
- Costs of remaining in business are high
- Many similar products
- Trend towards consolidation
- Old brands v new brands
- Numerous distribution channels
- Highly regulated
Bargaining power of customers
- Consumers do not really understand products
- IFA legally obliged to offer best deal
- Stakeholder pensions - no hidden costs, easy to switch
- Specialist adviser - professional purchasers
- Master distributors well competing products
- No 'hurried' purchase
Threat of substitute products
- Competition from new tax efficient products
- People may prefer to spend their money instead of saving
- Other forms of investments, eg antiques, art, property
- Stakeholder pensions

2.5 Micro environment Porter - 2010

(a) Threat of new entrants

- Wide availability of trained and experienced personnel
- Mature market
- Easy to acquire e-data on customers' profiles
- More efficient cost base
- Big players
- Economies of scale will exist
- Lower margins for some products

(b) Existing market

- Fewer but bigger suppliers
- European/global
- Increase in flexible products
- E-commerce main driver of business
- More direct selling methods by policy providers

- Pan European harmonisation of regulations
- Lower margins

(c) **Buyer power**

- Older population, fewer young people
- Buyers better informed
- European/global providers
- Wide product range
- Consumers will want value for money - affects profitability

(d) **Supplier power and threat of substitution**

Unchanged

Internal audit

2.6 **Corporate**

(a) **People**

- Rated excellent (5th and 6th) for various elements of customer service
- General lack of entrepreneurial behaviour – CM need more creative and innovative people if they are to compete
- FSA requires investment companies to show integrity, skill, care and diligence

(b) **Process**

- In 1999 total value of CMI business was sold through IFAs
- IFAs must select best product from across the market
- Distribution takes place through numerous channels and each company has its own customer administration, computer operations, human resources, finance and actuarial sections – this is inefficient

(c) **Finance**

- Regulation has added to costs in the industry
- If CMI is to pursue stakeholder pensions, major investment in IT is required
- CMI has relatively low expense ratio within the business, both for acquisition and other costs
- CMI has an AA rating according to Standard and Poor - 'very strong' financial security characteristics
- CMI made a loss in 1999 - may be attributed to prudence for long term provisions

2.7 **Marketing**

(a) **Strategy**

- CMI targets net worth individuals through IFAs with a more specialist range of products
- Marketing strategies are generally not clear in the industry. Most companies have a variety of products and spread management, marketing and financial resources too thinly across channel and customers

(b) **General marketing**

- Greater significance of marketing for stakeholder pensions - standardised products

- Current tend to is retain brands for particular product markets and customer types

(c) **Systems**

- Non-integrated customer database
- Legacy systems - policy based - makes it difficult to build customer based systems
- New and better IT platform required for stakeholder pensions

(d) **Productivity**

- Productivity of distribution channels affected by shake out due to FSA regulatory decisions

- CMI rank 16th for new business in the league tables over the last decade

2.8 **Mix**

(a) **Product**

Four main product areas

- Pensions - growth market, although business in this area has fallen by 5% for CMI over the 9 months to September 1999

- Group/corporate pension plans

- Life assurance (present under investments and pensions)

- Investments *plus* offshore investments

(b) **Price**

- Commission to intermediary
- High base costs so 20% of premiums are used to cover expenses
- No hidden cost with stakeholder pension - needs very efficient cost base

(c) **Distribution**

- Mainly IFAs (good rating)

- If IFAs are to retain dominant position, they will need to react quickly to the changes and pressures in the market

- Specialist advisers in international markets

- Master distributors in international markets

- Internet presence through Halifax

- Regulation has reduced distributors and constrained the industry

- Direct writers are attractive to politicians because they seem to offer a simple proposition

(d) **Promotion**

Internet, IFAs, recommendation/word-of-mouth, press - financial pages, public relations

2.9 CMI SWOT analysis

Strengths	Weaknesses
• Financial backing of the Halifax • Low expense ratio • Rated excellent for customer service • Brand image for upper class/professionals • AA rating by Standard and Poor • Presence in Europe and international markets	• Assume CMI has legacy systems • High base costs • Marketing strategies often not clear, lack of customer focus, segmentation • Possible lack of innovation, reflected by brand image • Relatively undifferentiated products • Only one route to market (IFAs)
Strong base to work from	Need to improve marketing orientation, and reduce costs
Opportunities	**Threats**
• Changing demographics • E-business/internet • Company pensions • International and European markets • Existing customer base - cross well • Stakeholder pensions could provide growth	• New 'branded' financial services providers • New agile players, no legacy IT, could exploit 'greenfield' opportunities • Pressure for very efficient cost base and economies of scale • Regulation compliance and subsequent costs • Government and public mistrust • Reliance on intermediaries
Produce a marketing plan	Increase product range and brand awareness

2.10 Mission statement

To be the trusted and preferred provider of life-time, flexible investment solutions through our commitment to customer service and quality products.

2.11 Aims

1 To continue to increase market share

2 To develop new distribution channels

3 To be perceived as a provider of modern and relevant investment products

4 To improve competitiveness through enhanced efficiency measures

Objectives

1 To increase market share to 6% by 2005(1)

2 To develop 20% of new business via non-IFA channels in the next four years (2)

3 To break even by 2001 and achieve £20 million in profit in 2003 (3 & 4)

4 To be in the top three companies in terms of investment product service ratings by 2005 (1 & 2 & 3 & 4)

2.12 Choice of strategy - differentiation

(a) Justification

- Broad market
- Cost leadership unwise in view of pressure for industry to reduce base costs and need for provisions
- Market characterised by relatively undifferentiated products and services

(b) Differentiating variables

- Customer focus, low costs base and good fund performance
- Image of trust, quality and excellent customer service

Segmentation

2.13 **Individuals**

(a) **Details**

- 21-45
- Male/female
- ABC1 + self employed
- £18k+

(b) **Targeting**

Above plus: buyer readiness, benefits sought, critical life events, attitude

(c) **Positioning**

Through IFAs, clear information, well-managed, efficient purchase process, added value via customer service

2.14 **Organisations - other group pensions only**

(a) **Details**

- Medium to large
- Clear information provision, trustworthy, integrity
- CRM and high level of service required
- Flexible, modern and relevant

(b) **Positioning**

Informative, trustworthy, excellent service, well managed, relevant.

2.15 **Brand components Clerical Medical - now**

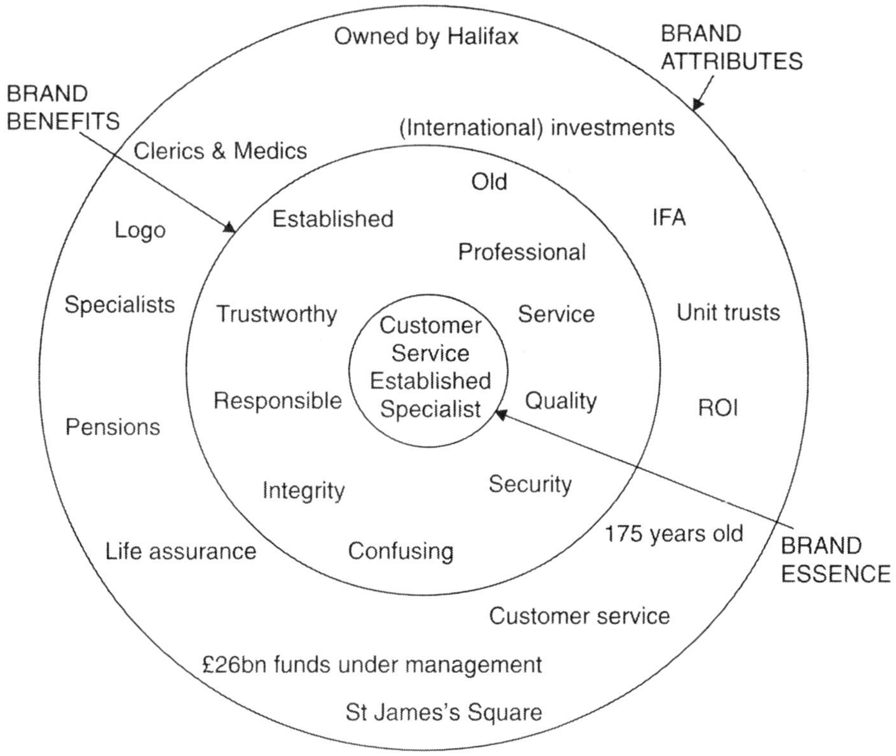

Clerical Medical - 'The choice of the professional'

2.16 Product/market expansion grid

Intensive growth strategies - Ansoff

	Current products	New products
Current markets	*Withdrawal - from selected markets* MARKET PENETRATION 1 Develop CRM with current customers to ensure life-long relationship 2 Develop CRM with IFAs to develop greater awareness of CM products 3 Consolidate through staff training and development in all service rating elements 4 Implement new IT system that allows data mining and targeting for cross sales	PRODUCT DEVELOPMENT 1 Develop more flexible products to suit people's changing lives 2 Introduce stakeholder pensions *3 Develop new products targeted at specific groups, eg ethical investments, pensions for females etc*
New markets	MARKET DEVELOPMENT *1 Target C2 DE social classes* 2 Target youngest age group (21-25) 3 Target Halifax customers 4 Develop new distribution channels, eg internet and direct sales options *5 Enter new countries in Europe* *6 Enter new 'other' countries*	*DIVERSIFICATION* *1 Acquisition of foreign companies* *2 Buying of IFAs*

Italics = Not selected

2.17 Clerical Medical - Marketing strategy and mix statements

Strategy	CRM to IFAs	CRM to end users	Launch stakeholder pensions	New distribution channels	Develop new and flexible products
Competitive advantage	Differentiation: • Customer focus • Financial strength • Good performance	Differentiation: • Customer focus • Low costs base • Good fund performance	Differentiation: • Customer focus • Low cost base • Trustworthy image	Differentiation: • Customer focus • Low costs base • Good fund performance	Differentiation: • Customer focus • Low cost base • Good fund performance
Target market	Registered IFAs	• ABC1 + self employed • 21-44 • Male/female • £18K • (Non actively to other end users via stakeholder pension)	• Companies with no previous interest in pensions - medium to large • Individual, via employers	• Individuals and businesses with little time. Confident not to seek advice. • Innovators, early adopters and young	• 21-44 but 21-25 in particular • ABC1 + self employed £18k
Positioning	Trusted provider of flexible investment solutions	For a lifetime of opportunities	Trusted provider of flexible investment solutions	Accessible, modern and relevant	Accessible, modern and relevant
Sales objectives	To increase market share to 6%		To increase market share to 6% by 2005: ready to market April 2001 Website/on-line applications by April 2001	To develop 20% of new business via non-IFA channels in the next four years	
Business direction	Market penetration	Market penetration	NPD	Market development	NPD
Product/service	Good performance Modern, relevant, accessible	Good performance Modern, relevant, accessible	Standardised - added value through customer service	Good performance Simple, accessible and relevant	Good performance Specialised, flexible and accessible
Price	Competitive packages	Competitive packages	Outlined by government but competitive due to customer service and low cost base	Competitive due to customer service	Competitive due to customer service
Place	Internet Direct mail	IFA Internet Direct mail Direct selling Halifax	IFAs Direct mail Direct selling Internet	Internet	IFAs Direct mail Direct selling Internet Halifax

Strategy	CRM to IFAs	CRM to end users	Launch stakeholder pensions	New distribution channels	Develop new and flexible products
Promotion - see communications table	Personal selling, PR, promotional literature Ads in sector magazine	Advertising in TV and press, promotional literature, PR Corporate advertising/ sponsorship Direct marketing	No specific advertising. Via IFAs to companies. PR. Promotional CD ROM to employers and employees	Corporate advertising to raise awareness. Clear, understandable promotional literature	Corporate advertising to raise awareness. Clear, understandable promotional literature
People	Trained in CRM techniques and products. Additional resource to support IT and key account management. All staff understand the brand and business aims.	Trained in CRM techniques and products. Additional resource to support IT development. All staff understand the brand and the business aims.	Trained in CRM techniques and stakeholder product. Additional resource to support IT development. All staff understand the brand and the business aims.	Excellent IT support and expertise required. All staff understand the brand and the business aims.	Innovators - new product development expertise Market analysis and CRM All staff understand the brand and the business aims.
Physical evidence	Clear and relevant literature. Modern, accessible, simple to use website. Logo	Clear and relevant literature. Modern, accessible, simple to use website. Help line IFAs, website, logo	Product literature IFAs, website, logo	• Logo • Website • Marketing communications	• Logo • Website • Marketing communications literature
Process	Key account management • Business process re-engineering to simply processes • Ease of access	Simple, clear, straightforward • Via IFA, internet or direct • Help line • Key account managers for IFAs	Customer visits website or IFA to gain further info and sign on	Simple, clear, straightforward • Additional resources to manage new business • Highly trained sales support staff	• Simple, clear, straightforward help line • Highly trained sales support staff

2.18 Clerical Medical - marketing strategy and communications statements

Strategy	CRM to IFAs	Launch stakeholder pensions	Y1	Y2	Y3	Y4	Budget - all years
Market research	3 month research to examine IFA requirements and feedback	Research into companies with nc pervious interest in group pensions - medium to large	→				£40k
Personal selling	Recruitment and training of key account managers	To IFAs to encourage sales of company pensions to those with no previous interest	→	→	→	→	£400k
CRM	Selection and installation of CRM software. Staff training in use	Via key account managers to IFAs and to employees via direct mail	→	→	→	→	£200k
E-commerce	Further development of website and extranet to accommodate communications between IFAs and CMI staff	Launch product on-line April 2001	→	→	→	→	million
Advertising	Corporate advertising and sector magazines	No TV or press advertising specific to stakeholder pensions	→	→			£100k
Corporate advertising	Raise awareness of the brand through TV and press advertising	Raise awareness of the brand through TV and press advertising	→		→		million
Internal marketing	All CMI training in CRM, business aims and brand values	All customer facing staff trained in stakeholder products. All staff trained in CRM, business aims and brand values	→	→	→	→	£200k
PR	PR in IFA magazines and national press	PR in IFA magazines and national press	→	→	→	→	£50k
Sponsorship	Sponsorship of sports relevant to 21-44 age group	Sponsorship of sports relevant to 21-44 age group	→	→	→	→	million
Exhibitions/ roadshows	Roadshows to promote CMI products and philosophy to IFAs. Awards. Corporate hospitality	Roadshows to promote CMI procucts and philosophy to IFAs. Awards. Corporate hospitality	→	→	→	→	million
Direct marketing	To launch the CRM/extranet	To target employers and employees with follow up from IFAs to employers	→	→	→		£50k

3 DETAILED MARKETING PLAN: EXAMPLE 2

Strategic marketing plan for Clerical Medical: 2000-2005

Contents

1.0 **Situation**

Clerical Medical has a strong market position and in recent years has grown dramatically. The market is mature and highly competitive and therefore in order to be able to increase their market share further, a strategic marketing plan must be drawn up and implemented.

2.0 **Mission statement**

'Our aim is to provide clear solutions for professionals seeking high quality, flexible and competitive pensions, investments and life assurance.'

3.0 **Assumptions**

3.1 The composition of Clerical Medical's portfolio is balanced and profitable

3.2 Clerical Medical's competence in investing on behalf of its customers is assumed to be comparable to that of its competitors

3.3 Barriers to international markets remain high for this 5 year period

3.4 Bases for segmentation apply across both corporate and consumer markets

4.0 **Broad aims**

4.1 To be recognised as the leading provider of pensions, investments and life assurance
4.2 To clearly communicate Clerical Medical's philosophy to all stakeholders
4.3 Improve and communicate the corporate image
4.4 To increase our customer base
4.5 To decrease our costs

5.0 **Corporate objectives**

5.1 Double market share to 6% by 2005
5.2 To achieve top 5 ranking by 2005
5.3 To introduce hi-tec IT system by end of 2000
5.4 Gain 60% of existing customer's new financial investments by 2005

6.0 **Strategic options and choice**

6.1 **Competitive forces** (ref to Porter's 5 forces, page 4)

By assessing the issues regarding competitive forces, it is easier to determine the strategic choice. The key points are as follows.

6.1.1 There is a threat of competition both in 2000 and 2010

6.1.2 Buyer power shows a changing population, in terms of lifestyles and preferences and there is a need to provide for these changes

6.1.3 The threat of substitutes emphasises the current availability of the state pension which the government is abolishing and replacing with the new stakeholder pensions

6.2 **Porter's generic strategies**

6.2.1 **Overall cost leadership**

This would not be a suitable strategy for Clerical Medical to pursue at this time as they are currently not the lowest cost producer, and their aim is to provide quality products which cannot be based in a low cost situation

6.2.2 **Differentiation focus**

This is the recommended strategy to adopt. It meets Clerical Medical's mission, aims and objectives which are to provide quality and flexible products and targets to a segmented audience

6.3 **Growth strategies: Ansoff matrix**

In order to achieve the objective of increasing market share to 6% by 2005, a market penetration strategy is recommended for short-term with a product development strategy and market development strategy for medium to long-term based on these points.

6.3.1 **Product development strategy**

There are certain points within this strategy which need to be considered in the short-term time scale such as the stakeholder pensions. These are new pensions due to commence this year and therefore will need promoting almost immediately. Other new products will be focused towards more long term strategies

6.3.2 **Market development strategy**

These strategies are certainly important and should be considered for medium to long term. Direct contact with consumers via the internet are certainly going to be the way forward but Clerical Medical need to focus on their current distribution channels at present. For new international markets, extensive research will need to be carried out before any major moves are made into new markets

6.3.3 **Market penetration strategy**

This is the key strategy for Clerical Medical at present. They need to focus on building up their customer base in their current market through product differentiation and CRM policies with IFAs

7.0 **Marketing objectives**

In addition to the corporate objectives set, there are some specific marketing objectives which need to be addressed and which will support the strategies outlined above.

7.1 Define the market segments in which to target Clerical Medical's product range

7.2 Define the bases for differentiation which will be attractive to the selected market segment

7.3 Determine the cost effective means of reaching and servicing the target market in order to retain the 5 star customer service ratings

7.4 Adopt a customer relationship management policy by 2002

7.5 Increase awareness within target market to 90% name recall by 2001

8.0 **Target audience**

From the analysis, it is clear that the basis for segmentation is on typology, age and socio-economic groups. From the information supplied on Clerical Medical we also know that the current target groups are 'high net worth' individuals. I think that it is also valid to consider the following issues.

8.1 **Benefits sought (from the product)**

8.1.1 Peace of mind for the future
8.1.2 Prestige company
8.1.3 Cash lump sums

8.1.4 Up to date information on policies
8.1.5 Convenient/simple/flexible products

8.2 **Buyer readiness (crisis events)**

8.2.1 Purchasing a house
8.2.2 Marriage
8.2.3 Starting a family
8.2.4 Higher education
8.2.5 Retirement
8.2.6 Death

9.0 **Targeting**

9.1 **Targeting strategy**

To target those individuals whose needs are not being met by the standardised products of our competitors.

Based on the segmentation analysis, Clerical Medical should be targeting the following defined segments.

9.2 Socio-economic group ABC1

9.3 Group profiled 'Active, seeking personalised solutions' which consists of self-employed, professionals, high income earners

9.4 Group profiled 'passive, brand loyal[therefore being able to cross sell to current customers which assists with the market penetration strategy

9.5 Age range 25-44

9.6 Targeting the above groups at various stages in the life (crisis events)

9.7 Research on the above should be carried out in order to assess the 'benefits sought' by the customer to enable targeting to be more successful

10.0 **Positioning**

10.1 **Positioning strategy**

To provide an all encompassing service focusing on supreme quality and expertise

This looks at how Clerical Medical is perceived by its customers.

10.2 **Competitive advantage**

Clerical Medical's current competitive advantages are as follows.

10.2.1 Quality service
10.2.2 Quality products

Clerical Medical should look to improving competitive advantage through:

10.2.3 Developing perceived advantage
10.2.4 Superior knowledge of market segment
10.2.5 Superior product benefits

10.3 **Branding**

Clerical Medical should consider a re-branding exercise in order to be positioned as follows.

10.3.1 Modern

10.3.2 Differentiated

10.3.3 Flexible

10.3.4 Relevant

10.3.5 Forward-thinking

10.3.6 Changing the company logo or introducing a new rap line would help towards altering the perception of the brand and create a more modern image, eg:

CLERICAL *Medical*

"Unique performance for your tomorrow"

11.0 **Marketing mix**

11.1 **Product/service strategy**

To provide clear, flexible and differentiated products with first class customer service

11.2 **Pricing strategy**

Price set to achieve perceived high quality and to be competitive

11.3 **Place strategy**

To continue to distribute through IFA channel with a long-term strategy being to distribute direct to consumers via the internet

11.4 **Promotion strategy**

To ensure that the target market are reached with an effective and relevant message through cost-effective communications

11.4.1 **Advertising**

All advertising to carry logos and strap line and generally portray the company image

11.4.2 **PR**

To deliver consistent corporate messages to the relevant target audience

11.4.3 **Selling**

To have an efficient and effective sales force to deliver the product and service package

11.4.4 **Direct marketing**

To deliver appropriate marketing materials/literature to the relevant target market

11.5 **People strategy**

To ensure qualified and experienced personnel are recruited and receive on-going training

11.5 **Physical evidence strategy**

To ensure Clerical Medical's tangible attributes, ie logs, brochures carry the company's image and perceived values

11.6 **Process**

To ensure that policies procedures are carried out with a professional approach and that information is up-to-date, accessible and is provided both efficiently and effectively

12.0 **Tactics**

12.1 **Advertising**

TV, trade and national press/magazines, poster sites, internet

12.2 **Sponsorship**

Events aimed at the target market, ie music/arts/theatre/university awards/teachers' conferences

12.3 **Direct mail**

By having a database with current customers on it, it is then possible to send them information on other products for various stages of the life (crisis events). If someone is buying a house, you can then contact them about a life assurance policy and a pension, then in a few years time contact them regarding an investment policy, which will mature for when they have a family or a policy which will mature when their child will go to university.

12.4 **Public relations**

Build close relations with journalists and provide them with information on new products, new personnel recruited or events which are being sponsored. It is important to keep Clerical Medical in the public eye so that when potential customers want life assurance then they will think of Clerical Medical.

12.5 **Customer relationship management**

It is essential that Clerical Medical adopts good CRM with IFAs in order to meet the objectives of increasing recommendations from IFAs. This can be achieved by:

12.5.1 Each key account to have its own relationship manager
12.5.2 Recruit an overall relationship manager
12.5.3 Provide IFAs with up to date literature
12.5.4 Regular visits to build relations and to advise and support IFAs
12.5.5 Organise hospitality events

12.6 **Web site**

Keep web site up to date and ensure that it is attractive to the target audience. The long term plan being to create an interactive web site. A web site officer will need to be recruited in order to achieve this.

12.7 **Exhibitions**

Attend yearly trade events in order to be see by IFAs.

12.8 **New IT system**

A new IT system must be reviewed in order to replace the current legacy system.

13.0 **Implementation**

Activity	**2001**	**2002**	**2003**	**2004**	**2005**
Advertising	****	***	**	***	***
Web site	**	**	**	**	**
Exhibitions	**	**	**	**	**
Direct mail	**	**	**	**	**
PR/sponsorship	**	**	**	**	**
Hospitality	**	**	**	**	**
Recruitment	****	****			
New IT system	****	****	**		
Re-branding	****	****	**	*	

* represents level of activity

14.0 **Budget**

Communications activity	**Budget**
Advertising	£90,000
Web site	£46,000
Exhibitions	£120,000
Direct mail	£70,000
PR/sponsorship	£120,000
Hospitality	£120,000
Business activity	**Budget for 2000**
Recruitment	£160,000
New IT system	£40,000
Re-branding	£75,000

The budget will be based on the **objective and task** method therefore we look at what activities we need to pursue and budget for them. The results should be monitored on a regular basis and the budget/ activity level adapted as and when necessary.

15.0 **Control**

15.1 Level of recommendations from IFAs
15.2 Level of publicity
15.3 Level of enquiries due to direct mail/internet/exhibitions
15.4 Feedback from IFAs and consumers

4 STAKEHOLDER PENSIONS: LAUNCH PLAN

4.1 Situation

(a) **External - macro**

(i) The government is promoting stakeholder pensions. Companies with over five employees have to offer the stakeholder pension as a company pension or give employees access to this personal pension. **Purpose**: to ensure that those on low-to-middle incomes have adequate income in retirement and to reverse the present balance of public and private provision, so that 60% of pensions are privately funded.

(ii) There are doubts in the industry over how many will market the new pensions to the full range of the government's target group - the 5m earning £9,000 - £18,000 a year who lack a private pension.

(iii) The government has upped the contribution to stakeholder pensions from £10 to £20 per month to allow people on lower incomes to build up an appropriate pension.

(iv) The management fee may not exceed 1% - considered to be very low and covering only the cost of basic financial advice.

(v) People who work for small companies (< 5 employees) will still be able to obtain them, but direct from pension companies. It is possible that they will not do anything.

(vi) Website launched in Jan 2001 for people to find out more about stakeholder concept.

(b) **External - micro**

(i) Stakeholder pensions are due to go on sale April/May 2001, but there are already some pension plans available offering stakeholder style low charges and flexibility (IFA with Friends Provident).

(ii) Nine of the UK's top 10 life companies and some key retail banks have decided to offer stakeholder pensions in spite of strong industry criticism of the scheme.

(iii) Big insurers intend to enter the market, eg Legal & General, CGU, Axa Sun Life, Zurich Financial Services and Friends Provident.

(iv) Those that have yet to make the decision: Standard Life (Europe's largest mutual group), NatWest and Barclays

(v) 'Bottom-end' product, not the dominant product (CEO, Norwich Union).

(c) **Internal**

(i) **Strengths**

- Low cost base, so can cover the small fund management charge of stakeholder pensions without serious risk to financial position

- Experience in the pensions market, a trustworthy image and well managed funds, which could work well for those people who have little money to invest but put their trust into CM for a decent return

(ii) **Weaknesses**

- Currently no other channels used but IFAs, a channel not used by people with lower incomes
- Image of targeting high earning professionals

(iii) Whether to sell stakeholders to individuals as opposed to groups through employers and affinity groupings. This could leave self-employed or those in small companies with little or no choice of providers.

4.2 **Objectives**

To increase market share to 6% by 2005 (corporate)

1	To develop a stakeholder pension product for individuals and companies ready to market in April 2001
2	To include the stakeholder pension product in our website and being able to offer online applications and account management by April2001
3	To achieve 80% awareness amongst IFAs (100% amongst our IFAs) of our stakeholder product by April 2001

4.3 **Strategy**

(a) Set up new **product project team** (cross departmental with senior involvement) to develop the stakeholder pension product; look at **competitor** developments and **government guidelines** to be one step ahead in terms of flexibility and service level

(b) Develop **Halifax website** (greenfield.co) further to include stakeholder pensions and to allow for online applications to be taken and online account management (this also reduces operations cost dramatically)

(c) Various forms of promotion to IFAs and customer relationship management

4.4 **Targets**

(a) Companies: all companies that neither show an interest in nor have other pension products

(b) Private individuals: all individuals that are not eligible for a company pension plan but will be made aware of stakeholder pensions by their employer

4.5 Tactics

	Individuals	Companies
Products	Standard but flexible product with good service level	Standard but flexible product with good service level
Price	1% management fee Low cost base for CM	1% management fee Low cost base for CM
Place	Individuals through Internet and direct channels	Companies through IFAs
Promotion	Target eligible companies (employees < 5) with information packs including CD ROM	Target eligible companies (employees > 5) with information packs and nearest IFA, followed up by CD ROM packs Product information packs to IFAs to create initial awareness Followed up by mailing with CD ROM with internet viewing once website has been completed No TV
Process	Customer visits website or IFA to gain further information and sign on for stakeholder pension	Customer visits website or IFA to gain further information and sign on for stakeholder pension
Physical evidence	Contact with CM, paperwork, statements	Contact with IFA, paperwork, statements
People		IFAs

4.6 Money (budget)

		£
Project team time (20 people, 1 day a week for 6 months)	520m/days	62,500
Website development (IT resource and development)		20,000
Information pack (development, print, postage)	200k × £1.50	300,000
Total launch		382,500

4.7 Men and women

As above

4.8 Minutes - time

Gantt chart (not included)

4.9 Measurement

- Are we ready for launch on 1 April 2001?
- What is the awareness amongst (our) IFAs about our stakeholder pension product?
- Can we take apps online?
- Can we service accounts online?

5 E-COMMERCE PLAN

5.1 Situation

Clerical Medical, like other traditional life companies, have systems known as 'legacy' systems. There is a system for each new product introduced and each system has to keep track of each client's product performance over a number of years. Clerical Medical currently has a basic website which acts as an on-line brochure.

Key issues

(a) Each system has its own way of collecting direct debits and tracking policies.

(b) Systems were set up by software engineers at different times, under different conditions with different technologies.

(c) Decision making was IT-driven not marketing-driven.

(d) With legacy systems it is difficult to build customer-based systems as systems are policy based which have difficulty in acquiring consumer profiles

(e) There is no time to 'stock the clock' and improve the old system due to system constraints within the design that have to be managed differently

(f) Competition from more established players armed with the latest technology could exploit 'greenfield' opportunities

5.2 **Aims**

1	To adopt a market driven approach
2	To build better relationships/communication channels with IFAs
3	To improve the quality of information available to all stakeholders

5.3 **Objectives**

1	To have an interactive website operational by end of 2001
2	To develop 20% of new business through IFA recommendation
3	To increase enquiry levels by 20% from both IFAs and consumers by 2000

5.4 **Strategy**

(a) **Market strategies**

A new IT system will assist with Clerical Medical's market strategy.

(i) **Market penetration**: will help to reach current/new customers in current markets

(ii) **Market development**: will allow Clerical Medical to reach new customers in new markets as this system will be a new distribution channel

(iii) **Product development**: will provide a more efficient service to IFAs and consumers

(b) **IT strategies**

Develop an IT support system for use both by internal employees and IFAs to assist with product selection and advice process

(i) **Intranet**

An internal (view only) network system enables employees to be aware of corporate issues. Helps with internal marketing.

(ii) **Extranet**

A way of servicing key accounts through the internet. IFAs will be able to view the internal network which in turn helps them to advise customers more effectively and efficiently. IFAs will not have access to the same level of information that the intranet provides as that information is confidential. Being provided with corporate information can often increase the level of loyalty from the IFAs

(iii) **Internet**

Provides general product and company information. Can act as a pull strategy to encourage consumers to request Clerical Medical products. More of an advertising/ PR tool which must be kept up to date.

5.5 **Personnel**

Clerical Medical will need to recruit an IT expert to oversee the implementation the running of this new IT system.

5.6 **Schedule**

	Year 1				Year 2			
Activity	**Q1**	**Q2**	**Q3**	**Q4**	**Q5**	**Q6**	**Q7**	**Q8**
Appoint IT personnel	→							
Liaise with IT/Web cos	——	→						
Trial systems			——	→				
Link with related websites					——	→		
Launch systems							——	→

5.7 **Budget**

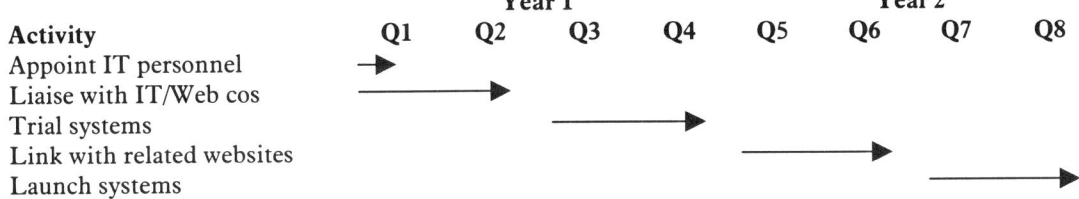

New and better IT platforms require major investment but this must be budgeted for, if Clerical Medical are to meet their objectives and be in a good competitive position. I estimate that a budget of £40,000 will be required to achieve the programme outlined above.

5.8 **Control**

- Assess the number of recommendations from IFAs
- Assess the quantity and quality of enquiries from IFAs and consumers
- Assess the number of hits to the web site

6 CUSTOMER RELATIONSHIP MANAGEMENT PLAN (1)

6.1 **Situation**

Clerical Medical currently only distributes through IFAs so it is crucial that a sound relationship is built up with the IFAs to ensure successful distribution through this channel.

6.2 **Aims/objectives**

1 To establish, maintain and enhance relationships with IFAs at a profit so that the objectives of the parties involves are met

2 To adopt a CRM strategy with IFAs by end of 2000

3 To be first choice for recommendation by IFAs

4 To improve and continue to provide excellent customer service to IFAs

5 To have the attitude as quoted by Gummerson 'firms need to enter wedlock rather than one night stands'.

6.3 **Strategy**

(a) **Marketing strategy continuum**

Transaction marketing ———————————— Relationship marketing

FMCGs — Consumer durables — Industrial goods — Services

This suggests that in certain contexts a one-deal-at-a-time approach, or transaction marketing, is the best strategy and in other contexts long-term relationship building is more appropriate. In this case, Clerical Medical are offering more of a service and therefore a relationship marketing strategy is required.

(b) Direct and regular contact is key in a service industry and requires long-term focus based on interactive marketing between buyer and seller. Close relationships are necessary where is changing technology, shorter product life cycles and increased competition and all these factors are facing Clerical Medical.

(c) **Types of relationship marketing**

- Transactions
- Repeated transactions
- Long-term relationships
- Buyer-seller partnerships
- Strategic alliances
- Network organisations
- Vertical integration

6.4 Establishing relationship marketing

(a) **Identify key IFAs meriting relationship marketing.** If it is the objective to develop relationship marketing with all of them the options are to put them in order of importance or if you have enough manpower, roll out the strategy to all of them at the same time.

(b) **Assign a skilled relationship manager to each IFA.** It is essential that personnel are skilled in this area.

(c) Develop clear **job descriptions** for relationship managers.

(d) Appoint an **overall manager** to manage the relationship managers.

(e) Each manager must develop long-range and annual cost relationship plans.

(f) Hospitality events would give Clerical Medical the opportunity to build relationships further and on more of a personal basis.

6.5 Personnel

More staff will be required by Clerical Medical in order to adopt a relationship marketing strategy. Relationship managers, an overall manager and a larger sales force will need to be recruited in order to build and sustain a portfolio of client relationship through which strategic advantage may be achieved.

6.6 Marketing mix

(a) **Hospitality** events to take place at least once per year.

(b) **Marketing packs** containing CD ROM, video and product literature to be provided for IFAs and kept up to date

(c) **Personal selling** - increased salesforce to visit IFAs on a regular basis. Salesforce to have regular training.

(d) The mix must be expanded to include **process** and **people** (as issues of customer care and service quality should become more prominent)

6.7 Control

Assess through number of IFAs who attend hospitality events plus research into how many IFAs are recommending Clerical Medical's products to their customers.

6.8 Conclusion

An advantage of CRM is reduced buyer risk, improve communication, problem solving and increased barriers to entry. By building strong relationships with IFAs they will become more aware of Clerical Medical and its products. By building up trust between Clerical Medical and the IFAs, the IFAs may be more inclined to recommend the products. Relationships are important but Clerical Medical must have the products to match.

7 CUSTOMER RELATIONSHIP MANAGEMENT PLAN 2

7.1 Situation

(a) **External (macro)**

- The Financial Services Act was passed in 1986 - IFAs must select best product from across the market
- FSA and PIA conduct rigorous checks and reviews of tied agents and IFAs
- Large numbers, particularly tied direct sales people have left industry
- Quality of advice has improved but costs of implementation means many small IFA businesses have gone
- All distributors have been required to increase resources for training and compliance
- Number of IFAs stood at around 21,000 for past 10 years
- The government feels that IFAs are mainly for the rich and lack professionalism
- The government is in favour of more direct selling methods because they are simpler
- Pressures for reductions in costs base
- Introduction of stakeholder fees with 1% management fee - not profitable
- Major investment required for new and better IT platforms (esp for stakeholder pensions)

(b) **Micro**

- Trend towards consolidation
- Highly competitive industry
- Mature market
- Relatively undifferentiated products
- IFAs have 60% market share of the business - doubled over the past five years
- Some IFAs have preferred suppliers
- Pressures for systems integration via use of technology
- Weaknesses of alternative channels in 1990s gave IFAs a relatively clear run - this will not last with new direct channels such as internet

- Consumer is changing - demanding more choice with less time. Also ageing population and changing work practices
- Direct customer links could more than halve present transaction costs

(c) **The structure of the IFA channel**

	Value %		
	1998	2005	
Nationals	30	35	• Consolidation will build national's share
Networks	15	20	• Small firms will move to networks/ties
Regionals	45	40	• Regionals will consolidate to no less than 40%
Small	10	5	

7.2 **Internal**

(a) **Strengths**

- Entire value of last year's business sold through IFAs - which suggests good relationships
- Good fund performance - something that IFAs look for
- Strong financial rating
- Excellence in customer service
- Low cost base - means they should have more money to differentiate their service
- Doubled market share to 6% since 1996

(b) **Weaknesses**

- Lack of entrepreneurial behaviour - new techniques will need to be learned
- Legacy systems are policy based - new systems must be introduced
- Marketing strategies often not clear, lack of customer focus, segmentation - as above
- Lack of strategy regarding alternative channels of distribution

(c) **Objectives**

1	To increase market share to 6% by 2005 (corporate)
2	To increase the share of business with each IFA by 5% by 2001
3	To win the IFA customer service award in 2001
4	To increase the number of IFAs selling CMI products by 10% in 2003

7.3 **Definition**

Consistent high quality customer support access across all communications channels and business functions and business partners.

7.4 If IFAs are to retain their dominant position, they need to react quickly to the changes and pressure in the market, eg:

- Be first choice for their clients
- Retain and source new clients
- Shift to professional status
- Move from commissions towards fees for remuneration
- Exploit the opportunities offered by e-commerce

- Build corporate business (advice on stakeholder pensions to be provided via companies then offer additional advice to pension scheme members)
- Cut costs and raise productivity

7.5 **Strategy**

Set up a cross-departmental project team with strategy, marketing and IT expertise to carry out the following tasks.

(a) Carry out research amongst IFAs to assess their requirements - customer insight
(b) Examine the customer/process dynamics in this area - customer interface
(c) Segment the IFA market
(d) Assess the organisational implications of introducing CRM - customer orientation
(e) Outline plan for introduction of CRM - customer innovation
(f) Assessment of likely costs and benefits
(g) Outline brief for CRM suppliers, especially IT

7.6 **Targets**

Registered, reputable and highly qualified IFAs with a good performance record and

(a) existing, new and potential users of CMI products
(b) high medium and low users of CMI products
(c) size of company - small, medium, large

Competitive advantage	Customer service. Current relationship with IFAs. All 1999 business sold through IFAs
Target market	IFAs
Positioning	Excellent customer service. Good fund performance. Financial strength
Sales objective	To increase market share to 6% by 2005

7.7 Assuming that we have completed stages 1-4 above we can assume that the likely findings will require:

Tactics

Communications tool	CRM with IFAs
Market research	Testing and selection of CRM software to integrate IFA and CMI information requirements and high levels of service. Hold IFA panels and find new value. Look for new ways to interface with IFAs. Analyse complaints. Use feedback to develop new products. Raise the profile of IFA satisfaction measures in the company.
Product	For existing products develop clear, understandable information provision. Seamless integration of electronic and human interface between IFA and CMI. Develop new products based on information from IFAs.
Price	Excellent customer service. Competitive fee payments. Good fund performance.
Place	Key account managers, direct mail. Provide information through extranet, CD ROMS, bulletins.
Promotion	Provide IFAs with an incentive to keep CMI informed. Advertising in specialist financial services magazines. Sponsorship of IFA awards. Launch a special service level for the best performing IFAs based on sales/market share %age and quality of service.
Process	Business process re-engineering. Target IFA with material and make personal contact via key account manager to develop relationship.
Physical evidence	Seminars, roadshows and briefings. Literature. Key account managers.
People	'Every contact with the customer is a critical episode.' Key training and development in areas of CRM and IT for CMI staff. Recruitment and training of key account managers to manage the interface between IFAs and the company. Cross company internal marketing to ensure that everyone in the business understands the brand positioning and business aims. Develop a culture of commitment to customers at CMI and an organisation structure to match. Recruit, motivate and retain employees and introduce reward systems. Develop new attitudes and approaches to customer innovations which involves IFAs.

7.8 Implementation of CRM

	Days
• Management 'buy' in to presentation	1
• Recruit internal project manager	28
• Recruit cross functional task force	28
• Develop market research requirements	35
• Management presentation and agreement	14
• Carry out market research of target IFAs	90
• Analyse data and make recommendations	14
• Develop spec for CRM/extranet requirements	30
• Management presentation and agreement	14
• Invite tenders from agencies	21
• Tender evaluation and selection	14
• Presentation of tenders	7
• Select successful tender	4
• Comments and further draft developed	21
• Begin recruitment and training of key a/c managers	30
• Final draft of CRM system prepared	21
• In-house presentation - CRM, IT and bus reprocess	1
• Business re-engineering process begins	30
• Internal marketing strategy developed	14
• Training of all staff with customer interface	30

	Days
• Testing of new system	21
• Final version developed and presented	14
• Management agreement	1
• Awareness mailshot to IFA	1
• Internal promotion	28
• New CRM system and philosophy goes live	1
• Training of IFAs	21

7.9 Control

Quantified objectives	Means of measuring	Frequency of measurement	Accountability	How much does it cost to measure	Action
To increase the share of business with each IFA by 5% by 2001	Compare with data for previous year	Quarterly	Key account managers Marketing IT	£40,000	
To win the IFA customer service award in 2001	Success in winning the award	Annually	Customer interface personnel Marketing IT	Nothing	
To increase the number of IFAs selling CMI products by 10% in 2003	Measure against IFA data for the previous year	Quarterly	Key account managers Marketing IT		

23 Clerical Medical Investment Group Ltd: The Examination Paper, Answers and Examiner's Comments

This chapter contains the following.

CLERICAL MEDICAL INVESTMENT GROUP LTD

THE EXAM QUESTIONS ARE ON THE NEXT PAGE

DO NOT LOOK UNTIL YOU ARE READY TO SPEND THREE HOURS ON DOING THESE AS A MOCK EXAM

1 THE EXAMINATION PAPER

Additional information - to be taken into account when answering the questions set.

> A new pensions survey recently published shows that just one in eight of existing 'stakeholder friendly' pension plans meets all of the criteria for the low cost retirement policies, which start officially in April 2001. It says that to call forty-eight out of fifty-three plans 'stakeholder friendly' is 'clearly misleading'. It appears that only seven plans out of fifty-three on offer meet all eight rules of acceptability as shown in the case. The Clerical Medical marketing team is considering this issue and debating it extensively.

Based on your analysis of Clerical Medical's position within the given industry sector, together with the detailed information that you have gathered as the appointed Marketing Consultant, you have been asked to prepare a report addressing the following questions.

Question 1

Produce a strategic marketing plan for Clerical Medical for the next three years, taking into account the changes that are taking place in the sector. Justify your recommendations. **(50 marks)**

Question 2

Analyse the demographic and savings patterns in the UK population and offer possible branding and communications positions to Clerical Medical. **(25 marks)**

Question 3

Given the nature of the life and pensions industry and Clerical Medical's position within it, how would you develop a sensible and coherent customer relationship management strategy? **(25 marks)**

2 SENIOR EXAMINER'S OVERVIEW OF ISSUES THAT MUST BE COVERED

Overview

2.1 The case

The case study has been based on a real organisation. The case poses real problems and takes into account the opportunities and difficulties a service based company with a long term perspective has in developing a coherent marketing strategy in a slow growing ever changing market. This case has no personalised comments, is factual and contains no 'red herrings'. Nonetheless, as usual, there is the usual problem of an extensive range of detailed information. There is a need to develop clear and concise insights into the key issues involved in developing a strategy.

2.2 This case was generally well appreciated by tutors and examiners. There was plenty of data for analysis. Although there were some concerns about the case for overseas candidates, there was no appreciable disadvantage as the problem were generic rather than pertinent to just one country.

2.3 New information on the day of the examination

A new pensions survey recently published shows that just one in eight of existing 'stakeholder friendly' pension plans meets all of the criteria for the low cost retirement policies, which start officially in April 2001. It says that to call forty-eight out of fifty-three plans 'stakeholder friendly' is 'clearly misleading'. It appears that only seven plans out of fifty-three on offer meet all eight rules of acceptability as shown in the case. The Clerical Medical marketing team is considering this issue and debating it extensively.

Key issues

(a) The changing market conditions, especially with mergers and acquisitions

(b) The long-term nature of the insurance industry

(c) Intensively competitive market

(d) The growth of bancassurers and other providers such as Virgin

(e) In the long term the industry will be faced with EC regulations and competition

(f) The strength and importance of the IFAs

(g) The importance the government is placing on stakeholder pensions

(h) The ageing population needing greater pension support

(i) The 'old style' brand image of Clerical

(j) Generally poor image of the sector amongst the government and consumers

(k) Regulatory factors

(l) Mature market

(m) The sector is quite fragmented

(n) Customer relationship management is a very important issue

(o) The curious juxtaposition of the old and new technologies giving new start-up companies a headstart

(p) The growth of the internet and the best way to utilise the opportunities offered by the medium

(q) Specialist service providers such as Clerical medical need to stand out from the generalist providers

(r) The company is under the 'friendly' umbrella of Halifax

(s) The company needs to understand the best way to CRM via IFAs

(t) The company rates well on service measures

(u) The structural changes in the industry favour the larger players

(v) Market segments are changing with more individuals moving towards self employment

(w) Many individuals are not very knowledgeable about financial matters

(x) The UK sales and international business are doing well compared to 1998. It also appears that the European business is growing

(y) The P&L shows a loss in 1999, perhaps showing that the company is paying out considerable sums on long term pensions

(z) The shareholder funds have grown as a result of a further issue of share capital - presumably through Halifax

The answers

2.4 This case is reasonably straightforward and does not contain many surprises. Therefore the following issues should be considered.

(a) The application of theory

(b) The amount of international marketing theory/application that the students applied to the case. The amount of communication theory that they applied.

(c) The candidates should be thinking strategically not tactically.

(d) The answers given must be realistic and practical.

(e) A degree of innovation and lateral thinking is rewarded.

(f) It is important that the questions were answered within the given context.

(g) The additional information is quite important in making a clearer assessment of the company's strategy. The information shows how the new stakeholder pensions are perceived by the market. This sector is likely to grow being pushed by the government.

Question 1

Produce a strategic marketing plan for the Clerical Medical Investment Group for the next three years, taking into account the changes taking place in the industry sector. Justify your recommendations.

2.5 This question requires students to use many of the strategic planning models used by marketers. These are McDonald, Andrews, Doyle etc. Candidates will then need to consider the following.

(a) Consider the objectives that they wish to set for Clerical Medical for the long and the short term. In the short term the company needs to consider how to improve its profitability. In the longer term it needs to position itself sensibly with clear segmentation analysis.

(b) Take into account the rate of technological changes and consider the degree of flexibility allowed by the plan.

(c) Take into account the fragmented nature of the products and the markets and map out the key growth areas.

(d) The possibility of expanding in the European market.

(e) The strategic vision should be based on the core values of the company and be reflected in the segments that are targeted.

(f) The strategy should take into account the financial status of the company. The company has boosted its shareholder funds by issuing new shares and not from revenues from profits.

(g) What market positioning strategies should the company adopt vis a vis the different markets? Appendix 1, 2 and 3 are quite important.

(h) The company needs to build on its excellent customer satisfaction profiles.

(i) The company needs to rethink its branding stance for the future.

(j) How are the different services to be positioned in the markets?

(k) The fragmented market means that the market shares of individual companies are quite small. So an incremental growth in share is important.

(l) The company has to work closely with IFAs in developing customer relationship management.

(m) Models such as Porter, Ansoff, BCG, GEC, Shell Directional and GAP could be used in the analysis of the case.

(n) What are the constraints to the given strategy? How can the company follow a market led strategy? What would be a realistic marketing budget?

(o) Which markets are the key priorities and why?

(p) As no organisation chart is provided, how should the company execute its marketing strategies?

(q) How much of the company's money should be directed towards developing an internet strategy?

(r) The regulatory issues surrounding stakeholder pensions need to be considered. We do not know from the case whether the company is one of the ones that satisfies all government rules.

(s) The company needs to consider how much it should be involved in Halifax's launch of Greenfield.co.

(t) How should the Internet be used?

(u) Developing and supporting the brand.

2.6 **Points in a strategic plan**

(1) Set corporate objectives
(2) Identify target markets
(3) Set marketing objectives
(4) Develop marketing strategy and tactics
(5) Organise control systems

2.7 Given the points above, the best answers will show a clear grasp of the following.

1	A good analysis of the current position
2	The development of a strategic plan with fully developed implementation strategies
3	A good justification of the strategies to be adopted

2.8 Yet again, this was a reasonable question and should have been anticipated by the candidates. Overall, it appears that the use of pre-prepared answers is decreasing. This is a good sign as candidates need to be able to answer the question on the day. The general concerns surrounded the lack of insights into strategic thinking and general basics such as structures, confusion between objectives and strategies, lack of justification for recommended strategies and failure to indicate resource implications such as marketing expenditures. Porter and Ansoff are used as a minimum for analysis, after that only the good candidates utilised other models effectively. The usual presentation faults were in evidence with some scripts containing several pages of unnecessary preliminaries which were basically regurgitations of the case. The sequencing and structure of plans was poor. In many instances the new information provided was ignored.

2.9 Pilot centres (limited use of pre-prepared material 15 marks allocated)

Overall, it appears that the students on the pilot study took their analyses very seriously and presented them well. The marks were generally higher. Candidates though, showed a mixed performance on the application of the analysis. The application was the real test of the understanding of the analyses. Some students just referred to a particular appendix, but then failed to explain why they had chosen a particular table or analysis to justify their approach. Others used them very well. On the whole the answers were of a better quality than the norm. Candidates also seem to understand the case better and concentrate on its as they have no other extraneous material with them in the examination room.

> **Question 2**
>
> Analyse the demographic and savings patterns in the UK population and offer branding and communications positions to Clerical Medical.

2.10 This question is based on a clear analysis of the appendix on consumer profiles. Clerical Medical offers services to a niche market of wealthy individuals and yet the government directives are for 'standardised' products such as 'stakeholder pensions'.

(a) The company has a distinct market position but a weak brand - low familiarity and consideration by potential clients.

(b) In the current branding strategy the company is seen as professional, old fashioned, masculine and gentlemanly. It is also seen as established, secure, of integrity and professional.

(c) The emotional rewards offered are those of security, aspiration fulfilment, peace of mind and responsibility. The company is seen to have heritage and as having a specialist offer. The company needs to consider whether these brand values are likely to prove successful in the future.

(d) Given these issues, the compete needs to consider the following.

(i) The changes required to reposition the brand with figure 1 being indicative of the possibilities compared to the current branding stance.

Figure 1

(ii) Whether the company chooses to aim itself at upmarket and younger contributors in line with the new branding philosophy.

(iii) Understanding the growing importance of the female market, that appears to be purchasing pension fewer schemes than the male market.

(iv) Understanding that although ABs are lucrative, more people in the C1 and C2 category have savings and protection products.

(v) The age group 25-45 is likely to offer the best changes for further growth.

(vi) The wealthy achievers offer scope for growth.

(vii) National savings are declining.

2.11 Professional people - their needs are determined by professional 'status' and life stage

IFAs need to broaden their appeal - and Clerical Medical has the same opportunity. 'Professional' must be inclusive and not 'elitist'.

Possible segments that could be considered

Self employed	From new to mature businesses
	Business builders
	Not just 'freelancers'
Professions	Traditional and modern professionals
	Long study prior to qualifying
	Become partners or own their practice
Managers/directors	Employed management/director positions
	High responsibility and transferable skills
	Includes specialists who are mobile
Professional women	From a mix of previous groups
	Includes singles, married, divorced etc
Career professionals	Teachers, policemen, nurses, radiographers, forces, librarians etc
	Clear defined career path *within* profession
	Bias to public sector
	Lower earning power than 'traditional' professionals
Student professionals	Under and post graduates studying a course which leads to a profession

These targets would be in line with the general positioning adopted since its inception.

2.12 Given the somewhat contradictory messages from the savings tables, it is important to be able to fashion a positioning and branding strategy that is modern and appeals to both the upper socio-economic groupings according to the Acorn classifications and also the C1 and C2s. The branding has to appeal to the aspirers in the future in order to build a degree of long term thinking into the business.

2.13 Also when developing all these ideas, the candidates should utilise the wealth of data contained in the case and look for the anomalies indicated above. The question should elicit a wide variety of interesting answers.

2.14 A good answer will take into the following:

- Analysis of the key issues
- Development of a branding and positioning strategies
- Links with the overall strategy

8 marks were allocated towards the pre-prepared material.

2.15 **Comments**

This question needed an appreciation of the details surrounding demographic and savings patterns and utilising them to answer the case. Many make no attempt to answer the first part of the question or made only a token effort to do so. Far too many students simply copied out a marketing communications plan and missed out considering brand values and attributes. Many also failed to utilise the brand triangle already given, in order to develop a brand triangle for the future! In many cases, links with the overall strategies advanced in question 1 were conspicuous by their absence. This was a key question in separating many passes from failures.

Candidates at the pilot centres generally performed better as they had actually undertaken segmentation, targeting and positioning exercises in their analyses and utilised them in the answers. Although it must be said that many candidates often failed to utilise their analyses effectively in answering this question.

> **Question 3**
>
> Given the nature of the life and pensions industry and Clerical Medical's role within it, how would you develop a sensible and coherent customer relationship management strategy?.

2.16 Customer relationship management is seen as the key marketing issue of the new millennium. The advent of the Internet adds greater impetus to issues surrounding CRM. It could be argued that at the key reason d'être of a company involved in the life and pensions industry is the good management of customer relationships if it is to be successful. Taking this and the internet into account, Clerical Medical should be considering the following points.

(a) The development of good relationships with the IFAs who provide them with the bulk of the business.

(b) This means that the company needs to consider its distribution policies through the IFAs in the following ways.

   (i) Provide IFAs with a range of support to ensure effective delivery of advice around the tailored products plus generic material around the professional sub-segments.

   (ii) Provide IFAs with a relationship management programme to use with their clients.

   (iii) Create a system for IFAs so that the broader definition of professional people know the CM name and recognise that CM has 'something specific for them'.

   (iv) Certain products are promoted very specifically at professional people - when they visit an IFA he/she should have all the back up material to talk about the product and tailor advice.

   (v) Ensure that the service is up to high professional standards so that people enjoy dealing with the company.

(c) Help IFAs recognise that the professional relationship which exists between them and Clerical Medical (CM) can be replicated between them and their clients - and they can use CM services to deliver this, probably through the Internet.

2.17 In addition to this, the company needs to consider:

(a) A feasibility study offering direct services to the customer via the Internet - hence developing a good CRM

(b) Ensure training for salesforce so that the business development consultants can provide training for customer service teams in the professional delivery of their service

(c)

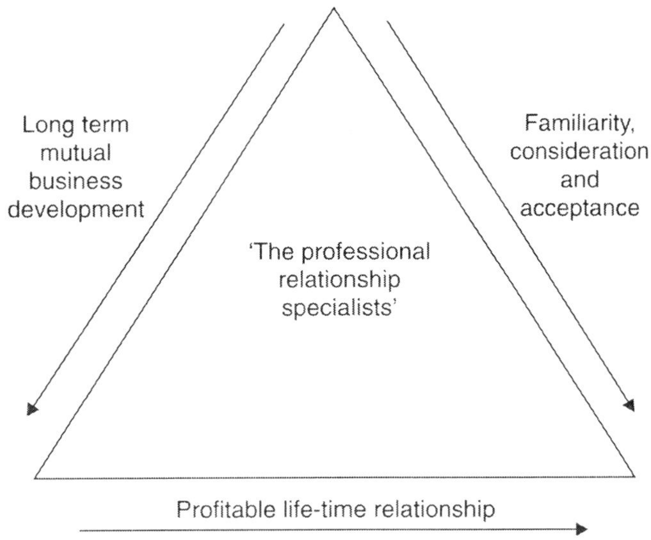

Figure 2 - Relationship building diagram

(d) The company needs to improve service and investment performance - toward the hygiene benchmarks.

(e) It needs to become better rated (financially sound) so that it gets a triple A rating.

(f) Current profitability needs to be improved and CRM strategies could play a large part in this.

The impact of e-commerce

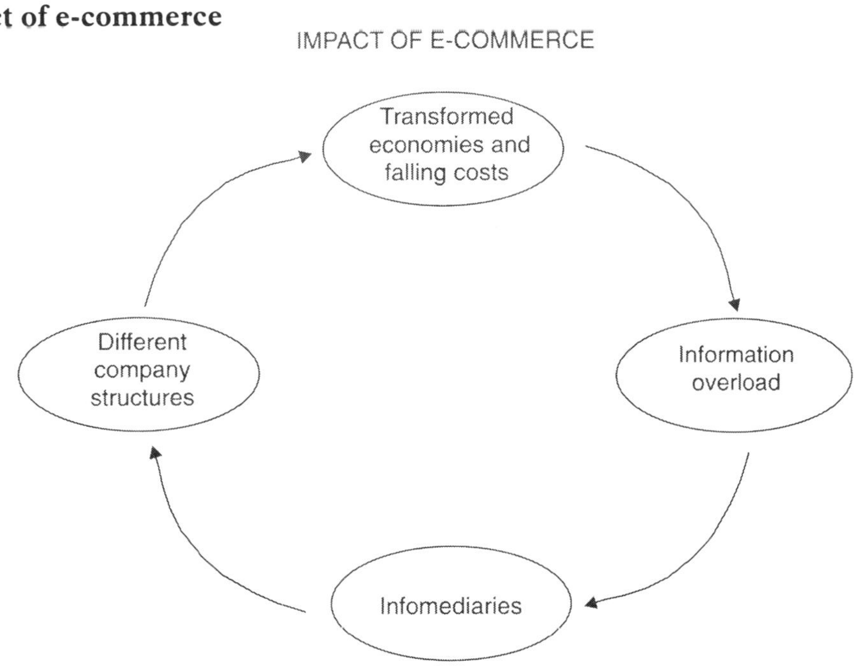

E-commerce affects the entire value chain

2.18 The growth of e-commerce is already changing the nature of purchasing. Many products can be viewed and bought on-line directly from the supplier. This means that the company needs to consider the internet as a key component of its CRM strategy, offering support to the IFAs and marketing to clients via IFAs with clearly defined stances on the services offered.

2.19 Customer relationship management is about building trust and in this respect CM is already doing well as many customers are very satisfied with their services as indicated in the appendices.

2.20 **General analysis of customer relationship management**

Many students understood the basic tenets of CRM, so reasonable marks were achieved. Some even elaborated on models that they were conversant with. Some overseas scripts had pre-prepared answers which followed a planning format. Some dug out information from standard texts and then found it difficult to cross-relate the themselves to Clerical Medical.

2.21 In many ways this was an easy question that students should have done well on.

2.22 The **pilot** centres performed well on this question as many had undertaken some segmentation analysis and also considered the role of IFAs in managing relationships.

2.23 As usual I would have liked to see coherence, strategic thinking, justification and detail featuring in the answers. The case was quite long and there was considerable amount of data so that candidates should have been able to fashion a range of interesting answers. Creativity and innovation, as usual was lacking.

2.24 Again we would urge centres to consider my triangle so that students follow what is exposed.

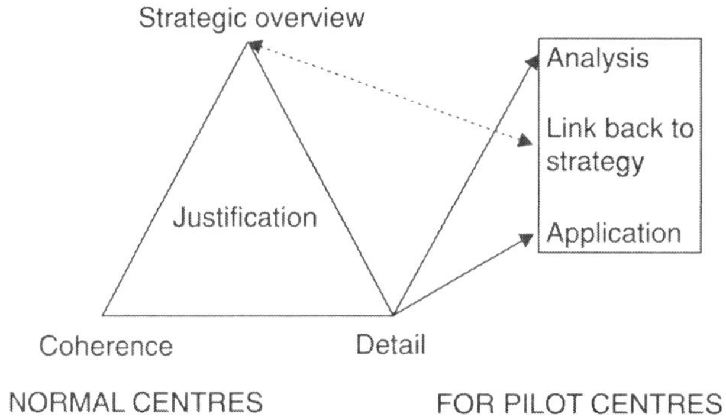

2.25 Pilot centres (limited use of pre-prepared material, 7 marks allocated)

For pilot centres it was important that the feedback loop from the analyses to the main text was followed through with clear justifications. The pilot has been successful in raising standards and the level of analysis was generally very good. The standard of work was very centre dependent and therefore varied. Overall pass rates were rather good. I suspect the variations may be tutor dependent. The main pleasing aspect of the pilot was the amount of effort that went into analysis was clear to see. The cleverer students used the analysis to good effect. The poorer students either regurgitated the analysis in the answers, ignored it or made broad rather than specific references to particular tables/ graphs. This case just like all the others underlines the necessity of preparation and application. Students also need a good grasp of all the other diploma subjects.

3 SPECIMEN ANSWERS WITH EXAMINER'S COMMENTS: SCRIPT 1

To: Mr James Broadbent, Marketing Director
From: Mr Don Sherwood, Marketing Consultant
Date: 16 June 2000

Subject: Report on development of future organisation plans

Contents:

Question 1 Strategic marketing plan for Clerical Medical for the next 3 years

Question 2 Recommendations on possible branding and communications positions for Clerical Medical

Question 3 Recommendations on a coherent customer relationship management strategy

3.1 Question 1

Strategic marketing plan for Clerical Medical for the next 3 years

Using information available to me, I am writing this report to recommend a strategic marketing plan for Clerical Medical over the next 3 years, give my recommendations on possible branding and communication positions for Clerical Medical and offer my advice on a sensible and coherent customer relationship management strategy.

Having analysed the market, there is a vast amount of further information that is required for accurate analysis and effective decision-making. In the absence of the actual information, certain assumptions have been made and these will be noted where appropriate. The following are some basic assumptions which shall apply throughout this report.

Assumptions

1 Sufficient funds are available for implementation of any plan proposed, given Clerical Medical's 'AA' financial strength rating and strong financial backing from Halifax.

2 The problems affecting the insurance industry in general applies equally to Clerical Medical (CM) unless there is clear evidence to the contrary provided in the case.

1 **Current situation analysis summary**

1.1 **Internal**

(a) CM is an old established company having vast experience in the insurance industry.
(b) It has a good reputation among its customers with a high score for service.
(c) However, it has become unfocussed and lacking in direction over the last few years.
(d) It offers a wide product range.
(e) It enjoys strong financial backing from Halifax who bought the company voluntarily in 1996.
(f) Brand awareness is low for its products in the market relative to newcomers like Virgin.

1.2 **External**

(a) Growing competition from old established players and new entrants into the market

(b) Market is changing with new technology and trends being introduced quickly

(c) Decline of mortgage related business for endorsement policies (a traditionally strong insurance product)

(d) Competition from new tax efficient products such as PEPs, TESSAs and ISAs

(e) Considerable pressure in the industry for cost reduction and product rationalisation

(f) Increased government regulation has constrained and added to the cost of the industry

(g) Poor image of the industry. Customer mistrust of product providers

1.3 **Market**

(a) Life assurance has reached a mature stage in the UK (7.3% of GNP)
(b) Fragmented market with over 200 authorised life insurers
(c) Market operates on long-term basis with premiums paid over 25 years
(d) Clerical Medical commend 3% share of the market

1.4 **Current portfolio analysis**

Insufficient information has been provided to produce a detailed portfolio analysis, eg using BCG matrix, but I have made the following observations.

(a) **Main product mix**

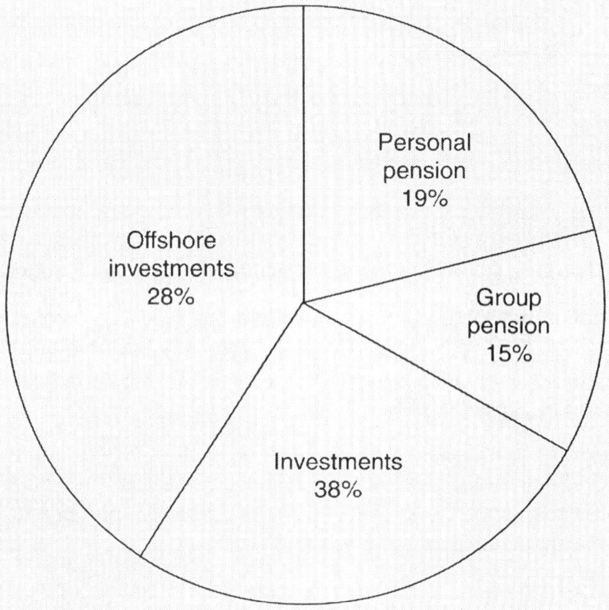

Clerical Medical generally target on the high earning consumers which have accounted for the slight bias in its portfolio towards investment products. In particular, offshore products have been popular with the better-off people as it offers the benefit of tax efficiency and growth of initial investments. There is also good potential for personal pensions and offshore investments as more people are expected to be self-employed and employment structure is shifting to more 'ABC1' type.

(b) **Wholesale market**

Clerical Medical currently holds a small market volume and this market is highly competitive. Not a very attractive product to sell.

(c) **Investment products in the international market**

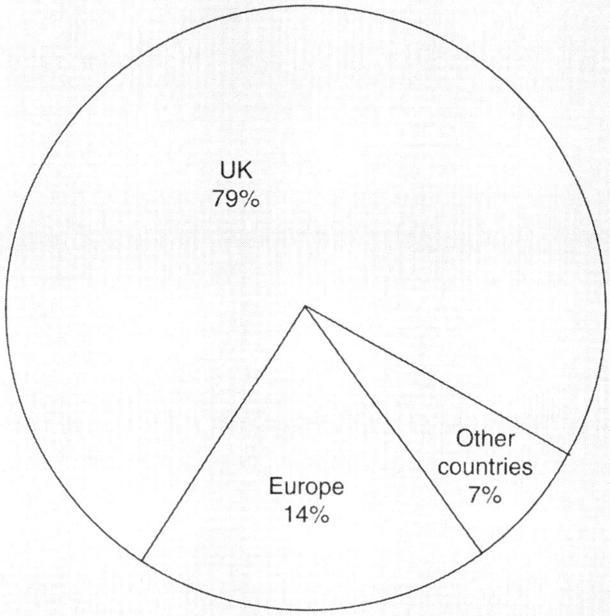

The bulk of business is in the UK. Good potential in European markets such as Germany and France which still have a low penetration of insurance products - 2.63% and 3.77% of GNP respectively.

1.5 **Product life cycle (life assurance industry)**

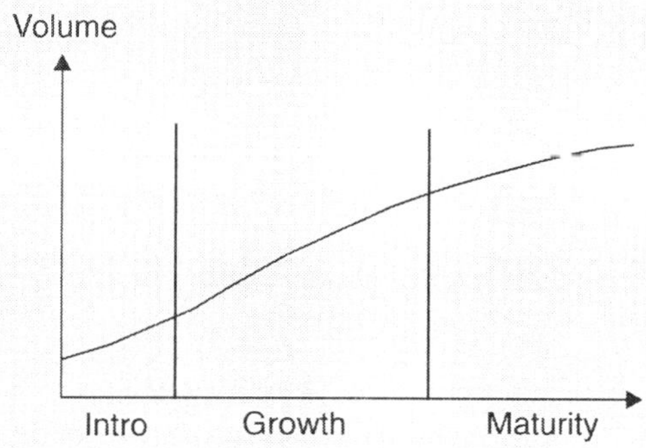

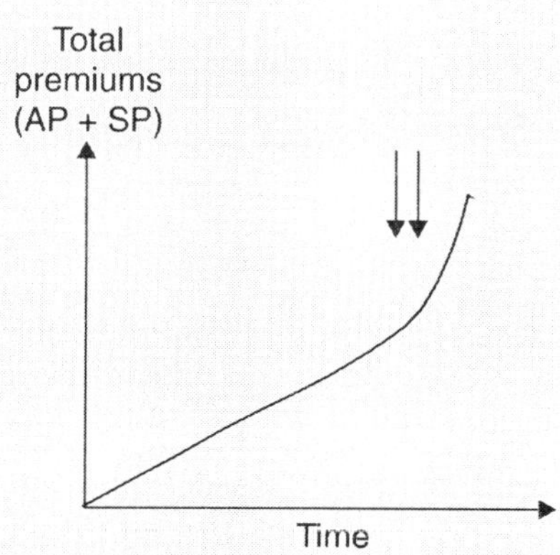

Although number of policies in force has stagnated, there is still a lot of growth potential in terms of sales value.

1.6 **Current positioning**

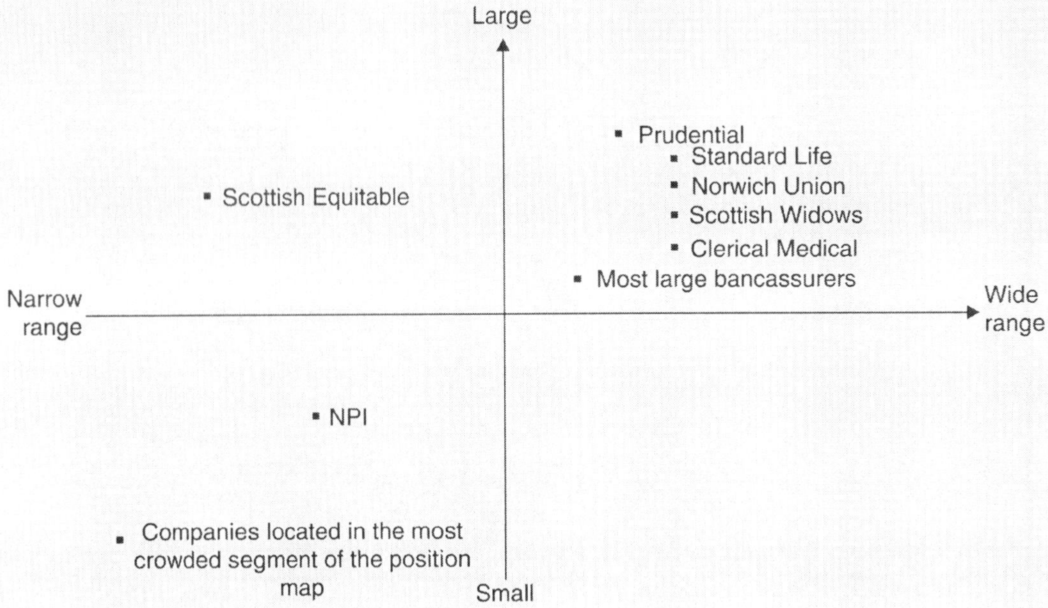

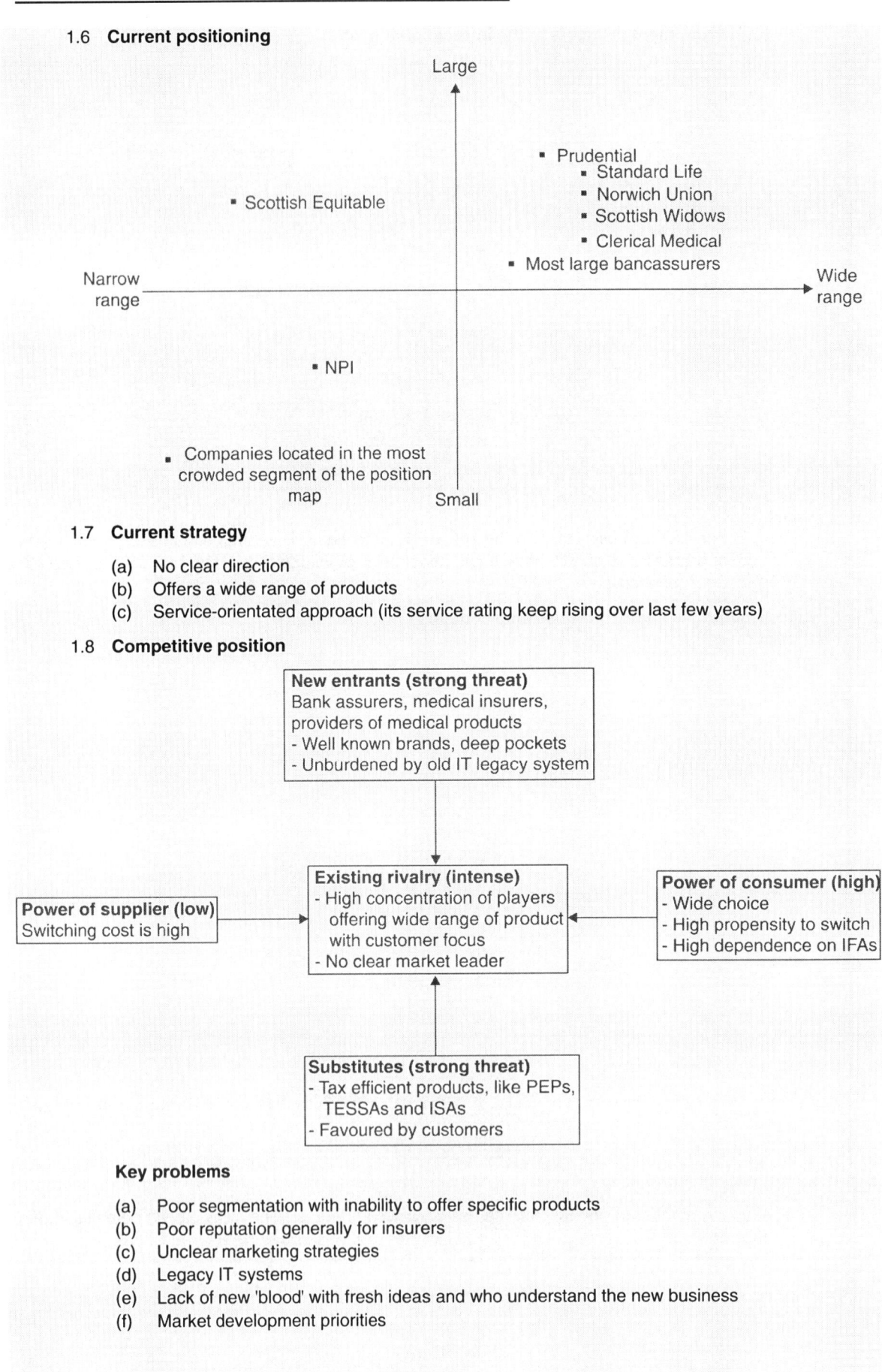

1.7 **Current strategy**

(a) No clear direction
(b) Offers a wide range of products
(c) Service-orientated approach (its service rating keep rising over last few years)

1.8 **Competitive position**

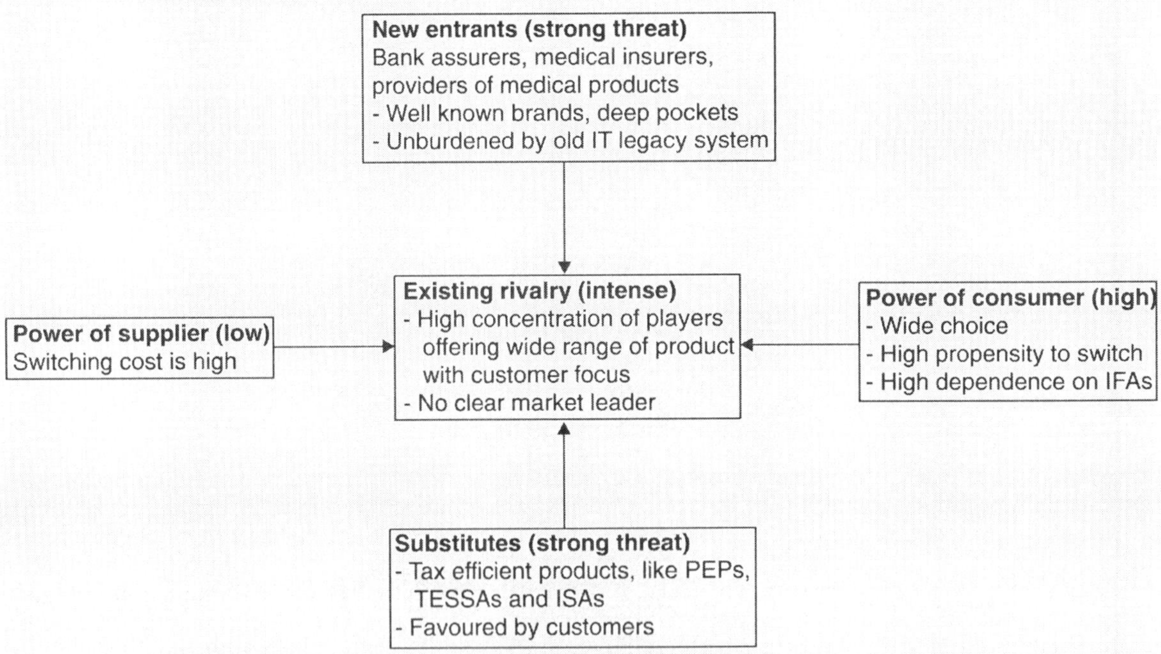

Key problems

(a) Poor segmentation with inability to offer specific products
(b) Poor reputation generally for insurers
(c) Unclear marketing strategies
(d) Legacy IT systems
(e) Lack of new 'blood' with fresh ideas and who understand the new business
(f) Market development priorities

2 **Corporate vision mission and values**

To address these problems, I suggest CM should clarify its strategic direction. My recommendations are:

2.1 **Vision**

To protect and grow the assets of every individual for his/her retirement and old age.

2.2 **Mission**

A mission statement would further focus activities as follows:

To be identified as the preferred supplier of personal pension and investment planning for our target customers.

2.3 **Brand values**

CM needs to move its corporate brand values to support a new position.

Unfocused - focused/specific
Untrustworthy - honest, good guarantee
Undifferentiated - high value for money

2.4 **Objectives**

In order to improve its competitive position, it is vital to increase existing revenue and turn its current loss into profits.

2.5 **Corporate objectives**

(a) **Quantitative**

(1) To break even or turn in a profit in a year's time
(2) To achieve growth of 5% above the industry average within 3 years

(b) **Qualitative**

(1) To be perceived as being focused and professional in our service to our customers

(2) To be in the top 3 in terms of service ranking in the next 3 years

3 **Strategies**

To achieve the objectives and in order to ensure survival in the increasingly difficult environment, CM needs to pursue a clear, consistent strategy.

3.1 **Choice of competitive strategy**

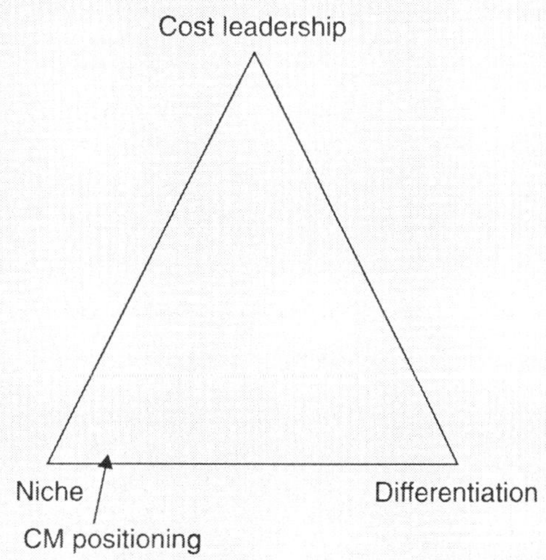

(a) CM will find it hard to achieve cost leadership as there are many other major players with huge financial reserves. It will also be difficult to realise a steady growth in returns using this strategy when the base costs are high and increasing government regulations have further added to cost.

(b) Given the market size and share, CM is unlikely to sustain differentiation across all markets/sectors due to limited resources.

(c) The only logical option is to move away from the field where the competition is most intense and adopt a more focused strategy. Besides, it will be better that CM concentrates its resources on a far specialised products and avoid duplicating any product which Halifax may want to offer.

Justifications

(a) This is both less costly and less risky strategically, than cost leadership

(b) A narrower product range will enable CM to serve its target customers better

(c) CM can better distinguish itself from other players offering a wide range of products and this will help to raise brand awareness of the customers for its products.

Product position

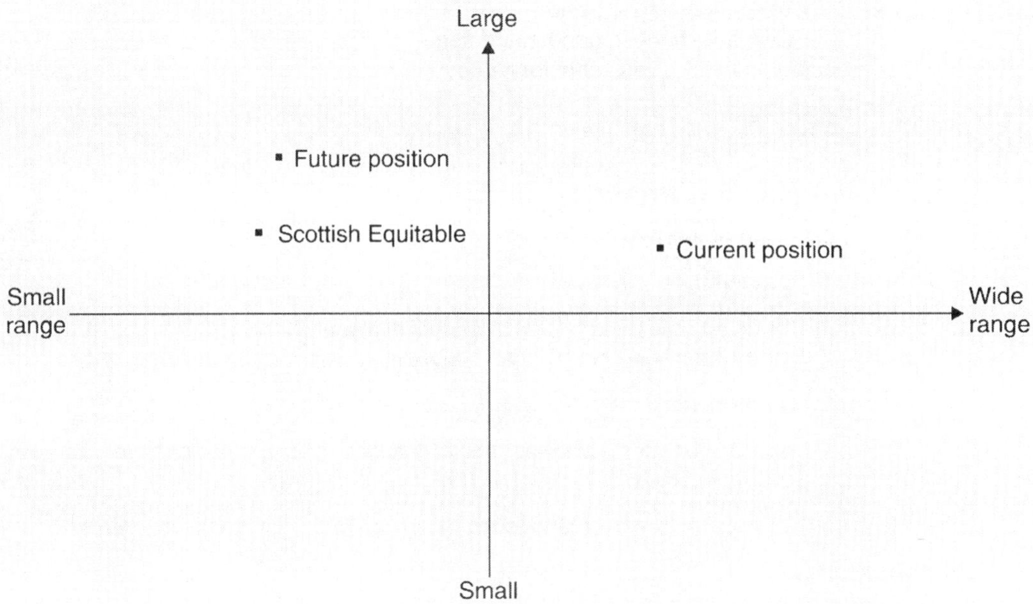

Currently there is only one strong player in this segment which is Scottish Equitable. This is an attractive segment as indicated by the high growth rate of Scottish Equitable of 1.8% (total new business/funds under management × 100) as compared to CM's current rate of 0.68%.

Implications

To effectively become a niche player, CM will need an effective market information system, in order to specialise effectively and create competitive advantage. Currently, CM is perceived as providing very good service. This can be used as a first competitive advantage over Scottish Equitable.

If CM accepts this competitive position, the company can then concentrate on the development of a more customer and market orientated strategy for the future.

3.2 **Segmentation and targeting**

Currently there is generally poor customer segmentation in the industry. To segment the market effectively, a look at the psychodemographics of the population may suggest evolving trends and also identify some of the unserved portions of the market.

Of particular note are the following populations:

(a) An ageing population

(b) More people are becoming self-employed

(c) The employment structure is moving towards more 'ABC1' type. This implies higher discretionary income.

(d) More professional women who have remained single or are divorced.

(e) Greater mobility among managers, directors and professionals with good transferable skills. This also implies that work will bring their skills across borders with the globalisation of the world economy.

The above are some of the segments which could form our target groups.

3.3 Evaluation of strategic alternatives

The Ansoff matrix shows the various options available to CM as its possible marketing strategies.

	Product *Existing*	*Product* *New*
Existing markets	**Market penetration** - self employed (personal pension) - ageing population (investments) - families/singles (personal investments)	**Product development** More flexible products, arrived at market penetration/ development segments
New markets	**Market development** - Europe (investment products) - Asia - highly mobile Professional	**Diversification** Not realistic at the moment

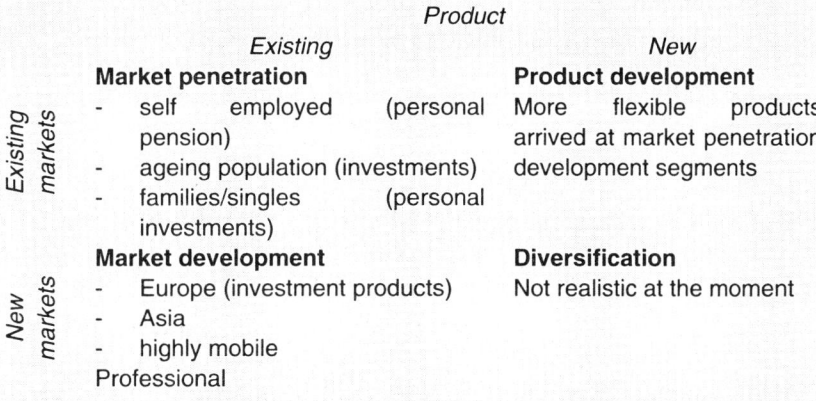

3.4 Clerical Medical's competitive strengths

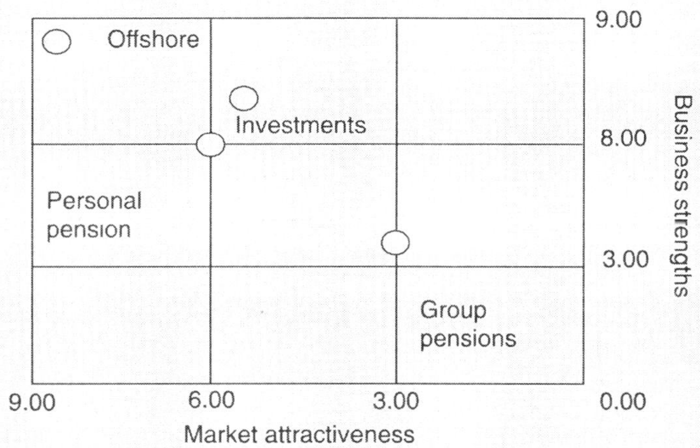

Some of the criteria used are

Business strengths
- Product range
- Market share
- Experience
- Financial capability
- Management
- Reaction time
- Brand identity
- Image

Market attractiveness
- Size of market in volume
- Size of market in value
- Number of competitors
- Ease of entry
- Easy of exit
- Cost of entry
- Cost of exit
- Learning experience change

The relative attractiveness of offshore investments, investments and personal pension in CM's product mix as reflected in the analysis using GE matrix further confirm that our market penetration/development strategies using a combination of both investments and personal pension to target our segment is sound.

Omission of stakeholder pension strategy

- Low returns since the charges are low. Hence unattractiveness
- Switching allowed – this makes it hard to get customer loyalty
- Many big players experienced to offer this – though competition
- 2/3 of Britain's employers will not have to make stakeholder pensions available – more will go for other options

4 MARKETING MIX

4.1 Product

A combination of personal pension, offshore investments and investments targeted at selected segments. Flexibility to be built into the product.

4.2 Pricing

Can opt for premium pricing but need to provide value-added service.

'Value for money' to customers.

Premium pricing service as added incentives to IFAs (those still on commission base) to push product.

4.3 Place

(a) Use IFAs to push product

(b) For international markets, use 'master distributors'

(c) E-commerce – customised product offerings online can help to target 'suspicious and confused' as well. Also offers choice to consumers between having a call back or live chat with licensed agent or IFA

4.4 Promotion

Need to create brand awareness. From emphasis on 'above the line' to 'refer the line' activities. More elaboration is provided later under brand strategy.

4.5 Process/people

(a) Online support to IFAs and overseas master distributors

(b) Integrated IT system to improve process of signing up for new payment (eg direct debiting of annual premium from using account with associated banks)

(c) Provide training for IFAs to inform about policy features

Implementation issues

In addition, the following key activities may be necessary to be carried out in order for CM to realise corporate objectives.

(1) Organisational change

- More market-orientated approach with support from top management
- More entrepreneurship encouraged through a proper internal marketing plan. Also through recruitment of 'new blood'

(2) Gradual by steady upgrading of IT system

Objective is to allow CM to execute more effective data mining and keep up with the latest legislative requirements and keep streamline operations

(3) Development of customer relationship management (CRM) with IFAs and other customers

(4) Schedule

Year	1	2	3
Organisational change	X		
IT system upgrade	X	X	
CRM	X		
Marketing penetration	X	X	
Product development	X	X	X
Marketing development			

6 **BUDGET**

I will assume that a significant sum (a reasonable figure of about 2% of sales) will be set aside to implement the promotional activities.

7 **EVALUATION AND CONTROL**

In order to measure the effectiveness of their plan, measurements should be performed against the objectives set with market data, eg profits and sales.

The actual results should be regularly measured against short-term targets and tactics modified where necessary to achieve goals.

Qualitative and quantitative measurements should be made with regard to customer perception and company positioning.

Constant maintaining and control will be required with regard to finance, HR development, marketing activities, status of organisational change and development of CRM programme.

Examiner's comments

This answer is well laid out and considers some of the key issues facing CM, especially with regards to positioning. However there could have been more analysis with models such as the GE matrix. The greatest weakness is the lack of proper financial analysis and estimates in the answer.

3.2 Question 2

Recommendations on possible branding and communications position for CM

1 **Situation**

(a) **Demographics**

A look at the demographics of the population may suggest evolving trends and some of these have already been highlighted in section 3.2 of Question 1.

Some of the observations:

- Ageing population
- More self-employed
- More 'ABC1' type
- More professional women. More single and divorced.
- Greater mobility of professionals

(b) **Savings pattern**

The saving pattern of the people show that buying of insurance is performed using discretionary income – not an immediate and important purchase.

The individuals who are buying are people who are working and the better off who have more discretionary income. The young are rather inactive in saving but represent a high potential market in the future. They are not a good target at the moment but will be good to tap later.

2 **Brand values**

It is necessary to influence the perception of the customers about its brand and not associate it with their general impression of the whole industry (which currently has got a bad reputation).

Focused/specific, honest/good guarantee and high value for money.

3 **Promotional activities**

There is a strong need to create brand awareness from emphasis on 'above the line' to 'below the line' activities.

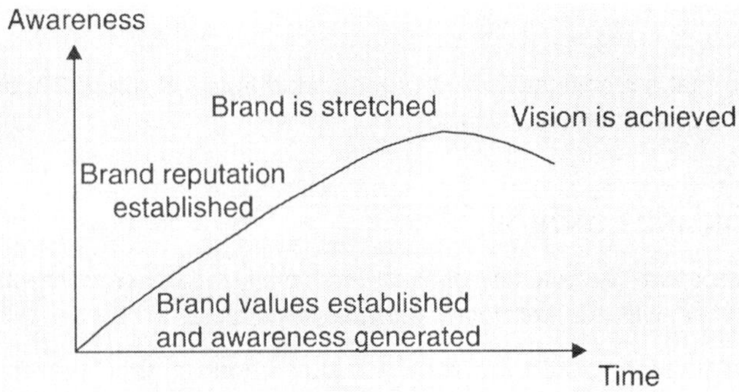

Above the line – mass media. The newspaper

Public relations – become a patron of a charitable organisation

Communications objectives: to create an image of being trustworthy, safe, caring and providing helpful service.

Below the line – focused advertising.

Eg direct marketing – use existing database. Can also tap database of Halifax.

(c) Seminars, investment talks

(d) Direct selling by IFAs (web-based or otherwise)

(e) Sales promotion – incentives (gifts for introduction) new client

The allocation of the funds may be proportioned as follows

Above the line – 60%
Below the line – 40%

The budget may be expected to be spent over the next 10 years as follows.

1st year – 40%
2nd year – 30%
3rd year – 30%

> **Examiner's comments**
>
> This is a fairly basic answer. It needs to consider the branding and positioning strategies as asked for in the question. The current CM brand is already given and one would have expected more in terms of a new branding triangle and also an interesting positioning strategy based on the analysis of the detailed figures given in the appendices.

3.3 Question 3

Recommendations on a coherent customer relationship management strategy

(1) **Situation analysis**

Life assurance is a service orientated industry. As such, customer service is of paramount importance. It is also an industry which operates on a long-term basis – meaning that premium can be paid over a long period, say 25 years. Hence, the customer life-time value is very important and customer loyalty has to be constantly cultivated in the face of other more tax efficient substitutes like PEPs, TESSAs and ISAs.

Competition is also getting keener with the influx of new 'muscular' entrants like the bancassurers and providers of consumer products. Hence it is critical to retain customers as trying to regain lost customers later will be a very expensive process.

Increasing government pressure for the industry to show integrity, skill, care and diligence further make it important for the industry to improve its public relationship not only with the end clients but also the government. The distribution channel with the greatest success has been the IFAs as the other channels are either outdated or ineffective. The situation is not likely to change much as the IFAs strive to improve their professionalism.

(2) **Key customers marketing relationship managers**

- IFAs
- Government
- End clients
- Halifax

(3) **Strategies to implement CRM with key customers**

(a) **IFAs**

(i) Maintain a partnership relationship with IFAs

(ii) Provide training to IFAs to inform about policy features. Knowing CM's policies well will enable them to provide better service and hence encourage them to push CM's products

(iii) Provide online support to IFAs

(iv) Provide internet links between CM's web portals and IFAs web sites

(v) Get constant feedback from IFAs

(b) **Government**

(i) Keep updated with latest government regulations. Prompt implementation into integrated IT system

(ii) Show integrity, skill, care and diligence in service to the clients in line with government expectations

(iii) Have regular meetings with government representatives

Caution. Since CM may not want to provide stakeholder pensions (a government initiative), it may be necessary to provide a variant on the scheme to please the government. However, they must take care not to be totally committed.

(c) **End consumers**

(i) Develop customer database
(ii) Include satisfaction questionnaire in all product packaging
(iii) Fast response to queries
(iv) Develop customer feedback system
(v) Value opinions and respond accordingly
(vi) Encourage comment

(d) **Halifax**

(i) Regular feedback and reporting to Halifax
(ii) Ensure no conflict of interest with the policies developed by Halifax
(iii) Encourage more frequent interaction between staff

(e) **International implementation**

- Top management to lead by example
- Proper communication of objectives to all staff
- Assign a skilled Relationship Manager to each key customer
- Develop clear job descriptions for relationship managers
- Have each relationship manager to develop annual and long-range customer relationship plans
- Appoint an overall manager to supervise the relationship manager
- Enough budget to be allocated to ensure success
- Get a time frame of 1-2 years and constantly monitor progress of each plan

Conclusion

I feel strongly that a niche strategy as outlined in the above report will be the best way forward for Clerical Medical for the foreseeable future. However, with the constantly changing landscape of the business environment which Clerical Medical is in, it may be important to modify some of the proposed plans as and when necessary. The need to introduce entirely new insurance products (new product development) or diversification to suit the demands of the customers is another distinct possibility for future plans. By constantly monitoring the environment and adopting a clear and consistent strategy, I believe that Clerical Medical will emerge as a strong financial service provider despite the current difficult environment.

Examiner's comments

This answer is better, but it needs to consider a clear diagrammatic representation of how CRM would be managed. The points on IFAs being crucial is well made. Also it is interesting to note that the writer justifies caution about stakeholder pensions, but does not take this further by saying that if stakeholder pensions are just standard products, does CRM hold any meaning?

4 SPECIMEN ANSWERS WITH EXAMINER'S COMMENTS: SCRIPT 2

REPORT

To: Mr James Broadbent, Marketing Director
From: Mr Don Sherwood, Marketing Consultant
Date: 16 June 2000

Section I

Subject: **Strategic marketing plan for Clerical Medical for the next three years with recommendations**

Section II Question 2

Section III Question 3

1.0 **Executive summary**

The strategic marketing plan for CMIG 2000 – 2003 covers the main goals of the company. To be a leader in financial services encompassing information technology, and to stay ahead of competitors in anticipating and satisfying customer needs.

The main competitors of CMIG are Standard Life, Norwich Union, Scottish Widows and Prudential among others. The smaller ones include Scottish Provident and National Mutual.

In order to achieve these goals I have recommended that CMIG increase revenues by 40% and reduce expenditure by 15% by 2003.

Summary of budget by 2003

	£million
Total expected income	10,114.19
Total expected expenditure	5,968.47
Surplus	4,145.72

To attain these targets CMIG needs to intensify its marketing and promotional activities, introduce internet and implement customer relationship management.

A marketing budget of 20% of the total revenues is that £829,150 million has been set aside for the achievement of these goals. For which £500,000 will consist of promotional activities.

For the successful implementation of this plan tight controls should be set that will minimise costs.

2.0 **Situational analysis**

2.1 **Marketing environment**

CM in operating in a very competitive environment. In spite of this, it has managed to double its market share to 3%.

2.2 With the development of new technology, competition is likely to become more intense in the domestic and global markets since competitors are investing in modern technology.

2.3 The political environment which CMIG is operating in is stable, although the government is introducing new policies which the financial sectors may be forced to adapt.

2.4 The social cultural aspect in which we are operating is fairly unvarying in the UK, but it will vary in the international market.

2.5 The legal aspect has changed since the signing of the Rome treaty in 1957, making member states become a common market, leading to liberalisation of goods and services among member states. The economic situation is fairly stable.

3.0 **SWOT analysis**

Strengths of CMIG

3.1 Strong financial base as it has been acquired by Halifax bank.

3.2 Targets only the net worthy individuals

3.3 Has ventured internationally to foreign nationals

3.4 Rated among the top 5 star in service providing

3.5 Good customer reputation

3.6 Wide range of products

3.7 Long period of existence

3.8 **Weaknesses**

3.8.1 Poor promotional plan. Initially targeted wide market, this has disappeared with time. Poor segmentation.

3.8.2 Liquidity is low as the company made a loss in the last accounting period

3.8.3 Brand is not well known

3.8.4 Staff promoted within the organisation

3.8.5 Lack of control over distributors

3.9 **Opportunities**

3.9.1 International market is growing enabling CMIG to venture overseas

3.9.2 Population age bracket 60 plus is bound to increase and gives CMI an opportunity to develop. Specialised products for this segment

3.9.3 Advances in technology will increase demand for CMIG in the market

3.9.4 Employ qualified staff who give added value to customers, and good image

3.9.5 Teleselling and direct marketing

3.9.6 Better relationships with IFAs through CRM

3.10 **Threats**

3.10.1 New entrants eg Virgin, Marks & Spencer

3.10.2 Distributors are selling other substitute products

3.10.3 Tax efficient products, eg PEPs, TESSAs

3.10.4 Constraining set by the government for the insurance industry

3.10.5 Organisations in financial services that are technologically advanced

3.10.6 Government attitudes towards IFAs having lack of professionalism, which may have an impact on CMI's image

3.10.7 Porter's forces of competition

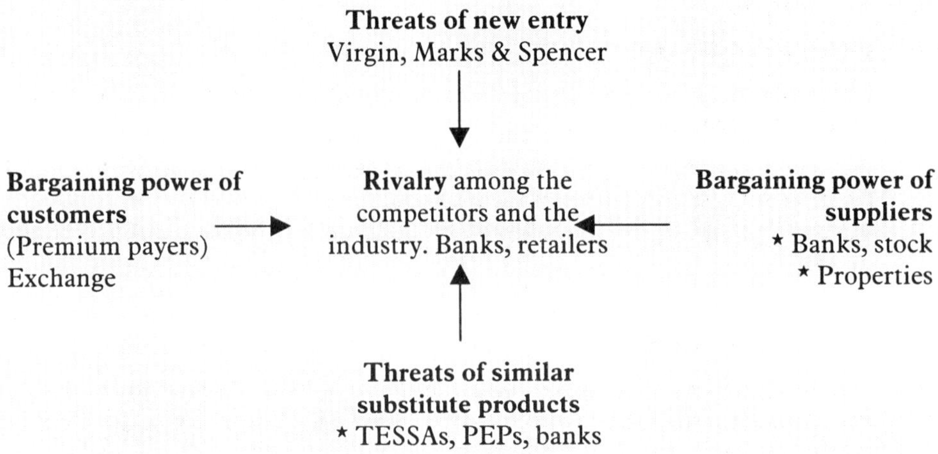

4.0 **Internal environment**

CMIG should look into its organisation structure, management structures and its employee selection criteria.

In order to achieve a competitive edge CMIG should adapt marketing philosophy on the following.

- Customer orientation and customer care
- Improve marketing information suppliers
- Adapt internal marketing
- Change management culture

I recommend that CMIG should have the following organisation structure that includes a marketing department customer service department and an export department.

4.1 **Organisation structure**

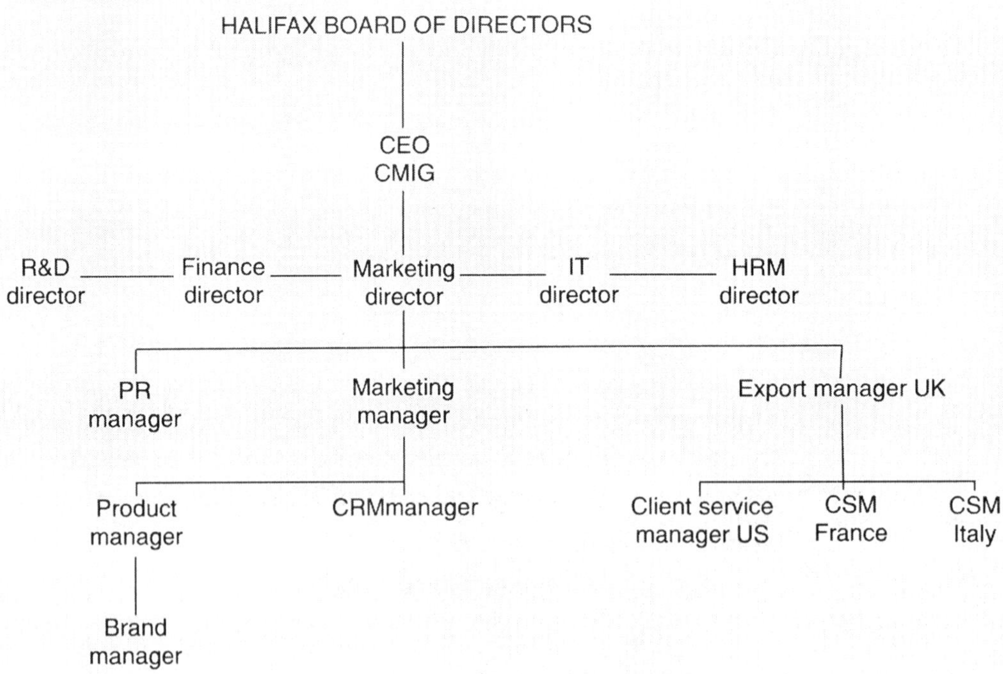

Structure of life industry

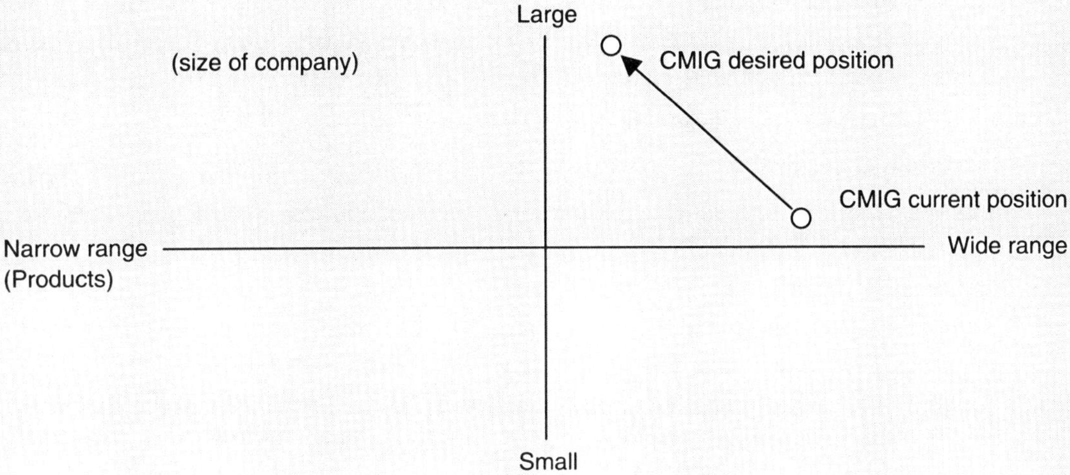

5 **Critical success factors**

5.1 Flexibility seems to be a critical success factor in a rapidly changing technological environment. Therefore CMIG should provide the following to its customers.

5.2 High quality services that will enhance their security

5.3 Relationship marketing

5.4 Offer technical advice in education on financial services

5.5 Increase confidence and trustworthiness through processing their returns in good time

6.0 **Corporate objectives**

I suggest the following objectives for CMIG.

6.1 The board of directors should meet and set objectives and how to achieve them. I recommend the following.

- Adopt a market oriented culture – employ qualified and experienced employees within 1 year
- Increase profitability by 20% in 3 years
- Exploit opportunities from Halifax Bank's plan to introduce internet banking
- Improve corporate image from 2000 onwards
- Strive to become a large financial service provider in the next 3 years

Structure of financial services

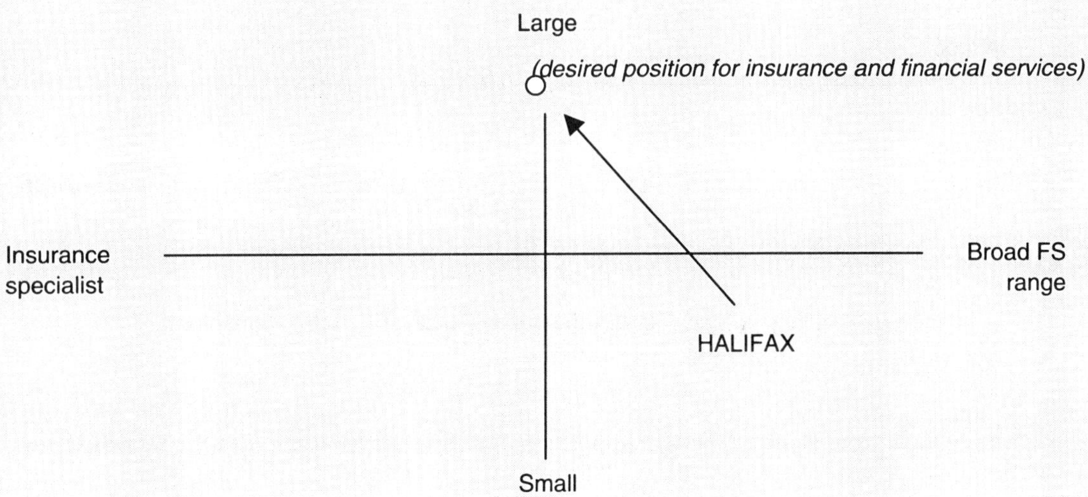

7.0 **Strategic planning gap**

Due to the current competitive situation and the fact that this is set to increase I would not want the planning to show an increase of 5% on ROCE.

8.0 **CMIG should have a vision/mission**

8.1 **Vision suggested**

To be the most eminent financial provider, encompassing new technology to be at the peak of excellence in financial services.

8.2 **Mission statement**

(a) To provide unique financial services that will provide security, safeguard the future, to improve quality of life to the society through the creation of economic value.

(b) Our aim is to be at the peak in customer service and retain best valued staff; through IT to stay ahead of our competitors in satisfying and anticipating our customer needs. Maximising benefit to our stakeholders.

9.0 **Marketing objectives**

9.1 Identify and meet customer needs, to build customer loyalty by 80% in the next 3 years

9.2 Develop products/services that appeal to target market AB, G, G2 target groups

9.3 Create awareness amongst customers; increase corporate image awareness by 50% in 2003 by intensive promotion.

9.4 Recruit qualified experienced staff from 2000 onwards.

9.5 Penetrate international markets by 2003 by the use of internet as a distribution channel.

9.6 Develop effective MkIS system to facilitate decision making in one year (database management)

9.7 Define CMIG target markets within 1 year

9.8 Reduce cost by 15% in the next 3 years

9.9 Review current distribution channels. Incorporate the use of internet for CMIG services utilising the Halifax systems for Greenfield – six months.

9.10 Adapt a customer relationship management strategy by establishing a marketing department immediately.

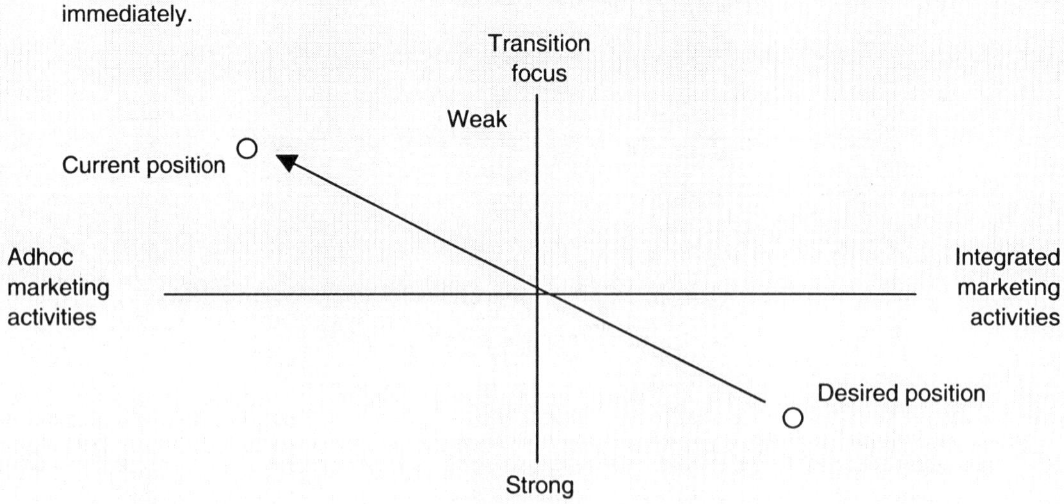

9.11 Improve relationships with our distributors especially IFAs within 5 months.

10 **Marketing strategies**

Having identified the gaps in the market several marketing strategies have to be employed as implemented. I have logged in the marketing strategies onto the Ansoff matrix.

Ansoff's matrix

	Existing products	**New products**
Existing markets	1 Market penetration • UK markets • Increases sales per customer	2 Product development • NPD • Branding • Redesign
New markets	3 Market development • USA market • EU market	4 Diversification • Medical scheme • Health care provider

10.1

Market penetration	Justification
Existing products in existing markets	This will create awareness, desire and stimulate customers to purchase CMIG products
CMIG should adapt a promotional strategy through the following. 10.1.1 Advertising • Press adverts • Radio, TV 10.1.2 Sales promotion Discounts on premium buyers paying promptly. Give gifts, organise competitions and undertake other promotional activities 10.1.3 Personal selling Offering technical advice and educate customers 10.1.4 PR strategy • Sponsoring events • Giving donations 10.1.5 Price differentiation strategy Different prices for different segments and markets 10.1.6 Distribution strategy • Improve relationships with IFAs, regionals and nationals • Use internet	Increase sales per customer through cross selling • Increase purchase frequency • Maintain targeted segments • To maintain customer base • Improve customer relationships Increase knowledge within our customers Customer relationship with links • Improve corporate image • CMIG will be socially responsible Offer clear plans for the younger in upmarket offering them long term annual payments and short term single payments for the older upmarket. Each group is motivated to purchase. • Build our area operations • Easy access to CMIG products • Increase efficiency • Transactions will be done faster

10.2

Strategy	Justification
Develop relationship marketing programmes	To build long term customer relationships hence increase new business and profits
10.2.1 Product/service development Modify our group pensions to maintain maturity level (give discounts or guaranteed interests)	CMIG will be able to get funds to maintain their services at maturity otherwise there is a risk of decline. Available fund for NPD.
10.2.2 Develop new package (policy for in PPP for the self employed, whole percentage is increasing 16-15% by 2005)	New business Self employed will be motivated to take pensions
10.2.3 Develop flexible, short term investment plan for 60 year plus in upmarket	Attract the hold and increase market share
10.2.4 Prepare new product catalogues	Inform and educate

10.3

Strategy	Justification
10.3 Market development • Export insurance products	Great opportunity to increase market share
10.3.1 Designing marketing mix (4Ps and 3Ps to suit target market)	• Encourage market orientation • Beat competition
10.3.1 Use Halifax internet to distribute internationally	Cost effective method
10.3.2 Target older generation in USA, France, Germany	Increase market share and get new segment for new business
10.3.3 Enhance promotional strategies abroad and adapt to the market	To reach target market reduces costs on planning
10.3.4 Diversification This strategy can only be implemented if CMIG is not successful in the financial service sector	This is a high risk strategy

Competitive strategy

10.4 In order to have competitive edge CMIG needs to produce a strategy that is consistent with its objectives and corporate image. Recommendations will be based on Michael Porter's three generic strategies to select a clear position.

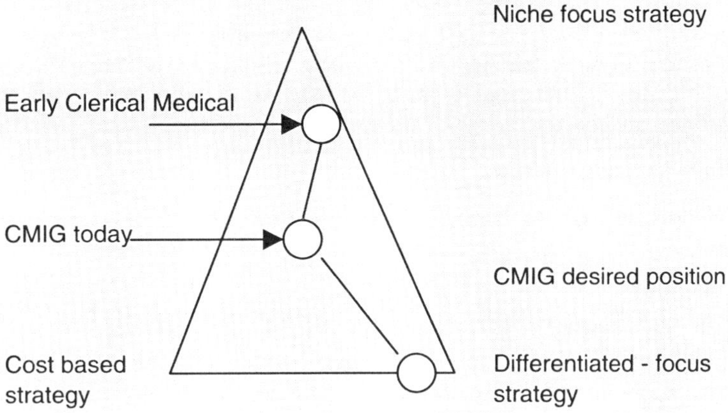

(a) CMIG should adopt differentiated strategy, differentiating their policies for selected market segments, eg social class AB, C1, C2 affluent high income earners and professionals.

Justifications

(b) Will make it possible to adapt marketing mix that is suitable for the selected segments preferred

(c) Reduce dependence on single sector

(d) Opportunity to exploit available segments like C1, C2 who are in the efficient category

(e) Can continue using premium pricing strategy and maintain corporate image and make its plans stakeholder friendly.

Implications

(f) Successful development and applications of MkIS

(g) Become market orientated

(h) Will reflect cost leadership strategy since it has expanded its customer base to professionals

11.0 **Action plan**

	Activity	**Time**	**Responsibility**	**Cost**
	Product development	6m - 2001	NPD manager	100,000
11.1	Maintain group pension maturity	Continuously 2000-2003	Product manager	40,000
11.2	Price	2003	Finance manager	30,000
	Achieve ROCE 5-04%	Intermediate	Marketing manager	
	Premium price	Maintained		
	Distributor/agent fees			
11.3	Place. Internet	6 months	IT manager	45,000
	• Export departments	Intermediate 2003	Export manager	
11.4	Promotion	6 months	Brand manager	500,000
	Brand names	6 months	IT Marketing	
11.5	Process MKIS	1 yr - 2003	PR manager	20,000
11.6	Physical evidence Mission/ internally	3 months	PR and marketing manager	10,000
11.7	People recruitment	By 2002 Continuous	HRM marketing manager	100,000
	TOTAL BUDGET			845,000

12.0 **Evaluation and control**

12.1 The corporate and marketing objectives provide the basis of the evaluation of performance. I recommend that the performance of cost reduction by CMIG takes priority. All activities suggested are monitored on a quarterly basis.

12.2 CMIG is in a poor financial state. Therefor there is risk of severe cash flow problems. It is advisable to seek assistance from Halifax. Annual evaluation should be conducted so that by 2003 CMIG should have established itself as a large and broad range, high quality financial service provider.

13.0 **Contingency planning**

Develop contingency plans that CMIG will consider should drastic change occur in the market place.

14.0 **Conclusion**

CMIG has proved to be in the trend of achieving success to continue this trend, the company needs to adapt more strategic approach and to focus the minimum resources available towards those segments which will provide the most stable long term future for the company.

Budget for 3 years

	2000	**2001**	**2002**
Income items	12%	14%	14%
Earned premiums	3,661.73	4,172.37	4,758.78
Investment income	1,677.20	1,912.01	2,179.69
Unrealised gains	2,384.59	2,718.43	3,099.01
Other technical income	59.02	67.29	76.71
Total expected	7,782.54	8,872.10	10,114.19
Expenditure items	3%	4%	8%
Claims received	1,522.42	1,461.52	1,344.60
Charge to provisions for claims	11.16	10.71	9.85
Change in technical provisions	1,876.76	1,801.69	1,657.55
Net technical provisions for linked liability	1,191.16	1,143.51	1,052.03
Net operating expenses	353.86	339.70	312.52
Investment expenses as charges	353.86	339.70	312.52
Tax attributable to long term business	112.62	108.11	99.46
Transfers to the funds for future	1,607.39	1,543.10	1,419.64
Total	6,757.82	6,487.49	5,968.47
Surplus	1,024.72	2,384.61	4,145.72

Assumptions – all products of CMIG have been taken up for the domestic and international market.

Income = strive to increase it by 40%

Expenditure = strive to reduce it by 15%

Strategic planning gap

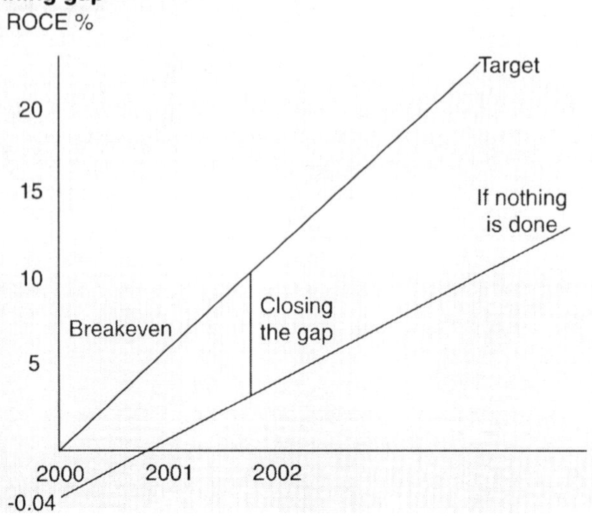

Examiner's comments

This answer, though slightly disjoined contains all the key issues that need to be considered for developing a marketing strategy for CM. The best part of the answer is the depth of the detail of how the candidate sees the financial growth to take place. It is also strong on considering performance measures. The question would have benefited from a more structured plan.

4.2 Question 2

14.0 The demographic and savings patterns in the UK population

Through the data provided CMIG should first segment the market and position its market segments before offering a branding strategy. Since CMIG is going to target the AB, C1, C2 groups then it will take a demographic and psychographic approach.

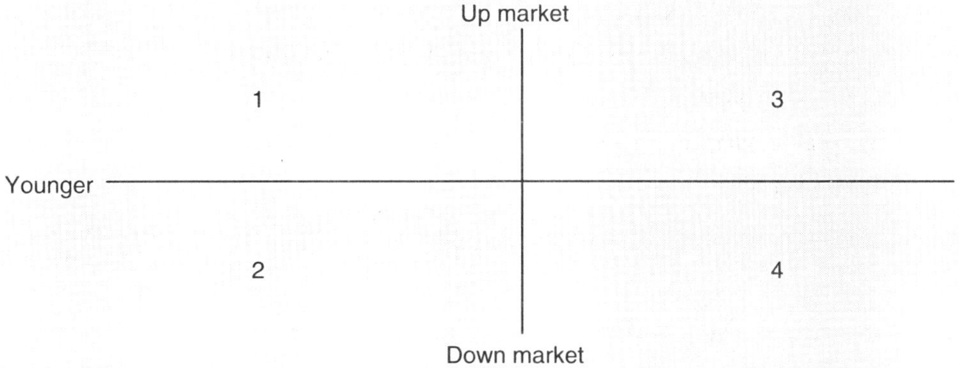

For the diagram above CMIG will take quadrant 1 and 3 as its target segments.

Quadrant 1

Demographic	Psychographic
24-34 years male female	Social class
35-44 years male female	AB, C1, C2

NB. The social class comprises of the efficient executives, wealthy achievers, well off workers and professionals.

Quadrant 2

Demographic	Psychographic
55-64 years male female	Social class AB

14.1 Justification of this segmentation

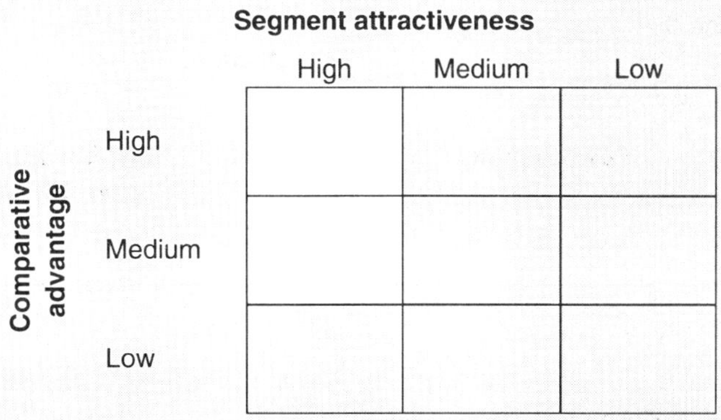

Quadrant 1 comprises of the high young earning individuals who are willing to invest now for future returns. This has high segment attractiveness and medium to high competitive advantage.

14.1.1 CMIG should make high profit margins
14.1.2 Design products as per customer needs
14.1.3 The growth of each segment is high

14.2 Quadrant 3

Assuming that it comprises of the older 55-64 years and above, social class AB w2ho are willing to invest in short term policies to supplement their pension scheme.

(a) This segment has not been catered for therefore a brand can be developed to suit them and increase market share.

(b) With increase in percentage of population of 60 years and over this segment has potential to grow in UK, USA and France.

(c) Competition is low in this segment.

(d) CMIG has the opportunity to produce innovative policies.

This will also assist CMIG to create a customer base in which it will help in developing brands that are suitable to the segments.

15.0 **Targeting for communications**

In year one CMIG will maintain status, as all strategies will not have been implemented. Targeting will assist CMIG communications and branding so as to maximise effort and resources in the necessary chosen segments.

15.1.1 This requires long term relationships with customers

15.1.2 Significant changes to distribution channels

Develop key account managers and teams – develop a key corporate brand

Positioning

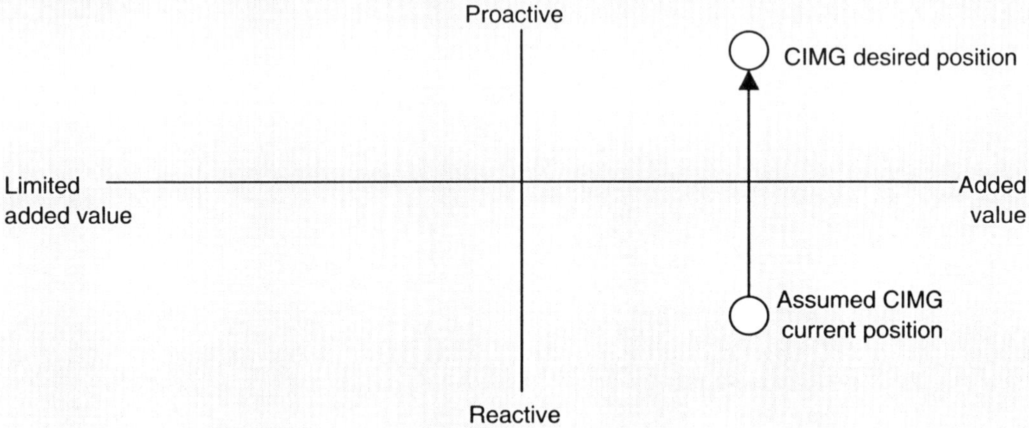

Customers need to believe that CM offers exclusive service compared to all other competitors in order to achieve substantial advantage. Communications should be focused to support the company's position in order to convince all parties of the company.

15.3 CMIG should be perceived as one of the best financial services providers offering customers innovative high quality policies and technical advice. Therefore its branding strategy should follow a similar line.

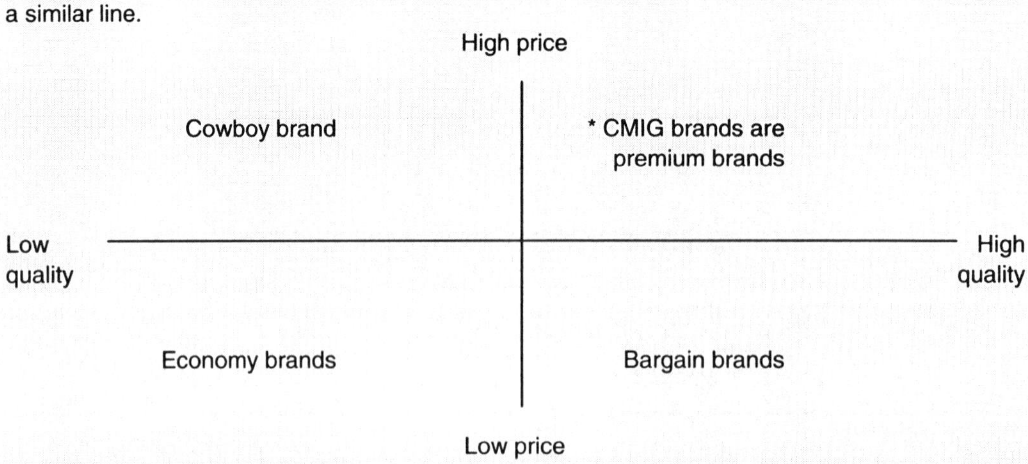

Therefore CMIG position is clear. Currently CMIG brand values are not well known compared to competitors. I recommend that CMIG come up with a corporate brand and give its products brand names.

Positioning will make our messages to the customer focused. Branding therefore will improve CMIG's corporate image, increase customer retention and loyalty.

Examiner's comments

This question is well answered with the positioning strategies clearly defined. The branding discussions would have benefited from a better understanding of the current brand triangle and a reasoned argument for the shape of a future triangle.

4.3 Question 3

16.0 Clerical Medical's position in the life and pensions industry faces intensive competition from all the financial service sector. CMIG has striven to be among the top 5 rated highly in providing good service. From the recommendations I have given CMIG will need to develop customer relationship management strategy in order to be successful in implementing all the strategies recommended.

Currently CMIG promotional activities and brands are not well known as compared to its competitors like Virgin and Marks and Spencer.

CMIG should come up with a corporate brand in order to uplift the corporate image. This will involve changing the internal culture of both management and staff, should understand and appreciate corporate values, and hence the brands that will be introduced should give its products brand names and implement a company trade name for its products.

Internal marketing strategy

- Intensify the 7Ss by making employees more customer focused

  Style, structure, staff/skills, systems, strategy, shared values

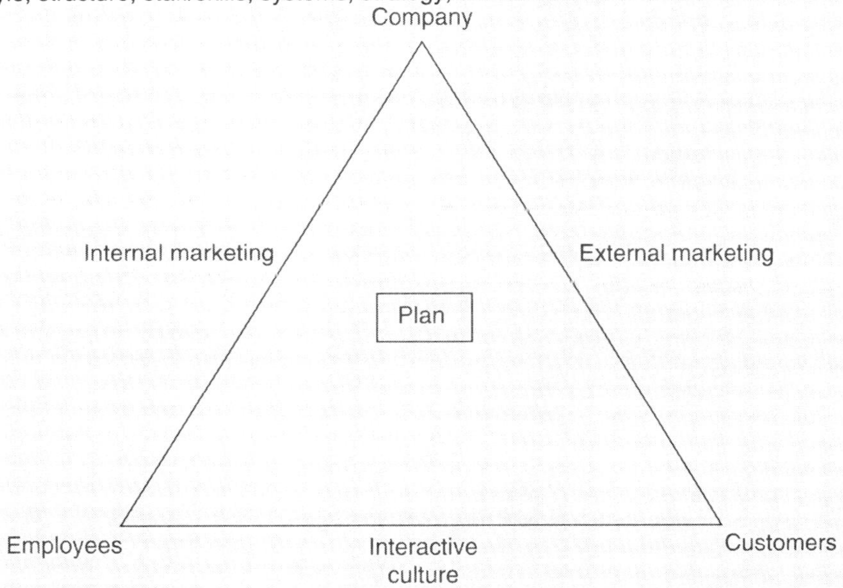

- Change attitudes, culture of the entire staff which will overflow to the customers' processes
- All staff should be aiming at effectiveness and efficiency

Physical evidence

The organisation should be based in suitable location and the ambience attractive to the customers.

Customer service

Train staff on customer care in order to create a good relationship with its customers.

CMIG should strive:

- To differentiate itself from competitors
- Increase retention and referrals by customers. Therefore creating loyalty to our products.
- We should be able to satisfy our customer emotionally and values.
- Develop an effective MkIS system that will encourage more information coming in hence the management will be able to make valid decisions for its improvement as an organisation for better service delivery

This will increase customer perceived value of CMIG products and brands.

Examiner's comments

This answer is very basic. It touches on issues surrounding CRM, but falls apart on the actual implementation. There appears to be very little cognisance of IFAs and the impact that have on CM's distribution network. At the end of the day who needs a CRM strategy most, IFAs or consumers? Internet developments mean that a CRM strategy needs to target some of the internal issues that need to be addressed for successful implementation.

Summary

Both these answers show different ways of attacking the case. One of the answers is very good on the control measures and detail surrounding performance. The other takes more of a strategic overview. Both cases reflect the need to be coherent and to justify the strategies taken. In both cases, however, there could have been more emphasis on teasing out segmentation positions from the wealth of data that was given. The case gave plenty of scope for differing strategic viewpoints.

5 A FINAL WORD

5.1 So how did it go? Hopefully your performance will have improved. Further practice is available should you need it. An order form for Solo Cases can be found at the back of this Tutorial Text.

Index

CIM Order

To BPP Publishing Ltd, Aldine Place, London W12 8AA

Tel: 020 8740 2211. Fax: 020 8740 1184

Mr/Mrs/Ms (Full name) ______

Daytime delivery address ______

Postcode ______

Daytime Tel ______ Date of exam (month/year) ______

	5/00 Texts	9/00 Kits	9/99 Tapes
CERTIFICATE			
1 Marketing Environment	£17.95 ☐	£8.95 ☐	£12.95 ☐
2 Customer Communications in Marketing	£17.95 ☐	£8.95 ☐	£12.95 ☐
3 Marketing in Practice	£17.95 ☐	£8.95 ☐	£12.95 ☐
4 Marketing Fundamentals	£17.95 ☐	£8.95 ☐	£12.95 ☐
ADVANCED CERTIFICATE			
5 The Marketing Customer Interface	£17.95 ☐	£8.95 ☐	£12.95 ☐
6 Management Information for Marketing Decisions	£17.95 ☐	£8.95 ☐	£12.95 ☐
7 Effective Management for Marketing	£17.95 ☐	£8.95 ☐	£12.95 ☐
8 Marketing Operations	£17.95 ☐	£8.95 ☐	£12.95 ☐
DIPLOMA			
9 Integrated Marketing Communications	£17.95 ☐	£8.95 ☐	£12.95 ☐
10 International Marketing Strategy	£17.95 ☐	£8.95 ☐	£12.95 ☐
11 Strategic Marketing Management: Planning and Control	£17.95 ☐	£8.95 ☐	£12.95 ☐
12 Strategic Marketing Management: Analysis and Decision (9/00)	£24.95 ☐		☐

SUBTOTAL £ ______

POSTAGE & PACKING

Study Texts

	First	Each extra	
UK	£3.00	£2.00	£
Europe*	£5.00	£4.00	£
Rest of world	£20.00	£10.00	£

Kits/Passcards/Success Tapes

	First	Each extra	
UK	£2.00	£1.00	£
Europe*	£2.50	£1.00	£
Rest of world	£15.00	£8.00	£

Grand Total (Cheques to *BPP Publishing*) I enclose a cheque for (incl. Postage) £ ______

Or charge to Access/Visa/Switch

Card Number ______

Expiry date ______ Start Date ______

Issue Number (Switch Only) ______

Signature ______

We aim to deliver to all UK addresses inside 5 working days. A signature will be required. Orders to all EU addresses should be delivered within 6 working days.

All other orders to overseas addresses should be delivered within 8 working days.

* Europe includes the Republic of Ireland and the Channel Islands.

REVIEW FORM & FREE PRIZE DRAW

All original review forms from the entire BPP range, completed with genuine comments, will be entered into one of two draws on 31 July 2000 and 31 January 2001. The names on the first four forms picked out on each occasion will be sent a cheque for £50.

Name: ______________________ **Address:** ______________________

____

____

How have you used this Text?
(Tick one box only)

- ☐ Home study (book only)
- ☐ On a course: college ______________
- ☐ With 'correspondence' package
- ☐ Other ______________

Why did you decide to purchase this Text?
(Tick one box only)

- ☐ Have used companion Kit
- ☐ Have used BPP Texts in the past
- ☐ Recommendation by friend/colleague
- ☐ Recommendation by a lecturer at college
- ☐ Saw advertising
- ☐ Other ______________

During the past six months do you recall seeing/receiving any of the following?
(Tick as many boxes as are relevant)

- ☐ Our advertisement in the *Marketing Success*
- ☐ Our advertisement in *Marketing Business*
- ☐ Our brochure with a letter through the post
- ☐ Our brochure with *Marketing Business*

Which (if any) aspects of our advertising do you find useful?
(Tick as many boxes as are relevant)

- ☐ Prices and publication dates of new editions
- ☐ Information on Text content
- ☐ Facility to order books off-the-page
- ☐ None of the above

Have you used the companion Practice & Revision Kit for this subject? ☐ Yes ☐ No

Your ratings, comments and suggestions would be appreciated on the following areas.

	Very useful	*Useful*	*Not useful*
Introductory section (How to use this text, study checklist, etc)	☐	☐	☐
Setting the Scene	☐	☐	☐
Syllabus coverage	☐	☐	☐
Action Programmes and Marketing at Work examples	☐	☐	☐
Chapter roundups	☐	☐	☐
Quick quizzes	☐	☐	☐
Illustrative questions	☐	☐	☐
Content of suggested answers	☐	☐	☐
Index	☐	☐	☐
Structure and presentation	☐	☐	☐

	Excellent	*Good*	*Adequate*	*Poor*
Overall opinion of this Text	☐	☐	☐	☐

Do you intend to continue using BPP Study Texts/Kits? ☐ Yes ☐ No

Please note any further comments and suggestions/errors on the reverse of this page.

Please return to: Kate Machattie, BPP Publishing Ltd, FREEPOST, London, W12 8BR

REVIEW FORM & FREE PRIZE DRAW (continued)

Please note any further comments and suggestions/errors below.

FREE PRIZE DRAW RULES

1 Closing date for 31 July 2000 draw is 30 June 2000. Closing date for 31 January 2001 draw is 31 December 2000.

2 Restricted to entries with UK and Eire addresses only. BPP employees, their families and business associates are excluded.

3 No purchase necessary. Entry forms are available upon request from BPP Publishing. No more than one entry per title, per person. Draw restricted to persons aged 16 and over.

4 Winners will be notified by post and receive their cheques not later than 6 weeks after the relevant draw date. Lists of winners will be published in BPP's *focus* newsletter following the relevant draw.

5 The decision of the promoter in all matters is final and binding. No correspondence will be entered into.